Cultural Anthropology

Cultural Anthropology

Second Canadian Edition

Barbara D. Miller

The George Washington University

Penny Van Esterik

York University

John Van Esterik

York University

PEARSON

Toronto

National Library of Canada Cataloguing in Publication

Miller, Barbara D., 1948–
   Cultural anthropology / Barbara D. Miller, Penny Van Esterik, John Van Esterik. — 2nd Canadian ed.

Includes bibliographical references and index.
ISBN 0-205-36575-2

1. Ethnology—Textbooks. I. Van Esterik, Penny II. Van Esterik, John III. Title.

GN316.M34 2003   306   C2003-900702-2

ISBN 0-205-36575-2

Vice President, Editorial Director: Michael J. Young
Executive Editor: Jessica Mosher
Developmental Editor: Matthew Christian
Senior Marketing Manager: Judith Allen
Production Editor: Cheryl Jackson
Copy Editor: Claudia Forgas
Proofreader: Lu Cormier
Production Manager: Wendy Moran
Formatter: Phyllis Seto
Art Director: Julia Hall
Interior and Cover Design: Monica Kompter
Cover Image: "Sister and Brother" by Lorraine Greenfield

1 2 3 4 5   08 07 06 05 04

Printed and bound in the United States

Contents

PART II Economic and Demographic Foundations

Preface from Barbara Miller

Why would anybody want to write an introductory cultural anthropology textbook? Such a project requires years of research, writing, and rewriting, and is a humbling task throughout as one continually faces how much material there is yet to read and how much more rethinking of categories and questions must be done. One catalyst for my undertaking the writing of this book was that over the three years of my teaching large classes in introductory cultural anthropology each spring semester at the University of Pittsburgh, my enrollments went from 100 in 1991 to 200 in 1992 to 300 in 1993. I figured that I must be doing something right.

On top of that experience, throughout the many years of my teaching introductory cultural anthropology—from my first course in 1979 to now—it has become clearer to me what I find unsatisfying in other cultural anthropology textbooks: They mainly treat the topic of social inequality and variation in just one chapter (usually on "social stratification"), rather than considering it as part of the whole range of topics in cultural anthropology. Thus, their treatment of material about economies, kinship, politics, religion, and language involved little attention to how they relate to social inequality and social variation. While I appreciate cultural similarities worldwide, I find differences more important since they are often what divides people in ways that are dangerous, hurtful, and changeable.

I am also keenly aware of how "dead" many of the longstanding subjects have become. I found it painful to teach many of cultural anthropology's core topics, especially kinship and language. The material presented in the textbooks seemed irrelevant to cultural anthropology's goal of understanding why people do what they do and think the way they do. These textbooks presented just definitions and categories.

Last, I found that my strong interest in culture change was poorly presented in the available books. They do not integrate attention to cultural change throughout but instead resort to a few standard cases such as "cargo cults" in the chapter on religion and perhaps a separate chapter on international development or urbanization. Closely related to this topic is the relevance of knowledge in cultural anthropology not just for understanding world problems but for contributing to preventing or solving them. While some textbooks now have boxes on "relevance" and "application," the treatment of these deeply important issues is just that—boxed and peripheral to the main material, which is largely the same as it always has been.

I live and teach in Washington, DC, a highly politicized and policy-focused environment. This niche impresses on me every day the need for cultural anthropology to be "relevant" to the contemporary world of power, policy, and change. My academic appointment at the George Washington University is located within the Elliott School of International Affairs and the Department of Anthropology. This double focus is important to me in terms of helping to integrate cultural anthropology into international affairs and promoting concerns with international policy debates within anthropology. Many of my students, both undergraduates and graduates, find paid or unpaid work at various governmental and nongovernmental institutes in some point during their training. I hope that *Cultural Anthropology* conveys a sense, either directly or indirectly, of the importance of anthropological research and learning for the understanding and potential amelioration of world problems such as poverty, hunger, violence, and illness. These issues, and a sense of policy relevance in cultural anthropology, thread through the book.

I set out to write a textbook that would reshape and enliven the teaching and learning of cultural anthropology along all of these lines. Whether you are interested in environmental studies, peace studies, international business, or health studies, knowing about the world's cultures is a crucial foundation for shaping a vision of what is both possible and appropriate in terms of goals and actions. *Cultural Anthropology*, to this end, presents interesting and informative material about "exotic" and distant cultures as well as pursuing a new direction in cultural anthropology by including substantial attention to "Western" cultures (primarily European and European-American). Readers coming from diverse cultural perspectives will be able to "make the strange familiar and the familiar strange," to use the powerful words of Melford Spiro (1990).

Barbara Miller

Preface to the First Canadian Edition

This is the first introductory textbook in anthropology to be adapted for Canadian students. We hope it will remind students of the role Canadian anthropologists are playing in international anthropology, and we have highlighted some of their contributions—past and present—in this Canadian edition.

In the 1960s, we were introduced to anthropology as students at the University of Toronto through American textbooks. As the subject was new to us, the content and approach seemed normal. Later, when we taught anthropology in Thai universities, we saw the same textbooks translated into Thai. In the 1970s we both taught Introduction to Anthropology at universities in the United States, so American texts fit the teaching contexts and indeed were normal. In the 1980s we returned to Canada and to teaching introductory anthropology. American textbooks were still being used, but their use seemed more problematic. By the 1990s we were teaching other courses in anthropology using texts by British, American, and Canadian anthropologists that reflected the diversity of the discipline. Our colleagues still used American textbooks for teaching introduction to cultural anthropology, but with growing dissatisfaction. It is appropriate to begin the new millennium with an anthropology textbook that includes Canadian experiences, research, and personalities.

Miller's text is an excellent choice for adaptation as it contains up-to-date materials on complex societies. Its strengths complement the interests of many Canadian anthropologists, and include a strong gender balance and focus, emphasis on the themes of social inequality and diversity, and a clear demonstration of the application of anthropology to contemporary issues such as health systems, migration, and development. Population and other statistical information now include Canadian data.

The practice and teaching of anthropology is shaped by context, both institutional and national. It matters to students and professors that Canadian anthropology is not the same as American anthropology. Its foundations were set in its long association with museums, First Nations research, anglophone and francophone dialogue,

and ethnohistorical studies. In the first chapter we have made some adjustments to the theoretical stance of the book in keeping with the British, European, and American roots of Canadian anthropology. To orient the students to the unique history of anthropology in Canada, we have added a feature on some developmental highlights of Canadian anthropology. We have sought out Canadian case studies—both new and classic—that may be more familiar to Canadian teachers and students, and resonate with Canadian understandings of the world, including references to First Nations groups, where appropriate. We have not included Canadian material gratuitously, nor have we removed all American examples. Rather, we have recontextualized American examples to become cross-cultural comparisons; American examples are no longer the benchmark defining "us" or "we." The reference materials at the end of each chapter include the work of some Canadian anthropologists who have contributed to the field, and similarly, the Web sites include Canadian material and sources. In short, we have tried to highlight the significant contributions Canadians and Canadian institutions have made to the discipline and practice of anthropology.

Frank Manning (1983:2) began a volume reviewing Canadian ethnology by referring to a mythical plan that would see Canada incorporating British politics, American technology, and French culture, but, by accident, the country was left with French politics, British technology, and American culture. That story reveals something of the ironic and irreverent Canadian style, both self-deprecating and ambivalent toward our ancestors. A number of American anthropologists say they regularly participate in Canadian anthropology meetings because they enjoy the civility and the intellectual style of Canadian anthropology. This style is what makes the *Royal Canadian Air Farce*, *Codco*, *Kids in the Hall*, and *This Hour Has 22 Minutes* recognizable as Canadian television entertainment. It helps explain why clowns and magicians have been known to perform at Canadian anthropology meetings over the years. But, like all attempts at cultural generalization, this elusive sense of style is best conveyed by the Canadian anthropologists we hope will enjoy teaching from this book.

Penny and John Van Esterik

Preface to the Second Canadian Edition

We are pleased with the reception of the first edition of this textbook in Canadian schools from British Columbia to the Maritimes. The book entered the marketplace as the first Canadian edition of an introductory textbook in anthropology. In addition to updating or adding the work of more Canadian anthropologists in this revised edition, we have streamlined the text in several ways, integrating the topics of politics, leadership, social order and social conflict into a single comprehensive chapter called "Politics, Conflict, and Social Order," and reducing the types of boxes used to illustrate key points. The key questions that open and close each chapter help students focus on the most important issues in each chapter. Maps have been added to help students locate the peoples and places referred to in the book. We hope we have done justice to the work of the many colleagues whose work has inspired us, and to the generations of students taking courses in introductory anthropology.

Distinctive Features of the Second Canadian Edition

The world has changed in the three years since the publication of the first Canadian edition of *Cultural Anthropology*, and anthropology has changed with it. The need for understanding the relation between social inequality and globalization has never been greater. This second edition makes these connections between the global and the local even clearer. Much more attention is given to **globalization** as a force of change worldwide and how **localization** of global forces can be seen in various domains of change including making a living, marriage and family, and religion. Each chapter contains material on such change as well as boxes discussing, for example, transnationalism, migration, cyberspace communities, and cultural pluralism.

To begin with, this textbook emphasizes the importance of studying **social inequality** and **social diversity** (including class, race, ethnicity, gender, and age) and we present material on these topics throughout the book with more in-depth attention in particular places. The major social categories of class, race, ethnicity, age, and gender are introduced in Chapter 1 as analytical categories, examined in Chapter 2 in terms of how they affect research methods and strategies, revisited in most chapters, and explored in greater depth in Chapter 10 ("Social Groups and Social Stratification").

Second, examples from **contemporary Canada** (and the "West") are integrated into the text, including the gender division of labour in Canadian farm households (Chapter 3), the use of credit cards in "middle-class" consumption patterns (Chapter 4), an examination of Western medical training (Chapter 7), "outlaw" motorcycle clubs and other countercultural groups (Chapter 10), play and leisure as forms of expressive culture (Chapter 14), and the variety of experiences of recent immigrants (Chapter 15).

Third, an up-to-date and lively chapter on **language and communication** (Chapter 13) is innovative in that it de-emphasizes more "formal" aspects of linguistic anthropology such as phonetics and phonemics and gives more material on everyday language in use: children's disputes, adolescent girls' "fat talk," and dress and looks as forms of communication. We also include current research on mass media and how it is culturally shaped: for example, an in-depth study of bias in news reporting.

Finally, this textbook offers two unique chapters, one on Medical anthropology (Chapter 7) and one on migration (Chapter 15). We know of no other introductory cultural anthropology book that devotes entire chapters to these important topics. Students will find much of interest, and much to inspire thought, in these chapters.

The pedagogy of this book is unique in the many ways that it promotes a **critical thinking approach** to the information provided. Instead of simply accepting what we hear or read, a critical thinking approach prompts us to ask questions. It establishes a dynamic relationship between the material and the reader rather than merely allowing for a passive form of information transferral. By providing a sense of engagement with the material, this approach promises to advance student thinking more effectively than traditional forms of learning.

How This Book Is Organized

Cultural Anthropology pursues its goal of promoting learning about the world's cultures in two ways, one that will be more familiar (the delivery of information) and another that may be unsettling and disturbing (asking questions about the information at hand that will make readers unsure of what they thought they knew).

In the first place, readers will encounter abundant, up-to-date *information* about what is known about cross-cultural lifeways: How do people in different parts of the world obtain food, conceive of their place in the universe, and deal with rapid cultural change? This substantive material of cultural anthropology begins with two chapters that establish a foundation for understanding what the discipline of anthropology in general is about, how cultural anthropology fits with it, and what the concept of *culture* means.

Chapter 1 ("Anthropology and the Study of Culture") establishes the importance of the themes of social diversity and inequality that will accompany us throughout the book, especially class, race, ethnicity, gender, and age. Chapter 2 ("Methods in Cultural Anthropology") takes us to the question of how one does research in cultural anthropology and how findings are analyzed and presented. Students will be able to link what they already know about general research concepts (for example, inductive versus deductive approaches, qualitative versus quantitative data) with what they learn here about how cultural anthropologists have used such concepts in their research and also come up with distinct approaches to data collection, analysis, and presentation.

Following these two chapters, the book moves into a consideration of cross-cultural ways of behaving and thinking in many domains from economics to religion. All aspects of life are interrelated and it is often difficult, in real life as well as in scholarly analysis, to separate them. Chapter 3 ("Economies and Their Modes of Production") and Chapter 4 ("Consumption and Exchange") appear at the beginning of the topical chapters as the foundation of culture. Reproduction, or "making people," can be usefully paired with the topic of production, "making a living." Therefore, treatment of reproduction is placed in Chapter 5, "Birth and Death," which immediately follows the two chapters on economics.

The book proceeds to the subject of the human life cycle in cross-cultural perspective (Chapter 6, "Personality and Human Development"), presenting material from the exciting subfield of psychological anthropology. This chapter connects with the introductory psychology courses that many students will have taken. The next chapter in this cluster about "making people" is Chapter 7, "Illness and Healing." A rare chapter in introductory cultural anthropology textbooks, this one will be partic-ularly interesting to the many students who are considering careers in health-related fields.

Next is a series of chapters dealing with various aspects of "people in groups," or social structures, beginning with Chapter 8, "Kinship Dynamics." This chapter incorporates up-to-date research that has enlivened the traditional core area of cultural anthropology. Although traditional categories and definitions are presented, the emphasis is on kinship in action, and on bringing kinship into a more relevant place in cultural anthropology. Chapter 9, "Domestic Groups," looks at how people are arranged into groups for everyday living. Chapter 10, "Social Groups and Social Stratification" widens the lens to examine social groups beyond the domestic situation, including clubs and cooperatives. It also addresses how, in different societies, groups may be arranged hierarchically in relation to one another (for example, in India's caste system). Chapter 11, "Politics, Conflict, and Social Order," presents cross-cultural material on the various forms of political organization and includes more than the usual amount of material on contemporary state-level societies. It also explores the subfield of legal anthropology, an area of interest to preprofessional students considering careers in law and law enforcement.

The next chapters move the reader toward the topics of ideology, belief systems, and values. All the previous chapters have related to belief systems and values in one way or another, but here, the focus becomes explicit, addressing three important subjects: Chapter 12, "Religion"; Chapter 13, "Communication," including verbal language, nonverbal language, and mass media; and Chapter 14, "Expressive Culture," which includes the arts, the representation of culture in museums, play, and leisure.

The final two chapters bring together many of the topics addressed in Chapters 3–14 in their examination of two of the most important aspects of contemporary cultural change: migration and international development. Each chapter is based on the growing body of anthropological data on the infrastructural, structural, and superstructural aspects of these two topics. Chapter 15, "People on the Move," provides insights about categories of migrants and detailed information on the "new immigrants" in North America. Chapter 16, "Development Anthropology" shows how cultural anthropologists have contributed to making international development projects and processes more culturally appropriate and less harmful to local people, especially marginalized indigenous peoples and minorities. Both Chapters 15 and 16 highlight the "action" aspect of cultural anthropology and underline how it can be relevant to policy issues in the contemporary world.

Boxed Features

The pedagogical goals of this book are advanced through the use of distinctive and original boxes. These features show the interconnection of anthropology to other disciplines and to career opportunities. "Food for Thought" questions now conclude the "Multiple Cultural Worlds" boxes and are designed to encourage critical thinking.

Given the book's underlying and pervasive theme of cultural variation and social inequality within and between cultures, **Multiple Cultural Worlds** boxes are used to present material that demonstrates cultural variation and, often, but not always, inequalities by class, race, ethnicity, gender, and age. For example:

- "Globalization and Tomato Production"
- "Cultural Cuing in the Medical Interview"
- "Urban Labour Migration of Girls in Ghana"

The book's commitment to giving students practice in how to think critically is carried out in each chapter through a **Critical Thinking** box. In most of these boxes, students will read about an issue and how it has been interpreted from two different, conflicting perspectives. The students are then asked to consider how the researchers approached the issue, what kind of data they used, and how their conclusions are influenced by their approach. Many of the boxes carry through on the three theoretical issues presented in Chapter 1 as characterizing contemporary cultural anthropology (biological determinism versus cultural constructionism, ideationism versus cultural materialism, and individual agency versus structurism). For example:

- "Adolescent Stress: Biologically Determined or Culturally Constructed?"

In other boxes, students are asked to reflect on "received wisdom" from a new angle:

- "Was the Invention of Agriculture a Terrible Mistake?"

New categories of analysis are introduced and old ones are reassessed:

- "Assessing One's Own Entitlement Bundle"
- "Photography and Anthropology"

The inclusion of "first-person" voices, especially those of minorities, women, and indigenous people emphasizes that the people anthropologists study, even the most marginalized, have their own active voices in which they describe their experiences and express their views. These **Voices** boxes help make the material come alive and add to its relevance. Examples include:

- "Homicide in Canada"
- "A Portugese Woman Trying to Make a Better Life in Toronto"
- "My Algonquin Vocabulary"

In-Text Pedagogy

We have included many pedagogical tools in the book to help students learn and to help teachers teach. Each chapter opens with an outline of the main topics to be covered, including the boxed features. Chapter introductions now include a "preview" paragraph that outlines the broad strokes of each chapter so students see how topics are connected and can navigate through the material more easily.

"The Key Questions" is a new feature located at the beginning of each chapter that identifies the three "key questions" students should keep in mind as they read the chapter. Each chapter concludes with "The Key Questions Revisited," a section that reviews concepts and provides answers to "The Key Questions" in a summary

format. This new feature makes key concepts clearer and more accessible to students.

Another exciting new feature of the second edition is the maps. A two-page map opens the text. In addition, seven locator maps within the text, integrated with the discussions of indigenous peoples and ethnographic material, enable students to locate the cultures discussed within their appropriate geographical contexts.

As in the first Canadian edition, a list of core concepts can be found at the end of each chapter. Each concept is listed along with the page number on which it appears. Concepts appear in boldfaced text throughout the chapter. Finally, each chapter ends with a list of suggested readings.

Supplements for Instructors

Accompanying this text is an array of supplements that will assist instructors in using the book. Contact your local Pearson Education Canada sales representative for information on how to obtain copies of the following items.

Instructor's Manual ISBN 0-205-35693-1

This manual includes teaching tips and classroom exercises that can be used to teach cultural anthropology, and suggestions on how to teach the many cases and examples included in the book.

Test Item File ISBN 0-205-35697-4

The test bank is available in both printed and computerized (TestGen) versions. The computerized version is contained on the Instructor's Resource CD-ROM. The test bank contains multiple choice, true/false, fill-in-the-blank, short answer/identification, and essay questions.

Instructor's Resource CD-ROM
ISBN 0-205-35694-X

The Instructor's Resource CD-ROM collects all of the materials useful to an instructor using *Cultural Anthropology,* Second Canadian Edition, in one place. A computerized version of the printed Test Bank (in TestGen format), PDF files of the Instructor's Manual, a set of graphic images from the text, and a series of PowerPoint® presentations arranged by chapter, can all be found on this one convenient resource.

The PowerPoint presentations for *Cultural Anthropology,* substantially revised for the second Canadian edition, combine graphics and text into chapter-based teaching modules. Using either Macintosh® or DOS/ Windows®, a professor can easily create customized visual presentations for lectures. PowerPoint software is not required to use this program; a PowerPoint viewer is included to access the images. These supplements will also be available on Instructor Central, Pearson Education Canada's online source for instructor resources. This password-protected site can be visited at www.pearsoned.ca/ instructor. First time users will find applying for a password online easy, quick and convenient.

Allyn & Bacon Interactive Video for Cultural Anthropology 2002 ISBN 0-205-34266-3

This five-part custom video introduces key concepts in foundations of cultural anthropology, with 30 video clips for about 90 minutes of viewing. It will help instructors launch lectures, spark classroom discussion, and encourage critical thinking. The video user's guide provides detailed descriptions of each video segment, specific tie-ins to the text, and suggested discussion questions and projects. Available free to adopters (some restrictions may apply).

Allyn & Bacon Video Library

Qualified adopters may select from a wide variety of high-quality videos from such sources as Films for the Humanities and Sciences and Annenberg/CPB. Contact your Pearson Education Canada sales representative for a complete list of videos.

Supplements for Students

FREE CD-ROM

The CD-ROM that accompanies each new copy of *Cultural Anthropology*, Second Canadian Edition, contains complete electronic and searchable PDF files of the text and hundreds of links to Web sites where you can find more information about some of the people, places, concepts, and cultures discussed in the book.

FREE Companion Website

Another innovative learning tool, this Companion Website (www.pearsoned.ca/miller) has been created to enable students to test their understanding of the material in the book. It offers numerous types of exercises and opportunities to monitor their own learning and prepare for class tests. These exercises are self-scoring, giving students instant feedback and results for each quiz.

Study Guide ISBN 0-205-35713-X

This student supplement offers practice quizzes and testing in a traditional printed format so students can test their understanding of key material presented in the text.

iSearch Guide for Anthropology (with Content Select Research Database Access Code)

This tool is designed to help students strengthen their research skills, and to quickly and easily find and cite reliable sources. Powered by EBSCO Information Services, the online database gives you immediate access to all of our journal database collections, conveniently organized by discipline. This guide can be packaged FREE with a new copy of this text. Teachers should contact your Pearson Education Canada sales representative for bookstore order ISBNs.

In Thanks—from Barbara Miller

This book has evolved out of my long relationship with cultural anthropology, which began with the first anthropology course I took as an undergraduate at Syracuse University in 1967. Agehananda Bharati was an important figure in my undergraduate training as were D. Glynn Cochrane, Michael Freedman, and cultural geographer David Sopher. Since then, and especially beginning with the writing of my dissertation, my theoretical perspectives have been most deeply influenced by the work of anthropologists Marvin Harris, Jack Goody, G. William Skinner, and economist Ester Boserup. My research in India has been enriched especially by the work of Pauline Kolenda, Stanley Tambiah, Gerry Berreman, and Sylvia Vatuk. The list of my many other favorite writers within and beyond anthropology is too long to include here, but much of their work is woven into the book.

Four anthropologists carefully reviewed drafts of the first edition of the book, and I will always be grateful to them for their contribution: Elliot Fratkin (Smith College), Maxine Margolis (University of Florida), Russell Reid (University of Louisville), and Robert Trotter II (University of Arizona). Their words of praise were just as welcome. By pointing out positive features of the book, they helped a sometimes discouraged author regain strength and continue writing and revising. Several other anthropologists offered comments about how I should revise this edition: William W. Donner, Kutztown University; Ed Robbins, University of Wisconsin; Leslie Lischka,

Maryhurst University; Diane Baxter, University of Oregon; Charles R. de Burlo, The University of Vermont; Wesley Shumar, Drexel University; and Katrina Worley, Folson Lake College. I have tried my best to incorporate their advice without sacrificing the original spirit of the book.

During the several years of research and writing for this book, many anthropologists have provided invaluable comments, encouragement, and even photographs, including Lila Abu-Lughod, Vincanne Adams, Catherine Allen, Joseph Alter, Donald Attwood, Christopher Baker, Nancy Benco, Marc Bermann, Alexia Bloch, Lynne Bolles, John Bowen, Don Brenneis, Alison Brooks, D. Glynn Cochrane, Jeffery Cohen, Carole Counihan, Liza Dalby, Loring Danforth, Patricia Delaney, Timothy Earle, Elliot Fratkin, Martin Fusi, David Gow, Curt Grimm, Richard Grinker, Daniel Gross, Marvin Harris, Michael Herzfeld, Barry Hewlett, Michael Horowitz, Robert Humphrey, Anstice Justin, Laurel Kendall, David Kideckel, Dorinne Kondo, Conrad Kottak, Ruth Krulfeld, Joel Kuipers, Takie Lebra, David Lempert, Lamont Lindstrom, Samuel Martínez, Catherine McCoid, Leroy McDermott, Jerry Milanich, Kirin Narayan, Sarah Nelson, Gananath Obeyesekere, Ellen Oxfeld, Hanna Papanek, Deborah Pellow, Gregory Possehl, Joanne Rappaport, Jennifer Robertson, Nicole Sault, Joel Savishinsky, Nancy Scheper-Hughes, Richard Shweder, Chunghee Soh, Martha Ward, James (Woody) Watson, Rubie Watson, Van Yasek, and Kevin Yelvington.

Many others have made important contributions to this book: Avery Andrews, Nathan Brown, Cynthia Deitch, Frances Gouda, Cynthia Harrison, Christopher Heaton, Cornelia Mayer Herzfeld, Alf Hiltebeitel, Jonathan Higman, James Hoag, Edward Keller III, Roshani Kothari, Lester Lefton, Craig Linebaugh, John Logsdon, Neal Oxenhandler, Gary Price, Jon Rohde, Carol Sigelman, Samuel Skogstad, Stanley Stevens, and Jeff Weinstein. These people, and no doubt many more whom I have failed to name, were helpful in a variety of ways, from offering periodic supportive comments to providing critiques of certain sections and sending material and photographs to include in the book.

Harry Harding, Dean of the Elliott School of International Affairs at the George Washington University, has helped my involvement with this book from its beginning by counting it as a valid research activity for a faculty member in his School and by allocating research assistance to me each year. My several assistants have tracked down library material and done reference checking: Joseph Mineiro, Han Quyen Thi Tran, Hena Khan, Omar McDoom and most recently, Carolyn Walkley, whose careful work and continuing good cheer saw me through this revision. The staff in the Elliott School dean's office, especially my executive assistant Ryan Matsuno, along with Karen Turney and Jennifer Lerner, have sent faxes, mailed packages, commented with humor on the first draft figures of "the head" when we tried to combine both tongue positions in one figure (see Chapter 13), and generally kept things bouyant even under stressful times.

My students have always been a key source of inspiration. In addition, students—far too many to name here—in my introductory cultural anthropology classes at George Washington University have provided helpful comments about aspects of the first edition and have offered corrections and additions to specific areas. They seem to enjoy and benefit from looking at cultural anthropology from a "critical thinking" perspective, thus giving me hope that this approach does indeed work. I thank them for their support and comments.

Sylvia Shepard, my development editor for the first edition, was a crucial factor in making this book happen. I can say with surety that, without Sylvia, this book would not exist. For this second edition, I was fortunate in being able to work with Lisa McLellan, editor at Allyn & Bacon, whose intelligent eye and deft editorial hand guided the revision process in a fruitful way. Series Editor Jennifer Jacobson has succeeded in making a smooth transition from her predecessor, Sarah Kelbaugh. Jennifer was a calm and helpful presence during the revision and production stages of this edition. The book's copy editor and "packager," Kathy Smith, provided her keen insights for editorial improvement of the text and a knack for discovering photographs to fit my sometimes bizarre-seeming specifications. Allyn & Bacon has, in all, provided a great home for me and my work. At the very "top" of the organizational hierarchy is Bill Barke, who has become a friend (and, simultaneously, one of my toughest critics) and I have enjoyed dinners with him and his wife Vicky when they are in Washington. An extra plus was the joy of having his daughter, Amber, in my introductory anthropology class in Fall 2001.

Bernard Wood has, for some time, been an indispensable daily support and source of perspective, with his wry sense of humor, on my writing and on life in general.

I also thank "the Millers"—my parents, siblings, aunts and uncles and nieces and nephews—for their interest and support throughout the years of the writing and revising. The same applies to "the Heatons"—my former in-laws, including parents-in-law, brothers- and sisters-in-law, and nieces and nephews. I thank my son, Jack Heaton, for being an inspiration to my writing, a superb traveling companion on our trip around the world with the Semester at Sea Program in 1996, and a delicately effective critic of my (occasional) excesses in thinking. This book is dedicated to him.

Barbara D. Miller
Washington, DC

In Thanks—from Penny and John Van Esterik

The task of Canadianizing Miller was made possible by our being situated in York University's very vibrant department of anthropology. Students and colleagues generously provided references, suggestions, words of wisdom, and warning; we thank them all, and are particularly grateful for the assistance of Naomi Adelson, Saul Cohen, Ruth King, Priti Kohli, Wendy Lawrence, Ken Little, David Lumsden, Kathy M'Closkey, Margaret MacDonald, Beth McGuire, Lynne Milgram, Lynn Morrison, Debra Pelletier, Lynne Phillips, Margaret Rodman, Andrea Walsh, and Daphne Winland.

At Pearson Education Canada, we would like to thank Jessica Mosher, Executive Editor, for pursuing this project, and selecting us for the undertaking. We thank Matthew Christian, Developmental Editor, for his patient efforts to keep us on schedule and focused, Claudia Forgas, for her careful copy editing, and Joe Zingrone, Cheryl Jackson and Wendy Moran for integrating all the pieces into an outstanding product. We would also like to thank Judith Allen, Senior Marketing Manager, for directing our marketing campaign, and the members of the sales team, who have given this project such support.

We are most grateful to the reviewers who made valuable suggestions during the process of preparing the second Canadian edition. Thank you to Douglass Drozdow–St. Christian of the University of Western Ontario, Deborah Woodman of the University of Guelph, Nadia Ferrara of McGill University, Lisa Mitchell of the University of Victoria and Marjorie Mitchell also of the University of Victoria. We regret the inevitable errors of omission and commission. Some of these we have been able to correct in this second Canadian edition.

Penny and John Van Esterik

Location of Places Discussed in This Text

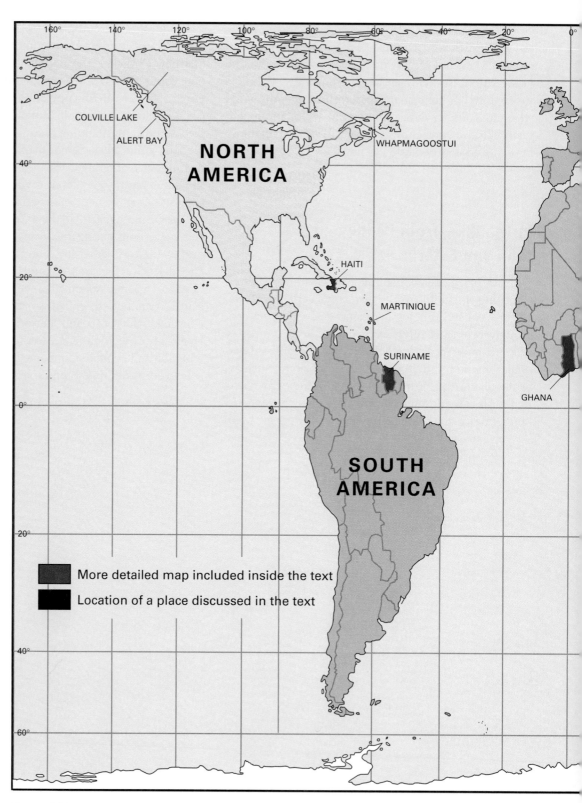

Source: This map was prepared for *Cultural Anthropology*, Second Canadian Edition. Map projection from *Peters Atlas of the World* (1990).

ASIA

OMAN

BAAN
NAA
SAKAE

TAMIL
NADU

MAYOTTE ISLAND

PAPUA
NEW GUINEA

IRIAN JAYA

TROBRIAND ISLANDS

AUSTRALIA

ANTARCTICA

ope

RICA

Chapter 1

Anthropology and the Study of Culture

CHAPTER OUTLINE

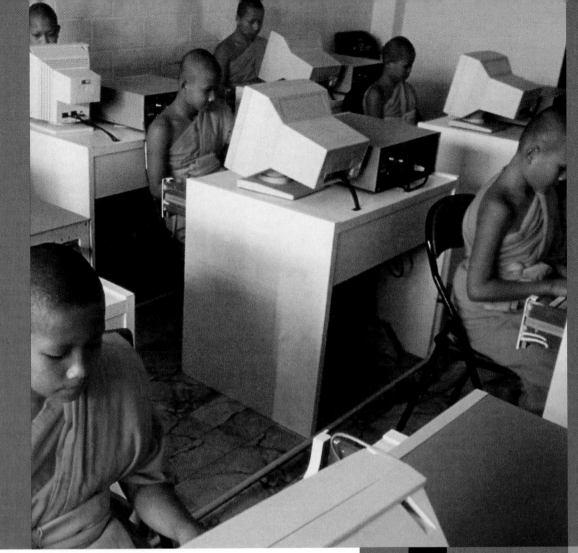

Education for Buddhist monks and novices in Thailand now involves learning to use a computer in addition to studying religious scriptures.

Key Questions

What is anthropology?

What is cultural anthropology?

What is culture?

The turn of the millennium brought a heightened awareness of the influence of globalization, a process of intensified economic and political connections among all nations that affects all people. Globalization increases the need for understanding human diversity and unity. It is hard to believe that in 1980, the terms HIV and AIDS didn't exist, yet now we are in the second generation of people afflicted with HIV/AIDS.

Old bones, Jurassic Park, cannibalism, hidden treasure, Indiana Jones and the Temple of Doom. In North America, the popular impression of anthropology is based mainly on movies and television shows that depict anthropologists as adventurers and heroes. Many anthropologists do have adventures, and some discover treasures such as ancient pottery, medicinal plants, and jade carvings. But most of their research is less than glorious, involving repetitive and tedious activities. What do anthropologists do, and why do people study anthropology?

This chapter offers an overview of general anthropology, an academic discipline devoted to the study of human life throughout history and in all its variations. General anthropology encompasses several subareas, or fields. After a brief overview of each field, we turn to the field that is the focus of this book: cultural anthropology, the study of *culture,* learned and shared patterns of behaviour and beliefs. We then examine cultural differences and ways to understand such differences. This chapter also explains the various characteristics of culture, and how culture relates to nature but is not the same as

nature. Class, race, gender, and other bases of cultural identity are introduced as important factors that will receive attention throughout this book.

The Fields of General Anthropology

Most anthropologists agree that the discipline of anthropology, or general anthropology, is divided into four fields:

- archaeology (or prehistory);
- physical anthropology (or biological anthropology);
- linguistic anthropology; and
- cultural anthropology (or social anthropology).

Most anthropologists say that training in anthropology ideally should involve knowledge in all four fields and awareness of the linkages between them because of anthropology's broad goal of understanding human behaviour and cultural change. In much of Europe and in countries whose educational systems were influenced by European colonialism, the term "anthropology" usually includes only the subject matter of socio-cultural anthropology.

Other anthropologists contend that the four-field approach is no longer relevant and should be abandoned. The sheer amount of knowledge in the various fields has increased over time, and apparently greater differences in theory, methods, and subject matter have emerged, making interchange across fields less frequent or useful. At least two Canadian universities have split their departments into anthropology and archaeology. About one-third of the departments of anthropology in Canada include the four subfields within one department, and most espouse in principle the ideal of four-field interchange. Linguistics is most likely to be omitted, reflecting the British university pattern of considering linguistics outside the scope of anthropology (Darnell 1998). The distinctly Canadian triad of archaeology, ethnology, and folklore may have its roots in government-supported museums rather than American departments of anthropology (Preston 1983:288). The following section provides a brief description of each field.

Primatologist Dian Fossey interacts with a gorilla during fieldwork in Rwanda.

Archaeology

This field is devoted to studying the life-ways of past cultures by examining material remains. Data include stone and bone tools, skeletal material, remains of buildings, and refuse such as pot shards (broken pieces of pottery) and coprolites (fossilized fecal matter). Since its beginnings in the mid-eighteenth century, archaeology has contributed knowledge about towns and villages, as well as the emergence of the great early states of Egypt, Phoenicia, the Indus Valley, and Mexico. New research is questioning some previous conclusions about "kingdoms." For example, excavations at a royal burial site of the Old Silla Kingdom of Korea, which extended from 57 BCE (Before Common Era) to 668 CE (Common Era), reveal that queens were often the rulers (Nelson 1993). This finding challenges the earlier generalization that centralized state systems always involve male political dominance.

An example of a relatively new area of research is archaeologists' examination of European colonialism and its impact on pre-colonial states (Graham 1998). In the Maya area, for example, where an interest in the civilization of the Classic Maya period has dominated research, archaeologists have documented intensive occupation from the time of the so-called Maya collapse, in the ninth century, to the end of the seventeenth century (Pendergast, Jones, and Graham 1993). This long sequence has enabled them to chart the changes that took place as the Spanish administrators and priests colonized the Maya world, and the result has been documentation of the continuity of cultural, social, and technological traditions from the ancient past to the modern times.

The archaeology of the recent past is another new research direction; an example is the "Garbage Project," which is being conducted by archaeologists at the University of Arizona at Tucson (Rathje and Murphy 1992). The "Garbage Archaeologists" are excavating the Fresh Kills landfill on Staten Island, near New York City. Its mass is estimated at over 90 million tonnes and its volume at 82 million cubic metres. Thus, it is one of the largest human-made structures in North America. Through excavation of artifacts such as pop-top can tabs, disposable diapers, cosmetic containers, and telephone books, the Garbage Archaeologists are learning about recent consumption patterns. These findings also provide lessons for the future. They reveal how long it takes for contemporary goods to decompose. Urban planners and other people interested in recycling may be surprised to learn that the kinds of garbage that people often blame for filling up landfills, such as fast-food packaging, polystyrene foam, and disposable diapers, are less serious problems than paper. Paper, especially newspaper, is the major culprit because of sheer quantity. This kind of information can help improve recycling efforts in North America.

Physical or Biological Anthropology

In seeking to understand human variation, adaptation, and change, physical anthropologists study many forms of life, human and nonhuman, past and present. This field deals with topics ranging from evolutionary theory to the human fossil record and the identification of human skeletal remains from crime scenes and accidents (Park 1996:vii). Genetics, anatomy, animal and human behavior, ecology, nutrition, and forensics are subject areas included in this field. Many physical anthropologists do research on animals other than humans in order to understand human origins or to use them as models for understanding contemporary human behaviour.

Within physical anthropology, the subfield of primatology is focused on studies of nonhuman primates and how their behaviour compares with that of human primates. Primatologists are well known for their pioneering work in studying nonhuman primates in their natural habitats (see the Multiple Cultural Worlds box). Jane Goodall's (1971, 1986) research on Tanzanian chimpanzees revealed rich details about their social relationships. Linda Fedigan (1992) has shown how females play significant roles in the social structure of primate groups, and provided a feminist critique of theories of primate and human evolution.

Physical anthropologists share many research interests with archaeologists, given their study of evidence from the past. One such area is the question of when human beings first emerged as *Homo sapiens*. An early population named the Neanderthals, dated about 130 000–30 000 years ago, are at the centre of this question. Some experts consider them the earliest humans ever discovered. Others say that they should not be considered *Homo sapiens*. The fossils are from a skull cap found in 1856 in Germany's Neander Valley (Park 1996:233). Key features that support the "humanness" of Neanderthals include large cranial capacity (skull size); evidence of tool making and tool use; and the ability to think symbolically, as suggested by burial of the dead, sometimes with offerings such as animal bones, tools, and maybe flowers. But differences are also notable. The Neanderthals' foreheads are sloped, the back of the skull is bulging, and brow ridges are large. Arguments about "humanness" rest on which features are more important and should carry more weight. One conclusion is that it is impossible to draw a hard-and-fast line between humans and prehumans because humans evolved gradually over millions of years: There was no "moment in time" when "modern humans" sprang forth from our primate ancestors.

Another area linking physical anthropology with archaeology is paleopathology, the study of diseases in prehistoric times. Analysis of trace elements in bones, such as strontium, provides surprisingly detailed information

Biruté Galdikas and the Orangutans of Borneo

Primatologist Biruté Galdikas first went to Indonesia to study orangutans in 1971 (Galdikas 1995). She soon became aware of the threat to the orangutans from local people who, as a way of making a lot of money, capture them for sale to zoos around the world. These poachers separate the young from their mothers, often killing the mothers in the process. Sometimes local police locate and reclaim these captured orphans. They try to return them to the rain forest, but the transition into an unknown niche is extremely difficult and many do not survive.

Orangutan juveniles are highly dependent on their mothers, maintaining close bodily contact with them for at least two years and nursing until they are eight. Because of this long period of orangutans' need for maternal contact, Biruté set up her camp to serve as a way station for orphans and she became the maternal figure. Biruté's first "infant" was an orphaned orang, Sugito, who clung to her like its own mother for years.

Biruté Galdikas's intense involvement with the orangutans and her lengthy stays in Indonesia affected her personal life, especially her marriage and family life. She and first husband, Rod Brindamour, raised their son, Binti, with orangs for friends instead of humans. He had no human companions his own age during most of his childhood. While Binti was still a child, Rod fell in love with Binti's Indonesian babysitter and he, she, and Binti moved to Canada. There, Binti could at least have human friends. Biruté Galdikas visited him every year when she went to Canada to teach anthropology at Simon Fraser University in Vancouver. Biruté subsequently fell in love with and married Pak Bohap, an Indonesian man of the Dyak tribe. She and he and their children live at Camp Leakey. In order to try to gain some distance from the orangutans and find some privacy at Camp Leakey, they have discouraged orangutans from coming into the house and dining hall. But they are still prominent features of everyday life. If you visit, you may walk along a path and suddenly find yourself hand-in-hand with an orangutan.

Due to extensive logging and mining, in addition to poaching, orangutans in Borneo are in serious danger of becoming extinct. Biruté Galdikas is focusing her efforts on preventing this from happening. She says, "I feel like I'm viewing an animal holocaust and holocaust is not a word I use lightly... The destruction of the tropical rainforest is accelerating daily. And if orangutans go

Biruté Galdikas in Indonesia. She has been studying the orangutans for over three decades and is an active supporter of conservation of their habitat.

extinct in the wild, paradise is gone" (Dreifus 2000:D3). Like Biruté Galdikas, many primatologists and other anthropologists and environmentalists find themselves as guardians of preservation, a position that may put them in direct conflict with local people whose interests, such as those of the Indonesian poachers, lie in other directions.

FOOD FOR THOUGHT

What are some of the ethical, personal, and culutrsal consequences of long-term fieldwork conducted far from home?

about the diets, activities, and health of prehistoric people, including whether they were primarily meat eaters or vegetarians and how their diets affected their health. Marks on bones provide information on changing work patterns; for example, skeletons of nineteenth-century voyageurs from a fur trade post in Alberta show evidence of arthritis of the spine, shoulder, and elbow, and robust muscle attachments compatible with paddling heavy freight canoes (Lovell and Lai 1994). We can also learn age at death, age at birth of first child for a woman, and birth rate per woman. Data from several time periods provide clues about how the transition to agriculture altered people's health and longevity (M. N. Cohen 1989; Cohen and Armelagos 1984; Cohen and Bennett 1993).

Linguistic Anthropology

Linguistic anthropology explores the relation between culture and language, mainly, but not exclusively, among humans. It is integral to cultural anthropology since language is the primary means for transmitting culture. How we classify relatives, honour our ancestors, and describe beauty make visible beliefs and values. Descriptive linguistics examines the structure of languages, while historical linguistics traces the origin and development of related languages, and how they change through time. Sociolinguistics explores the relation between language and social interaction.

Early philologists such as Horatio Hale (1817–1896), who worked with the elders in the Six Nations Reserve near Brantford, Ontario, in the 1870s, recorded and analyzed disappearing First Nations languages, concluding, for example, that Tutelo was related to Siouan language stock, that Mohawk was the senior language of the original Five Nations, and that Huron was nearer proto-Iroquoian than Mohawk. Today, most "disappearing" languages have either been recorded or lost, and most previously unwritten languages have been transferred into written form. Because language change goes on all the time, anthropologists document and analyze what kinds of changes are occurring and why. Many changes are related to politics and conflict worldwide. For example, in Moldova, a former Soviet republic, speakers of Russian and Ukrainian in eastern Moldova have been in conflict since 1992 over the official language policy of Moldova. Instead of having a shrinking area of study, linguistic anthropology is broadening its scope to include many aspects of communication such as the media, electronic mail, popular music, and advertising. These new research directions connect linguistic anthropology with psychology, journalism, television and radio, education, and marketing.

Cultural Anthropology

Cultural anthropology is devoted to studying how cultures differ from or resemble one another, and why, and how different cultures influence each other. (The debates around the meaning of culture, the "core concept" in cultural anthropology, are reviewed in detail in the next section, pages 15–20. Ultimately, cultural anthropology decentres us from our own cultures, teaching us to look at ourselves from the "outside" as somewhat "strange." Melford Spiro (1990) aptly asserts that the work of anthropology is to "make the strange familiar and the familiar strange." A good example of "making the familiar strange" is the case of the Nacirema, who were first described in 1956:

> They are a North American group living in the territory between the Canadian Cree, the Yaqui and the Tarahumare of Mexico, and the Carib and the Arawak of the Antilles. Little is known of their origin, though tradition states that they came from the east. According to Nacirema mythology, their nation was originated by a culture hero, Notgnihsaw, who is otherwise known for two great feats of strength—the throwing of a piece of wampum across the river Pa-To-Mac and the chopping down of a cherry tree in which the Spirit of Truth resided. (Miner 1965 [1956]:415)

The anthropologist goes on to describe the unusually intense focus of Nacirema culture on the human body, its beauty, and its wide variety of private and personal rituals. He gives a detailed account of one ritual that is performed daily within the homes at a specially constructed shrine area:

> The focal point of the shrine is a box or chest which is built into the wall. In this chest are kept the many charms and magical potions without which no native believes he could live. These preparations are secured from a variety of specialized practitioners. The most powerful of these are the medicine men, whose assistance must be rewarded with substantial gifts.... Beneath the charm box is a small font. Each day every member of the family, in succession,

enters the shrine room, bows his head before the charm box, mingles different sorts of holy water in the font, and proceeds with a brief rite of ablution. (415–416)

If you don't know this tribe, try spelling its name backwards! (One note: Please forgive Miner for his use of the masculine pronoun in describing Nacirema society in general; his writings are now about a half-century old.)

Cultural anthropology encompasses all aspects of human behaviour and beliefs. Its subject matter includes making a living and distributing goods and services, reproduction and group formation, political patterns, religious systems, forms of communication, and expressive aspects of culture such as art, dance, and music. In addition, cultural anthropologists consider how change occurs in all of these areas.

Applied Anthropology: Separate Field or Crosscutting Focus?

Applied anthropology, or practising anthropology, involves the use or application of anthropological knowledge to help solve social problems. Richard Salisbury (1983), who developed applied anthropology at McGill University in Montreal, saw applied work as the growth point of anthropology in Canada, and trained many Canadian anthropologists to put their research to practice in fields such as Native land claims, health care, and ethnic diversity. Active engagement with First Nations peoples and rural communities characterized the work of Francophone anthropologists in the 1960s. Many anthropologists in small colleges and universities engaged in community-based applied research. One of the defining features of Canadian anthropology is the integration of basic and applied research. From the earliest work of nineteenth-century ethnologists to the expert witnesses in current land claim issues, we find the widely shared assumption that anthropological research should not be morally or ethically neutral (Darnell 1998:155). Advocacy roles, however, require sensitivity to complex moral and political contexts.

Application of knowledge to help solve particular social problems is, and should be, part of all four fields. Just like theory, application is a valid aspect of every branch of the discipline. Many archaeologists in Canada are employed, for example, in Cultural Resource Management (CRM), undertaking professional assessments of possible archaeological remains before construction projects such as roads and buildings can proceed. Physical anthropology has many applied aspects. For example, forensic anthropologists participate in criminal investigations through labwork identifying bodily remains. Others work in the area of primate conservation (see Multiple Cultural Worlds box). Applied linguistic anthropologists consult with educational institutions about how to improve standardized tests for bilingual populations, or they may do policy research for governments. Development anthropology refers to an aspect of applied anthropology concerned with how so-called developing countries change and how knowledge in anthropology can play a role in formulating and implementing more appropriate kinds of change.

Many anthropologists are concerned that applied anthropology should be addressing more directly and with greater force the effects of globalization, particularly some of its negative consequences such as the increasing wealth gap between powerful industrialized countries and less powerful, less industrialized countries (Hackenberg 2000). This need takes anthropologists in a challenging direction since it involves the study of global-local interactions and change over time, both important parts of cultural anthropology's focus. Moreover, it asks that cultural anthropologists abandon an attitude of non-involvement in change. One anthropologist goes so far as to state, "Can anthropology in the 21st century be anything except applied anthropology?" (Cleveland 2000:373).

Cultural Anthropology's Distinctive Features

Several features of cultural anthropology have traditionally distinguished it from other disciplines. Scholars in other disciplines, however, have been adopting anthropological approaches. Thus, while cultural anthropology's traditional characteristic features may no longer be unique to the field, they are still part of its identity and character.

Ethnography and Ethnology

Cultural anthropologists approach the study of contemporary human life in two basic ways. The first is in-depth study of one culture. This approach, **ethnography**, meaning "culture writing," provides a first-hand, detailed description of a living culture based on personal observation. Ethnography is usually presented in the form of a full-length book. It is based on experiences gained by going to the place of study and living there for an extended period. As cultural anthropologist Richard Shweder says,

> An ethnography begins with an ethnographic experience: with your eyes open you have to go somewhere.... The first thing that strikes an anthropologist in the field are details that seem alien. It is April 5, 6 A.M., 90 degrees Fahrenheit, and I'm in a remote region of India on a tennis court fashioned out of the earth of termite mounds. Music, cacophonous to a foreign ear, is blaring over a loudspeaker. In India, the gods and ancestral spirits, who are not hard of hearing but are sometimes a long way off, not only like to eat food offerings, they also like to be entertained. To a foreigner for whom the gods don't exist, in the midst of a tennis match at six in the morning on a very hot day, the magnified blare is a nuisance. After two sets my Indian doubles partner finally takes off his heavy wool sweater. (1986:1, 38)

In the first part of the twentieth century, early ethnographers wrote about "exotic" cultures located far from the homes of European and North American anthropologists. Classics of this phase of ethnography include A. R. Radcliffe-Brown's *The Andaman Islanders* (1964 [1922]), a study of people living on a group of small islands off the coast of Burma; Bronislaw Malinowski's *Argonauts of the Western Pacific* (1961 [1922]), concerning a complex trade network linking several islands in the South Pacific; and Reo Fortune's *Sorcerers of Dobu* (1959 [1932]), which describes a culture in the Western Pacific islands, with a focus on its social and religious characteristics. Although early Canadian ethnographies were not considered classics, it is interesting that the mammoth ethnography, *The Bella Coola Indians* by T. F. McIlwraith, the first professional anthropologist to hold an academic position at a Canadian University, was ready in draft form in 1925, but not published until 1948 because the editors judged the material to be obscene (Barker 1987).

For several decades, ethnographers tended to treat a particular tribal group or village as a bounded unit. The era of "village studies" in the ethnography of India, extending from the 1950s through the 1960s, is an example of this trend. Dozens of anthropologists went to India for fieldwork, and each typically studied in one village and then wrote an ethnography describing that village. These anthropologists were inspired by the perspective of **holism**, the view that says cultures consist of integrated features such as economy and religion and one must study all of the features to have a complete picture. Examples of village studies include Adrian Mayer's *Caste and Kinship in Central India* (1960), S. C. Dube's *Indian Village* (1967), and Gerald Berreman's *Hindus of the Himalayas* (1963). The topics of concern were caste, agricultural practices, kinship, and religion. Little attention was given to exploring links between villages, or to determining the effects of world forces such as nineteenth-century colonialism or twentieth-century post-colonialism on the villagers' lives. Berreman's book is an exception. It includes a detailed chapter on "The Outside World: Urban Contact and Government Programs."

Recent ethnographies, from 1980 onward, differ from earlier ethnographies in several ways. First, they are more likely to treat local cultures as embedded within regional and global forces. Francis Henry's *Victims and Neighbors: A Small Town in Nazi Germany Remembered* (1984) examines social relations between Jews and Christians in a town in Germany where Henry grew up during the 1930s. The ethnography combines intensive interviews in 1979 about events in the 1930s to document acts of kindness in the context of state-encouraged hatred. This study demonstrates the importance of local context in understanding events of global importance such as World War II. Second, many contemporary ethnographies are focused on one topic of interest and avoid a more holistic approach. Cultural anthropologists in this category feel that holism is an impossible goal, since no one can perceive cultures from all their complex angles (see the Voices box). A third trend is expanded interest in incorporating attention to history. Philip Gulliver and Marilyn Silverman's *Merchants and Shopkeepers: A Historical Anthropology of an Irish Market Town* (1995) examines a town in southeast Ireland that has been a site of commerce for nearly 800 years. As a regional trade centre, the location provides an opportunity to analyze shopkeeping and entrepreneurial strategies over a long duration. A fourth trend is for an increasing number of ethnographic studies to be situated in Western, industrialized cultures. Philippe Bourgois's research in East Harlem in New York City for his book *In Search of Respect: Selling Crack in El Barrio* (1995) explores how people in one neighbourhood cope with poverty and dangerous living conditions. Daniel Wolf's research on a biker gang in Alberta, *The Rebels: A Brotherhood of Outlaw Bikers* (1991) provides another example of urban ethnographic work close to home.

While these topics may superficially resemble something that a sociologist might study, the approach of a cultural anthropologist provides a unique perspective that is more richly detailed from the everyday perspective of the people.

Many factors explain these new trends in ethnography, including the expanded number of anthropologists seeking research topics and areas of theoretical importance; social changes in the world that provide new topics for study; varying strengths and interests of anthropology doctoral programs that shape the theoretical and regional focus of their students; and trends in funding institutions' interests and budgetary priorities.

Richard Lee (left) asks several Ju/wasi men about food plants of the Kalahari desert in Botswana. This photograph was taken in 1968.

In contrast to ethnography, **ethnology** is cross-cultural analysis, or the study of a particular topic in more than one culture using ethnographic material. Ethnologists have compared such topics as marriage

James Peacock, "Holism: Impossible but Necessary"

James Peacock, cultural anthropologist and former president of the American Anthropological Association, is a professor at the University of North Carolina at Chapel Hill.

> Holism is an important but impossible ideal. You cannot see everywhere or think everything. You must select and emphasize. To do this, you must categorize and make distinctions. Only in this way can you analyze and understand.
>
> In the physical world, it is relatively easy to do this. Here is a house, there is a road... We can describe the size of the house (so many square or cubic feet), the size of the land (so many acres), and the length of the road (so many miles). We could even analyze the ratio of one measurement to another if we found that useful... When we try to dissect human experience this way, we run into trouble [because] culture is not a physical thing but an attitude, or way of viewing the world... We can describe indications of a certain cultural pattern—people hurrying or loitering as clues to their assumptions about time, for example—but culture itself is an abstraction that we make based on such indications. There is nothing wrong with an abstraction as long as we recognize it for what it is. But inevitably we are tempted to treat the abstraction as a thing. (1986:19–20)

FOOD FOR THOUGHT

If holism is impossible, should cultural anthropologists relinquish it as an ideal?

forms, economic practices, religious beliefs, and child-rearing practices in order to examine patterns of similarity and variation and possible causes for them.

Ethnography and ethnology are closely linked endeavours. Ethnographic studies provide in-depth information that can be compared with other ethnographic reports to reveal more general theoretical issues. These questions in turn demand further ethnographic research.

Cultural Relativism

Most people grow up thinking that their culture is the way of life and that other ways of life are strange, perhaps even inferior. Other cultures may even be considered less than human. Cultural anthropologists have labelled this attitude **ethnocentrism:** judging other cultures by the standards of one's own culture rather than by the standards of that particular culture. Ethnocentric views have fuelled centuries of efforts at changing "other" people in the world, sometimes in the guise of religious missionizing and sometimes in the form of secular colonial domination. Looking back to the era of European colonial expansion beginning in the fifteenth century, it is clear that exploration and conquest were intended to extract wealth from the colonies. In addition to plundering their colonies, the Europeans also imposed their culture on indigenous groups. The British poet Rudyard Kipling reflected the dominant view when he said that it was "the white man's burden" to spread British culture throughout the world. Christian missionaries played a major role in European attempts to transform non-Christian cultures into a European model. Many contemporary Western powers hold similar attitudes, making foreign policy decisions that encourage the adoption of Western economic, political, and social systems.

The opposite of ethnocentrism is **cultural relativism,** the idea that each culture must be understood in terms of the values and beliefs of that culture and should not be judged by the standards of another culture. Cultural relativism assumes that no culture is better than any other. How does a person gain a sense of cultural relativism? Besides living with other people, ways to develop a sense of cultural relativism include travelling, especially extended periods of study abroad, taking a course such as this, eating different foods, listening to music from Appalachia or Brazil, reading novels by authors from other cultures, making friends who are "different" from you, and exploring the multicultural world on your campus. In sum, exposure to "other" ways, with a sympathetic eye and ear to appreciating differences, is the key.

Can a person ever completely avoid being ethnocentric? The answer is probably no, because we start learning about other cultures from the position of the one we know first. Even the most sensitive person who has spent a long time living within another culture still carries an original imprint of her or his native culture. As much as we might say that we think we are viewing Culture B from the inside (as if we were natives of Culture B), that is a logical impossibility because everything about Culture B—the language, dress, food habits, social organization, work habits, leadership patterns, and religion—was learned in relation to or in comparison with what we already knew about Culture A.

One way that many anthropologists have interpreted cultural relativism is to use **absolute cultural relativism,** which says that whatever goes on in a particular culture must not be questioned or changed because no one has the right to question any behaviour or idea anywhere—it would be ethnocentric to do so. The position of absolute cultural relativism can lead, however, in dangerous directions. Consider the example of the Holocaust during World War II in which millions of Jews and other minorities in much of Eastern and Western Europe were killed as part of the German Nazis' Aryan supremacy campaign. The absolute cultural relativist position becomes boxed in, logically, to saying that since the Holocaust was undertaken according to the values of the culture, outsiders have no business questioning it. Can anyone feel truly comfortable with such a position?

Critical cultural relativism offers an alternative view that poses questions about cultural practices and ideas in terms of who accepts them and why, and who they might be harming or helping. In terms of the Nazi Holocaust, a critical cultural relativist would ask, "Whose culture supported the values that killed millions of people on the grounds of racial purity?" Not the cultures of the Jews, Gypsies, and other victims. It was the culture of Aryan supremacists, who were one subgroup among many. The situation was far more complex than a simple absolute cultural relativist statement takes into account because there was not "one" culture and its values involved. Rather, it was a case of **cultural imperialism,** in which one dominant group claims supremacy over minority cultures and proceeds to change the situation in its own interests and at the expense of the other cultures.

By taking a close look at a practice or value attributed to a "culture," critical cultural relativism recognizes oppressors and victims, winners and losers, and struggles over practices and values within particular cases. Critical cultural relativism is situated within the general framework of cultural relativism in which we try to view all cultures empathetically from the inside. A growing number of cultural anthropologists seek to critique (meaning to probe underlying power interests, not just to come up with negative comments as in the general usage of the term criticism) the behaviour and values of groups from the standpoint of some set of more or less generally agreed-on human rights. As prominent French anthropologist Claude Lévi-Strauss commented, "No society is perfect" (1968:385), even when considered from what that society claims as moral values. While considering the "imperfections" of any and all cultures, cultural anthropologists should examine and discuss their own biases, and then try to treat all cultures equally. This means looking equally critically at all cultures—their own and those of "others."

Valuing and Sustaining Diversity

Most anthropologists value and are committed to cultural diversity just as environmentalists value and are committed to biological diversity. Anthropologists contribute to the preservation of cultural diversity and knowledge by describing cultures as they have existed, as they now exist, and as they change. Many have become activists in the area of cultural survival. Since 1972, an organization named Cultural Survival has been working with indigenous people and ethnic minorities to deal as equals in their interactions with industrial society. As printed on the inside cover of their publication *Cultural Survival Quarterly* (1998), Cultural Survival's guiding principle is as follows:

> We insist that cultural differences are inherent in humanity; protecting this human diversity enriches our common earth. Yet in the name of development and progress, native peoples lose their land, their natural resources, and control over their lives. The consequences often are disease, destitution, and despair—and war and environmental damage for us all. The destruction is not inevitable.

To that end, Cultural Survival sponsors programs to assist indigenous peoples and ethnic minorities to help themselves in protecting and managing natural resources, claiming and reclaiming land rights, and diversifying their means of livelihood. We will return to these issues in the last chapter of this book.

Contemporary Debates

Within cultural anthropology, enduring theoretical debates both divide the discipline and provide threads that give it coherence. Contemporary theoretical approaches include cultural materialism, interpretive, symbolic, and political ecology, neo-Marxism, and postmodernism. Although different departments of anthropology in Canada tend to have specific theoretical orientations, Canadian anthropologists in general tend to avoid extremely deterministic interpretations of human behaviour. They seek to explain difference as well as similarity, and address questions that crosscut theoretical (and national) borders. Three important contemporary debates, explained briefly here, will resurface throughout the book. Each is concerned with cultural anthropology's basic question of why people behave and think the way they do.

Biological Determinism versus Cultural Constructionism **Biological determinism** gives priority to such biological features as people's genes and hormones in explaining human behaviour and ideas. Thus, biological determinists search for the gene or hormone that might lead to certain forms of behaviour such as homicide, alcoholism, or adolescent stress (see the Critical Thinking box and the Voices box). They also examine cultural practices in terms of how they contribute to the "reproductive success of the species," or how they contribute to the gene pool of subsequent generations through promoting the numbers of surviving offspring produced in a particular population. Behaviours and ideas that have reproductive advantages logically are more likely than others to be passed on to future generations. Biological determinists, for example, have provided an explanation for why human males apparently have "better" spatial skills than females. They say that these differences are the result of evolutionary selection because males with "better" spatial skills would have an advantage in securing both food and mates. Males with "better" spatial skills impregnate more females and have more offspring with "better" spatial skills.

Adolescent Stress: Biologically Determined or Culturally Constructed?

Margaret Mead, one of the first trained anthropologists of North America, went to eastern Samoa in 1925 to spend nine months studying child-rearing patterns and adolescent behaviour. She sought to answer these questions: "Are the disturbances which vex our adolescents due to the nature of adolescence itself or to the civilisation? Under different conditions does adolescence present a different picture?" (1961 [1928]:24). She observed and interviewed fifty adolescent girls of three different villages. Her conclusion, published in the famous book *Coming of Age in Samoa* (1961 [1928]), was that, unlike the typical experience in the United States, children in Samoa grew up in a relaxed and happy atmosphere. As young adolescents, they made a sexually free and unrepressed transition to adulthood. These findings had a major impact on thinking about child rearing in North America, prompting attempts at more relaxed forms of child rearing in the hope of raising less-stressed adolescents.

In 1983, five years after Mead's death (at which point she had no chance for response), Derek Freeman, an Australian anthropologist, published a strong critique of Mead's work on Samoa. Freeman said that Mead's findings on adolescence were wrong. Freeman, a biological determinist, believes that universally, adolescents are driven by hormonal changes that cause social and psychological upheavals. He claims that Mead's work was flawed in two major ways. First, he says her fieldwork was inadequate because she spent a relatively short time in the field and she had insufficient knowledge of the Samoan language. Second, he says that her theoretical bias against biological determinism led her to overlook or under-report evidence that was contrary to her interests. In addition, he marshalls statistical evidence against Mead's position. He compares rates of adolescent delinquency in Samoa and England and finds that they are similar in both cultures. On the basis of this result, he argues that sexual puritanism and social repression also characterized Samoan adolescence. In other words, Samoa is not so different from the West with its supposedly pervasive adolescent problems.

Because of Mead's reputation, Freeman's critique prompted a vigorous response from scholars, mostly in defence of Mead. One response in defence of Mead came from Eleanor Leacock, an expert on how colonialism affects indigenous cultures. Leacock claimed that Freeman's position failed to take history into account: Mead's findings apply to Samoa of the 1920s while Freeman's analysis is based on data from the 1960s. By the 1960s, Samoan society had gone through radical cultural change due to the influence of World War II and intensive exposure to Western influences, including Christian missionaries. Freeman's data, in her view, do not contradict Mead's because they are from a different period.

CRITICAL THINKING QUESTIONS

Mead felt that finding one "negative case" (no adolescent stress in Samoa) was sufficient to disprove the view that adolescent stress is a cultural universal. Do you agree that one negative case is sufficient?

If an anthropologist found that a practice or pattern of behaviour was universal to all cultures, does that necessarily mean that it is biologically driven?

Cultural constructionism, in contrast, is a position that says that human behaviour and ideas are best explained as products of culturally shaped learning. In terms of the example of "better" male spatial skills, cultural constructionists would provide evidence that such skills are passed on culturally through learning, not genes. They would say that parents socialize their sons and daughters differently in spatial skills and that boys are more likely to gain greater spatial skills through learning than girls, in general. Anthropologists who favour cultural construction and learning as an explanation for behaviours such as homicide and alcoholism also point to the role of childhood experiences and family roles as being more important than genes or hormones.

Interpretive versus Cultural Materialism

Interpretive anthropology considers how people use symbols to make sense of the world around them, and how these meanings are negotiated. Interpretive anthropologists view culture as a contested domain, not a given. They favour an approach to ethnography that constructs a rich complex description emerging from the insider's point of view. Interpretive anthropology tries to communicate this complexity, and rejects approaches that are reductionistic, externalist, and controlling. For example, if Hindus in India say they don't eat cows because cows are sacred, interpretivists would explore the meaning of food and eating within the Hindu religion. Similarly, interpretivists such as Mary Douglas argue that pigs cannot be eaten by Jews because of their taxonomical definition in Jewish belief as defined in the rules of Leviticus. The pig is a hoofed animal that does not chew its cud, unlike cows and sheep, and is categorized as anomalous and thus impure. Materialists have rejected such reasoning because the rules of Leviticus are untestable (Harris and Ross 1987:60).

Cultural materialism, on the other hand, is the theoretical school in cultural anthropology that emphasizes the importance of material conditions in studying and explaining human behaviours and ideas. Cultural materialists take as basic the material features of life, such as the environment, natural resources, and ways of making a living. Infrastructure is the term that refers to these crucial material factors. **Infrastructure** largely shapes the other two domains of culture: **structure** (social organization, kinship, and political organization) and **superstructure** (ideas, values, and beliefs). Cultural materialists seek explanations for behaviour and ideas by looking first and primarily at infrastructural factors. For example, a materialist explanation for a taboo restricting the eating of a particular animal first considers the possibility that such an animal plays a more important role alive, such as cows' utility in agricultural work in India.

Individual Agency versus Structurism

This debate concerns the question of how much individual will, or **agency,** has to do with why people behave and think the way they do versus the power of forces, or "structures" that are beyond individual control. Western philosophical thought gives much emphasis to the role of agency. The individual is supposed to be able to choose how to behave and think. In contrast, **structurism** emphasizes that "free choice" is an illusion since choices are structured by larger forces such as the economy, social and political institutions, and ideological systems. Explaining why people are poor, unemployed, or on welfare has been approached from both positions by cultural anthropologists and others. Some observers who emphasize the power of agency in explaining behaviour and ideas say, for example, that people are poor, unemployed, or on welfare because of their own choices. On the other hand, agency could mean indi-

Homicide in Canada

Canadian anthropologist Elliott Leyton has written several books on violence, including those on serial murderers and children who kill their parents. He comments on the reasons for the relatively low level of homicidal violence in Canada:

> The essential thing for the public to understand... is that fear of violent crime is not based on any statistical reality, but rather it is manipulated by a variety of self-serving special interest groups that stand to benefit from it in significant and material ways... [With a homicide rate of 2.9 per 100 000, Canada is] in the lowest quarter of industrial nations [far below] the

United States at 21.9 per 100,000. This appears to be partly a function of the low societal toleration for violence at any level, personal or governmental... Our low homicide rates are also a function of the cultural devaluation of aggressivity. The extirpation of aggression begins in the nursery.... Putting our money into justice enforcement that is often counter-productive, spending hundreds of millions of dollars on attention-distracting tactics such as "getting tough on crime" and gun control, will not calm the relations among our citizens. Where such funding belongs is in the radical ex-

pansion of a truly professional day care system for overworked and harassed parents; in the establishment of a sophisticated educational enterprise aimed at inculcating in our youth a distaste for aggressive display; and in meaningful job creation. (1996)

FOOD FOR THOUGHT

How could a biological determinist explain the difference in homicide rates between Canada and the United States? What roles does Leyton suggest are played by individual agency and structurism?

viduals and groups can manipulate, resist, and negotiate around structures. The poor or marginalized can develop a voice and agency and need not be the passive victims of welfare bureaucracies or large corporations. Structurists would say that the poor and unemployed are trapped by larger forces and cannot escape these traps. They would argue that the people at the bottom of the economic ladder have, in reality, little opportunity to exercise choice. The tensions between structurism and agency are visible in contemporary ethnographies because many anthropologists are concerned that their work not be read as either denying agency or ignoring structures.

The Concept of Culture

The question of how to define culture has intrigued anthropologists for over a century. Even now, spirited discussions take place between animal scientists and cultural anthropologists about whether nonhuman animals have culture and if so, how it resembles or differs from human cultures (McGrew 1998). This section overviews approaches to defining culture in cultural anthropology, characteristics of culture, and several bases for cultural identity formation.

Definitions of Culture

Culture is the core concept in cultural anthropology, so it seems likely that cultural anthropologists agree about what it is. This may have been the case in the early days of the discipline when there were far fewer anthropologists. In the 1950s, two anthropologists, Alfred Kroeber and Clyde Kluckhohn (1952), gathered 164 definitions of culture that had appeared in anthropological writings since the 1700s. Over the past 200 years, there has been continuing tension in the use of the terms between culture as a means for attaining certain ends or goals or culture as ideas, a division that persists to the present.

The first definition was proposed by British anthropologist Edward Tylor in 1871. He said that "Culture, or civilization . . . is that complex whole which includes knowledge, belief, art, law, morals, custom, and any other capabilities and habits acquired by man as a member of society" (Kroeber and Kluckhohn 1952:81). The phrase "that complex whole" is the most longstanding feature of this proposition. It has contributed to commitment to the perspective of holism, which emphasizes the importance of looking at cultures as complex systems that cannot be fully understood without attention to their different components—including economics, social organization, and ideology. Two other features of Tylor's definition have not stood the test of time. First, most anthropologists now avoid the use of *man* to refer generically to all humans and instead use generic words such as *humans* and *people*. While you may argue that the word *man* can be used generically according to its linguistic roots, many studies indicate that this usage can be confusing. Second, most anthropologists no longer equate culture with civilization. The term civilization implies a sense of "highness" versus non-civilized "lowness" and sets up an invidious distinction placing "us" (the so-called civilized nations of Europe and North America) in a superior position to "them"—the other societies.

In contemporary cultural anthropology, the theoretical positions of the interpretive anthropologists and the cultural materialists correspond to two different definitions of culture. Interpretive anthropologists state that culture includes symbols, motivations, moods, and thoughts. This definition focuses on people's perceptions, thoughts, and ideas, and does not focus on behaviour as a part of culture but, rather, seeks to explain behaviour. Interpretive anthropologists stress the idea that culture is contested and negotiated, and not always shared or imposed. Cultural materialist Marvin Harris states that "A culture is the total socially acquired life-way or life-style of a group of people. It consists of the patterned repetitive ways of thinking, feeling, and acting that are characteristic of the members of a particular society or segment of society" (1975:144). Like Tylor's definition of over 100 years ago, Harris's definition pays attention to both behaviour and ideas (beliefs). The definition of culture used in this book follows this more comprehensive approach.

Culture, as all learned and shared behaviour and ideas, is found universally among human beings. Thus, it exists in a general way as something everyone has. Some anthropologists have referred to this universal concept of culture as Culture with a capital *C*. Culture also exists in a more specific way because all cultures are not the same. **Local culture** refers to distinct patterns of learned and shared behaviour and ideas found in localized regions and among particular groups. These may include ethnic groups, racial groups, genders, and age categories. **Macroculture** refers to learned and shared ways of behaving and thinking that cross local boundaries, such as a sense of national culture that some governments seek to promote to enhance unity, or the global consumer culture that pervades upper-middle and upper-class groups transnationally.

Characteristics of Culture

Getting a clear idea of what culture is and how it affects our lives cannot come simply from a short definition. This section provides some characteristics of culture in order to help you get closer to this elusive concept. Major characteristics include culture as adaptive, culture as related to nature but not the same as nature, culture as based on symbols, culture as something that is learned, culture as integrated, and culture as something that changes.

Culture Is Adaptive

The concept of **adaptation,** which derives from the Darwinian biological evolutionary model, refers to a process of adjustment that plants and animals make to their environments that enhances their survival and their reproduction. According to Darwinian theory, the process of evolution proceeds through the selective survival of plants and organisms with the most successful patterns of adaptation, leading over time to improvements in the population. This occurs through changes, often interrelated, in human biological characteristics and human culture.

Fossil and archaeological evidence have revealed some of the changes in human physical and cultural characteristics that have occurred over the millions of years of human evolution. For instance, cranial capacity has increased, allowing for enhanced symbolic thought and communication abilities. Bipedalism, or two-footed movement, replaced walking on all fours and freed the upper arms for other activities. These physical changes are related to cultural changes such as the evolution of verbal language that depends on certain physical formations in the larynx and certain forms of tool use that depend on having an "opposable thumb" (meaning that the thumb can touch the little finger).

Human economic systems (ways of making a living) are a primary form of cultural adaptation. The earliest forms of subsistence were most directly dependent on the physical environment. While hunting certain animals could be done only where those animals existed, for example, many economic strategies now are independent of context. For example, a computer software specialist is able to work in a wide variety of geographical settings. However, other occupations are still environmentally limited; being a ski instructor requires the presence of snow or a snowmaking machine and some hills. Besides ways of making a living and providing food and shelter, human cultures that promote certain forms of social organization, intergroup communication, and even leisure behaviour are adaptive within their contexts. In many ways, culture can be viewed as humanity's most powerful strategy for survival.

Culture Is Not the Same as Nature

The relationship between nature and culture is of basic interest to cultural anthropologists in their quest to understand people's behaviour and thinking. Cultural anthropology emphasizes the importance of culture over nature, while recognizing that in some instances, nature shapes culture. For example, biological traits that affect people's behaviour and lifestyles are aspects of physiology, including certain diseases such as sickle-cell anemia or hemophilia. But even in these cases, it is not easy to predict how a person possessing them in Culture A will resemble or differ from a person possessing them in Culture B.

Another way of seeing how culture diverges from nature, even though related to it, is to see how basic "natural" demands of human life are met in different ways because of culturally defined variations. The universal human functions that everyone must perform to stay alive are eating, drinking, sleeping, and eliminating. (Requirements for shelter and clothing vary, depending on the climate. Procreation is not necessary for individual survival, although it is for group survival, so it is not included in this discussion.) In all cultures, people will eat, drink, sleep, and eliminate. But beyond this, we cannot predict how, when, or where these functions will be fulfilled. Nor can we say much about the meanings that they all have in various cultures without in-depth study.

Eating. Culture shapes what one eats, how one eats, and when one eats, and influences ideas about eating. The human body requires certain nutrients for survival, but they can be provided in many ways. For example, eating meat is not a necessity for survival. Many vegetarian societies have avoided eating meat of any sort for centuries.

Two Ethiopian women dining at an Ethiopian restaurant. The main meal consists of several meat and vegetable dishes, cooked with special spices and laid out on *injera* bread, a soft, flat bread which is torn into small pieces and used to wrap bite-sized bits of meat and vegetables. The entire meal can be eaten without utensils.

Preferences about what tastes good vary markedly, and many examples exist of foods that are acceptable in one culture and not in another. In China, most people think that cheese is disgusting, but in France, most people love cheese. One distinction exists between eating animals that are alive and animals that are dead. In a few cultures, consumption of live, or nearly live, creatures is considered a gourmet specialty; for example, a Philippine dish includes ready-to-be-born chicks. In many cultures where hunting and fishing are dominant ways of procuring food, people believe that the freshness of the catch is important. They consider canned meat or fish highly undesirable. Although some scientists and anthropologists have attempted to delineate universal taste categories into four basic types (sweet, sour, bitter, and salty), cross-cultural research disproves these as universals. Among the Weyéwa people of the highlands of Sumba, an island in Eastern Indonesia, categories of flavours are sour, sweet, salty, bitter, tart, bland, and pungent (Kuipers 1991).

How to eat is also an important area of food behaviour. Rules about eating are one of the first things you will confront when entering another culture. Proper dining manners in India require that a person eats using only the right hand because the left hand is reserved for elimination purposes. A clean right hand (one that has been rinsed in water, preferably) is believed to be the cleanest dining implement, since silverware, plates, and glassware that have been touched by others, even though washed, are never truly pure.

Food has culturally endowed meaning. Everyday food patterns and ceremonial food use may express ethnic and religious identity, promoting in-group cohesion and setting boundaries in relation to other groups. Adhering to cultural rules about food preparation and consumption

MULTIPLE CULTURAL WORLDS

Globalization and Tomato Production

Every food item creates complex relations of production and consumption. Consider the tomato. The Tomasita Project (Barndt 1999) traced the journey of a tomato from the Mexican field to a Canadian fast food restaurant. The tomato was chosen as a symbol of globalization and the shifting roles of women as producers and consumers of food. With collaborators from Canada, Mexico, and the United States, women told their stories about making and producing food. One story told of the members of a Canadian family working at McDonald's, often on different shifts, so that they seldom ate together; other stories tell of the peasant and indigenous labourers working on tomato plantations in Mexico, making US$4 a day, barely able to afford their traditional tortillas and beans. These stories bring out a North-South contradiction: while fresh tomatoes come north, fast food restaurants like McDonald's are moving south, at a faster rate since NAFTA was implemented in January 1994. Tomatoes have complex metaphorical meanings and fit into culturally constructed recipes and meals. When multinational corporations control food production, tomatoes also become commodities.

Source: Barndt 1999.

can be a defining feature of who is a "good" member of a particular group. Eating is also shaped by economic and political forces (see the Multiple Cultural Worlds box).

Drinking. The cultural elaboration of drinking is as complex as for eating. Every culture defines the appropriate substances to drink, when to drink, and with whom. French culture allows for consumption of relatively large amounts of table wine with meals. In Canada, water is commonly consumed during meals, but in India one takes water only after the meal is finished. Different categories of people drink different beverages. In cultures where alcoholic beverages are consumed, men tend to consume more than women. Coffee is the liquid of choice among "housewives" in the United States, while martinis might be the choice for male corporate executives. The meaning of particular drinks and the style of drinking and serving them are heavily influenced by culture. If you were a guest and the host offered you water, you might think it odd. If your host then explained that it was "sparkling water from France," you might be more impressed. Social drinking, whether the beverage is coffee, beer, or vodka, creates and reinforces bonds.

Sleeping. Going without sleep for an extended period would eventually lead to insanity and even death. Common sense might say that sleep is the one natural function that is not shaped by culture, because people tend to do it every 24 hours, everyone shuts their eyes to do it, everyone lies down to do it, and most everyone sleeps at night. But there are many cultural aspects to sleep, including the question of who sleeps with whom. Cross-cultural research reveals varying rules about where infants and children should sleep: with the mother, with both parents, or by themselves in a separate room. Among indigenous cultures of the Amazon, mothers and babies share the same hammock for many months, and breastfeeding occurs whenever the baby is hungry, not on a schedule. Culture also shapes the amount of time a person sleeps. In rural India, women sleep fewer hours than men since they have to get up earlier to start the fire for the morning meal. In fast-track, corporate North America, "A-type" males sleep relatively few hours and are proud of that fact—to have slept too much is to be a wimp.

Elimination. This subject takes the discussion into more private territory, but it cannot be overlooked as it is one of the major biological necessities of human life. How does culture affect the elimination process? Anyone who has travelled internationally knows that there is much to learn about elimination when you leave familiar territory. The first question is: Where to eliminate? Differences emerge in the degree to which elimination is a private act or can be done in more or less public areas. Public options include street urinals for males but not for females, as in Paris. Cultures tend to allow males to urinate in public, but not females. In most villages in India, houses do not have interior bathrooms. Instead, early in the morning, groups of women and girls leave the house and head for a certain field where they squat and chat. Men go to a different area. No one uses toilet paper; instead everyone carries in their left hand a small brass pot full of water with which they splash themselves clean. This practice has ecological advantages because it adds fertilizer to the fields and leaves no paper litter. Westerners may consider the village practice unclean, but village Indians would think that the Western system is unsanitary because paper does not clean one as well as water.

In many cultures, the products of elimination (urine and feces) are considered dirty, polluting, and disgusting. People do not try to keep such things, nor do they in any way revere them. In Papua New Guinea, in the South Pacific, people take great care to bury or otherwise hide their fecal matter. They fear that someone will find it and use it for magic against them. A negative assessment of the products of elimination is not universal, however. In some cultures, these substances are believed to have positive effects. Among First Nations cultures of the Pacific Northwest, urine, especially women's urine, was believed to have medicinal and cleansing properties and was considered the "water of life" (Furst 1989). In certain death rituals, it was sprinkled over the corpse in the hope that it might rejuvenate the deceased. People stored urine in special wooden boxes for ritual use, including the first bath that a baby was given (the urine was mixed with water for this purpose).

Culture Is Based on Symbols Making money, creating art, and practising religion all involve symbols. A **symbol** is an object or other sign that has a range of culturally significant meanings. Symbols are arbitrary (bearing no necessary relationship with that which is symbolized), unpredictable, and diverse. Because symbols are arbitrary, we cannot predict how a particular culture will symbolize any particular thing. Although we might predict that people who are hungry would have an ex-

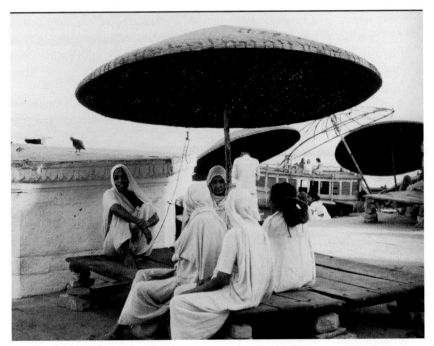

In India, a white sari (women's garment) symbolizes widowhood. To these women, the Western custom of a bride wearing white would seem inauspicious.

pression for hunger involving their stomach, no one could predict that in Hindi, the language of much of northern India, a colloquial expression for being hungry says that "rats are jumping in my stomach."

Culture Is Learned Because culture is based on arbitrary symbols, it cannot be predicted or intuited, but must be learned. Cultural learning, or **enculturation**, begins from the moment of birth, if not before (some people think that an unborn baby takes in and stores information through sounds heard from the outside world). A large but unknown amount of people's cultural learning is unconscious, occurring as a normal part of life through observation. Schools, in contrast, are a formal way to learn culture. Not all cultures throughout history have had formal schooling. Instead, children learned appropriate cultural patterns through guidance from elders and observation and practice. Hearing stories and seeing performances of rituals and dramas are other longstanding forms of enculturation.

Cultures Are Integrated To state that cultures are internally integrated is to assert the principle of holism.

Thus, studying only one or two aspects of culture provides understanding so limited that it is more likely to be misleading or wrong than more comprehensively grounded approaches. Consider what would happen if a researcher were to study intertribal warfare in Papua New Guinea and focused only on the actual practice of warfare without examining other aspects of culture. A key feature of highland New Guinea culture is the exchange of pigs at political feasts. To become a political leader, a man must acquire many pigs. Pigs eat yams, which men grow, but pigs are cared for by women. This division of labour means that a man with more than one wife will be able to produce more pigs and rise politically by giving more feasts. Such feasting enhances an aspiring leader's status and makes his guests indebted to him. With more followers attracted through feasting, a leader can gather forces and wage war on neighbouring villages. Success in war brings gains in territory. So far, this example pays attention mainly to economics, politics, and marriage systems. But other aspects of culture are involved, too. Supernatural powers affect the success of warfare. Painting spears and shields with particular designs helps increase their power. At feasts and marriages, body decoration, including paint, shell ornaments, and elaborate feather headdresses, is an important expression of identity and status. It should be obvious that looking at just warfare itself will yield a severely limited view of its wider cultural dimensions.

The fact of cultural integration is also relevant to applied anthropologists who are involved in analyzing cultural change. Attempting to introduce change in one aspect of culture without giving attention to what its effects will be in other areas is irresponsible and may even be detrimental to the survival of a culture. For example, Western missionaries and colonialists in parts of Southeast Asia banned the practice of headhunting. This practice was embedded in many other aspects of culture, including politics, religion, and psychology (a man's sense of identity as a man sometimes depended on the taking of a head). Although stopping headhunting might seem like a good thing to readers of this book, it had disastrous consequences for the cultures in which it had been a practice. This book will consider such controversial issues and examples.

Cultures Interact and Change Cultures interact with and affect each other in many ways, through trade networks, telecommunications, education, migration, and tourism. Interaction and change can occur from the local level to the global, a process called **globalization.** Also, global trends can be transformed within the local context to something new, a process called **localization.** When Jamaican reggae singer Bob Marley started singing in Jamaica, he was first popular locally, in Kingston, and then on the entire island. Subsequently, his popularity expanded to the regional (Caribbean) level, and finally he gained international fame. From the international level, reggae and Bob Marley have filtered down into localities where they have been subject to reinterpretation.

The culture of dominant groups often serves as the "index culture" for other groups. Index cultures are found at all levels: a village elite, a city compared to a rural area, and global capitals, which influence cultures in the periphery. In Bolivia, many indigenous Aymara women migrate from the rural highlands to the capital city of La Paz, where they work as domestic servants for the wealthy (Gill 1993). In the city, they stop wearing their traditional dress and adopt the urban styles of skirts, hats, and haircuts. In Kathmandu, Nepal, the index culture for hairstyles among some upper-class women is Parisian (Thompson 1998).

Global cultural dominance, or hegemony, as a driving force of international change is influenced by the material and political interests of the powerful nations and international business corporations. The spread of American merchandise, including well-known items such as Coca-Cola and Marlboro cigarettes and less well-known but economically important items such as pharmaceuticals, is part of conscious marketing. Many cultural anthropologists question the value of much of this marketing since it often does more to enhance the profits of Western businesses than to improve human health and welfare. The promotion of American cigarettes to adolescents in the United States and in developing countries, as a compensation for the declining adult market in America, is an

alarming case of cultural hegemony and inhumane mercantilism. Defenders of these practices argue that global marketing simply increases people's choices and stress that ultimately it's up to individuals to decide whether to purchase a particular item.

Multiple Cultural Worlds

As mentioned earlier in this chapter, numerous local cultures exist within every macroculture. Much of this internal cultural differentiation is structured by the categories of class, race, ethnicity, gender, age, region, and institutions. A particular individual fits in to several categories, but may identify more or less strongly with one, say a teenager, a woman, a member of a visible minority. Memberships may overlap or they may be related to each other hierarchically. The contrast between difference and hierarchy is important. People and groups can be considered different from each other on a particular criterion, but not unequal. For example, people with blue or brown eyes might be recognized as different, but this difference does not entail unequal treatment or status. In other instances, such differences do become the basis for inequality.

Class

Definitions of class depend on one's theoretical perspective. **Class** may refer to a category based on people's economic position in society, usually measured in terms of income or wealth and exhibited in terms of lifestyle. Class societies may be divided into upper, middle, and lower classes. An earlier definition of class associated with Karl Marx and Friedrich Engels says that class membership is determined by people's relationship to the "mode of production," or how people make a living. Separate classes are, for example, the working class (people who trade their labour for wages) and the landowning class (people who own land on which they or others labour). In either sense, classes are related in a hierarchical system, with certain classes dominating others. According to Marx and Engels, class struggle is inevitable as those at the top seek to maintain their position while those at the bottom seek to improve theirs. People at the bottom of the

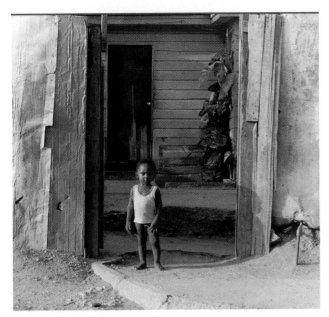

A view into the yard of a house of a low-income neighbourhood of Kingston, Jamaica. People in these neighbourhoods prefer the term *low-income* to *poor*.

amounts of body hair were associated with "barbarian" races and the lack of "civilization." Chinese writers typified male missionaries from Europe, with their beards, as "hairy barbarians." Even in the twentieth century, some Chinese anthropologists and sociologists divided humans into evolutionary stages on the basis of their body hair. One survey of humankind provided a detailed classification on the basis of types of beards, whiskers, and moustaches.

Physical features do not explain or account for behaviour or ideas. Instead, the fact of being placed in a particular racial category and the status of that category in society are what explain "racial" behaviours and ideas. Rather than being a biological category, race in the anthropological view is a cultural or social category just like class. People's perceptions about race and their use of racial differences may result in discrimination and marginality of certain groups. Racial differentiation has been the basis for some of the most invidious oppression and cruelty throughout history. A concept of racial purity inspired Hitler to pursue his program of exterminating Jews and others who were not of the Aryan "race." Racial apartheid in South Africa denied citizenship, security, and a decent life to all those labelled non-White (including, for example, "Blacks" and "Coloureds").

class structure may attempt to improve their class position by gaining access to resources and by adopting aspects of upper-class symbolic behaviour such as speech and dress, leisure and recreation.

Class is a key basis of cultural differentiation and stratification in most contemporary states, but it is a relatively recent social development in human history. For example, in precontact tribal groups in the Amazonian region, all members had roughly equal wealth. In complex and large capitalist states, however, classes are prominent forms of cultural differentiation. Some scholars say that global systems of cultural integration now mean that indigenous tribal groups, which themselves have little internal class differentiation, have become part of a global class structure, with their position being at the bottom.

Race

Race is a pervasive, though not universal, basis for social differentiation. However, race is a culturally constructed category, not a biological reality. In South Africa, race is mainly defined on the basis of skin colour. In pre-twentieth-century China, however, the basis of racial classification was body hair (Dikötter 1998). Greater

Ethnicity

Ethnicity refers to a sense of group affiliation based on a distinct heritage or worldview as a "people," for example, Caribbean Canadians or Italian Canadians, the Croats of Eastern Europe, and the Han peoples of China. This sense of identity can be vigorously expressed through political movements or more quietly stated. It can be a basis for social ranking, claimed entitlements to resources such as land or artifacts, and a perceived basis for defending or retrieving those resources. Compared to the term race, ethnicity is often used as a more neutral or even positive term. But ethnicity has often been a basis for discrimination, segregation, and oppression. The "ethnic cleansing" campaigns conducted in the early 1990s by the Serbs against Muslims in the former Yugoslavia is an extreme case of ethnic discrimination. Expression of ethnic identity has been politically suppressed in many cultures, such as the Tibetans in China. Tibetan refugees living outside Tibet are struggling to keep their ethnic heritage alive. Among First Nations groups in contemporary Canada, a shared ethnicity is one basis for cultural and spiritual revival.

Gender

Gender refers to patterns of culturally constructed and learned behaviours and ideas attributed to males, females, or sometimes a blended or "third gender." Thus gender variability can be contrasted to sex, which uses biological markers to define the categories of male and female. Sex determination relies on genital, chromosomal, and hormonal distributions and thus depends on Western science to determine who is male or female. Cultural anthropology shows that a person's biological makeup does not necessarily correspond to gender. A simple example is that in the West, people tend to associate the activity of sewing with women, but in many other areas of the world, sewing (or tailoring) is mainly men's work. The task, in other words, has nothing to do with biology. Only a few tasks are more related to biology, such as nursing babies. Cross-culturally, gender differences vary from societies in which male and female roles and worlds are largely shared, with few differences, to those in which genders are sharply differentiated. In much of rural Thailand, males and females are about the same size, their clothing is quite similar, and their agricultural tasks are complementary and often interchangeable (P. Van Esterik 2000). Among the Hua of the New Guinea Highlands, extreme gender segregation exists in almost all aspects of life (Meigs 1984). The rafuri, or men's house, physically and symbolically separates the worlds of men and women. The men live in strict separation from the women, and they engage in rituals seeking to purge themselves of female influences and substances: nose or penis bleeding, vomiting, tongue scraping, sweating, and eye washing. Men possess the sacred flutes, which they parade though the village from time to time. If women dare to look at the flutes, however, men have the right to kill them for that transgression.

First Nations Pow Wows provide an opportunity for socializing and celebrating. Here, men of the Mystic River Nation compete in the drumming competition at the Heartbeat of Nations Pow Wow at Red River Park in Winnipeg.

Strict rules also govern the kinds of food that men and women may eat.

In many cultures, the lives of gay and lesbian people are adversely affected by discrimination based on gender identity and sexual preferences. In general, Southeast Asian cultures, such as Thailand and Indonesia, are less repressive about homosexuality than Western cultures.

Age

The human life cycle, from birth to old age, takes a person through a range of cultural stages that change dramatically and for which appropriate behaviour and thinking must be learned anew. Special rituals marking physical maturation, marriage, or the end of a period of learning are found in all societies, with varying degrees of elaboration. Depending on the cultural context, each life stage places a person in a new position within the culture. Age categories intersect with other categories, such as class and gender, to define a person's status in relation to other people and groups. In many African herding societies, elaborate age categories for males define their roles and status as they move from being boys with few responsibilities and little status, to young men who are warriors and live apart from the rest of the group, to finally becoming adult men who are allowed to marry, have children, and become respected elders.

In many cultures, adolescents are in a particularly powerless category since they are neither children, who have certain well-defined rights, nor adults. Given this "threshold" position, many adolescents behave in ways of which the larger society disapproves and defines as deviance, crime, or even psychopathology (Fabrega and Miller 1995). Youth gangs in North America are an example of a situation in which adolescents have a marginal social position associated with signs of psychological deviance. Concerning women, cross-cultural research shows that in many pre-industrial societies, middle-aged women have the highest status in their life cycle if they are married and have children (J. Brown 1982).

Region

Region refers to a distinct spatial area with a name and cultural characteristics that separate it from other areas. These characteristics may include the more obvious ones such as speech, dress, and food, as well as deeper patterns of social interaction, political behaviour, and religious values. Environmental features often play an important role in defining the boundaries of a region, such as the Tibetan plateau of inner Asia or the Andean region of Latin America.

The study of regional cultures has been somewhat neglected by cultural anthropologists in their pursuit of holistic understanding of small, bounded communities. Two pioneers in this endeavour are William Skinner and Jack Goody. Skinner (1964) did work on how the role of markets and trade shaped regional integration in China. His work showed that people who live in seemingly isolated rural villages in fact may have far-reaching contacts. Jack Goody formulated generalizations about regional cultures of Europe, Asia, and Africa and how they compare to each other in terms of economic systems, marriage, food culture, and even the cultivation and use of flowers. His work, for example, revealed the more prominent role of women in crop production in Africa than in Europe and Asia. Regional studies may have to sacrifice local depth for comparative breadth (although they are based on in-depth local studies in generating their wider pictures), but their findings provide meaning to localized studies by placing them in a wider context.

Institutions

Institutions, or enduring group settings formed for a particular purpose, have their own cultural characteristics. Institutions include hospitals, boarding schools and universities, and prisons. Anyone who has entered such an institution has experienced that feeling of strangeness, of not "knowing the ropes." Until you gain familiarity with the often unwritten cultural rules, you are likely to make mistakes that offend or perplex people, that fail to get you what you want and make you feel marginal, just as if you went to a land where people are speaking a language that you don't know and are doing things that you don't understand.

Hospitals are excellent examples of institutions with their own cultural rules. Melvin Konner, an anthropologist who had studied among a group of indigenous hunting-gathering people of southern Africa and had taught anthropology for many years, decided to become a doctor. In his book *Becoming a Doctor* (1987), he reports on his experience in medical school, providing an anthropologist's insights about the hospital as a particular kind of cultural institution. One of his most striking conclusions is that medical students undergo training that in many ways functions to dehumanize them, numbing them to the pain and suffering that they will confront each day. Medical training involves, for example, the need to memorize massive amounts of material, sleep deprivation, and the learning of a special form of humour and vocabulary that seems crude and even cruel. Some special vocabulary items are *boogie*—a verb meaning to move patients along quickly in a clinic or emergency room (as in "Let's boogie!"); a *dud*—a patient with no interesting findings; and a *gomer*—an acronym for Get Out of My Emergency Room, referring to an old, decrepit, hopeless patient whose care is guaranteed to be a thankless task, usually admitted from a nursing home.

Relationships of power and inequality exist within institutions and between different institutions. These relationships crosscut other criteria, such as gender. Recent claims by women prisoners in North America of rape and abuse by prison guards are an example of intra-institutional inequality linked with gender inequality. Within and between universities, rivalries are played out in the area of competition for large research grants as well as in athletics. Within the classroom, studies document that many professors are not egalitarian in the way

Foundations of Canadian Anthropology

The roots of Canadian anthropology are anchored in both the British/European tradition of social anthropology and American cultural anthropology. Many people contributed to the institutional development of a distinguished independent anthropological tradition in Canada, regardless of place of birth, education, citizenship, or where fieldwork was conducted. For example, Americans Edward Sapir and Franz Boas both contributed to the professionalization of anthropology in Canada. Concerns about an American bias in Canadian anthropology often downplay the influence of social anthropology and the Anglo-French tradition in American universities such as Chicago, which had a strong influence on Canadian anthropologists (Darnell 1998:163). In addition, the Francophone tradition of anthropology in Canada is not American based.

Canadian anthropology was shaped by ethnohistorical and advocacy work with First Nations peoples, strong relations with museums, community studies, and a global perspective independent of Canadian political agendas. Contemporary Canadian anthropology reflects the distinct histories and nature of the colleges, universities, and museums where the subject is taught.

Landmarks of Canadian Anthropology

- Father Brebeuf describes Huron dwellings in 1635 in letters to France, recorded in the *Jesuit Relations* (Mealing 1963):

  I cannot better express the fashion of the Huron dwellings than to compare them to bowers or garden arbors, some of which, in place of branches and vegetation, are covered with cedar bark, some others with large pieces of ash, elm, fir, or spruce bark; and, although the cedar bark is best, according to common opinion and usage, there is, nevertheless, this inconvenience, that they are almost as susceptible to fire as matches. Hence arise many of the conflagrations of entire villages. There are cabins or arbors of various sizes, some two brasses [about 3.4 metres] in length, others of twenty, of thirty, of forty; the usual width is about four brasses, their height is about the same.

- Horatio Hale, trained at Harvard, was a philologist and ethnologist for the Wilkes Pacific Expedition of 1837–42. He married a Canadian and lived in Ontario, returning to ethnological work in the 1870s and 1880s. He was an early cultural relativist, attacking developmental stage theories of evolutionary progress. In addition to linguistic work in the Six Nations Reserve near Brantford, he studied the oral traditions of the elders and published the *Iroquois Book of Rites* in 1883.

- In 1853, Sir Daniel Wilson, a Scottish archaeologist, was appointed professor of English literature and history at University College, Toronto. He introduced the term "prehistory" into the English language and published *Prehistoric Man: Researches into the Origin of Civilizations in the Old and New World* in 1862.

- Sir John William Dawson, born in Nova Scotia, was principal of McGill University from 1855 to 1893. Trained as a geologist, he brought a strong natural history perspective into all his work. From his work on local archaeology, he concluded that cultures of different levels of complexity coexisted in North America. He published *Fossil Men and Their Modern Representatives* in 1880.

- In 1884, the BAAS (British Association for the Advancement of Science) met in Montreal and established a committee to study the peoples of the Northwest Coast of Canada, chaired by British anthropologist E. B. Tylor. Franz Boas's influential work on the Northwest Coast begun in 1888 was sponsored by the BAAS and the Bureau of American Ethnology.

- From 1910 to 1925, Boas's student Edward Sapir headed the Anthropology Division of the Geological Survey of Canada (established in 1842), funded by the Canadian government. This is generally recognized as the beginning of professional anthropology in Canada. Sapir published major theoretical work during this period and built the Anthropology Division into a major research centre.

- Sapir hired Marius Barbeau, trained at Laval University, Quebec, and Oxford, England, to carry out ethnological research. His work with the Tsimshian of the Northwest Coast, and on rural Quebec folklore established a strong ethnological research program that was influenced by European traditions. His work led to the establishment of a position in folklore at Laval University.

- Diamond Jenness, a New Zealander who also received an Oxford diploma in 1910, joined the National Museum under Sapir to study the Inuit and Athapaskans. The results of his ethnological research were published in the much-reprinted book *The Indians of Canada* (1932), a survey of all Native cultures in the country.

- T. F. McIlwraith, hired by the University of Toronto in 1925, was the first full-time anthropology appointment in Canada. Educated at McGill and Cambridge, his major research was based on year-long research among the Bella Coola of the Northwest Coast. Teaching at the University of Toronto and the Royal Ontario Museum until his retirement in 1964, he contributed substantially to the growth of academic anthropology in Canada.

MUSEUMS

Canadian anthropology developed in close relationship to its national and regional museums.

1841 Queen Victoria grants £1500 for a geological survey of the provinces of Canada.

1877 Geological Survey was mandated to make botanical, zoological and ethnological collections.

1894 Alexander Chamberlain (raised in Peterborough, Ontario) was awarded the first North American Ph. D. in anthropology under the supervision of Boas.

1910 The Geological Survey began linguistic and ethnological survey of First Nations communities in Canada.

1927 The establishment of the National Museum of Canada.

1934 The first Canadian Ph. D. in anthropology was awarded from the University of Toronto.

1968 National Museum of Man was established as an amalgamation of other museums of natural sciences and technology.

1986 National Museum of Man becomes the Canadian Museum of Civilization and opens to the public in 1989.

they call on and respond to students, depending on their gender, race, or "looks." In the Kilimanjaro region of north Kenya, a lesson about proper sexual behaviour directed to secondary school students advised boys to "preserve your bullets" and girls to "lock your boxes" (Stambach 2000:127–30). The surface message is that boys should learn to control their mental processes and girls should look after their possessions, which they keep in a metal trunk beneath their bed. The underlying message is that boys should learn to control their sexual desire and that girls should protect their bodies. The separate metaphors, bullets and boxes, for the boys and the girls, reflect and reinforce gender differences in moral codes and expected behaviour.

Anthropology: A Dynamic Discipline for a Changing World

Anthropology, and its four fields, has to be a discipline that is itself adaptive and changing because its subject matter—human life—is constantly adapting and changing. Lying somewhere between "pure" science and "pure" art, anthropology studies and seeks to understand why we all do what we do and think what we do. There is no other discipline with this goal.

What is anthropology?

Anthropology is an academic discipline, like history or economics. It comprises four interrelated fields in its attempt to explore all facets of human life from its very beginnings until the present: archaeology, physical or biological anthropology, linguistic anthropology, and cultural anthropology. Each field contributes a unique but related perspective. Each has a capability of making both theoretical and applied contributions. Cultural anthropology is mainly concerned with describing and analyzing contemporary people's learned and shared behaviours and beliefs.

What is cultural anthropology?

Cultural anthropology is the field within general anthropology that focuses on the study of contemporary human culture, or patterned and learned ways of behaving and thinking. It has several distinctive features that set it off from both the other fields of general an-

thropology and other academic endeavours. It uses ethnographical and ethnological approaches, supports the view of cultural relativism, and values cultural diversity. Key debates characterize the field: between biological determinism and cultural constructionism, between interpretive and cultural materialism, and between individual agency and structurism.

What is culture?

Culture is the key concept of cultural anthropology. Some anthropologists define culture as both shared behaviour and ideas, while others equate culture with ideas alone and exclude behaviour as a part of culture. Important characteristics of culture are that it is adaptive, related to nature but not the same as nature, based on symbols, and learned. Cultures are integrated within themselves. They also interact with other cultures and thereby change. Culture is found at different levels and people participate in cultures of different levels, including global macrocultures and local cultures shaped by such factors as class, race, ethnicity, gender, age, and institutions.

Core Concepts

absolute cultural
    relativism, p. 11
adaptation, p. 16
agency, p. 14
biological determinism,
    p. 12
class, p. 20
critical cultural relativism,
    p. 11

cultural constructionism,
    p. 13
cultural imperialism,
    p. 11
cultural materialism,
    p. 14
cultural relativism, p. 11
culture, p. 4
enculturation, p. 19

ethnicity, p. 21
ethnocentrism, p. 11
ethnography, p. 9
ethnology, p. 10
gender, p. 22
globalization, p. 20
holism, p. 9
infrastructure, p. 14
institutions, p. 23
interpretive anthropology,
    p. 13

local culture, p. 15
localization, p. 20
macroculture, p. 16
race, p. 21
region, p. 23
structure, p. 14
structurism, p. 14
superstructure, p. 14
symbol, p. 18

Suggested Readings

William I. Adams, *The Philosophical Roots of Anthropology*. Stanford, CA: CSLI Publications, 1998. This book considers five ideas as roots of North American anthropology: progressivism, primitivism, natural law, Indianology (the study of First Nations), and German idealism. These ideas help explain why North American anthropology, compared with British anthropology, for example, retained the four-field structure.

Stanley Barrett, *Anthropology: A Student's Guide to Theory and Method*. Toronto: University of Toronto Press, 1996. This helpful handbook for undergraduate anthropology students provides a useful overview of the development of the discipline, and links methods to past and present theories.

Robert Borofsky, ed., *Assessing Cultural Anthropology*. New York: McGraw-Hill, 1994. This collection includes over 30 essays by prominent cultural anthropologists representing diverse views of the discipline and its concept of culture, the value of the comparative perspective, contemporary priorities for research and theory, and the application of anthropological perspectives to world problems.

Marvin Harris, *Our Kind: Who We Are, Where We Came From and Where We Are Going*. New York: HarperCollins, 1989. This book contains 100 thought-provoking essays on topics in general anthropology's four fields, including early human evolution, tool making, Neanderthals, food preferences, sex, sexism, politics, animal sacrifice, and thoughts on the survival of humanity.

F. Manning, ed., *Consciousness and Inquiry: Ethnology and Canadian Realities*. Ottawa: National Museum of Man, 1983. CES paper 89e. In this edited volume, eminent Canadian anthropologists present overviews or historical perspectives on their areas of specialization, including applied anthropology in Canada.

Pearl T. Robinson and Elliott P. Skinner, eds., *Transformation and Resiliency in Africa: As Seen by Afro-American Scholars*. Washington, DC: Howard University Press, 1983. Framed by an introductory essay on Black scholarship on Africa and a conclusion that looks towards the future, nine chapters explore different areas of African culture, including labour migration in Kenya, politics and government in Nigeria, religion in the Ivory Coast, religion and popular art in urban Africa, and the transformation of African music.

George W. Stocking, Jr., *The Ethnographer's Magic and Other Essays in the History of Anthropology*. Madison: University of Wisconsin Press, 1992. This book provides a detailed examination of the emergence of cultural anthropology from Tylor through Boas and Mead, with a summary chapter on major paradigms in the history of general anthropology.

Eric R. Wolf, *Europe and the People without History*. Berkeley: University of California Press, 1982. This book examines the impact since 1492 of European colonial expansion on the indigenous cultures with which they came into contact. It also traces various phases of trade relationships, including the slave trade and goods such as fur and tobacco, and the emergence of capitalism and its effects on the movement of people and goods between cultures.

Your *Cultural Anthropology*, Second Canadian Edition Media Edition CD-ROM contains many Web sites relevant to this chapter. Use it to explore the Web and to expand your knowledge of anthropology.

Chapter 2

Methods in Cultural Anthropology

CHAPTER OUTLINE

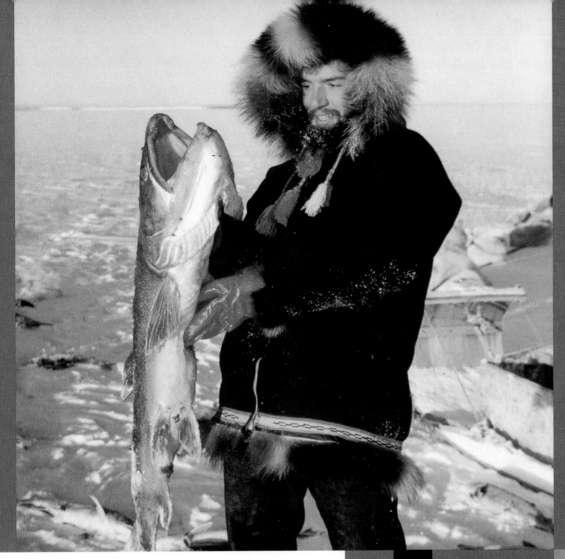

During the course of winter travels with the Hare Indians, anthropologist Joel Savishinsky holds an 11-kilogram lake trout. His dog team is resting behind him.

Key Questions

How do cultural anthropologists conduct research on culture?

What does fieldwork involve?

What are some special issues in cultural anthropology research?

31

Tau, Manu'a

March 24, 1926

This will be my last bulletin from Manu'a and very probably the last from Samoa. I'll probably leave Manu'a in about three weeks....

At dawn on March 8th, a boat arrived from Ofu and lured by thoughts of ethnological gain I decided to go back with the boat—a 15-foot [4.5-metre] rowboat... I decided it would be expensive but pleasant. So we set out in the broiling sun with a crew of some nine Samoans. The girls were desperately seasick but I rested my head on a burlap bag of canned goods, and... enjoyed the three-hour pull in the open sea. The swell is impressive when viewed from such a cockleshell of a boat. The Samoans chanted and shouted....

The whole conduct of the malaga *[ceremonial visiting party] was charming. My two companions were my talking chiefs, functionally speaking. They made all the speeches, accepted and dispersed gifts, prepared my meals, etc.... And these were merry companions. Even when they went to wash my clothes, one carried the clothes but the other carried the ukelele.... There were some slight difficulties. Once I killed 35 mosquitoes inside my net in the morning, and all had dined liberally. (Mead 1977:55–57)*

*T*here are many important differences between being a tourist and doing research in cultural anthropology, as this excerpt from one of Margaret Mead's letters from Samoa demonstrates. Most cultural anthropologists gather data by doing **fieldwork,** that is, going to "the field," which includes any place where people and culture are found (Robson 1993). A cornerstone method of fieldwork in cultural anthropology is **participant observation,** in which an anthropologist simultaneously lives in and studies a culture for a long period of time.

Compared to the other three fields of general anthropology, cultural anthropology is most associated with participant observation as its primary technique for gathering data. Because archaeologists work mainly with artifacts from bygone cultures, they cannot truly participate in the cultures they study. Many physical anthropologists, especially primatologists, live in primate habitats

for long periods of time, but the limited degree to which humans and nonhuman primates can communicate with each other constrains true participation. Linguistic anthropologists who work with contemporary populations most resemble cultural anthropologists in their use of fieldwork. They are able to both observe and participate in the same ways that cultural anthropologists do.

In this chapter we explore the way that cultural anthropologists learn about culture through fieldwork and participant observation. The entire process of fieldwork is considered, from coming up with an idea for research to leaving the field, analyzing the data, and writing up one's findings. Later on in the chapter, we consider some special topics such as the importance of ethics and doing fieldwork in dangerous situations. Throughout this chapter, you might try to keep in mind the similarities and differences between research in cultural anthropology and research in other areas of study such as psychology, economics, or history.

The History of Fieldwork in Cultural Anthropology
From the Armchair to the Field

Research in cultural anthropology one hundred years ago was not based on fieldwork and participant observation. Referred to as the "armchair approach," it involved reading reports from travellers, missionaries, and explorers and then providing an analysis. Edward Tylor (1871), who proposed the first definition of culture, was an armchair anthropologist. So was Sir James Frazer, another famous founding figure of anthropology, who wrote *The Golden Bough* (1978 [1890]), a multi-volume collection of myths, rituals, and symbols from around the world compiled from reading other people's reports. In the second stage of the late-nineteenth and early-twentieth centuries, some anthropologists moved out from their homes and libraries and travelled to foreign countries, where they spent time living near, but not with, the people they were studying. This pattern is nicknamed the "verandah approach" because typically the anthropologist would send out for "native" informants to come to the verandah for interviewing. Verandah anthropology was practised by many anthropologists who worked for colonial governments. They lived within colonial settlements, not with the indigenous people. The third stage is the current one of fieldwork and participant observation.

The field can be practically anywhere: a school, a rural community, a corporation, a clinic, an urban neighbourhood, in any part of the world. In some ways, the field is equivalent to a scientist's lab. A cultural anthropologist, however, does not perform experiments, but follows a less obtrusive approach.

The Origin of Participant Observation

The first lessons about the value of participant observation came from nineteenth-century observations of Iroquoian groups by Lewis Henry Morgan, and lesser known Horatio Hale. Both were nineteenth-century lawyers who lived near Iroquoian groups in New York State and Brantford, Ontario, respectively. Neither did participant observation in the sense of living for a long time, say a year or two, with the people, but both made field trips to Iroquois settlements. This experience, though brief, provided important insights into the lives of the Iroquois and formed the basis for Morgan's book, *The League of the Iroquois* (1851), and Hale's *Iroquois Book of Rites* (1883). The books helped dismantle the prevailing Euro-American perception of the Iroquois as "dangerous savages."

Bronislaw Malinowski is generally considered the "father" of participant observation because he first placed it in the centre of cultural anthropology methods while studying the people of the Trobriand Islands in the South Pacific during World War I. "For two years, he set his tent in their midst, learned their language, participated as much as he could in their daily life, expeditions, and festivals, and took everything down in his notebooks" (Sperber 1985:4). Malinowski made the crucial step of learning the local language, and therefore was able to dispense with interpreters. Direct communication brings the researcher much closer to the lived reality of the people being studied, as is evident in his ethnography about the Trobrianders, *Argonauts of the Western Pacific* (1961 [1922]).

In the late 1800s and early 1900s, a primary goal was to record as much as possible of a people's language, songs, rituals, and social life because many cultural anthropologists believed that cultures were disappearing.

Given the assumption that small, localized cultures could be studied in their totality, early cultural anthropologists focused on gaining a holistic view of a single group. Today, few isolated cultures remain to be studied. The integration of most cultures into wider economic and political spheres has prompted new research topics and revised methods of study that can take in both local and global factors.

Several examples of contemporary ethnographies demonstrate the simultaneous attention to local patterns and wider cultural links. Harriet Rosenberg's *A Negotiated World: Three Centuries of Change in a French Alpine Community* (1988) examines 300 years of changes in a small Alpine village in southwestern France, tracing its shifting position in the political and economic transformations of French state formation. She combined historical study with ethnographic observations to explain contemporary social life and the complexity of social change.

Margaret Lock explored the cultural construction of menopause in *Encounters with Aging: Mythologies of Menopause in Japan and North America* (1993). In it she combines individual narratives about the aging symptoms associated with the end of menstruation, medical discourses about female mid-life, and the politics of aging in Japan and North America. This combination of popular and professional accounts is a powerful ethnographic approach in medical anthropology.

A methodological innovation that helps cultural anthropologists take globalization, complexity, and change into account is **multi-sited research,** or fieldwork in more than one location. Cultural anthropologists are beginning to use this approach particularly in studies of migrant populations. Studying migration has challenged traditional cultural anthropology's focus on one village or neighbourhood and created the need to take into account national and global economic, political, and social forces (Lamphere 1992; Basch, Glick Schiller, and Szanton Blanc 1994). They study why people move and analyze their adjustments to living in a new place, especially the challenges and opportunities of maintaining their culture or constructing a new cultural identity.

Camilla Gibb (2002) studied the Harari, a dispersed community of Muslim Ethiopians, in the city of Harar and in Toronto. Since a third of the Harari are scattered across the globe, a key component of her study included discussions taking place on H-Net, an e-mail-based discussion group where aspects of community and identity were defined and debated. Use of this new media revealed differences among diasporic generations about eventual return to Ethiopia.

Another anthropologist conducted research among Chinese Americans in the San Francisco Bay area and then in the Pearl River Delta region in Guangdong Province in the People's Republic of China (Louie 2000). The research in China focused on a youth festival that attracts young Chinese Americans seeking to find out about their homeland. At the same time, the festival allows the Chinese people to reframe and restate their sense of national identity. These studies reveal the importance of **transnationalism,** or national identity that crosses nation-states and is created through the flow of people, goods, and ideas.

Beginning the Fieldwork Process

This section covers important activities that characterize the early stages of all cultural anthropology research: project selection, project funding, and preparing for the field.

Project Selection and Funding

The first step is deciding on the research topic, since no one goes to the field without an idea of what they want to learn. Cultural anthropologists often find a topic to research by reviewing reports on what has been done already. Through library research, also called *secondary research*, they may find a gap that needs to be filled. For example, in the 1970s, many cultural anthropologists began to focus on women because they realized that little previous research had addressed women's lives (Miller 1993). Other topics have emerged because of historical events. The discovery of the AIDS virus and its social dimensions stimulated interest from cultural anthropologists, many working within the subfield of medical anthropology. The recent rise in the numbers of immigrants and refugees in North America prompted studies of the adaptation of these groups of people. The fall of state socialism in Russia and Eastern Europe shifted attention to that region. Conflicts in Ireland, Rwanda, for-

mer Yugoslavia, and other places have spurred cultural anthropologists to ask what keeps states together and what makes them fall apart. Even luck can lead to a research topic. While conducting fieldwork in southwestern Ontario on contemporary Mennonite efforts to articulate a renewed vision of peoplehood, Daphne Winland came across a small congregation of Hmong refugees from Laos who had been sponsored by the Mennonite community in Kitchener-Waterloo, Ontario. These refugees, who had decided to convert to Christianity (specifically Mennonitism), not only provided a fascinating example of the role of religion in refugee adjustment, but also a perfect case study through which to examine the central theme of her research, Mennonite struggles over their long-established identity as an ethnoreligious enclave (Winland 1992).

"Re-studies" are another way to design a research project. Decades of previous anthropological field studies provide us with a base of information. In 2001, John and Penny Van Esterik returned to their fieldsite, a village

Penny and John Van Esterik re-studied a central Thai community in Uthong district 30 years after their first fieldwork. Their informants now own a shop in the village; the man used to be a barber.

TROBRIAND ISLANDS

Losuia

GOODENOUGH ISLAND

FERGUSSON ISLAND

NEW GUINEA

NORMANBY ISLAND

in Central Thailand, to see how the community had changed in 30 years. It makes sense for contemporary anthropologists to go back to a place that had been studied earlier to examine the changes that have occurred, or to look at the culture from a new angle. For her dissertation research, Annette Weiner (1976) decided to go to the Trobriand Islands, following in the footsteps of Malinowski. She was surprised at what she discovered about Trobriand women's lives, a subject Malinowski had almost entirely overlooked (see the Critical Thinking box).

Over the past several decades, the regional focus of research in cultural anthropology has shifted. These changes are not random, but occur in response to underlying factors such as funding sources or security interests (Shankman and Ehlers 2000). Some funding sources support domestic research by applied anthropologists on issues such as homelessness and HIV/AIDS. But when

CRITICAL THINKING

Shells and Skirts in the Trobriand Islands

A lasting contribution of Malinowski's ethnography, *Argonauts of the Western Pacific* (1961 [1922]), is its detailed examination of the *kula*, a trading network linking many islands in the region in which men have longstanding partnerships with other men for the exchange of both goods such as food and highly valued necklaces and armlets. More than half a century later, Annette Weiner (1976) travelled to the Trobriand Islands to study woodcarving. She settled in a village not far from where Malinowski had done much of his research and began making startling observations: "On my first day in the village, I saw women performing a mortuary [death] ceremony in which

they distributed thousands of bundles of strips of dried banana leaves and hundreds of beautifully decorated fibrous skirts. Bundles of banana leaves and skirts are objects of female wealth with explicit economic value" (xvii).

She decided to investigate women's activities and exchange patterns. Weiner discovered a world of production, exchange, social networks, and influence that existed among women, but that Malinowski and other earlier (male) observers had overlooked. Men, as Malinowski described, exchange shells, yams, and pigs. Women, as Weiner discovered, exchange bundles of leaves and intricately made skirts. Power and prestige derive from both.

Reading Malinowski alone informs us about the dramatic and exciting world of men's status systems. But that is only half the picture. Reading Weiner's *Women of Value, Men of Renown* (1976) provides an account of the linkages between domains of male and female power and value. Weiner shows how understanding of one domain requires understanding of the other.

CRITICAL THINKING QUESTIONS

How did Malinowski miss the importance of women's exchange patterns?

Do the findings of Annette Weiner simply provide another one-sided view?

Anthropologist Margaret Rodman researches colonial housing on an island in Vanuatu as part of an ethnography of colonial culture.

the research site is more "foreign" and "exotic," the researcher gains more status and prestige (Gupta and Ferguson 1997). Nevertheless, some of the most significant and policy-relevant anthropological research in Canada is conducted "at home." (See, for example, Scott 2001; Asch 1997; Glasser and Bridgeman 1999; Winland 1992; Davis 1989; Culhane Speck 1987; and Adelson 2000.) Private or government foundations provide research funding on a competitive basis. A research proposal is usually required for consideration by the funding source. It describes the project; explains why it is important; and provides information about how the research will be conducted, how much it will cost, and what the results will be—a book, scholarly papers, a film, or a detailed report. Canadian funding for anthropological research comes primarily from the Social Science and Humanities Research Council (SSHRC), Canadian

International Development Agency (CIDA) awards programs, and area-specific foundations such as the Shastri Indo-Canadian Institute and the Japan Foundation.

Preparing for the Field

Once the project is defined and funding secured, it is time to begin preparing to go to the field. Visas, or formal research permission from the host government, may be required and may take a long time to obtain. On the other hand, they may not be needed if the research is conducted in one's native country. The government of India, for example, is highly restrictive about research by foreigners, with "sensitive" topics such as "tribal people" or family planning being off limits. Some nations have been completely closed to anthropological research for decades and are only now relaxing their restrictions. China's restrictions against allowing foreign anthropologists to do research there have been lifted only in the past 15 years or so, and Russia's restrictive policies have changed even more recently.

Preparation may involve buying equipment, such as a tent, arctic sleeping bag, or special clothing. Health preparations may involve having a series of shots for immunization against contagious diseases such as yellow fever. For research in malaria-endemic areas, individuals are advised to start taking anti-malaria pills weeks before arrival to build up immunity. If the project is to take place in a remote area far from adequate medical care, a well-stocked medical kit is essential. Research equipment and supplies are other important aspects of preparation. Cameras, video recorders, tape recorders, and laptop computers are becoming basic field equipment, reflecting technological changes in doing fieldwork from the days of the simple notebook and pen.

If a researcher is unfamiliar with the local language, intensive language training before going into the field is a necessity. If a particular language is not taught anywhere in the anthropologist's home country, intensive language study should be started on arrival in the country where the research will be done. Even with language training in advance, cultural anthropologists often find that they need to learn the local version of the more standardized language they studied in a classroom. Many cultural anthropologists rely on help from a local interpreter.

Working in the Field

Fieldwork in cultural anthropology is a difficult and lengthy social process that involves the researcher's coming to terms with an unfamiliar culture. The anthropologist attempts to learn the language of the people, live as they do, understand their lives, and often be a friend.

Site Selection

The researcher often has a basic idea of the area where the fieldwork will occur—for example, a *favela* (shanty town) in Rio de Janeiro or a village in Scotland—but it is difficult to know exactly where the project will be located until after arriving. Selecting a research site depends on many factors. For example, it may be necessary to find a large village if the project involves looking at social class differences in work patterns and food consumption, or a clinic if the study concerns health care behaviour. Locating a place where the people welcome the researcher and the project, which offers adequate housing, and which fits the requirements of the project may not be easy.

Jennifer Robertson's (1991) selection of Kodaira as a research site in Japan for her study of urban residents and immigrants was based on a combination of good advice from a Japanese colleague, available housing, a match with her research interests, and the happy coincidence that she already knew the area:

> I spent my childhood and early teens in Kodaira [but] my personal past did not directly influence my selection of Kodaira as a fieldsite and home.... A colleague, Matsumura Mitsuo of the Institute for Areal Studies in Tokyo, suggested that the Mutashine region in central Tokyo prefecture would be an ideal locus for a historical anthropological study of village-making (mura-zakuri), the substance of my initial research proposal. That I wound up living in my old neighborhood in Kodaira was determined more by the availability of a suitable apartment than by a nostalgic curiosity about my childhood haunts. As it turned out, I could not have landed at a better place at a better time. (6)

Gaining Rapport

Rapport refers to the relationship between the researcher and the study population. In the early stages of research,

the primary goal is to establish rapport, probably first with key leaders or decision makers in the community who may serve as gatekeepers (people who formally or informally control access to human or material resources to the group or community). Gaining rapport involves trust on the part of the study population, and their trust depends on how the researcher presents herself or himself. In many cultures, local people will have difficulty understanding why a person would come to "study" them, since they may not know about universities and research and cultural anthropology. They may provide their own often inaccurate explanations, based on previous experience with outsiders whose goals differed from those of cultural anthropologists, such as tax collectors, missionaries, family planning promoters, and law enforcement officials.

Much has been written about the problem of how the anthropologist presents herself or himself in the field and how the local people interpret "who" the anthropologist is and why the anthropologist is there at all (see the Voices box on page 38). Stories about such role assignments can be humorous. Richard Kurin (1980) reports that in the earliest stage of his research among the Karan in the Punjab region of northwest Pakistan, the villagers thought he was a spy—from America, Russia, India, or China. After he convinced them that he was not a spy, the villagers came up with several other acceptable roles for him—first as a "teacher" of English because he was tutoring one of the village boys, then as a "doctor" because he was known to dispense aspirin, then as a "lawyer" who could help villagers in negotiating local disputes because he could read court orders. Jean Briggs was adopted as a daughter in an Inuit community in the Canadian Arctic. This role raised the problems of losing her outsider status, depletion of her supplies, and loss of privacy.

Exchanges and Gift Giving

Giving gifts to local people can help the project proceed, and they are sometimes an expected part of exchange relationships in the culture. Gifts should be culturally and ethically appropriate. Many cultural anthropologists working in developing countries have provided basic medical care, such as wound dressing, as a regular part of their interactions. Some have taught in the local school part time. Others have helped support individuals in

In my first months on the block, though, I was not debating complex theoretical points.... I was primarily concerned with how to persuade Primo, the manager of the crack house on my block—known as the Game Room—that I was not an undercover police officer. I remember vividly the night I first went to the Game Room. My neighbor Carmen—a thirty-nine-year-old grandmother who I had watched over the past three months become addicted to crack and transform herself into a ninety-nine pound harpie... —brought me over to the manager of the Game Room and told him in Spanish, "Primo, let me introduce you to my neighbor, Felipe...."Staring out into the street, he asked Carmen in English, loud enough for me to hear, "What precinct did you pick him up at?" I hurriedly mumbled an embarrassed protest about not being "an undercover" and about wanting to write a book..... I had the good sense not to impose myself, however, and instead slunk into the background after buying a round of beers. Even in my largesse, I managed to prolong the awkwardness by purchasing the wrong kind of beer—an unstreetwise brand whose taste Primo did not like....

Despite my inauspicious first evening, it took less than two weeks for Primo to warm up to my presence. . . . It was not until two years later at 2 a.m. in the stairwell of Primo's mother's high-rise project . . . that they told me what their first impressions of me at the Game Room had been: When I first met you, Felipe, I was wondering who the hell you were, but you sounded interesting so, of course . . . te recibi como amigo, con respeto [I welcomed you as a friend, with respect].

Source: Bourgois 1995:39–43.

obtaining a higher education degree outside their homelands.

Learning the local rules of exchange is important, including what constitutes an appropriate or inappropriate gift, how to deliver the gift (timing, in private or public, wrapped or unwrapped), and how to behave as a gift giver (for example, should one be modest and emphasize the smallness of the gift?). Richard Lee, who conducted fieldwork among the !Kung San Bushmen (Ju/wasi), wrote a classic article on the complexities of gift giving and reciprocity. After a year in the field, he used the custom of slaughtering a huge fat ox at Christmas to repay in part the community for their hospitality. Because of the disparity between his inventory of canned food and the Bushmen's scant supplies of food, he fell open to accusations of being stingy, a hard-hearted miser:

> The Christmas ox was to be my way of saying thank you for the cooperation of the past year; and since it was to be our last Christmas in the field, I determined to slaughter the largest, meatiest ox that money could buy, insuring that the feast and transcendence would be a success. (Lee 1969:26)

Following his purchase of a huge ox, community members began complaining about the scrawny, bony animal he had chosen. Even after the carcass was cut open, the complaints continued:

> "Hey /gau," I burst out, "that ox is loaded with fat. What's this about the ox being too thin to bother eating? Are you out of your mind?" "Fat?" /gau shot back, "You call that fat? The wreck is thin, sick, dead!" And he broke out laughing. So did everyone else. They rolled on the ground, paralyzed with laughter. Everybody laughed except me; I was thinking. (28)

Following two days of feasting, Lee was still troubled by people's response to his generosity. He asked:

> "Why did you tell me the black ox was worthless, when you could see that it was loaded with fat and meat?"

> "It is our way," he said smiling. "We always like to fool people about that. Say there is a Bushman who has been hunting. He must not come home and announce like a braggart, 'I have killed a big one in the bush!' He must first sit down in silence until I or someone else comes up to his fire and asks, 'What did you see today?' He replied quietly, 'Ah, I'm no good for hunting. I saw nothing at all [pause] just a little tiny one.' Then I smile to myself," /gaugo continued, "because I know he killed something big."

> "But," I asked, "why insult a man after he has gone to all that trouble to track and kill an animal and when he is going to share the meat with you so your children will have something to eat?"

> "Arrogance," was his cryptic answer.

> "Arrogance?"

"Yes, when a young man kills much meat he comes to think of himself as a chief or a big man, and he thinks of the rest of us as his servants or inferiors. We can't accept this. We refuse one who boasts, for someday his pride will make him kill somebody. So we always speak of his meat as worthless. This way we cool his heart and make him gentle."…

The pieces now fell into place. I had known for a long time that in situations of social conflict with Bushmen I held all the cards. I was the only source of tobacco in a thousand square miles [2500 square kilometres], and I was not incapable of cutting an individual off for non-co-operation. Though my boycott never lasted longer than a few days, it was an indication of my strength. People resented my presence at the water hole, yet simultaneously dreaded my leaving. In short I was a perfect target for the charge of arrogance and for the Bushmen tactic of enforcing humility. I had been taught an object lesson by the Bushmen; it had come from an unexpected corner and had hurt me in a vulnerable area. For the big black ox was to be the one totally generous, unstinting act of my year at /ai/ai, and I was quite unprepared for the reaction I received.

As I read it, their message was this: There are no totally generous acts. All "acts" have an element of calculation. One black ox slaughtered at Christmas does not wipe out a year of careful manipulation of gifts given to serve your own ends. After all, to kill an animal and share the meat with people is really no more than Bushmen do for each other every day and with far less fanfare. (29)

Factors Influencing Fieldwork

An anthropologist's class, race, gender, and age all affect how he or she will be interpreted by local people. It is clear from Bourgois's commentary in the Voices box on page 38 that race was a dominant factor in people's initial response to him. An anthropologist who is a young, unmarried female studying child-rearing practices may not be taken seriously because since she is not herself a mother, how could she possibly understand? Or, bearded males who look like "hippies" may alienate local people whose experiences with true hippies have not been positive.

Class In most fieldwork situations, the anthropologist is generally more wealthy and powerful than the people studied. This difference is obvious to the people. They know that the anthropologist may have spent hundreds or thousands of dollars on education and travel to the research site. They see the expensive equipment (camera, tape recorder, video recorder, even a vehicle) and valuable trade items (stainless steel knives, cigarettes, flashlights, canned food, medicines). This class difference affects how people in the field relate to the researcher. When Ernestine Friedl (1986) and her husband did fieldwork in a Greek village, their status as "professors" influenced people's behaviour. Village men would refrain from telling sexual jokes or swearing when the professor was present (213).

This pattern—of the anthropologist having more wealth and status than the people being studied—has typified cultural anthropology throughout its history. Laura Nader (1972) has urged a departure from this typical pattern. She says that some anthropologists should "study up" by doing research among powerful people such as business elites, political leaders, and government officials. Cultural anthropologists who "study up" find themselves in research situations in which they are less wealthy and less powerful than their informants. Dorinne Kondo's (1997) research on the high-fashion industry of Japan placed her in touch with many members of the Japanese elite, influential people capable of taking her to court if they felt she wrote something defamatory about them. Many people being studied are now able to read the book or articles that the anthropologist writes. Thus, the anthropologist has to be extremely careful about what goes into the ethnography. But all anthropologists, regardless of the research context, should be respectful of their informants and take extreme care in their writing.

Race For most of its history, cultural anthropology has been dominated by Euro-American White researchers who have studied "other" cultures, most often non-White and non-Euro-American. The effects of "Whiteness" on role assignments range from the anthropologist being labelled as a god or ancestor spirit to his or her being reviled as a representative of a colonialist past. While doing research in Jamaica, Tony Whitehead (1986) learned how race and status interact. For Whitehead, an African American, being essentially the same "race"—of African descent—did not automatically create solidarity between him and the African-descent residents of Haversham, Jamaica. The people of Haversham have a complex status system that relegated Whitehead to a higher social status position that he did not predict. Similarly, David Murray working in Martinique recognized that his "presence as a 'white' man may have censured the expression of other beliefs, feelings or opinions among both gay and straight Martinican men as the white/black racial dyad has a major structuring influence on Martinican social life" (Murray 2002:12).

Gender The literature on the impact of gender on fieldwork is large and growing (for example, Golde 1986; Whitehead and Conway 1986). Generally, if a female researcher is young and unmarried, she is likely to face more difficulties than a young unmarried male or an older female, married or single, because a young, unmarried female who is on her own is often an anomaly (Warren 1988:13–15). Rules of gender segregation may dictate that a young unmarried woman should not move about freely without a male escort and her status may prevent her from attending certain events or being in some places. Gender boundaries exist cross-culturally to varying degrees, and a researcher probably can never fully overcome them. A woman researcher who studied a secretive male gay community in the United States comments:

> I was able to do fieldwork in those parts of the setting dedicated to sociability and leisure—bars, parties, family gatherings. I was not, however, able to observe in those parts of the setting dedicated to sexuality—even quasi-public settings such as homosexual bath houses.... Thus my portrait of the gay community is only a partial one, bounded by the social roles assigned to females within the male homosexual world. (Warren 1988:18)

Gender segregation limits male researchers from gaining access to a full a range of activities as well, especially in the domestic domain. In an unusual study, Liza Dalby (1983) lived with the geishas of Kyoto, Japan, and trained to be a geisha. Through this, she learned more about the inner workings of this local culture than a man ever could.

Age Typically, adult anthropologists are responsible for studying people in all age categories. Although some children and adolescents readily welcome the participation of a friendly adult in their daily lives and respond to

Liza Dalby in full geisha formal dress in the person of Ichigiku.

questions openly, others are much more tentative. Margaret Mead (1986) commented that "Ideally, a three-generation family, including children highly trained to understand what they experience, would be the best way to study a culture" (321). She recognized that each age category has its own cultural rules and age-specific language, and needs to be studied on its own terms. Although Mead paid a great deal of attention to children and adolescents, few contemporary anthropologists consider children except in discussions of the family and motherhood. Recently a number of Canadian anthropologists explored the complexity of children's lives, including the media depiction of children, the intimacy of children's play, and the cultural politics revealed in post-war parliamentary debates about family allowances and "the right kind of children" (Helleiner 2001). Virginia Caputo (2001) studied children's musical practices in

Toronto and showed how their play allowed them to resist adult definitions of childhood. When Pamela Downe asked children to choose a research name for themselves, she learned about how important names are to children's identity. Seven-year-old Kizzy from Bridgetown, Barbados, explains: "Sometimes I feel very tiny... Like I [could] fit in a thimble, like the tooth fairy— but all's I gotta do is imagine someone calling my name and I be feeling big again. That is why I like thinking about what name you should call me in your notes" (Downe 2001:167).

Ethnographies of children also demonstrate how clichés like "the innocent child" mask differences among children according to age, gender, race, class, and location.

Other Factors

The fieldworker's role is affected by many more factors than the characteristics listed above, including language, dress, and religion. Being the same religion as the elderly Jewish people at the Aliyah Center in California helped Barbara Myerhoff (1978) in establishing rapport in her first meeting with members of the Center. This is evident in her conversation with one elderly woman named Basha:

"So, what brings you here?"

"I'm from the University of Southern California. I'm looking for a place to study how older Jews live in the city."

At the word university, she moved closer and nodded approvingly. "Are you Jewish?" she asked.

"Yes, I am."

"Are you married?" she persisted.

"Yes."

"You got children?"

"Yes, two boys, four and eight," I answered.

"Are you teaching them to be Jews?" (14)

Myerhoff was warmly accepted into the lives of people at the Center, and her plan for one year of research grew into a longstanding relationship.

In a study of women who were denied the *get,* or Jewish divorce document, Lisa Rosenberg (1996) was aware that although she was a Jewish woman, as a non-Orthodox woman she might be perceived as an outsider by those within the Orthodox community. She was often subject to scrutiny that was, at times, quite overt. More than once she was asked, "What synagogue do you belong to?" It was also common for her to have to speak about her Jewish education and her knowledge of Jewish law.

Culture Shock

Culture shock refers to persistent feelings of uneasiness, loneliness, and anxiety that often occur when a person has shifted from one culture to a different one. The more "different" the two cultures are, the more severe the shock is likely to be. Culture shock happens to many cultural anthropologists, no matter how much they have tried to prepare themselves for the field. Culture shock can happen to students who study abroad, overseas volunteers (CUSO, WUSC), or anyone who spends a significant amount of time living and participating in another culture. It can range from problems with food to the language barrier. Food differences were a major problem in adjustment for a Chinese anthropologist who came to the United States (Shu-Min 1993). American food never gave him a "full" feeling.

For Martha Ward (1989), who went to an island in the Pacific named Pohnpei to study the interactions between social modernization and high blood pressure, language caused the most serious adjustment problems. She spent much time in the early stages of her research learning basic phrases and vocabulary, and she reports on the frustration she felt:

...when even dogs understood more than I did.... The subtleties and innuendo I wanted to express (and could in English) were impossible. For months, I sweated profusely when I had to carry on a full conversation in Pohnpeian. It was no gentle perspiration, either; it was the sweat of hard, dirty work. Nonetheless, I will never forget the elation of deciphering and using relative clauses and personal pronouns. Nor will I forget the agony of stepping on a woman's toes. Instead of asking for forgiveness, I blurted out, "His canoe is blue." (14)

A psychological aspect of culture shock is the feelings of reduced competence as a cultural actor. At home, the anthropologist is highly competent. Everyday tasks like shopping, talking with other people, mailing a letter, or sending a fax can be done without thinking. In a new culture, the most simple task becomes difficult and one's sense of self-efficacy is undermined. In extreme cases, an anthropologist may have to abandon a project because of an inability to adapt to the fieldwork situation. For most, however, culture shock is a temporary affliction that subsides as the person becomes more familiar with the new culture.

"Reverse culture shock" can occur on returning home. Alan Beals (1980) describes his feelings on returning to San Francisco after a year of fieldwork in a village in India:

> We could not understand why people were so distant and hard to reach, or why they talked and moved so quickly. We were a little frightened at the sight of so many white faces and we could not understand why no one stared at us, brushed against us, or admired our baby.
>
> We could not understand the gabble of voices on the television set. When we could understand people, they seemed to be telling lies. The trust and warmth seemed to have gone out of life to be replaced by coldness and inhumanity. People seemed to have no contact with reality. All of the natural human processes—eating, sleeping together, quarreling, even playing—seemed to be divorced from earth and flesh. Nowhere could we hear the soft lowing of cattle or the distant piping of the shepherd boy. (119)

Fieldwork Techniques

Fieldwork is devoted to collecting data for subsequent analysis. The main approaches to data collection, **quantitative research** and **qualitative research,** provide different kinds of data and follow different analytical routes (Bernard 1995; Hammersley 1992). Quantitative data and analysis include numerical information, counting, and the use of tables and charts in presenting results. Qualitative methods generate detailed descriptions rather than counting or quantifying. Some researchers concentrate on quantitative data, some rely on qualitative data, and others use a combination of both. Regardless of these

variations, participant observation is the basic research method through which the data are collected.

Theoretical Considerations

The choice of methods for data gathering and the subsequent interpretation and analysis of the data depend on the anthropologist's theoretical perspective. **Deductive research** methods involve posing a research question or hypothesis, gathering data related to the question, and then assessing the findings in relation to the original hypothesis. Thus, fieldwork should be devoted to the collection of detailed observational and interview data in order to learn what people do as well as how people explain what they do and why they do it. Data analysis also involves interpreting the disjuncture between what people say and their actions, as well as cross-cultural comparison.

Inductive research approaches avoid hypothesis formation in advance of the research and instead take their lead from the culture being studied. An important source of detailed information on insiders' views is **discourse**—people's talk, stories, and myths. People's discourse reveals their perceptions of important themes and concepts. Cross-cultural comparison is less significant since each system of local knowledge makes sense only in itself. Understanding other people's subjective meanings is an important part of inductive research strategies.

These distinctions also relate to the concepts of "emic" and "etic," terms which emerge from linguistics and philosophy, but have been adapted to refer to different approaches to ethnographic explanation. The term **emic** (adapted from the last two syllables of "phonemic") refers to what insiders do and perceive about their culture. It includes their perceptions of reality and their explanations for why they do what they do. One goal of cultural anthropology fieldwork is to gain as much knowledge of emics as possible. The term **etic** (adapted from the last two syllables of "phonetic") refers to the analytical framework and tools used by outsiders in searching for patterns and regularities of the insider's culture.

A philosophically interesting question arises about whether a truly emic ethnographic representation of a culture can be provided by anyone—either insider or outsider—because the very concept of ethnography is etic. Ethnography, even of the most descriptive kind, necessarily involves the abstraction of selected aspects of a culture. Even when an insider (or native) of a culture writes an ethnography about it, etic categories are likely to appear, such as "kinship" or "social inequality." No pure etic exists, either. A cultural anthropologist's etic framework logically is part of that particular person's emic world. Nevertheless, these two terms are "shorthand" reminders of different ways to understand what people do and think, and why.

Whether an anthropologist is guided by materialist or interpretive theory, adopts an emic or etic approach, or uses more deductive or inductive methods during fieldwork, all cultural anthropologists seek to know about a culture from multiple perspectives. A cultural anthropologist circles around a culture, moving from person to person and context to context. The researcher sees the culture from multiple viewpoints and has the privilege, later, of sitting back from the data and analyzing how it all fits together. Most individuals, in their normal lives, do not have the opportunity of doing such intensive research and analysis of their own lives and cultures.

Participant Observation

Once in the field, cultural anthropologists use particular **research methods** or strategies and techniques to learn about culture. Within the overall approach of participant observation, many different methods are available. Being a participant means that the researcher tries to adopt the same lifestyle as the people being studied as much as possible, living in the same kind of housing, eating similar food, wearing similar clothing, learning the language, and participating in the daily round of activities and in special events. Participation over a long period improves the quality of the data. The more time the researcher spends living a "normal" life in the field area, the more likely it is that the people being studied will also live "normal" lives. However, ethnographers are part of—and therefore always influence—any social situation they enter.

While participating in everyday life, the researcher carefully and thoroughly observes everything that is going on: who lives with whom, who interacts with whom in public, who are leaders and followers, what work people do, how people organize themselves for different activities, and far more. (See the Multiple Cultural Worlds box for a novel way of doing participant observation.) The range of topics that a participant observer must pay attention to is vast. Obviously, not everything can be cov-

ered. Unstructured observations form the basis for a daily field-note diary in which the researcher attempts to record as much detail as possible about what has been observed. This process generates masses of qualitative data.

More formal methods of gathering quantitative observational data involve planned observations of a particular activity. One type of quantitative observational research is time allocation study, which can be an important tool for understanding people's behaviour: work and leisure patterns, social interactions and group boundaries, and religious activities. This method relies on using Western time units as the basic matrix and then labelling or coding the activities that occur within certain time segments (Gross 1984). Each coding system responds to its particular context. For example, activity codes for types of "garden labour" designed for a horticultural society—burning, cutting, fencing, planting, soil preparation, weeding, and harvesting—would not be useful in a time allocation study in a retirement home. Observation may be continual, at fixed intervals (for instance, every 48 hours), or on a random basis.

Compared to other techniques for finding out about how people spend their time, observational methods are very time-consuming. Continuous observation limits the number of people that can be observed because it is so time-consuming. Spot observations may inadvertently miss important activities. In order to increase coverage, time allocation data can be collected by asking people to keep daily logs or diaries. Of course, self-reporting may include intentional or unintentional biases, but observations can help correct some of these.

Interviews and Questionnaires

In contrast to observing and recording events as they happen, an **interview,** or the gathering of verbal data through questions or guided conversation, is a more purposeful approach to research. An interview involves at least two people, the interviewer and the interviewee, and more during "group" interviews. Cultural anthropologists use varying interview styles and formats, depending on the kinds of information they seek, the amount of time they have, and their language skills. The least structured type of interview is called "open-ended." In an open-ended interview, the respondent (interviewee) takes the lead in setting the direction of the conversation, the topics to be covered, and the amount of time to be spent on a particular topic. The interviewer does not

Researching a Hakka Community in Cyberspace

Computer-mediated communication (CMC), such as e-mail, allows people who have never met to communicate with each other (Cheung 1998). It allows people to express opinions and share information in a participatory, rather than "top-down" way as in the case with television or journalism. CMC creates virtual social networks and contributes to the formation of new cultural patterns. Eriberto Lozada, a doctoral dissertation student at Harvard University, studied a "Hakka community in cyberspace" (1998:148). Many years ago, the Hakka people of southern China were mainly village-dwelling agriculturalists. Now, Hakka communities can be found in many countries, including Canada, the United States, Indonesia, and Malaysia. Lozada has done participant observation in a Hakka village in China in addition to studying the Hakka Global Network (HGN).

Hakka people worldwide are actively building Web sites about Hakka culture and promoting transnational communication at levels that would not have been imagined 10 years ago. Lozada conducted what he calls participant observation over the Internet for nearly two years. Using a search engine (WebCrawler), he searched for Web sites that had the word "Hakka" and found five listings. He joined one Web site and soon began receiving numerous messages. Over the years, he collected many e-mail messages, which form his data set. His analysis was of the messages themselves, not the people, since he had little data on the people other than that they tend to be highly educated people scattered around the world. Thus, this is a study of discourse and its possible meanings for the people involved. Lozada's analysis of the messages involved the search for persistent themes. Overall, he found that the prominent theme is preservation of Hakka culture in the face of global forces of change. Many of the messages provided announcements about television or radio broadcasts carrying items about Hakka culture; others included discussions of the Hakka language, origins, and customs. Many people requested information, such as the person who wrote about his grandfather who had immigrated to Borneo and died in a certain village; he asked if anyone knew the location of that village (158).

What can a cultural anthropologist learn about cyberspace Hakka culture from studying these Web sites and discussions and exchanges taking place between people who have never met? One conclusion of Lozada's is that through HGN, the Hakka are creating a "local global community," a new form of cultural organization that helps them deal with the present and shape the future in ways that no one can predict.

FOOD FOR THOUGHT

How does traditional participant observation differ from the participant observation that Lozada conducted?

What ethical problems might Lozada face in conducting this research?

---

interrupt or provide prompting questions. In this way, the researcher discovers what themes are important to the respondent.

Surveys and questionnaires administered during an interview session, in contrast, are more formal since they involve structured questions. Structured questions limit the range of possible responses, for example, by asking informants to rate their positions on a particular issue as very positive, positive, negative, very negative, or "no opinion." Ideally, the researcher should have enough familiarity with the study population to be able to design a formal questionnaire or survey that makes cultural sense. One anthropologist (Beyene 1989) dedicated time to an exploratory research phase in order to obtain background information before beginning formal interviews in her comparative study of women's reproductive experiences in Mexico and Greece:

During this initial phase of participant observation, I obtained data on women and their roles and activities, conducting unstructured and informal interviews with persons in the communities. Unstructured interviews were conducted with key informants such as older women, traditional healers, midwives, and medical personnel in the health services and clinics that served the villagers. As the process of participant observation and informal interviewing unfolded, a series of culturally relevant categories and information was developed around the issues of the menopausal experiences of women in the villages, which became the topics for the formal interviews. (6)

Marjorie Shostak (right) during fieldwork among the Ju/wasi of Botswana in 1975. Shostak focused her research on women's lives and wrote about Nisa, a Ju/wasi woman.

Researchers who take ready-made questionnaires to the field with them should, at the minimum, ask another researcher who knows the field area to review the instrument to see if it makes cultural sense. Additional revisions of the questionnaire may be required in the field to make it more appropriate to local conditions. A pilot survey, or trial run, before proceeding with a formal survey will reveal areas that need to be changed before the final version is used and should be considered an essential step.

Combining Watching and Asking

Many cultural anthropologists agree that formal interviews and questionnaires must be complemented by observational data on what people actually do (Sanjek 2000). Consider this example of a study that relied on interview data alone to examine the relationship between personal characteristics and participation in a fishing cooperative in Newfoundland (Jentoft and Davis 1993). The Canadian and Norwegian researchers conducted formal interviews with a questionnaire among 51 members of the fishing cooperative. Questions probed such issues as whether members were willing to donate their time

to cooperative projects, and what they valued most about the cooperative. On the basis of their responses, the researchers categorized the members into two basic groups: "rugged individualists" and "utilitarians." The people in the first group tended to be older and less educated than those in the latter group. According to the questionnaire responses, the rugged individualists were more willing to donate time to cooperative activities compared to the utilitarians. Since observational studies were not conducted, however, there is no way to know whether the respondents' self-reported participation in the cooperative corresponded to their actual involvement. Other research on the Canadian fishing industry examines the discourse of fishing. Adlam's study of "fish talk" among Mi'kmaq fishers of the Miramichi River, New Brunswick, (2002) contrasts the traditionalist with the modernist conception of the rapidly changing fishing economy.

Other Data-Gathering Techniques

Besides participating, observing, and asking questions of various types, cultural anthropologists use many other methods to gather data to fit their project goals. This section provides a sample of some of these methods.

Kinship Data One of the oldest field methods in cultural anthropology involves collecting data on **kinship**, or people's knowledge and beliefs about who is related to whom and how. In most cases, kinship information can be obtained through structured interviews. But, it is sometimes difficult to obtain accurate information. When Judith Okely (1993 [1984]) was doing research on Gypsies in England, a Gypsy friend warned her during her research that she "could be burned" for writing down a family history (4). Kinship information can be useful for examining systems of inheritance, marriage choices, and even political relationships.

Life History A **life history** is a qualitative, in-depth portrait of a single life experience as narrated by that person to the researcher. A life history provides the most intimate possible perspective on a culture. For example, in *Life Lived Like a Story*, three First Nations women living in the Yukon recount their life experiences through family genealogies, personal recollections, and traditional stories (Cruikshank 1990).

Anthropologists differ in their views about the value of the life history as a method in cultural anthropology, however. Early in the twentieth century, Franz Boas rejected this method as too unreliable since informants might lie or exaggerate (Peacock and Holland 1993). One of his students, Paul Radin, disagreed, however. He believed that "personal reminiscences and impressions" would throw light on the "workings of the mind" (1963 [1920]:2). Radin's publication of the autobiography of a Winnebago Indian of Wisconsin, referred to only by his initials S.B., reveals much about how his life course was affected by involvement in the Peyote Cult that was active in Nebraska. He provides vivid descriptions of the visions and feelings he had while under the influence of the drug peyote: "Now this is what I felt and saw. The one Earthmaker (god) is a spirit and that is what I felt and saw. All of us sitting there, we had all together one spirit or soul; at least that is what I learned. I instantly became the spirit and I was their spirit or soul. Whatever they thought of, I (immediately) knew it" (59).

Current understanding of cultural variation throws into question the possibility of ever finding people who are representative of an entire culture. Thus, some anthropologists seek informants who occupy a particular social niche; for example, Gananath Obeyesekere's book, *Medusa's Hair: An Essay on Personal Symbols and Religious Experience*, presents the life histories of four Sri Lankan people, three women and one man (1981). Each one became a religious devotee and ascetic, physically distinguished by their thickly matted hair, which became mysteriously twisted in a snake-like fashion. According to these four people, they cannot comb out their hair: It is permanently matted. The devotees explain that the god's presence is in their hair. Using material in the life histories of these people, Obeyesekere provides an interpretation suggesting that they all suffered deep psychological afflictions, including sexual anxieties. Their matted hair symbolizes this suffering and provides them with a special status as holy and thus outside the bounds of normal married life and sexual relations.

Alternatively, life histories of several people within one social category can be collected to provide a picture of both shared experiences and individual differences. James Freeman's book, *Hearts of Sorrow* (1989), is an example of this approach. It presents "cuts" from several life stories of Vietnamese refugees living in southern California. Together, the story cuts portray both a shared sadness of the refugees about the loss of their homeland

One of the Sri Lankan women whose life story Gananath Obeyesekere analyzed, a priestess to the deity Kataragama, stands in the shrine room of her house holding her long, matted hair.

and a range of adaptive experiences of the different individuals.

The ability of informants to "present" a story of their lives varies, depending on the cultural context. An attempt to gather life histories from women on Goodenough Island of Papua New Guinea was difficult because telling one's life story is a masculine style of presentation and the women were reluctant to adopt it (M. Young 1983). Marjorie Shostak (1981), in contrast, found a willing and extremely expressive informant for a life story in Nisa, an indigenous woman of the Ju/wasi of the Kalahari Desert in southern Africa. Nisa's book-length story, presented in her voice, includes rich details about her childhood and several marriages.

Texts Many cultural anthropologists, especially interpretive anthropologists, emphasize the value of collecting and analyzing texts. The category of "text" includes written or oral stories, myths, plays, sayings, speeches, jokes, and transcriptions of people's everyday conversations. In the early twentieth century, Franz Boas collected thousands of pages of texts from First Nations groups of the Northwest Coast of Canada, including myths, songs, speeches, and accounts of how to perform rituals. These texts are useful records of cultures that have changed since the time of his fieldwork. More recently, First Nations communities have made use of early ethnohistorical texts to assist them in recovering forgotten aspects of their culture.

Historical Sources
History is culture of the past, and it therefore has much relevance to understanding contemporary cultures. Ann Stoler (1985, 1989) made excellent use of archival resources in her study of Dutch colonialism in Java. Her research has exposed rich details about colonial strategies, the culture of the colonizers themselves, and their impact on indigenous Javanese culture. Most countries have libraries and historical archives in which written records of the past are maintained. Local official archives are rich sources of information about land ownership, agricultural production, religious practices, and political activities. London, Paris, and Amsterdam contain records of colonial contact and relations. The National Archives of Canada, provincial archives, and mission reports provided valuable evidence on the development of residential schools for Native Peoples in Canada (D. Smith 2001). Meticulous record keeping in France meant that Harriet Rosenberg (1988) had access to information about dowries, wills, marriage contracts, court cases, land survey registers, tax rolls, and family histories for reconstructing the history of a village in the French Alps.

Fieldwork among living people can also yield rich historical information. Several methods exist to help the anthropologist delve into the cultural past. When investigating the recent past of Native American culture in New England, William Simmons (1986) knocked on doors of houses where the mailboxes had names that seemed of possible Native American heritage. He sometimes discovered long-forgotten diaries and family memorabilia tucked away in the closets and attics of these homes. Interviewing older informants about what they remember can often reveal not only events about their earlier lives but also history that they were told by their parents and grandparents.

Anthropologists study patterns of what people remember and what they don't, how culture shapes their memories, and how their memories shape their culture. Information on how memory is shaped exists in collections of letters, diaries, and family photograph albums. The importance of memory, not simply as a record of history but as interpretive reconstruction, is increasing in anthropology (Antz and Lambek 1996) and in the public domain.

Multiple Research Methods and Team Projects
Most cultural anthropologists use several different methods for their research, since just one would not provide all the kinds of data necessary to understand a given problem. For example, a small survey of 40 households provides some breadth of coverage, but adding some life histories (of five men and five women, perhaps) provides depth. **Triangulation** is a technique that involves obtaining information on a particular topic from more than one angle or perspective (Robson 1993:290). Asking only one person something provides information from only that person's viewpoint. Asking two people about the same thing doubles the information and often reveals that perspectives differ. The researcher may then want to check other sources on the same topic, such as written records or newspaper reports for additional perspectives.

In Canada, team research may also involve several anthropologists and students working together with members of First Nations communities to document land claims or assess the consequences of new hydroelectric development projects for their communities. The James Bay Cree Project, which began in 1971 at McGill University in Montreal, trained graduate students in anthropology to do research for local agencies representing indigenous groups, providing information useful in settling the James Bay land claim (Trigger 1997; Salisbury 1986).

Another way of gaining a more complex and complete view is through team projects that involve cultural anthropologists and researchers from other disciplines to provide additional skills. A research project designed to assess the effects of constructing a dam on the agricultural and fishing practices of people in the Senegal

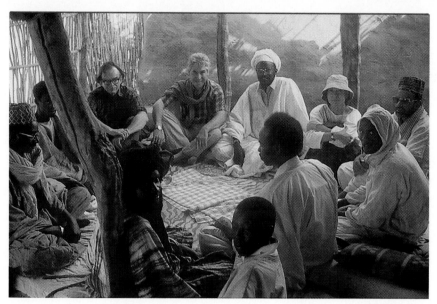

A multidisciplinary team consisting of anthropologists, engineers, and agricultural experts from North America and Senegal meet to discuss a resettlement project.

and needs no elaboration. But when you are in the field for a year—even for a month—you will find that "just" taking notes is quite complicated. After discussing note taking, we turn to other forms of recording data including tape recording, photography, and video.

Field Notes

The classic impression of anthropological research is that of the cultural anthropologist observing a ritual, with notebook and pen in hand. From the beginning of cultural anthropology, field notes have been the basic way to record observations. Field notes include daily logs, personal journals, descriptions of events, and notes about those notes. Ideally, researchers should "write up" their field notes each day. Otherwise, a backlog piles up of daily "scratch notes," or rough jottings made on a small pad or note card carried in the pocket (Sanjek 1990a:95–99). Trying to capture, in the fullest way possible, the events of a single day is a monumental task and can result in dozens of pages of handwritten or typed field notes each day. The bulk of an anthropologist's time in the field is probably spent taking rough notes by hand. The invention of the laptop computer now allows anthropologists to enter many of these notes directly into the computer.

River Valley, West Africa, included cultural anthropologists, hydrologists, and agronomists (Horowitz and Salem-Murdock 1993). In another project, a cultural anthropologist and a nutritionist worked together to study the effects of adopting new agricultural practices in the Amazon (Gross and Underwood 1971).

Recording Culture

Imagine the cultural anthropologist in the field—participating, observing, conducting interviews, and using other techniques such as asking people to keep records of their time allocation. How does the anthropologist keep track of all this information and record it for future analysis? As with everything else about fieldwork, things have changed since the early times when a typewriter, index cards, and pencils were the major recording tools. Still, there is continuity: Taking copious notes is still the trademark method of recording data for a cultural anthropologist. This section begins with a discussion of note taking, a process that you may think is simple

Tape Recording, Photography, Videos, and Films

Tape recorders are an obvious aid to fieldwork because they allow the accurate recording of much more information than taking notes by hand. However, tape recording may raise problems such as informants' suspicions about a machine that can capture their voices, and the ethical issue of maintaining anonymity of informants whose actual voices are preserved on tape. María Cátedra (1992) reports on her use of tape recording during research in rural Spain in the 1970s:

At first the existence of the "apparatus," as they called it, was part wonder and part suspect. Many had never seen one before and were fascinated to hear their own voice, but all were worried about what I would do with the tapes.... I tried to solve the problem by explaining what I would do with the tapes: I would use them to record correctly what people told me, since my memory was not good enough and I could not take notes quickly enough.... One event helped people to accept my integrity in regard to the "apparatus." In the second braña *[small settlement] I visited, people asked me to play back what the people of the first* braña *had told me, especially some songs sung by a group of men. At first I was going to do it, but then I instinctively refused because I did not have the first people's permission.... My stand was quickly known in the first* braña *and commented on with approval. (21–22)*

A problem with tape recordings is that they have to be transcribed (typed up), either partially or completely. Each hour of recorded talk takes between five to eight hours to transcribe, on average. Even more time is needed if the recording is garbled, many voices are heard at once, or complications in translation arise.

Like tape recordings, photographs, films, or videos may catch and retain more detail than rough notes. Any researcher who has watched people doing a ritual, taken rough notes, and then tried to reconstruct the details of the ritual later on in more detailed field notes knows how much of the sequencing and related activity is lost to memory within just a few hours. Reviewing photographs or a video recording of the ritual provides a surprising amount of forgotten, or missed, material. But there is a trade-off. Using a camera or video recorder precludes taking notes simultaneously. Since field notes are invaluable, even if the video is also available, it is best to use a team approach. Kirsten Hastrup (1992) provides an insightful description of her use of photography—and its limitations—in recording the annual ram exhibition in Iceland that celebrates the successful herding in of the sheep from mountain pastures. Hastrup took many photographs. After they were developed, she was struck by how flat they were and how little of the totality of the event they conveyed. Photographs and films, just like field notes and other forms of recorded culture, provide only partial images of a cultural event.

Rosalind Morris (1994a) examined ethnographic films of the Northwest Coast of Canada. From the earliest films made of the Northwest Coast (1914), the Kwakwaka'wakw, Nootka, Tsimshian, and Haida, in addition to other First Nations peoples, have been represented by outsiders who made films that drew attention to potlatches, feasts, totem poles, and wood carvings. More recently, films have been made by and for First Nations communities, and they focus more on land-claim disputes and other struggles with provincial and federal governments (Morris 1994a:118). Clearly, films are no more objective than any other form of recorded culture since it is the researcher who selects what the camera will capture. (See the Critical Thinking box for a discussion of the interpretation of ethnographic photographs.)

Data Analysis

During the research process, a vast amount of data in many forms is collected. The question is how to use these data to increase our understanding of human societies. Ethnographic research mostly entails qualitative, prose-based analysis, in combination with quantitative (numeric) data where appropriate. Qualitative data can be rendered in quantitative terms, and reporting on quantitative results necessarily requires descriptive analysis of local conditions to accompany graphs, charts, and computations.

Analyzing Qualitative Data

Qualitative data include descriptive field notes, informants' narratives, myths and stories, and songs and sagas. Relatively few set guidelines exist for undertaking qualitative analysis of qualitative data. One general procedure of qualitative analysis is to search for themes, or regularities, in the data. This approach involves exploring the data, or "playing" with the data, either "by hand" or with the use of a computer. Jennifer Robertson's analysis of her Kodaira data was inspired by writer Gertrude Stein's approach to writing "portraits" of individuals, such as *Picasso* (1959). Robertson says that Stein was a superb ethnographer who was able to illuminate the nature of her subjects and their worlds through a process that Stein referred to as "condensation." To do this, "she scrutinized her subjects until, over time, there emerged for her a repeating pattern of their words and actions. Her literary

Photography and Anthropology

Since books were first written in anthropology, many authors illustrated their ethnographies with black and white photographs of their "subjects." *Anthropology and Photography 1860–1920* (Edwards 1992) examines the parallel development of anthropology and photography as cameras enabled "exotic" peoples to be viewed by an external audience. Contemporary ethnographies continue this practice, hopefully with more sensitivity and reflection about the representation of others.

Textbooks in anthropology also use illustrations to draw the eyes and interests of students (and to break up the text), to illustrate abstract principles in the discipline, and to provide visual images of the people discussed in the text. Photographs relate to textual arguments in distinctive ways; they may supplement, complement, or even contradict written accounts. They may be arranged in groups to suggest comparison, or juxtaposed in a striking manner to illustrate change. They often document a technical process or a material object that may be unfamiliar to the reader and difficult to describe in words.

Photographs may be "worth a thousand words," but they never speak for themselves. Their meanings are shaped by the interaction between the producer of the image, the subject of the image, and the viewer. You may have a personal response to a photograph that may be quite unlike the response the photographer intended. The choice of photograph to be inserted into the text is determined by the authors and publishers; thus, the set of photographs in a textbook already represents a selection of what others think is instructive. Even captions draw attention to how you are expected to analyze photographs. Thus, the photograph is never a snapshot of reality, but something that must be interpreted.

CRITICAL THINKING QUESTIONS

To improve your "visual literacy," consider each of the photographs used in this textbook:

What questions does the photograph raise for you?

How might the presence of the camera alter the event recorded in the photo?

How do you think the community or subject of the photograph would react to the use of the photo in a textbook of anthropology?

What ethical issues are raised by the use of this photograph?

Select a photograph that illustrates rapport, ethnocentrism, gender inequity, racism, globalization, acculturation, or other concept.

Suggest an alternative caption for the photograph.

What does the photograph say about the culture portrayed and the representing culture?

---

portraits… were condensations of her subjects' repeatings" (Robertson 1991:1). Like Stein, Robertson reflected on all that she had experienced and learned in Kodaira, beginning with the years when she lived there as a child. Emerging from all this was the dominant theme, *furusato*, which literally means "old village." References to *furusato* appear frequently in people's accounts of the past, conveying a sense of nostalgia for a more "real" past. Many qualitative anthropologists use computers to help sort for **tropes** (key themes). Computer scanning of data offers the ability to search vast quantities of data more quickly and perhaps more accurately than the human eye. The range of software available for such data management, for example ETHNO and The Ethnograph, is expanding. Of course, the quality of the results depends on, first, careful and complete inputting of the data and,

second, an intelligent coding scheme that will tell the computer what it should be scanning for in the data.

The ethnographic presentation of qualitative data relies heavily on the use of quotations of informants—their stories, explanations, and conversations. Although most ethnographies also include analytical commentary, some provide just the informants' words. Lila Abu-Lughod followed this approach in her book, *Writing Women's Worlds* (1993). She presents Bedouin women's stories and conversations within a light authorial framework that organizes the stories into thematic clusters such as marriage, production, and honour. Although she provides a rather traditional, scholarly introduction to the narratives, she offers no conclusion. In her view, a conclusion would give a false sense of authorial control over the narratives. She prefers to prompt readers to think for themselves about the meanings of the stories and what they say about Bedouin life.

Some anthropologists question the value of interpretive analyses on the ground that they lack verifiability or reliability: Too much depends on the individual selection process of the anthropologist, and too much is built around too few cases. Most anthropologists would respond that verifiability in the scientific sense is not their goal and it is not a worthwhile goal for cultural anthropology in general. Instead, they seek to provide a plausible interpretation, an evocation, or new understanding that has detail and richness as its strengths rather than replicability. They would criticize purely quantitative research for its lack of richness and depth of understanding, even though it has the appearance of validity.

Analyzing Quantitative Data

Analysis of quantitative, or numeric data, can proceed in several directions. Some of the more sophisticated methods require knowledge of statistics, and many require the use of a computer and a software package that can perform statistical computations. In Barbara Miller's (1987a) research on low-income household budgeting patterns in Jamaica, she used computer analysis first to divide the sample households into three income groups (lower, medium, higher). She then used the computer to calculate percentages of expenditures in the three categories on individual goods and groups of goods such as food, alcohol, dry goods, housing, and transportation. Because the number of households in the study was relatively small (120), the analysis could have been done "by hand." However, using the computer helped the analysis proceed more quickly and more accurately.

Writing about Culture

Ethnography, or writing about culture, is one of the main projects of cultural anthropology. Ethnographies range across a continuum from realist to reflexive. Realist and reflexive ethnographies both provide insights about culture, and both are valid presentations of something about culture by someone from another culture who is participating in the culture being described. In realist ethnographies, authors include less material about themselves directly in the text. In a realist ethnography, a single author typically narrates the findings in a dispassionate, third-person voice. The ethnography includes attention to the behaviour of members of the culture, theoretical analysis of certain features of the culture, and usually a brief account of why the work was undertaken. The result is a description and explanation of certain cultural practices. Realist ethnographies appear to follow a more scientific approach and attempt to present findings that more than one person would be able to discover about another culture. Most early works by such anthropologists as Malinowski, Mead, and Radcliffe-Brown are in the category of realist ethnography, which is still the predominant form of ethnography. For example, Katherine Verdery's study of economic and political change in Romania, *What Was Socialism, and What Comes Next?* (1996), is a realist ethnography. In this book she presents both description and analysis about how Romanian socialism operated politically and economically and how its effects are now being felt in terms of Romanian nationalism and nationalist sentiments in the post-socialist era. A clear argument threads through the descriptive material: Verdery says that socialism did not cause the current conflicts and sentiments about Romanian nationhood, but it did contribute to them by perpetuating and intensifying them.

In contrast, reflexive ethnographies explore the research experience itself, in addition to generating or presenting wider theoretical arguments and analysis: "The story itself… is a representational means of cracking open the culture and the fieldworker's way of knowing it" (Van Maanen 1988:103). Reflexive ethnographies are distinguished by the degree to which the authors include their fieldwork experience as an important part of the ethnography. They are thus characterized by highly personalized styles and findings. In contrast to realist ethnographies, reflexive ethnographers frequently use the word "I" in their writings. Reflexive ethnographers offer more poetically insightful perspectives that might not be perceived or grasped by anyone except the particular anthropologist involved. An example in this category is Vincent Crapanzano's (1980) classic study, *Tuhami*, which explores the life history of a Moroccan man who believed he was possessed by spirits. Crapanzano interweaves the effects of his own presence and perspectives into an understanding of the ethnography. Crapanzano explains, "As Tuhami's interlocutor, I became an active participant in his life history…. Not only did my presence, and my questions, prepare him for the text he was to produce, but they produced what I read as a change of consciousness in him. They produced a change of consciousness in me, too" (11).

Ethics and Responsibility in Cultural Anthropology

Ethical Concerns in Perspective

Anthropology was one of the first disciplines to devise and adopt a code of ethics. Two major events in the 1950s and 1960s led American anthropologists to reconsider their role in research in relation to both the sponsors (or funders) of their research and the people whom they were studying. The first was the infamous "Project Camelot" of the 1950s. Project Camelot was a plan of the United States government to influence political leadership and stability in South America (Horowitz 1967). To further this goal, the United States government employed several anthropologists, who were to gather detailed information on political events and leaders in particular countries without revealing their purpose, and then report back to their sponsor (the United States government) about their findings. It is still unclear whether the anthropologists involved were completely informed about the purposes to which their data would be put.

The second major event was the Vietnam War (or the American War, as it is called in Vietnam). This brought to the forefront conflicts about government interests in ethnographic information, the role of the anthropologist, and the protection of the people studied. American anthropologists were recruited and funded to provide information that could help subvert communism in Vietnam and Thailand (Wakin 1992). The Vietnam War affected Canadian anthropology, as many anthropologists participated in teach-ins and anti-war protests, and many departments of anthropology absorbed American draft resistors as graduate students and professors, aligning some Canadian departments more closely with American ones.

In 1970, a standard code of ethics was adopted by the American Anthropological Association (AAA). This code states that the anthropologist's primary responsibility is to ensure the safety of the people being studied. A related principle is that cultural anthropology does not condone covert or "undercover" research. The people being studied should be informed that they are being studied and the purposes for which they are being studied. Long a practice in biomedical research, the principle of **informed consent** requires that the researcher fully inform the research participants of the intent, scope, and possible effects of the study and seek their consent to be in the study. Anthropologists have adapted the concept of informed consent to make it applicable to the varied contexts in which cultural anthropologists work (Fluehr-Lobban 1994).

Canadian anthropologists face new ethical demands as they must now conform to the ethics policies of cross-disciplinary research agencies, in addition to meeting university and anthropology standards. Many anthropologists say that the nature of anthropological research often makes it difficult to apply the strict standards of informed consent that are used in medical settings. For example, people in nonliterate societies may be frightened by being asked to sign a typed document of consent that they cannot read. Given that the intent of informed consent is a good one—people should be aware of the purpose and scope and possible effects of a study involving them—each anthropologist should consider some way to achieve this goal. Holding a "town meeting" with all community members present and explaining the research project is one approach.

In presenting the results of one's research, whether in a book or a film, all efforts should be made to protect the anonymity of the people in the study unless they give permission for their identities to be revealed. The usual practice in writing ethnographies has been to change the name of the specific group, area, or village, blur the location, and use made-up names for individuals mentioned.

Some topics are more sensitive than others, and some topics are sensitive to some groups and not others (Lee and Renzetti 1993). Governments may decree that certain subjects are simply off limits for research by foreigners. Strictly speaking, an anthropologist should abide by the ethical guideline stating that rulings of host governments are to be respected. Sometimes, such rules can be highly restrictive. For example, the Indian government allows no foreigners to visit the Nicobar Islands, and it has strict regulations that limit how long foreigners—tourists or anthropologists—can spend in the Andamans (only 30 days). Major factors influencing the extreme sensitivity of

Sex Is a Sensitive Topic

Richard Parker went to Brazil to study the historical and political aspects of Carnaval (1991). As he explored the festival and got to know participants, he began to realize how closely linked it is to sexual symbolism and sexuality, both heterosexual and homosexual. Simultaneously, he realized how important an understanding of these topics was to a better understanding of Brazilian culture in general. As his research continued, he began to be trusted by both heterosexuals and gay men and lesbians, and therefore gained access to their multiple cultural worlds. The quality of his personal relationships with his some 30 participants was the key factor in the success of the study. Parker mentions passing "a set of initial barriers," though he does not elaborate on these (177).

Parker's focus on sexual culture, in fact, supported a shared sense of breaking the rules of social decorum, something that would not arise out of a study of a nonsensitive topic, such as work roles or family life. Parker found that, once he had gained people's trust, "informants often seemed to take a certain pleasure in being part of a project which seemed to break the rules of proper decorum… that while they often resisted, understandably, speaking too directly about their own sexual lives, they seemed to enjoy (and, at times, to take a positive delight in) the opportunity to speak freely about the question of sex more generally" (177).

Parker's personal skills and rapport with his informants are evident in the rich data that he collected on such taboo topics as masturbation, oral sex, and anal sex. Thus, the sheer sensitivity of a topic does not always prevent its study—as long as the researcher is sensitive, too.

A street scene during Carnaval in Rio de Janeiro, Brazil. Cultural anthropologists often focus on festivals and other special events as important expressions of values and identity.

FOOD FOR THOUGHT

How would you respond if a cultural anthropologist wanted to interview you about your sexual practices?

---

the Indian government about foreigners in the Andaman and Nicobar Islands include the islands' strategic location near Myanmar (Burma) and Indonesia, and the need to protect the indigenous peoples from unwanted contact.

Anthropologists researching First Nations communities in Canada must follow stringent guidelines and be approved by band councils, as well as obtaining the usual ethics approvals discussed above. Research is conducted in partnership with the council and community, and the results of research are expected to be shared with the community, although individuals retain the right to privacy.

Sexual behaviour is another important example of a potentially sensitive research topic, more from the point of view of informants than host governments. Sexual practices and ideas cannot be researched in depth without excellent rapport. In most cultures, homosexuality is even more difficult to research than heterosexuality because it may contravene mainstream norms or even laws (see the Multiple Cultural Worlds box).

Danger in the Field

Fieldwork can involve serious physical and psychological risks to the researcher and to members of his or her family if they are also in the field. A pervasive value on "the anthropologist as hero" has muffled, to a large degree, both the physical dangers and psychological risks of fieldwork. Attention to fieldwork safety has recently been addressed by an inquiry into the hazards faced by anthropologists while conducting fieldwork, including mental health problems (Howell 1990). Howell's book (based on the experiences of anthropologists) ends with specific recommendations about how fieldworkers can prepare themselves more effectively for risks they might face. Some departments (including many in Canada) require students to submit a form indicating that they are aware of possible risks in the field and have taken precautions to ensure that their fieldwork will be as safe as possible. Dangers from the physical environment can be fatal. The slippery paths of the highlands of the Philippines caused the death in the early 1980s of Michelle Zimbalist Rosaldo, one of the major figures in contemporary cultural anthropology. Disease is another major risk factor. Many anthropologists have contracted contagious diseases, such as malaria and typhoid, which stay with them throughout their lives. Bernard Deacon (Gardiner 1984), a young British anthropologist who went to Malekula, a South Pacific island, was a victim of tropical disease. His memoir, composed of letters he wrote from the field and published after his death by the woman he would have married on his return, records his observations of the prevalence of disease among the Malekulans:

> I am terribly overstrained, my work here seems all to be going to bits. There seems nothing here but Death—a man was dead in the village this morning of dysentery.... In one village of 20, 9 died in one week.... It's not like death in war or crisis—it is the final death, the death of a people, a race, and they know it more clearly than we do.... Spanish influenza has wiped out whole villages in Santo, Pentecost & Malekula, one might say districts. As for work, I despair & despair again. (34–35)

A few days before he was to leave the field, Deacon caught blackwater fever, which caused his death at the age of 24.

Social violence in the field figures prominently in some recent ethnographic research experiences. During the five years that Philippe Bourgois lived in East Harlem, he witnessed a shooting outside his window, a bombing and machine-gunning of a numbers joint, a shoot-out and police car chase in front of the pizza parlour where he was eating, the aftermath of a fire-bombing of a heroin house, a dozen serious fights, and "almost daily exposure to broken-down human beings, some of them in fits of crack-induced paranoia, some suffering from delirium tremens, and others in unidentifiable pathological fits of screaming and shouting insults to all around them" (1995:32). He was rough-handled by the police several times because they could not believe that he was "just a professor" doing research, and he was mugged for the sum of $8. Bourgois's research placed him in physical danger as well as psychological risk. Nevertheless, it also enabled him to gain understanding of oppression from the inside.

New Directions: Towards Participatory Fieldwork

The freedom of a cultural anthropologist to represent a culture as she or he perceives it is a power issue that is increasingly being brought into question, especially by indigenous peoples who read about themselves in Western ethnographies. The people that anthropologists have traditionally studied—the non-elites of rural India, Ireland, and Papua New Guinea—are now able to read English, French, and German. They can therefore critique what has been written about their culture. Annette Weiner (1976) learned from people in the Trobriand Islands that some Trobrianders who had read sections of *Argonauts of the Western Pacific* thought that Malinowski had not gotten things right (xvi).

One of the newest directions in cultural anthropology fieldwork is the attempt to involve the study population in actively shaping the data collection and presentation. This change reflects an interest on the part of anthropologists to refrain from treating people as "subjects" and to consider them more as collaborators in writing culture. However, anthropologists must continue to take full responsibility for the effects that their work may have on the communities they study.

Key Questions Revisited

How do cultural anthropologists conduct research on culture?

Cultural anthropologists conduct research by doing fieldwork and using its characteristic method called participant observation. Fieldwork and participant observation became the cornerstones of cultural anthropology research after Malinowski's fieldwork in the Trobriand Islands during World War I. These methods emphasize the importance of living for an extended period of time with the people being studied and learning the local language.

What does fieldwork involve?

Some basic steps in doing fieldwork have been established since the time of Malinowski. They include site selection, gaining rapport, and dealing with culture shock. Depending on one's theoretical perspective, specific research techniques may emphasize quantitative or qualitative data gathering. Cultural materialists tend to focus on quantitative data while interpretive anthropologists gather more qualitative data. Taking notes by hand has always been the hallmark of data recording, but now it is complemented by other methods, including laptop computers, photography, and audio and video recording. Data analysis and presentation, like data collection, are guided by the anthropologist's theoretical orientation and goals. Emphasis on quantitative or qualitative techniques of data collection shape the way the data are organized and presented, for example, whether statistics and tables are used.

What are some special issues in cultural anthropology research?

Questions of ethics have been paramount to anthropologists since the 1950s. American anthropologists developed a set of ethical guidelines for research in 1970 to address their concern about what role, if any, anthropologists should play in research that might harm the people being studied. The first rule listed in the AAA code of ethics states that the anthropologist's primary responsibility is to maintain the safety of the people involved. Thus, anthropologists should never engage in covert research and should always endeavour to explain their purpose to the people in the study and maintain anonymity of the location and individuals. Other special issues include the role, responsibility, and safety of anthropologists who are conducting research in dangerous conditions.

Core Concepts

culture shock, p. 41
deductive research, p. 42
discourse, p. 42
emic, p. 42
etic, p. 42

fieldwork, p. 32
inductive research, p. 42
informed consent, p. 52
interview, p. 43
kinship, p. 45

life history, p. 45
multi-sited research, p. 33
participant observation, p. 32
qualitative research, p. 42
quantitative research, p. 42

rapport, p. 37
research methods, p. 43
transnationalism, p. 34
triangulation, p. 47
tropes, p 50

Suggested Readings

H. Russell Bernard, *Research Methods in Cultural Anthropology: Qualitative and Quantitative Approaches*. 2nd edition. Newbury Park, CA: Sage Publications, 1995. This is a sourcebook of anthropological research methods—from how to design a research project to data analysis and presentation.

Sidney C. H. Cheung, *On the South China Track: Perspectives on Anthropological Research and Teaching*. Hong Kong: Hong Kong Institute of Asia-Pacific Studies, 1998. Thirteen chapters explore aspects of anthropological research and teaching in Chinese cultures including Hong Kong, China, Taiwan, and Singapore.

S. Cole and L. Phillips, *Ethnographic Feminisms*. Ottawa: Carleton University Press, 1995. This book of readings explores how feminist anthropologists have approached ethnography, and includes experimental approaches to writing ethnography in innovative ways.

Peggy Golde, ed., *Women in the Field: Anthropological Experiences*. 2nd edition. Berkeley: University of California Press, 1986. This text provides 15 chapters on fieldwork by women anthropologists including Margaret Mead's fieldwork in the Pacific, Laura Nader's fieldwork in Mexico and Lebanon, Ernestine Friedl's fieldwork in Greece, and Jean Briggs's fieldwork among the Inuit of the Canadian Arctic.

Bruce Grindal and Frank Salamone, eds., *Bridges to Humanity: Narratives on Anthropology and Friendship*. Prospect Heights, IL: Waveland Press, 1995. The 14 chapters of this text explore the "humanistic" dimension of fieldwork, in which the anthropologist reflects on the friendships established in the field, how they contributed to the fieldwork, and how or if they can be continued once the anthropologist leaves the field.

Joy Hendry, *An Anthropologist in Japan: Glimpses of Life in the Field*. London: Routledge, 1999. This book is a first-person account of the author's third research project in Japan, including information on her original research design, how the focus changed, and how she reached unanticipated conclusions.

Carolyn Nordstrom and Antonius C. G. M. Robben, eds., *Fieldwork under Fire: Contemporary Studies of Violence and Survival*. Berkeley: University of California Press, 1995. After an introductory chapter discussing general themes, examples are provided of fieldwork experiences in dangerous situations including Palestine, China, Sri Lanka, United States, Croatia, Guatemala, and Ireland.

Roger Sanjek, ed., *Fieldnotes: The Makings of Anthropology*. Ithaca: Cornell University Press, 1990. This text includes 16 chapters by cultural anthropologists on taking and using field notes in ethnographic research in diverse settings.

 Your *Cultural Anthropology*, Second Canadian Edition Media Edition CD-ROM contains many Web sites relevant to this chapter. Use it to explore the Web and to expand your knowledge of anthropology.

Chapter 3

Economies and Their Modes of Production

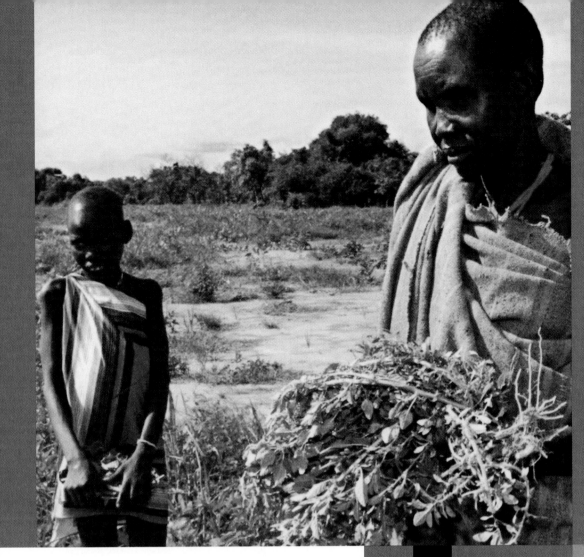

During a time of food shortage in 1999, a Sudanese mother and her daughter collect edible leaves.

Key Questions

What is the scope of economic anthropology?

What are the characteristics of the five major modes of production?

What are some directions of change in the five modes of production?

*F*or thousands of years of human life, people made their living by gathering food and other basic necessities from nature. Everyone had equal access to life-sustaining resources. We now live in a rather different cultural world. In October 2000, the press carried a story about how a woman in Florida had established the name of the Yanomami, an Amazonian tribe who live in the rain forest in Venezuela, for a Web site address, www.yanomami.com, and was auctioning it for $25 000. When leaders of the 26 000 Yanomami people heard about this, they were not happy. While the Yanomami themselves do not yet have access to the Internet, they may soon. At that point, they may want to use their own tribal name for their site. But to do so, they will have to buy it. Private property has now moved into the virtual realm. Cultural anthropologists have long studied economic systems cross-culturally. In this globalizing world, they have to study that and much more: the new global economy, e-commerce, and how these changes affect economic systems that have been around for thousands of years.

In this chapter we explore how people cross-culturally make a living. This topic fits within the scope of the subfield of economic anthropology, which is the cross-cultural study of **economic systems.** Economic systems include three major areas: **production,** or making goods or money; **consumption,** or using up goods or money; and **exchange,** or the transfer of goods or money between people or institutions. This chapter looks at the first area. We review the characteristics of the five major **modes of production,** or the dominant way of making a living in a society, and we consider examples of change in each of these modes.

Cultural Anthropology and Economic Systems

This section discusses two basic features of the study of production in cultural anthropology. The first is a brief introduction to the important modes of production, along with a discussion of how they are useful as categories but, like all categories, they are not perfect. These categories provide the conceptual foundation for all the material that appears in subsequent chapters of this book, so you must know them well. Second, this section raises the question of whether people in all cultures make a sharp conceptual distinction between "culture" and "nature" as most people in Western/European cultures do. It appears that whether or not people do this is related to the kind of economic system in which they live.

Modes of Production

In their study of production cross-culturally, cultural anthropologists have gathered rich data that are then placed into analytical categories, called modes of production. Categorizing a certain society as having a particular mode of production implies an emphasis on that type of production and does not mean that it is the only kind of production undertaken. In a given society, not everyone will necessarily be involved in the dominant mode of production. Also, a particular individual may be involved in more than one; for example, a person could be both a farmer and a herder. In most cultures, however, a dominant mode of production exists that analysts use as a basis for classification. These categories blend with and overlap each other, but they are nonetheless useful as broad generalizations.

The modes of production are discussed in order of their historical appearance in the human record. Please note, though, this continuum does not mean that a particular mode of production evolves into the one following it—for example, foragers do not necessarily transform into horticulturalists—and so on, across the continuum. Nor does this ordering imply any kind of judgment about level of sophistication or superiority of the more recent modes of production. Even the oldest system involves complex and detailed knowledge about the environment that a contemporary city dweller, if transported to a rain forest, would find difficult to learn as a basis for survival. Furthermore, none of these systems of production is "frozen in time," for they have all undergone change.

Nature, Modes of Production, and Thought

In its most basic sense, human economic adaptation must deal with what nature has to offer in terms of resources and the constraints it places on satisfying human material needs. A general finding about Western **capitalism** is that it has a dualist view that separates the concepts of nature and culture and places culture as dominant over nature. Cultural anthropologists debate about whether such nature/culture **dualism** is a cultural universal.

Sherry Ortner (1974) proposed that a nature/culture distinction is universal and that culture is always more highly valued than nature. She pairs that distinction with another that she says is universal: male and female, with a similar higher valuation on the male than the female. The simple formula she generated says that "nature:culture:female:male" or, "nature is to culture as female is to male." She asserts that females in all cultures are thought to be closer to nature because their reproductive physiology involves childbirth and related domestic roles. Men, in contrast, are thought to be involved in "the projects of culture." Ortner explains that "in reality," women are not any closer to nature than men, but that is the model that all cultures have constructed.

Since the time of Ortner's theoretical proposition, many cultural anthropologists have considered the question of the universality of the nature/culture duality. Cross-cultural data indicate that many cultures do not have a dualist view of nature and culture, they do not liken culture and nature to gender categories, and they do not place culture in a dominant position. For example, the Hagen people of highland Papua New Guinea divide the world into three categories: humans and human activity, spirits, and the wild (M. Strathern 1980). None of these categories match the English terms "nature" and "culture." There is no strict gender match-up with these categories since males and females can be found in all three. There is no hierarchical relationship among the three. In another example that is nondualist, the Nayaka, a South Indian tribal group, conceive of the natural environment with metaphors that involve relatedness and not separateness, as in the Western model (Bird-David 1993). The Nayaka's image of relatedness is based on the caring relationship between an adult and a child: nature, like a parent, gives generously to its children. In ritual and everyday talk, the Nayaka frequently describe and address the forest as a parent and thank it for affection and food. Other tribal cultures also have relatedness metaphors concerning the natural environment, including the Cree of North America, the Western Desert Aborigines of Australia, and the Ju/wasi of southern Africa. This evidence strongly suggests that relatedness metaphors, compared to binary/hierarchical metaphors, are common in nonindustrial, noncapitalist cultures.

The dualist and nondualist ideologies seem correlated with different environmental outcomes. The Western binary distinction between culture and nature supports resource exploitation in the global competition for economic growth. The nondualistic conceptualizations of nature relatedness correspond to economies and lifestyles that demand less from the environment in terms of resources and contribute to sustainability in the long term.

Globalization and the World Economy

The emergence and evolution of capitalism has had far-reaching effects on all modes of production. According to one social theorist, global capitalism involves world trade in goods and transfers of labour and resources. Global capitalism creates a "world-economy" (Wallerstein 1979). Competition among capitalist nations—and socialist nations as well—for markets, resources, and labour has led to ever-increasing incorporation of so-called "peripheral" societies by the "core" societies. A third category is "semi-peripheral" societies, which are either declining core societies or rising peripheral societies (Hall 1996). Core societies specialize in manufacturing, while periphery nations provide labour and raw materials. Core societies tend to have strong governments and play a prominent role in the affairs of periphery societies. Periphery societies have weak governments and are heavily influenced by core societies. This system works to the advantage of core nations and the disadvantage of periphery nations. Thus, core nations experience economic growth and become more wealthy and developed, while periphery nations are trapped in poverty and dependency. This chapter examines several modes of production that, over time, have been increasingly affected by the power and influence of globalized economies, especially capitalism.

Foraging

Foraging means searching for and collecting food that is available in nature (fruits, vegetables, nuts, animals, fish), either by gathering, fishing, or hunting. It is the oldest economic system, having existed since the appearance of *Homo sapiens* between 300 000 and 100 000 years ago. Other systems, discussed below, did not emerge until about 10 000 years ago. While foraging stood the test of time for millennia, it is now in danger of extinction as a "pure" form. Very few people—roughly only a quarter of a million people—support themselves predominantly from foraging. European colonialism and contemporary industrial development have drastically changed their life-ways. Foragers now are mostly located in what are considered marginal areas, such as deserts, the circumpolar region, and some dense tropical forest regions. Many people living in other types of economies use foraging as a supplement to their main strategy for obtaining food. Foraging survived as the predominant mode of production for 90 per cent (or more) of human existence because it maintains a general balance between resources and lifestyle.

Foraging is no simple matter, since doing it successfully requires substantial and sophisticated knowledge of the natural environment: how to find particular roots buried deep in the ground, how to follow animal tracks and other signs, and how to judge the weather and water supply. It also relies on the use and maintenance of tools to aid in the processing of wild foods, including nutcrackers, seed-grinders, and cooking containers. Depending on the environment in which foragers live, the main activities include gathering such food as nuts, berries, roots, honey, insects, and eggs; trapping or hunting birds and animals; and fishing. Foragers do not grow food in gardens or keep domesticated animals. Their tools include digging sticks for removing roots from the ground and for penetrating the holes dug by animals in order to get the animals out, bows and arrows, spears, nets, and knives. Baskets of many types are important for carrying foodstuffs. For processing raw materials into edible food, foragers use stones to mash, grind, and pound. Meat can be dried in the sun or over fire, and fire is used for cooking either by boiling or by roasting. In sum, for foragers, obtaining and processing food requires few nonrenewable fuel sources beyond wood or other combustible substances for cooking.

Foraging is an **extensive strategy**, a mode of production involving temporary use of large areas of land and much spatial mobility. It makes little sense for people to construct elaborate and durable shelters in one place. Before they were contained in reservations and settled into agricultural contexts, the Ju/wasi of southern Africa moved several times during a year, depending on the seasonal availability of water sources. Each cluster of families would return to "their" territory, reconstructing or completely rebuilding their shelters with sticks for frames and leaf or thatch coverings. Sometimes the shelters were attached to two or three small trees or bushes for support. Among the Ju/wasi, the amount of investment of time, labour, and material in constructing shelters is modest.

In contrast to foragers of temperate climates, those of the circumpolar regions of North America, Europe, and Asia had to devote more time and energy to food procurement and providing shelter. The specialized technology of circumpolar peoples includes making spears, nets, and knives as well as building sleds and using domesticated animals to pull them. Sled dogs or other animals that are used to pull sleds are an important aspect of circumpolar peoples' economic technology, just as

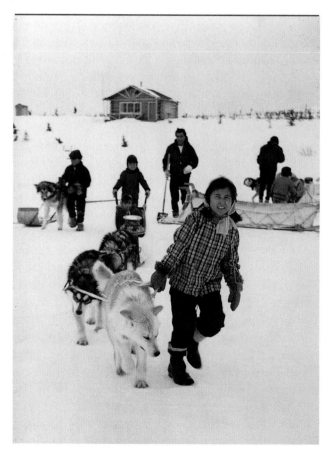

Hare Indian children use their family's sled and dogs to haul drinking water to their village from Colville Lake, Northwest Territories.

The Dene of Colville Lake

The Colville Lake community consists of 75 members of a First Nations people, the Dene (Savishinsky 1974). To distinguish them from other Dene, outsiders arbitrarily call them the Hare Indians because they hunt hares. They survive by hunting, trapping, and fishing in one of the harshest environments in the world. Joel Savishinsky's major research interest was to analyze the experience of stress, tension, and anxiety among this isolated group and observe how they cope with it. Ecological stress factors include "extreme temperatures, long and severe winters, prolonged periods of isolation, hazardous weather and travel conditions, an often precarious food supply, and the constant need for mobility during the harshest seasons of the year" (xiv). Social and psychological stress factors also exist, including contact with White people: fur traders and missionaries.

Savishinsky discovered the importance of dogs in relation to the economy and psychological well-being:

[L]ater in the year when I obtained my own dogteam, I enjoyed much greater freedom of movement, and was able to camp with many people whom I had previously not been able to keep up with. Altogether I travelled close to 600 miles [1000 kilometres] by dogsled between mid-October and early June. This constant contact with dogs, and the necessity of learning how to drive, train and handle them, led to my recognition of the social and psychological, as well as the ecological significance of these animals in the lives of the people. (xx)

Among the fourteen households, there are a total of 224 dogs. Some households have as many as 4 teams, with an average of 6.2 dogs per team, corresponding to people's estimation that 6 dogs are required for travel. More than being only economically useful, dogs play a significant role in people's emotional lives. They are a frequent topic of conversation: "Members of the community constantly compare and comment on the care, condition, and growth of one another's animals, noting special qualities of size, strength, color, speed, and alertness" (169). Emotional displays, not generally common among the Hare, are significant between people and their dogs:

The affectionate and concerned treatment of young animals is participated in by people of all ages, and the nature of the relationship bears a striking resemblance to the way in which people treat young children. Pups and infants are, in essence, the only recipients of unreserved positive affect in the band's social life, all other relationships being tinged with varying degrees of restraint and/or negativism. (169–170)

FOOD FOR THOUGHT

Do you know of another culture in which animals are a focus of such intense human interest? Or a culture in which people have no interest in animals?

---

tractors are for contemporary farmers (see the Multiple Cultural Worlds box above). Considerable amounts of labour are needed to construct durable igloos or permanent log houses, which are necessary adaptations to the cold temperatures. Protective clothing, including warm coats and boots, is another feature of circumpolar economic adaptation.

Labour

Among foraging peoples, occupational specialization (assigning particular tasks to particular people) exists to varying degrees and depends mainly on gender and age. Among foraging cultures located in temperate climates, a minimal gender-based division of labour exists. Most people get the majority of their food by gathering roots, berries, grubs, small birds and animals, and fish. One difference is that, when hunting is done, men are more likely to be involved in long-range expeditions to hunt large animals. However, hunting large animals provides only a small portion of the diets of temperate-climate foragers. In contrast, hunting large animals, including seals, whales, and bears, and capturing large fish is an important part of food provision in circumpolar groups, and gender-based specialization is therefore more marked.

Many anthropologists have emphasized a "Man the Hunter" model for prehistoric humans and contemporary foragers in general (for example, G. R. Lee 1979). This view takes men's hunting roles in some foraging groups and uses them as the model for all foraging groups, both now and in the past. These roles were also used as the basis for theories about social patterns of male dominance in the past and the present. Comparative studies of foragers around the world indicate that greater male involvement in hunting is found in more depleted and resource-limited environments (Hiatt 1970). The implication is that men's hunting of large game is an adaptation to increasing resource scarcity in recent times and thus was not necessarily a predominant practice throughout the long history of foraging. In contrast to the "Man the Hunter" model, some cultural anthropologists have proposed a "Woman the Gatherer" model (Slocum 1975). This model seems to make more sense, since the bulk of everyday food in most foraging systems came from gathering, the primary work of women. Among the Ju/wasi, for example, women's gathering provides 75 to 80 per cent of the diet, while large game provided by men accounted for the rest. In some cultures, women have roles in hunting game similar to those of men, as among the Agta of the Philippines (Estioko-Griffin 1986; Estioko-Griffin, Goodman, and Griffin 1985). The Agta pattern is that some of the women go out hunting while other women stay at the camp caring for the small children, thus disproving the proposition that women's maternal roles universally prevent them from hunting. Most cultural anthropologists would now agree that the "Man the Hunter" model is an example of male bias in interpretation. However, the "Man the Hunter" model is still strong in much popular thinking and is perpetuated through textbook images and museum displays of gender-specific roles in human evolution (Wiber 1997).

Age is a basis for task allocation in all societies since children and the aged generally spend less time in food provision. In foraging societies, both boys and girls perform various tasks that North Americans would label as "work," particularly gathering food. Among the Ju/wasi, young boys begin practising hunting skills through the games they play with small bows and arrows. They gradually take on more adult skills as they mature. Among the Agta of the Philippines in which women hunt, both girls and boys learn to hunt along with their mothers.

Property Relations

The concept of private property in the sense of owning something that can be sold to someone else is not found in foraging societies. Instead, the term **use right** is more appropriate. It means that a person or group has socially recognized priority in access to particular resources such as gathering regions, hunting and fishing areas, and water holes. This access, however, is willingly shared with others by permission. Among the Ju/wasi, certain family groups are known to control access to particular water holes and the territory surrounding them (Lee 1979:58–60). Visiting groups are welcome and will be given food and water. In turn, the host group, at another time, will visit other camps and be given hospitality there. In the Andaman Islands, family groups each control known offshore areas for fishing. Again, sharing is a common practice if permission has been given. Encroaching on someone else's area without permission is a serious misdemeanour that could result in violence. While some instances of conflict between foraging groups over territory and other resources have been documented by anthropologists, the level of conflict is less intense and less likely to be lethal than in settled groups with rules of private property. In foraging groups, use rights are generally invested in the collective group and passed down equally to all children who are members of the group.

Foraging as a Sustainable System

When untouched by outside influences and with abundant land available, foraging systems are sustainable, meaning that crucial resources are regenerated over time in balance with the demand that the population makes on them. Evidence of the sustainability of foraging systems comes from many places, but the Andaman Islands provide the clearest case because their island habitats have been "closed" systems with little, if any, outmigration from specific areas of habitation in recent centuries. The few hundred Andamanese living on Sentinel Island, which has never been entered by outsiders, seem to have been able to maintain their lifestyle within a fairly limited area since earliest observations of them (from a distance) by the British in the late nineteenth century.

One reason for the sustainability of foraging is that foragers' needs are modest. Some anthropologists have typified the foraging lifestyle as the "original affluent society" because needs are satisfied with minimal labour efforts. This term is used metaphorically to signal the fact that foraging economies should not be dismissed as poor and inadequate attempts at making a living. That is an ethnocentric judgment made from the perspective of a consumer culture with different economic and social values. Highly industrialized societies may be maladaptive in the long run because they promote overconsumption of nonrenewable resources. In the 1960s, when the Ju/wasi of the Kalahari desert were still a foraging system, the major food source was the mongongo nut, which was so abundant that there was never a shortage (Howell 1986). In addition, hundreds of species of plants and animals were considered edible. Yet the people were very thin and often complained of hunger, year round. Their thinness may be an adaptation to seasonal fluctuations in food supply. Rather than maximizing food intake during times of plenty, they minimize it. Mealtime is not an occasion for stuffing oneself with treats until there is no room for anything more. Ju/wasi culture taught that one should have a hungry stomach, even in the midst of plentiful food.

Since foragers' needs for goods are not great, minimal labour efforts are required to satisfy them. They would typically work fewer hours a week than the average employed North American. In traditional (undisturbed) foraging societies, people spend as few as five hours a week "working," so they have more leisure time that they spend in activities like storytelling, playing games, and resting. Foraging populations also traditionally enjoyed good health records. During the 1960s, the age structure and health status of the Ju/wasi compared to that of the United States of around 1900—without any modern medical facilities (Lee 1979:47–48). They were described as a "healthy and vigorous population with a low incidence of infections and degenerative diseases." The high level of needs satisfaction and general health and well-being of foragers is the basis of their being called the "original affluent societies."

Changing Cultural Worlds of Foragers: The Tiwi

The Tiwi live on two islands off the north coast of Australia (Hart, Pilling, and Goodale 1988). As foragers, the Tiwi survived through gathering food, especially vegetables (such as yams) and nuts, grubs, small lizards, and fish. Women provided the bulk of the daily diet with their gathered vegetables and nuts that were ground and cooked into a kind of porridge. Occasionally men would hunt kangaroos, wildfowl, and other game such as *goanna*, larger lizards. Vegetables, nuts, and fish were abundant the year around. The Tiwi lived a more comfortable life than Aboriginal groups of the mainland where the environment was less hospitable.

The Tiwi have long been in contact with different foreign influences, beginning in the 1600s with the arrival of the Portuguese, who were attracted to the islands as a source of iron. Later, in 1897, an Australian buffalo hunter named Joe Cooper came to the islands and kidnapped two native women to train as mainland guides in the Tiwi language. Cooper and his entourage greatly changed the Tiwi by introducing a desire for Western goods, especially tobacco. Later, Japanese traders arrived, offering manufactured goods in return for Tiwi women. In the early 1900s, the French established a Catholic mission on Bathurst Island. The mission disapproved of the traditional Tiwi marriage pattern of polygamy (multiple spouses, in this case a man having more than one wife) and promoted monogamy in its place. The year 1942 brought World War II to the Tiwi as the Japanese bombed

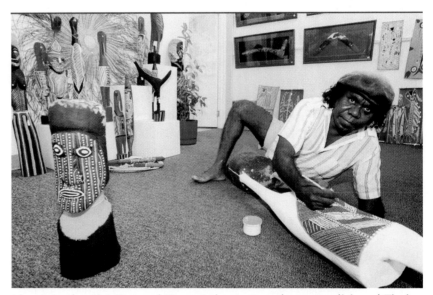

Aboriginal artist Eymard Tungatalum retouches a traditional Tiwi carving in an art gallery in Australia's Northern Territory. Tungatalum's carvings, along with songs and poems, are an important part of the aboriginal people's efforts to revive their culture.

and strafed an American airstrip in nearby Darwin in what is called the "Australian Pearl Harbor." Military bases were prominent on the islands. Tiwi dependency on Western manufactured goods increased.

Today, they are incorporated in the modern world as a part of the Australian nation. Over these many decades of contact, Tiwi residence patterns changed substantially. From mobile hunter-gatherers, the Tiwi changed into settled villagers living in houses built of corrugated iron sheets. Tiwi men now participate on football (soccer) teams, competitive javelin throwing, and water polo. Tiwi art, especially carving and painting, is highly regarded in Australia and, increasingly, internationally. Tiwi are active in public affairs and politics, including the aboriginal rights movement. Another major factor of change is international tourism, a force that the Tiwi are managing with dignity and awareness. As an anthropologist who has studied among the Tiwi for many years reports, "With increasing numbers of non-Tiwi as tourists coming to know the people and county of Melville and Bathurst islands, it is also possible, as one Tiwi told me in 1986, 'that white people too will learn to live with and survive in the country'" (Hart, Pilling, and Goodale 1988:144–145).

Horticulture

Both horticulture and pastoralism emerged only within the last several thousand years of human existence. They both involve an emerging dependence on the **domestication** of plants and animals, or their control by humans in terms of both their location and reproduction. No one is sure as to when and where domestication first occurred, and whether the domestication of plants and animals occurred at the same time or sequentially. At this point, some evidence seems to favour plant domestication coming first.

Horticulture is the cultivation of domesticated crops in gardens with simple hand tools. It emerged first around 12000 BCE in the Middle East. A horticultural economy is based mainly on food crops that people plant and harvest. The food grown in gardens is often supplemented by foraging for wild foods and trading with pastoralists for animal products. Horticulture is still practised by many thousands of people mainly in sub-Saharan Africa; South and Southeast Asia, including the Pacific island of Papua New Guinea; Central and South America; and some parts of the Caribbean islands. Prominent horticultural crops include yams, corn, beans, grains such as millet and sorghum, and several types of roots, all of which are rich in proteins, minerals, and vitamins.

Horticulture involves the use of hand-held tools, such as digging sticks, hoes, and carrying baskets. Rain is the sole source of moisture, and there are no artificial sources. Horticulture requires rotation of garden plots in order to allow used areas to regenerate and thus is also termed "shifting cultivation." Crop yields from horticulture can be great and can support denser population levels than foraging. Surpluses in food supply emerge as a new element of this mode of production. These surpluses enable trade relationships to increase and cause greater affluence for some people. In some cases, horticulture was the foundation for complex civilizations; for example, in Central Africa and in the Mayan civilization of Central America. Average plot sizes are less than one-half hectare, and one hectare can support a family of five to eight members for a year. Yields are sufficient to support semi-permanent village settlements of 200 to 250 people. Overall population density per square kilometre is low because horticulture, like foraging, is a land-extensive strategy. But horticulture is more labour-intensive than foraging because of the energy required for plot preparation and food processing. Horticulturalists supplement their diets by fishing or hunting, or both, or perhaps by trade with nearby foragers.

Anthropologists distinguish five phases in the horticultural cycle:

- *Clearing:* To start the garden area, a section of the forest is cleared, either partially or completely. Common techniques are cutting trees and brush down, then setting the area on fire to burn off other growth. This burning creates a layer of ash that is rich fertilizer. Sometimes people refer to horticulture as "slash and burn cultivation" because of the importance of the two stages of cutting and burning.

- *Planting:* This is accomplished either with a digging stick to loosen the soil into which seeds or slips of plants are placed or through the broadcasting method of simply scattering the seeds by hand over the surface of the ground.

- *Weeding:* Weeds are a relatively minor problem because of the ash cover and somewhat shady growing conditions.

- *Harvesting:* This phase requires labour mainly to cut or dig crops and carry them to the residential area.

- *Fallowing:* After cultivating the same garden plot for a certain number of years (which varies depending on the environment and the type of crop grown), the land has to be left unused, or fallow, for a period of time before it can be gardened again with any success.

Labour

As with foraging groups, no class differences exist in terms of work in horticultural societies. A family of husband, wife, and children form the core work group for cultivation, but groups of men form for hunting and fishing expeditions, and women often work in collective groups for food processing. Gender is the key factor structuring the organization of labour, with male and female work roles often being clearly differentiated. Male and female roles fall into three general patterns (Martin and Voorhies 1975). Most commonly, men do the clearing, and men and women plant and tend the staple crops that are the basis of the people's everyday diets. This pattern exists in Papua New Guinea, much of Southeast Asia, and parts of West and East Africa. In the second pattern, men do the clearing and women cultivate the staple crops; men cultivate prestige crops (used in ceremonies and for exchange) and may also hunt. Many horticultural societies of East Africa fit this pattern. This pattern is, however, reversed in some cultures, notably the precontact Iroquois of upstate New York. Iroquois women were in charge of cultivating maize, the most important crop, and their economic importance was reflected in the overall social and political importance accorded to women (J. K. Brown 1975). In the third pattern, which is the least common, men do both the clearing and the cultivating. The Yanomami of the Amazon (Chagnon 1992) are an example of this male-dominated horticultural production system. Yanomami men clear the fields, plant and maintain the gardens, and harvest the crops. Yanomami women are not idle, however. They work, on average, more hours than men because they are responsible for performing the arduous and time-consuming tasks involved in processing manioc. Manioc, the main food source, is a starchy root poisonous to humans unless put through a lengthy process of soaking in water, which is carried from the river by teams of women. Once soaked, the manioc is grated by hand and cooked before it is ready for consumption.

While no simple explanation exists for why these three patterns developed in particular areas, each one does have implications for female status in society. Peggy Sanday (1973) examined the relationship between women's roles in horticulture and their social status as indicated in terms of women's economic and political rights: female control over produce, the value placed on female produce, female participation in political activities, and female organizations devoted to female economic or political interests. She found evidence to support a correlation between women's contribution to horticulture and their social status. For example, both are high among the (precontact) Iroquois, among the Yoruba of West Africa, and in Samoa in the South Pacific. Where women's contribution was low, their status was also low, as in South America. A complication in the correlations appeared, however: Women's status was not always high in societies in which women's horticultural roles were significant. The conclusion is that female contribution to subsistence is a "necessary but insufficient" cause of high female status. A major role in production does not necessarily bring high status if one does not have control over the goods that are produced, as in systems of slavery (Friedl 1975).

Children do much productive work in horticultural societies, perhaps more than in any other type of economy. A famous comparative research project, the "Children of Six Cultures" study (Whiting and Whiting 1975), examined children's roles in different modes of production. The Gusii of Kenya were the most dependent on horticulture. Compared to children in the other five cultures, Gusii children were assigned more tasks at younger ages. Both young boys and girls were responsible for caring for siblings, fetching fuel, and hauling water. The reason horticultural societies involve children in "responsible" adult-like tasks more than other societies has to do with the fact that in most horticultural societies, adult women's time allocation to work is very high and children's labour serves as a replacement in the domestic domain.

Among the Ariaal, herders of Kenya, men are in charge of herding camels. Here, an Ariaal herder watches over two baby camels.

Property Relations

As in foraging societies, the concept of private property as something that an individual can own and sell is not operable in horticultural societies. Use rights are important and more clearly defined than in foraging societies. By clearing and planting an area of land, an individual puts an indisputable claim on it and its produce. With the production of surplus goods, the possibility of social inequality in access to goods and resources emerges. Rules about group sharing may decline or even disappear as some people gain access to higher status.

Horticulture as a Sustainable System

Crop rotation and fallowing are crucial factors in the sustainability of horticulture. Crop rotation varies the demands made on the soil. Fallowing allows the plot to rest completely and recover its nutrients. It also promotes soil quality and helps prevent compaction by allowing the growth of weeds, whose root systems help keep the soil loose. Once the fallow period is over, the weeds are burned off, providing a layer of ash that serves as a rich source of natural fertilizer. The benefits of a well-managed system of shifting cultivation are clear.

A major constraint in horticulture is the time required for fallowing in situations of pressure on the land. In general, seven years or more of fallow time are required for a year of cultivation. Reducing fallowing time quickly brings negative consequences, including soil nutrient depletion and soil erosion. Several factors contribute to reusing plots that should be left fallow (Blaikie 1985):

- reduced access to land due to incursions from ranchers, miners, farmers, tourists;

- government pressure on horticulturalists to intensify production for cash in order to pay taxes and other fees;

- interest of horticulturalists in boosting production for cash in order to buy manufactured commodities; and

These girls are in charge of herding water buffaloes to the Ganges River, at Banaras, India.

Helen Sekaquaptewa, "Corn Is the Staff of Life"

A Hopi woman, Helen Sekaquaptewa was born in 1898 in northern Arizona. When she was 70 years old, she narrated her life history, which contains descriptions of how the Hopi people practised agriculture in the dry environment of Arizona. This passage reveals how, when the annually awaited floodwaters arrived from the mountains, the Hopi people gathered to work communally to channel the water to their corn fields:

> Corn was literally the "staff of life" in olden days. The Hopis knew how to make their corn grow in sandy, arid soil. Farmers unfamiliar with the situation, who had to depend on the corn they could raise, would surely starve. We had our own native varieties— sweet corn, field corn, blue corn, and yellow corn, red, white, and mixed corn. One aimed to have on hand a supply of corn, enough to last two years, so that if there was a dry year, one's family wouldn't starve. A desperate fear that it might not rain and mature the corn was ever with us. No edible thing was ever wasted. When I was a little girl there were times when we went for weeks without having enough to eat. Then, when the corn was ripe, the whole family would move out and camp at the cornfield and eat corn on the cob three times a day and be glad to have it....

> When the warm spring days started to melt the snow back in the mountains, the floodwaters could be seen approaching for miles. A watcher would give the word, and the town crier would give the order from his housetop: "Everybody report for work down in the valley." Men and women, boys and girls, even little children (I remember working there when I was no more than six years old) were required to respond to the call. Very old women and mothers of very young children remained in the village to care for the little ones and to prepare food for the workers. The few men who were herding the sheep were also exempted....

> When the corn was harvested and stored, it was a time of joyous thanksgiving. Years of bountiful harvest were happy years. (Udall 1969)

FOOD FOR THOUGHT

Are there occasions in your experience in which everyone in the group pitches in and works together the way the Hopi did when the floodwaters came?

- pressure from population growth when outmigration is not an option.

The last factor, population growth, is often blamed as the sole culprit, but often, it is not involved at all. For example, in one case in eastern India, the major causes of land degradation were heavy government taxes and fees and growing indebtedness to merchants in the plains:

> Up to thirty years ago, the hill area occupied by the Sora was covered by dense jungle, while today the hillsides are near-deserts of raw red soil. Shifting agriculture is practised with only three to four year fallow periods, as opposed to over ten years some generations ago. The population has grown only slowly, and certainly at a much slower rate than the rapidly increased destruction of the environment might suggest. (Blaikie 1985:128)

Changing Cultural Worlds of Horticulturalists: The Mundurucu

Outside economic and political factors have made major impacts on horticultural societies. The rubber industry's impact on indigenous peoples of the Amazon ranges from the complete loss of traditional life-ways to comparatively moderate change. The Mundurucu illustrate two patterns of change (Murphy and Murphy 1985). After the arrival of rubber planters in the Brazilian Amazon in the late nineteenth century, many Indians began to work for the Brazilian planters as latex tappers. For over a century, Mundurucu men combined their traditional horticultural life with seasonal work in the rubber area collecting latex. Cultural retention survived over a century of this kind of interaction. Marked cultural change occurred later when many Mundurucu opted to leave their traditional villages, migrating to live in the rubber area year-round.

In the traditional villages, men live in a separate house at one side of the village, with husbands visiting wives and children in their group houses. In the rubber settlement, husbands and wives live in their own houses and there is no separate men's house. In the traditional villages, women's communal work groups shared water-carrying. Such groups do not exist in the rubber settlement villages. So, the husbands have taken over the task of carrying the water and thus, men work harder than in the traditional village. Women continue to work more hours per day than men, however, but they believe that life is better in the rubber settlement area because they like living in the same house with their husbands.

Pastoralism

Pastoralism is a mode of production based on the domestication of animal herds and the use of their products such as meat and milk for 50 per cent or more of the pastoral society's diet. Pastoralism has long existed in the "old world"—Europe, Africa, and Asia, especially in regions where rainfall is limited and unpredictable. In the Western hemisphere, pastoralism did not exist until the Spanish colonialists introduced it during the fifteenth century. Some First Nations groups, especially in the southwestern United States, still rely on herding animals. Pastoralism may be based on a wide variety of animals, including cows, sheep, goats, horses, camels, and reindeer, but most pastoralists specialize in one main type of animal. Pastoralism can succeed in a variety of environments, depending on the animal involved. For example, reindeer herding is popular in the circumpolar regions of Europe and Asia, and cattle and goat herding is common in India and Africa.

Pastoralism is geared to providing daily food, primarily milk. Thus, this mode of production is limited in what it can provide, so pastoralist groups forge trade links with settled groups. In this way, they can secure food and other goods they cannot produce themselves, particularly grains and manufactured items like cooking pots in return for their animals, hides, and other animal products. Pastoralism may seem to resemble contemporary large-scale ranching operations, but in fact, ranches resemble modern industry more than traditional pastoralism (Fratkin, Galvin, and Roth 1994; Loker 1993). The primary purpose of ranching is to provide meat for sale, whereas pastoralism provides many animal products. Also, pastoralism involves the movement of animals to pasture, while ranching moves the fodder to the animals.

A common problem for all pastoralists is the continued need for fresh pasture for their animals. This need makes pastoralism, like foraging and horticulture, an extensive form of economic adaptation. Herds must move or else the pasture area will become depleted. A useful distinction is made between pastoralists depending on whether they move their herds for short or long distances (Fratkin, Galvin, and Roth 1994). The Nuer are an example of short-distance herders. E. E. Evans-Pritchard's (1965 [1947]) classic study describes the Nuer, cattle herders of Sudan in the late 1930s. Depending on the availability of water, the Nuer would spend part of the year in settled villages and part in temporary camps. Cows provided food for the Nuer from their milk, meat, and blood (the Nuer, and other pastoralists, extract blood from the cow's neck, which they then drink). They provided hides, horn, and other materials for everyday use and were the medium of exchange for marriage and payment of fines. The economic and social importance of cattle is reflected in the Nuer's detailed vocabulary for naming types of cattle on the basis of their colours and markings.

Pastoralist systems vary greatly in terms of their level of wealth and the degree of political organization among groups. Environmental setting seems to explain much of this variation. The Qashqai of Iran are long-distance sheep herders and camel drivers (Beck 1986). This area of the Middle East is relatively lush, with a rich and varied natural resource base that supports agriculture and urban centres, including the important city of Shiraz. The nomadic pastoralism of the Qashqai involves seasonal migration to remote pastures, separated by about 500 kilometres. Long-distance herding makes the Qashqai vulnerable to raids and requires negotiation with settlements along the way for permission to cross their land. This vulnerability prompted them to develop a confederacy of tribes into a centralized political organization for protection. The Qashqai thus show how ecology, economy, and political organizations are linked within an environment well-endowed with resources and with many settled communities. In areas with fewer resources and sparser settlements, such as Mongolia in Central Asia or the circumpolar region, pastoralist groups are less politically organized and less wealthy than the Qashqai.

Labour

The pastoralist division of labour is not structured by class differences. Families and clusters of related families are the basic unit of production. Gender is an important factor in the allocation of work. In many pastoralist cultures, little overlap exists between male and female tasks. Men are often in charge of the herding activities—moving the animals from place to place. Women tend to be responsible for processing the herd's products, especially the milk. A cultural emphasis on masculinity characterizes many herding populations. Traditional reindeer herding among the Sami of Finland was connected to male identity (Pelto 1973). The definition of being a man was to be a reindeer herder. As traditional herding practices declined and many men no longer made their living from herding, they had to redefine their sense of identity. In contrast, women are the predominant herders among the Navajo of the American Southwest. Navajo men traditionally had little to do with herding the sheep. Instead, their major role is crafting silver jewellery.

The size of the animal involved appears to be a factor in the gender division of labour. Women are often the herders of smaller animals, perhaps since smaller animals need to graze less widely and can be kept penned near the house. Men tend the animals that are pastured at longer distances. This difference suggests the emergence of a distinction between men's wider spatial range than women's, something that becomes further accentuated in many agricultural systems.

Children often play important roles in tending herds. Among the cattle-herding Maasai of Kenya and Tanzania, parents prefer to have many children so that they can help with the herds. Before boys in these pastoralist societies advance to the "warrior" stage, beginning around adolescence, their main task is herding.

Property Relations

The most important forms of property among pastoralists include animals, housing (such as tents, or yerts), and domestic goods (rugs, cooking ware). Use rights regulate pasture land and migratory routes. Some sense of private property exists with the animals since they may be traded by the family head for other goods. A family's tent, or yert, is also theirs. However, no private rights in land or travel routes exist; instead, these are generally accepted informal agreements. Many pastoral societies emphasize male ownership of the herds, and sons inherit herds from their fathers. In other societies, such as the sheepherding Navajo of the southwestern United States, women are the primary herders and they pass the herds from mother to daughter.

Pastoralism as a Sustainable System

Pastoralism is a highly extensive system, requiring the ability of groups to range widely with their herds in search of grass and water. Pastoralists have been able to develop successful and complex cultures in extremely limited environments; an example is the Mongolian herders, who created a vast and powerful empire. As such, pastoralism can be a highly successful and sustainable economic adaptation that functions complementarily with other economic systems. As with horticulture, however, when outside forces begin to squeeze the space available for migration, overexploitation of the environment results and pastoralism then becomes accused of depleting the environment. Many forms of outside pressure, including national interests to "sedentarize" (settle down) pastoralists so that they will be easier to tax, and commercial interests in pastoralists' land threaten the sustainability of pastoralism.

Changing Cultural Worlds of Pastoralists: Mongolian Nomads

In the early 1990s, cultural anthropologist Melvyn Goldstein and physical anthropologist Cynthia Beall (Goldstein and Beall 1994) were allowed to do fieldwork among herders in Mongolia, a landlocked and mountainous country located between Russia and China. Mongolia has the highest ratio of livestock to people of any country in the world. Currently, 70 per cent of its agricultural production comes from cattle raising, although goat, sheep, and horse herding are also important—they had traditionally been the most important herd animals. Goldstein and Beall wanted to study how the transformation from a socialist, collectivized economy to a capitalist, market system was affecting the people.

> As our truck crossed a ridge and descended the rough dirt road onto a broad plain, two herders on horses not much bigger than American ponies emerged from a ravine, driving hundreds of sheep across our path. They rode grandly, integral extensions of their horses, as they fluidly darted back and forth constraining stragglers and urging the herd forward. Their effortless skill reminded us that we had come to this remote place because these were the descendants of the brilliant Mongol nomad cavalry who had terrorized much of Eurasia 750 years earlier, conquering a vast empire that stretched from the Pacific Ocean to the Danube River. (15)

Since the 1950s, the communist party of the then USSR ruled Mongolia and sought to transform it from a herding system into an agricultural and industrial state. The USSR established several urban centres. The population changed from being 78 per cent rural in 1956 to 42 per cent rural in 1989. In addition, given USSR policies against private property, ownership of herds was socialized. The state provided all social services such as health and education. There was no homelessness or unemployment. The transition was not smooth or easy: Collectivization first resulted in a 30 per cent reduction of livestock and produced a revolt in the western part of the country (Barfield 1993:169). Subsequently, policy was altered and the people were allowed to control some of their own animals. Nevertheless, the predominant organization of pastoralism was collectivized and labour was organized along the lines of a factory system.

Starting in the late 1980s, the transition away from socialist economic policies spread throughout Russia, including Mongolia. By the early 1990s, **privatization**, a process of transferring the collective ownership and provision of goods and services under **socialism** to a capitalist system of private ownership, was the government's policy guideline. In Mongolia, this took the form of ending collective ownership of herds and reinstating family-organized production. At the same time, the government cut back on state-provided services.

Goldstein and Beall wanted to learn about the reactions to these changes among more traditional Mongols, herders who still lived in *ger*, tents made of felt. They headed for Moost district in the Altai Mountain area in the southeastern part of the country. The district includes over 25 000 square kilometres of mountain and valley land, of which 99.9 per cent is pasture. The area contains about 4000 people and about 115 000 head of livestock. Goldstein and Beall set up their *ger* and were immediately welcomed by an invitation to have milk-tea, a hot drink made of tea, water, milk, butter, and salt. During their stay, they spoke with many of the nomads, participated in their festivals, and learned about perceptions of economic change.

Changes in the wider Mongolian economy during privatization created serious problems for the herders. Their standard of living declined markedly in the early 1990s. Goods such as flour, sugar, candy, and cooking oil were no longer available. Prices for meat fluctuated widely, and the nomads had to learn to adjust to the vagaries of the market versus the security of state-controlled

In parts of Mongolia and Siberia, many pastoralists continue to herd reindeer as a major part of making a living.

prices. Lower meat prices resulted in fewer herd animals being slaughtered. Larger herd sizes increased the potential for exceeding the carrying capacity of the grasslands. Beall and Goldstein close their book with this statement: "As we said our final good-byes to the herders in August of 1992, we had mixed emotions—sadness mingled with respect and hope. It was sad to have witnessed such a sudden and dramatic decline in the nomads' standard of living. The feasts of 1990 were no more and no one thought they would return soon. An era had ended" (164). On a somewhat brighter note, another expert on pastoralism in central and inner Asia comments that the cultural identity of the descendants of Genghis Khan "is so closely tied to the history of great deeds by men on horseback that even as their number declines, their role as symbols of a proud way of life will grow" (Barfield 1993:176).

Agriculture

Both horticulture and **agriculture** emphasize food growing over food gathering. A major difference between the two is that agriculture is an **intensive strategy** of production. Intensification involves new techniques that allow the same land to be used repeatedly without losing its fertility. Key inputs include more labour power for weeding, conscientious use of fertilizers, and control of water supply. The earliest agricultural systems are documented from the time of the neolithic period, beginning around 10 000 BCE in the Tigris-Euphrates valley, India, and China. Agricultural systems now exist on all continents except for Antarctica.

Agriculture involves the use of domesticated animals for plowing, transportation, and organic fertilizer—manure or composted materials. It also relies on irrigation as a source of water and the construction of elaborate terraces and other ways of increasing the amount of land available for cultivation. Settlements are permanent and houses are not movable. Permanent homes, investment in private property, and increased yields all promote larger family size as a way of further increasing production through the use of household labour. Population density increases substantially in agricultural societies, and urban centres of thousands of people develop. Occupational specialization increases. Instead of people repairing their own tools and weapons, some people take on this work as a full-time job and no longer grow their own food but become dependent on trading their skills for food with farmers. Other specializations that emerge as full-time occupations are political leaders, religious leaders or priests, healers, artisans, potters, musicians, and traders. Four major types of agriculture are described here.

Family Farming

Over one billion people, or about one-fourth of the world's population, belong to households involved in family farming (what cultural anthropologists formerly termed "peasant agriculture"). In family farming, farmers "produce much of their own subsistence as well as some food or fibre to sell, supplying labour largely from their own households, and possessing continuing, heritable rights to their own resources" (Netting 1989:221). Family farming is always part of a larger market economic system (E. Wolf 1966:8). It is found throughout the world, but is more prevalent in primarily agrarian countries such as Mexico, India, Poland, and Italy than in more industrialized countries. Family farmers exhibit much cross-cultural variety: They may be full-time or part-time farmers, they may be more or less closely linked to urban markets, and they may or may not grow cash crops such as coffee or sugar cane. Major tasks include plowing,

planting seeds and cuttings, weeding, caring for terraces and irrigation systems, harvesting, and processing.

Labour The family (or household) is the basic unit of production. Gender and age are important factors around which productive roles are organized. A gender-based division of labour tends to be marked in most family farm economies. Cross-cultural analysis of gender roles in 46 family farm societies revealed that men perform the "bulk" of the labour in 38, or more than three-fourths of the sample (Michaelson and Goldschmidt 1971). The few societies in which females predominate in agriculture were located in Southeast Asia. In general, men work more hours in agricultural production than in the previous systems considered, and women's work tends to be more devoted to activities near the home, such as processing food and child care (Ember 1983). This division of labour has been typified as the basis of the **public/private dichotomy** in family farm societies, in which men are more involved with the nondomestic world and women are increasingly involved in activities in or near the home.

Analysis of time allocation data for men and women in horticultural and agricultural societies reveals that both men's and women's work hours are substantially higher in agricultural economies, but in differing proportions to inside and outside work (Ember 1983). The data indicate that women's contribution to production is not less in agriculture. Instead, the shares of time devoted to particular activities shift. Women's inside work hours increase absolutely and relatively (compared to men's), and their outside work hours increase absolutely, but decline relative to those of men. Why do many family farm agricultural systems increase men's workloads and increase women's involvement in the domestic domain? One hypothesis is based on the importance of plowing fields in preparation for planting, and the fact that plowing is almost exclusively a male task (Goody 1976). This fact has led some anthropologists to argue that men plow simply because they are stronger than women or have the advantage of greater "aerobic capacity" (the ability of the circulatory system to nourish the blood through processing air). In south-central India, weather patterns require that plowing be accomplished in a very narrow time band (Maclachlan 1983). Assigning the task to the physically stronger gender ensures that it can be done more quickly and is thus an adaptive strategy because it optimizes chances for a good crop. Another hypothesis says that women are not involved with plowing and other fieldwork because such tasks are incompatible with child care (J. K. Brown 1970).

Yet another view emphasizes that agriculture increases the demand for labour within and near the house (Ember 1983). Winnowing, husking, grinding, and cooking of agricultural products such as rice are extremely labour-intensive. The high demand for family labour in agriculture prompts people to want many children, so child care becomes a more demanding task that is relegated to women. As women become isolated from other women within their households, they are less able to depend on labour contributions from other women than in modes of production where women live and work collectively.

In some farming systems, females play an equal or even more important role in agricultural production and distribution than males. Such "female farming systems" are numerically fewer than male farming systems. Most are found in Southeast Asia, a region where **wet rice agriculture** is practised. This is a highly labour-intensive way of growing rice that involves starting the seedlings in nurseries and transplanting them to flooded fields. Males play a role in the initial plowing of the fields, but this work is less arduous than in dry-field agriculture, since the earth is wet. Women's labour and decision making are the backbone of the operations. Why women predominate in wet rice agriculture is a question that has intrigued anthropologists and economists (Bardhan 1974; Goody 1976; Winzeler 1974), but no one has provided a solid explanation for this pattern yet. Its consequences are clearer than its causes: Where female farming systems exist, women are more likely to have access to rights to land ownership, a greater role in household decision making, more autonomy, and higher status in general (Dyson and Moore 1983; Stivens et al. 1994).

A third variation in the gender division of labour in family farming involves complementary and balanced task allocations between males and females, with males involved in agricultural work and females involved in food processing and marketing. This form of gender division of labour is common among highland communities of Central and South America. For example, among the Zapotec Indians of southern Mexico's state of Oaxaca (pronounced "wah-haka"), men grow maize, the staple crop, and cash crops—bananas, mangoes, coconuts, and sesame (Chiñas 1992). Zapotec women contribute substantially to household income by selling produce in the town markets and by making tortillas and selling them from their houses. The farming household thus derives its income from the labour of both genders working interdependently on different aspects of the production process. Male and female status is also relatively balanced.

Children's roles in agricultural societies range from being prominent to rather minor, depending on the context (Whiting and Whiting 1975). The "Children of Six Cultures" study found lower rates of child work in the North Indian and Mexican agricultural villages, compared to the horticultural village in Kenya. But in some agricultural societies, children's work rates are very high, as shown through detailed observations of children's activities in two Asian villages, one in Java and the other in Nepal. In these villages, an important task of children, even as young as six to eight years old, is tending the farm animals (Nag, White, and Peet 1978), and children spent more time caring for animals than adults did. In both villages, girls aged six to eight spend more time than adults in child care. Some of the Javanese children in the six- to eight-year-old group worked for wages. In general, girls did more hours of work daily than boys at all ages.

Property Relations The investments in land such as clearing, terracing, and fencing that agriculture requires are linked to the development of firmly delineated

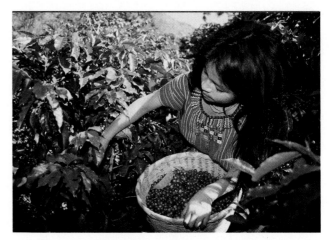

Child labour is prominent in many modes of production. In this photograph, a girl picks coffee beans in San Juan La Laguna, Atitlan, Guatemala.

and protected property rights. Rights to land, the most important resource, can be acquired and sold. Clear guidelines exist about inheritance and transfer of rights to land through marriage. Social institutions such as law and police emerge to protect private rights to resources. The more marked gender division of labour in many family farming systems often means that men have access to the more highly valued tasks and to goods that have value in the outside world. The women are more involved with food processing, child bearing and child rearing, and family maintenance, tasks that generate no income and have no exchange value.

This division of labour is related to gender-differentiated inheritance systems. In family farming systems where male labour and decision making predominate, women and girls tend to be excluded from land rights and other forms of property control. Conversely, in female farming systems, inheritance rules tend to regulate the transmission of property rights more often through females (see the Multiple Cultural Worlds box). Class distinctions become more rigid, and there are greater gaps between those who have access to resources and those who do not.

Changing Cultural Worlds of Family Farmers: Zinacantan and Abries Some applied anthropologists and other development specialists have said that peasants in closed communities are "risk averse" because they avoid adopting innovations such as new techniques for cultivation, new seed varieties, or new forms of fertilizer. Economic anthropologists have shown, in contrast, that such conservatism may be adaptive. Family farmers have intimate knowledge of the systems within which they work, and they are capable of

MULTIPLE CULTURAL WORLDS

Malay Women Farmers Lose Rights to Land

Interventions by Western development experts have promoted changes in family farming systems worldwide. One feature of this change is towards increasing male economic roles. Many projects ignore women's traditional agricultural roles, assuming that men are always the farmers (Rogers 1979). Projects have targeted men for receiving new tools and techniques regardless of the actual division of labour.

Economist Ester Boserup (1970) pointed out decades ago that colonial governments often undermined women's status by denying them formal rights to land. Access to land is a major determinant of wealth and social status, especially in developing countries where most sources of income are related to the land. Women's access to land is even more crucial than men's because women have less access to other forms of income such as wage labour (Stivens et al. 1994). In Malaysia, gender inequality is less severe than in many parts of the world. Daughters traditionally inherited land equally with sons. In terms of labour force participation, women again ranked high. Women's economic rights produced a significant degree of autonomy for rural women.

But this has changed. Both colonialism and international development programs have brought disadvantages to Malay women that did not exist before. British colonial officials registered land in the name of men only, regardless of whether the property was owned by a woman, or jointly owned by a husband and wife. With independence, agricultural development programs in Malaysia, as elsewhere, have been aimed at males. The Green Revolution promoted mechanized rice farming and displaced thousands of female workers from their jobs. Rodolphe De Koninck (1992) studied the impact of the Green Revolution in Malaysia and reports how men have become entrepreneurs borrowing money and purchasing mechanized harvesters. One man used land owned by his sisters and mother without compensation to support his harvester rental business (128). In 100 years, the gender division of labour and women's economic rights and status have been steadily transformed from one in which women had high status to one in which men now have dominant roles.

FOOD FOR THOUGHT

Do you think the decline of the roles of women in farming under colonialism and more recent development policies is inevitable?

assessing costs and benefits of innovations. These contrasting perspectives both emphasize the farmers' agency as decision makers, determining whether they should change in certain directions. On the other hand, development projects such as the construction of roads, global patterns in demand for certain products, and labour opportunities shape the choices that farmers have to consider, as the following two examples demonstrate. The two examples share some features, which are characteristic of such change in all parts of the world. Each example has unique features as well.

Several outside influences have led to major changes in family farming as Frank Cancian's (1989) study of economic change in rural Mexico shows. In 1960, Cancian first went to the village of Zinacantan to study the economy of the Maya Indians in the southern state of Chiapas. The Zinacantecos mostly earned their living by growing corn and selling part of their crops in a nearby city. When Cancian returned in the 1980s, significant economic change had occurred because of government road building that linked rural communities with urban market centres. The number of households that relied solely on growing corn had declined substantially. Many farmers had been displaced from the land they had rented by the landowners, who put the land into cattle production, and by the construction of a dam. These farmers began to take up wage work in the area that was created by these changes. Others began to participate in labour migration to nearby cities for wage work for up to a year or two at a time.

Harriet Rosenberg's study of Abries village in the French Alps also reveals how external economic changes and opportunities affected a family farm system. Two hundred years ago Abries supported a population of close to two thousand people based on an economy of sheep raising. Villagers made a good living trading sheep and selling ewes' milk, butter, and cheese. "Women played an active decision-making role in family economic enterprises and were expected to know about agricultural matters" (H. Rosenberg 1988:27). The worldwide depression of the 1930s hit the village hard. The Swiss corporation Nestlé paid low prices for the farmers' milk and people attempted to peddle milk products directly to lowlanders. After World War II, the villagers were encouraged to adopt mechanized agriculture by the French government, but the continued unprofitability of agriculture forced people to move away until the village sup-

ported only 200 people. In the 1990s, winter tourism had come to the village. But local people are employed at the bottom of the pay scale and reap few benefits from tourism. "Decisions made around the world influence life in Abries but the Abriesois have no control over them. The policies of the European Economic Community are not negotiated with villages; neither are the budgets of multinational corporations such as Nestle" (H. Rosenberg 1988:210). The people comment that their children must leave the village because they have no future if they stay.

Plantation Agriculture

Plantation agriculture involves concentrated ownership of land, with the means of production in the hands of one family or corporation, the use of hired labour, and mono-crop production for sale. As a form of production, the plantation system exhibits some of the most severe inequalities between owners and workers of any production system. Plantation workers worldwide endure some of the most deplorable working conditions. Many have started to organize in order to improve these conditions. Anthropological studies of plantation agriculture have tended to take a historical view and have focused on slavery (forced and unpaid labour) and the slave trade that developed as means to provide labour to support this system as well as an economic end in itself (E. Wolf 1982). Archaeological research in the United States and the Caribbean has revealed much about how plantations worked in the past (Armstrong 1990). However, participant observation studies of contemporary plantation systems are difficult to conduct because plantations do not welcome close study.

The plantation mode of production is still prominent in some of Europe's former colonies. Plantations exist, for example, in Sri Lanka, the small island off the southern coast of India, where plantations still produce tea, coffee, rubber, and coconuts. British colonialists first developed coffee plantations there in the late 1880s and brought in labourers from South India. Sri Lanka is now well known as having an excellent human welfare record, by far the best in South Asia. Social programs since World War II led to admirable national health and literacy achievements. A survey study of the plantation sector reveals significant disparities between it and the non-plantation sector (Jayawardena 1984). Sri Lanka's plantation sector is the largest contributor to the Gross

National Product (GNP) and the largest source of employment. As tea and rubber cultivation developed, women labourers were especially brought in to pick tea leaves and to tap rubber. The plantation labour force in Sri Lanka is now over half female. Children aged 14 to 16 years are a legal part of the labour force, while younger children often help their mothers on an unpaid basis. The plantation workers' health status is far worse than the national level, however. Among the plantation population, infant malnutrition rates and mortality rates are higher than in the general population. Housing is crowded, and most households occupy only one or two rooms. Child care facilities for working mothers are non-existent, poorly run, or located at a distance too far from the place of work. Illiteracy is high among plantation workers, while the general population in Sri Lanka has the highest literacy rate in the region.

Industrial Agriculture

Industrial agriculture produces crops through means that are "capital-intensive, substituting machinery and purchased inputs such as processed fertilizers for human and animal labor" (Barlett 1989:253). It is practised in the capitalist countries of the United States, Canada, Germany, Russia, and Japan; it is increasingly being exported to developing nations such as India and Brazil; and it is also found in socialist countries such as China. Thus far, few cultural anthropologists have studied this form of production.

Corporate Farming in Canada In Canada the rural population continues to dwindle. In 1999, approximately 900 000 Canadians or only about 3 per cent of the total population lived on farms (Statistics Canada 2002). The use of new technology has contributed to this decline. For example, in Quebec in the 1930s the advent of the motor car allowed farm labourers to leave farming communities and cut ties with farmer employees (Verdon 1980:120). The growing involvement of farmers in the market economy also meant that farmers and labourers no longer exchanged labour as kin within the community.

On many farms in Canada, there is a clear gender division of labour. The husband is usually primarily responsible for daily farm operations, usually involving extensive use of machinery, while wives' participation ranges from equal to that of husbands to minimal (Barlett 1989:271–273). Wives are generally responsible for managing the domestic domain. Because of their domestic and farm duties, women's daily work hours are 25 per cent more than those of men. A new trend is for farm women to take salaried jobs off the farm to help support the farm. In Canada, 50 per cent of farm wives, in addition to their domestic and farm chores, also work off the farm (Bollman and Smith 1988). Children are not formally employed in farm work, but many family farms rely on children's contributions on weekends and during summer vacations. Amish farm families rely to a significant extent on contributions from all family members (Hostetler and Huntington 1992).

Industrial agriculture has brought the advent of a new subcategory of **corporate farms**, huge enterprises that produce goods solely for sale and that are owned and operated by companies who rely entirely on hired labour. Studies reveal four aspects of

This farmer works near a highly urbanized area of Kyoto. In Japan, farming now often combines elements of industrial mechanization and intensive labour.

First Nations Migrant Labour in Southern Alberta

From the 1950s to the mid-1980s the sugar beet industry in southern Alberta worked closely with the federal and provincial governments to develop a source of migrant labour from First Nations reserves. A series of paternalistic and coercive tactics were used to recruit labour to this form of industrial agriculture production (Laliberte and Satzewich 1999). The authors criticize assumptions that First Nations peoples reside mainly on reserves and that few people from reserves have employment in the wider society. It is only partially true that First Nations peoples on reserves have not been part of capitalist production in Canada. One example was the effort to involve people on reserves in sugar beet production in southern Alberta.

The sugar beet is a major industrial agricultural product in Alberta. Unlike other crops like wheat, sugar beet production requires a large amount of hand labour for thinning and hoeing.

With technology, wheat and other grain production can dispense with hired labour and make do with family labour. When sources of hired labour dried up in the 1950s, the sugar beet producers began lobbying the government to mobilize the labour resources of First Nations reserves of northern Alberta and Saskatchewan. Canada Manpower Centres carried out the recruitment for seasonal employment in sugar beet farming. People travelled many hundreds of kilometres from their reserves to southern Alberta to work in the sugar beet fields. Throughout the 1970s and into the early 1980s, the federal government absorbed part of the travel costs and assisted farmers with housing for migrant labourers. However, living conditions for the farm labourers were often deplorable. "In some cases, [they lived] in chicken coops or converted granaries. In one instance, the farmer moved the chickens out just before the work-

ers arrived, and, later, the chickens tried to return home for the night" (65). All agricultural workers in Canada are explicitly excluded from benefits enjoyed by other workers and thus the First Nations farm labourers had no protection from exploitation. One way to encourage First Nations peoples to work the sugar beet fields was for the government to terminate welfare payments during May and June, the peak period for sugar beet labour. Many tried to find work on the reserves to cover this loss, but usually found they had no option but to work in the sugar beet fields.

FOOD FOR THOUGHT

To your knowledge, are agricultural workers treated this unfairly in your community?

To your knowledge, are First Nations peoples treated this unfairly in your community?

---

the evolution of industrial agriculture over the past 150 years:

- The increased use of complex technology, including machinery, chemicals, and genetic research on new plant and animal varieties.

- The increased use of **capital** (wealth used in the production of more wealth—either in the form of money or property). Industrial agriculture uses the most capital per unit of production of any farming system (Barlett 1989:260). The high ratio of capital to labour has enabled farmers to increase production, but it reduces flexibility. If a farmer invests in an expensive machine to harvest soybeans and then the price of soybeans drops, the farmer cannot quickly change from growing soybeans to potatoes.

- The increased use of energy—primarily fossil fuels to run the machinery and provide nitrates for fertilizer—

to grow crops, often exceeds the calories of food energy yielded in the harvest. Calculations of how many calories of energy are used to produce a calorie of food in industrial agricultural systems reveal a very high ratio of perhaps 2.5 calories of fossil fuel to harvest one calorie of food, and more than 6 when processing, packaging, and transport are counted (Barlett 1989:261). In this sense, industrial agriculture is a less efficient mode of production than foraging, horticulture, and pastoralism.

- The decline of the family farm. In Canada, family farms were the predominant pattern until a few decades ago. Now, experts speak of "the death of the family farm." Increasing numbers of family farms have fallen into debt and cannot compete with industrial farms. In Canada, foreclosure notices to family farms tripled between 1984 and 1990 (Young and Van Bers 1991).

A key difference between corporate farms and family farms is that corporate farms depend completely on hired labour rather than on family members. Much of the labour demand in industrial agriculture is seasonal, creating an ebb and flow of workers, depending on the task and time of year (see the Multiple Cultural Worlds on page 78). Large ranches hire seasonal cowboys for round-ups and fence mending. Crop harvesting is another high-demand point. Leo Chavez (1992) studied the lives of undocumented (illegal) migrant labourers from Central America who work in the huge tomato, strawberry, and avocado fields owned by corporate farms in southern California. Many of these migrants are Indians from Oaxaca, Mexico. They sneak across the border to work in the United States as a way of making ends meet. In the San Diego area, they live temporarily in shantytowns, or camps that Chavez describes as resembling Third World living conditions (63). Here is what a camp, where all male workers live, is like on Sunday when the men do not go out to work in the fields:

On Sundays, the campsites take on a community-like appearance. Men bathe, and wash their clothes, hanging them on trees and bushes, or on lines strung between the trees. Some men play soccer and basketball, using a hoop someone has rigged up. Others sit on old crates or tree-stumps as they relax, talk, and drink beer. Sometimes the men talk about fights from the night before. With little else to do, nowhere to go, and few outsiders to talk to, the men often drink beer to pass the time on Saturday nights and Sundays. Loneliness and boredom plague them during nonworking hours. (65)

Another recent change in corporate agriculture has been the introduction of genetically engineered crops. A few large agribusiness corporations and government agencies encouraged this change in Canada. This process has been largely hidden from the bulk of the Canadian population who are now consuming great quantities of genetically altered food especially in processed items using canola and soybean. Brewster Kneen, a former farmer and food ac-

tivist, has been concerned about the consequences of industrial agriculture in Canada for many years. He argues that there are substantial differences between the ways farmers selected plants and animals in the past, and the use of genetic technology. He argues that farmers were not imposing genetic uniformity, but rather required diversity. He writes:

We were not violently forcing plants or microorganisms to conform to our model of what they should be in order to maximize our profits. We were encouraging transformations to be sure, but they were gradual, subtle ones that we could only observe after the fact.... we do not really know what the long-term consequences of genetic engineering will be, and are not prepared to move slowly and take the time to find out, [this] means that a grand experiment is taking place, and the outcome is anyone's guess. (Kneen 1999:5–8)

Collectivized Agriculture in Romania

Collectivized agriculture is a form of industrialized agriculture that involves nonprivate control of land, technology, and goods produced. Collectivism is inspired by the work of social theorists Marx and Engels (1964 [1848]), whose call: "Workers of the world unite," in *The*

This Romanian collective farm work team is sorting potatoes. Note the feminization of agricultural labour. Teams were composed of close friends, relations, and neighbours so that farms could take advantage of local social relations to satisfy their labour needs.

Communist Manifesto inspired many social movements. Collectivism's basic goal was to provide for greater economic equality and a greater sense of group welfare than is possible under competitive capitalism. A variety of collective agriculture arrangements have been used in places such as Russia and Eastern Europe, China, Vietnam, Laos, Cambodia, Tanzania, Ethiopia, and Nicaragua. David Kideckel conducted one of the few anthropological studies on collectivization in a Romanian community in two periods: first, in 1974 during a period of optimism for socialism, and later in 1990, after the revolution that brought socialism's end (Kideckel 1993).

Socialism in Romania involved an extensive state plan with the most comprehensive and centralized system in Eastern Europe. The state oversaw nearly every aspect of society, from university enrollments to the production of steel and tractors. With the completion of agricultural collectivization in the early 1960s, about 30 per cent of the land was in state farms, 60 per cent in collectives, and 10 per cent privately held. Workers on state farms were employees and were paid wages. They received a small garden for their own use. The state farm provided services such as child care facilities and shopping centres. Collective farms, in contrast, were "ostensibly" owned and controlled by their members, who pooled land, labour, and resources. Their earnings were determined by total farm production, and their wages tended to be lower than state farm worker wages. Collective farm workers were entitled to a "use plot" of the collective land. These plots could provide up to three-fourths of subsistence needs. Most of the private land existed in mountain zones where ecology limited the feasibility of collectivization.

In spite of the socialist rhetoric proclaiming equality between all workers, there were economic distinctions between males and females. Women were relegated to agricultural and reproductive labour, while rural men moved into industry. Women were the mainstay of collective farm labour, but they were underrepresented among the leadership. Nevertheless, women's increased involvement in wage-earning, and their roles in cultivating household use plots strengthened their influence in the household and the community. Overall, the gender division of labour involved substantial overlap between male and female roles in the rural sector.

The 1980s brought serious economic decline to Romania, and in December 1989, the Romanian revolution began. By 1991, about 80 per cent of the farm land had reverted to private ownership. The transition to private land was not easy. State farms gave up land reluctantly, and many collective farmers had second thoughts about private agriculture:

> One couple in their early forties were horrified when they heard a rumor that people were to be required to take back the land.... They had no desire to work in agriculture, and to them the half hectare to which they were entitled was a burden. (Kideckel 1993:221–222)

The Sustainability of Agriculture

Agriculture, as we have seen, requires more in the way of labour inputs, technology, and the use of nonrenewable natural resources than the other systems discussed earlier. The ever-increasing spread of corporate agriculture is displacing other longstanding economic systems, including foraging, horticulture, and pastoralism. It is resulting in the destruction of important habitats, notably rain forests, in its search for agricultural land (along with commercial ranching and other aspects of industrialism, discussed next), and for water and other energy sources to support its enterprises. Intensive agriculture itself is unsustainable, and it is also undermining the sustainability of other systems. Anthropologists have pointed to some of the social costs of agriculture as well (see the Critical Thinking box).

Industrial and Post-Industrial Economies

Industrialism refers to the production of goods through mass employment in business and commercial operations. In industrial capitalism, the form of capitalism found in most industrialized nations, the bulk of goods produced are not for basic needs, but to satisfy consumer demands for nonessential goods. Employment in agriculture decreases while jobs in manufacturing and the service sector increase. In some industrialized countries, the number of manufacturing jobs are declining, with more people being employed in service occupations and in the growing area of "information processing" (such as computer programming, data processing, communications, and teaching). Some experts feel that Canada, for

Was the Invention of Agriculture a Terrible Mistake?

Most Euro-Americans have a "progressivist" view that agriculture is a major advance in cultural evolution because it brought with it so many things that Westerners admire—cities, centres of learning and art, powerful state governments, and monumental architecture:

> Just count our advantages. We enjoy the most abundant and varied foods, the best tools, and material goods, some of the longest and healthiest lives, in history.… From the progressivist perspective on which I was brought up, to ask "Why did almost all our hunter-gatherer ancestors adopt agriculture?" is silly. Of course they adopted it because agriculture is an efficient way to get more food for less work. (Diamond 1994 [1987]:106)

Another claim about the advantage of agriculture is that it allows more leisure time, so art could flourish. Why would one rather be a hunter-gatherer, struggling every day to make ends meet?

On the other hand, many scholars raise serious questions about the advantages of agriculture. These "revisionists" argue that agriculture may be "the worst mistake in the history of the human race," "a catastrophe from which we have never recovered" (105–106). Some of the "costs" of agriculture include social inequality; disease; despotism; and destruction of the environment from soil exhaustion and chemical poisoning, water pollution, dams and river diversions, and air pollution from tractors, transportation, and processing plants. With agriculture, life did improve for many people, but not all. Elites emerged with distinct advantages, but the gap between the haves and the have-nots increased. Health improved for the elites, but not the landless poor and labouring classes. With the vast surpluses of food created by agricultural production, elaborate state systems developed with new forms of power exercised over the common people.

CRITICAL THINKING QUESTIONS

What is your definition of the "good life"?

Given your definition, how does life in pre-agricultural societies compare to life in contemporary agricultural and industrial societies?

What are the benefits and costs of achieving the good life among the Ju/wasi compared to contemporary agricultural and industrial societies?

Who gets the good life in each type of economy?

example, is moving out of the industrial age and into the "information age."

Within industrial capitalism an important distinction exists between the **formal sector,** which is salaried or wage-based work registered in official statistics, and the **informal sector,** which includes work that is outside the formal sector, not officially registered, and sometimes illegal. If you have done babysitting and were paid cash that was not formally recorded by your employer (for tax deduction purposes) or by you (for income tax purposes), then you have participated in the informal sector. Informal sector activities that are illegal are referred to as being part of the "underground economy."

The Formal Sector

The formal sector comprises a wide array of occupations, ranging from stable and lucrative jobs in what has been labelled the "primary labour market" to unstable or part-time and less lucrative jobs in the "secondary labour market" (Calhoun, Light, and Keller 1994). Cultural anthropologists could conduct research in any number of domains ranging from huge multinational corporations to neighbourhood beauty parlours. Some anthropologists have pursued the former direction, but the tendency has been to focus on small-scale organizations, especially factories. Factory studies are an important genre in cultural anthropology. They apply the tools and insights of anthropology into the domain of a work-focused institution. Fieldwork techniques in factory studies include conducting interviews with workers and managers in the plant and in their homes, and observing plant operations. Their findings shed light on how people adapt to this environment and stresses that arise.

One study used a team approach of cultural anthropologists and graduate students and focused on the role of ethnicity in shaping social relationships in a Miami clothing factory (Grenier et al. 1992). The clothing plant, a subsidiary of the largest U.S. clothing manufacturer, employs about 250 operators, mainly women. The majority of employees are Cuban women who immigrated to Miami many years ago. The workers are organized into a union, but members of the different ethnic groups have more solidarity with each other than with the union. Interethnic rivalry exists around the issue of management's treatment of members of different groups. Many non-Cuban workers claim that there is favouritism towards Cuban employees. Some supervisors and managers expressed ethnic stereotypes, but not always consistent ones: "Depending on whom one listens to, Haitians are either too slow or too fast; Cubans may talk too much or be extraordinarily dedicated workers" (75). The management sees ethnic-based competition and lack of cooperation as a key problem that they attempt to deal with by enforcing an environment that downplays ethnicity. For example, management banned workers from playing personal radios and installed a system of piped-in music supposedly by a radio station that alternates between "American" and "Latin" songs.

The Informal Sector

Studying the informal sector presents several challenges. People who work in the informal sector may not be "organized" in one location, like a factory. Often, workers are involved in illegal activities, which means they are even less willing than other people to be "studied." In general, it is easier to do research on aspects of people's lives of which they are proud. Informal economy work may yield a sense of pride less often than formal economy work. On the other hand, some research advantages also arise. People involved in the informal economy, compared to a CEO of a multinational corporation, may have more time to share with the anthropologist. This is not always the case, however, since many informal sector workers are involved in more than one enterprise in an attempt to make ends meet, as well as being responsible for child care.

The illegal drug industry is an important part of the globalized informal economy. Neither international drug dealers nor street sellers pay income tax on their profits, and their earnings are not part of the official GNP of any nation. In the United States and Canada, many young males are drawn into the drug economy as sellers (see

MULTIPLE CULTURAL WORLDS

Street Youth in Edmonton

Stephen Baron's (2001) research in Edmonton's downtown core illustrates that street youth find government support inadequate for their needs, and that most find they must participate in illegal activities to survive. Most of the 200 young people he interviewed (average age 19) left school after grade 9, leaving low-paying entry-level jobs their only option. They eventually gave up the search for better jobs and came to rely on welfare and crime. The youth claimed free trade policies encouraged many manufacturing industries to move to Mexico and elsewhere, leaving few available well-paid jobs. Illegal ac-

tivities like dealing drugs, breaking and entering, and violent crimes gave them an income that far outstripped the legal sources of support available to them. They claimed that these informal, illegal activities also gave structure to their lives and provided excitement in an otherwise hopeless existence. Government support is an alternative income source, but it is often not enough. Baron reported some of the youths' views of their needs:

> [On welfare] you have enough to live on… have enough to survive (but) you can't do anything like go to a movie. You should go into the drug-

dealing business for one year… I was dealing dope, I didn't need to work. I'd make more in a day than they do in a week… Looking for work you just get broke and have no place to live. (Baron 2001)

FOOD FOR THOUGHT

Do you think the wider society should take responsibility for the growth in the number of street youth who feel criminal activity is their only option? What can government agencies or other community groups do about this situation?

the Multiple Cultural Worlds box). Their lives are fractured with danger and violence. Some anthropologists have undertaken research in such settings, including Philippe Bourgois (1995), who reports on his findings about Hispanic crack dealers in Harlem:

> Regular displays of violence are necessary for success in the underground economy—especially at the street-level drug-dealing world. Violence is essential for maintaining credibility and for preventing rip-off by colleagues, customers, and hold-up artists. Indeed, upward mobility in the underground economy requires a systematic and effective use of violence.... Behaviour that appears irrationally violent and self-destructive to the middle class (or the working class) outside observer, can be reinterpreted according to the logic of the underground economy, as a judicious case of public relations, advertising, rapport building, and long-term investment in one's "human capital development." (29)

In many parts of the world, prostitution is illegal, but exists as part of the informal sector. In Thailand, the sex industry, although illegal, is the leading sector of the economy (Skrobanek, Boonpakdee, and Jantateero 1997). In 1990, Thailand's sex industry accounted for about 10 per cent of Thailand's GNP, following closely behind income from all agricultural imports. Much of the income derives from Thailand's international popularity as a place for "sex tourism," which is travel that includes a "sex package." Thai prostitutes are also part of the international "export" sex industry. Over 200 000 Thai prostitutes live in Europe, while many others live in Japan, Hong Kong, Taiwan, Singapore, Canada, the United States, Saudi Arabia, and Kuwait. Child sex work in Thailand is an increasingly important part of this informal economy. The number of child prostitutes under 16 years old is estimated to be about 800 000, or 40 per cent of the total prostitute labour force. Recent changes, especially the fear of AIDS, have stepped up the demand for ever-younger prostitutes, since people associate child sex with safe sex. Health risks are high for prostitutes.

In Thailand, statistics show that AIDS is increasing rapidly among child prostitutes. Many international organizations have become involved in focusing attention on the issue of child prostitution in Thailand.

Changing Cultural Worlds of Industrial Workers: Barberton

Increased mechanization is a major aspect of change in industry worldwide, and it has marked impacts on labour. Unemployment and manufacturing declines in America's Rust Belt are well-known trends in industrial life-ways. Gregory Pappas (1989) studied unemployment in Barberton, a working-class Ohio town. A tire company that had been the town's major employer closed in 1980, eliminating 1200 jobs. Pappas lived in Barberton for a year, interviewing many people and sending a questionnaire to over 600 displaced workers for further information. His work sheds light on how unemployed workers cope either by migrating or by finding new ways to spend their time in Barberton. These people are faced with having to construct a new identity for themselves: "For factory workers the place of employment is crucial; their identities are bound up in a particular place, and plant shutdowns compromise their ability to understand themselves" (83). As one unemployed man commented, "I don't know who I am anymore." In this context of decline, levels of stress and mental disorder have increased for many people.

Many experts question the current and future sustainability of a mode of production that relies so heavily on the use of nonrenewable resources and that is also polluting the very planet that thus far has provided those resources. Others suggest that new forms of energy will be discovered and many planets besides earth will be able to provide both resources and places of human habitation. Given the global interconnections of industrialism—its demand for raw materials, markets, and labour, and its social and environmental effects—cultural anthropologists are now being challenged to devise new theories and methods to study such complexity.

What is the scope of economic anthropology?

Like the discipline of economics, economic anthropology encompasses the study of production, consumption, and exchange. But economic anthropology approaches these processes from a cross-cultural perspective and does not assume that Western economic patterns and values are universal. Economic anthropologists study a wider range of modes of production, or ways of making a living through goods or money, than economists study. The five modes of production anthropologists address are foraging, horticulture, pastoralism, agriculture, and industrialism. Anthropologists propose that the Western dualist notion of nature as separate from culture, with culture dominant, fits with capitalist economics and the economic exploitation of nature.

What are the characteristics of the five major modes of production?

The five modes of production involve the factors of labour, property relations, and sustainability. In foraging societies, the division of labour is based on gender and age, with temperate foragers having more gender overlap in tasks than circumpolar foragers. Property is shared, with all people having equal rights to resources such as land and water holes. These resources are managed by family groups and shared with others as needed. With its strategy of limited exploitation of local resources in combination with seasonal migration, foraging has long-term sustainability when not affected by pressure from the outside world.

Horticulture and pastoralism are also extensive strategies, requiring the sequential fallowing of plots in horticulture and migration of animals to fresh pastures in pastoralism. We cannot easily generalize about the division of labour in these modes of production because they include those in which men do most of the work, those in which women do most of the work, and those in which

workloads are shared more evenly. As with foraging peoples, use rights are the prominent form of property relations, but increased levels of production through the domestication of plants and animals yield more food and goods as well as heightened interest in protecting group rights to land. Given the mobile strategies of shifting use of plots in horticulture and shifting use of pasture land in pastoralism, these modes of production have long-term sustainability when not affected by encroachments from other economic systems.

Early agriculture, like many agricultural contexts now, was family-based in terms of labour. Most family farming systems involve more male labour in the fields and more female labour in the domestic domain, although some examples of dominant female roles in field labour exist. Plantation agricultural systems, which are quite recent, involve the use of hired labour, both male and female, as does corporate farming. Socialist states created another form of labour organization for farming through the collective, which organized workers into teams regardless of family affiliation or gender. In collectivized agriculture, men and women were supposed to have equal roles, but women tended to have lower status positions than men. With settled agriculture came the emergence of private property, and social control and laws to protect private interests. Social inequality in access to the primary means of production, land, emerged along with gaps between the rich landed people and the poor landless people. Agriculture's sustainability is limited by the need to replenish the land, which is used continuously for crops and animals.

In industrialism, labour is highly differentiated by class in addition to gender and age. Widespread unemployment is found in many industrial economies. In capitalist industrial societies, private property is the dominant pattern, with high rates of imprisonment for people who violate the rules. Socialist industrial societies have attempted to distribute property among all people, but most such attempts have not been successful. Given its intensive and ever-expanding exploitation of nonrenewable resources, industrialism lacks long-term sustainability.

What are some directions of change in the five modes of production?

Foragers are being incorporated into more settled economies as their access to large amounts of land is decreased by outside economic forces. Many former foraging people now work, for example, as farm labourers, jobs typically of low status in the mainstream cash economy. Others are participating in the revitalization of their culture in the new global economy, producing art for sale on the world market or developing cultural tourism opportunities for outsiders. While horticulture and pastoralism exist on a larger scale than foraging, these land-extensive systems are also under great pressure from the competing economic forms of agriculture and in-dustrialism. Many former horticulturalists have migrated to plantations or urban areas and become part of the cash economy. States have pressured pastoralists to settle down or to become collectivized in some contexts and then de-collectivized. In many parts of the world, family farms are declining in number as corporate farms increase. The labour force changes from being family-based to being dependent on migrant labourers who are often transnationals. A possible sixth mode of production is emerging with the information age and economic processes being carried out via the Internet. E-commerce is creating new ways of making a living, new labour patterns, new forms of property, and new questions about sustainability. Cultural anthropologists are just beginning to address this latest stage in economic change.

Core Concepts

agriculture, p. 72
capital, p. 78
capitalism, p. 60
collectivized agriculture, p. 79
consumption, p. 60
corporate farms, p. 77
domestication, p. 66

dualism, p. 61
economic systems, p. 60
exchange, p. 60
extensive strategy, p. 62
foraging, p. 61
formal sector, p. 81
horticulture, p. 66

industrial agriculture, p. 77
industrialism, p. 80
informal sector, p. 81
intensive strategy, p. 72
modes of production, p. 60
pastoralism, p. 70
plantation agriculture, p. 76

privatization, p. 72
production, p. 60
public/private dichotomy, p. 73
socialism, p. 72
use right, p. 64
wet rice agriculture, p. 74

Suggested Readings

Anne Allison, *Nightwork: Sexuality, Pleasure and Corporate Masculinity in a Tokyo Hostess Club.* Chicago: University of Chicago Press, 1994. Based on the author's participant observation, this book explores what it is like to work as a hostess in a club that caters to corporate male employees and discusses how that culture is linked to men's corporate work culture.

Frances Dahlberg, ed., *Woman the Gatherer.* New Haven: Yale University Press, 1981. These path-breaking essays examine the role of women in four different foraging societies, provide insights on human evolution from studies of female chimpanzees, and give an overview of women's role in human cultural adaptation.

Elliot Fratkin, *Ariaal Pastoralists of Kenya: Surviving Drought and Development in Africa's Arid Lands.* Boston: Allyn and Bacon, 1998. Based on several phases of ethnographic research among the Ariaal beginning in the 1970s, this book provides insights about pastoralism in general and the particular cultural strategies of the Ariaal, including attention to social organization and family life.

John G. Galaty and Pierre Bonte, eds., *Herders, Warriors, and Traders: Pastoralism in Africa.* Boulder, CO: Westview Press, 1991. This collection of readings examines the ability of pastoralists in Africa to maintain their way of life despite years of droughts and war.

David Uru Iyam, *The Broken Hoe: Cultural Reconfiguration in Biase Southeast Nigeria.* Chicago: University of Chicago Press, 1995. Based on fieldwork among the Biase people by an anthropologist who is a member of a Biase group, this book examines changes since the 1970s in the traditional forms of subsistence—agriculture, fishing, and trade—and related issues such as environmental deterioration and population growth.

Richard Lee and Richard Daly, eds., *The Cambridge Encyclopaedia of Hunters and Gatherers. Cambridge:* Cambridge University Press, 1999. This comprehensive book, written by recognized leaders in the field, outlines and evaluates anthropological knowledge on hunters and gatherers worldwide.

Katherine S. Newman, *Falling from Grace: The Experience of Downward Mobility in the American Middle Class.* New York: The Free Press, 1988. This book provides ethnographic research on the downwardly mobile of New Jersey as a "special tribe," with attention to loss of employment by corporate managers and blue-collar workers, and the effects of downward mobility on middle-class family life, particularly women.

Richard H. Robbins, *Global Problems and the Culture of Capitalism.* Boston: Longman, 1999. Robbins takes a critical look at the role of capitalism and global economic growth in creating and sustaining many world problems such as poverty, disease, hunger, violence, and environmental destruction. The last section includes extended case studies to support the argument.

 Your *Cultural Anthropology*, Second Canadian Edition Media Edition CD-ROM contains many Web sites relevant to this chapter. Use it to explore the Web and to expand your knowledge of anthropology.

Chapter 4

Consumption and Exchange

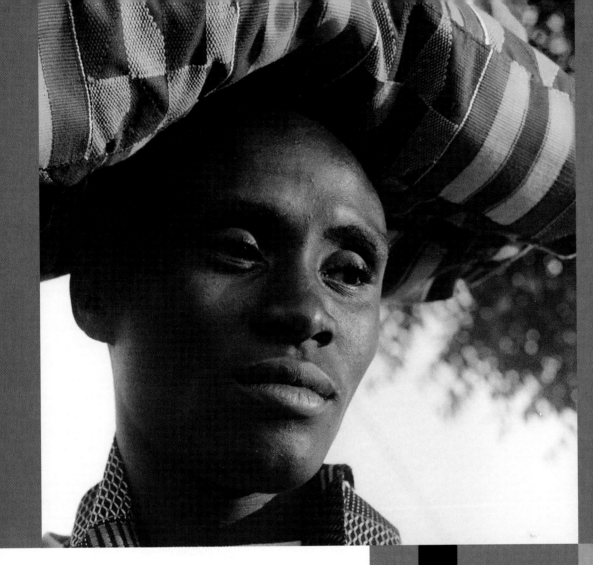

An itinerant cloth peddler, rural Ghana.

Key Questions

How do modes of production relate to consumption?

How do modes of production relate to exchange?

What are some examples of how contemporary global economic change affects nonmarket modes of consumption and exchange?

I *magine that it is the late eighteenth century and you are a member of a Kwakwaka'wakw village in British Columbia. Along with the rest of your local tribal group, you have been invited to a* **potlatch,** *a grand feast in which guests are invited to eat and to receive gifts from the hosts (Suttles 1991). Be prepared to eat a lot because potlatch guests are given abundant helpings of the most honourable foods: eulachon oil (oil from the eulachon fish, which has high fat content), high-bush cranberries, and seal meat, all served in ceremonial wooden bowls. The chief will present the guests with many gifts: hand-embroidered blankets, canoes, and carefully crafted household articles such as carved wooden boxes and woven mats, and food to be taken back home. The more the chief gives, the higher his status will rise, and the more his guests will be indebted to him. Later, when it is the guests' turn to hold a potlatch, they will try to give away as much as—or more than—their host did, thus shaming him into giving the next potlatch. Before the arrival of the Europeans, peoples throughout the Pacific Northwest were linked with each other through a network of potlatching relationships. The Europeans tried to stop potlatching because they thought it was "wasteful," and because it contained elements that offended Christian principles they were trying to promote. In spite of the fact that the Canadian government banned potlatching and the Winter Ceremonials in 1884, potlatches continued to be held furtively and openly among some groups, and are being revived by others.*

The Kwakwaka'wakw retained their ceremonial and feasting tradition throughout the sporadically enforced ban. However, potlatching among the Haida and Tlingit disappeared with relatively little resistance. Potlatches are no longer illegal, but a long battle was required to remove restrictions.

Contemporary reasons for giving a potlatch are similar to those in past times: naming children, mourning the dead, transferring rights and privileges, marriages, and the raising of totem poles and houses. The length of time devoted to planning a potlatch has shortened. Elders recall that several years were involved in planning a proper potlatch. Still, much property must be accumulated to make sure that no guest goes away empty handed, and the guest list may include between 500 and 1000 people. The kinds of goods exchanged are different today: Typical potlatch goods now include crocheted items such as cushion covers, afghans, and potholders, glassware, plastic goods, manufactured blankets, pillows, towels, articles of clothing, and sacks of flour and sugar (Webster 1991).

Potlatches figure prominently in ethnographic descriptions of the Northwest Coast and anthropologists have applied many theoretical approaches to interpreting the potlatch. For example, **functionalist theories** examine how a given practice or belief contributes to cultural continuity. According to this theory, potlatch networks provided a food safety net for people in the region (Piddocke 1969). Because of local annual fluctuations in food supply, a particular group might have a substantial surplus of fish, berries, and nuts during one year, but a deficit in the next year. Foodstuffs could not be saved for long enough to deal with this unevenness. Instead of saving food, people "banked" food through potlatching: A group experiencing an abundant season would be inspired to potlatch its neighbours and distribute its surplus to others. In the future, a former

Villagers assemble gifts in preparation for a potlatch, held before 1914 in Alert Bay, Vancouver Island.

host group would be the guests at a neighbouring group's potlatch when they had a surplus.

This sketch of potlatching demonstrates how closely linked production, consumption, and exchange are. Potlatches relate to levels of production; they are opportunities for consumption; and they involve exchange of goods among groups. This chapter considers the areas of economic anthropology that deal with modes of consumption, or the predominant patterns within a culture of using up goods and services, and modes of exchange, or the predominant patterns within a culture of transferring goods, services, and other items between and among peoples and groups (see Figure 4.1).

Culture and Consumption

What Is Consumption?

In this section, we examine the concept of consumption and we review various modes of consumption in rela-

tion to modes of production (see Chapter 3). We also look at several consumption funds, or areas to which people devote resources, such as basic needs and social needs.

Consumption has two senses: First, it is a person's "intake" in terms of eating or other ways of using things; second, it is a person's "output" in terms of spending or using resources. Thus, consumption includes eating habits and household budgeting practices. People consume many things: Food, drink, clothing, and shelter are the most basic consumption needs. Beyond that, they may acquire and use tools, weapons, means of transportation, computers, books and other items of communication, art and other luxury goods, and energy for heating and cooling one's residence.

In order to consume, one must have something to consume or to trade for something consumable. In a market economy, most consumption depends on having cash. A person's ability to consume would thus be measured in terms of cash income. Economists who study consumption in cash-based market economies often use

FIGURE 4.1 Modes of Consumption and Exchange

FORAGING	HORTICULTURE	PASTORALISM	AGRICULTURE	INDUSTRIALISM (CAPITALIST)
Mode of Consumption Minimalism Finite needs				*Mode of Consumption* Consumerism Infinite needs
Social Organization of Consumption Equality/sharing				*Social Organization of Consumption* Class-based inequality
Primary Budgetary Fund Basic needs				*Primary Budgetary Fund* Rent/taxes, luxuries
Mode of Exchange Balanced exchange				*Mode of Exchange* Market exchange
Social Organization of Exchange Small groups, face-to-face				*Social Organization of Exchange* Anonymous market transactions
Primary Category of Exchange The gift				*Primary Category of Exchange* The sale

data on people's cash income or expenditures as measures of consumption. However, cultural anthropologists are interested in all economic systems, not just market economies, so the categories they use for analysis of economic processes must be more broadly applicable. In all economies, people expend something to satisfy their needs. In nonmarket economies, instead of expending cash, people "spend" time, labour, or trade goods in order to provide for their needs. While it may seem odd to consider time or labour as equivalent to cash, this conceptual framework allows for cross-cultural comparison of people's access to resources and their consumption and exchange patterns.

The relationship between the processes of consumption and exchange also differs between nonmarket and market systems. In nonmarket economies, many consumption needs are satisfied without any exchange at all, or only to a limited degree. In market economies, most consumption items are not self-produced and must be purchased. Thus, aspects of consumption and exchange overlap substantially. For example, when a horticulturalist grows food for home consumption using seeds saved from the previous year, no exchange is involved in providing for consumption. If a farmer purchases seeds and fertilizer to grow food, then exchange has become an essential part of providing for consumption needs. In nonmarket economies, relatively few goods must be obtained through exchange, while in market economies most goods are obtained this way.

Modes of Consumption

Using cross-cultural evidence on consumption, we can construct a general picture of **modes of consumption** or dominant patterns of using things up or spending one's resources in order to satisfy demands. Modes of consumption correspond generally with the production continuum (see Figure 4.1 on page 91). At the opposite ends of the continuum, two contrasting modes of consumption exist, defined by the relationship between demand (what people want) and supply (the resources available to satisfy demand) (Sahlins 1972). **Minimalism** is a mode of consumption that emphasizes simplicity and is characterized by few and finite (limited) consumer demands and an adequate and sustainable means to achieve them. At the other end of the continuum is **consumerism,** in which people's demands are many and

infinite and the means of satisfying them are, therefore, insufficient and become depleted in the effort to meet demands. Minimalism is most clearly exemplified in (free-ranging) foraging societies, while consumerism is the distinguishing feature of industrial cultures (of the capitalist variety). In between these two extremes are blended patterns, with a decreasing trend towards minimalism and an increasing trend towards consumerism as one moves from left to right. Changes in the mode of production influence the transformation in consumption. Notably, the increase of surpluses and the ability to store wealth for long periods of time allow for a more consumerist lifestyle to emerge.

The social organization of consumption also changes as one moves across the continuum. As noted in Chapter 3, social inequality in access to resources increases as one moves from foraging to agricultural and industrial (especially capitalist) societies. In foraging societies, everyone has access to all resources. Food, land, water, and materials for shelter are usually communally shared as among the traditional Ju/wasi of southern Africa:

> Food is never consumed alone by a family; it is always (actually or potentially) shared out with members of a living group or band of up to 30 (or more) members. Even though only a fraction of the able-bodied foragers go out each day, the day's return of meat and gathered foods are divided in such a way that every member of the camp receives an equitable share. The hunting band or camp is a unit of sharing, and if sharing breaks down it ceases to be a camp. (Richard Lee 1979:118)

The distribution of personal goods, such as clothing or "leisure" items such as musical instruments or smoking pipes, is also equal. In horticultural and pastoral societies, group sharing is still a prevalent ethic, and it is the duty of leaders to make sure that everyone has food and shelter.

At the other end of the continuum, we find the leading consumerist cultures of the world. Consumption levels in the United States, since the 1970s, have been the highest of any society in human history. Consumerism is widely promoted as a good thing, a path to happiness. Increasing one's consumption level and quality of life is a primary personal goal of most people, and of the government, too. Many other nations around the world have growing economies that allow some of the population to demand consumer goods and have the energy capa-

A view of Seoul, the capital of the Republic of Korea. The demand for electricity in urban centres worldwide has prompted the building of many high dams to generate power. Food must be shipped to urban markets. In general, cities have high energy costs compared with rural areas.

bilities to support a luxury lifestyle (cars, air conditioning, and other appliances). These countries include the rapidly developing nations of Asia, such as China, the Republic of Korea, and Vietnam, and many countries in Africa and Latin America. For example, in the 1990s Ghana's economy grew at about 5 per cent a year. During the same period, electricity consumption increased almost 11 per cent a year in the nation and in Accra, the capital, at over 13 per cent a year. At this rate, national consumption of electricity will double in five years. The increase is the result of both industrial growth and increased consumer demand. Once unattainable luxuries—electrical appliances and other gadgets such as fans, refrigerators, televisions, stereos, air conditioners, VCRs, computers, and fax machines—are increasingly common in Ghanaian homes (*The Economist* 1994:45).

In all, the amount of goods that the world's population consumed in the past 50 years equals what was consumed by all previous generations in human history. Minimalism was sustainable over hundreds of thousands of years. In contrast, many experts have provided data documenting the non-sustainability of consumerism. Some nations, such as Sweden, have taken steps to control consumerism and its negative environmental effects:

Stockholm is attempting to reduce the dependence on cars. The city is laid out to encourage walking, bicycling, and, in the long winter, cross-country skiing. Continuous paths through parklands encircle many of the islands on which the city is built, and Stockholm's commercial district is laced with bicycle routes, wide sidewalks, and pedestrian zones. Buses move swiftly through the metropolis, and the national bus and railway depot is in the heart of the city. People commute not only by foot and cycle, but also by kayak through the city's dozens of channels and waterways. (Durning 1993:23)

Consumption Funds

A **consumption fund** is a category of a person's or household's budget used to provide for their demands. Cross-cultural analysis of expenditures (including time or labour and cash) reveal that expenditure patterns differ according to the mode of production and the amount of surplus goods available in the society. In a forager's "budget," the largest share of expenditures goes into the **basic needs fund**, which includes food, beverages, shelter, fuel, clothing, and the tools needed to obtain these items. In other words, foragers "spend" the largest proportion of their "budget" on fulfilling their basic needs, including repair and maintenance of tools and baskets, weapons, and shelter. Smaller amounts of expenditure are made to the **entertainment fund**, for personal leisure, and the **ceremonial fund**, for public events beyond the immediate group such as a potlatch. No funds go to the **tax/rent fund** (payments to a government or landowner for civic responsibilities or use of land or housing).

Consumption budgets in consumerist cultures differ in the overall size of the budget and in the proportions allocated to particular funds. First, the budget size is larger. People in agricultural and industrial societies work longer hours (unless they are unemployed); thus, they "spend" more time and labour than foragers. However, the very poor may simply not be able to meet their basic needs. This change follows a well-known economic principle that says: Budgetary shares for food and housing decline as income rises. People with higher incomes may spend more on food and housing in an absolute sense than people with lower incomes, but the proportion of their total budget devoted to food and housing is less. For example, someone who earns a total of $1000 a month and spends $800 on food and housing, expends 80 per cent of his budget in that category. Someone who makes $10 000 a month and spends $2000 a month on food and housing, expends only 20 per cent of her budget in this category, even though she spends more than twice as much as the first person, in an absolute sense. People living in agricultural and industrial cultures devote the largest proportion of their budget to the tax/rent fund. In some agricultural contexts, tenant farmers and share-croppers provide one-third or one-half of their crops to the landlord as rent. Income taxes constitute over 50 per cent of income in countries such as Japan, Sweden, the Netherlands, and Italy (Pechman 1987). Consumers in industrial countries are also placing increasing importance on the entertainment fund, which is used for recreation such as attending movies and sports events, travel, and buying "home entertainment" appliances.

Consumption Inequalities

Amartya Sen (1981), an economist and a philosopher, developed the concept of **entitlements,** which are socially defined rights to life-sustaining resources, in order to explain why some groups suffer more than others during a famine. In this book, we will extend the use of the concept of entitlements to nonfamine situations as well, as a way of looking at consumption inequalities in everyday life. Also, Sen's original use of the entitlement concept was in terms of intrasocietal patterns, but we will use it at three levels: global, national, and household. The concept of entitlements helps us understand how social inequality works and can change.

According to Sen, a person possesses a set or "bundle" of entitlements. A person may own land, earn cash from a job, be on welfare, or live off an inheritance, for example. Through these entitlements, people provide for their consumption needs. A crucial factor in entitlement theory is that some kinds of entitlements are more secure and more lucrative than others, and thus they provide more secure and luxurious levels of consumption (see the Critical Thinking box). **Direct entitlements** are the most secure form of entitlement; in an agricultural society, for example, owning land that produces food is a direct entitlement. **Indirect entitlements** are ways of gaining subsistence that depend on exchanging something in order to obtain consumer needs—for example, labour, animal hides, welfare cheques, or food stamps.

Indirect entitlements entail dependency on other people and institutions, and they are thus riskier bases of support than direct entitlements. For example, labour or animal hides may drop in value or no longer be wanted, and food stamps may cease to be awarded. People who have no direct entitlements and only one or two forms of indirect entitlements in their bundle are in the most vulnerable position during economic recession, famine, or other times when access to resources becomes squeezed.

In foraging societies, everyone has the same entitlement bundles and, except for infants and the very aged, the bundles are direct (infants and the aged are dependent on sharing from members of the group for their food and shelter and so could be said to have indirect entitlements). In industrial capitalist societies, entitlement bundles, in terms of access to food and resources, are preponderantly indirect. The few people who still grow their own food are a small proportion of the total population, and even they are dependent on indirect entitlements for electricity and other aspects of maintaining their lifestyle. In the highly monetized cash economies of industrialized societies, the most powerful entitlements are those that provide a high and steady cash income such as having a good job, savings, and a retirement fund.

Entitlements at Three Levels

Applied globally, entitlement theory allows us to differentiate among nations that have more or less secure and direct access to life-supporting resources. Nations with strong rates of food production have a stronger entitlement to food than nations that are dependent on imports, for example. Growing cash crops rather than food crops puts a nation in a situation of indirect entitlement to food. The same applies to access to energy sources that may be important for transportation to work or for heating homes. Direct access to energy resources is preferable to indirect access. The current structure of the world economy, as noted in Chapter 3, places some countries in far more secure positions than others.

In a parallel way, the entitlement concept can be applied at the level of the household to examine within-household entitlement structures. In contemporary industrial societies, having a job, owning a business or farm land, owning a home, or having savings and in-

Assessing One's Own Entitlement Bundle

Do you own land on which you grow your own food? If yes, then a basic part of your entitlement bundle consists of direct entitlements to food.

Or, do you buy your food? If so, where do you get the money to buy food? If parents or other relatives give you money to buy food, then your entitlement bundle consists of indirect entitlements of two sorts: cash transfers from other people and then exchange of cash for food. Maybe you work for someone who pays you cash in return for

your labour. That's an indirect entitlement, too.

What would you do if every cafeteria, restaurant, and grocery store declared that they no longer would accept money in exchange for food?

Do you have any other entitlements in your bundle that you could use to get food? You might take some of your personal goods, such as your bicycle or computer, to trade for food. You might see if some of your friends or relatives have some stored-up supplies that they would give you

or lend you. If you own land, you might start planting food crops, but that would not help in the short run. In an extreme situation in which none of these options worked, you might be driven to stealing food, but theft is not considered an entitlement because it is illegal.

If none of these strategies succeeds, you have experienced "entitlement failure" and the end result could be starvation.

---

vestments puts a person in a more secure position. This means that often adult members, and males more than females in most industrial societies, have more secure entitlements than other household members. Depending on the cultural context, inheritance practices may ensure that certain children receive entitlements to certain assets (the family business, for example) while other children are left out, thus passing on entitlement bundles over time.

Famine as Entitlement Failure

Famine is massive death resulting from food deprivation in a geographically widespread area. It tends to reach a crisis point and then subside. Famines have been recorded throughout history for all parts of the world, including Europe (Dando 1980:113). Between the year 10 and 1850, 187 famines were recorded in what is now the United Kingdom. India, Russia, and China experienced major famines in the twentieth century. Most recently, famines have occurred mainly in the Sahel: the Sahelian famine of 1969–1971, the Ethiopian famine of 1982–1984 and 2000, the Sudan and Somalian famines of 1988–1992, and the North Korean famine (or near-famine) of 1996–1997.

Most people think that famines are caused by "too many people to feed," or natural disasters such as droughts and floods. Neither overpopulation nor natural

disasters are sufficient explanations for famine. First, calculations of world food supply in relation to population indicate that there is enough food produced every year to feed the world's population. Second, natural factors are

Civil war in southern Sudan in 1998 contributed to the spread of famine. Here a sister and brother await medical treatment in a Doctors Without Borders relief compound.

often catalysts of famines, but natural disasters happen in many parts of the world and are not necessarily followed by famine. For example, Florida's devastating Hurricane Andrew did not cause a statewide famine. The answer to what causes famine lies in entitlement failures at three levels: global, national, and household.

Global Entitlement Structures

Throughout history, many countries that were colonized by external powers are now more resource-depleted than before and more dependent on food imports. Colonization changed local production from that of food crops for the farmers themselves to cash crops for sale. Thus, massive replacement of direct entitlements to food to indirect entitlements occurred. International relations in contemporary times often involve the "politics of food." As a journalist reported on the Sudan in 1988: "There is, cruelly, food to be had. The land is fertile, the rains were good, and this year's harvest will be the best in a decade. But four million people are starving because of a civil war.... On both sides the terrible weapon is increasingly food, not bullets" (Wilde 1988:43). The northern army blocked the delivery of food aid to the south, and the food that did get through was often diverted by the southern rebel troops. Norway donated substantial amounts of maize, but the United States was slow to get involved because it did not want to upset its diplomatic relationship with the Sudanese government.

Global politics were a key causal factor in the Bengal famine of 1943–44. This massive famine was related to British efforts during World War II to stop the Japanese forces from advancing into India from Burma. The region of Bengal at that time included what is now a state of India (named West Bengal) and the nation of Bangladesh (called East Bengal when it was part of British India). Bengal was a lush food-producing region located adjacent to Burma. As the Japanese moved closer to India, the British devised and implemented a plan to destroy food supplies in Bengal that could be used by the advancing enemy. The British burned standing crops and seeds that were being stored, and destroyed fishing boats as well (Greenough 1982; Sen 1981). This policy succeeded in stopping the Japanese, but at a terrible cost to thousands of Bengalis. The United States has also used food as a political weapon, including the trade embargo, much to the dismay of human rights groups in the United States and elsewhere.

National Entitlement Structures

Within nations, entitlement inequalities lead to particular patterns of suffering. In no famine has everyone in the affected area starved. Instead, many people grow wealthy by hoarding food and selling it at inflated prices. During the Bengal famine, the people who were most affected were those lacking direct entitlements to food: the landless poor who normally worked as labourers for the landowners and were paid in cash food shares, and fishing people who could not fish without boats (Sen 1981). In the meantime, rich landowners and merchants bought up the rice that existed and secretly stored it. As food prices rose astronomically during the famine, they grew even richer by selling hoarded rice.

Intrahousehold Entitlement Structures

Within households, famine conditions force decisions about how to allocate scarce resources or deal with the absence of any resources at all. No cultural anthropologist was on the scene during the Bengal famine, studying intrahousehold decision making. However, indirect historical evidence of how decisions were made can be found in records kept by the Bengal Relief Committee about people who came to their centres for relief, mainly in the form of food, but also medicine and clothing (Greenough 1982). These records contain information about the households of those who appeared at the centres for help. One of the clearest findings is that the famine caused the breakup of households. In Bengali culture, males are valued over females and adults are valued over children. In the household, the senior male is the head of household and has the highest authority and responsibility. These values are reflected in resource allocation choices during times of scarcity.

During the famine, spouses frequently separated, with the husband either leaving the wife behind or sending her away. The relief records show a high number of abandoned married women. Women who were interviewed said that "their husbands were unable to maintain them at the present moment and asked them to go elsewhere to search for food" (Greenough 1982:220). Many of these women migrated to cities, such as Calcutta, where their options for survival were limited to dependency on relief handouts, begging, or prostitution. Some women and girls were sold by their families into prostitution. Children were sold by desperate families either in hope that someone else could give them food or for the immediate pur-

Homeless children rest by a storefront grate in Ho Chi Minh City, Vietnam. The transition from socialism to capitalism has altered people's entitlement bundle in Vietnam.

pose of obtaining cash. Many children were simply abandoned by the roadside. The pre-eminence and importance of the male head of household and the emphasis on preservation of the family line through males in Bengal shaped this pattern of decision making that differentially deprived women and children from household support.

Consumption Categories

People's consumption patterns are also shaped by class, gender, race, and age. These intersecting categories influence entitlement bundles and ways of consuming resources (see the Voices box).

Class

Class differences, which are defined in terms of levels of income and wealth, are reflected in class-specific consumption patterns. In societies with class structures, upper-class people spend more on consumption than the poor. The poor, however, spend a higher percentage of their total income on consumption than the rich, especially on basic needs such as food, clothing, and shelter. Class differences in consumption in contemporary industrial societies may seem so obvious that they are scarcely worth studying. A team of French researchers, however, undertook a national sample survey with over 1000 responses to study class differences in consumer preferences and tastes (Bourdieu 1984). The results revealed strong class patterns in, for example, choice of

Harriet Nalubwame, "Micro-Finance Loans Changed My Life"

Harriet Nalubwame is a 17-year-old single mother living in Mbigi, Uganda. She told her story to a credit officer at MED-Net (Micro-Enterprise Development Network), a micro-finance lending institution started by World Vision, which has disbursed loans to more than 10 000 people—mainly women—since its beginning in 1997.

I don't know when I got infected with HIV but I was told of my seropositive status in 1996... I received treatment for six months be-

fore I was told there were no more drugs for me if I did not pay. I felt very dejected and thought that my time to die was drawing near. I was worried about my child... A neighbor who saw me in agony introduced me to a group of women who were borrowing money from MED-Net's Kampala/Mbigi branch. The women visited me several times and provided moral support... They later invited me to borrow money from MED-Net. The initial amount of money that I borrowed was US$130....

At first it was hard, but with a lot of encouragement from two other women in my loan group, I began to pick up the shattered pieces of my life. My retail shop that I had neglected for so long gradually began to pick up... I am now able to look after my child without relying on aid. I am also able to pay for my medical bills and spend a good part of the day without actually thinking about the disease. (Nalubwame 2000:3) favourite painters or pieces of music, most closely associated with people's level of education and their father's occupation. An overall pattern of "distance from necessity" in tastes and preferences characterized members of the educated upper classes, who were more likely to prefer abstract art. In comparison, the working classes, given their economic position, were closer to "necessity" and their preference was for realist art. Bourdieu provides the concept of the "game of distinction," in which people of various classes take on the preferences of higher income people in order to enhance their own standing. Education, according to Bourdieu, provides the means for learning how to play the "game of distinction" to acquire symbolic capital.

Gender

In many societies, especially those where males and females have highly demarcated roles and status, consumption patterns are clearly gender-marked as well. Specific foods may be thought to be "male foods" or "female foods." In places where alcoholic beverages are consumed, the overwhelming pattern is that males drink more than females. Following is a vivid example of differences in food consumption between males and females in highland Papua New Guinea where males generally have higher status than females. This example begins with the eruption of a mysterious disease, with the local name of *kuru*, among the Fore (pronounced "for-ay"), a highland foraging group (Lindenbaum 1979). Between 1957 and 1977, about 2500 people died of *kuru*, but the victims were mostly women.

> An initial shivering tremor usually progresses to complete motor incapacity and death in about a year. Women, the prime victims of the disease, may withdraw from the community at the shock of recognizing the first symptoms— pain in the head and limbs, and a slight unsteadiness of gait. They resume their usual gardening activities a few weeks later, struggling to control their involuntary body movements until forced by gross physical incoordination to remain at home, sedentarily awaiting death. (Lindenbaum 1979:9–10)

The Fore believed that *kuru* was caused by sorcery, but a team of medical researchers and cultural anthropologist Shirley Lindenbaum showed that *kuru* was a neurological disease caused by the consumption of the flesh of deceased people who were themselves *kuru* victims. Who was eating human flesh, and why? Among the Fore, it was considered acceptable to cook and eat the flesh of a deceased person, although it was not considered a preferred form of food. Some Fore women were turning to eating human flesh because of the increased scarcity of the usual sources of animal protein in the region. Population density had increased, areas under cultivation had increased, forest areas had decreased, and wild animals as a protein source were scarce in the Fore region. This scarcity acted in combination with the Fore's strongly male-preferential system of consumption: Preferred protein sources go to men. Some women, therefore, turned to consumption of less-preferred foods and thereby contracted *kuru*.

Race

The racial apartheid that was a matter of national policy in South Africa until recently is one of the world's clearest examples of explicit definition of racial inequalities in consumption. Whites owned property, had wealth, and lived prosperous lives that included good food, housing, and educational opportunities for their children. Blacks were denied all of these things. The current government in South Africa is still attempting to redress decades of deprivation linked to racial categories and now has to face the additional burden of widespread HIV/AIDS.

In the United States, as in Canada, racial differences in consumption and welfare exist. One area in which racial discrimination affects consumption is housing, a subject that has been studied by cultural anthropologists and other social scientists (B. Williams 1988; Yinger 1995; Hacker 1992). Access by Blacks to housing in integrated neighbourhoods in American cities is limited by the tendency of Whites to move out as more Black families move in. A 1992 survey conducted in Detroit found that most Blacks prefer to live in an integrated neighbourhood, but nearly half of the Whites surveyed said they would move out if the neighbourhood were one-third Black (Farley 1993, cited in Yinger 1995:7).

Nova Scotia's Black population arrived in the late 1700s and following the war of 1812. Segregated on small farm lots on rocky, marginal land, the settlers formed Canada's earliest and largest Black settlement, Africville. The community had no plumbing, sewage, running water, or paved roads, and was identified as early as 1917 as a slum requiring clearance. It was cleared in the 1960s, with property owners compensated or re-housed. Today the descendants of Africville view the destruction of their community as racially motivated and seek redress for the injustices of community destruction and relocation (Millward 1996). On July 5, 2002, Africville was designated a national heritage site as a reminder of the need for racial respect.

Age

Different age categories also have characteristic consumption patterns that are culturally shaped. In different contexts, certain foods are believed appropriate for infants, young children, adolescents, adults, and the aged. Consider the category of "the aged." Biologically, the elderly have "more critical and unique nutritional needs" than other age groups (Shifflett and McIntosh 1986–1987). In spite of these special needs, in many cultures, the very old fall into a category with declining entitlements and declining quality of consumption. In North America, the elderly tend to decrease their physical activities, and they tend to omit important food groups, especially fruits and vegetables. Little exercise and inadequate diet lead to increased obesity and reduced resistance to disease. Elderly men or women living alone may eat junk food and meals prepared with the least effort.

Aging affects everyone, regardless of class level, but wealth can protect the elderly from certain kinds of marginalization and deprivation. The class effects of aging are somewhat reduced in Canada by community care programs that gear community-based care and long-term institutionalized care to income and the Canada Pension Plan, as well as universal access to health care.

Culture and Household Budgeting

Intrahousehold decisions about resource allocations respond to cultural rules and thus vary, depending on the cultural context. Cross-cultural data indicate that household resources are often not evenly divided. This statement contrasts with a model long prevalent in economics that sees the household as an egalitarian unit that treated all members equally in the overall interest of the unit as a whole (Becker 1964). This model assumed egalitarian intrahousehold relationships as a given, without considering the possibility that viewing the household as an unexamined "black box" (Folbre 1986) might be inaccurate in many cases. A more appropriate hypothesis is that in particular cultural contexts, household decision makers may treat various members differently in order to maximize socially constructed individual and collective goals. Cultural anthropologists who have studied the internal dynamics of households look first at decision-making patterns, and then at the results of the decisions.

Patterns of Budgetary Decision Making

Four major categories of decision making about household budgeting have been found cross-culturally, based on studies of husband-wife units (Pahl 1980, 1983):

- *Male budgetary control:* This form of budgetary management is found in cultures where the husband is sole or main earner and he retains financial control of his income, giving his wife a set amount for household purchases. It is common in Western societies, the Middle East, and India, and in urban, elite cultures around the world that have been influenced by westernization. About one-fourth of all households in the United Kingdom follow this system. In urban Zambia, husbands "dole out" money to their wives. Husbands argue that this arrangement is necessary because their wives are careless with their money. For instance, one husband, a university graduate and senior civil servant explained, "I keep all the money myself and give [sic] my wife when necessary. If you entrust money to a wife, you invite trouble" (Munachonga 1988:187).

- *Female budgetary control:* This form of budgetary management is found where both the wife and the husband are earners, but all earnings are placed under the management of the wife, who gives the husband an allowance for personal expenses. This pattern is common throughout Southeast Asia, including the Philippines, Indonesia, and the mainland. A common belief in Indonesia is that women are more practically minded than men and thus are better money managers.

- *Pooling system:* Both partners place whatever earnings they make into a common fund, both are responsible for managing the common pool, and both may take personal spending money out of the pool. This system is found mainly in dual-income households in Europe and North America.

- *Nonpooling system:* Partners keep their earnings separate and they do not have access to each other's funds; each is responsible for certain expenditures, although there may be transfers between husband and wife (Guyer 1988). The nonpooling system is common in African cultures south of the Sahara.

How do these different organizational models affect intrahousehold decisions about consumption spending? Not enough data are available to answer this question conclusively, but some evidence suggests that women as budgetary managers tend to favour allocations to basic needs and child welfare more than men, who are more likely to shift expenditure shares away from basic needs to personal expenditures (Bruce and Dwyer 1988:5–6). Barbara Miller's (1987a) data on household budgets in Jamaica support this generalization. Budgetary shares for food and housing were larger in households headed by women than in households headed jointly by a man and woman (Miller 1987a).

More anthropologists are now studying intrahousehold distribution of resources. Biased distribution of food, money, and even affection, may be based on the child's gender, birth order, "looks," or a combination of these things. Inequality of some sort tends to be the norm, even when parents say that their intention is to treat all children equally. Gender is a major distinguishing factor, with son preference a common phenomenon worldwide. Evidence from a few cultures—the United States, Peru, and Malaysia—reveals a sort of "gender alliance," with mothers favouring daughters and fathers favouring sons (Thomas 1991).

Biases regarding particular adult family members have also been documented. In Ghana, West Africa, a bias in expenditures in favour of adult males occurs in both urban and rural areas, and in different regions and religious groups (Deaton 1987). A study in western Nepal reveals that mothers there have the most limited food shares within the household (Gittelsohn 1991).

Forbidden Consumption: Food Taboos

Anthropologists have a longstanding interest in trying to explain culturally specific food **taboos,** or rules of prohibition. This interest has generated several conflicting theories, with the strongest difference between cultural materialists, and those who favour symbolic or meaning-centred theories.

Cultural Materialism and Food Taboos

Marvin Harris (1974) asks why there are Jewish and Muslim taboos on eating pig when pig meat is so enthusiastically consumed in many other parts of the world. He says, "Why should gods so exalted as Jahweh and Allah have bothered to condemn a harmless and even laughable beast whose flesh is relished by the greater part of mankind?" (36). Harris proposes that we consider the role of environmental factors during early Hebrew times and the function of this prohibition in terms of its fit to the local ecology:

> *Within the overall pattern of this mixed farming and pastoral complex, the divine prohibition of pork constituted a sound ecological strategy. The nomadic Israelites could not raise pigs in their arid habitats, while for the semi-sedentary and village farming populations, pigs were more of a threat than an asset…. The pig has a further disadvantage of not being a practical source of milk, and of being notoriously difficult to herd over long distances…. Above all, the pig is thermodynamically ill-adapted to the hot, dry climate of the Negev, the Jordan Valley, and the other lands of the Bible and the Koran. Compared to cattle, goats, and sheep, the pig has an inefficient system for regulating its body temperature. Despite the expression "To sweat like a pig," it has recently been proved that pigs can't sweat at all. (41–42)*

Raising pigs in this context would be a luxury. On the other hand, in "pig-loving" cultures of Southeast Asia and the Pacific, climatic factors including temperature, humidity, and the presence of forest cover (good for pigs) promote pig raising. There, pigs offer an important protein source in people's diets that complements yams,

Preparations for a feast in the highlands of Papua New Guinea, where people place much value on consuming high-status foods such as roasted pig meat.

sweet potatoes, and taro. In conclusion, Harris acknowledges that not all religiously sanctioned food practices can be explained ecologically, and he allows that food practices do have a social function in promoting social identity. But first and foremost, analysis of food consumption should consider ecological and material factors of production.

Food Taboos as Systems of Meaning

Mary Douglas (1966) argues that what people eat has to do with the value of food as a way of communicating symbolic meaning as well as with the material conditions of life, including hunger. For Douglas, people's mental categories provide a psychological ordering of the world. Anomalies, or things that don't fit into the categories, become reminders to people of moral problems or things to avoid.

She uses this approach of ordered categories and disordered anomalies in her analysis of food prohibitions in the Old Testament book of Leviticus. One rule is that people may eat animals with cloven hoofs and that chew a cud. Several tabooed animals are said to be unclean, such as the camel, the pig, the hare, and the rock badger.

Among a pastoral people, she says, it is logical that the model food animal would be a ruminant (a cloven-hoofed, cud-chewing, four-footed animal such as a cow, bison, goat, and sheep). In contrast, a pig is a four-footed animal with cloven hoofs, but it does not chew a cud; thus the pig is an anomaly and taboo as food. In this way, Leviticus sets up a system that contrasts sacred completeness and purity (the animals one can eat) with impurity and sinfulness (the animals one cannot eat) to remind people of God's holiness and perfection and people's responsibility towards God.

Anthropologists studying food systems try to consider both the material aspects of food practices and the communicative, symbolic meaning of food in order to explain food prohibitions and preferences, acknowledging that there is more to food than just eating.

Culture and Exchange

Cultural anthropologists have done much research on gifts and other forms of exchange, starting with the early twentieth century studies by Malinowski of the *kula* of the Trobriand Islands (described later in this chapter) and Boas's research on the potlatch of the Pacific Northwest. We know that in all economic systems, individuals and groups exchange goods and services with others, so exchange is a cultural universal. But cultural variations arise in several areas: in what is exchanged, in how exchange takes place, and in when exchange takes place (see the Multiple Cultural Worlds box on page 102).

What Is Exchanged?

Exchange involves the transfer of something that may be material or immaterial between at least two persons, groups, or institutions. The items exchanged may be purely utilitarian or they may carry meanings and have a history, or "social life," of their own (Appadurai 1986). In contemporary industrial societies, money is a key item of exchange. In many other economies, money plays a less important role and valued items such as time, labour, and goods are prominent exchange items.

But nonmonetary exchange exists in contemporary industrial societies, too. Hosting dinner parties, exchanging gifts at holiday times, and sharing a bag of potato chips with a friend are examples of common forms

Favours and Gifts in China

While doing fieldwork in urban China, Mayfair Yang (1994) learned about the pervasive importance of guanxixue (pronounced "guan-shee-shwe"), or the exchange of gifts, favours, and banquets in order to cultivate mutual obligation and indebtedness. Yang went to China with the intention of doing research in a factory, but she was never given clearance to do that work. In the process of trying to gain permission, she learned about the many levels of bureaucracy that were involved in getting permission for the fieldwork. In order to pass through each of these stages, simple and straightforward requests would not be enough: Much guanxixue would be needed. Given the importance of guanxixue in Chinese social relationships, Yang decided to shift her research focus to that topic. She writes that "Guanxixue is a ubiquitous theme; it appears in economic transactions; in political and social relationships; in literature, newspapers, academic journals, theater, and film.... Compared with other social practices,

there also seems to be a greater cultural elaboration of vocabulary, jokes, proverbs, and etiquette surrounding guanxixue" (6).

Guanxixue involves getting what one wants through giving. If you give someone a gift and they accept it, or if you invite someone to dinner, then—later—you can ask a favour of the person and the rules of guanxixue prescribe that your favour will be granted. Guanxixue is not the same as bribery because it is indirect and usually handled discreetly. Yang describes one interaction that is less discreet since the first, discreet attempt failed:

A worker wanted to get a few authorized days off from work to attend to some personal business. He first tried to give presents in private to the factory manager, but the latter declined. So he cunningly worked out a way to make the manager accept. He waited for an opportunity when the manager was in the presence of many other workers to give the gift

to him.... He said to the manager, "Here is the gift which my father, your old comrade-in-arms... asked me to deliver to you. Please accept it so his feelings are not hurt." Both the worker and the manager knew that the story about his father being an old friend of his was made up, so the real aim of the gift was apparent to the manager. In front of so many people, however, the manager was in danger of losing face if he refused to accept the gift unless he could come up with a good reason." (133–134)

The manager did not want to say in public that he would not accept the gift because that would appear to be ungenerous. And he did not want to call the worker a liar because the worker would lose too much face. The manager was forced to accept the gift. Later, when the inevitable request for authorized days off work arrived, he would have to say yes or else the factory people would talk about his lack of generosity.

of nonmonetary exchange. Some people would even include giving caresses, kisses, loyalty, and glances (Blau 1964).

Material Goods Food is one of the most common exchange goods in everyday life and on ritual occasions. Marriage arrangements often involve complex stages of gifts and countergifts exchanged between the groom's family and the bride's family. Wedding exchanges among the Nias of northern Sumatra, Indonesia, provide a good illustration. From the betrothal onward to the actual marriage, there is a scheduled sequence of events at which gifts are exchanged between the families of the bride and groom (Beatty 1992). At the first meeting, the prospective groom expresses his interest in a betrothal. He and his party visit the bride's house and are fed: "The guests are given the pig's lower jaw (the portion of honour) and

take away with them raw and cooked portions for the suitor's father" (121). Within the next week or two, the groom brings a gift of three to twelve pigs to confirm the betrothal. He also returns the container used for the pig meat given to him on the previous visit, filled with a certain kind of nut. The groom gives pigs and gold as the major gift that seals the marriage. Gifts will continue to be exchanged between the two families over many years. Exchanges of food are important in signalling and reaffirming friendships. Among friends, food exchanges involve largely unconscious rules of etiquette (see the Multiple Cultural Worlds box on page 103).

Exchanging alcoholic beverages is an important feature of many communal, ritual events in Latin America. In an Ecuadorian village called Agato, the San Juan fiesta is the high point of the year (Barlett 1980). The fiesta consists of four or five days during which small groups of celebrants move from house to house, dancing and drinking. The anthropologist reports on the event:

> I joined the groups consisting of the president of the community and the elected alcaldes (councilmen and police), who were accompanied by their wives, a few friends, and some children. We met each morning for a hearty breakfast at one house, began drinking there, and then continued eating and drinking in other homes throughout the day and into the evening.... Some people drink for only one or two days, others prefer to make visits mainly at night, while some people drink day and night for four days.... The host or hostess greets the group with a bucket of chicha (home-made corn beer) and a dipper or bottle of trago (purchased cane liquor) and a shotglass. One member of the group, often the oldest man, accepts the liquor and distributes drinks to the entire party. Participants are urged to "do their share" to consume the liquor, but refusals are also accepted easily. After several rounds of drink, the server returns the empty bottle or bucket to the host, the group choruses goodbyes and hurries into the street. (118–119)

Guests who drink at someone's house will later serve their former hosts alcohol in return. In this way, social ties are reinforced. (See the Multiple Cultural Worlds box below for another example.)

Symbolic Goods Intangible valuables such as myths (sacred stories) and rituals (sacred practices) are sometimes exchanged in ways similar to material goods. In lowland areas of Papua New Guinea, men trade myths, rituals, dances, flutes, costumes, and styles of body decoration for the pigs of highland men (Harrison 1993). Certain secret spells were some of the most prestigious trade items. In the Balgo Hills region of Australia, long-standing exchange networks transfer myths and rituals among groups of women (Poirier 1992). Throughout the region, the women may keep important narratives and rituals only for a certain time and then must pass them on to other groups. One such ritual is the *Tjarada*, a love-magic ritual with an accompanying narrative. The *Tjarada* came to the women of Balgo Hills from the north. They kept it for about 15 years and then passed it on to another group in a ceremony that lasted for three days. During the

The Rules of Hospitality in Oman

In much of the Middle East, where women spend little time in the public domain, social visits among women are much anticipated and carefully planned events with complex rules about what should be served (Wikan 1982). In the town of Sohar, in Oman, men go out to work, while women spend most of their time at home. When women do venture outside, they wear head veils, face masks, and full-length gowns. Their main social activity outside the home involves visits to other women in their homes. A typical visit involves sitting, chatting, and eating snacks. Social etiquette dictates what should be served and how:

Dates and coffee compose the traditional food of entertainment between close neighbors. Nowadays, biscuits, inexpensive caramels, and popcorn tend to be favored substitutes. Between neighbors who interact on a daily basis, or nearly so, a single dish will do. But all other visitors, even solitary ones, should be offered at least two plates, with different contents, or the hostess is thought stingy. If the guests are more numerous, the amounts or variety must be increased, up to a minimum of four plates. Three or four plates may also be offered to one or two guests when the hostess wishes to honor them.

The rules of etiquette require that approximately half of the food served be left for the hostess' household. (130–132)

Cooked food, such as meat and sweets, is served when entertaining more important guests, or for weddings, seasonal feasts, and burials. With cooked food, though, the hosts may never eat with their guests: "Even if the consequence is that the guest must eat all alone, in a separate room, it would be disrespectful to arrange it otherwise" (133).

event. Later, when another family needs help, they call on the same people.

Money **Money,** or currency, refers to things that can be exchanged for many different kinds of items (Godelier 1971:53). Besides being a medium of exchange, money can be a standard of value and a store of value or wealth (Neale 1976). Anthropologists have labelled as money

A Guatemalan woman works at her hand loom. Maya weaving is closely linked with identity and ethnicity. This association is especially evident in women's embroidered blouses, *huipiles* (pronounced "hu-wee-PEEL-es"), which convey messages about the wearer's wealth, age, and home region. Three decades of civil war have threatened Maya culture in Guatemala, but many Maya groups are now revitalizing their traditions, including weaving.

time that the Balgo Hills women were custodians of the *Tjarada,* they incorporated some new elements into it. These elements are retained even after its transfer to the next group. Thus, the *Tjarada* contains bits of local identity of each group that has had it. A sense of linked community and mutual responsibility thereby develops and is sustained among the different groups that have held the *Tjarada.*

Labour In labour-sharing groups, people contribute labour to other people on a regular basis (for seasonal agricultural work such as harvesting) or on an irregular basis (in the event of a crisis such as the need to rebuild a barn damaged by fire). Labour-sharing groups are part of what has been called a "moral economy," since no one keeps formal records on how much any family puts in or takes out. Instead, accounting is socially regulated. The group has a sense of moral community based on years of trust and sharing. In Amish communities of North America, labour sharing is a major factor of production, infrastructure maintenance, and social cohesion. When a family needs a new barn or faces repair work that requires group labour, a barn-raising party is called. Many families show up to help. Adult men provide manual labour, and adult women provide food for the or currency such diverse items as shells, salt, cattle, furs, and iron hoes. Compared to other exchange items, money or currency is a relatively recent innovation. Although no one knows when money first appeared, one of the earliest forms of coined money was in use by the Greeks in Asia Minor (Turkey) in the seventh century BCE. Precoin money undoubtedly existed well before that time.

Items that can be exchanged for only a few other items are called **limited-purpose money.** Canadian Tire "money," for example, can only be used to buy goods in Canadian Tire stores. Raffia cloth serves as limited-purpose money among the Lele of central Africa (Douglas 1962). Raffia cloth, made from the fibres of a certain kind of palm, is a medium of payment for certain ritual and ceremonial events, such as a marriage, and as a payment of compensation for wrongdoing. It is not used for commercial transactions such as buying food or houses or for renting or buying land. Modern money is **multipurpose money,** or a medium of exchange that can be used as payment for all goods and services available.

Rights in People
Throughout history, some people have been able to gain control of other people and treat them as objects of exchange, as in systems of institutionalized slavery and in underground, criminal activities even today. The particular topic of women as "items" of exchange in marriage is a puzzling one in anthropology and has attracted much debate. Lévi-Strauss proposed many years ago that the exchange of women between men is one of the most basic forms of exchange in human culture. His argument about exchange is based on the universality of some sort of "incest taboo," which he defines as a rule preventing a man from marrying or cohabiting with his mother or sister (1969 [1949]). Such a rule, he says, is a logical motivation for equal exchange: "the fact that I can obtain a wife is, in the final analysis, the consequence of the fact that a brother or father has given her up" (62). According to this theory, men are thus impelled to develop exchange networks with other men. This process increases social solidarity between groups. For Lévi-Strauss, the incest taboo is the basis of the original form of exchange and thereby the emergence of an important aspect of culture.

Some anthropologists say that this theory, while intriguing, is male-centred and denies agency to the women involved. In an influential essay called "The Traffic in Women," Gayle Rubin (1975) says that it disregards the many foraging societies in which men do not have rights in women and in which women choose their own male partners. Evidence from horticultural and agricultural societies of Southeast Asia has been put forward as further refutation of a universal model of men exchanging women (Peletz 1987). In these systems, the focus of marriage arrangements is on the exchange of men and control of their labour power and productivity. Adult women arranged their daughters' marriages, selecting the groom themselves.

Modes of Exchange

All societies devise systems for the exchange of resources that are not consumed by producers. The most common modes of exchange include reciprocity (generalized and balanced), redistribution, and the market system. While generalized reciprocity occurs in all societies, it is the dominant **mode of exchange** within foraging, horticultural, and pastoral societies. **Market exchange** becomes increasingly important in agricultural societies when surplus is produced, and in industrial economies where production for sale is the primary goal.

Reciprocity
Reciprocity is the mutual exchange of goods and services, or gifts and favours. **Generalized reciprocity** is a transaction that involves the least conscious sense of interest in material gain or thought of what might be received in return. When, or if, a possible return might be made is not calculated. Such exchanges often involve goods and services of an "everyday" or mundane nature, such as a cup of coffee. Generalized reciprocity is the predominant form of exchange between people who know each other well and have a high degree of trust in each other. It is the predominant form of exchange in foraging societies and it is also found among close kin and friends cross-culturally. **Balanced reciprocity** is the exchange of approximately equally valued goods or services, usually between people of roughly equal social status; the exchange may occur simultaneously from both parties, or an agreement or understanding may exist that stipulates the time period within which the exchange will be completed. This aspect of the timing contrasts with generalized reciprocity, in which there is no fixed time limit for the return. In balanced reciprocity, if the second party fails to complete the exchange, the relationship will break down. Balanced reciprocity is less personal than generalized reciprocity and, according to Western definitions, more "economic." The

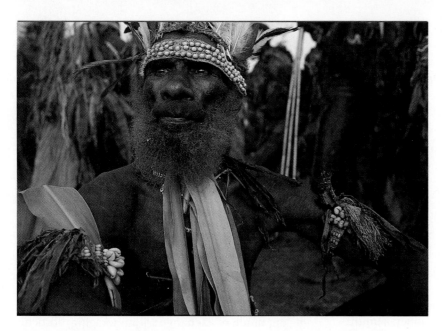

Shell ornaments are important items to be worn at ceremonial events, as shown on this man of the Sepik River area of Papua New Guinea.

The *kudu* ("clinching gift") will come later and balance the original gift. The equality of exchange ensures a tight social bond between the trading partners and a statement of social equality and mutual trust. When a man sails to an area in which there may be danger because of previous raids or warfare, he can count on having a friend to receive him and give him hospitality. Although most attention has been on men's *kula* exchanges, Annette Weiner (1976) pointed out the importance of women's exchanges of food, bundles of banana leaves, and woven skirts for mortuary ceremonies.

Redistribution Redistribution is a form of exchange that involves one person collecting goods or money from many members of a group, then, at a later time, "returning" the pooled goods to everyone who contributed. In comparison to the two-way pattern of reciprocity, redistribution involves some sort of "centrality." It contains the possibility of institutionalized inequality since what is returned may not always equal what was contributed. The pooling group may continue to exist in spite of inequality because of the leadership skills of the person who mobilizes contributions.

In the New Guinea Highlands, political leadership involves redistribution in a system of contributions and ritual feasts called *moka* that may take several years to organize (discussed in chapter 11). Formal taxation systems of industrial societies can be considered a form of redistribution. People pay taxes to a central institution, and they receive services from the government in return. Depending on the context, the return may or may not appear to be satisfactory to the contributors. In Canada, the federal government redistributes tax revenues to the provinces in the form of equalization payments that favour the poorest provinces. The degree of personal contact in different redistributive systems varies just as with forms of reciprocity. Similarly, the contexts in which greater personal interaction is involved tend to be more egalitarian and less exploitative than the impersonal forms.

form of exchange whereby the giver tries to "one up" or get the better of the exchange at the expense of the partner is sometimes referred to as *negative reciprocity*.

The *kula* is an example of a system of balanced reciprocity. Men of many different Trobriand groups participate in the exchange of necklaces and armlets, giving them to their partners after keeping them for a while. The trading includes local trading partners who are neighbours and people in faraway islands who are visited via long canoe voyages on high seas. Men are distinguished by the particular armlets and necklaces that they trade, since certain armlets and necklaces are more prestigious than others. However, the *kula* social code dictates that "to possess is great, but to possess is to give." Generosity is the essence of goodness and stinginess is the most despised vice. The higher the man's social rank, the more he must give. *Kula* exchanges should involve items of equivalent value. If a man trades a very valuable necklace with his partner, he expects to receive in return a very valuable armlet as a *yotile* (equivalent gift). At the time, if one's partner does not possess an equivalent item, he may have to give a *basi* (intermediary gift). The *basi* stands as a token of good faith until a proper return gift can be given.

Market Exchange Marketing is the buying and selling of commodities under competitive conditions in which the forces of supply and demand determine value (Dannhaeuser 1989:222). In a market transaction, the people involved may not be related to or know each other at all. They may not be social equals, and their exchange is not likely to generate social bonding. Many market transactions take place in a marketplace, a physical location in which buying and selling occur. Markets evolved from other, less formal contexts of **trade**, a formalized exchange of one thing for another according to set standards of value. In order for trade to develop, someone must have something that someone else wants.

Specialization in producing a particular good promotes trade between regions. Particular products are often identified with a town or region. In Oaxaca, Mexico, different villages are known for blankets, pottery, stone grinders, rope, and chili peppers (Plattner 1989:180–181). In Morocco, the interior city of Fez is famous for its blue-glazed pottery, while the Berber people of the southern mountain region are known for their fine blankets, rugs, and other woven goods. Specialization also develops with illegal commodities, such as Jamaican marijuana or BC bud. Such market exchanges may be based on the exchange of goods or money.

The periodic market, a site for market transactions that is not permanently set up but takes place regularly, emerged with the development of agriculture and urban settlements. As Stuart Plattner (1989) points out, however, a periodic market (or what Plattner calls a "peasant market") is more than just a place for buying and selling; it is also a place of social activity:

> [C]rowds come from the countryside to sell their farm products and buy manufactured goods and foodstuffs from other areas. Government officials often visit on market days, and local places of worship hold services so that farm families can combine economic, political, and religious activities at one time and place. Peasant market arenas… have much of the excitement of a fair, with friendships made, love affairs begun, and marriages arranged. In many societies, the end of market day is often marked by drinking, dancing, and fighting. (171)

Worldwide, permanent markets situated in fixed locations have long served the everyday needs of villages and neighbourhoods. Permanent markets throughout China, for example, have long provided for the everyday needs of local people (Skinner 1964). The persistence of the role of such localized markets can be seen in the number of neighbourhood shops in the city of Shanghai (Lu 1995). Shanghai is the most westernized city in China, but in the back streets and neighbourhoods, small-scale and personalized marketing still prevails with small shops selling sesame-cakes, hot water, wine, traditional Chinese medicine, coal, tobacco, paper, soy sauce, and locally produced groceries. More contemporary, less personalized forms of permanent marketplaces in North America include shopping malls and stock exchanges. The Internet and "eBay" is the least personalized way to shop.

Unbalanced Exchanges Several forms of unbalanced exchange exist that involve the transfer of goods from one person or institution to another without an

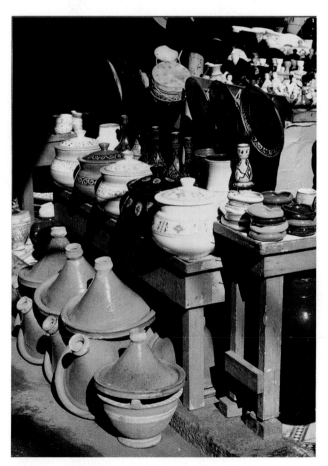

Moroccan pottery is for sale here in a regular market in Marrakech.

In China, many marketers are women. These two women display their wares in a regular neighbourhood food market in a city about an hour from Shanghai.

equivalent return. In extreme instances, no social relationship is involved; in others, sustained unequal relationships are maintained over time between people. These forms range from the extreme example of giving something with no expectation of return to taking something with no expectation of return. These forms of unbalanced exchange can occur anywhere along the continuum of economic systems, but they are more likely to be found in large-scale or culturally complex societies where more options for other than face-to-face, balanced exchange exist.

The pure gift. A **pure gift** is something given with no expectation or thought of a return. The pure gift could be considered an extreme form of generalized reciprocity. Examples of a pure gift may include donating money for a food drive, in which the giver never knows or sees the receiver, or donations to famine relief, blood banks, and religious organizations. Some people say that a truly pure gift does not exist since one always gains something, no matter how difficult to measure, in giving—even if it is just the good feeling of generosity. Parental care of children is often considered a pure gift since most parents do not consciously calculate how "much" they have spent on their children with the intention of "getting it back" later on. In Thailand, expectations for reciprocity be-

tween parents and children are made explicit in the ordination ritual; a son ordains as a monk to pay for the gift of his mother's milk (J. Van Esterik 1996). Those who do not consider parental care a pure gift say that even if the "costs" are not consciously calculated, parents have unconscious expectations about what their children will "return" to them, whether the return is material (care in old age) or immaterial (making the parent feel proud).

Theft. Theft is taking something with no expectation or thought of returning anything to the original owner for it. It is the logical opposite of a pure gift. The study of theft has been neglected by anthropologists, perhaps because it might involve danger. One insightful analysis considers food stealing by children in Africa (Bledsoe 1983). During fieldwork among the Mende of Sierra Leone, Caroline Bledsoe's research focus was on child fostering (placing a child in the care of friends or relatives, usually so they can receive apprenticeship training or education in a city school). She learned that children who are fostered out, especially older ones, receive less food at meal times than children living with a biological parent, specifically less meat and leafy green sauces. The nutritional status of fostered children, however, was not as low as their limited food shares would indicate. Further investigation revealed a widespread pattern of children foraging for wild food and a "clandestine economy" of food stealing. Bledsoe at first dismissed cases of food stealing as rare exceptions, "But I began to realize that I rarely walked through town without hearing shouts of anger from an adult and cries of pain from a child being whipped for stealing food" (2). Since her goal was to assess children's nutritional status, she needed to know about how much food children were gaining from foraging and stealing. Her discussion of methods for this kind of research is illuminating:

> *I focused on eliciting information primarily from children themselves. This required careful effort, because children wanted to avoid getting in trouble. Most were reluctant*

at first to divulge their strategies. However, as children saw that I regarded their efforts as they themselves did—as almost an art—they disclosed some of their more creative techniques of "tiefing" ("TEEF-ing") as petty stealing is referred to in Sierra Leone Creole… Another technique I tried was meal simulations in which people showed me how children "tiefed" even at meal time, both when the food was being prepared as well as while groups of children were seated together, eating rice and sauce with their hands out of a communal bowl, as most people eat. Since this was simulation, people greatly enjoyed demonstrating the subtleties of "tiefing" and bad etiquette." (2)

Bledsoe had the children participate in simulations of meal preparation and meal serving. In both situations, children revealed to her subtle methods of tiefing. She also asked them to keep diaries to elicit information on "tiefing." At first, children wrote about more legitimate ways they acquired food, such as doing errands for small tips, playing soccer games for stakes, soliciting relatives for "munching" money, asking friends to share snacks with them, and visiting friends at meal times. From an analysis of these diaries, she found that fostered children and children temporarily placed in the care of friends or relatives participate more in food stealing than children living with their natal families. Food stealing can be seen as children's attempts to compensate for their less-than-adequate food shares at home. They do this by claiming food that is not part of their rightful entitlement, by "tiefing."

Stealing as a conscious attempt to alter an unfair entitlement system underlies an analysis of the "looting" that occurred in Los Angeles in 1992 following the Rodney King verdict (Fiske 1994). This looting can be seen to be rooted in the economic inequities faced by the African American community of South Central Los Angeles at the time of the Rodney King decision.

Between 1982 and 1989, 131 factories closed in LA with the loss of 124,000 jobs.… The jobs that were lost were ones that disproportionately employed African Americans… in the four years before 1982, South Central, the traditional industrial core of LA, lost 70,000 blue-collar jobs. In Black eyes, this pattern is produced not by a raceless free market, but by racism encoded into economics: To them the 50 percent Black male unemployment in South Central does not look like the result of neutral, let alone natural, economic laws. (469–470)

The North American culture of consumption presumes equality among all consumers. In South Central Los Angeles, this is not the case: "For the deprived, shopping is not, as it is for the wealthy, where success in the sphere of production is materially rewarded: It is an experience of exclusion and disempowerment. Shopping is painful" (481). How does all of this relate to exchange? The "looting" during the Los Angeles uprising can be seen as an expression of deep-seated resentment about economic discrimination. "Looting" could instead be termed "radical shopping" in the sense that it was political protest, just as consumer boycotts are protests of a different sort. The politics of language emerge: The media's use of the word "looting" linked the uprising to the domain of crime, leaving prison as the only solution. By constructing the uprising as a law-and-order issue only, the public's interpretation was diverted from seeing its roots in severe economic discrimination.

Obviously, much theft that occurs in the world is motivated by greed, not economic deprivation or oppression. The world of theft in expensive commodities such as gems, drugs, and art has not been extensively researched by cultural anthropologists.

Exploitation. Exploitation is getting something of greater value for less in return; it is extreme and persistent unbalanced exchange. Slavery is a form of exploitation in which people's labour power is appropriated without their consent and with no recompense for its value. Slavery is rare among foraging, horticultural, and pastoral societies. Social relationships that involve sustained unequal exchange do exist between members of different social groups that, unlike pure slavery, involve no overt coercion and a certain degree of return by the dominant member to the subdominant member (see the Multiple Cultural Worlds box). Some degree of covert compulsion or dependence is likely to be present, however, in order for relationships of unequal exchange to endure.

Relationships between the Efe, who are "pygmy" foragers, and the Lese, who are farmers, in Congo (formerly Zaire) is an example of sustained unequal exchange (Grinker 1994). The Lese live in small villages located along a dirt road. The Efe are seminomadic, and they live in temporary camps near Lese villages. Men of each group maintain long-term hereditary exchange partnerships with each. Members of the two groups describe their relationship simply: The Lese give cultivated foods and iron to the Efe and the Efe give meat, honey, and other forest goods to the Lese.

Each Efe partner is considered a member of the "house" of his Lese partner, although he lives separately. Their main link is the exchange of food items, a system conceptualized by the Lese not as trade, per se, but as sharing of co-produced goods, as if the two partners were a single unit with a division of labour and a subsequent division or co-sharing of the goods produced. Yet there is evidence of inequality in these trading relationships, with the Lese having the advantage. The Efe provide much-wanted meat to the Lese, but this role gives them no status, for it is the giving of cultivated foods by the Lese to the Efe that conveys status. In fact, the Lese claim that the Efe are *their* dependents, denying that their interest in Efe meat supplies actually makes them dependent. Another area of inequality is in marital and sexual relationships. Lese men may marry Efe women, and sometimes do, and the children are considered Lese. Efe men cannot marry or have sexual intercourse with Lese women.

Theories of Exchange

Here we look at two theories that seek to explain why people participate in patterned processes of exchange. The first is a functional view that sees exchange as creating social and economic safety nets for people, along the lines of the potlatch explanation provided at the beginning of the chapter. The second is a critical theory that points to how patterns of exchange create and sustain social inequality.

Exchange and Risk Aversion

At the beginning of this chapter the potlatch system was presented as an exchange network with an economic security function. By linking together with other groups, the unevenness of a particular local economy could be "smoothed" out to a certain extent. Many more such examples can be found cross-culturally.

Carol Stack (1974) was perhaps the first cultural anthropologist to study how exchange patterns among kin and friends in urban America serves as a social safety net. She did research in "The Flats," the poorest section of a Black community in a Midwestern city that she calls

Jackson Harbor. Jackson Harbor is marked by racial inequality with, for example, a much higher proportion of Blacks than Whites living in deteriorating or severely dilapidated housing. Stack's approach differed from earlier studies of the Black family in America by avoiding negative comparisons with middle-class White lifestyles. She instead looked at the Black family members' strategies for dealing with poverty and uncertainty.

> *I found extensive networks of kin and friends supporting, reinforcing each other—devising schemes for self-help, strategies for survival in a community of severe economic deprivation…. Their social and economic lives were so entwined that not to repay an exchange meant that someone else's child would not eat. People would tell me, "You have to have help from everybody and anybody," and "The poorer you are, the more likely you are to pay back." (28)*

Stack spent nearly three years in The Flats, studying the complex exchange system. She also became involved in the system: "If someone asked a favor of me, later I asked a favor of him. If I gave a scarf, a skirt, or a cooking utensil to a woman who admired it, later on when she had something I liked she would usually give it to me. Little by little as I learned the rules of giving and reciprocity, I tried them out" (28). Timing is important in the "swapping system." The purpose is to obligate the receiver over a period of time; thus, swapping rarely involves simultaneous exchange. The swapping system of The Flats lies between the categories of generalized and balanced reciprocity, both of which are related to the maintenance of social bonds.

Exchange and Social Inequality

In addition to strengthening social relations, exchange may also support and perpetuate social inequalities. Paul Bohannan (1955), an early economic anthropologist, studied the economy of the Tiv, horticulturalists of Nigeria, before European monetary systems entered their economy. He learned that, besides gift exchange, three spheres of market exchange existed in which items of equivalent value are traded for each other. Each of the three spheres carried different levels of prestige. The lowest ranking sphere is the arena of women's trade. It includes chickens, hoes, baskets, pots, and grain. This domestic sphere has the most frequent activity, but no prestige.

The second ranking category included brass rods, special white cloth, guns, cattle, and slaves. While slavery had been abolished at the time of Bohannan's research and the brass rods were increasingly rare, the Tiv still talked about the relative value of these items. For example, one brass rod was equivalent to one large piece of white cloth, and five rods or pieces of cloth were equal to a bull, while ten equalled a cow. Young men seeking marriage would accumulate such goods in order to enhance their prestige and to impress elder males.

The top-ranking exchange sphere contains only one item: rights in women. This category ranks highest in the Tiv moral sphere since a male's highest goal is to gain and maintain family dependents (wife and children). As Bohannan (1955) says, "The drive toward success leads most Tiv, to the greatest possible extent, to convert food into prestige items; to convert prestige items into dependents—wives and children," a process of up-trading he terms "conversion." Subsequent analyses have pointed out that the Tiv spheres of exchange, like those of many other African cultures, support the power structure of elder males (Douglas and Isherwood 1979). They maintained dominance over the entire social system by keeping tight control over marriageable women. This forces younger males into competition for marriage and for eventual entry into the ranks of the elders.

Bohannan's analysis dealt with how exchange relationships within one culture strengthen the power position of certain social groups and keep others in subordinate positions because they cannot participate in the highest form of exchange. At the global level, many examples of exchange between powerful and nonpowerful groups show how the powerful groups use exchange to maintain their position and how difficult it is for the nonpowerful groups to escape their position of subordination. Few Canadians may be familiar with the stories about the whalers who harvested the once abundant beluga whales in Hudson's Bay to satisfy the lucrative European market for whale oil; the street lamps of England were lit with the rendered fat of these whales no longer available to Cree hunters (Adelson 2000:38).

Anyone who has grown up in North America has probably heard the tales of European colonialists trading a string of glass beads for the island of Manhattan, and of the colonialists' plying Native Americans with "fire water," alcoholic drinks, and thus creating their dependency and acquiescence. The current heavy alcohol consumption among many indigenous peoples worldwide is testimony to the continuing power of alcohol as part of the mode of exchange of colonialism and its modern forms. The introduction of alcohol to the indigenous people of Australia, for example, has created a culture—especially among men—of binge drinking and depletion of cash earnings to buy alcohol (Saggers and Gray 1998). Before the coming of outsiders to Australia, the Aborigines had nothing like alcohol. It arrived with the British. Despite much effort in recent decades to reduce alcohol consumption among Aboriginal peoples, no decline is apparent. One interpretation is that economic marginalization and social discrimination support continued high levels of alcohol consumption, along with the assurance of a continued supply of alcohol from the global market.

Changing Patterns of Consumption and Exchange

Several trends are notable in the transformation of consumption and exchange. The powerful market forces of the first world are the predominant shapers of global change. At the same time, local cultures variously adopt and adapt to global patterns of consumption and exchange, and sometimes resist them outright.

The Lure of Western Goods

There is now scarcely any human settlement that does not engage in exchanges beyond its boundaries to acquire new consumer goods (Gross et al. 1979). The northern Cree have embraced many technological changes in the last few decades: "Satellite dishes, fax machines, computers and web sites are as much a part of northern living as skidoos, rifles, and the ubiquitous Northern Stores (formerly the Hudson's Bay Company Posts)" (Adelson 2000:11). Forest-living foraging groups in the Brazilian Amazon also embraced manufactured goods with amazing enthusiasm. They appreciated the efficacy of a steel machete, axe, or cooking pot. In the early decades of the twentieth century, when the Brazilian government sought to "pacify" Amazonian groups, they used manufactured goods. They placed pots, machetes, axes, and steel knives along trails or hung them from trees. Once the Indians have grown accustomed to these new items, the next step is to teach them that these gifts will not be repeated. The Indians are now told that they must work to earn money or must manufacture goods for trade so that they can purchase new items. Unable to contemplate returning to life without steel axes, the Indians begin to produce extra arrows or blowguns or hunt additional game or weave baskets beyond what they normally need so that this new surplus can be traded. Time that might, in the past, have been used for other tasks—subsistence activities, ceremonial events, or whatever—is now devoted to production of barter goods (Milton 1992:40).

Adoption of Western foods has negatively affected the nutrition and health of indigenous peoples. Cree health and strength is intimately connected to eating Cree bush food. Now that there is a greater variety of processed foods available for sale, it is often consumed to excess (Adelson 2000:103). In the Amazon, "The moment manufactured foods begin to intrude on the indigenous diet, health takes a downward turn" (Milton 1992:41). The Indians have begun to use table salt, which they have been given by outsiders, and refined sugar.

Previously, they consumed small quantities of salt made by burning certain leaves and collecting the ash. The sugar they consumed came from wild fruits, in the form of fructose. Sucrose tastes "exceptionally sweet" in comparison, and the Indians get hooked on it. As a result, tooth decay, obesity, and diabetes become new health risks (see the Multiple Cultural Worlds box).

Cash Cropping and Declining Nutrition: You Can't Eat *Sisal*

Increasing numbers of horticultural and agricultural groups have been persuaded to change over from growing crops for their own use to cash crop production. Intuition might tell you that cash cropping should lead to a rising standard of living. Some studies show, to the contrary, that often people's nutritional status declines with the introduction of cash cropping. A carefully documented analysis of how people's nutritional status was affected by introducing *sisal* (a plant that has leaves used for making rope) as a cash crop in Brazil is one such case (Gross and Underwood 1971). Around 1950, *sisal* was widely adopted in arid parts of northeastern Brazil. The traditional economy was based on some cattle raising and subsistence farming. Many poor subsistence farmers gave up farming and took up work in the *sisal* processing plants. They thought that steady work would be preferable to being dependent on the unpredictable rains in this dry region.

Processing *sisal* leaves for rope is an extremely labour-consuming process. One of the most demanding jobs is being a "residue man," whose tasks include shovelling soggy masses of fibre, bundling fibre, and lifting bundles for weighing. In families that contained a "residue man," the amount of money required for food was as much as what the *sisal* worker earned. In one case study household, the weekly budget was completely spent on food. The greatest share of the food goes to the *sisal* worker himself because of his increased energy output in *sisal* work.

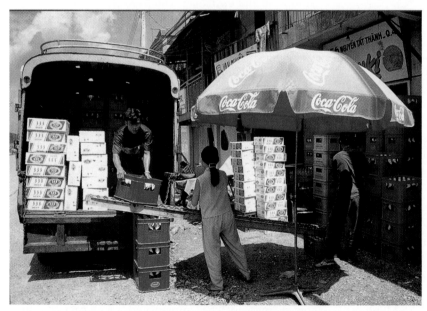

Cases of locally produced beer, "333," are unloaded near the port of Ho Chi Minh City, Vietnam, where logos of many Western products are familiar sights in the growing capitalist economy.

The White Bread Takeover in Ecuador

A cross-cultural analysis of food cultures, with attention to contemporary change, revealed an enduring and growing distinction between bread and porridge (Goody 1977). Bread is associated with dominant, colonizing cultures, and porridge is associated with dominated and colonized cultures.

A contemporary illustration of this dichotomy comes from rural Ecuador (Weismantel 1989). In the village of Zumbagua, bread has been a high-status, special-occasion food for many years. Recently, children have begun pressuring parents to serve bread regu-larly to replace the usual barley gruel for breakfast. Children prefer bread. The anthropologist reports, "Many of the early morning quarrels I witnessed in Zumbagua homes erupted over the question of bread. This conflict arises between young children and their parents. Pre-school children, especially, demand bread as their right" (93). But "Zumbagua adults do not feel that bread is appropriate for everyday meals because it is a part of a class of food defined as wanlla. Wanlla is anything that is not part of a meal… bread is the wanlla par excellence. It is the univer-sally appropriate gift" (95). Importantly, bread consumption requires cash income. The husband (more frequently than the wife) works for wages in the city. He often returns with a gift of bread for the family, while the wife provides the traditional boiled grain soups or gruels.

Children's demands for bread increase the role of purchased foods. This in turn leads to increased dependence on the cash economy and on male wages rather than on traditional female provisioning.

Analysis of data on the nutritional status of several hundred children in *sisal*-processing areas showed that: "Some *sisal* workers in northeastern Brazil appear to be forced systematically to deprive their dependents of an adequate diet… if they did not they could not function as wage earners. In those cases where the workers' dependents are growing children, the deprivation manifests itself in attenuated growth rates" (736).

Privatization's Effects: The New Rich and the New Poor of Russia and Eastern Europe

As the countries of the former Soviet Union dismantle socialism and enter the market economy, income inequality is rising. The new rich are enjoying unprecedented levels of comfortable living. The influx of Western goods, including sugared soft drinks and junk food, nicknamed "pepsistroika" by an anthropologist who did fieldwork in Moscow (Lempert 1996), allows people to change their traditional diets in ways that nutritional guidelines in North America would advise against.

At the same time, consumption levels have fallen among the newly created poor. Historically, average reported levels of food intake in what is now Russia and Eastern Europe have exceeded those of most middle-income countries (Cornia 1994). Between 1961 and 1988, consumption of average calories, proteins, and fats rose and were generally higher than those recommended by the World Health Organization. These countries were also characterized by full employment and low income inequality, so the high consumption levels were shared by everyone. This is not to say that diets were perfect. Characteristic weaknesses, especially in urban areas and among low-income groups, were low consumption of good-quality meat, fruits, vegetables, and vegetable oils, while people tended to overconsume cholesterol-heavy products (eggs and animal fats), sugar, salt, bread, and alcohol.

Now there are two categories of poor people: "the ultra-poor" (those whose incomes are below the subsistence minimum, or between 25 and 35 per cent of the average wage) and "the poor" (those whose incomes are above the subsistence minimum but below the social minimum, or between 35 and 50 per cent of the average wage). The largest increases in the number of ultra-poor occurred in Bulgaria, Poland, Romania, and Russia where, in 1992, between 20 to 30 per cent of the population could be classified as ultra-poor and another 20 to 40 percent as poor. Overall calorie and protein intake diminished significantly. People in the ultra-poor category are substituting less expensive sources of nutrients, so now they consume more animal fats and starch, and less milk, animal proteins, vegetable oils, minerals, and

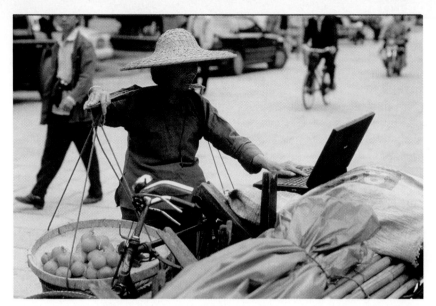

In China, a market vendor weighs her produce and calculates the price using a laptop computer.

vitamins. These changes are affecting the growth rates of children. In Bulgaria, the prevalence of growth stunting among infants rose from under 2 per cent in 1989–1990 to 17 per cent in 1991. Rates of low-birth-weight babies rose in Bulgaria and Romania, reflecting the deterioration in maternal diets. The rate of childhood anemia has also risen dramatically in Russia.

Buying with Credit Cards

Throughout the world, certain markets have long allowed buyers to purchase goods on credit. Such informal credit purchasing was usually based on personal trust and face-to-face interaction. It is only recently, however, that the credit card has made credit purchasing a massive, impersonal phenomenon in North America and many other parts of the world: "New electronic technology in the 1970s and deregulation in the 1980s offered retail bankers exciting opportunities to experiment with credit as a commodity, and they did experiment, wildly, at 'penetrating the debt capacity' of varied groups of Americans" (B. Williams 1994:351). Among middle-class people in North America, the use of credit cards is related to their attempts to maintain a middle-class lifestyle:

The primary users of installment credit appear to be those between ages twenty-five and forty-four whose incomes are stagnant or falling. Many have relied on credit to shape an appropriately classed life course: to attend college, purchase durables and set up households, meet the needs of kin, and launch children.… They have served like domestic partners to some who cannot live on one income. Thus, for the last ten years, many normative middle-class people have not been able to support the households they want when they want them, or to organize their lives, without loans and liens. (B. Williams 1994:353)

People's attitudes about their credit card debts vary. Some people express feelings of guilt similar to having a drug dependency. One woman reported, "Last year I had a charge-free Christmas. It was like coming away from drug abuse" (354). Others who are in debt feel grateful: "I wouldn't be able to go to college without my credit card" (355). Williams suggests that, no matter what people's attitudes are, credit cards are sinking many people deeply into debt. The cards buy a lifestyle that is not actually affordable, and therefore they "mask" actual economic decline in North America.

The culture of electronic credit is a subject that cultural anthropologists will no doubt be devoting more attention to in the future, since credit card use is expanding around the world.

Key Questions Revisited

How do modes of production relate to consumption?

We can contrast modes of consumption in nonmarket versus market-based systems of production. In the former, minimalism is the dominant mode of consumption, with finite needs. In the latter, consumerism is the dominant mode of consumption, with infinite needs. Foraging societies typify the minimalist mode of consumption. Industrial capitalist societies typify the consumerist mode of consumption. The modes of production that emerged between foraging and industrialism exhibit varying degrees of minimalism and consumerism.

How do modes of production relate to exchange?

The mode of exchange corresponds to the modes of production and consumption. In foraging societies, the dominant mode of exchange is reciprocity, with the goal of keeping the value of the items exchanged roughly equal over time. This balanced mode of exchange involves people who have a social relationship with each other. The relationship is reinforced through continued exchange. In the context of market exchange, the goal of making a profit through exchange overrides social relationships. In market exchange, the people involved in the transaction are less likely to know each other or to have a social relationship. In fully marketized economies, most transactions are anonymous, that is, no social relationship is involved at all, as in e-commerce.

What are some examples of how contemporary global economic change affects nonmarket modes of consumption and exchange?

Globalizing capitalism appears to be shaping most of the changes in consumption and exchange occurring around the world. Cultural anthropologists critique this process as being better for capitalism than it is for the people of nonmarket cultures being swept into the global economy. Western-inspired goods, such as steel axes and white bread, are now in high demand by people in non-Western, nonindustrialized contexts. Such goods must be purchased, a fact that impels people to work for cash so that they can buy things. Nutritional status of many nonindustrial groups has fallen with the adoption of Western-style foods containing large amounts of sugar and salt. The demand for cash has prompted many people to switch from growing food for their own use to growing crops for sale. This transition means that farmers have relinquished a direct entitlement for an indirect entitlement, thus putting themselves at risk when the market price drops for the crop they grow. Throughout post-Soviet countries, average health and nutrition levels dropped after perestroika, and they continue to decline.

Core Concepts

balanced reciprocity, p. 105
basic needs fund, p. 93
ceremonial fund, p. 93
consumerism, p. 92
consumption fund, p. 93
direct entitlements, p. 94
entertainment fund, p. 93

entitlements, p. 94
famine, p. 95
functionalist theories, p. 90
generalized reciprocity, p. 105
indirect entitlements, p. 94

limited-purpose money, p. 105
market exchange, p. 105
minimalism, p. 92
modes of consumption, p. 92
mode of exchange, p. 105
money, p. 104
multi-purpose money, p. 105

potlatch, p. 90
pure gift, p. 108
reciprocity, p.105
redistribution, p. 106
taboos, p. 100
tax/rent fund, p.93
trade, p. 107

Suggested Readings

Elizabeth Cashdan, ed., *Risk and Uncertainty in Tribal and Peasant Economies*. Boulder, CO: Westview Press, 1990. Twelve chapters explore links between environment and diet, food-sharing networks, and risk-management strategies among different foraging, horticultural, and agricultural societies.

Jane I. Guyer, ed., *Money Matters: Instability, Values and Social Payments in the Modern History of West African Communities*. Portsmouth, NH: Heinemann/James Currey, 1995. A collection of chapters by historians and cultural anthropologists examining topics such as why people in rural Gambia do not save money in banks, money as a symbol among the Yoruba, and the impact of colonial monetization in Nigeria and elsewhere.

Betsy Hartmann and James Boyce, *Needless Hunger: Voices from a Bangladesh Village*. San Francisco: Institute for Food and Development Policy, 1982. Evidence from fieldwork in rural Bangladesh shows that poverty and hunger in Bangladesh are primarily caused by severe class inequalities in economic entitlements. The text includes a critique of the role of foreign aid in perpetuating inequalities, as well as suggestions for change.

Grant McCracken, *Culture and Consumption*. Bloomington: Indiana University Press, 1988. This book examines consumption in history, theory, and practice in relation to different consumer goods, including a consideration of clothing as language.

Sidney W. Mintz, *Sweetness and Power: The Place of Sugar in Modern History*. New York: Penguin Books, 1985. Combining historical and anthropological techniques, this book traces an important part of the story of world capitalism—the transformation of sugar from a luxury item to an omnipresent item of consumption worldwide.

Lidia D. Sciama and Joanne B. Eicher, eds., *Beads and Bead Makers: Gender, Material Culture and Meaning*. New York: Berg, 1998. Over a dozen articles on beads including early international trade in Venetian beads, the relationship between beads and ethnicity in Malaysia, beads and power at the New Orleans Mardi Gras, and rosaries in the Andes, all providing insights about gender roles and meanings.

Joseph J. Tobin, ed., *Re-Made in Japan: Everyday Life and Consumer Taste in a Changing Society*. New Haven: Yale University Press, 1992. After an introduction by the editor, 12 essays address different aspects of Japanese consumption trends, including drinking patterns, interior decoration, Tokyo's Disneyland, department stores, and a Japanese-French restaurant in Hawaii.

James L. Watson, ed., *Golden Arches East: McDonald's in East Asia*. Stanford: Stanford University Press, 1997. This book contains five case studies, preceded by an introduction written by the editor and an afterword by Sidney Mintz, noted cultural anthropologist of food and food-ways. Case studies are located in China, Taiwan, Korea, and Japan, and address topics such as how McDonald's American culture becomes localized, dietary effects on children, eating etiquette, and how food choices relate to national identity.

 Your *Cultural Anthropology*, Second Canadian Edition Media Edition CD-ROM contains many Web sites relevant to this chapter. Use it to explore the Web and to expand your knowledge of anthropology.

Chapter 5

Birth and Death

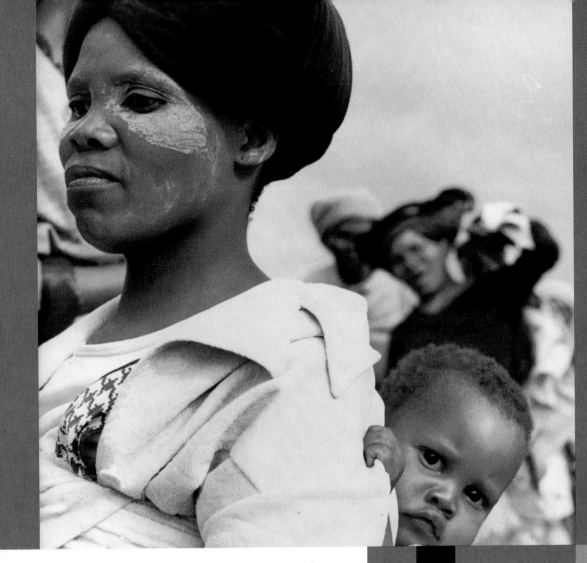

A mother and her infant, South Africa.

Key Questions

How is reproduction related to modes of production?

How does culture shape fertility in different contexts?

How does culture shape mortality in different contexts?

- *A common belief among Hindus in India is that men are weakened by sexual intercourse because semen is a source of strength, and it takes a long time to replace even a drop. Yet India has a high rate of population growth.*

- *The Chinese government policy of urging parents to have only one child significantly decreased the population growth rate. It also increased the death rate of female infants to the extent that there is now a shortage of brides.*

- *The highest birth rates in the world are found among the Mennonites and Hutterites in the United States and Canada. In these Christian groups, women on average bear nine children.*

*Such "population puzzles" can be understood using anthropological theories and methods. Population dynamics, along with many other examples of human variation in births and deaths, are an important area of life that is culturally shaped and that changes over time in response to changing conditions. This chapter provides a glimpse into some aspects of **demography**, or the study of population dynamics, and how it is culturally regulated. Demography, along with economics, lies within the category of infrastructure (Harris 1995:61; and see Chapter 1). It is hard to say whether economics influences demography or vice versa because they interact so strongly. Economic factors may have the edge in shaping demography, however, which is why it was covered first in this book.*

Demography includes three areas: *fertility* (births, or rate of population increase from reproduction), *mortality* (deaths, or rate of population decline in general or from particular causes), and *migration* (movement of people from one place to another). Many cultural anthropologists examine these processes, focusing on small populations and samples and examining the relationships between population dynamics and other aspects of culture such as gender roles, sexual beliefs and behaviour, marriage, household structure, child care, and health and illness. While demographers compile statistical reports, cultural anthropologists contribute understanding of what goes on behind the numbers and provide insights about the causes of demographic trends. For example, demographers may find that fertility rates are falling more rapidly in one nation than in another. They may be able to correlate certain factors with it such as changing literacy rates or economic growth. A cultural anthropologist involved in studying these issues would take a closer look at the causes and processes involved in the declining birth rates, including some that might not be included in official censuses or other statistical sources. They would gather information on household-level, and also individual-level behaviour and attitudes.

This chapter starts by discussing aspects of demography in relation to the modes of production (see Chapter 3). It then proceeds to show how and to what extent culture shapes the important natural processes of birth and death in different contexts.

Culture and Reproduction

Every human population has had culturally constructed ways to either promote or limit population growth. Anthropologists are interested in the cultural factors that influence birth and death rates. This chapter examines the relationship between **reproduction,** or the "making of people," and production, or the "making of things."

Archaeologists and cultural anthropologists have provided enough data to allow the construction of general models of reproduction corresponding with different means of livelihood. Three general models of reproduction are proposed. The foraging model of reproduction, which lasted for most of human history, had low population growth rates because of a combination of moderate birth rates and moderate death rates. Fertility was controlled by the low-fat diets of women, combined with their heavy workloads and long periods of breastfeeding. Life expectancy was low and maternal mortality high. In the agricultural model, children's labour was highly valued. Sedentary ways of life produced increased food surpluses to support more people. Birth rates increased over death rates and high population densities were reached in agricultural societies such as India and China. In the industrialized countries of Europe, Japan, and the United States, population growth rates declined because of falling birth rates and declining death rates. Horticulturalists and pastoralists possess some features of the foraging model of reproduction and the agricultural model, depending on specific conditions. Industrialized societies have developed both special methods of contraception and of fertility enhancement. Life expectancy is high and maternal mortality rates are low, except among some marginalized classes and groups.

Reproduction in Foraging Societies

Archaeological evidence about prehistoric populations, from about six million years ago to the Neolithic era of agricultural development around 10 000 years ago, indicates that population growth rates among foragers remained low over millions of years. Foraging societies' need for daily and seasonal spatial mobility would call for a relatively small number of children to facilitate movement. The low population growth rates over thousands of years were likely the result of several factors, of more or less importance in different contexts, that would suppress fertility: high rates of spontaneous abortion because of heavy workloads of women, the seasonality of diets that created reproductive stress on women, long breastfeeding of infants, induced abortion, and **infanticide** (deliberate killing of offspring). Low birth rates appear to be more important in leading to population stability than mortality. In the few relatively undisturbed contemporary foraging societies, low population growth rates are still typical.

Nancy Howell (1979) conducted research on the demography of the Ju/wasi that sheds light on how population homeostasis is achieved. Howell's data show that birth intervals (the time between one birth and a subsequent birth) among the Ju/wasi are often several years in duration. What accounts for the long birth intervals? Two factors emerge as most important among the Ju/wasi: breastfeeding and women's low levels of body fat. Frequent and long periods of breastfeeding inhibit progesterone production and suppress ovulation. Also, a certain level of body fat is required for ovulation (Frisch 1978). Ju/wasi women's diets contain little fat. Their body fat level is also kept low through the physical exercise their work entails. The combination of diet and exercise maintained Ju/wasi women's body fat at low levels, suppressing ovulation.

Thus, ecological factors (food supply—including breastfeeding—and diet) and economic factors (women's workloads) are basic determinants of Ju/wasi demography. This mode of reproduction can be interpreted as highly adaptive to the Ju/wasi environment and sustainable over time. Among the Ju/wasi who have given up foraging and become sedentarized farmers or labourers, fertility levels have increased, perhaps because of higher consumption levels of grains and dairy products.

Reproduction in Agricultural Societies

Settled agriculture promotes and supports the highest fertility rates of any mode of production. **Pronatalism,** an ideology promoting many children, emerges as a key value of farm families. It is prompted by the need for a large labour force to work the land, care for animals, process food, and do marketing. In this context, having many children is a rational reproductive strategy related to the mode of production. Thus, people living in family farming systems cross-culturally have their own "family planning"—which is to have many children—including the Mennonites and Hutterites of the United States and Canada (Stephenson 1991).

In rural North India, sons are especially important, given the gender division of labour. Men provide the crucial work of plowing the fields and protecting the family in the case of village quarrels over land rights and other matters. When Western family planning agents first visited the village of Manupur in northern India in the late 1950s to promote small families, the villagers did not see the value of their ideas (Mamdani 1972). To them, a large family equals wealth and success, not poverty and failure. Mahmoud Mamdani describes the villagers' responses to the family planning agents:

> One group displayed an air of amused tolerance which was typified by the weaver who told me he thought the "outsiders" were just plain "ignorant." Then there were those who were genuinely puzzled about the motives of the study. Consider the following inquiry, one that I encountered several times during my stay in Manupur: "It's strange they offered to give free medicine to stop women from bearing children, but had nothing to help those who could not bear children. That's where medicine could be of use to us."

> The final response represented a rather serious charge… [one] farmer, gently stroking his young son's hair, told me: "These Americans are enemies of the smile on this child's face. All they are interested in is war or family planning." (147)

Members of an Amish household sit around their kitchen table.

Western family planning agents, with their anti-natalist agenda, made the mistake of thinking that non-Western people had no thoughts of their own about what constitutes the desired family size and that they could simply provide modern contraceptive techniques to an interested market. The key point is that having many children in a family farming system "makes sense." Mechanization, the availability of cheap hired labour, and socialized agriculture may encourage farm families to opt for smaller numbers of children because it makes less sense to have many children.

Reproduction in Industrial Societies

In industrial societies, either capitalist or socialist, reproduction tends to decline to the point of **replacement-level fertility** (the number of births equals the number of deaths, leading to maintenance of current population size) or **below-replacement-level fertility** (the number of births is fewer than the number of deaths, leading to population decline). Below-replacement-level societies include Canada (Quebec's birth rate is lower than the national average); Japan; several European countries such as Austria, Belgium, Hungary, Denmark, and Norway; and some countries that the United Nations categorizes as "developing." The 2000 World Population Data Sheet (Washington D.C. Population Reference Bureau) lists 48 developed and developing countries with below-

replacement-level fertility. Children are considered less useful in production because of the changing labour demands of industrialism. Furthermore, children are required to attend school and cannot work for their families as much. Parents respond to these changes by having fewer children and by "investing" more resources in the fewer children they have.

Changes during the industrial mode of reproduction correspond to what demographers call the **demographic transition**, which refers to a change from the high fertility and high mortality of the agricultural mode of reproduction to the low fertility and low mortality of industrialized societies. This model proposes two phases. In the first phase, mortality declines due to improved nutrition and health, leading to high rates of population growth. The second phase is reached when fertility also declines, resulting in low rates of population growth. Cultural anthropologists have critiqued the demographic transition model as being too narrowly focused on the role of industrialism and not allowing for alternative models (Ginsberg and Rapp 1991). They claim that industrialism, with its reduced need for labour, is not the only factor that reduces pronatalism. China, for example, began to reduce its population growth rate before widespread industrialism (Xizhe 1991). Instead, strong government policies and a massive family planning program were key factors: "China's transition has been, by and large, not a natural process, but rather an induced one" (281) because its motivation came mainly from the government rather than from couples themselves. Nevertheless, reduced population growth in China is consistent with the government's program of stepping up the level of industrialization and reducing the demand for agricultural labour.

One prominent characteristic of capitalist industrial states is their socially stratified demographies. Middle- and upper-class people tend to have few children, with high survival rates. Among the poor, both fertility and mortality rates are unusually high (see the Voices box on page 124). Brazil, a newly industrializing state with the most extreme inequality of income distribution in the world, also has extreme differences in demographic patterns between the rich and the poor. Another characteristic of industrial countries is population aging. In Japan, for example, the total fertility rate declined to replacement level in the 1950s, and subsequently reached the below-replacement level (Hodge and Ogawa 1991:vii). Japan is currently experiencing a decline in population growth of about 15 per cent per generation. At the same time, Japan is experiencing a rapid aging of the population. Many people are moving into the senior category, creating a population bulge not matched by population increases in younger age groups. A third distinguishing feature of industrial demographies is the high level of involvement of scientific (especially medical) technology in all aspects of pregnancy: preventing it, achieving it, and even terminating it (Browner and Press 1995, 1996). The growing importance of the "new reproductive technologies" (NRTs) such as *in vitro* fertilization is a major part of a growing market in scientific reproduction. This technologization of reproduction is accompanied by increasing levels of specialization in providing the new services.

Culture and Birth

Cultures shape human reproduction from its very beginning, sexual intercourse itself. Cultural practices and beliefs about pregnancy and birth affect the viability of the fetus during its gestation as well as the infant's fate after birth.

Sexual Intercourse

Anthropological research on sexuality and sexual practices is particularly difficult to undertake. Sexuality involves private, sometimes secret, beliefs and behaviours. The ethics of participant observation disallow intimate observation or participation, so data can be obtained only indirectly. Biases in people's reports to an anthropologist about their sexual beliefs and behaviour are likely for several reasons. They may be too shy to talk about sex in the first place, too boastful to give accurate information, or simply unable to remember answers to questions such as "How many times did you have intercourse last year?" If people do provide detailed information, it might be inappropriate for an anthropologist to publish it because

of the need to protect confidentiality. Malinowski (1929) wrote the first anthropological study of sexuality, based on his fieldwork in the Trobriands. He discusses the sexual lives of children; sexual techniques; love magic; erotic dreams; husband-wife jealousy; and a range of topics related to kinship, marriage, exchange, and morals. Since the late 1980s, cultural anthropologists have paid more attention to the study of sexuality, given the increase in cases of sexually transmitted diseases (STDs), including HIV/AIDS.

When to Begin Having Intercourse

Biologically speaking, sexual intercourse between a fertile female and fertile male is normally required for human reproduction, although artificial insemination is an option in some contexts. Biology also defines the time span within which a female is fertile: from menarche (the onset of first menstruation) to menopause (the final cessation of menstruation). Globally, average age at menarche is between 12 and 14 years, with earlier ages found in the industrial nations and later ages in developing nations, presumably because of different diets and activity patterns. Average age at menopause varies more widely, from the forties to the fifties, with later ages in industrialized societies (the higher fat content of diets in industrialized nations may account for this difference).

Cultures socialize children about the appropriate time to begin sexual intercourse. Guidelines for initiating sexual intercourse may differ by gender, class, race, and ethnicity. In many cultures, menarche marks the beginning of adulthood for a girl. She should marry soon after menarche, and she should become pregnant as soon as possible in order to demonstrate her fertility. Rules more strictly forbid premarital sexual activity of girls than boys. In Zawiya, a traditional Muslim town of northern Morocco, as in much of the Middle East, the virginity of the bride—but not the groom—is highly valued (Davis and Davis 1987). The majority of brides conform to the ideal. Some unmarried young women do engage in premarital sex, however, and if they choose to have a traditional wedding, then they must somehow deal with the requirement of producing blood-stained wedding sheets. How do they do this? If the bride and the groom have been having premarital sexual relations, the groom may assist in the deception by nicking a finger with a knife and bloodying the sheets himself. Another option is to buy fake hymeneal blood in the drugstore.

Fatma, who works as a maid in Cairo, told her life history to ethnographer Wédád Zenié-Ziegler (1988). Fatma is the maid of a journalist. She is the second wife of her husband Ahmed, who, according to Fatma, spends most of his time with his first wife.

I have three children: two sons, Wahib, twelve, Khaled, six, and a daughter, Nagua, eleven. With us, women sometimes have eight to ten children, but I stopped at three. After the birth of the first, I did not want another child, but I found myself pregnant again. I did everything to get rid of it. I banged my stomach against walls, ran up and down stairs, took boiling hot baths, had a very heavy woman press down on my hips with all her weight... I was afraid to go to an abortionist. Lots of women have died that way. I also had an injection, but it didn't work.

Nowadays they talk about the pill. It's sold in chemists [drugstores] everywhere. I tried it, but it tired me. One day, I didn't feel well, so I didn't take it any more. It was a disaster: I became pregnant for the third time...

Thanks to God my children's health has never caused me any worry...

they study hard and they also help me at home... I don't want to hear another word about having children. Enough is enough. (53-55)

FOOD FOR THOUGHT

Given this brief narrative, do you think Fatma sounds like an unusual Egyptian woman? How would you go about discovering how typical or atypical Fatma's fertility history is, compared to other women in Cairo? Does Egypt have a class-stratified fertility pattern?

In many societies, a high value is placed on a woman becoming pregnant soon after she reaches menarche, making "teenage pregnancy" a desired condition instead of a "social problem," as perceived by many experts in North America (Ginsberg and Rapp 1991:320). The concept of a 30-year-old first-time mother would shock villagers in Bangladesh, for example, as to both its physical possibility and its social advisability. Commonly in South Asia, Africa, and elsewhere, a married woman's status depends on her having children. The longer she delays, the more her spouse and in-laws might suspect her of being infertile. In that case, they might send her back to her parents or bring in a second wife.

How Often Should One Have Intercourse? Cross-cultural studies indicate a wide range in frequency of sexual intercourse, confirming the role of culture in shaping sexual desire (see the Multiple Cultural Worlds box). However, the relationship between sexual intercourse frequency and fertility, the subject of this section, is not simple. A common assumption is that people in cultures with high rates of population growth must have sexual intercourse frequently. Without "modern" birth control, such as condoms, coitus interruptus, or the "rhythm method," intercourse frequency would seem to lead to high rates of fertility.

A comparison of reported intercourse frequency for Euro-Americans in the United States and Hindus in India reveals that Indians had intercourse far less frequently (less than twice a week) than the Euro-Americans did (two to three times a week) in all age groups (Nag 1972). Several features of Indian culture limit sexual intercourse. The Hindu religion teaches the value of sexual abstinence, thus providing ideological support for limiting sexual intercourse. Hinduism also suggests that one should abstain from intercourse on many sacred days: the first night of the new moon, the first night of the full moon, and the eighth day of each half of the month (the

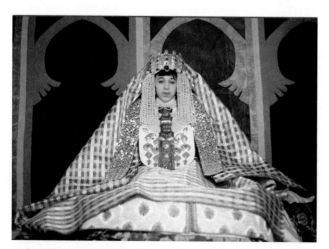

A bride wearing traditional wedding clothing in the city of Meknes, Morocco.

light half and the dark half), and sometimes not on Fridays. As many as 100 days each year could be observed as non-sex days. A more subtle psychological factor may be what Morris Carstairs (1967) termed the "lost semen complex" to explain the beliefs of Gujerati men: "Everyone knew that semen was not easily formed; it takes forty days and forty drops of blood to make one drop of semen.... Semen of good quality is rich and viscous, like the cream of unadulterated milk. A man who possesses a store of such good semen becomes a superman.... Celibacy was the first requirement of true fitness, because every sexual orgasm meant the loss of a quantity of semen, laboriously formed" (83–86, quoted in Nag 1972:235).

The fact remains, however, that fertility is higher in India than in many other parts of the world where such restrictions on sexual intercourse do not exist. Obviously, sheer frequency of intercourse is not the explanation. It takes only one act of sexual intercourse at the right time of the month to create a pregnancy.

The point of this discussion is to show that "reverse reasoning" from high fertility to assuming that people have nothing better to do than have sex is wrong. In fact, the cultural dynamics of sexuality in India function to restrain sexual activities and thus may keep fertility lower than it otherwise would be.

The Politics of Fertility

This section explores power issues related to decision making about fertility at three levels: the family level, the national level, and the global level. Within the context of the family unit, decision makers weigh factors influencing why and when to have a child. What choices do women have for controlling their own reproduction? At the national level, governments seek to plan their over-

The Dani Low-Energy Sexual System in Perspective

The Dani are horticulturalists of Irian Jaya, the Indonesian-controlled part of the island shared with Papua New Guinea in the South Pacific. Karl Heider (1976) studied among the Dani in the 1970s, and offered his interpretation that the Dani have "low" rates of sexual intercourse and relatively little interest in sex. He reports that Dani men express little frustration over the cultural rule against having sex with one's wife for four to six years after she has given birth: "Most people have no alternative sexual outlets." No one, according to Heider, shows signs of unhappiness or stress during the period of abstinence (188). The Dani, like many other horticultural groups, probably have the longest **post-partum taboos**, or rules stating how long a couple should abstain from having sexual intercourse after the woman has given birth.

Heider's assessment of low sexual interest implies a comparison with some "norm" of, say, an "average-energy sexual system," although what that might be is unstated. The comparatively short post-partum taboo in North America of six weeks, and the apparent high interest in sex in North American popular culture (as evidenced, at least, in the content of many television shows) would suggest, in contrast to the Dani, a high-energy sexual system.

Because of the scarcity of anthropological studies of sexuality, we cannot say much about whether the Dani's low-energy sexual system is characteristic of other horticulturalist societies of New Guinea or elsewhere. One explanation for the existence of this system is its contribution to suppressing population growth. Cross-cultural analysis of the relationship between the length of

the post-partum taboo and fertility rates does indicate a relationship, although a weak one, between longer periods of post-partum abstinence and lower fertility rates (Nag 1963). This would be a logical conclusion: no sex, no conceptions. We might wonder why the relationship is not stronger. One reason may be that the analysis depends on reported norms about sexual abstinence rather than data on whether people actually abstain.

FOOD FOR THOUGHT

How would a cultural anthropologist go about studying sexual abstinence in contrast to reported norms about sexual abstinence? (See the Multiple Cultural Worlds box "Sex Is a Sensitive Topic" in Chapter 2).

all population level on the basis of particular goals that are sometimes pronatalist and sometimes antinatalist. What strategies do they employ and how successfully are they enacted? At the global level, we can see that powerful economic and political interests are at work influencing the reproductive policies of individual nations and, in turn, families and individuals within them.

Family-Level Decision Making
At the family level, parental and other family members' perceptions about the value and costs of children influence their reproductive decision making (Nag 1983). Assessing the value and costs of children is a complex matter, involving many factors. It is difficult to know how much any of these factors affect reproductive decision making in any particular society. Four variables are most important in affecting the "demand" for children in different cultural contexts: children's labour value, children's value as old-age support for parents, infant and child mortality rates, and the economic costs of children.

In the first three, the relationship is positive: When children's value is high in terms of labour or old-age support, fertility is likely to be higher. When infant and child mortality rates are high, fertility rates also tend to be high in order to "replace" offspring who do not survive. Costs—including direct costs (for food, education, clothing) and indirect costs (employment opportunities that the mother gives up)—have a negative relationship. Higher costs promote the desire for fewer children. Industrial society alters the value of children in several ways: "Industrialization, improvement in income, urbanization, and schooling are likely to reduce the labour value of children" (Nag 1983:58) and greatly increase their costs. Provision of old-age security and pension plans by the state may reduce that fertility incentive, although few developing countries have instituted such policies thus far. A reduction in infant and child mortality rates is correlated with subsequent declines in overall fertility as parents gain confidence that their children will survive.

Depending on the gender division of labour and other social features related to gender, sons or daughters may be relatively more valued. Son preference is widespread, especially in Asia and the Middle East, but it is not a cultural universal. In some societies, people prefer a balanced sex ratio in their offspring, while in others daughters are preferred. Daughter preference is found in some Caribbean populations, in Venezuela, and some parts of Africa south of the Sahara. Longitudinal research

from 1956 to 1991 among the Tonga of Gwembe District, Congo, documents a female-biased population system that has persisted for at least the second half of the twentieth century (Clark et al. 1995). This study finds that "at most ages, men's death rates in Gwembe are higher than those of women" (104). Differences in mortality are especially great for the very young and the elderly, among whom males die at twice the rate of females the same age. The authors link this female-survival advantage to both the **matrilineal** kinship system of the Tonga, through which property is passed down from mother to daughter and the fact that the groom makes a valuable payment of bridewealth to the bride's father, which means that daughters bring wealth into the family.

In Japan, during the Tokugawa period of 1702 to 1872, husbands and wives had different fertility preferences based on the different value to them of sons versus daughters (Skinner 1993). Tokugawa wives, as is still common in Japan, preferred to have "first a girl, then a boy." This preference is related to the benefit in having a girl to help the mother in her work and to care for subsequent children, especially the boy it was hoped would come next. Husbands prefer a son-first strategy since a son helps them with their work. William Skinner hypothesized that husbands and wives would each try to achieve their goals with the one method available: **sex-selective infanticide,** or the killing of offspring on the basis of sex. Depending on their relative power position, either the husband or wife would be able to dominate the decision making about whether a child born would be kept. In order to test this hypothesis, Skinner needed information on the relative power of husbands and wives. He was lucky to have data on the ages of spouses at the time of marriage. Age differences in Japan are a key indicator of status. Seniority requires deference, respect, and obedience. Working with this principle, Skinner devised three categories of marital power based on age differences at the time of marriage: low husband power (when the wife is older than the husband), intermediate husband power (when ages are about equal), and high husband power (when the husband is older than the wife). Over one-third of the marriages involved men who were at least 10 years older than their wives, about 60 per cent were in the intermediate category, and less than 6 per cent were in the low husband-power category. Was the gender of children related to marital power relations? Results in Figure 5.1 clearly show that parental preferences about having a girl or boy did exist and were acted on, depending on whose values would win out.

In a highland village in the Oaxacan region of southern Mexico, men and women have different preferences about the number of children they wish to have (Browner 1986). Men are more pronatalist than women. Among women with only one child, 80 per cent were content with their present family size. Most men (60 per cent) who were satisfied with their present family size had four or more children. Carole Browner, the anthropologist who studied husband-wife differences in fertility preferences, offers further insights:

Women with large families said they resented the demands of child care and the limitations it placed on them. Many saw children as a burden. They considered them too much work, too hard to raise, a source of problems.... They viewed children as pesky disturbances who kept them tied to the house. One woman told me, "[The people of the community] want us to have many children. That's fine for them to say. They don't have to take care of them and keep them clean. My husband sleeps peacefully through the night, but I have to get up when the children need something. I'm the one the baby urinates on; sometimes I have to get out of bed in the cold and change both our clothes.

They wake me when they're sick or thirsty, my husband sleeps through it all." (714)

At the National Level National governments play key roles in decreasing or increasing rates of population growth within their boundaries, shaped by their concerns about providing employment and public services, maintaining the tax base, filling the ranks of the military, maintaining ethnic and regional proportions, and dealing with population aging. The former Soviet Union faced significant planning challenges created by the contrasts between the below-replacement fertility of the "European" areas and high fertility rates in the Central Asian and Muslim regions such as Tajikistan and Kyrghizstan. Some governments, including Japan and France, which are concerned about declining population growth rates, have urged women to have more babies. The Quebec government is aware of the province's low birth rate, and has developed policies to provide extra supports for families, including subsidies and low-cost child care. Israel is openly pronatalist, given its interest in boosting its national population level as a political statement of strength.

In the Philippines in the 1970s, Marcos's government initiated the export of Filipino workers overseas. By 1994, 60 per cent of the migrants were women. In Canada, Filipina nannies and caregivers provide domestic serv-

FIGURE 5.1 Gender of First-Born Child According to Spouse-Power in the Household, Tokugawa, Japan

Percent Male Offspring

- Low Husband Power: 34%
- Medium Husband Power: 53%
- High Husband Power: 84%

Note: under normal conditions, one would expect roughly equal percentages of male and female births.

Source: Skinner 1993.

Residents of the Oaxaca region, Mexico, at the Sunday market in Tlacalula. Oaxaca is a distinctive cultural region and the scene of a vigorous movement for indigenous people's rights.

ices for many Canadian families. In the process of be-having like mothers to Canadian children, they leave their own children in the care of their parents and struggle to visit them on occasion. Remittances sent to their children sometimes result in their children becoming self-indulgent (Barber 1997).

At the Global Level The broadest, most far-reaching layer that affects decision making about fertility occurs at the international level, where power structures such as the World Bank, pharmaceutical companies, and religions influence national and, ultimately, individual priorities about fertility. For example, religious positions in the global politics of family planning were visible at the 1994 Cairo Population conference. Roman Catholic and Islamic leaders opposed promoting birth control technology in developing countries. Many European and North American groups support selected aspects of modern family planning. Population policies of the govern-

Reproductive Rights or Wrongs

Beginning in the 1980s, serious criticism of Western family planning programs in relation to reproductive rights emerged from several directions. In the United States, the conservative Reagan administration opposed support of abortion and other forms of population control at home and abroad. (In November 1999, the United States government again refused to pay its estimated $1.5 billion in unpaid United Nations dues, an estimated 80 per cent of all unpaid dues, because of Republican demands for conditions that ban spending any American funds to support family planning clinics offering abortions in other countries.) At the same time, critics on the left claimed that the Western-supported and Western-styled family planning programs in developing countries were a form of neocolonialism. Areas of debate included sterilization of women and the use of incentives such as cash payments, radios, or clothing to attract people into being sterilized.

Betsy Hartmann, an early critic of Western family planning promotion in developing countries, wrote an influential book called *Reproductive Rights and Wrongs* (1987). In the mid-1970s, she did fieldwork in a village in Bangladesh. Two key lessons about women's reproductive freedom emerged. First, in one area, there were women who were satisfied with the number of children they had, and they wanted to adopt some form of "modern" contraception, but none was available. Second,

in other areas of Bangladesh, population control programs were in full force, indiscriminately putting women on the pill, injecting Depo-Provera, or inserting IUDs without offering adequate medical screening, supervision, or follow-up. As a result, many women experienced negative side-effects and became disillusioned with contraception. The government's response was not to reform the program to meet women's needs, but instead to further intensify its population control efforts by pushing sterilization. (x-xi)

A family planning clinic in Egypt. Throughout much of the world, provision of Western-style family planning advice is controversial because it may conflict with local religious and other beliefs about the value of having many children and women's duty to be child bearers.

ments of donor countries affect the welfare of people in developing countries since funding for particular programs may wax or wane depending on political currents. The policy of the Canadian International Development Agency (CIDA) is to support women's reproductive health programs in developing countries in the context of family health, safe motherhood, women's nutrition, and quality family-planning services (see the Critical Thinking box below).

Techniques of Fertility Control

All cultures throughout history have had ways of influencing their fertility, including ways to increase it, reduce it, and regulate child spacing. Some of these are direct, such as using certain herbs or medicines that induce abortion. Others are indirect, such as long periods of breastfeeding, which reduce chances of conception. In Indonesia, for example, breastfeeding probably

In both instances, women were denied control over their own reproduction. Hartmann pursued the topic of reproductive freedom by reading the available literature, corresponding with many experts involved in family planning and health, and contacting reproductive rights activists. By the mid-1980s she was involved in exposing the United States's involvement in sterilization abuse in Bangladesh. She argued that sterilization was being heavily targeted at the poorest women and involved "coercive" incentives. The incentive given to a man or woman for sterilization was Taka 175, equivalent to several weeks' wages. Women also received a *sari* (women's clothing worth about Taka 100), and men received a *lungee* (men's clothing worth about Taka 50). In some cases, food incentives were given. Poor women who approached local government officials for wheat as part of a special food aid program were told that they would get wheat if they had the "operation." Food aid was withheld from women who refused. The number of sterilizations increased during the autumn months when food was scarcest. Doctors and clinic staff received a

bonus for each sterilization. Some family planning workers who failed to meet the sterilization quota for the month suffered pay cuts. However, others have argued that the "compensation payment does not appear to be an important influence on the decision as to whether or not to get sterilized" (Pillsbury 1990:181).

In the mid-1980s, over 60 health advocacy groups formed a coalition to block the approval of the injectable hormone Depo-Provera for use as a contraceptive in Canada. An effective contraceptive when injected every three months, activists were concerned that Depo-Provera had been used for years in family planning programs in developing countries and refugee camps before having been approved for use in Canada. They raised concerns over safety issues, including considerations of risk-benefit for women, and informed consent, since Depo-Provera had been administered to mentally handicapped women, women with disabilities, First Nations women, addicted women, and women prisoners, often without informed consent, screening, or follow-up care. Because of the potential for abuse and concerns about

safety, the coalition managed to delay approval of the drug's use as a contraceptive in Canada until 1997 (Tudiver 1997). It is currently used successfully in Canada and in overseas programs.

CRITICAL THINKING QUESTIONS

How might an anthropological approach provide specific information on the role of structural influences on individual decision making concerning family planning choices?

How might anthropological fieldwork provide more information on the role of agency and individual decision making concerning family planning choices?

If you were a population policy-maker for CIDA, would you support family planning programs using incentives such as cash payments or the use of Depo-Provera without informed consent? How would you justify your position?

Was the delay in approving Depo-Provera use as a contraceptive in Canada justified considering its widespread and effective use today in Canada and in developing countries?

accounts for more child spacing than all other forms of contraception combined (Rohde 1982).

Hundreds of indigenous fertility control methods are available cross-culturally. One study conducted in Afghanistan, for example, found about 500 fertility-regulating techniques in just one region of the country (Hunte 1985). In Afghanistan, as in most pre-industrial cultures, the women are mainly the holders of this information. Certain specialists, such as midwives or herbalists, provide further guidance and expertise. Of the total number of methods in the Afghanistan study, 72 per cent were aimed at increasing fertility, 22 per cent were contraceptives (preventing fertilization of the ovum by the sperm), and 6 per cent were used to induce abortion. These methods predominantly involve plant and animal substances prepared in different ways. Herbs are made into tea and taken orally, some substances are formed into pills, some steamed and inhaled as vapours, some vaginally inserted, and others rubbed on the woman's stomach.

Contemporary medical research reveals the efficacy of many indigenous fertility regulating methods. For example, experiments on animals show that some 450 plant species worldwide contain natural substances that prevent ovulation, block fertilization, stop implantation, or reduce fertility in some other way. In the history of Tibet, the population was stable for long periods of time. The Tibetans subsisted mainly on barley and peas. When mice were fed a diet of 20 per cent peas, litter sizes dropped by half. At 30 per cent peas, the mice failed to reproduce at all.

Induced Abortion Direct intervention in a pregnancy may be resorted to in order to prevent fetal development and lead to abortion (expulsion of the fetus from the womb). Induced abortion, in its many forms, is probably a cultural universal. A review of ethnographic literature on about 400 societies indicates that it was practised in virtually all societies (Devereaux 1976). It is usually done either by the woman herself or with assistance from another woman, perhaps a midwife. Attitudes towards abortion range from acceptability to conditional approval (abortion is acceptable under specified conditions), to tolerance (abortion is regarded with neither approval nor disapproval), to opposition and punishment for offenders. Methods of inducing abortion include hitting the abdomen, starving oneself, taking drugs (such as *kava*), jumping from high places, jumping up and down, lifting heavy objects, and doing hard work.

Motivation for inducing abortion. Economic and social factors largely explain why people induce abortion (Devereaux 1976:13–21). Nomadic women, for example, work very hard and have to carry heavy loads, sometimes for long distances. This lifestyle does not allow women to care for many small children at one time. Poverty is another motivating factor: When faced with another birth in the context of limited resources, abortion may appear to be the most rational choice. Culturally defined "legitimacy" of a pregnancy, along with possible social penalties for bearing an illegitimate child, has been a prominent reason for abortion in Western societies.

Some governments have intervened in family decisions to regulate access to abortion in varying ways, sometimes promoting it, and other times forbidding it. Since the late 1980s, China has pursued one of the most rigorous campaigns to limit population growth (Greenhalgh 1994). Its One-Child Policy, announced in 1978, allowed most families—particularly in cities—to have only one child. It involved strict surveillance of pregnancies, strong group pressure towards women pregnant for the second time or more, and forced abortions and sterilizations. Although there are regional differences in enforcement, this policy inadvertently led to an increase in female infanticide as parents, in their desire for a son and with only one child allowed to them, opted to kill daughters born to them.

Religion and abortion. There is no simple relationship between what a particular religion teaches about abortion and what people actually do. Catholicism forbids abortion, but thousands of Catholic women have sought illegal abortions throughout the world. Islamic teachings forbid abortion and female infanticide, yet sex-selective abortion of female fetuses is known to be practised covertly in Pakistan and by Muslims in India. Hinduism teaches *ahimsa,* or nonviolence towards other living beings, including a fetus whose movements have been felt by the mother ("quickening"). Yet, thousands of Hindus seek abortions every year, and many of them are specifically to abort a female.

In contrast, Buddhism provides little in the way of overt rulings against abortion. In fact, Japanese Buddhism teaches that all life is fluid and that an aborted fetus is simply "returned" to a watery world of unshaped life and

People regularly visit and decorate statues in memory of their aborted or "returned" fetuses in Japan.

may, some time later, come back to live with humans (LaFleur 1992). This belief fits well with the fact that abortion has, in recent years at least, been the most commonly used form of birth control in Japan as it passed through its demographic transition, since other forms of contraception were less available. For example, contraceptive pills were only approved in 1999.

The new reproductive technology. Women's reproductive rights are an important and contentious contemporary issue. In one context, these rights may involve the choice of seeking abortion, while in another, the right to bear a child. They include the issue of the right to decide the gender or other characteristics of one's unborn child. Since the early 1980s, new forms of reproductive technology have been developed and been made available in many places around the world.

One important new development is the ability to gain genetic information about the fetus, which can be used by parents in decision making about whether to keep or abort it. In North America and some European countries, amniocentesis is a legal test used to reveal certain genetic problems in the fetus such as Down's syndrome or spina bifida. Experts have begun to question the social equity involved in this testing and the ethical issues related to the ever-growing role of technology in birth and reproduction. For example, Rayna Rapp's research (1993)

among poor women on Medicare in New York City demonstrated that new technology such as amniocentesis overpowered rather than empowered women.

In 1989, the federal government of Canada appointed a commission to explore the social, ethical, and medical implications of the new reproductive technologies. After four years of research and public hearings, the Royal Commission on New Reproductive Technologies released its report in November 1993. The committee recommended banning surrogate motherhood; sex-selection procedures for non-medical purposes; the buying and selling of human eggs, sperm, embryos, and fetal tissue; and genetic alteration such as the creation of human-animal hybrids. *In vitro* fertilization producing "test-tube babies" would only be available to women with blocked fallopian tubes. Procedures such as artificial insemination and *in vitro* fertilization should only be performed in public, non-profit clinics. The commission also upheld the rights of a pregnant woman over the rights of her fetus; no woman should face civil liability for harm done to her fetus during pregnancy.

Culture and Death

Cultural anthropologists have done many studies on fertility, but their research on mortality is relatively scant (Bledsoe and Hirschman 1989). This difference is partly because mortality is more difficult to research in a typical fieldwork period in the traditional fieldwork setting of a village or urban neighbourhood. In a year, several births might occur in a village of 1000 people, while fewer infant deaths will occur and perhaps no murders or suicides. (Of course, if one did fieldwork in a home for the aged, then death would be far easier to study than birth.) Another reason for the difference in research emphasis between fertility and mortality is the greater availability of funding for fertility studies, given the worldwide concern with population growth and family planning.

Death may occur randomly and from biological causes that impair the body's functioning. However, cultural factors often put certain people more at risk of dying from a certain cause and at a particular age than others. Consider statistics on deaths from car accidents. According to many studies, the rate of severe accidents is higher among men, and men exhibit more high-risk driving behaviour, such as driving at high speeds and driving under the influence of alcohol (Hakamies-Blomqvist 1994). A study of fatal accidents in older male and female drivers in Finland finds a clear increase among older female drivers. The analysis found that older women drivers had substantially less driving experience in terms of mileage and conditions, compared to older men drivers. The lower experience level of women drivers, in turn, was related to more men having held jobs to which they commuted. Women's relative lack of driving experience places women at a disadvantage when it comes to coping with the effects of aging on driving. If the division of labour were to change and more women had jobs to which they commuted, the accident pattern of older women drivers might also change.

Causes of death can be analyzed on several levels. For example, if an infant living in a poor, tropical country dies of dehydration, what might be the cause? Levels of causality considered in population studies are proximate, intermediate, and ultimate causes. A proximate cause is the one that is closest to the actual outcome. In the case of the infant death, dehydration was the proximate cause of death and one that might be written on the death certificate. Why was the baby dehydrated? A closer look into the situation might show that the baby was malnourished. Malnutrition leads to diarrhea and subsequent dehydration. Malnutrition could be considered the intermediate cause of death. Why was the baby malnourished? This question takes us down a complex pathway of inquiry—perhaps the baby was not breastfed, and the family was poor and tried to bottle feed using expensive breast milk substitutes that were over-diluted with dirty water (P. Van Esterik 1989); perhaps the baby died during a period of extreme food scarcity in the area; or maybe the baby was an unwanted third daughter and was fed less than she needed in order to thrive. The question of ultimate causation takes the inquiry out of the realm of medical and nutritional experts and into an analysis of the ultimate, or deeper economic, political, and social factors that put a particular individual at increased risk of dying.

In the next sections, we review how culture shapes death at several points in the human life cycle, beginning with infancy and proceeding to suicide and then death by violence and warfare. This organization is somewhat misleading, however, in placing death through violence and warfare in the later, more "adult" sections of the chapter since violence and warfare also take the lives of many infants and children (Lerer 1998; Olujic 1998) as does the indirect violence of poverty (Bourgois 1998).

Infanticide

Deliberate killing of offspring has been widely documented, although it is not usually a frequent or common practice in any particular society (Dickemann 1975, 1979; Divale and Harris 1976; Scrimshaw 1984; Harris 1977). **Direct infanticide** is the death of an infant or child resulting from actions such as beating, smothering, poisoning, or drowning. **Indirect infanticide,** a more subtle process, may involve prolonged practices such as food deprivation, failure to take a sick infant to a clinic, or failure to provide warm clothing in winter, that bring about the death of an infant. The most frequent motive for direct infanticide reported in the cross-cultural record is that the infant was "deformed" or very ill (Scrimshaw 1984:490–91). Other motives for infanticide include sex of the infant, an adulterous conception, an unwed mother, the birth of twins, too many children in the family already, and poverty. Psychologists Martin Daly and Margo Wilson (1984) offered a sociobiological explanation for 148 cases of infanticide in Canada from 1961 to 1979, arguing that mothers convicted of killing their offspring were likely to be young and unmarried, and may thus have had fewer supportive resources to help them.

Family Resource Constraints and Child "Fitness" In all cultures, parents have expectations for their children—what roles they will play as children, their future marital status, and their roles as adults. If an infant appears to be unable to meet these expectations, parental disappointment and detachment may occur. When family resources are extremely limited, parents may opt for infanticide. As yet, no general theory has been formulated to explain precisely the relationship between resource constraints and perceived child "fitness." Not all people living in poverty practise infanticide, nor do all people practise infanticide when a child is born with certain disabilities.

This Pakistani mother allowed her twin son exclusive access to her breastmilk, while not breast-feeding her twin daughter. The girl died the day after this photo was taken. The mother told her doctor to use the picture if it would help others avoid making the same mistake.

Culturally accepted infanticide has long existed among the Tarahumara, a group of about 50 000 indigenous peoples living in the rugged mountainous area of northern Mexico (Mull and Mull 1987). Most live in log houses with dirt floors and no running water and electricity. They make their living by growing corn and beans and raising sheep and goats, mainly for their own use. Human strength is valued in adults as well as in children, since children begin helping with herding and child care early in their lives. Dorothy and Dennis Mull first learned of the possible existence of culturally sanctioned infanticide when Dennis was working as a volunteer physician in a hospital. A 12-month-old girl who had been admitted several months earlier had developed a complication necessitating the amputation of half her foot. During the course of her recovery in the hospital, her mother's visits became less frequent, to the point of being only a few minutes long while she was in town on other errands. In conversations with the medical staff, the mother expressed a restrained but deep anger about the fact that her daughter had lost half her foot. The Mulls learned later that the child had been dismissed from the hospital. A few weeks later she reportedly "failed" and died. One member of the community interpreted her death this way: "Well, after all, with only half a foot she'd never be able to walk right or work hard. She might never find a husband" (116–117).

Interviews with 20 Tarahumara women about their knowledge of infanticide revealed that all of the women had heard of at least one case of infanticide in the area, 95 per cent of the women knew of at least one case of infanticide when the mother had no husband or had "too many children," 55 per cent knew of at least one case of infanticide of a "damaged" child, and 10 per cent knew of at least one case in which a sickly infant had been killed.

Among the poor of urban Brazil, a similar pattern of indirect infanticide exists that is driven by poverty (Scheper-Hughes 1993). Life is hard for the poor residents of the shantytown called Bom Jesus. Life expectancy is low, although precise information on mortality is not available for these shantytown dwellers (116–117).

Available data on infant and child mortality rates in Bom Jesus since the 1960s lead anthropologist Nancy Scheper-Hughes to coin the ironic phrase, the "modernization of mortality." The modernization of mortality in Brazil refers to a deep division between mortality patterns of the rich and the poor. Recent economic growth in Brazil has brought rising standards of living for many. The national **infant mortality rate** (deaths of children under the age of one year per 1000 births) has declined substantially in recent decades. However, such developments have been unevenly distributed. Instead, there has been a concentration of high death rates among the poorest classes of society and a concentration of infant deaths (under one year of age) as a proportion of all child deaths, with infant death almost replacing child death. Poverty and class differentiation are at the base of these trends. Poverty forces mothers to selectively (and unconsciously) neglect babies that seem sickly or weak, sending them to heaven as "angel babies" rather than trying to keep them alive with the inadequate resources available. The people's religious beliefs, a form of Catholicism, provide ideological support for this practice of indirect infanticide since it allows mothers to believe that their dead babies are now safe in heaven.

Female Infanticide When the infant's sex is the basis for infanticide, females tend to be the target (Miller 1997 [1981]:42–44). Among foraging groups, sex-selective infanticide is rare, being found mainly among some Inuit groups. While early ethnographers such as Boas and Rasmussen attribute high rates of female infanticide to the need to reduce the number of non-food producers, more recent reports emphasize the decline in infant mortality rates among the Inuit as health care improved (Frideres 1998:401). Among horticultural societies, a correlation exists between the level of intergroup warfare and the practice of female infanticide (Divale and Harris 1976). Warfare puts a premium on raising males, to the detriment of investing care and resources in females.

Indirect female infanticide exists in contemporary times in much of China, the Republic of Korea, Hong Kong, India, Pakistan, and parts of the Middle East (see the Multiple Cultural Worlds box). In these countries, female infanticide is related to a complex set of factors, including the gender division of labour and marriage practices and costs.

Suicide

Suicide, or the taking of one's own life, is known in all societies, but the degree to which it is viewed as a positive or negative act varies. In some cultures, suicide is legally or religiously defined as a crime. Catholicism defines suicide as a sin, and suicide rates tend to be lower in Catholic countries than in Protestant countries (Durkheim 1951 [1897]:152). Buddhism does not condone suicide, nor does it consider it a punishable crime. Indeed, Buddhists have sometimes resorted to suicide as a political statement. Several suicides of Buddhist priests and nuns by self-immolation during the Vietnam War were protests of the Catholic president's persecution of Buddhism.

Throughout much of Asia and the South Pacific, suicide is considered a noble and honourable act. When Cheyenne Brando, daughter of Marlon Brando and Tahitian actress Tarita, committed suicide in Tahiti, the local mayor called her suicide "a beautiful gesture" (Gliotto 1995:70). Aged 25 years old at the time of her death, she had been depressed for many years, especially after the death of her fiancé, who was killed by Cheyenne's brother, Christian, in what he claims was an accidental shooting. Honourable suicide is also found in Japan, where it seems to result from a strong commitment to group goals and a feeling of failure to live up to those goals (Lebra 1976). In this way, suicide is a way of "saving face."

Sati (pronounced "SUT-TEE"), or the suicide of a wife upon the death of her husband, has been practised in parts of India for several hundred years and, on occasion, into the present. According to Hindu scriptures, a woman whose husband dies does an act of great personal and group honour if she voluntarily joins his corpse on the funeral pyre and thus burns to death. No one knows for sure how common this was in the past, but its ideal is still upheld by conservative Hindus. The most recent reported *sati* occurred in the northern state of Rajasthan in 1987 by a young widow named Roop Kanwar. Historians and social scientists have debated the degree of voluntarism involved in such suicides, as there is evidence of direct coercion in some cases—the widow was drugged, or physically forced onto the pyre. Indirect coercion is also culturally embedded in the belief that a woman whose husband dies is to blame for his death. Perhaps she didn't serve him with enough devotion, pray or fast for him enough, or she ate too much and didn't give him enough food. The life of surviving widows is difficult, involving loss of status, shame, and material deprivation. Knowing this, a new widow may decide she would be better off dead.

In terms of sheer numbers, suicide is more prevalent in the industrialized, urbanized societies of Europe than elsewhere. However, in several developing nations, such as Sri Lanka and Samoa, suicide rates have risen steeply in recent decades. The general explanation proposed for the cross-cultural variation in suicide rates is that the rapid social changes brought about by industrialism, the spread of education, and global change in consumer values are often not matched by people's ability to satisfy these new aspirations. French sociologist Emile Durkheim (1951 [1897]) used the term *anomie* to refer to the feelings of dislocation and dissatisfaction caused by rapid social change and thwarted ambitions. The concept of anomic suicide seems to apply well to the rising trend

Female Infanticide in India

In North India in the eighteenth century, direct female infanticide was fairly widespread, with upper-caste Hindu groups such as Rajputs, Jats, and Brahmans often keeping none or few of the daughters born to them. Entire villages were reported with no daughters at all. Census data for 1871 revealed that there were between 115 and 120 boys per 100 girls among the Hindu population in a large region of northern India. Over 100 years later, similar juvenile sex ratios persist in this region in spite of increased economic development, literacy, and communication (Miller 1987b). Today, the Indian population has 55 million fewer females than males. Much of this gap, although precisely how much is not known, is caused by indirect female infanticide and sex-selective abortion. Baby girls are breastfed less often and for a shorter period of time than baby boys, and they are taken to clinics for treatment of illnesses less frequently. Hospital admissions in the North are 2:1 boys to girls, and that is not because more boys are sick than girls, but because parents and grandparents are more willing to allocate time and money for the health of boys than girls (Miller 1997 [1981]).

Why is discrimination against daughters and in favour of sons in terms of household allocations of food, health care, and even attention more marked in northern India than in its southern and eastern regions? This pattern corresponds with two features of the economy: production and marriage exchanges. The northern plains are characterized by dry-field wheat cultivation, which requires intensive labour inputs for plowing and field preparation and then moderate amounts of field labour for sowing, weeding, and harvesting, with women assisting in the latter tasks as unpaid family labour. Production in southern and eastern India relies more on wet rice cultivation, in which women form the bulk of the paid agricultural labour force. In much of southern India, women of the household may even participate on an equal footing with men in terms of agricultural planning and decision making.

Paralleling this regional difference in labour patterns is a contrast in costs related to marriage. In the North, marriage typically requires, especially among the propertied groups, **groomprice** or **dowry**—the transfer of large amounts of cash and goods from the bride's family to the groom's family (Miller 1997 [1981]). Marriage costs in the South among both propertied and unpropertied groups were more likely to emphasize **brideprice**—the transfer of cash and goods from the groom's side to the bride's father, along with a tradition of passing gold jewellery through the female line from mother to daughter. From a parent's perspective, the birth of several daughters in the northern system is a financial drain. In the South, a daughter is considered a valuable labourer and source of wealth. Importantly, much of northern dowry and southern bridewealth circulates: An incoming dowry can be used to finance the marriage of the groom's sister, and bridewealth received in the South at the marriage of a daughter can be used for the marriage of her brother. Logically, in the North, the more sons per daughter in the household the better, since more incoming dowries will allow for a "better" marriage of a daughter.

The economic costs and benefits to a household of having sons versus daughters in India also varies by class. This variation relates to both work patterns and marriage patterns. Middle- and upper-class families, especially in the North, tend to keep girls and women out of the paid labour force more than the poor. Thus, daughters are a greater economic liability among the better-off than among the poor where girls, as well as boys, may earn money in the informal sector, for example, doing piece-work at home. This class difference is mirrored in marriage costs. Among the poor, marriage costs are less expensive than among the middle and upper classes, and sometimes involve more balanced exchange between the bride's and groom's families. Thus, marital costs of daughters are lower and the benefits of having sons are not that much greater than having daughters.

Poverty is therefore not the major driving factor of female infanticide or female-selective abortion in India. It is more related to a drive to maximize family status and wealth by having sons and avoiding having daughters: If one has two sons and one daughter in the North Indian marriage system of huge dowries, then two dowries will come in with the brides of the sons and only one dowry will be expended. Incoming dowries can be used to finance the dowry of one's own daughter, so one can provide a huge outgoing dowry that will attract a "high quality" husband. If, on the other hand, one has two daughters and one son, the ratio of incoming to outgoing wealth changes significantly. This situation would impoverish a family rather than enrich it.

FOOD FOR THOUGHT

Have you experienced, or has anyone you know experienced, a feeling of being less valued as a child than other children in the family? If you are an "only child," you will need to ponder experiences you may have heard from friends.

of youth suicide worldwide. In Canada, the suicide rate for adolescent males between 15 and 19 years has risen fourfold since 1960, from 5 to 19.9 per 100 000 in 1997. Suicide rates among First Nations youth are six times higher than the rates in the rest of Canada (Frideres 1998:182).

Violence

Violent death can be the result of private, interpersonal conflict or it can occur in a public arena, either through informal conflict between individuals or groups, such as gang fights, or through formal conflict, such as war. Throughout history, millions of people have died from private and public violence. Often their deaths have culturally defined patterns.

Private Violence: Spousal Abuse Throughout the world, private violence resulting in death is all too common. One example, infanticide, was discussed earlier. Lethal spousal violence is known to exist throughout most of the world in varying degrees, although it is difficult to pinpoint cross-cultural rates because statistics are undependable or unavailable. Far more women are killed by husbands or male partners. Anecdotal, case-by-case evidence suggests that in much of the Middle East, a husband may kill his wife or daughter with a fair amount of impunity, as if it is within his rights in terms of protecting family honour. In Canada in 1997, one in eight women living with a man was abused at some time, according to the Canadian Department of Justice. Anthropological studies of the dynamics of domestic violence cross-culturally are discussed later in this book.

In India, beginning in the 1980s, many cases of an apparently new form of femicide were reported in the media. Called *dowry death*, such murders were characteristically committed by a husband, often in collusion with his mother, and carried out by throwing a flammable substance over the victim and then lighting her on fire. These murders are especially prevalent in northern cities, among the middle and upper classes. They are spurred by an obsessive material interest in extracting wealth from the wife's family through first her dowry and later, a continuing stream of demanded gifts. If the bride's family cannot comply with these demands, the bride is harassed, and her life is endangered. This form of **femicide**, or murder of a person based on the fact of being female, is related to the overall low value of women in India, es-

Refugees from the late 1990s violence in Rwanda on their way to neighbouring Democratic Republic of Congo (Zaire). Many refugees did not survive the ordeal, although adequate statistics are not available to assess the mortality rate of refugees.

pecially in the North and among the status-aspiring middle and upper classes.

Public Violence Warfare is a common form of public violence (political aspects of warfare are discussed in Chapter 11). The few studies that have addressed mortality from warfare cross-culturally reveal that among horticultural societies, warfare accounts for the highest proportion of male deaths and can thus be seen to function as a major mechanism of population control in such societies (Divale and Harris 1976). Horticulture's requirement for large territories puts many groups in conflict with one another. In recent decades, conflicts with outsiders have increased; for example, the Yanomami of the Brazilian and Venezuelan Amazon region are squeezed by outsiders such as cattle ranch developers and miners (R. Ferguson 1990). This external pressure impels them to engage in intergroup raids that often result in the deaths of male fighters, but also sometimes women, who may be captured and then killed. In some especially vulnerable groups of Yanomami, it has been reported that up to one-third of all adult males die as a result of intergroup raids and warfare.

In contrast, in industrialized societies, the death rates of males actively involved in warfare constitute a much smaller proportion of total death rates, being replaced by such causes as automobile accidents or heart disease. Canadian casualties totalled 138 166 in World War I, and 53 145 in World War II, according to the Canadian Department of National Defence and Veterans Affairs.

Some scholars distinguish **ethnocide,** destruction of a culture without physically killing its people, from **genocide,** the destruction of a culture and its people through physical extermination (Chalk and Jonassohn 1986:180). The Chinese occupation of Tibet, the Khmer Rouge's massacres in Cambodia, the Serbian-Bosnian conflict, the Hutu-Tutsi conflict in Rwanda, and the Indonesian government's actions in East Timor are examples of politically motivated genocide (Maybury-Lewis 1997).

The history of Native American demography can also be interpreted as one of genocidal destruction and has been called "the American holocaust." It is likely that well over 50 million Amerindians died as a result of contact with the Europeans from 1492 through the seventeenth century (Stannard 1992). For example, the conquest of Mexico by Hernando Cortés had the following demographic results:

> Tenochtitlán, with its 350,000 residents, had been the jewel of an empire that contained numerous exquisite cities. All were destroyed. Before the coming of the Europeans, central Mexico, radiating out from the metropolitan centers over many tens of thousands of square miles, had contained about 25 million people—almost ten times the population of England at that time. Seventy-five years later hardly more than one million were left. And central Mexico, where 60 out of a hundred people perished, was typical.… In western and central Honduras 95 percent of the native people were exterminated in half a century. In western Nicaragua the rate of extermination was 99 percent—from more than one million people to less than 10,000 in just sixty years. (430)

In another example of genocidal destruction, the Beothuk, the Aboriginal inhabitants of Newfoundland were actively hunted and killed primarily by British farmers, fishers, and trappers who settled on the bays that had been the Beothuk's summer camps. The Beothuk had been pushed further inland, away from their resources from the time of the island's discovery in 1497. With no intermediaries such as traders or missionaries interested in interacting with them, and weakened by diseases such as bubonic plague, small pox, and tuberculosis, the population decreased from approximately 345 in 1768, to 72 in 1811; the "last" Beothuk, Shanawdithit was captured and brought to St. John's in 1823, where she died of tuberculosis in 1829 (J. Price 1979; I. Marshall 1996).

Key Questions Revisited

How is reproduction related to modes of production?

Reproduction, or the dominant ways in a society that people come into the world and leave the world, are everywhere shaped by culture. More specifically, the various modes of production are basic structures to which reproduction responds. For thousands of years, foragers maintained a balanced level of population through direct and indirect means of fertility regulation. As sedentarization increased and food surpluses became more available and storable, population increased as well, culminating in the highest rates of population growth in human history among settled agriculturalists.

How does culture shape fertility in different contexts?

Cross-culturally, many techniques exist for increasing fertility, reducing it, and regulating its timing. Anthropological studies of indigenous fertility regulating mechanisms reveal hundreds of different methods, including the use of herbs and other natural sources for inhibiting or enhancing fertilization, and for inducing abortion if an undesired pregnancy occurs. In non-industrial societies, the knowledge and practice of fertility regulation was largely unspecialized and available to all women. Early specializations included midwives and herbalists. In the industrial mode of reproduction, scientific and medical specialization abounds, and most knowledge and expertise is no longer in the hands of women themselves. Class-stratified access to fertility-regulating methods exists globally and within nations.

How does culture shape mortality in different contexts?

Population growth and change are also affected through the cultural shaping of death. The practice of infanticide is of ancient origin, and it still exists today. It may be done in response to familial resource limitations, perceptions of "fitness" of the child, or preferences about the gender of offspring. Deaths from suicide, and from public and private violence, also reflect particular cultural patterns that "target" certain people or groups. In a specific mode of production, death at a certain age or from a particular cause is more likely than it would be in a different mode of production. Thus, far from being random, natural events, birth and death are cultural events to a large extent.

Core Concepts

below-replacement-level fertility, p. 122
brideprice, p. 135
demographic transition, p. 122
demography, p. 120
direct infanticide, p. 132
dowry, p. 135
ethnocide, p. 137
femicide, p. 136
fertility, p. 120
genocide, p. 137
groomprice, p. 135
indirect infanticide, p. 132
infant mortality rate, p. 133
infanticide, p. 121
matrilineal, p. 126
migration, p. 120
mortality, p. 120
post-partum taboos, p. 125
pronatalism, p. 121
replacement-level fertility, p. 122
reproduction, p. 120
sex-selective infanticide, p. 126

Suggested Readings

Caroline Bledsoe and Barney Cohen, eds., *Social Dynamics of Adolescent Fertility in Sub-Saharan Africa*. Washington, D.C.: National Academy Press, 1993. An anthropologist and a demographer examine national survey data on cultural factors related to high fertility rates among adolescents in sub-Saharan Africa. Attention is given to patterns of adolescent sexuality, attitudes towards marriage, women's status, knowledge and practice of contraception, and the role of education in change.

Thomas E. Fricke, *Himalayan Households: Tamang Demography and Domestic Processes*. New York, Columbia University Press, 1994. An example of demographic anthropology, this is a local study of population patterns and change in one region of Nepal. The book includes chapters on the subsistence economy, fertility and mortality, the life course, household dynamics, and recent changes.

W. Penn Handwerker, ed., *Births and Power: Social Change and the Politics of Reproduction*. Boulder, CO: Westview Press, 1990. An overview chapter by the editor is followed by 11 case studies, including studies of the Inuit of Canada, the Bariba of West Africa, the Mende of Sierra Leone, teen pregnancies in the United States, and people who have AIDS in Africa.

Nancy Howell, *Demography of the Dobe !Kung*. New York: Academic Press, 1979. This classic book describes the demography of a group of South African foragers before they were sedentarized. The text considers how anthropological methods contribute to demographic analysis of small-scale societies, causes of illness and death, fertility and sterility, and population growth rates.

Marcia C. Inhorn, *Infertility and Patriarchy: The Cultural Politics of Gender and Family Life in Egypt*. Philadelphia: University of Pennsylvania Press, 1996. Based on fieldwork in Alexandria, this book uses narratives from several infertile Egyptian women to show the different ways these women and their families deal with cultural pressures to bear children.

Nancy Scheper-Hughes, *Death without Weeping: The Violence of Everyday Life in Brazil*. Berkeley: University of California Press, 1993. This book is a landmark "ethnography of death," based on fieldwork in a Brazilian shantytown over several periods of time. The author argues that poverty drives a demographic system of very high infant mortality rates and high fertility.

 Your *Cultural Anthropology*, Second Canadian Edition Media Edition CD-ROM contains many Web sites relevant to this chapter. Use it to explore the Web and to expand your knowledge of anthropology.

Chapter 6

Personality and Human Development

CHAPTER OUTLINE

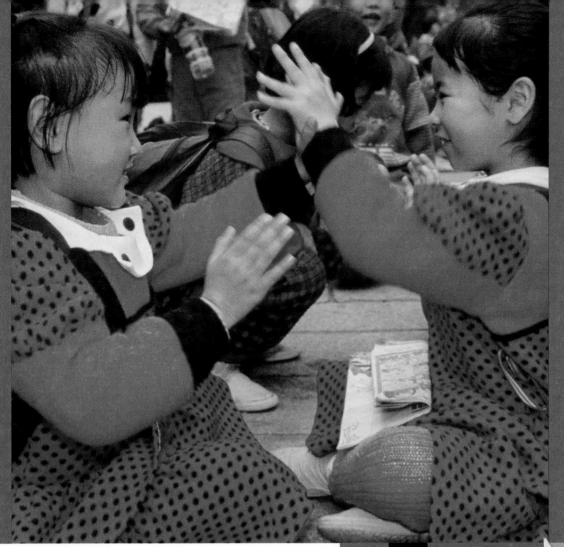

Girls in China playing a clapping game with each other. Games, and play in general, are an important way that children learn cultural values and ways of interacting with others.

Key Questions

How does culture shape personality during infancy and childhood?

How does culture shape personality during the transition from childhood to adulthood?

How does culture shape personality during adulthood?

The Mehinaku are peaceful horticulturalists of the Brazilian Amazon whose society, thus far, is mainly intact (Gregor 1981). Nonetheless, the Mehinaku are aware of the presence and power of Brazilians (non-Indians). An analysis of 385 dreams of the Mehinaku indicates that they have deep anxieties about the outsiders. Of the total set of dreams, over half contained indications of some level of anxiety. In 31 of the dreams, Brazilians were central characters, and of these, 90 per cent of the dreams were tinged with fear, evidencing a clear focus of anxiety on the outsiders. Recurrent themes in the dreams with outsiders as key characters were fire, assault, and disorientation. While the Mehinaku's land and culture are so far intact, their inner tranquility is gone.

The study of people's dreams in different cultural contexts is just one of the many approaches that psychological anthropologists pursue in their attempt to understand psychological processes.

Psychological anthropology addresses many of the topics of contemporary Western psychology: learning, perception, cognition, memory, intelligence, the emotions, sexuality and gender, personality, and mental health problems. Studying these topics cross-culturally has revealed the ethnocentrism involved in applying Western psychological concepts universally, including definitions of what is "normal." An enduring question in psychological anthropology is whether and how much human psychology is the same cross-culturally or whether variation overrides universals.

This chapter provides a general background on how cultural anthropology has approached the study of the individual within culture, particularly how cultures shape **personality,** an individual's patterned and characteristic way of behaving, thinking, and feeling. We then review the major life-cycle stages, noting key anthropological findings about the role of culture in human development. This chapter focuses on "normal" human development, as defined culturally. Problematic aspects of human development, including what Western psychology defines as mental illness, are discussed in Chapter 7.

Culture and Personality

Cultural anthropologists have mainly pursued the line of argument that personality is formed through **enculturation,** or socialization, the process of transmitting culture to infants and other new members of society. They seek answers to the question: How do different cultures enculturate their members into different personalities?

The Culture and Personality School

The American-based culture and personality school began in the 1930s and persisted through the 1970s. Culture and personality studies began with Franz Boas's interest in the individual, developed through his fieldwork on the Northwest Coast and the Central Arctic. The school was further developed through his students. Members of the school adopted some aspects of Freudian theories, including the importance of childhood experiences in shaping personality, and the symbolic analysis of dreams. Boas's student, Edward Sapir shared his interest in the relation between language and culture. In spite of Boas and Sapir's important role in institutionalizing Canadian anthropology, culture and personality as a "school" was never strongly developed in Canada, partly because of the influence of British social anthropology in the country. American influence in Canadian anthropology was most visible in the 1960s when many American professors taught in Canadian anthropology departments. By that time, culture and personality was no longer an important theoretical orientation in the United States. Meanwhile, Canadian anthropologists began collaborating with psychologists and psychiatrists to explore transcultural psychiatry. In 1955, Transcultural Psychiatric Studies was established at McGill University to explore the effects of culture on psychiatric disorders.

Personality and Child Rearing In the early 1930s, Margaret Mead went with her husband, anthropologist Reo Fortune, to the Sepik River area of northern New Guinea. Her subsequent publication, *Sex and Temperament in Three Primitive Societies* (1963 [1935]), revealed striking differences in how male and female roles and personalities were defined and acted out. Once again, Mead's findings seemed to prove that nature is subservient to culture, in this case with culture, not nature dictating what is male and what is female. Among the Arapesh, the first group she studied, both men and women had nurturant and gentle personalities. Both valued parental roles and both participated equally in child care. Arapesh males and females all behave according to what is stereotypically defined as "feminine" in Western cultures. Among the Mundugumor, in contrast, both

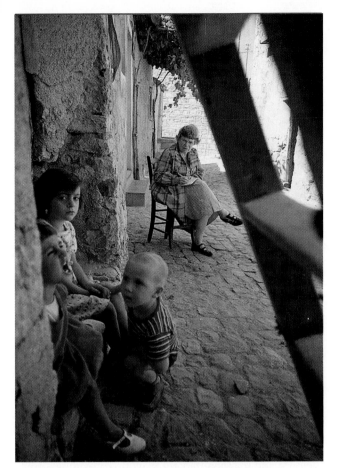

Margaret Mead, during some of her later years of fieldwork, observes children's interactions in Sicily.

males and females corresponded to the Western stereotype of "masculine" behaviour. Adults in general were assertive, aggressive, loud, and even fierce. Children were treated indifferently by their parents, with neither mothers nor fathers expressing nurturance. The situation among the Tchambuli was equally surprising to Mead and her readers: The men fussed about their looks, gossiped with each other most of the day, and did little in the way of productive work. The women were competent and responsible, providing most of the food through fishing and gardening, and managing the household. Among the Tchambuli, women played a dominant role in the culture, and their personalities reflected this importance. In all, these findings show that gender is an arbitrary matter, defined culturally and shaped through child-rear-

ing patterns. Mead's detailed analysis of variations in child care, including differences in degrees of tenderness or neglect during breastfeeding, provide evidence of how children in different contexts learn patterns of personality formation from an early age.

Cultural Patterns and National Character

Ruth Benedict, a leading figure of the culture and personality school, argued that cultures promote distinct personality types. In her book *Patterns of Culture* (1959 [1934]), she proposed that descriptions of cultures might be integrated around the unconscious selection of a few cultural traits from the "vast arc" of potential traits. For example, one culture may emphasize monetary values while another overlooks them. The selected traits "interweave" to form a cohesive pattern, a **cultural configuration**, characteristic of people's thoughts and behaviours in that culture. Benedict first formulated her theories while doing research on Native American cultures. In her view, the Pueblo Indians of the American Southwest had personalities that exemplified a "middle road," involving moderation in all things and avoiding excess and violence. She termed the Pueblo an "Apollonian" culture, after the Greek deity Apollo. In contrast, she labelled the Kwakwaka'wakw (the group Boas called Kwakiutl) of the Pacific Northwest, "Dionysian," after the Greek god of revelry and excess, because of their individualism and high levels of expressive emotionality, mainly expressed through their potlatches.

Benedict's portrait of the Kwakwaka'wakw has been criticized for its over-reliance on Boas's data on just one group of southern nobility after European contact, its selective ignoring of the amiable, playful side of their life, and for ignoring ecological factors (Harris 1968:310). Similar criticisms have been levelled against Ruth Landes, a student of Boas and Benedict, for her portrayal of the Ojibway of northwestern Ontario. Her work stressed the extreme individualism and atomistic behaviour of the Ojibway, their lack of political organization, and severe anxiety neuroses manifested in cannibalism and violence. Anthropologists have criticized her work for questionable ethnographic accuracy and for failing to place the Ojibway in historical context reflecting the changed economic conditions after government suppression of political and religious organizations (Lovisek, Holzkamm, and Waisberg 1997).

During World War II, the United States Office of War Information commissioned Benedict to analyze Japanese personality structure and submit reports to the government to help defeat the Japanese. During the war, she could not do fieldwork, and so she consulted secondary sources (newspapers, magazines, movies) and interviewed Japanese Americans. Her book, *The Chrysanthemum and the Sword* (1969 [1946]), presents a set of essential features of Japanese character: importance of *on* (obligation, the necessity to repay gifts and favours), the concept of virtue, the value of self-discipline, keeping one's name "clear" or honourable, and rules of etiquette. Following Benedict's work on Japan, **national character studies** that defined basic personality types and core values of nations declined in importance and are now criticized for three main reasons: (1) they are ethnocentric, classifying cultures according to Western psychological values and features; (2) they are reductionist, emphasizing only one or two features; and (3) they are totalizing, obscuring intranational variation in their construction of a single national character (e.g., *the* French, *the* English, *the* Japanese).

Class Position and Personality

Two cultural anthropologists of the mid-twentieth century came up with theories about poverty and personality formation. George Foster (1965), who did research among small-scale farmers in Mexico, proposed his model of a world view called the **image of the limited good.** People who have this world view believe that the resources or wealth available within a particular social group are finite. If someone increases his or her wealth, other people will necessarily lose out. The pie analogy illustrates how the image of the limited good works. If a group of eight people equally divides a pie into eight pieces, everyone gets the same share. But if one person takes two pieces, only six pieces remain for everyone else. One person's gain is another's loss. The image of the limited good, according to Foster, is found along with a "status quo" mentality that prevents people from trying to improve their economic condition. Major personality traits associated with the image of the limited good are jealousy, suspiciousness, and passivity.

Oscar Lewis (1966) proposed a related concept, the **culture of poverty,** to explain personality and behaviour among the poor and why poverty persists. He typified poor Mexican people as, among other things, "improvident," lacking a future time-orientation, and sexually promiscuous. He argued that because of these personality traits, poor people are trapped in poverty and cannot change their situation.

The models proposed by Foster and Lewis have been rejected by contemporary anthropologists as products of American capitalistic culture, which places a highly positive value on aggressive self-assertion, competitiveness, and a belief that resources are infinite. The marital values expressed in their models are based on a Euro-American puritan tradition. The personality traits they attributed to the poor and the negative value they attached to these traits can be seen as ethnocentric, self-serving, and a form of "blaming the victim."

New Directions

Recent studies of personality formation in particular economic niches have tried to be less ethnocentric in their interpretations. For example, one ethnography of a poor Black neighbourhood in a city in the Midwestern United States uses words such as "resourceful" and "resilient" in describing how people adapt to difficult circumstances (Stack 1974). Other work in cultural anthropology considers the many cases of revolution and resistance among the poor and marginalized of the world, providing a complete reversal of the models proposed by Foster and Lewis about passivity.

At the opposite end of the class spectrum, psychological anthropologists are beginning to "study up" the class structure. An examination of how corporate culture shapes personality in Japan is a landmark in this new direction in showing how child care patterns and demands of the business world fit together to create compliant male workers (see the Multiple Cultural Worlds box).

Personality Formation during Infancy

In North America, commonly accepted life stages include infancy, childhood, adolescence, middle age, and old age (psychologists and other experts concerned with human development construct even finer substages). Western

Corporate Personality Formation: The Making of Salarymen in Japan

Research in Japan on the personality of "salarymen," males employed in the fast-paced corporate world, links male personality with the demands of the business world (Allison 1994). Salarymen work long hours for the company. They leave home early in the morning and return late at night and thus are nicknamed "7-11 men." Many Tokyo salarymen eat dinner with their family only a few times a year. After work, they typically spend many hours with fellow workers at expensive nightclubs. Groups of about five to ten men go out together after work. A few drinks and light snacks can result in a tab in the hundreds of dollars for one hour. The corporation picks up the bill. At the club, men relax and have fun after a long day at work. This is ensured by having a trained hostess sit at the table, keeping the conversation moving along in a lightly playful tone. Her job is to flatter and flirt with the men and to make them feel good.

In order to learn about this night world, Anne Allison did participant observation while working as a hostess.

She found that conversations are full of teasing and banter, with much of it directed at the hostess and most of it derogatory: The hostess's breasts are too small, her hair is not right, and so on. The hostess must take all of this with a smile, and even joke along with it: "Yes, I have no breasts at all." Allison calls this type of banter "breast talk." How should this focus on the female breast be interpreted? Salarymen's night club behaviour appears to be linked with their upbringing. Given the near total absence of the father from the home scene, children are raised mainly by the mother. The concentration of maternal attention is especially strong towards sons and their school achievements. The goal is that the boy will do well in school, get into a top university, and then gain employment with a large corporation. These corporations pay well, guarantee lifelong employment, and provide substantial benefits after retirement. In the corporation, hierarchies are clear, total loyalty is required, work hours are long, and

the pressure to perform is high. Regular socializing at the club solidifies bonds between salarymen and strengthens their loyalty to the corporation.

Salarymen's behaviour in night clubs can also be viewed as a reaction to their upbringing, with its total control by the mother. Club culture puts the man in control, reversing the power differential of his childhood. At the club, he has guaranteed control over a desirable woman who flatters him and flirts with him. She will never control him because after an hour or so of fun, he leaves and there is no enduring relationship. Club culture provides only temporary ego gratification for a salaryman: He needs to return again and again for reinforcement. This fact keeps salarymen away from their homes, leaving their own sons in the isolated care of the mother.

FOOD FOR THOUGHT

How are males and females in Canadian society socialized to be compliant corporate employees?

life-cycle stages are based on biological features such as the ability to walk, puberty, and parenthood (Bogin 1988). However, these stages and their associated features are not cultural universals.

Birth

Cultural anthropologists have asked whether the style and ambience of the event of birth itself have psychological effects on the infant. Through their cross-cultural research, they have discovered variations in the birth experience that may affect an infant's psychological development. Brigitte Jordan (1983), a pioneer in the cross-cultural study of birth, conducted research on birth practices in Mexico, Sweden, Holland, and the United States. She studied the birth setting, including its location

and who is present, the types of attendants and their roles, the birth event, and the post-partum period. Among Maya women in Mexico, the midwife is called in the early stages of labour. One of her tasks is to give a *sobada* (massage) to the mother-to-be. She also provides psychological support by telling stories, often about other women's birthing experiences. The husband is expected to be present during the labour, so that he can see "how a woman suffers." The woman's mother should be present, along with other female kin such as mother-in-law, godmother, sisters, and friends. Compared to many other birthing contexts, the Maya mother is surrounded by a large group of supportive people.

A study exploring natural childbirth in Toronto, including Lamaze preparation as an alternative to medical control, showed that mothers wanted more control over the childbirth experience and less dependence on technological interventions such as induced labour, anesthesia, episiotomies, and fetal heart monitoring (Romalis 1981). Nevertheless, over 99 per cent of births in Canada in 1996 took place in hospitals, according to the National Population Health Survey. The newborn infant is generally taken to a nursery where it is wrapped in cloth, placed in a crib under bright lights, and fed with sugar water rather than being left with the mother to be fed. Critics argue that the Western hospital-based system of highly regulated birth is extremely technocratic and "too managed," alienating the mother—and the father as well as other members of the family and the wider community—from the birthing process and the infant (Davis-Floyd 1992). Criticism of the Western birth process and the subsequent physical separation of the infant from the mother has led to consideration of how to improve the way birth is conducted and the context it sets (or doesn't set) for maternal support and infant bonding. For example, the Baby-Friendly Hospital Initiative supported by UNICEF and many non-governmental organizations (NGOs) identifies hospital practices that will encourage mother-infant bonding and successful breastfeeding, including initiating breastfeeding immediately after birth, allowing mothers and infants to room together, discouraging the use of pacifiers, and refusing monetary donations and free supplies from the infant formula industry. In 1999, the Brome-Missisquoi-Perkins Hospital in Cowansville, Quebec, became the first Canadian hospital to be designated as "Baby-Friendly," joining over 14 000 Baby-Friendly Hospitals worldwide.

Some Western psychologists argue that immediate contact and early skin-to-skin contact is crucial for the development of parental feelings of bonding and if it is not established early, then it will not develop later. Oddly enough, given these theories, many Western-based hospital practices separate infants from mothers. Explanations for juvenile delinquency or other unfavourable child development problems often include reference to lack of proper infant bonding at birth.

Nancy Scheper-Hughes (1993), whose research in a Brazilian shantytown was discussed in Chapters 5 and 7, questions Western bonding theory. She argues that bonding does not necessarily have to occur at birth to be successful. Her observations in Bom Jesus show that many mothers do not exhibit bonding with their infants at birth. Bonding occurs later, if the child survives in-

fancy, when it is several years old. She proposes that this pattern of later bonding is related to the high rate of infant mortality among the poor of Brazil. If women were to develop strong bonds with their infants, they would suffer untold amounts of grief. Bonding is adaptive in low-mortality/low-fertility societies in which strong maternal attachment is reasonable because infants are likely to survive.

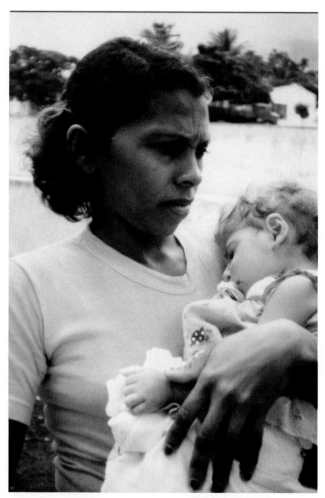

In Bom Jesus, a shantytown in northeastern Brazil, this mother was told by a doctor at the local clinic that her son was dying of anemia and that she needed to feed him red meat. The mother said, "Now where am I going to find the money to feed my hopeless son rich food like that?" Western mother-infant bonding theory does not appear to apply in all cultures.

Sleeping Patterns

Related to bonding theory is the question of where and with whom the infant sleeps. The practice of infants and children sleeping beside their parents is found in most societies. Recent research by physical anthropologist James McKenna (1993) demonstrates the advantages of sleeping in close contact with at least one other person, including possible protection against SIDS (sudden infant death syndrome). His research demonstrates the importance of a co-sleeping environment, rather than a solitary environment, for infant well-being.

The Basque people of northern Spain favour long periods of co-sleeping (Crawford 1994). Interviews with 217 Basque mothers probed topics such as their attitudes about parenting, religious beliefs, dreams, personality characteristics, and the mother's childhood sleeping patterns. Of these women, 167 had slept in their parents' room for two to three years. Compared to the women who had not been co-sleepers as children, women who had been co-sleepers had both greater ego strength and a greater sense of connectedness. This study suggests that co-sleeping does not necessarily prevent the development of a strong ego.

Gender and Infancy

As noted in Chapter 1, cultural anthropologists distinguish between sex and gender. In the view of Western science, sex has three biological markers: genitals, hormones, and chromosomes. Males are defined as people who have a penis, more androgens than estrogens, and the XY chromosome. Females have a vagina, more estrogens than androgens, and the XX chromosome. Increasingly, however, scientists know that these two categories are not definitive. In all populations, some people are born with indeterminate genitals, similar proportions of androgens and estrogens, and chromosomes with more complex distributions than simply XX and XY. Thus, continuum models of sex and gender might be more accurate than strictly binary models.

Gender refers to the learned behaviour and beliefs associated with maleness and femaleness, and thus is culturally constructed (Miller 1993). Individuals acquire their gender identity, roles, and status through learning, much of which is unconscious. From the moment of birth, an infant's life course is shaped by whether it is labelled male or female and what the defined roles and status of "male" and "female" are in a particular culture. Most cultural anthropologists acknowledge the high degree of human "plasticity," as demonstrated by Mead's early work on gender roles and personality in New Guinea, and that gender socialization can to a large extent "override" sex-linked features such as hormones.

Many other researchers continue to insist on a wide range of supposedly sex-linked personality characteristics as being innate. A major problem arises in how to test for innate characteristics. First, one needs data on infants before they are subject to cultural influences. But culture starts shaping the infant from the moment of its birth through handling and treatment (some scholars say that socialization could begin even in the womb through exposure to sound and motion). Second, studying and interpreting the behaviour of infants is fraught with potential bias. Studies of infants have focused on assessing the potential innateness of three major Euro-American personality stereotypes: (1) whether infant males are more aggressive than infant females, (2) whether infant females are more social than infant males, and (3) whether males are more independent. Boy babies do tend to cry more than girl babies, and some people believe this is evidence of higher levels of inborn aggression in males. An alternative interpretation is that baby boys on average tend to weigh more than girls. They therefore are more likely to have a difficult delivery from which it takes time to recover, so they cry more, but not out of aggressiveness. In terms of socialness, baby girls smile more often than boys. Does this mean girls are born to be people pleasers? Evidence of caretakers smiling more at baby girls shows that the more frequent smiling of girls is a learned, not innate response. In terms of independence or dependence, studies thus far reveal no clear gender differences in how upset babies are when separated from their caretakers. Studies seeking to document innate gender differences through the behaviour of infants are not convincing. However, some anthropologists continue to explore the possibilities of innate neurophysiological differences in the central nervous systems of male and female infants in pre- and perinatal development as one of many factors explaining differences in violent aggression/nurturance and spatial acuity/verbal acuity polarities (Laughlin 1989). Two questions continue to be important. First, if gender differences are innate, why do cultures go to so much trouble to instill them? Second, if gender differences are innate, then they should be similar throughout history and cross-culturally which, of course, they aren't. Throughout the rest of this chapter, cultural constructions of gender at various stages of the life cycle are explored.

Socialization during Childhood

The concept of "the child" as a special age category may have emerged first in Europe in the last few centuries (Ariès 1962). In art, portraits of children became commonplace only in the seventeenth century. Other changes occurred at the same time: new interests in children's habits, more elaborate terminology about children and childhood, and special clothing for children instead of small-sized versions of adult clothing. The special focus on "the child" is associated with the emergence of industrial capitalism's need for an ever-expanding market. "The child" becomes a new niche for sales, which allowed for the production and sale of clothes, books, and toys specifically for that niche. In less industrialized cultures, "the child" is not regarded as having such specialized needs. In these societies, children are expected to take on adult tasks at an earlier age. These different expectations about what a child should do and be have implications for personality formation.

Mode of Production and Child Personality

The "Six Cultures Study" is a renowned cross-cultural study designed to provide comparative data on children's personalities in relation to their activities and tasks (Whiting and Whiting 1975). Researchers observed a total of 67 boys and 67 girls between the ages of three and eleven years. They recorded many forms of behaviour, such as being supportive of other children; hitting other children; and performing tasks such as child care, cooking, and errands. These behaviours were analyzed in the following personality dimensions: "nurturant-responsible" or "dependent-dominant." Nurturant-responsible personalities are characterized by more caring and sharing acts towards other children. The dependent-dominant personality involves fewer acts of caring and sharing towards other children, and more acts that asserted dominance over other children. Six teams of researchers were trained in the methodology and conducted intensive research in six contexts (see Table 6.1).

TABLE 6.1 Modes of Production and Child Personality: Six Cases

Culture	Location	Nurturant-Responsible (High Scores)/ Dependent-Dominant (Low Scores) Personality
Group A: Horticulture, Small-Scale Family Farming		
Gusii	Kenya	+1.14
Oaxaca	Mexico	+0.54
Tarong	Philippines	+0.48
Group B: Intensive Agricultural or Industrial		
Taira	Japan	−0.24
Rajputs	India	−0.75
Orchard Town	United States	−1.04

Source: Whiting and Whiting 1975:71.

The Gusii children of Kenya had the highest prevalence of a nurturant-responsible personality type, while the children in Orchard Town had the lowest. Orchard Town children had the highest prevalence of the dependent-dominant personality type. The range of variation in the prevalence of these dimensions followed a general pattern correlating with the economy. The six cultures fit into two general groups, economically and in terms of child tasks and personality development. "Group A" cultures (Kenya, Mexico, Philippines) all had more nurturant-responsible children. Their economies are similar: They are more reliant on horticulture and other forms of less intensive production. The economies of "Group B" cultures (Japan, India, and the United States) were based on either intensive agriculture or industry.

How does the mode of production influence child tasks and personality? The key underlying factor is differences in women's work roles. In Group A cultures, women are an important part of the labour force and spend much time working outside the home. In these cultures, children take on more family-supportive tasks and thereby develop personalities that are nurturant/responsible. When women work mainly in the home, as in Group B cultures, children have fewer tasks and less re-

Sibling caretaking, as shown here in Ghana, is a common task of older children cross-culturally, but especially so in pre-industrial societies.

sponsibility. They develop personalities that are more dependent/dominant. Gusii children were responsible for the widest range of tasks and at earlier ages than in any other culture in the study, often performing tasks that an Orchard Town mother does. While some children in all six cultures took care of other children, Gusii children (both boys and girls) spent the most time doing so. They also began taking on this responsibility at a very young age, between five and eight years old.

This study has implications for Western child development experts. In one direction, we can consider what happens when the dependent-dominant personality develops to an extreme level—into a **narcissistic** personality. A narcissist is someone who constantly seeks self-attention and self-affirmation, with no concern for other people's needs. The Western consumer-oriented economy supports the development of narcissism through its inculcation of identity formation through ownership of self-defining goods (clothing, electronics, cars) and access to self-defining services (vacations, therapists, fitness salons). The Six Cultures Study's findings suggest that involving children in more household responsibilities might result in less self-focused personality formation.

Informal Learning

Most of the world's children under age five spend these years within the family, learning informally from family members. In recent years, institutionalized care in daycare centres has increased in many parts of the world. Parents send their child to preschool as a substitute for family care while they are working, for social enrichment, or as a way to "fast-track" the child intellectually.

Children enrolled in daycare and early childhood programs in Canada in 1994–1995 were found to have a head start in school, including having better communication, learning, and math skills regardless of family income or mother's education level, according to a Statistics Canada study. As another researcher noted, kids who attended day care were taught to share cookies, not to be the Marlborough Man.

Toys and games also shape children's personalities. Among hunting peoples such as the Yanomami, young boys learn to be future hunters by shooting small arrows from small bows at small targets such as beetles. They learn to kill animals without sentimentality. In contrast, caring for animals as pets is a prominent part of child socialization in the West, where many animals are taboo as food. Some games, such as chess, teach strategic thinking that appears to be correlated with social-political patterns of hierarchy and obedience.

The media is another important area for child socialization and personality acquisition. Generations of Canadian children watched the "Polka Dot Door" and "Mr. Dressup," shows that attempt to break down gender and racial stereotypes. However, American cartoon shows are also aired on Canadian television. One study considered children's cartoon shows aired on American television in the 1980s (B. Williams 1991). Content analysis reveals two types of shows, one featuring interpersonal relationships aimed at little girls and one featuring battles aimed at little boys.

Formal Schooling

Universal primary education exists in most nations, but not all. For example, in Mali, one of the world's poorest

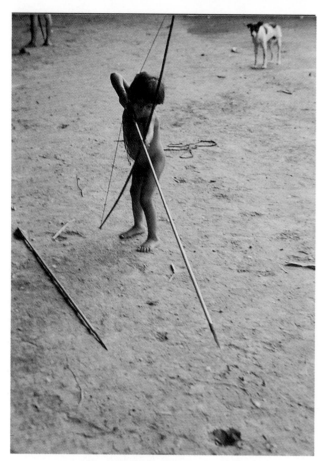

Yanomami boys acquire skills necessary for hunting and warfare at an early age through play.

countries, only 25 per cent of children attend primary school (United Nations Development Program 1994). Poorer children cross-culturally face more problems enrolling and remaining in school. In some countries, the school system is inadequate, with too few local schools available. In poor families, children are needed to work. The schooling experience is also diminished for the poor because malnourished and exhausted children have more difficulty concentrating during class. Their level of achievement is likely to be lower than better-off children because of economic factors. Teachers, however, may interpret their performance as a sign of "bad attitude," apathy, and laziness.

In Malawi, a poor nation of southern Africa, all children face obstacles in completing primary education, but it is especially difficult for girls (Davison and Kanyuka 1992). An ethnographic study of this situation included 80 students (40 boys and 40 girls) at two grade levels. It was conducted in four poor rural districts where girls' school participation rates were among the lowest and their drop-out rates the highest. Most of the children came from agricultural families. Both boys and girls face the same constraints in terms of the quality of the schools and teachers. Girls also have to contend with negative attitudes from male teachers about the value of schooling for them. This discouragement of their academic achievement in the schools is mirrored by their home situation, where parents indirectly discourage girls from valuing

Charles James Nowell, "Play Potlatches"

Charles James Nowell is a Kwakwaka'wakw man born in 1870 at Fort Rupert, in what is now British Columbia. He was interviewed in English in 1940.

When I was a boy we used to give potlatches of small canoes to imitate the potlatches of older people. I had small canoes made for me just the shape of the big ones. My second brother made some of them, and I paid other older people tobacco and things to make some others for me. When I have

enough to give my potlatch, I go around to all the boys of the other tribes at Fort Rupert. I call my own tribe boys to come in front of my house and to count these small canoes and put them in rows according to the rank of the fathers of the boys....

Our fathers and brothers teach us to give these potlatches, and help us do it, telling us all about what we should do to do it right. That is just like teaching what we should do when

we get grown up and give real potlatches. My older brothers were the ones who taught me, but they didn't come and watch us while we gave them. They only heard about it and how we did afterwards. When I come home, they tell me that is fine. They are the ones that started it—I wouldn't have done it if they hadn't started it—and they helped me all the time with my play potlatches.

Source: Hirschfelder 1995:103–104.

schooling and instead instill in them the values of domesticity. Girls are supposed to learn to assume the traditional roles of wife and mother. The combination of school systems that offer little in the way of creative learning experiences, home situations that are unsupportive of girls' achievement, and conservative political elements in the wider society combine powerfully to constrain both cognitive achievements and the attainment of independent, autonomous personalities among women. Tracking female students into domestic roles still characterizes formal education throughout much of the world, especially in conservative cultures. The students in these situations may experience conflicts about such tracking and resist it to varying degrees.

In Israel, all-girl Zionist-Orthodox boarding schools are aimed at strengthening the religiosity of girls and preparing them for family life. They also emphasize academic excellence, and the girls are highly motivated to achieve. The curriculum includes lectures, lessons, religious activities, and volunteer community work. Religious study excludes the canonic texts, promoting instead everyday religious practice and emphasis on morality, wifehood, child rearing, and purity. The strong emphasis on family roles conflicts with the simultaneous pressure for academic achievement. Some girls resolve the dilemma of career aspirations and achievement versus the domestic role by opting for career paths that will accommodate their family role, or by giving up further studies (Rapoport, Garb, and Penso 1995).

In school, children learn much about how they should behave and think, both formally through the curriculum and informally through clubs, peer pressure, and sports. Illustrations in textbooks may further socialize children into particular roles and personality patterns.

Adolescence and Identity

Puberty is a time in the human life cycle that occurs universally and involves a set of biological markers. In males, the voice deepens and facial and body hair appear; in females, menarche and breast development occur; in both males and females, pubic and underarm hair appear and sexual maturation is achieved. **Adolescence,** in contrast, is a culturally defined period of maturation from around the time of puberty until adulthood is at-

tained, usually marked by becoming a parent, getting married, or becoming economically self-sufficient.

Is Adolescence a Universal Life-Cycle Stage?

Some scholars say that all cultures define a period of adolescence. One comparative study using data from 186 societies indicated the universality of a culturally defined phase of adolescence (Schlegel 1995; Schlegel and Barry 1991). Cultures as diverse as the Navajo and the Trobriand Islanders, among others, have special terms comparable to the term "adolescent" for a person between puberty and marriage. Sociobiologists have generated a theory that views adolescence as a "training" for becoming a parent (Schlegel 1995:16).

In contrast to the sociobiological view, another perspective views adolescence as culturally constructed. Historical and anthropological studies of the life cycle question the universality of adolescence and its function as reproductive training. In many cultures, there is no recognized period of adolescence. In others, recognition of an adolescent phase is recent. Moroccan anthropologist Fatima Mernissi (1987), for example, states that adolescence was not a recognized life-cycle phase for females in Morocco until the late twentieth century. She says that "The idea of an adolescent unmarried woman is a completely new idea in the Muslim world, where previously you had only a female child and a menstruating woman who had to be married off immediately so as to prevent dishonorable engagement in premarital sex" (xxiv).

In different cultures, the length of the period of adolescence, or whether it exists at all, can be related to constructions of gender. In many horticultural or pastoral societies where men are valued as warriors, as among the Maasai, a lengthy period between childhood and adulthood is devoted to training in warfare and developing solidarity among males. Females, on the other hand, move directly from being a girl to being a wife. For example, a Maasai girl learns her adult roles while she is a child, assisting in the care of cattle and doing other tasks. In other cultures, females have long periods of separation between girlhood and womanhood, marked by seclusion from general society, during which they learn special skills and lore, and then re-emerge into society as marriageable (J. K. Brown 1978). Such evidence of variation seems to speak against any theory that assumes universality.

The fact that adolescence is found in many pre-industrial societies puts into question the explanation that adolescence is a by-product of industrial economies. A cultural materialist approach looks at the relationship between adolescence and the mode of production, suggesting that a prolonged period of adolescence is likely to be preparation for culturally valued adult roles as either workers, warriors, or reproducers. For example, the definition of adolescence for females in many pre-industrial societies, accompanied by years of training and seclusion, is found where adult females have high rates of participation in food production (J.K. Brown 1978). This correlation can be explained by the need to train young women for their adult roles. Likewise, certain areas of employment in industrialized societies, especially in most of the professions such as medicine and law and the upper echelons of the corporate world, require a university education. The many years of study can be considered a key part of the adolescent period preceding the assumption of adult roles.

A comparison of adolescence in pre-war Japan and post-war Japan demonstrates the emergence of a clearly defined period of adolescence in the latter period, a change related to economic transformations of that time (Hogan and Mochizuki 1988). Adolescence for most Japanese youth in contemporary Japan, especially for males, corresponds with a period of formal education in high school and college. This new pattern is consistent with the rapid development of a powerful corporate economy requiring university-trained employees. In Japan, female employment is less often full-time or as highly professionalized as that of males (Brinton 1993). They spend fewer years in formal schooling than males and get married at a younger age than males, meaning that they have a shorter period of adolescence.

During the latter half of the twentieth century, industrialization and economic globalization were accompanied by the spread of Western notions of adolescence among the middle and upper classes in countries around the world. The age at marriage has risen as young people attempt to finish their educations and find employment before starting a family (Xenos 1993). At the same time, clear class differences exist. Those who are poor tend to have shorter adolescent phases; they spend less time in formal education, and they are likely to become parents at younger ages.

Coming of Age and Gender Identity

Margaret Mead made famous the phrase "coming of age" in her book, *Coming of Age in Samoa* (1961 [1928]). It can refer generally to the period of adolescence or specifically to a ceremony or set of ceremonies that marks the boundaries of a period of adolescence. What are the psychological aspects of this phase of life when children become adults?

Among the Sambia, a highland New Guinea group, people do not believe that a young boy will "naturally" grow into a man (Herdt 1987). Instead, a boy's healthy maturation requires that he join an all-male initiation group. In this group, he becomes a partner of a senior male, who regularly transfers his semen to the youth orally. The Sambia believe that ingesting semen nourishes the youth and provides for his healthy growth. After a period in this initiation group, the youth will rejoin society and take up a heterosexual relationship and raise children.

Ceremonies that provide the transition from youth to adulthood often involve marking of the body in some way to impress the person undergoing it with a clear sense of gender and group identity. Such marking includes scarification, tattooing, and genital surgery. (A discussion of ritual and symbolic aspects of puberty rituals appears in Chapter 12.) In many societies, adolescent males undergo genital surgery that involves removal of part of the skin around the tip of the penis (see the Voices box on page 153). Without this operation, the boy would not be considered a full-fledged male.

For girls, the physical fact of menstruation is marked by rituals in some cultures; in others it is not noted publicly at all. In Turkey, and elsewhere in the Middle East, menstruation is not even mentioned to young girls, who are thus surprised and shocked at menarche (Delaney 1988:79). Turkish girls may therefore feel ashamed and embarrassed by menstruation. Their Islamic culture teaches them that menstruation is the result of Eve's disobedience against Allah. Eve allowed herself to be persuaded by Satan to eat a forbidden fruit, and so was punished by being made to bleed monthly. In contrast, elaborate feasts and celebrations for girls are held upon their first menstruation in South India, although not in the North (Miller 1997 [1981]). In the absence of studies on the psychological impact of these differences, one can only speculate at this point that being made the person of

Tepilit Ole Saitoti, "My Initiation as a Maasai Warrior"

Three days before the ceremony my head was shaved and I discarded all my belongings, such as my necklaces, garments, spear, and sword. I even had to shave my pubic hair....

I was summoned to the main cattle gate, in my hand a ritual cowhide from a cow that had been properly slaughtered during my naming ceremony.... I laid the hide down and a boy was ordered to pour ice-cold water, known as engare entolu (ax water), over my head. It dripped all over my naked body and I shook furiously. In a matter of seconds, I was summoned to sit down. A large crowd of boys and men formed a semicircle in front of me; women are not allowed to watch male circumcisions and vice-versa. That was the last thing I saw clearly. As soon as I sat down, the circumciser appeared, his knives at the ready. He spread my legs and said, "One cut," a pronouncement necessary to prevent the initiate from claiming that he had been taken by surprise. He splashed a white liquid, a ceremonial paint called enturoto, across my face. Almost immediately, I felt a spark of

pain under my belly as the knife cut through my penis' foreskin. I happened to choose to look in the direction of the operation. I continued to observe the circumciser's fingers working mechanically. The pain became numbness and my lower body felt heavy, as if I were weighed down by a heavy burden. After fifteen minutes or so, a man who had been supporting me from behind pointed at something, as if to assist the circumciser. I came to learn later that the circumciser's eyesight had been failing him and that my brothers had been mad at him because the operation had taken longer than was usually necessary. All the same, I remained pinned down until the operation was over. I heard a call for milk to wash the knives, which signaled the end, and soon the ceremony was over....

I was carried inside the house to my own bed to recuperate.... I stopped bleeding after about half an hour but soon was in intolerable pain. I was supposed to squeeze my organ and force blood to flow out of the wound, but no one had told me, so

the blood coagulated and caused unbearable pain. The circumciser was brought to my aid and showed me what to do, and soon the pain subsided.

In two weeks I was able to walk and was taken to join other newly circumcised boys far away from our settlement.... Our heads were shaved, we discarded our black cloaks and bird headdresses and emerged as newly shaven warriors, Irkeleani.

As long as I live, I will never forget the day my head was shaved and I emerged a man, a Maasai warrior. I felt a sense of control over my destiny so great that no words can accurately describe it.

Source: Saitoti 1986:67–71.

FOOD FOR THOUGHT

Have you gone through a ceremonial marking that has made you feel like a different person than you were before? If so, what was involved and how did you feel before and afterwards?

honour at a celebration would have positive effects on a girl's sense of self-esteem, whereas ignoring or linking menstruation with shamefulness would have the opposite effect.

The term **female circumcision** refers to a range of genital cutting practised on females, including the excision of part or all of the clitoris, part or all of the labia, and the least common practice, infibulation, stitching together of the vaginal entry leaving a small aperture for drainage of menstrual blood (Shell-Duncan and Hernlund 2000). These procedures are usually performed when the girl is between seven to fifteen years of age. Some form of genital cutting is most common in the Sahelian countries of Africa, from the west coast to the east coast.

It is also found in Egypt, in some groups of the Middle East (particularly among Bedu tribes), and among some Muslim groups in South and Southeast Asia. The distribution of some form of genital cutting encompasses many groups in which female labour participation is high, but others where it is not. In terms of religion, genital cutting is often associated with people who are Muslim, but not always. In Ethiopia, for example, some Christian groups practise it. As yet, no one has presented a clear explanation for the regional and social distribution of female genital cutting.

Many young girls have been reported to look forward to the ceremony so that they will then be freed of having to do childhood tasks and can take on the more respected

Cultural Relativism, Human Rights, and Female Circumcision

Indigenous views supporting female genital cutting say that, like male circumcision, it is a necessary step towards full womanhood (Ahmadu 2000). It is required for a woman to be considered marriageable in societies in which marriage is the normal path for women. Fathers say that an uncircumcised daughter is unmarriageable and will bring no brideprice. Aesthetically, supporters claim that removal of the labia makes a woman beautiful and, removing "male" parts, makes her a complete woman.

The Western view, which is increasingly shared by many people who traditionally practised what many Western health experts and feminists term "female genital mutilation" (FGM), is that it is both a sign of low female status and an unnecessary cause of women's suffering. Feminists worldwide claim that cutting of the female genitals constitutes a violation of basic human rights and is a patriarchal "sado-ritual" that should be banned everywhere (Daly 1978).

Female circumcision has been linked with a range of health risks, including those related to the surgery itself (shock, infection), and future genito-urinary complications. Infibulation causes scarring and malformation of the vaginal canal that obstruct delivery and cause lacerations to the mother and even death of the infant and mother. The practice of having a new bride's husband "open" her, using a stick or knife to loosen the aperture, is both painful and an opportunity for infection. After giving birth, a woman is usually reinfibulated, and the process begins again. Health experts have suggested that the repeated trauma to the woman's vaginal area could increase the risk of contracting HIV/AIDS. The Western view argues that the effects on a woman's sexual enjoyment of both clitoridectomy and infibulation are highly negative, that clitoral orgasm, for one thing, is no longer possible.

Fuambai Ahmadu, born and raised in Washington, D.C., and descended from a powerful Kono lineage in Sierra Leone, travelled to Sierra Leone in 1991 with her mother and several other family members for what she refers to as her "circumcision." In a powerful and insightful chapter, she describes Kono culture as gender-complementary, with strong roles for women. She also describes her initiation and subsequent reflections. While the physical pain was excruciating (in spite of the use of anesthetics), "the positive aspects have been much more profound" (Ahmadu 2000:306). Through the initiation she became part of a powerful female world. Her discussion addresses the effects on health and sexuality and argues that Westerners have exaggerated these issues by focusing on infibulation (which she says is rarely practised) rather than the less extreme forms. If, however, global pressures against the practice continue, she would go along with it and support "ritual without cutting" (308).

CRITICAL THINKING QUESTIONS

Why is female circumcision, in the eyes of many human rights groups, a more controversial practice than male circumcision?

Where do you stand on this issue and why?

What information on female circumcision, other than the material presented in this chapter, have you gathered in order to form your opinion?

---

roles of an adult woman. In other cases, anthropologists have reported hearing statements of resistance. Among the Ariaal, pastoralists of northern Kenya, a new bride undergoes circumcision on the day of her wedding (Fratkin 1998:60). The Ariaal practice involves removal of the clitoris and part or all of the labia majora. At one wedding, a bride-to-be was heard to say: "I don't want to do this, I don't even know this man, please don't make me do this." The older women told her to be strong and that it would soon be over. The bride-to-be is expected to emerge in a few hours to greet the guests and join the wedding ceremony.

In 1999, Senegal joined Sudan, Somalia, Kenya, Togo, Ghana, and Burkina Faso in banning female genital cutting. Fewer issues have forced the questioning of cultural relativism more than female genital mutilation (see the Critical Thinking box above).

Sexual Identity

Puberty is the time when sexual maturity is achieved and sexual orientation becomes more apparent. Anthropologists, unlike psychologists, have tended to avoid arguments about whether sexual preferences are

New Legal Rights for Gay and Lesbian Couples in Canada

Affirming equal rights for gays and lesbians in provincial and federal law has been a long process. Gay and lesbian organizations emerged in the 1960s, promoting varied agendas including legal reforms, civil rights through human rights codes, and social support. In 1969, the federal government amended the Legal Code to exempt from prosecution two consenting adults engaged in sexual activity. Decriminalization was accompanied with Prime Minister Trudeau's comment that "the state has no place in the bedrooms of the nation." Nevertheless, in the more right-wing climate of the 1970s and 1980s, city bathhouses were raided in Toronto, and their occupants arrested and charged as "found-ins." In 1986, the Ontario government added "sexual orientation" to its human rights code.

In October 1999, the Ontario legislature granted new rights to gay and lesbian couples. Bill 5 gives same-sex couples the same rights and responsibilities as heterosexual common-law couples. The new law follows a supreme court decision that ordered the province to end discriminatory treatment of gays and lesbians under the Family Law Act. The law amends 67 provincial statutes to add the new category of same-sex partner to every statute that refers to common-law spouses, without changing the legal definition of marriage or spouse. Critics of the bill argue that gay and lesbian couples should have been included in the definition of "spouse"—not separated into a new class. In July 2002, the Ontario courts ordered the provincial government to recognize same-sex marriage. It remains to be seen how provincial and federal laws will respond to this and other legal challenges.

FOOD FOR THOUGHT

What effect do you think legal changes will have on attitudes towards same-sex relationships and sexual identity in your community?

---

biologically determined (somehow mandated by genetic or hormonal factors) or culturally constructed and learned. Biological anthropologist Melvin Konner (1989) argues that both factors play a part, but simultaneously warns us that no one has a simple answer to the question of "who becomes gay":

> Neither science nor art has yet produced a single answer. Yet perhaps that in itself is the answer: that anything so complicated and various and interesting could have a single origin seems wrongheaded. Socrates and Tennessee Williams, Sappho and Adrienne Rich, to take only four people, representing only two cultures, seem so certain to have come to their homosexuality in four such different ways as to make generalizations useless. (60)

Lesbian feminist poet Adrienne Rich's (1980) approach combines attention to both biology and culture in her view that all people are biologically bisexual, but that patriarchal cultures try to mold them into being heterosexual. This "compulsory heterosexual project," she says, will never be completely successful in overcoming innate bisexuality, and so some people will always opt out of the heterosexual mold and become either homosexual or bisexual.

Anthropologists generally examine how cultural context shapes the form, interpretation, and expression of same-sex sexuality, emphasizing socialization and childhood experiences as the most powerful factors shaping sexual orientation. Support for this position comes from a study in the United States that later-born children are more likely to be homosexual than earlier-born children (Blanchard et al. 1995). This result applies more strongly for gay men, about whom more studies have been conducted. For lesbians, fewer studies are available, but those available indicate that lesbians tend to be later-born and to have more sisters than heterosexual women. In terms of birth order and socialization of sexual orientation in the United States, a hypothesis worth investigating is whether parents unconsciously promote "girl"-like behaviour in the last-born when they have a string of sons in order to have a child to fulfill female roles, and the "boy"-like behaviour in a last-born girl who follows several sisters.

Another indication of the relatively weak role of biology is that many people change their sexual orientation more than once during their lifetime. In the Gulf state of Oman, the *xanith* is a male who becomes more like a female, wearing female clothing and having sex with other men, often for several years, but then reverting to a standard male role by marrying a woman and having children (Wikan 1977). Similar fluidity during the life cycle between homosexuality and heterosexuality occurs among Sambia males (Herdt 1987). These examples indicate that a person can assume different gender identities over time.

No matter what theoretical perspective one takes on the causes of sexual preferences, it is clear that homosexuals are discriminated against in many cultural contexts where heterosexuality is the norm of mainstream society. Homosexuals in North America have been the frequent victims of violence, problems in the workplace, housing discrimination, and legal bias (see the Multiple Cultural Worlds box). They often suffer from being stigmatized by parents, other students, and the wider society. The psychological damage done to their self-esteem is reflected in the fact that homosexual youths in North America have substantially higher suicide rates than heterosexual youths.

Many cultures explicitly allow for more than two strictly defined genders and permit the expression of varied forms of sexual orientation without societal condemnation. Most "third genders" are neither purely "male" nor "female," according to a particular culture's definition of male and female. They are ways for "males" to cross gender lines and assume more "female" behaviours, personality characteristics, and dress. Parallel institutionalized third gender roles that allow "females" to cross over into "male" territory have been less documented in the anthropological literature.

The **berdache** constitutes an accepted and admired third gender role in many First Nations groups. A berdache is a male (in terms of genital configuration) who opts to wear female clothing, may engage in sexual relations with a man, and performs female tasks such as basket-weaving and pottery-making. Current research suggests that the berdache is a better example of gender crossing than of institutionalized same-sex sexuality. Some people say that parents, especially if they have several sons, choose one to become a berdache. Others say that a boy who shows interest in typically female activities or who likes to wear female clothing is then allowed to become a berdache. Such a child is a focus of pride for the family, never disappointment or stigma. The impact of Euro-American culture on the institution of the berdache was negative, however. Native Americans became aware of Euro-American disapproval and derision of the berdache (Roscoe 1991), and it was suppressed as a cultural pattern. In the 1980s, as Native American cultural pride resurged, so has the open presence of the berdache.

First Nations in general continue to be more tolerant of homosexuality than mainstream Euro-American society (see the Multiple Cultural Worlds box).

In India, the counterpart of the berdache is termed a **hijira**. Hijiras dress and act like women, but are neither truly male nor truly female (Nanda 1990). Many hijiras were born with male genitals, or with genitals that were not clearly male or female. Hijiras have the traditional right to visit the home of a newborn, inspect its genitals and claim it for their group if the genitals are neither clearly male nor female. Some evidence exists that hijiras may forcibly claim or steal babies in order to increase their population. Hijiras born with male genitals may opt to go through an initiation ceremony that involves cutting off of the penis and testicles. Hijiras roam large cities of India, earning a living by begging from store to

A Zuni berdache, We'wha, wearing the ceremonial costume of Zuni women and holding a pottery bowl with sacred cornmeal.

Culture Contact and the Native American Berdache

Throughout decades of contact between Euro-American colonizers, including Christian missionaries, and Native American cultures, the institution of the berdache was the focus of disapproval and ridicule by the outsiders (Roscoe 1991). Under the influence of the negative reactions of the Euro-Americans, many **Native American** cultures began to suppress their berdache traditions in favour of "mainstream" values and practices that promote less gender fluidity.

In the 1980s, as Native American cultural pride began to grow, the open presence of the berdache, and the **amazon,** or a woman who takes on male roles and behaviours, has returned. Native American cultures in general remain accepting of gender role fluidity and the contemporary concept of being gay:

> Younger gay Indians, upon coming out to their families, will sometimes have an elderly relative who takes them aside and tells them about the berdache tradition. A part-Choctaw gay man recalls that his full-blooded Choctaw grandmother realized he was gay and it was totally acceptable.... This respectful attitude eliminates the stress felt by families that harbor homophobia. (225)

FOOD FOR THOUGHT

Do you think that changes have occurred in Euro-American attitudes towards people who change their gender or towards gay people as a result of coming into contact with more tolerant First Nations peoples? Why or why not?

---

store (and threatening to lift their skirts if not given money). Because women rarely sing or dance in public, the hijiras play an important role as performers in public events, especially as dancers or musicians. Given this public role and the hijira's association with prostitution, people in the mainstream do not admire or respect hijiras, and no family would be delighted to hear that their son has decided to become a hijira. In contrast to the berdache among First Nations peoples, the hijiras form a separate group from mainstream society.

In Thailand, three basic gender categories have long co-existed: *phuuchai* (male), *phuuying* (female), and *kathoey* (transvestite/transsexual/hermaphrodite) (Morris 1994b; P. Van Esterik 2000). Like the berdache and hijira, a kathoey is "originally" a male who crosses into the body, personality, and dress defined as female. Kathoeys represent a "third gender," and may be heterosexual, homosexual, or bisexual in orientation. In contemporary Thailand, sexual orientation does not confer a fixed gender identity, nor is it legally regulated. The discourse on HIV/AIDS is shaping the way sexual identities are talked about and labelled, and terms derived from English are appearing. For example, the words for lesbian include *thom* (from the word *tomboy*) and *dee* (from *lady*). As in many parts of the world, reflecting the widespread presence of patriarchal norms, lesbianism is a more suppressed form of homosexuality than male homosexuality, and there has been less research on women's same-sex relationships.

Adult Personality

Adulthood for most of the world's people means the likelihood of some form of marriage (or long-term domestic relationship) and having children. This section discusses how selected aspects of adulthood, such as parenthood and aging, affect people's personality and psychological status.

Becoming a Parent

More studies have been done of how cultures shape maternal roles than paternal roles. Biologically, a woman becomes a mother when she gives birth to an infant: She is transformed from a pregnant woman to a mother. Like adolescence, the culturally defined and shaped phase of motherhood varies in terms of its beginning, duration, and meaning. In some cultures, a woman is transformed into a mother as soon as she thinks she is pregnant. In others, she becomes a mother and is granted full maternal status only when she delivers an infant of the "right" sex, a male in much of northern India.

In pre-industrial cultures, becoming a mother occurs in the context of supportive family members. Some cultures promote prenatal practices such as abiding by particular food taboos. Such rules make the pregnant woman feel that she has some role in helping to make the pregnancy turn out right. In the West, medical experts during the twentieth century have increasingly defined the prenatal period as an important phase of becoming a mother, and they have issued many scientific and medical rules for potential parents (Browner and Press 1995; 1996). Pregnant women are urged to seek prenatal examinations; be under the regular supervision of a doctor who monitors the growth and development of the fetus; follow particular dietary and exercise guidelines; and undergo a range of tests such as ultrasound scanning. Some anthropologists think that such medicalized pregnancies lead to the greater likelihood of post-partum depression among mothers as a result of their lack of control in the birthing process.

Cultural definitions of what constitutes "motherhood" change over time, providing an argument against fixed, innate features of the role. Maxine Margolis (1984) traced changes in how the maternal role was defined in the United States from the late 1700s to the present. The amplification or constriction of women's maternal and domestic roles was a clear function of the wider economic demands for female labour. During World War II, when many men were away in the armed forces, women's motherhood roles were downplayed as they replaced men in the factories. When the war ended and the men returned, public rhetoric exhorted women to return to the home and to child care duties. The 1950s brought the creation of a highly intensified domestic role for mothers in North America, involving time-consuming devotion to housekeeping and child rearing.

Becoming a father is usually less socially noted than becoming a mother. The practice of **couvade** is an interesting exception to this generalization. Couvade refers to "a variety of customs applying to the behaviour of fathers during the pregnancies of their wives and during and shortly after the births of their children" (Broude 1988:902). The father may take to his bed before, during, or after the delivery. He may also experience pain and exhaustion during and after the delivery. More common is a pattern of couvade that involves a set of prohibitions and prescriptions for male behaviour. For example, an expectant father may not hunt a certain animal, eat cer-

An Aka father and his son. Aka fathers are affectionate caretakers of infants and small children. Compared to mothers, they are more likely to kiss and hug children.

tain foods, cut objects, or engage in extramarital sex. Early theories of why the couvade exists relied on Freudian interpretations that men were seeking cross-sex identification (with the female role) in contexts where the father role was weak or fathers were absent. Cross-cultural examination of the existence of couvade indicates the opposite: Couvade occurs in societies where paternal roles in child care are prominent. This interpretation views couvade as one phase of men's participation in parenting: Their good behaviour as expectant fathers helps ensure a good delivery for the baby. Another interpretation of couvade is that it offers support for the mother. In Estonia, a folk belief is that a woman's birth pains will be less if her husband helps by taking some of them on himself (Oinas 1993).

Most cultural anthropologists agree that child care is predominately the responsibility of women worldwide—but not universally. While breastfeeding is exclusively a female act of nurturance and care, other aspects of child care can be taken over by caretakers besides the biological mother. In many cultures of the South Pacific, child care is shared across families, and women breastfeed other women's babies. Paternal involvement varies as well. Among the Aka pygmy hunter-gatherers of Central Africa, paternal child care is prominent (Hewlett 1991). The Aka are an exceptional case, perhaps even unique, in comparison with other societies because of the high involvement of fathers in child care. Aka fathers are intimate, affectionate, and helpful, spending about half of their time each day holding or within arm's reach of their infants. While holding their infants, they are more likely to hug and kiss them than mothers are. Good fatherhood among the Aka means being affectionate towards children and assisting the mother when her workload is heavy. Among the Aka, a prevailing ideology of gender equality exists and violence against women is unknown; the high level of paternal involvement in child care probably helps explain this pattern.

Middle Age

Perceptions of the boundaries of "middle age" have changed in industrial countries as the life span has increased. A generation ago, people in their thirties were considered middle aged, while now a turning point is more likely to be the fortieth birthday. One possible reason behind this relatively new emphasis on 40 as a turning point is that it reflects the current midpoint of a "typical" lifespan for a middle-class North American.

Menopause is a significant event of middle age for women in some, but not all, cultures. A comparative study examined differences in perception and experience of menopause among Maya women of Mexico and rural Greek women (Beyene 1989). Among the Maya women, menopause is not a time of stress or crisis. They associate menstruation with illness and look forward to the time when they no longer have menses. Menopause among these women is not associated with physical or emotional symptoms. In fact, none of the women reported hot flashes or cold sweats. Among the Maya women, menopause brought no associated role changes. In contrast, Greek women in the village of Stira recognized menopause as a natural phenomenon that all women experience and one that causes temporary discomfort, *exapi,* which is a phase of hot flashes especially at night, that may last about a year. The women did not think *exapi* was terribly serious, certainly nothing worthy of medical attention. Postmenopausal women emphasized the relief and freedom they felt. Postmenopausal women can go into cafés by themselves, something they

would never do otherwise, and they can participate more fully in church ceremonies.

In Canada, debates about surgical menopause and the safety of hormone replacement therapy confirm the medicalization of an event that is physiologically universal, but that carries diverse cultural meanings. Patricia Kaufert (1986) studied the transition to menopause in women in Manitoba, and found that the rate of estrogen use was low, and that it was used intermittently and possibly with reluctance. These variable findings raise the question of how much perceived suffering from menopause in North America is **iatrogenic,** that is, an affliction caused by medical definition or intervention.

The Senior Years

The "senior" life cycle stage may be a particular development of contemporary human society because, like most other mammals, our early ancestors rarely lived beyond their reproductive years (Brooks and Draper 1998 [1991]). The category of the aged, like several other life-cycle stages discussed, is variably recognized, defined, and valued. In many cultures, elders are highly revered, and their life experiences are valued as the greatest wis-

Much research indicates that people living in retirement homes benefit psychologically from having animal companions.

dom. In others, aged people become burdens to their families and to society. In general, the status and well-being of the elderly cross-culturally is higher where they continue to live with their families (Lee and Kezis 1979). This pattern is more likely to be found in pre-industrial societies than in highly industrialized ones, where the elderly are increasingly experiencing a shift to "retirement homes." In such age-segregated settings, people have to create new social roles and ties and find new ways of gaining self-esteem and personal satisfaction. Being allowed to have pets seems to have a positive effect on people's adjustment to retirement homes (Savishinsky 1991).

The Final Passage: Death and Dying

It may be that no one in any culture welcomes death, unless he or she is in very poor health and suffering greatly. Contemporary North America, with its dependence on medical technology, appears to be particularly active in resisting death, often at very high costs. In many other cultures, a greater degree of acceptance is common. A study of attitudes towards death and dying among Alaskan Inuit revealed a pervasive feeling that people are active participants in their death rather than passive victims (Trelease 1975). The usual pattern for a person near death is that the person calls friends and neighbours to-

gether, is given a Christian sacrament, and then, within a few hours, dies. The author comments, "I do not suggest that everyone waited for the priest to come and then died right away. But the majority who did not die suddenly did some degree of planning, had some kind of formal service or celebration of prayers and hymns and farewells" (35).

In any culture, loss of a loved one is accompanied by some form of sadness, grief, and mourning. The ways of expressing such emotions vary from extended and public grieving that is expressively emotional to no visible sign of grief being presented. The latter pattern is the norm in Bali, Indonesia, where people's faces remain impassive at funerals and no vocal lamenting occurs (Rosenblatt, Walsh, and Jackson 1976). Different modes of expression of a universal experience of loss might affect the actual experience of loss itself (Brison and Leavitt 1995). Does highly expressive public mourning contribute to a "faster" healing process, or does a quietly repressed sense of grief play an adaptive role, as Scheper-Hughes (1993) argues for the poor of Brazil? The domain of emotional suffering surrounding death is a relatively new area of study for psychological anthropologists, one that promises to provide intriguing insights. The expression of grief surrounding death is also of interest to anthropologists who study religion (Bowen 1998). Research shows that beliefs about the dead, and how the dead may affect the living, shape people's experience of death and mourning.

How does culture shape personality during infancy and childhood?

Human psychological development begins from the moment of birth, if not before. Margaret Mead was a pioneer in showing how infant care practices such as breastfeeding, how the baby is held, and how much contact the infant has with others, can affect personality formation, including gender identity. Her study of the Arapesh, Mundugumor, and Tchambuli peoples of New Guinea indicates that gender is a largely "plastic" (or malleable) aspect of human personality. Cross-cultural studies show that children's work roles and family roles correspond to personality patterns. Informal and formal learning, depending on cultural context, shapes young people's sense of identity.

How does culture shape personality during the transition from childhood to adulthood?

Adolescence, a culturally defined time around puberty and before adulthood, varies cross-culturally from being nonexistent to being long in duration and involving detailed training and elaborate ceremonies. "Coming of age" ceremonies sometimes involve bodily cutting, which denotes membership of the initiate in a particular gender. In contrast to the sharp distinction between "male" and "female" laid out in Western science and folk belief, many cultures have longstanding traditions of third gender identities, most prominently for males or people of indeterminate biological sex markers, to become more like females in those cultures.

How does culture shape personality during adulthood?

Following the fact that more women tend to be more involved in child care than males, cultures generally provide more in the way of enculturation of females for this role. In nonindustrial societies, learning about motherhood is embedded in other aspects of life and knowledge about birthing and child care is shared among women. In industrialized cultures, science and medicine play a large role in defining the maternal role. This change reduces women's autonomy and fosters their dependence on external, non-kin-based structures.

The senior years in nonindustrialized societies are shorter, in general, than in industrialized societies in which lifespan tends to be longer. Elder men and women in nonindustrial cultures are treated with respect, considered to know the most, and retain a strong sense of their place in the culture. Increasingly in industrialized societies, elderly people are removed from their families and spend many years in age-segregated institutions. This transition tends to have negative implications for their psychological well-being.

Core Concepts

adolescence, p. 151
amazon, p. 157
berdache, p. 156
couvade, p. 158

cultural configuration, p. 143
culture of poverty, p. 144
enculturation, p. 142

female circumcision, p. 153
hijira, p. 156
iatrogenic, p. 159
image of the limited good, p. 144

narcissistic, p. 149
national character studies, p. 144
personality, p. 142
puberty, p. 151

Suggested Readings

Evalyn Blackwood, ed., *The Many Faces of Homosexuality: Anthropological Approaches to Homosexual Behavior*. New York: Harrington Park Press, 1986. This text contains chapters on anthropological writings about lesbianism, and case studies of ritualized male homosexuality in Irian Jaya, the berdache in North America, hijiras of India, lesbian relationships in Lesotho, and Mexican male homosexual interaction patterns in public.

Jean Briggs, *Never in Anger*. Cambridge, MA: Harvard University Press, 1970. This classic study explores the ethnographer's experience with the Inuit of the Canadian Arctic through a perceptive and reflective examination of family life.

Jean Briggs, *Inuit Morality Play*. New Haven, CN: Yale University Press, 1998. A wonderful introduction to the use of psychoanalytic anthropology, this book details the "dramas" in the life of a three-year-old Inuit girl. (Winner of the Boyer Prize in psychoanalytic anthropology for 1999).

Michael Moffatt, *Coming of Age in New Jersey: College and American Culture*. New Brunswick, NJ: Rutgers University Press, 1991. Based on a year's participant observation in a college dormitory in a university in the eastern United States, this study presents insights on sexuality, race relations, and individualism.

Mimi Nichter, *What Girls and Their Parents Say about Dieting*. Cambridge, MA: Harvard University Press, 2000. The author collected and analyzed interview data with adolescent girls in the United States focusing on girls' perceptions of their weight, their attachment to dieting, and influences of their mothers' views and comments on weight.

Richard Parker, *Bodies, Pleasures, and Passions: Sexual Culture in Contemporary Brazil*. Boston: Beacon Press, 1991. This ethnographic study of contemporary sexual culture in Brazil addresses such topics as sexual socialization, bisexuality, sadomasochism, AIDS, prostitution, samba, the symbolism of breasts, courting, and the Carnaval.

 Your *Cultural Anthropology*, Second Canadian Edition Media Edition CD-ROM contains many Web sites relevant to this chapter. Use it to explore the Web and to expand your knowledge of anthropology.

Chapter 7

Illness and Healing

164

Mentawai healers treat a woman suffering from a toothache on Siberut Island, Indonesia.

Key Questions

What does medical anthropology contribute to understanding illness cross-culturally?

What does medical anthropology contribute to understanding healing systems cross-culturally?

How are illness and healing changing during increasing globalization?

*P*rimatologist Jane Goodall witnessed a polio epidemic among the chimpanzees she was studying in Tanzania (Foster and Anderson 1978:33–34). A group of healthy animals watched a stricken member try to reach the feeding area, but did not help him. Another badly paralyzed chimpanzee was simply left behind when the group moved on. Humans also sometimes resort to isolation and abandonment, as seen in the traditional Inuit practice of leaving aged and infirm people behind in the cold; the stigmatization of HIV/AIDS victims; and the ignoring of the homeless mentally ill in North American cities. Compared to our nonhuman primate relatives, however, humans have created more complex and variable ways of interpreting health problems and highly creative methods of preventing and curing them.

Since the 1970s, medical anthropology has been one of the fastest growing areas of inquiry in all of anthropology's four fields. From the perspective of cultural anthropology, medical anthropology encompasses five major foci: (1) the interaction of biological and social factors in disease causation; (2) the analysis of Western and non-Western health systems; (3) illness and healing as systems of meaning; (4) the political economy of health; and (5) the application of anthropological knowledge to improving health care (Joralemon 1999). This chapter addresses each of these areas, in addition to examining how contemporary globalization changes patterns of illness and healing.

Nature, Culture, and the Distribution of Illness

The **ecological/epidemiological approach** examines how aspects of the natural environment and social environment interact to cause illness. For example, in learning about an infestation of hookworm in a village in China, researchers discovered that only rice cultivators had the disease because they worked the padi fields where night soil (human waste) was used as a fertilizer. Thus, environment and work were causally related. In their study of Inuit living along the west coast of Hudson's Bay, Kaufert and O'Neil explored how the epidemiological language of "risk" with regard to neonatal mortality was used to justify a policy change requiring pregnant women to be evacuated to southern hospitals to give birth (Kaufert and O'Neil 1990).

This section on culture and disease occurrence focuses on forms of infectious disease. First, we look at what are called "the new infectious diseases," especially HIV/AIDS. Next, we look at how European colonialism spread certain infectious diseases around the world. Last, we consider how current practices in international development that affect the environment in turn contribute to the spread of old and new infectious diseases.

The New Infectious Diseases

The 1950s brought hope that infectious diseases were being controlled through Western scientific advances such as antibiotic drugs, vaccines against childhood diseases, and improved technology for sanitation. In North America, deaths from infections common in the late nineteenth and early twentieth centuries were

Women working in padi fields near Jinghong, China. Agricultural work done in standing water increases the risk of hookworm infection.

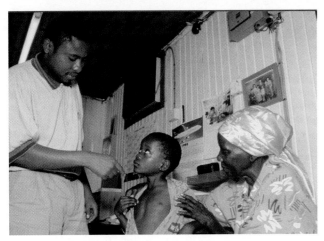

A woman takes her eight-year-old grandson who has HIV/AIDS to a clinic in Dar es Salaam, Tanzania. Throughout the world, increasing numbers of children are infected and are, at the same time, orphans because their parents have died of the disease.

no longer major threats in the 1970s. In tropical countries, pesticides lowered rates of malaria by controlling the mosquito populations. Since the 1980s, however, confidence that infectious diseases have been controlled has been shaken. Besides the spread of the HIV/AIDS epidemic, another challenge is presented by the fact that many infectious microbes have reappeared in forms that are resistant to known methods of prevention and treatment. New contexts for exposure and contagion are being created through increased international travel and migration, expansion of populations into previously uninhabited forest areas, changing sexual behaviour, and overcrowding in cities. Several new and re-emerging diseases are caused by unsafe technological developments. For example, the introduction of soft contact lenses has caused eye infections from the virus *acanthamebiasis*. In the early 1980s, many women in North America were diagnosed with a new disease, toxic shock syndrome, caused by a bacterial toxin possibly related to dioxins, a by-product of the chlorine bleaching process used to bleach tampons.

Many medical anthropologists are contributing their expertise to understanding the causes for and distribution of the new infectious diseases through studying social patterns and cultural practices. Research about HIV/AIDS addresses factors such as intravenous drug use, sexual behaviour, and condom use among different groups and how intervention programs could be better designed and targeted (see the Critical Thinking box).

Colonialism and Disease

Anthropologists have applied the ecological/epidemiological approach to the study of the impaired health and survival of indigenous peoples as a result of colonial contact. A basic question is how the introduction of European *pathogens* (disease-producing organisms) varies on the basis of size of the indigenous populations involved (Larsen and Milner 1994). Overall, findings about the effects of Western colonial contact are negative, from the worst examples being quick and outright extermination of indigenous peoples, to other groups showing resilience within drastically changed conditions.

In the Western hemisphere, European colonialism brought a dramatic decline in the indigenous populations they contacted, although disagreements exist about the numbers involved (Joralemon 1982). Medical anthropologists have tried to estimate, in coordination with archaeologists and colonial historians, the role of disease in depopulation compared with other factors such as warfare, harsh labour practices, and general cultural disruption, and to discover which diseases were most important. Research along these lines indicates that the precontact New World was largely free of the major European infectious diseases of smallpox, measles and typhus, and perhaps also syphilis, leprosy, and malaria. The exposure of indigenous peoples to these infectious diseases, therefore, was likely to have a massive impact, given the people's complete lack of resistance. One analyst compared contact to a "biological war":

> Smallpox was the captain of the men of death in that war, typhus fever the first lieutenant, and measles the second lieutenant. More terrible than the conquistadores on horseback, more deadly than sword and gunpowder, they made the conquest by the whites a walkover as compared to what it would have been without their aid. They were the forerunners of civilization, the companions of Christianity, the friends of the invader. (Ashburn 1947:98, quoted in Joralemon 1982:112)

This quotation emphasizes the importance of the three major diseases in Latin American colonial history: smallpox, typhus, and measles. A later arrival, cholera,

HIV/AIDS and Medical Anthropology

Between 1981, when AIDS was first identified, and 2002 the epidemic has infected over 58 million people, killing 22 million of them. Of the people living with HIV/AIDS, 95% live in developing countries. Few anthropologists have the clinical training to relieve pain or the laboratory experience to develop drugs and vaccines. But while clinical research may produce new treatments for symptoms, it cannot address the suffering of people with HIV/AIDS. Medical anthropologists look at HIV/AIDS cases within the larger matrix of culture, history, and political economy, the domain of anthropology.

What role do medical anthropologists play in the fight against HIV/AIDS? They bring special observational methods to HIV/AIDS research teams, often living among people with HIV/AIDS in order to understand barriers to HIV/AIDS prevention and treatment. Ultimately, medical anthropologists help make prevention and treatment programs more appropriate to the local context and language, and thus more effective. They combine qualitative and quantitative methods to explore complex and sensitive issues such as the interaction between gender, body image, and sexuality. They study the links between individual practices, cultural systems, and the larger political and economic forces shaping the disease. For example, this holistic approach has been effective in showing how AIDS relates to poverty.

The following examples show the kind of issues anthropologists are exploring in HIV/AIDS research, particularly on the topics of local perception of disease and on improving prevention and treatment programs.

- In the late 1980s, when HIV/AIDS was first recognized in Haiti, many Haitians thought it was a "disease of the city," contracted through sexual intercourse, or a "jealousy sickness" brought on one poor person by another through magic (Farmer 1990). The first explanation emphasizes the conventional biomedical definition of HIV/AIDS as an infectious disease; the second speaks to the Haitians' recognition of the social, political, and economic influences that render particular individuals or groups susceptible to illnesses of all kinds.

- San Jose prostitutes also recognize HIV/AIDS as an infectious disease, but locate it as part of a complex of contagion that includes drug abuse, diabetes, and violence (Downe 1997). While they are ready to embrace biomedicine—specifically "germs"—as a way to explain this contagion, they refuse to be defined as the vectors of the disease.

- A study assessing attitudes towards condom use among White, African American, and Hispanic respondents in the United States (Bowen and Trotter 1995) found that Whites were more likely to use condoms, followed by Hispanics, with lowest use among African Americans. Across all groups, people with "main partners" compared to "casual partners" were more likely to use condoms, as were older people and people classified as having a higher level of personal assertiveness. Recommendations for increasing condom usage include targeted self-awareness programs and assertiveness training, especially for younger people in casual relationships.

- Dennis Willms, a medical anthropologist from McMaster University, has worked in Kenya, Uganda, Malawi, and South Africa helping to develop HIV/AIDS prevention and intervention programs based on qualitative ethnographic research. In Uganda, research demonstrated that the reasons many long-distance truck drivers have unsafe sex are related to poverty, marriage practices, and fatalism. Educational intervention on HIV/AIDS for traditional healers in Zimbabwe and Malawi helped faith communities provide more supportive care in their communities (Higginbotham, Willms, and Sewankambo 2001).

- Even preventive programs that emphasize social conditions can be ineffective in practice if bureaucracies stigmatize and target marginal groups, especially low-caste and ethnic minority sex workers. Stacey Pigg (2001) learned from researching HIV/AIDS prevention programs in Nepal that groups working on AIDS prevention and treatment operate within political contexts which do not challenge power relations that perpetuate patterns of ill health.

- Research on HIV infections among intravenous cocaine users in Montreal and Vancouver demonstrated that needle exchange programs alone cannot stem the spread of HIV. By integrating qualitative participant observation methods into the substance abuse and HIV prevention studies, anthropologist Philippe Bourgois and epidemiologist Julie Bruneau (2000) were able to show the broader social and economic context of needle exchange programs for street addicts in Montreal and Vancouver. Bourgois likens the Canadian drug policy to abusive parents who alternatively whip and pamper their children.

CRITICAL THINKING QUESTIONS

Many Canadian medical anthropologists have been involved in HIV/AIDS research in Canada and internationally, including some cited above. Look up the work of Stacey Pigg, Pamela Downe, Richard Lee, Dennis Willms, and Lynn Morrison in the library or on the Web.

What concepts and skills have medical anthropologists brought to interdisciplinary health teams at home and internationally?

"Being Alive Well" in Whapmagoostui

The Cree word *miyupimaatisiiu* translates as "being alive well" and encompasses practices of Cree daily living such as hunting, eating the right foods, keeping warm, and balancing human relationships. Naomi Adelson's research (2000) with the Whapmagoostui Cree living along the Great Whale River in northern Quebec demonstrated that understanding health means understanding what it means to be Cree, as her informants explain:

> Twenty years ago, I was sick enough to be in the hospital for two years and I have lost a lot of my miyupimaatisiiun because of my illness. Even today, I see a doctor once in a while to see how my health is because of

my sicknesses and because I am not very well.... (61)

What I use in my body that helps me to be miyupimaatisiiu, that is food that I can eat and drink... taking my age which is over fifty years old, I use the food we call Iyimiichim (from Iyiyuu=Cree and miichim=food) more than I do the food of the whiteman or food that is purchased from the store. That is what I like which is what I have seen when I was growing up. All that I ate was food that had been gotten off the land. Still at my age, what I prefer to eat is the food that the Iyiyuu kills to eat and every kind of food that is considered iyimichim.... (63)

The things that children ate in the past, that was what made them strong and miyupimaatisiiu—because they ate only wildlife food, because they only killed what they needed for food. With the whiteman's food, sometimes it doesn't do a person well in his system if he eats just whiteman's food for long time. But if he eats half wildlife food and half whiteman's food, that would do him all right. (102)

FOOD FOR THOUGHT

Why do you think that the Cree changed their traditional eating practices?

---

also had severe effects since its transmission through contaminated water and food finds an ideal context in areas of poor sanitation. In Canada, the two greatest epidemics affecting Aboriginal health were smallpox in the sixteenth and seventeenth centuries, and tuberculosis, which continues to be a major problem today (Waldram, Herring, and Young 1995). First Nations groups in Canada today also face the chronic diseases of the twentieth century, such as diabetes and heart disease. Some of these diseases may be linked to disruptions in traditional diets, a key component of maintaining health (see the Voices box).

Diseases of Development

Another area of research that traces the spread of illnesses with attention to the links between ecological factors and social factors is the study of **diseases of development,** diseases that are caused or increased by economic development activities that affect the environment and people's relationship with it. Examples of diseases in this category are schistosomiasis, river blindness, malaria, and tuberculosis (Foster and Anderson 1978:27).

In many developing countries, dramatically increased rates of schistosomiasis (a disease caused by the presence of a parasitic worm in the blood system) have been traced to the construction of dams and irrigation systems. It is estimated that over 200 million people suffer from this debilitating disease (Inhorn and Brown 1997:41). The larvae of this particular form of worm hatch from eggs and mature in slow-moving water such as lakes and rivers. Upon maturity, they can penetrate human (or other animal) skin with which they come into contact. People who wade or swim in infected waters are highly likely to become infected. Once inside the human body, the adult schistosomes breed in the veins around the human bladder and bowel. They send fertilized eggs through urine and feces into the environment, which then continue to contaminate water in which the eggs hatch into larvae. Anthropologists' research has documented dramatic increases in the rates of schistosomiasis that have occurred at high dam sites and artificial lakes, over the past four decades of dam construction in developing countries (Scudder 1973; Heyneman 1984). This heightened risk is caused by the dams slowing the rate of water flow. In stagnant water systems, as opposed to the undisturbed rapid flow, an ideal environment emerges for the development of the larvae. Many anthropologists have used this information to speak out against the construction of large dam projects.

Formerly unidentified diseases of development continue to appear. One of these is Kyasanur Forest disease, or KFD (Nichter 1992). This viral disease was first identified in 1957 in southern India:

> Resembling influenza, at onset KFD is marked by sudden chills, fever, frontal headaches, stiffness of the neck, and body pain. Diarrhea and vomiting often follow on the third day. High fever is continuous for five to fifteen days, during which time a variety of additional symptoms may manifest themselves, including gastrointestinal bleeding, persistent cough with blood-tinged sputum, and bleeding gums. In more serious cases, the infection progresses to bronchial pneumonia, meningitis, paralysis, encephalitis, and hemorrhage. (224)

In the early 1980s, an epidemic of KFD swept through over 30 villages in a part of Karnataka state near the Kyasanur Forest. During this time, mortality rates in hospitals ranged between 12 and 18 per cent of those admitted. Investigation revealed that KFD especially affects agricultural workers and cattle-tenders who were most exposed to newly cleared areas near the forest. In the cleared areas, international companies established plantations and initiated cattle-raising. Ticks, which had long existed in the local ecosystem, increased in number in the cleared area and found inviting hosts in the cattle and their tenders. Thus, human modification of the ecosystem through deforestation and introduction of cattle-raising caused the epidemic and shaped its social distribution.

Ethnomedicine

Medical anthropologists used to refer to the study of medical systems of non-Western societies as **ethnomedicine**. In fact, all medical systems—including biomedicine—are "ethnomedicine," as they are grounded in particular social, historical, and cultural contexts and are culturally constructed. Different ethnomedical systems have their own approaches to the body as a locus for health and illness, methods of identifying and classifying illness, health concepts and practices, preventative and therapeutic approaches (including magico-religious techniques, use of medicinal substances, and mechanical techniques such as dentistry and surgery), and specialists in treating illness.

Perceptions of the Body

Medical anthropologists have found that cultural perceptions of the body have implications for how people maintain health, respond to illness, and approach healing. The highland Maya of Chiapas, southern Mexico, have a detailed vision of the exterior body, but do not focus much attention on internal organs, a fact related to the nonexistence of surgery as a healing technique among them (Berlin and Berlin 1996). Western logic of mind-body dualism has long pervaded popular and scientific thinking about health and illness. Thus, Western medicine has a special category called "mental illness," which addresses certain health problems as if they were located only in the mind. In many cultures where such a mind-body distinction does not exist, the category of mental illness does not occur either.

Cross-cultural variation exists in perceptions of which bodily organs are most critically involved in the definition of life versus death. In the West, a person may be declared dead while the heart is still beating if the brain is judged "dead." In Japan, for example, organ transplant from a brain-dead donor remains an unacceptable medical practice (Lock 1996). The definition of brain dead is not accepted in Japan, perhaps an indication of the relatively great value accorded to the brain in Western culture (Ohnuki-Tierney 1994).

In Japan, negative attitudes about cutting the body help explain the much lower rates of surgery there than in North America. The Japanese concept of *gotai* refers to the value of maintaining bodily intactness in life and death. "Even today ear piercing is uncommon.... Newspapers reported that one of the qualifications of a bride for Crown Prince Naruhitao was that she not have pierced ears" (Ohnuki-Tierney 1994:235). Historically, the warrior's practice of beheading the victim was the ultimate form of killing because it violated the integrity of the body and prevented the enemy's rebirth. *Gotai* is also an important reason for the widespread popular resistance to organ transplantation in Japan (although recently some Japanese people, including many physicians, have begun to reject *gotai* in favour of promoting transplant surgery).

Another area of interest for medical anthropologists is the relationship between the physical body and the social body in matters of health, illness, and healing. Western biomedicine typically treats only the physical body or only the mind, as they are thought to be completely separate from each other and from the social and cultural milieu of the patient. Health is also closely related to the body politic (recall the Voices box, where Cree from northern Quebec reflect on recent changes in their way of life and health). Most medical systems recognize a relationship between mind and body, and between individuals and their social contexts. Strained social relations—including those with supernatural beings—may cause illness; healing is intended to address and alleviate problems in the social body as well as the physical body. A cure is brought about by holding a family or community ritual that seeks to regain correct social relations or that will appease the deities. For example, the Lao residing in Laos and those who settled as refugees in North America perform a communal ritual called *sukhwan* to "tie" the 32 components of an individual's spirit essence permanently into the body with sacred strings tied around the wrist. This ritual draws the individual, who may have been ill or frightened, more tightly into the community (P. Van Esterik 1992).

Defining Disease

Western biomedicine defines and labels diseases according to its own diagnostic criteria. Other medical systems emphasize different symptoms or attribute disease to different causes. Locally specific disorders not easily assigned to Western categories of disease are sometimes called **culture-bound syndromes** or "folk illnesses" (see the Multiple Cultural Worlds box on page 172). A culture-bound syndrome is a collection of signs and symptoms that is restricted to a particular culture or a limited number of cultures (Prince 1985:201). While Western psychiatrists would label these afflictions psychiatric disorders, in fact, they do not match that category well. It should not be thought that non-Western perceptions of illness are "wrong." Like Western perceptions, they are embedded in their own social context and "make sense" within the cultural system.

Culture-bound syndromes are one way of looking at the cultural interpretation of *dis*-ease and stress. For example, *susto*, or "fright disease," is a widely distributed culture-bound syndrome of Latino cultures. People afflicted with *susto* attribute it to shock, such as loss of a loved one or experiencing a frightening accident (Rubel, O'Nell,

and Collado-Ardón 1984). In the Chiapas area of Mexico, one woman reported that her *susto* was brought on by an accident in which a lot of pottery she had made got broken on its way to market, while a man said that his *susto* came on after he saw a dangerous snake. *Susto* symptoms include appetite loss, loss of motivation, breathing problems, generalized pain, and nightmares. Analysis of many cases of *susto* in three villages showed that the people most likely to be afflicted were those who were in some way socially marginal or experiencing a sense of role failure. The woman whose pottery had broken, for example, had also suffered two spontaneous abortions and was worried that she would never have children. People who fall ill with *susto* have higher mortality rates than the unafflicted population, a finding that suggests that a deep sense of social failure (culturally diagnosed as a discrete event such as broken pottery) places the afflicted person at a higher risk of dying. Thus, some culture-bound syndromes are not only "psychological" problems.

Medical anthropologists first studied culture-bound syndromes in non-Western cultures, and this focus has led to a bias in thinking that all culture-bound syndromes are found in "other" cultures. Now it is recognized that some afflictions of the West could also be interpreted as culture-bound syndromes, such as *agoraphobia*, or an obsessive fear of leaving one's home and going to public places, or eating disorders such as anorexia nervosa and bulimia (see the Multiple Cultural Worlds box).

Preventive Practices

Many different practices based in either religious or secular beliefs exist cross-culturally for preventing misfortune, suffering, and illness. Among the Maya of Guatemala, one major illness is called *awas* (Wilson 1995). This illness is especially likely to occur among infants. Difficult labour may precede *awas* in the infant, and stillbirths and infant deaths are attributed to this disease. Children born with *awas* show symptoms such as lumps under the skin, marks on the skin, or albinism. Causes of *awas* are related to events that happen to the mother during her pregnancy: She may have been denied food that she desired or pressured to eat food she didn't want, or she may have encountered a rude, drunk, or angry person (usually a male). In order to help prevent *awas* in babies, the Mayas go out of their way to be care-

Culture-Bound Syndromes

Some medical anthropologists have been concerned about labelling locally specific complaints as culture-bound syndromes or culturally interpreted disorders because the label may reinforce stereotypes and result in dismissing the complaints of women, refugees, or First Nations patients. A focus on static categorization may also obscure how meanings are linked to larger social and political contexts, and how diseases and disorders may be a form of resistance. The following work relevant to Canadian medical anthropology demonstrates some of the debates around deciding whether a label names a unique cultural product or a local manifestation of a more general disease process.

- **"Old Hag"—Newfoundland:** The "Old Hag" is a local term for a condition of sleep paralysis and hallucinations accompanied by the feeling that a great weight is pressing on the chest. Attacks of the "Old Hag" are not considered manifestations of mental illness, but rather normal occurrences, possibly caused by occupationally derived sleeplessness related to the demands of family fishing in Newfoundland (Firestone 1985).

- *Anfechtung*—**Hutterites in Manitoba:** *Anfechtung* is identified as a culture-bound syndrome characterized by a withdrawal from social contact, a feeling of having sinned, and concerns with religious unworthiness. Through the Hutterite baptism of blood, disciples experience the suffering of Christ as an inner suffering of doubt and despair (Stephenson 1991:28). Stephenson reminds us that the stereotypes of Hutterites as dour, sober-faced authoritarians struggling under religious oppression influence the way illnesses are interpreted by health professionals.

- *Pibloktoq* (Arctic Hysteria)— **Inuit:** Arctic hysteria is widely cited as a culture-bound syndrome characterized by brooding, depressive silences followed by convulsive hysterical seizures, followed by collapse and recovery with amnesia for the experience. Possible explanations for the syndrome include the ecology of long, dark, cold days, crowded conditions in confined houses, shamanistic beliefs, and dietary conditions such as calcium and vitamin D deficiency, and hypervitaminosis A. Marine animals contain high, toxic concentrations of vitamin A in their livers, kidneys, and fat, which are then consumed in large quantities by Inuit (Landy 1985). Landy argues that biological and cultural factors are inseparable, and taken together, may offer a biocultural approach to explaining emotional disturbances.

- **Windigo—Cree and Ojibwa:** "Windigo psychosis," long identified as a classic culture-bound syndrome, is described as a condition characterized by depression, nausea, distaste for usual foods, and feelings of being possessed by a cannibalistic spirit. The condition is attributed to the Cree, Ojibwa, and other subarctic First Nations groups in northeastern Canada. Early reports hypothesized that the condition developed as a result of the stress of a diminishing or uncertain food supply. Landes's (1938) description of Ojibwa Windigo as a severe anxiety neurosis manifested as obsessive cannibalism has been criticized. However, others argue that the more significant question is, Under what conditions is a person likely to be accused of being a Windigo (Marano 1982)? While Windigo beliefs may structure how anxieties and psychoses are talked about, as reflected in the analysis of Cree "cannibalistic" myths (Turner 1977), actual cases of can- nibalistic psychotic behaviour are absent or very few in number.

- **Evil Eye (*Mal Ojo*)— Mediterranean and Latin American Hispanic groups:** Fitful sleep, cry without apparent cause, diarrhea, vomiting, and fever in a child or infant may be attributed to a fixed stare from an adult. An adult, usually female, may also be harmed by the evil and envious eye of another. Magliore (1983) looked at evil eye beliefs among Sicilian immigrants in Ontario, arguing that the term may refer to causes of general misfortune or specific illness. Carroll (1984) has linked evil eye beliefs to the weaning conflict and the loss of the maternal breast, setting up an emotional pattern that carries into adult life.

- **Nerves (*Nervios, Nevra*)—widespread in Euro-American contexts:** "Nerves" is a general term to refer to a culturally acceptable way of describing psychosocial distress to family and health professionals. Symptoms include headaches, dizziness, chest pain, trembling, disorientation, fatigue, lack of appetite, and feelings of melancholy and despair. Dona Davis (1984) reported cases of middle-aged women from the outports of Newfoundland complaining of bad nerves to their doctors and being given prescriptions for tranquilizers. In the local fishing communities, "woman the worrier" is a noble role and carries a wide range of meanings. Similarly, the narratives of first-generation Greek immigrant women in Montreal stressed their experiences of isolation, discrimination, and marital discord expressed through complaints of *nevra* (Lock and Wakewich-Dunk 1990). In both cases, nerves may be thought of as a form of communication about living with stress, poverty, and deprivation.

Anorexia Nervosa

Anorexia nervosa and a related condition called bulimia used to be considered examples of syndromes found predominantly among Euro-American adolescent girls of North America. More recently, cases have also been documented among African American girls, and a small number of cases have appeared in Japan, Hong Kong, South Africa, Argentina, and urban India (Fabrega and Miller 1995; Nasser, Katzman, and Gordon 2001). Anorexia nervosa's cluster of symptoms include aversion to food, distorted body image, hyperactivity, and, as it progresses, continuous wasting of the body and often death. Fat phobia or self-perceptions of fatness are often absent in Asian patients, a reminder that there are many routes to anorexia.

Eating disorders are difficult to cure with either medical or psychiatric treatment. Pinpointing the cultural causes has not proved easy. Many experts point to the societal pressures on young girls in North America towards excessive concern with their looks, especially body weight. Others feel that anorexia is related to girls' unconscious resistance to overcontrolling parents. To such girls, food intake may appear to be the one thing they control. This need for self-control through food deprivation becomes addictive and entrapping. The highly controversial Montreux Clinic in Victoria, BC, proposed a causal model of psychological negativity that "forbade" sufferers to eat. Although the primary cause of anorexia may be rooted in culture, the affliction becomes intertwined with the body's biological functions. Extreme fasting leads to the body's inability to deal with ingested food. A starving anorexic literally may no longer be able to eat and derive nourishment from food. Some medical treatments therefore include in-hospital monitored feeding or intravenous feeding to override the biological block. Other interventions by Canadian hospitals and advocacy groups include the following:

- support groups for parents of children with eating disorders
- out-patient treatment programs to develop coping strategies and improve self-acceptance
- individual psychotherapy focusing on issues such as control or body image
- family counselling
- publicity concerning the early signs of eating disorders
- public education such as National Eating Disorders Week (first week of February) and Internet resources

---

ful around pregnant women. A pregnant woman, like land before the planting, is considered sacred and treated in special ways. She is always given the food she wants, and people behave with respect in her presence. In general, the ideal is to keep a pregnant woman in a state of *kalkab'il*, or peace, contentment, and optimism.

Common forms of ritual health protection include charms, spells, and strings tied around parts of the body. After visiting a Buddhist temple in Japan, for example, one might purchase a small band to tie around the wrist to prevent future problems related to health and fertility. Wrist ties are commonly placed on infants in rural areas in India, especially by Hindus. Sukhwan rituals among the Lao also strengthen children and adults by the use of protective wrist strings. An anthropologist working in Thailand learned of the display of carved wooden phalluses (see photo on page 174) as protection against a certain form of sudden death among men (Mills 1995). In 1990, fear of a widow ghost attack spread throughout a wide area of northeastern Thailand. The fear was based on national news and radio reports of unexplained deaths among Thai migrants working in Singapore. Local people, many of whom had family and friends employed in Singapore, interpreted these sudden deaths as caused by widow ghosts. Widow ghosts are known to roam about, searching for men whom they take as their "husbands." Mary Beth Mills was conducting research in Baan Naa Sakae village at the time of the fear:

I returned to Baan Naa Sakae village after a few days' absence to find the entire community of two hundred households festooned with wooden phalluses in all shapes and sizes. Ranging from the crudest wooden shafts to carefully carved images complete with coconut shell testicles and fishnet pubic hair, they adorned virtually every house and residential compound. The phalluses, I was told, were to protect residents, especially boys and men, from the "nightmare deaths" (lai tai) at the hands of malevolent "widow ghosts" (phii mae maai). (249)

Wooden phalluses in a household compound in a village in northeastern Thailand are displayed to protect men from sudden death.

In Isan culture, and wider Thai culture too, spirits (*phii*) are a recognized source of illness, death, and other misfortunes. One variety of *phii,* a widow ghost, is the sexually voracious spirit of a woman who has met an untimely and perhaps violent death. When a seemingly healthy man dies in his sleep, a widow ghost is blamed. The wooden phalluses hung on the houses were protection against a possible attack. Mills reports:

> [I]nformants described these giant penises as decoys that would attract the interest of any phii mae maai *which might come looking for a husband. The greedy ghosts would take their pleasure with the wooden penises and be satisfied, leaving the men of that household asleep, safe in their beds. (251)*

As radio and other news coverage of the deaths in Singapore diminished over several weeks, so did concerns about widow ghosts, and villagers quietly removed the protective phalluses.

Diagnosis

If an affliction has been experienced and the person with the condition decides to seek help for it, diagnosis is the first stage in treatment. Diagnosis attempts to find out what is wrong and to label the affliction in order to determine the proper form of treatment. It includes magical-religious techniques such as **divination,** in which a specialist uses techniques to gain supernatural insights, and secular techniques such as asking the ill person to supply detailed descriptions of symptoms. Among the Navajo, three types of diagnostic techniques exist: hand trembling, star gazing, and listening (W. Morgan 1977). The hand trembling diagnosis works this way: The specialist enters the *hogan,* or the sacred home, of the afflicted person and, with friends and relatives present, discusses the problem. The specialist sits facing the patient, closes his eyes, and thinks of all the possible causes. When the correct one comes to mind, the specialist's arm involuntarily shakes, revealing the diagnosis. In all three forms of Navajo diagnosis, the specialist goes into a trance-like state that lends authority to the outcome since people believe that the diagnosis has been given by the supernaturals.

Among the urban poor of Bahia in Brazil, a flexible approach exists to ascertaining the cause of disease (Ngokwey 1988). In Feira de Santana, the second-largest city in the state of Bahia, with a population of about a quarter of a million people, traditional etiological (causal) systems consider both supernatural and secular factors. In the poorer neighbourhoods, unemployment is high. Those who work are bricklayers, plumbers, seamstresses, vendors, and labourers. Health problems are common in northeastern Brazil, the poorest region in the nation, including nutritional deficiencies; infectious diseases such as diarrhea, tuberculosis, measles, ascaridiasis, and schistosomiasis; and chronic diseases. Illness theories in Feira de Santana include natural, socioeconomic, psychological, and supernatural causes. Natural causes include exposure to the environment. Thus, "too much cold can provoke gripe; humidity and rain cause rheumatism; excessive heat can result in dehydration.... Some types of winds are known to provoke *ar do vento* or *ar do tempo,* a condition characterized by migraines, hemiplegia, and 'cerebral congestion'" (795). Other natural explanations for illness take into account the effects of aging, heredity, personal nature (*natureza*), and gender.

Heredity is a common explanation for mental retardation. Contagion is another "natural" explanation, as are the effects of certain foods and eating habits. Popular knowledge connects the lack of economic resources, proper sanitation, and health services with illnesses. "One informant said, 'There are many illnesses because there are many poor'" (796).

Psychosocial factors such as emotions may contribute to disease: "Anger and hostile feelings (*raiva*), anxiety and worry are possible causes of various illnesses ranging from *nervoso*, a folk illness characterized by 'nervousness,' to heart problems and *derrame* (cerebral hemorrhage)" (796). Illness is also attributed to supernatural causes such as spirits and magical acts.

The African-Brazilian religious systems of the Bahia region encompass a range of spirits who can inflict illness, including spirits of the dead and devil-like spirits. Some spirits cause specific illnesses, while others bring general misfortune. Spells cast by envious people with the evil eye are a well-known cause of illness. People also recognize multiple levels of causality. In the case of a stomach ache, for example, a quarrel (the ultimate cause) prompted the aggrieved party to seek the intervention of a sorcerer, who cast a spell (the instrumental cause), which led to the illness. This multiple etiology then calls for multiple treatments.

People's own (emic) perceptions of symptoms and explanations for why illness occurs often exist in direct contradiction to the teachings of Western biomedicine. This divergence may lead, on one hand, to people's rejection of Western biomedicine and, on the other, to frustration among medical care providers who accuse such people of "noncompliance."

For example, a study of emic perceptions related to breast cancer carried out in the rural south of the United States found that African American women with breast cancer come to medical clinics for treatment late in the course of the disease, and are likely to reject a medical diagnosis of breast cancer because the women have a model of the body and health that emphasizes balance in the blood (Mathews, Lannin, and Mitchell 1994). Women connect "dirty" or "bad" blood with the growth of lumps or knots in the body. In addition, they are practising Christians and believe that health and illness are properly in the hands of God. These women therefore do not go to the clinic when they notice a small lump in their breasts. Later, when the symptoms are more advanced, they may see a doctor, but even then most reject the diagnosis of breast cancer and also reject biomedical treatment.

Ways of Healing

This section considers two ways of conceptualizing and dealing with healing. They include the public and participatory group healing of the Ju/wasi and the humoral system of bodily balance through food intake in Malaysia. We also consider healers and healing substances.

Community Healing Systems
A general distinction can be drawn between private and public healing, with the former addressing bodily ailments more in isolation and the latter emphasizing social context as key to healing. Compared to Western biomedicine, many non-Western systems involve greater use of public healing and community involvement. An example of public or **community healing** comes from the Ju/wasi foragers of the Kalahari Desert in southern Africa. Ju/wasi healing emphasizes the mobilization of community "energy" as a key element in the cure:

> The central event in this tradition is the all-night healing dance. Four times a month on the average, night signals the start of a healing dance. The women sit around the fire, singing and rhythmically clapping. The men, sometimes joined by the women, dance around the singers. As the dance intensifies, num or spiritual energy is activated by the healers, both men and women, but mostly among the dancing men. As num is activated in them, they begin to kia or experience an enhancement of their consciousness. While experiencing kia, they heal all those at the dance.... The dance is a community event at which the entire camp participates. The people's belief in the healing power of num brings substance to the dance. (Katz 1982:34–36)

An important aspect of the Ju/wasi healing system is its openness—everyone has access to it. The role of healer is also open. Healers have no special privileges. In fact, more than half of all adult men and about 10 per cent of adult women are healers.

Humoral Healing Systems
Humoral healing systems are based on a philosophy of balance among certain natural elements within the body (McElroy and Townsend 1996). Food and drugs have different effects on the body and are classified as either "heating" or "cool-

A Ju/wasi healer in a trance, in the Kalahari Desert, southern Africa. Most healers are men, but some are women.

In Malaysia, several different humoral traditions co-exist, reflecting the region's history of contact with outside cultures. Malaysia has been influenced by trade and contact between its indigenous culture and that of India, China, and the Arab-Islamic world for around 2000 years. Indian, Chinese, and Arabic medical systems are similar in that all define health as the balance of opposing elements within the body, although each has its own variations (Laderman 1988:272). Indigenous belief systems may have been especially compatible with these imported models because they also were based on concepts of heat and coolness.

Insights about what the indigenous systems were like comes from ethnographic accounts about the Orang Asli, aboriginal peoples of the Malaysian interior who are relatively less affected by contact. A conceptual system of hot-cold opposition dominates Orang Asli cosmological, medical, and social theories. The properties and meanings of heat and coolness differ from those of Islamic, Indian, or Chinese humoralism in several ways. In the Islamic, Indian, and Chinese systems, for example, death is the ultimate result of too much coolness. Among the Orang Asli, excessive heat is the primary cause of mortality. Heat emanates from the sun, and it is associated with excrement, blood, misfortune, disease, and death. Humanity's hot blood makes people mortal, and their consumption of meat speeds the process. Heat causes menstruation, violent emotions, aggression, and drunkenness. Coolness, in contrast, is vital for health. Health is protected by avoiding the harmful effects of the sun by staying in the forest shade. This belief justifies the rejection of agriculture by some groups because it exposes people to the sun. Treatment of illness is designed to reduce or remove heat. If someone were to fall ill in a clearing, the entire group would relocate to the coolness of the forest. The forest is also a source of cooling leaves and herbs. Healers are cool:

[H]ealers' bodies are superhumanly cool, and they take steps to retain their coolness by bathing in cold water and sleeping far from the fire. Their eyes are especially cool, enabling them to see the true nature of things, hidden to ordinary people. After removing their patients from the hot clearing to the cool jungle, they blow their cooling breath upon their patients' backs, treat them with cooling medications, call upon beneficent spirits to assist them in magically infusing the sick body with refreshing (sometimes invisible) liquid, which they draw from a bowl placed under hanging leaf ornaments. (275)

ing" (the quotation marks indicate that these properties are not the same as thermal temperatures per se). Diseases are classified as being the result of bodily imbalances—too much heat or coolness, which must then be counteracted through dietary changes or medicines that will bring back balance.

Humoral healing systems have been practised for thousands of years in the Middle East, the Mediterranean, and much of Asia and were spread to the New World through Spanish colonization. They have shown substantial resilience in the face of Western biomedicine, often incorporating it into their own framework, for example, in the classification of biomedical treatments as either heating or cooling. Humoral logic persists in Euro-American public culture in advice such as "feed a cold; starve a fever."

Extreme cold, however, can be harmful. Dangerous levels of coolness are associated with the time right after birth since the mother is believed to have lost substantial heat: "She must avoid decreasing her heat further by refraining from drinking or bathing in cold water. She adds to her heat by tying sashes containing warmed leaves or ashes around her waist, bathing herself and her newborn child in warm water, and lying near a fire" (275–276).

Healers

In an informal sense, everyone is a "healer" since self-treatment is always the first consideration in dealing with a perceived health problem. Yet, in all cultures some people become recognized as having special abilities to diagnose and treat health problems. Notable forms of specialists include midwife, bonesetter (someone who resets broken bones), **shaman** (a healer who mediates between humans and the spirit world), herbalist, general practitioner, psychiatrist, acupuncturist, chiropractor, and dentist. Cross-cultural evidence indicates some common features of healers: selection (certain individuals may show more ability for entry into healing roles); training (this often involves years of observation and practice, and the training may be arduous); certification (this may be either legal or ritual); professional image (the role is demarcated through behaviour, dress, and markers such as the white coat in the West or the Siberian shaman's tambourine for calling the spirits); and expectation of payment (compensation is expected in kind or cash) (Foster and Anderson 1978:104–115).

Healing Substances

Around the world, many different natural or manufactured substances are used as medicines for preventing or curing health problems. Anthropologists have spent more time studying the use of medicines in non-Western cultures than in the West, although a more truly cross-cultural approach is emerging that examines the use of Western pharmaceuticals as well (van der Geest, Whyte, and Hardon

1996). **Ethnobotany** is an area of inquiry exploring the cultural knowledge of local plants, including the use of plants as medicines. Increasing awareness of the range of potentially useful plants worldwide has provided a strong reason for protecting both biodiversity and indigenous cultural knowledge of plant uses. For example, Marilyn Walker (1984) made an inventory of edible forest plants of the Northwest Territories. Leaves of the coca plant have for centuries been a key part of the medicinal systems of the Andean region, although it has broader uses in ritual, in covering hunger pains, and in combatting the cold (Carter, Mamani, and Morales 1981). Coca is used for gastrointestinal problems, and next most commonly for sprains, swellings, and colds. A survey of coca use in Bolivia showed a high prevalence rate: Of the 3501 people asked if they use coca medicinally, about 85 per cent answered *yes*. The leaf may be ingested alone (chewed), and it is frequently combined with other substances in a *maté*, or drink composed of herbs in a water

A Korean mansin performs the Tale of Princess Pari, a female hero who braves the perils of the underworld in quest of an herb that will restore her dying parents. Twenty years ago, this segment of the *kut* for the dead would have been performed outside the house gate. In urban Korea, it is performed inside to avoid complaints about noise and traffic obstruction.

base. Specialized knowledge about preparing some of the *matés* is reserved for trained herbalists. One *maté*, for example, is for treating asthma. Made of a certain root and coca leaves, it should be taken three to four times a day until the patient is cured.

Minerals are also widely used for prevention and healing. For example, bathing in sulphurous waters or water that contains high levels of other minerals has wide popularity for promoting health and curing several ailments, including arthritis and rheumatism. About 40 000 people a year go to the Dead Sea, which lies beneath sea level between Israel and Jordan, for treating skin diseases (Lew 1994). The adjacent sulphur springs and mud from the shore are believed to be helpful for people with skin ailments such as psoriasis. German studies conclude that it is more cost effective to pay for a trip to the Dead Sea than it is to hospitalize a psoriasis patient.

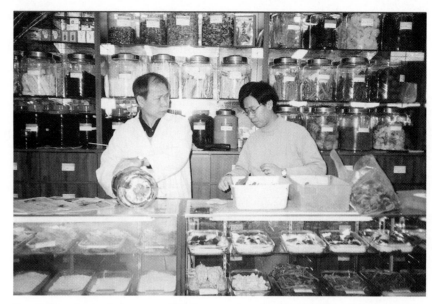

Traditional medicines available in a shop in Toronto include dried ingredients and patent medicines from Hong Kong, Taiwan, and mainland China.

Western patent medicines have gained popularity worldwide. There are benefits to the use of these medicines, as well as detriments, including use without prescription and overprescription. Often, sale of patent medicines is unregulated, and they are available for purchase from local markets by self-treating individuals. The popularity of capsules and even injections has led to misuse and overuse in many cases. Multinational pharmaceutical companies aggressively market medicines, and even "dump" out-of-date and recalled products not permitted for sale in North America. Medical anthropologists are assessing the distribution channels of medicines, the increased commodification of medicine, and cross-cultural perceptions of the efficacy of patent, herbal, and Western pharmaceuticals, among other important topics.

The Interpretive Approach

Interpretive approaches to health systems consider how people in different cultures label, describe, and experience illness and how healing offers meaningful responses to in-

dividual and communal distress. An important direction in interpretive medical anthropology has been to focus on the explanatory models and illness narratives of individual sufferers in order to understand the cultural realities of individual patients (Kleinman 1988). Illness and healing as dialectical processes involve the interaction between physical processes and social, cultural, and psychological contexts. Kleinman argued that Western biomedicine fails to recognize this, unlike many non-Western medical systems, which consider sufferers in their sociocultural context.

Interpretive approaches also pay attention to symbolic aspects of healing, such as ritual trance. Claude Lévi-Strauss, in a classic essay called "The Effectiveness of Symbols" (1967), examined how a song sung during childbirth among the Cuna Indians of Panama lessens the difficulty of childbirth. His main point was that healing systems provide meaning to people who are suffering. The provision of meaning offers psychological support and courage to the afflicted and may enhance healing through what Western science calls the **placebo effect** (a healing effect obtained through the positive power of believing that a particular method is efficacious). Anthropological research suggests that between 10 and 90 per cent of the efficacy of medical prescriptions lies in the placebo effect (Moerman 1979, 1983, 1992). Several features may be involved: the power of the person prescribing a particular treatment, the very act of prescription, and concrete details about the medicine such as its colour, name, and place of origin (van der Geest, Whyte, and Hardon 1996). For example, many international migrants prefer to obtain medicines from their homelands. In other situations, the prestige of a medicine from Sweden or Switzerland is an important factor.

Margaret Trawick (1988), in her study of Ayurvedic healing in India, examines the enduring efficacy and appeal of Ayurvedic treatments—treatments that are increasingly available in Canadian cities as well. Ayurvedic medicine is a widely used Indian health system based on texts composed from the beginning of the Christian era to about 1000 CE. Based on humoral principles, Ayurvedic diagnoses take into account bodily "channels" controlling the flow of life forces through the human body, and whether these are blocked or open and clear. Trawick transcribed an interview between an 80-year-old Ayurvedic physician and an old woman of a poor caste group. The transcription reveals the themes of channels, processes of flow, points of connection (the heart is believed to be the centre of all channels), and everyday activities that regulate the flow of life. After the interview, the doctor offers dietary prescriptions, such as avoidance of tamarind since that causes "dullness," and consumption of light food. Finally, he gently tells her that, basically, she is growing old. In this interaction, the meanings conveyed through the interview offer the client a sense that she is being taken seriously by the caregiver and a measure of self-efficacy in that there are things she can do to alleviate her distress, specifically carefully following a dietary regime (Trawick 1988:138–139).

Critical Medical Anthropology

Critical medical anthropology considers the way economic and political structures shape people's health status, their access to health care, and the prevailing healing systems. Critical medical anthropologists examine how economic and political systems create and perpetuate social inequality in health status. They have also exposed the power of **medicalization,** or the labelling of a par-

ticular issue or problem as medical and requiring medical treatment when, in fact, it may be economic or political. Critical medical anthropologists examine how larger structural forces determine the distribution of illness and people's responses to it. They are also concerned to see how individuals may, through personal agency, resist such forces.

Another area of research in critical medical anthropology addresses Western biomedicine, assessing it as a global power structure, critiquing medical training, and looking at doctor-patient relationships as manifestations of social control rather than social liberation. For example, Canadian medical anthropologist Pamela Downe (1999) analyzed how street prostitutes in Costa Rica medicalize the violence and discrimination in their lives, but resist and cope through their own brand of humour and jokes.

Many Canadian medical anthropologists favour a critical medical anthropology approach, reflecting, perhaps, their experience with debates around universal health care and the social safety net. Margaret Lock and Gilles Bibeau (1995) link Canadian debates about language, national identity, and multiculturalism to the eclecticism and pluralism of method characteristic of medical anthropology in Canada.

The Role of Poverty

Broad distinctions exist between the most prevalent afflictions of the richer, more industrial nations and the poorer, less industrial nations. In the former, the major categories of death include circulatory diseases, malignant cancers, AIDS, alcohol consumption, and tobacco consumption (United Nations Development Programme 1994:191). For developing countries, a different profile appears: tuberculosis, malaria, and AIDS. Substantial empirical evidence says poverty is a major cause of morbidity and mortality in both industrial and developing countries. It may be manifested in different ways, for example, by causing extreme malnutrition in Chad or Nepal, and high death rates from street violence among the poor of affluent nations.

Throughout the developing world, rates of childhood malnutrition are inversely related to income. As income increases, calorie intake as a percentage of recommended daily allowances also increases (Zaidi 1988:122). Thus, increasing the income levels of the poor may be the most direct way to influence health and nutrition. Yet, in contrast to this seemingly logical approach, many health and nutrition programs around the world have been focused on treating the outcomes of poverty rather than its causes.

The widespread practice of "treating" the health outcomes of poverty and social inequality with pills or other medical options has been documented by anthropologists. An example is Nancy Scheper-Hughes's research in Bom Jesus, a poor area of northeastern Brazil mentioned in Chapter 5 of this book (1993). She found that people who experienced symptoms of weakness, insomnia, and anxiety were given pills by a local doctor. Her interpretation is that instead of needing pills, the people were instead hungry and needed food. This system serves the interests of pharmaceutical companies in the first place, and, more generally, helps to keep inequitable social systems in place. Similar critical analyses have shown how psychiatry treats symptoms and serves to keep people in their places, rather than addressing the root causes of affliction, which may be powerlessness, unemployment, and thwarted social aspirations in general. High rates of depression among women in Western societies, treated with a range of psychotropic drugs and personal therapists, are a notable example.

Western Medical Training Examined

Since the 1980s, critical medical anthropologists have pursued the study of Western biomedicine as a very powerful cultural system. Much of their work critiques the dehumanization of medical school training and the overriding emphasis on technology. They often advocate for greater recognition of social factors in diagnosis and treatment, reduction of the spread of biomedical technology, and diversification of medical specialists to include alternative healing such as massage, acupuncture, and chiropractry (Scheper-Hughes 1990).

Robbie Davis-Floyd (1987) examined the culture of obstetric training in the United States. She interviewed twelve obstetricians, ten male and two female. As students, they absorbed the technological model of birth as a core value of Western obstetrics. This model treats the body as a machine. The physician-technician uses the assembly-line approach to birth in order to promote efficient production and quality control. One of the residents in the study explained: "We shave 'em, we prep

'em, we hook 'em up to the IV and administer sedation. We deliver the baby, it goes to the nursery and the mother goes to her room. There's no room for niceties around here. We just move 'em right on through. It's not hard to see it like an assembly line" (292). The goal is the "production" of a healthy baby. The doctor is in charge of achieving this goal, and the mother takes second place. One obstetrician said, "It is what we all were trained to always go after—the perfect baby. That's what we were trained to produce. The quality of the mother's experience—we rarely thought about that. Everything we did was to get that perfect baby" (292).

This goal involves the use of sophisticated monitoring machines. One obstetrician said, "I'm totally dependent on fetal monitors, 'cause they're great! They free you to do a lot of other things.... I couldn't sit over there with a woman in labor with my hand on her belly, and be in here seeing 20 to 30 patients a day" (291). In addition, use of technology conveys status: "Anybody in obstetrics who shows a human interest in patients is not respected. What *is* respected is interest in machines" (291).

How does obstetrical training socialize medical students into accepting this technological model? First, medical training involves a lengthy process of "cognitive retrogression" in which the students go through an intellectual hazing process. During the first two years of medical school, most courses are basic sciences; learning tends to be rote, and vast quantities of material must be memorized. The second phase, which could be termed dehumanization, is one in which medical school training succeeds in overriding humanitarian ideals through its emphasis on technology and objectification of the patient (Davis-Floyd 1987:299). Since midwifery was legalized in Ontario in 1994, even midwives are using more medical technology to fulfill their professional obligations and to respond to the choices of their clients (MacDonald 2001).

Medical training can offer a particular challenge to women, as Perri Klass documents in *A Not Entirely Benign Procedure: Four Years as a Medical Student* (1987). She was especially challenged in making it through the "initiation" of medical school because she was pregnant during part of it and then a mother. Cynthia Carver (1981) provides an insider's view of medical training at the University of Toronto, where she saw her fellow students become more rigid, goal-oriented, disciplined, authoritarian, and more concerned with finances. Even in innovative medical schools such as McMaster Medical School in Hamilton, students learn careful self-presentation to convince others of their developing competence and professionalization (Haas and Shaffir 1982).

Similar studies of other biomedical specialists, such as surgeons, make the same point (Cassell 1991) and show how the power of the physician is correlated with the complexity of the technology they use. Other studies reveal the problem of reliance on technology when the healing issue requires human understanding and interaction rather than machines (Fadiman 1997).

Clinical Medical Anthropology

Clinical medical anthropology refers to the application of anthropological knowledge to further the goals of health care providers; that is, in improving doctor-patient understandings in multicultural settings, making recommendations about culturally appropriate health intervention programs, and providing insights about factors related to disease that medical practitioners do not usually take into account. For example, making use of ethnographic work on Ojibway concepts of disease categories, a successful treatment program for diabetes was developed for Ojibway in Toronto. The program was effective because it acknowledged the historical and social context of the disease and emphasized personal control over lifestyle in the rapidly changing urban environment of Toronto (Hagey 1984).

While critical medical anthropology and clinical medical anthropology may seem diametrically opposed to each other (with the first seeking to critique and even limit the power and range of the medical establishment and the second seeking to make it more effective), some medical anthropologists are building bridges between the two perspectives.

An example of a clinical medical anthropologist who combines the two approaches is Robert Trotter (1987), who conducted research on lead poisoning among children in Mexican American communities. The three most common sources of lead poisoning of children in the United States are eating lead-based paint chips, living near a smelter where the dust has high lead content, and eating or drinking from pottery made with an improperly treated lead glaze. The discovery of an unusual case of lead poisoning by health professionals in Los Angeles in the early 1980s prompted investigations that produced understanding of a fourth cause: the use of a traditional healing remedy, *azarcon*, which contained lead, by people of the Mexican American community. *Azarcon* is given for the treatment of *empacho,* which is a combination of indigestion and constipation, believed to be caused by food sticking to the abdominal wall. Trotter then investigated the availability and use of *azarcon* in Mexico, and its distribution in the United States. His work resulted in restrictions on *azarcon* to prevent its further use, recommendations about the need to provide a substitute remedy for the treatment of *empacho* that would not have harmful side-effects, and ideas about how to advertise this substitute. Throughout his involvement, Trotter combined several roles: researcher, consultant, and program developer, all of which brought anthropological knowledge towards the solution of a health problem.

Much work in clinical medical anthropology involves health communication (Nichter and Nichter 1996:327–328). Anthropologists can help health educators in the development of more meaningful messages through

- addressing local images of ethnophysiology and acknowledging popular health concerns;

- taking seriously local illness terms and conventions;

- adopting local styles of communication;

- identifying subgroups within the population that may be responsive to different types of messages and incentives;

- monitoring the response of communities to health messages over time and facilitating corrections in communication when needed; and

- exposing possible victim-blaming in health messages.

These principles helped health care officials understand local response to public vaccination programs in several countries of Asia and Africa (Nichter 1996). Vaccination programs, such as those promoted by UNICEF, are often introduced in countries with much fanfare, but they are sometimes met with little enthusiasm or trust by the target population. In India, for example, some people are suspicious that vaccination programs are clandestine family planning programs. In other instances, fear of foreign vaccines prompts people to reject inoculations. Overall, acceptance rates of vaccination have been lower than expected by Western public health planners. Health communication is often required to explain side-effects of a vaccination, such as fever, so that family members do not perceive the vaccination as negative. Key features in the overall communication strategy are to promote trust of the public health establishment and to provide locally sensible understandings of what the vaccinations do and do not do.

Communication through audio teleconferencing has also provided support to people in more remote or rural areas. In Newfoundland, women with a history of breast cancer found teleconferencing to be invaluable in dealing with the emotional upheaval of the disease. They needed to talk with other women who knew what living with breast cancer was about, particularly long-term survivors. With teleconferencing, one participant explained, the community didn't have "to know my business" (Church, Curran, and Solberg 2000:22).

Cross-cultural communication is also important in multicultural health settings in Canada, an issue addressed in the book *Cross-Cultural Caring: A Handbook for Health Professionals in Western Canada* (Waxler-Morrison, Anderson, and Richardson 1990). The authors provide culturally sensitive advice about the cultural context of disease to help practitioners make sense of their patients' distress. However, cultural sensitivity and even ethnic matching of patients and practitioners does not guarantee good health care.

Globalization and Change

Other than the capitalist market system itself, perhaps no other aspect of Western society has so permeated the rest of the world as Western biomedicine. As biomedicine is adopted in other contexts, it undergoes localization and change. A task that faces medical anthropologists is the study of how and why such change occurs and what the effects are on the people involved.

Globalization trends in the past decade have brought not only economic and political changes, but also medical changes. The flow of influence has mainly gone in the direction of spreading aspects of Western biomedicine to many parts of the world. Changes have also resulted in the increasing appreciation in the West for some aspects of non-Western healing such as acupuncture. In this section we consider the concept of **medical pluralism**, the simultaneous existence of more than one model of prevention, diagnosis, and cure in a society, and **applied medical pluralism**, in which governments or health development agencies attempt to create a blended system of health care that selects traits from several systems.

Plural Medical Systems

Medical pluralism provides both options and complications. First, something may be classified as a health problem in some cultures and not in others. For example, spirit possession is welcomed in some cultures, but would be considered schizophrenia according to Western psychiatry. Second, the same symptoms may be classified as having different causes (such as supernatural versus germ theories) and therefore require different treatments. Third, certain treatment modalities may be rejected because they violate cultural rules. All of these issues affect how a particular culture will react to exogenous medical practices.

In some cases, alternative forms of healing that offer clients a range of choices coexist, while in others cases, conflicting explanatory models of illness and healing result in serious misunderstandings between healers and clients. Traditional Chinese medicine, particularly acupuncture, is available in most Canadian cities as complementary treatment.

Selective Pluralism: The Case of the Sherpas
The Sherpas of Nepal offer an unusual example of a newly capitalizing context in which preference for traditional healing systems remains strong, along with the adoption of certain aspects of biomedicine (V. Adams 1988). Former pastoralist-farmers, the Sherpas are now heavily involved in providing services for international tourism. They work as guides, porters, cooks, and administrators in trekking agencies, and in hotels and restaurants. Thus, many Sherpas are well acquainted with the cosmopolitan cultures of international travellers (506). The wide variety of healing therapies available in the Upper Khumbu region fit into three general categories: (1) orthodox Buddhist practitioners, such as lamas, who are consulted for both prevention and cure through their blessings and *amchis,* who practise Tibetan medicine, a system largely derived from India's Ayurvedic

Among the many forms of medical treatment available to the Sherpa of Nepal, shamanic healing remains a popular choice.

some situations people do not eat three meals a day and thus unwittingly do not follow the doctor's prescription.

One anthropological study of a case in which death ultimately resulted from cross-cultural differences shows the complexity of communication across medical cultures. The F family are Samoan immigrants living in Honolulu, Hawaii (Krantzler 1987). Neither parent speaks English. Their children are "moderately literate" in English, but speak a mixture of English and Samoan at home. Mr. F was trained as a traditional Samoan healer. Mary, a daughter, was first stricken with diabetes at the age of 16. She was taken to the hospital by ambulance after collapsing, half-conscious, on the sidewalk near her home in a Honolulu housing project. After several months of irregular contact with medical staff, she was again brought to the hospital in an ambulance, unconscious, and she died there. Her father was charged with causing Mary's death through "medical neglect." Nora Krantzler analyzes this case from the perspectives of the Western medical providers and Samoan culture.

Mary was diagnosed with juvenile-onset diabetes mellitus and treated in a hospital. She and her family were taught how to give insulin injections and urine tests. However, Mary did not keep her appointments and returned to the hospital four months later, blind in one eye. Although told of the need for compliance, her father also insisted on preparing a potion to supplement the insulin. The medical experts increasingly judged that "cultural differences" were the basic problem, and that in spite of all their attempts to communicate with the F family, her family was basically incapable of caring for Mary.

The family's perspective, in contrast, was grounded in *fa'a Samoa*, the Samoan way. In the family's opinion, Mary never had a single physician responsible for her care and they were never given adequate explanation of her problem and its treatment. Thus, the family lost trust in the hospital and began to rely on the father's skill as a healer.

While cultural differences may cause problems of communication, they may also marginalize certain groups and deny them adequate health care services. Dara Culhane Speck's ethnography of the politics of health care in a First Nations community on Alert Bay, adjacent to the northeastern end of Vancouver Island, British Columbia, is a powerful indictment of Native-White relations and the consequences of the destruction of an indigenous health care system. *An Error in Judgement* (1987)

medicine; (2) unorthodox religious or shamanic practitioners, who perform divination ceremonies for diagnosis; and (3) biomedical practitioners, who initially used their diagnostic techniques and medicines for tourists, and then established a permanent medical facility in 1967. Canadian medical anthropologist Stacey Pigg (1996) found that shamanic healing is also central to experiences of modernity in Kathmandu, Nepal, where ritual healing thrives alongside biomedical services.

Communication and Marginalization

Many anthropologists have documented the disjuncture between biomedicine and local cultural patterns. In some instances, miscommunication occurs between biomedical doctors and clients in matters as seemingly simple as a prescription that should be taken with every meal. The doctor assumes that this means three times a day, but in documents the death from an undiagnosed ruptured appendix of Renee Smith, an 11-year-old Nimpkish girl. The island's sole medical practitioner was considered responsible for the girl's death through his negligence, alcoholism, and racism; nevertheless, community members were reluctant to lose access to the doctor and the community hospital.

The family and leaders of the Nimpkish band wrote to the Attorney General of British Columbia, the Provincial Minister of Health, and the College of Physicians and Surgeons to complain about the quality of health care on the island and to request an inquiry into the deaths of band members. In 1974, the British Columbia Medical Association published a report on *Native Health*, stressing that Natives fail to recognize early symptoms of illness; have a higher tolerance for pain and discomfort and a fatalistic acceptance of things as they are; and present themselves in the acute and often fatal stages of an illness (Culhane Speck 1987:100).

The report perpetuated the idea that Natives were responsible for the quality of health care they received. In 1980, the Government of Canada Inquiry into Indian Health and Health Care in Alert Bay was convened. According to the Nimpkish Band Council, the community wanted to know why their rates of hospitalization and death were so high: "…why is our life expectancy so low? Why is our survival threatened? What is the quality of our health care services? Why have so many or our people lost confidence in the health care we have been receiving?" (Culhane Speck 1987:234).

Applied Medical Pluralism

Since 1978, the World Health Organization (WHO) has endorsed the incorporation of traditional medicine, especially healers, in national health systems (Velimirovic 1990). This policy emerged in response to increasing levels of national pride in local medical traditions and to the shortage of trained biomedical personnel. Debates continue about the synthesis of traditional and modern biomedicine, and the relative efficacy of many traditional medical practices compared to biomedicine. For instance, opponents of the promotion of traditional medicine claim that it has no effect on such infectious diseases as cholera, malaria, tuberculosis, schistosomiasis, leprosy, and others. They insist that it makes no sense to allow for or encourage ritual practices against malaria, for example, when a child has not been inoculated against it. Supporters of traditional medicine as one aspect of a planned, pluralistic medical system, point out that biomedicine neglects a person's mind and soul while traditional medicine is more holistic. Also, indigenous curers are more likely to know clients and their families, thus facilitating therapy. Nevertheless, critical medical anthropologists point out that international health policy still has the power to define what is traditional and therefore worthy of being included in WHO training programs.

One area where progress has been made in maintaining positive aspects of traditional health care is in midwifery. WHO assists many developing country governments with training programs that equip traditional birth attendants (TBAs) with rudimentary training in germ theory and provide them with basic "kits" that include a clean razor blade for cutting the umbilical cord. The many thousands of TBAs working at the grassroots level around the world thus are not squeezed out of their work, but continue to perform their important role with some enhanced skills and tools.

What does medical anthropology contribute to understanding illness cross-culturally?

The relatively young subfield of medical anthropology, within cultural anthropology, has pursued several directions of research. In the first, which emphasizes the links between ecological or environmental factors and social factors, medical anthropologists have shown how certain categories of people are at risk of contracting particular diseases, within various contexts in historical times and the present. Research on ethnomedicine reveals both differences and similarities across medical systems in perceptions of illness and symptoms. Culture-bound syndromes are illnesses that appear not to be universal in the way they cluster symptoms. The interpretive approach addresses health and illness as sets of meanings. Critical medical anthropologists reveal where social inequality and poverty contribute to certain kinds of illnesses. Clinical medical anthropologists work to apply information on cultural practices and beliefs about illness to improve how health care is provided.

What does medical anthropology contribute to understanding healing systems cross-culturally?

Research in ethnomedicine shows how perceptions of the body differ cross-culturally. Ethnomedical studies of healing modalities, healers, and healing substances encompass a wide range of approaches. Community healing systems are more characteristic of nonindustrial societies and they emphasize group interaction and treating the individual within the social context. In industrial societies, biomedicine emphasizes the body as a discrete unit, and treatment addresses the individual body or mind. The interpretive approach places in the forefront the study of meaning in illness and healing. Medical anthropology research in this area shows how, cross-culturally, the definitions of affliction and suffering are embedded in meaning and so are methods of prevention and healing. This approach places a high value on looking at the placebo effect in different cultural contexts. Critical medical anthropology locates healing and healers in systems of control and power. They have pointed to two trends: the medicalization of problems that are social, and the exclusion of the poor from health care. In their examination of Western medicine, critical medical anthropologists show how this system, rather than being one of purely humanitarian care, is part of powerful structures that put the physician in the role of a controlling, detached, technical expert. In contrast to critical medical anthropology, clinical medical anthropology seeks to make biomedicine more effective by providing cultural information to its practitioners. Clinical anthropologists are at the forefront of helping biomedical clinicians prevent diagnostic and communication errors when dealing with people who have alternative medical models.

How are illness and healing changing during increasing globalization?

Medical cultures everywhere are constantly changing in the face of the spread of Western biomedicine, a process that has prompted reconsideration of "traditional" medicine and its potential. Along with the growth and expansion of global market economics and political structures, Western biomedicine is also spreading. One result is that most countries now are characterized by medical pluralism through which people can choose to consult healers from one or more systems.

Core Concepts

applied medical
    pluralism, p. 182
clinical medical
    anthropology, p. 181
community healing
    systems, p. 175
critical medical
    anthropology, p. 179
culture-bound
    syndromes, p. 171
diseases of
    development, p. 169
divination, p. 174
ecological/epidemiological
    approach, p. 166
ethnobotany, p. 177
ethnomedicine, p. 170
humoral healing systems,
    p. 175
medical pluralism, p. 182
medicalization, p. 179
placebo effect, p. 178
shaman, p. 177

Suggested Readings

Elois Berlin and Brent Berlin, *Medical Ethnobiology of the Highland Maya of Chiapas, Mexico.* Princeton: Princeton University Press, 1996. This detailed report discusses the range of gastrointestinal diseases classified by the highland Maya, including the diarrheas, abdominal pains, and worms, and how the Maya use knowledge of plants to treat them within a humoral system.

Paul Farmer, *AIDS and Accusation: Haiti and the Geography of Blame.* Berkeley: University of California Press, 1992. This text combines attention to the global structures related to the spread of HIV/AIDS with in-depth study in one village in Haiti where HIV/AIDS is locally interpreted as one more phase in people's long-term exposure to afflictions and suffering.

Richard Katz, *Boiling Energy: Community Healing among the Kalahari Kung.* Cambridge: Harvard University Press, 1982. This account of the healing practices of the Ju/wasi (!Kung) of the Dobe area between Namibia and Botswana focuses on several different healers, their training, and styles.

Emily Martin, *The Woman in the Body: A Cultural Analysis of Reproduction.* Boston: Beacon Press, 1987. This text explores how Western medical texts represent women's reproductive experiences and how they compare to a sample of Baltimore women's perceptions and experiences of menstruation, childbirth, and menopause.

Carol Shepherd McClain, ed., *Women as Healers: A Cross-Cultural Perspective.* New Brunswick: Rutgers University Press, 1989. This collection of 11 studies is preceded by a general overview. Case studies include Ecuador, Sri Lanka, Mexico, Jamaica, the United States, Serbia, Korea, southern Africa, and Benin.

Sherry Saggers and Dennis Gray, *Dealing with Alcohol: Indigenous usage in Australia, New Zealand and Canada.* New York: Cambridge University Press, 1998. This comparative study looks at structural issues such as European colonialism and interests of liquor companies in creating and sustaining high rates of alcohol consumption among many indigenous groups, and people's own understanding of their situation.

J. Waldram, A. Herring, and K. Young, *Aboriginal Health in Canada: Historical, Cultural and Epidemiological Perspectives.* Toronto: University of Toronto Press, 1995. This volume offers very comprehensive coverage of First Nations health issues and includes discussions of current health problems, an overview of health and health care from an historical perspective, and ideas on what future changes need to be made.

 Your *Cultural Anthropology*, Second Canadian Edition Media Edition CD-ROM contains many Web sites relevant to this chapter. Use it to explore the Web and to expand your knowledge of anthropology.

Kinship Dynamics

A wedding procession of a Minangkabau couple in Sumatra, Indonesia. The bride wears an elaborate gold headdress, typical of the Minangkabau, as is the groom's turban.

Key Questions

How do cultures define kinship through descent?

How do cultures define kinship through sharing?

How do cultures define kinship through marriage?

Gathering data on kinship is basic to most anthropological research projects because one of the first fieldwork tasks is to learn "who is who." Areas of questioning include asking informants about who they live with, whether or not they are married, how many children they have, and who in their family may have died. In many cultures, the researcher finds that people openly provide such information. In other situations, gathering accurate kinship data may be difficult. In Canada, an example of potential bias in gathering kinship data relates to rules about the welfare system. Among low-income people on welfare, a woman is eligible for welfare payments only if she is not married (either formally or through common law). In order to protect her eligibility for welfare payments, a married woman may report herself as living alone even if she has a permanent, co-resident partner.

Anthropologist Napoleon Chagnon has studied among the Yanomami since 1964. During his first year of fieldwork, the Yanomami gave him false information about dead relatives.

Napoleon Chagnon (1992) learned about a taboo against saying the names of certain relatives during his fieldwork among the Yanomami. During his first several months of fieldwork, Chagnon gathered kinship data from many respondents and carefully recorded it in his notebooks. Once, when visiting a village about 10 hours' walk from his research area of Bisassi-teri, he was chatting with the village headman about the headman of Bisassi-teri. Chagnon's mention of the headman's name was greeted by gales of laughter. In this way, he learned that his informants in Bisassi-teri had given him misinformation about their names and those of their relatives. Out of sheer mischief, many had provided people with fake names that were silly and rude such as "asshole" or "fart breath." Eventually, he was able to obtain the "real" names for people. Still, Chagnon had problems getting people to say the names of dead relatives. He discovered that the Yanomami have a taboo against speaking the name of deceased kin, so they would invent a fake name. In order to construct a full picture of kinship relations, Chagnon was determined to learn about these dead relatives. He came up with an idea that worked. He would take a Polaroid photograph of an informant with him to a nearby village, show them the picture, and ask them to provide the names of the photographed person's relatives, dead or alive. This did not break their taboo, and so Chagnon was able to construct a solid data set of many people's kin.

The closest and most intense human relationships often involve people who consider themselves related to each other through kinship. All cultures have ideas about what defines a kinship relationship and rules for appropriate behaviour between kin. These rules can be informal or formally defined by law, such as a law forbidding marriage between first cousins. Everyone begins learning about his or her particular culture's **kinship system** (the combination of ideas about who are kin and what kinds of behaviour kinship relationships involve) from infancy. Like one's first language, one's kinship system becomes so ingrained that it tends to be taken for granted as something "natural" rather than cultural.

Learning another culture's kinship system is as challenging as learning another language. This was true for Robin Fox (1995 [1978]) during his research among the

Tory Islanders of Ireland. Some of the Irish kinship terms and categories he encountered were similar to American English usage, but others were not. For example, the word *muintir* can mean "people" in its widest sense, as in English. It can also refer to people of a particular social category, as in "my people" that refers to close relatives. Another similarity is with *gaolta*, the word for "relatives" or "those of my blood." In its adjectival form, *gaolta* refers to kindness like the English word *kin*, which is related to "kindness." Tory Islanders have a phrase meaning "children and grandchildren," also like the English term *descendants*. The word for *friend* on Tory Island is the same as the word for *kin*, reflecting the cultural circumstances on Tory Island with its small population, all living close together: Everyone is related by kinship, so, logically, friends are kin.

Studying kinship systems offers surprising discoveries. In some cultures, an uncle has a closer relationship with his sister's children than with his own children. In others, a child considers his or her mother's sisters as mothers and is close to all of them. Cousins, including first cousins (offspring of one's mother's and father's siblings), are preferred as marriage partners in much of the Middle East and in parts of South Asia where cousin marriages are both common and legal. In Canada first cousin marriage is legal but not preferred. In the United States some states allow first cousin marriage; others forbid it on the assumption that first cousin marriage may result in the birth of children with genetic defects. In some cultures, a person may have more than one spouse. Increasing numbers of people in Europe and North America choose to cohabit with a partner and never get married.

In all cultures, kinship links modes of production, reproduction, and ideology. Depending on the type of economy, it accordingly shapes children's physical growth and personality development, influences a person's marriage options, and affects the status and care of the aged. In small-scale pre-industrial cultures, kinship is the primary, and often only, principle that organizes people into coherent and meaningful groups. In such contexts, the kinship group performs the functions of ensuring the continuity of the group through arranging marriages; maintaining social order through setting moral rules and punishing offenders; and providing for the basic needs of members through regulating production, consumption, and distribution. In large-scale industrial societies, kin-

ship ties exist, but many other forms of social affiliation draw people together into groups that have nothing to do with kinship.

The Study of Kinship

Early anthropologists documented the importance of kinship in the societies they researched. Lewis Henry Morgan and others argued that kinship was the most important organizing principle in pre-state cultures. While taking some form of kinship as a cultural universal, they also discovered that definitions of who counts as kin differed from those of contemporary Europe and North America. Western cultures emphasize "blood" relations as primary, that is, relations between people linked by birth from a biological mother and father (Sault 1994). Ties through marriage are secondary. This model is expressed in the English-language adage: "blood is thicker than water." Not all cultures define who is a "blood" relative in the same way. In some, males in the family are of one "blood" (or "substance"), while females are of another. This contrasts with the Euro-American definition that all biological children of the same parents share the same "blood." In yet other cultures, a more important criterion for kinship is breastfeeding: Babies who were nursed by the same woman are considered related and cannot marry each other. The popular Western view of kinship as based on "blood" relationships and its contemporary grounding in a genetic relationship with the birth mother and "procreative father" (the male who provides the semen that fertilizes the female's ovum) is so widely accepted as real and natural that understanding other kinship theories is difficult for Westerners.

Kinship Diagrams, Genealogies, and Terminology

Early anthropological work on kinship tended to focus, as Chagnon did, on finding out who is related to whom and in what way. Typically, the anthropologist would interview one or two people, asking questions such as: What do you call your brother's daughter? Can you (as a man) marry your father's brother's daughter? or What is the term you use to refer to your mother's sister? In another approach, the anthropologist would interview an individual and ask him or her to name all their relatives, explain how they are related to them, and provide the terms by which they refer to them. From this kind of reported information, the anthropologist would construct a **kinship diagram**, a schematic way of presenting data on the kinship relationships of an individual, called "ego" (see Figure 8.1 below). It depicts all of ego's relatives, as remembered by ego and reported to the anthropologist. Strictly speaking, information gained from the informant for his or her kinship diagram is not supplemented by asking other people to fill in where ego's memory failed (as opposed to a genealogy, see below). In cultures where kinship plays a greater role in social relations, it is likely that an informant will be able to provide information on more relatives than in one where kinship ties are less important in comparison to other networks such as friendships and work groups.

In contrast to a kinship diagram, a **genealogy** is constructed beginning with the earliest ancestors (rather than starting with ego and working outward) that can be traced and working down to the present. The Tory Islanders were not comfortable beginning with ego when Robin Fox was attempting to construct kinship diagrams. They preferred to proceed genealogically, so he followed their preference. Tracing a family's complete genealogy may involve archival research in the attempt to construct as full a record as possible. Many cultures have trained genealogists whose task is to help families discover or main-

tain records of their family lines. In Europe and North America, Christians often record their "family tree" in the front of the family Bible.

Decades of anthropological research have produced a mass of information on kinship terminology, or the terms that people use to refer to people they consider to be kin of various types. For example, in Euro-American kinship, children of one's father's sister and brother and one's mother's sister and brother are all referred to by the same kinship term: cousins. Likewise, one's father's sister (aunt) and brother (uncle) and one's mother's sister and brother have the same terms. And the terms "grandmother" and "grandfather" can refer to the ascending generation on either one's father's or mother's side. In some cultures, different terms are used for kin on one's mother's and father's side. In North India, one's father's brother is called *chacha,* and one's mother's brother *mama*; one's father's father is *baba* and one's mother's father is *nana.* Another type of system emphasizes solidarity along lines of siblings of the same gender so that one's mother and mother's sisters all have the same term, which translates as "mother." This system is found among the Navajo, for example. Anthropologists have classified the cross-cultural variety in kinship terminology into six basic types, named after groups that were first discovered to have that type of system; for example, there is an "Iroquois" type and an "Eskimo" type (see Figure 8.2). Cultures that have similar kinship terminology are then placed into

FIGURE 8.1   Symbols Used in Kinship Diagrams

Characters		Relationships		Kin Abbreviations	
◯	female	=	is married to	**Mo**	mother
△	male	≈	is cohabiting with	**Fa**	father
⌀	deceased female	≠	is divorced from	**Br**	brother
◮	deceased male	≉	is separated from	**Z**	sister
●	female "ego" of the diagram	⊙	adopted-in female	**H**	husband
▲	male "ego" of the diagram	◬	adopted-in male	**W**	wife
■	"ego," regardless of gender	|	is descended from	**Da**	daughter
		⊓	is the sibling of	**S**	son

FIGURE 8.2   Two Kinship Naming Systems

Eskimo Kinship Terms

Eskimo kinship terminology, like that of most Euro-Americans, has unique terms for kin within the nuclear family that are not used for any other relatives: mother, father, sister, brother. This fact is related to the freestanding aspect of the nuclear family. Another feature is that the same terms are used for relatives on both the mother's and father's sides, which is related to bilineal descent.

Iroquois Kinship Terms

Iroquois kinship terminology operates in unilineal systems. One result is that there are different terms for relatives on the mother's and father's sides and distinctions between cross and parallel cousins. Another feature is the "merging" of one's mother with one's mother's sister (both are referred to as "mother") and one's father with one's father's brother (both are referred to as "father").

one of the six categories. The Yanomami would, in this way, be identified as having an Iroquois naming system. (Our perspective is that memorizing these six types of terminology is not a fruitful way to promote understanding of actual kinship dynamics, the focus of this chapter, so this text avoids going into detail on them.)

Getting Beyond Diagrams and Terms

The formalism of early kinship studies led many students of anthropology—and some of their professors—to think that kinship is a boring subject. Fortunately, a renewed interest in kinship is occurring that considers it in relation to other topics such as power relations, reproductive decision making, women's changing work roles, and ethnic identity (Carsten 2000). While we can leave much of the terminology behind, some of the complexity of kinship systems cross-culturally must be faced. Margaret Trawick (1992) offers these insights in her book on Tamil kinship in South India:

> Tamils and neighboring peoples have a very elegant set of ways of organizing their families and larger kin groups into patterned systems. Any person trying to understand South Indian culture must eventually come round to examining and trying to comprehend these elegant patterns

FIGURE 8.3 Economies and Kinship

FORAGING	HORTICULTURE	PASTORALISM	AGRICULTURE	INDUSTRIALISM (CAPITALIST)
Descent and Inheritance				*Descent and Inheritance*
Bilateral		Unilineal (matrilineal or patrilineal)		Bilateral
Marital Residence				*Marital Residence*
Neolocal or bilocal		Matrilocal or patrilocal		Neolocal
Household Type				*Household Type*
Nuclear		Extended		Nuclear or single-parent or single-person

of kinship organization.… I would argue that South Indian people create such patterns not only because they "work," not only because they perform some necessary social "function," but also because, in their beauty, they give their creators pleasure.… Kinship patterns can be understood as objects of artistic appreciation, in the same way that mathematical proofs or car engines are, for some people, such objects. Opening the hood of a fancy sports car, some of us will see nothing but a confusing jumble of ugly machinery. Others, who understand such things, will be perfused with bliss. It is the same with kinship patterns. (117–118)

As anthropologists attempt to study kinship as a dynamic aspect of life, they are increasingly turning to varied sources of data gathering, rather than simply interviewing informants. Participant observation is extremely valuable for learning about who interacts with whom, how they interact with each other, and why their relationship has the content it has. Observations can provide understanding, for example, of the frequency and intensity of people's kinship interactions and the degree to which they have supportive social networks. Another approach, the life history method (see Chapter 2), reveals changes through an individual's lifetime and the way they are related to other events such as migration, a natural disaster, or political change. Focused life histories are useful in target-

ing key events related to kinship such as marriage or cohabitation, divorce, or widowhood/widowerhood. Anthropologists interested in population dynamics, for example, use focused life histories, interviews, and questionnaires to gather information on personal demographics to learn at what age a woman commenced sexual relations, how many pregnancies she had, if and when she had an abortion or bore a child, whether the child lived or died, and when she stopped having children.

Descent

Descent is the tracing of kinship relationships through parentage. It is based on the fact that everybody is born from someone else. Descent creates a line of people from whom someone is descended, stretching through history. But all cultures do not reckon descent in the same way. Some cultures have a bilateral descent system, in which a child is recognized as being related by descent to both parents. Others have a **unilineal descent** system, which recognizes descent through only one parent, either the father or mother. The distribution of bilateral and unilineal systems is roughly correlated with different modes of production (see Figure 8.3). This correspondence makes sense because economies—production, consumption, and exchange—are closely tied to the way people and their labour power are organized and how commodities are used and transferred. This section begins with the descent system that is the most prevalent cross-culturally.

Unilineal Descent

Unilineal descent systems are the basis of kinship in about 60 per cent of the world's cultures, making some form of unilineality the most common form of descent. In general, unilineal systems characterize societies with a "fixed" resource base such as crop land or herds over which people have some sense of ownership. Inheritance rules that regulate the transmission of property through only one line help maintain cohesiveness of the resource base. Unilineal systems thus are most associated with horticultural, pastoralist, and agricultural modes of production. Unilineal descent systems have higher frequencies of **extended families** than bilateral cultures (discussed in Chapter 9).

Two patterns of unilineal descent are **patrilineal descent** (kinship is traced through the male line alone) and **matrilineal descent** (kinship is traced through the female line alone). In a patrilineal system, only male children inherit the major forms of property. Female children "marry out" and become members of the husband's lineage. The same applies in matrilineal descent systems, in which only daughters are considered to carry on the family line. These descent systems also affect the organization of labour through their determination of marital residence. After marriage in a patrilineal descent system, it is likely that the new couple will live with or near the groom's family, and the groom will continue to be a part of his family's work force with the addition of the bride.

Jack Goody (1976), a leading kinship theorist of the later twentieth century, advanced our thinking in this area. He developed a comparative approach that reveals differences between the descent systems of rural sub-Saharan Africa and Eurasia. In sub-Saharan African groups that rely on horticultural production, women are prominent as producers, reproducers, marketers, and decision makers. Their matrilineal descent system recognizes and perpetuates the importance of women. In rural Eurasia, in contrast, plough agriculture has long been the characteristic mode of production. As discussed in Chapter 3, males are primarily involved with plough agricultural systems, while women play complementary roles in animal care, food processing, weeding, and harvesting. The patrilineal descent system often associated with this mode of production does not give women's tasks high value. The question of why a particular culture is matrilineal or patrilineal has not been resolved, but at least we have some ideas about implications of patrilineality and matrilineality for the relative status of men and women in each system. Members of the gender that controls the resources (both productive and reproductive) tend to have higher status. Thus, in general, women have higher status in matrilineal societies and men have higher status in patrilineal societies.

Patrilineal Descent Patrilineal descent is found among about 44 per cent of all cultures. It is prevalent in most pastoral societies, most of India, East Asia, the Middle East, Papua New Guinea, northern Africa, and some horticultural groups of sub-Saharan Africa. Cultures with patrilineal descent tend to have ideologies that are consistent with that concept. For example, theories of how conception occurs and how the fetus is formed give priority to the male role. Among the Kaliai people of Papua New Guinea, people say that an infant is composed entirely of *aitama aisuru*, the "father's water" or semen, which is channelled to the fetus. The mother is an "incubator" who contributes nothing substantial to the developing fetus. The mother's relationship with the infant develops later, through breastfeeding.

Margery Wolf's book, *The House of Lim* (1968), is a classic ethnography of a patrilineal system. She lived for two years with the Lims, a Taiwanese farming household (see Figure 8.4 on page 196). In her book, she first describes the village setting and then the Lims' house, giving attention to the importance of the ancestral hall with its family altar, where the household head meets guests. She then provides a chapter on Lim Han-ci, the father and household head, and then a chapter on Lim Hue-lieng, the eldest son. She next introduces the females of the family: wives, sisters, and an adopted daughter. The ordering of the chapters reflects the importance of the "patriarch" (senior, most powerful male) and his eldest son who will, if all goes according to plan, assume the leadership position as his father ages and then dies. Daughters marry out into other families. In-marrying females (wives, daughters-in-law) are always considered outsiders, never fully merged into the patrilineage. The Lims' kinship system exemplifies strong patrilineality in that it heavily weights position, power, and property with males. In such systems, girls are raised "for other families" and are thus not fully members of their natal (birth) family; however, they never become fully merged into their marriage family, always being considered somehow "outsiders." Residence of married couples is typically **patrilocal,** with or near the husband's natal family. The world's most strongly patrilineal systems are found in East Asia, South Asia, and the Middle East (see the Multiple Cultural Worlds box).

Matrilineal Descent Matrilineal descent exists in about 15 per cent of all cultures. It traces kinship through the female line exclusively, and children belong to their mother's group. Less common than patrilineal descent, it is found among many Native North American groups, across a large band in central Africa; among many groups of Southeast Asia, the Pacific, and Australia; parts of eastern and southern India; in a small pocket of north-

ern Bangladesh; and in localized areas of the Mediterranean coast of Spain and Portugal. Matrilineal societies vary greatly, from foragers such as the Tiwi of northern Australia to settled ranked societies such as the Nayar of southern India (Lepowsky 1993:296). The majority, however, are found in horticultural systems where women have primacy in production and distribution of food and other goods. Married couples tend to reside matrilocally; that is, with or near the wife's natal family. Often, but not always, matrilineal kinship is associated with recognized public leadership positions for women, as among the Iroquois or Hopi. In general, women's status is likely to be higher in matrilineal descent systems than in patrilineal descent systems.

In matrilineal cultures, ideologies about conception give primacy to female contributions to the fetus. Among the Malays of Langkawi island, people say that children are created from the seed of their father and the blood of their mother (Carsten 1995:229). The seed spends 40 days inside the body of the father. The first, fifteenth,

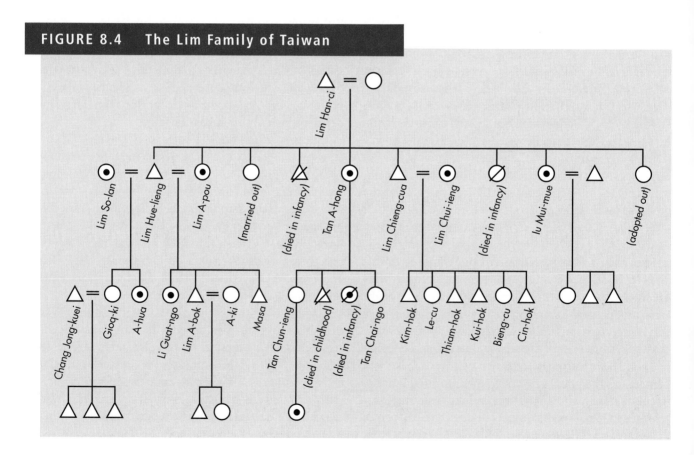

FIGURE 8.4   The Lim Family of Taiwan

The Named and the Nameless in a Cantonese Village

The village of Ha Tsuen is located in the northwest corner of a rural area of Hong Kong's New Territories (Watson 1986). About 2500 people live in the village. All the males belong to the same patrilineage and have the same surname of Teng. They are descended from a common ancestor who settled in the region in the twelfth century. In Ha Tsuen, as in its wider region, kinship is reckoned patrilineally. Daughters of Ha Tsuen marry out of the village. Sons of Ha Tsuen marry brides who come in from other villages, and marital residence is patrilocal. In Ha Tsuen, as in most strongly patrilineal systems, women do not own property, and they have no direct control of the means of production. Few married women are employed in wage labour; rather, they depend on their husbands for financial support. Local politics is a male domain, as is all public decision making. Women's primary role is in reproduction, especially of sons. A woman's status as a new bride is low; indeed, the transition from daughter to bride can be difficult psychologically. As a woman bears children, especially sons, her status in the household increases.

The naming system reflects the greater power, importance, and autonomy of males. A child is first given a name referred to as his or her ming when it is 30 days old. Before that time, the mother and infant are secluded to prevent soul loss in the infant. The 30th-day ceremony is as elaborate as the family can afford if the baby is a boy, including a banquet for neighbours and village elders, and the presentation of red eggs to everyone in the community. For a girl, the 30th-day ceremony is likely to involve just a special meal for close family members. Paralleling this bias towards sons in monetary expenditure is the amount of thinking that goes into the selection of the ming and its meaning. A boy's ming is more distinctive and flattering, perhaps having a literary or classical connection. A girl's ming often has a negative connotation, such as "Last Child," "Too Many," "Little Mistake," or "Joined to a Brother," which implies hope that this daughter will be a lucky charm to bring the birth of a son next. Uncomplimentary names may be given to a boy, but the goal is for protection: to trick the spirits into thinking he is only a worthless girl so that they won't take him. Thus, a precious son may be given the ming "Little Slave Girl."

Marriage is the next formal naming occasion. When a male marries, he is given or chooses for himself a tzu or marriage name. Gaining a tzu is an integral part of the marriage ceremony and a key marker of male adulthood. The tzu is not used in everyday address, but appears mainly on formal documents. A man will have a wai hao, "outside name," which is his public nickname. As he enters middle age, he may also take a hao, or courtesy name, which he chooses and which reflects his self-aspirations and self-perceptions. In the case of a woman, her ming ceases to exist upon marriage. She no longer has a name, but instead her husband refers to her as nei jen, "inner person," since now her life is restricted to the domestic world of household, husband's family, and neighbourhood. In her new world of kin, she is referred to by **teknonyms** (names for someone based on their relationship to someone else), such as "Wife of So and So" or "Mother of So and So." Her personhood and identity are rigidly defined by the kinship system and her names will be derived from her place in that system. In old age, she becomes ah po, "Old Woman," like every other aged female in the village.

Throughout their lives, men accumulate more and better quality names than women, and they can choose them themselves. Over the course of their lives, women have fewer names than men. Women's names are standardized rather than personalized, and they have no control over them.

FOOD FOR THOUGHT

Do you know of any examples of naming biases determined by a child's gender, birth order, or other basis?

and thirtieth days of the month are the days on which "the seed falls." Then the seed "descends to the mother." There it mixes with her menstrual blood. It has only to mix with the mother's menstrual blood once in order to conceive. After that, the seed is nourished in the mother's womb from her blood.

The Minangkabau (pronounced "mee-NAN-ka-bow," the last syllable rhyming with "now") of Indonesia are the largest matrilineal group in the world (Blackwood 1995). They are primarily rural agriculturalists, producing substantial amounts of surplus rice, but many of them also participate in migratory labour, working for wages in Indonesian cities for a time, then returning home. In their matrilineal kinship system, women hold power through their control of lineage land and its products and of agricultural employment on their land and through their pre-eminent position in business (especially having to do with rice). Inheritance passes from mothers to daughters, making the matrilineal line the enduring controller of property. Each submatrilineage, constituting perhaps four generations, lives together in a lineage house or several closely located houses. The senior woman has the power—her decisions are sought in terms of all economic and ceremonial matters. She is called *Bundo Kanduang,* "womb mother" or "elder woman" or "wise woman." Her advice is respected by all, although group consensus (not dictatorial power of the senior woman) is the guiding principle in group dynamics and is shaped by all senior members. The senior male of the sublineage has the role of representing its interests to other groups, but he is only a representative, not a powerful person in himself.

Matrilineal kinship appears to be declining worldwide in the face of globalized Western/European cultural forces such as colonialism and neocolonialism, which have had a strong effect in establishing patrilineal kinship norms through the spread of Western education, religion, and law. European colonial rule in Africa and Asia contributed to the decline in matrilineal kinship by registering land and other property in the names of assumed male heads of household, even where females were the heads (Boserup 1970). This process effectively eroded women's previous rights and powers. Western missionary influence throughout much of the world also transformed matrilineal cultures into more patrilineal systems (Etienne and Leacock 1980). European influences have led to the decline of matrilineal kinship among Native North Americans, which have long constituted one of the largest distributions of matrilineal descent worldwide (although not all Native North American groups were or are matrilineal). A comparative study of kinship among three diverse areas of the Navajo reservation in Arizona shows that matrilineality exists where conditions most resemble the pre-reservation era (Levy, Henderson, and Andrews 1989). In the case of the Minangkabau of Indonesia, matrilineal kinship is being undermined by the combined forces of Dutch colonialism, which promoted the image of male-led nuclear families as an ideal; the Islamic faith, which currently promotes female domesticity and male household dominance; and the modernizing Indonesian state, which insists on naming males as heads of households (see Chapter 9) (Blackwood 1995).

Double Descent

A minority of cultures have **double descent** systems (also called *double unilineal descent*) that combine patrilineal and matrilineal descent. In these systems, offspring are believed to inherit different personal attributes and property from both their father's line and their mother's line. Many early anthropologists mistook this mixed system for a patrilineal system, demonstrating once again the power of ethnocentrism in interpretation. For example, the Bangangté of Cameroon in West Africa have a double descent system, although it was first described by anthropologists as patrilineal (Feldman-Savelsberg 1995). This misrepresentation was probably the result of interviewing only men and focusing on the inheritance of land property rather than on other traits. "While Bangangté, in their conversations with inquisitive anthropologists, first list the property and titles they inherit from their fathers, they present a much more complex picture to those who listen further" (486). Research among married women uncovered double descent. Through the maternal line, one inherits movable property (such as household goods and cattle), personality traits, and a type of witchcraft substance that resides in the intestines. Patrilineal ties determine physical resemblance and rights to land and village residence. Matrilineally related women tend to bond together and visit each other frequently, consulting on marriage partners for their children, advising on child naming choices, and supporting each other in times of trouble.

Bilateral Descent

Bilateral descent traces kinship from both parents, more or less equally, to the child. Family groups tend to be nuclear, with strong bonds between father, mother, and their children. Marital residence is predominantly neolocal. Both residence types offer more flexibility than what is usual in unilineal systems. Inheritance of property from the parental generation is allocated equally among all offspring regardless of their gender. In bilateral descent systems, conception theories emphasize an equal biological contribution to the child from the mother and father. For example, contemporary Western science states that the sperm contributed by the male and the ovum contributed by the female are equally important in the formation of a new person.

Bilateral descent is found in less than one-third of the world's cultures (Murdock 1965 [1949]:57). The highest frequency of bilateral descent is found at the opposite ends of the production continuum (refer back to Figure 8.3 on page 194). For example, the Ju/wasi have bilateral descent, and most people think bilateral descent is the prevalent pattern in North America (see the Critical Thinking box). A minority pattern of bilateral descent is called **ambilineal descent.** This system recognizes that a person is descended from both parents, but allows for choice in determining which descent group to be more affiliated with and is therefore characterized by bilocal residence (a choice is available between living near or with the family of either the groom or the bride). For example, in Tahiti, newly married couples choose to live either with or near either the bride's or the groom's family with no particular preference involved (Lockwood 1993).

Given that most of the world's people recognize some connection between a baby and both parents, it is puzzling as to why the majority of kinship systems (which are unilineal) emphasize only one parent. Evolutionists of the late 1800s claimed that in early societies, the father was not known. Bilateral kinship, they said, emerged as "higher civilization" and male dominance emerged, granting the male greater recognition in paternity. Thus, unilineal kinship systems are remnants of earlier times. This argument is weak on two grounds. First, it is ethnocentric to claim that contemporary bilateral cultures, especially Euro-American culture, represent the only source of knowledge of the father's biological role. Evidence from many unilineal cultures indicates widespread understanding of this fact. Second, foraging peoples tend to have bilateral kinship, suggesting that the world's earliest peoples may have also had bilateral kinship.

CRITICAL THINKING

How Bilateral Is "American Kinship"?

"American kinship" refers to a general model based on the bilateral system of Euro-Americans of the 1960s (Schneider 1968). According to this model, children are considered to be descended from both mother and father, and general inheritance rules suggest that property would be divided equally between sons and daughters. Given the rich cultural diversity of the United States and Canada, most would now consider the label "American kinship" and its characterization as bilateral to be overgeneralized. Biases are often prominent towards either patrilineality or matrilineality. Indicators of patrilineality include the prevalent practice of a wife dropping her surname at marriage and taking her husband's surname, and the use of the husband's surname for offspring. Although inheritance is supposedly equal between sons and daughters, often it is not. In

many business families, the business is passed from father to sons, while daughters are given a different form of inheritance such as a trust fund. On the other hand, a certain degree of **matrifocality** (a domestic system in which the mother is the central figure) arises from another source: high rates of divorce and the resulting trend of young children living with the mother more often than the father. A matrifocal emphasis creates mother-centred residence and child-raising patterns, but may not affect inheritance patterns.

In order to explore descent patterns in Canada, each student in the class should draw his or her own kinship diagram. Students should note their ethnicity at the top of the chart, choosing the label with which they feel most comfortable. Then, each student should draw a circle around the rela-

tives who are "closest" to "ego," including parents, grandparents, aunts, uncles, cousins—whoever fits in this category as defined by ego. As a group, students in the class should then consider the following questions about the kinship diagrams.

CRITICAL THINKING QUESTIONS

How many students drew equal circles around relatives on both parents' sides?

How many emphasized the mother's side? How many emphasized the father's side?

Do ethnic patterns emerge in terms of the circled kin?

From this exercise, what can be said about "American kinship"?

In attempting to explain the relative scarcity of bilateral systems, cultural materialists offer a theory that looks to the mode of production as influencing the type of kinship system. They point out that bilateral kinship systems are associated mainly with two modes of production: foraging and industrialism. Both modes of production rely on a flexible gender division of labour in which both males and females contribute, relatively equally, to production and exchange. Logically, then, a bilateral kinship system recognizes the strengths of both the mother's and father's side. Bilateral kinship is also an adaptive system for members of foraging and industrial populations because it allows for small family units that are spatially mobile. Bilateral kinship offers the most flexibility in terms of residence, keeping open opportunities related to making a living. As the world becomes increasingly urbanized and industrialized, and if the gender division of labour and resource entitlements were to become more equal, then bilateral kinship might increase in distribution.

As noted earlier, residence rules often match the prevailing "direction" of descent rules (see Figure 8.3 on page 194). Thus, in most patrilineal societies, marital residence is patrilocal (with or near the male's kin). In most matrilineal societies, it is matrilocal (with or near the woman's kin) or **avunculocal** (with or near the groom's mother's brother). Common in Western industrialized society is the practice of **neolocality.** These residence patterns have political, economic, and social implications. The combination of matrilineal descent and matrilocal residence, for example, is often found among groups that engage in long-distance warfare (Divale 1974). Strong female household structures maintain the domestic scene while the men are absent on military campaigns, as among the Iroquois of upstate New York and the Nayar of southern India. Patrilineal descent and patrilocal residence promote the development of cohesive male-focused lineages that are associated with frequent local warfare, which requires the presence of a force of fighting men on the home front.

Sharing

A growing number of studies indicate that many cultures give priority to kinship that is not based on biologically defined birth, but through acts of sharing and support. These relationships may be informal or formally certified, as in legalized adoption. Ritually formalized kinship also fits in this category, including *godparenthood* (kinship based on ritual ties) and *blood brotherhood* (kinship based on sharing of "blood" or some other substance).

Food Sharing

Cultural anthropologists have devoted relatively little attention to studying food-based kinship, but examples are increasing in the literature. Among the Kaliai, as noted above, fathers are said to be related to their children by descent, while mothers are related to them through breastfeeding. Sharing-based kinship is common throughout much of Southeast Asia, New Guinea, and Australia (Carsten 1995). On an island of Malaysia, the process of developing sharing-based relatedness starts in the womb and continues throughout a person's life. The first food sharing is when the fetus is fed by the mother's blood. After birth, the infant is fed from its mother's breast. Breast milk is believed to derive from the mother's blood and thus "blood becomes milk." This tie is crucial. A child who is not breastfed will not "recognize" its mother. Breastfeeding is the basis of the incest rule:

> [K]in who have drunk milk from the breast of the same woman may not marry.... The salience of a prohibition on marriage between milk siblings is rendered greater by the fact that many children spend a considerable part of their childhood in houses other than their maternal ones. The frequency of formal and informal fostering arrangements... substantially increases the possibility that a child may drink the milk of a woman who is not its birth mother.... It is quite easy to imagine that a child who has been casually put on the breast of a neighbor or distant kinswoman might later marry her child. This ever-present threat looms large in the minds of villagers and runs through their discourse on incest. (227)

After the baby is weaned, its most important food is cooked rice. Sharing cooked rice, like breast milk, becomes another way the kinship ties are created and maintained, especially between mothers and children. Men are often away—on fishing trips, in coffee shops, or at the mosque—and so they are less likely to have these rice-sharing bonds.

Adoption and Fostering

Transferring children from their birth parent to the care of others through adoption and fostering is found in all cultures. Adoption offers a cultural solution to the natural unevenness in human reproduction. Common motivations for adopting a child include infertility and the desire to obtain a particular kind of child (often a son). Motivations for the birth parent to transfer the child to someone else's care include a premarital pregnancy in cultures that do not condone children being born outside a marriage relationship, having "too many" children as defined in that culture, or having "too many" of a particular gender of child. For example, among the Maasai, if a woman had several children, she might "give" one of hers to a friend, neighbour, or aged person who had no children or no one to care for them.

Fostering a child is sometimes similar to a formal adoption in terms of permanence and a developed sense of a close relationship. Or it may involve a temporary placement of a child with someone else for a specific purpose, with little development of a sense of kinship. Such "child transfers" (relocating a child's residence and primary care from one social unit to another) often fall midway between what Westerners would consider formal adoption and fostering. Given these several options for defining relations between adults and children, several questions arise for cultural anthropologists: How do different kinship systems deal with the issue of adoptive (or otherwise "transferred") offspring? Do adopted and fostered children have special problems constructing their personal identity and sense of self? Does this vary by culture? How do adopted offspring gain a sense of belonging if they are raised by people other than their birth parents? For the most part, these questions await in-depth research.

Legalized Adoption in North America
Currently, about one of every ten couples in Canada is infertile, and many of these couples would like to have children. Some use fertility drugs, *in vitro* fertilization, or surrogate child bearing. Many people, including those who have biologically recognized children, choose to adopt. Since the mid-1800s, adoption has been a legalized form of child transfer in Canada. It is "a procedure which establishes the relationship of parent and child between persons not so related by nature" (Leavy and Weinberg 1979, v, quoted in Modell 1994:2). Judith Modell, cultural anthropologist and adoptive parent, studied people's experiences of adoptees, birth parents, and adoptive parents. According to Modell, the biological relationship of kinship is so pervasive in that the legal process of adoption attempts to construct the adoptive relationship to be as much like a biological one as possible. The adopted child is given a new birth certificate. After adoption, the birth parent ceases to have any relationship with the child. This pattern is called "closed adoption." A recent trend is towards "open adoption," in which adoptees and birth parents have access to information about each other's identity and have freedom to interact with one another. Of the

An orphanage in Shanghai, China. Human rights activists have claimed that abuse was widespread in Chinese orphanages, especially of children with physical handicaps. Following this allegation, foreign media were invited to visit the Shanghai Children's Welfare Institute.

28 adoptees Modell talked with, not all were interested in searching for their birth parents:

> A few said they were "mildly curious" about their birth-parents while others had requested birth and medical records. Ten had established some kind of relationship with a birth family.... No one said they thought searching was bad. Those who did not want to find any more information were convinced that all adoptees had a "right to know." Four told me they would never consider searching. "I would just never go looking for her [birth mother] or my father. It just isn't something I consider important enough for me to do—in the first place, she could have passed away." One admitted that he had a "burning curiosity," but considered it would be "a selfish move on my part" to find out anything further. Another who said she had no "desire to go looking," added, "I wish I could see a photograph of my parents without meeting them." A fourth said, in an uncertain tone of voice, "Maybe I am just not curious enough." (144–145)

For many adoptees, a search for birth parents involves an attempt to discover "who I really am." It is a search for an identity that is believed to lie in genealogical roots. For others, such a search is backward-looking and not a path towards formulating one's identity. Given this diversity of views, it is not possible to formulate firm generalizations. The momentum of the movement for open adoption signifies many people's adherence to the biological model of selfhood and identity. Thus, in North America, we could interpret the system of legal adoption as one that legalizes sharing-based kinship, but does not completely replace a sense of descent-based kinship for everyone involved. This statement also applies to many birth parents who seek to reconnect with the children they gave up for adoption.

Ritually Established Sharing Bonds

Ritually defined "sponsorship" of children descended from other people is common throughout the Christian—especially Catholic—world from South America to Europe and the Philippines. Relationships between godparents and godchildren often involve strong emotional ties and financial flows from the former to the latter. In Arembepe, a village in Bahia state in northeastern Brazil, "Children asked their godparents for a blessing the first time they saw them each day. Godparents occasionally gave cook-ies, candy, and money, and larger presents on special occasions" (Kottak 1992:61). In wealthier, more urbanized contexts, godparents can provide major financial support, including costs of education. They may be expected to assume the role of "adoptive" parents in the event of death of the child's birth parents (Woodrick 1995:223).

In the village of Santa Catalina in the Oaxaca Valley of southern Mexico, godparenthood is both a sign of the sponsor's status and the means to increased status (Sault 1985). A request to be a sponsor is acknowledgement of a person's ability to care for the child. The prestige of being asked to be a sponsor reflects well on one's entire family. It also gives the godparent influence over the godchild. Because the godparent can call on the godchild for labour, being a godparent of many children increases power through the ability to amass a major labour force when needed. In Santa Catalina, the majority of sponsors are male-female couples, but a notable number of sponsors were women alone, while no male alone was a sponsor. This difference is related to the relatively important role and high status of women in the Maya culture of the Oaxaca region.

Marriage

The third major basis for forming close interpersonal relationships is through marriage or other forms of "marriage-like" relationships such as long-term cohabitation. This section presents anthropological material mainly on formal marriage (other domestic arrangements are discussed in Chapter 9).

Towards a Definition

Anthropologists recognize that some form of **marriage** exists in all cultures, with different form and functions. However, what constitutes a cross-culturally valid definition of marriage is open to debate. A standard definition from 1951 is now discredited: "Marriage is a union between a man and a woman such that children born to the woman are the recognized legitimate offspring of both parents" (Barnard and Good 1984:89). This definition says that the partners must be of different genders. It implies that a child born outside a marriage is not socially recognized as legitimate. Exceptions exist to both these features cross-culturally. Same-gender marriages are now legal in Denmark, Norway, and Holland. In the United States in 2000, the state of Vermont passed a law giving legal rights to same-sex couples, as did Ontario in 1999. Policy debates are ongoing about whether same-gender "domestic partners" are eligible for "spousal" employment benefits. Even the question of whether marriage always involves two people is salient, given ethnographic examples of ritual marriages between people and gods and people and trees.

Marriage patterns among the matrilineal Nayars and the patrilineal Nambudiri brahmans of Kerala, in South India, have forced anthropologists to stretch their concept of what marriage is. The Nayars are well known in anthropology for their high levels of female education, female autonomy, and complex marriage patterns (Fuller 1976; Mencher 1965; Gough 1959). In the traditional pattern, no longer followed, a young Nayar woman would be married to a Nayar man according to the proper ritual rules, and the marriage would be sexually consummated after the ceremony. From then on, the wife would wear a *tali*, gold wedding necklace. Complexity arises, however, because Nayars are of the kshatriya caste cluster (traditionally a warrior category). Nayar men, in the past, went away for many years, fighting battles in distant regions. The Nayars followed the residence rule of **matrilocality** (a married Nayar woman continued to live with her mother and her line of relatives including aunts and uncles, nieces and nephews). During the husband's absence, it was considered perfectly appropriate for a married Nayar woman to enter into "side marriages" called *sambandhan* relationships with other men. These relationships were often arranged by a woman's father or brothers. *Sambandhan* relationships could include Nambudiri brahman men.

The Nambudiri brahmans were the local priestly caste and also rich landowners. In contrast to their neighbouring Nayars, they have patrilineal kinship and they practised **primogeniture,** whereby only the eldest son could inherit the family property. Another Nambudiri rule was that only the oldest son was allowed to marry a Nambudiri bride. Younger brothers' only option for marriage was through *sambandhan* relationships with Nayar women. They did not live with their Nayar wives, however, but maintained a visiting relationship with them. Any child born to a Nayar woman was said to be born from a Nayar man.

Thus, later-born Nambudiri sons were excluded from contributing reproductively to their lineage. What happened to the "surplus" of marriageable Nambudiri girls? According to Hindu cultural principles, a key parental duty is to see to the proper marriage of daughters. Spinsterhood is not a respectable option. Furthermore, Nambudiris were the highest status group in the area, and it would not have been acceptable for them to marry anyone lower than they. These rules combine to create a serious bind: A Nambudiri girl must marry, she cannot marry beneath her status, and there are not enough first sons among the Nambudiris to go around. The solution was found in ritual marriage. Many Nambudiri girls were married to a tree believed to be a deity. A marriage ceremony, complete with the bride circling the "groom" seven times as in any Hindu marriage ceremony, was performed and she would then wear the marriage tali. This ritual effectively placed Nambudiri females into a position parallel to a Catholic nun who "marries" Jesus and pledges herself to lifelong celibacy. Over time, these relationships between the matrilineal Nayars and the patrilineal Nambudiris have declined, mainly because of the decline of Nayar military service and legal changes made by the national government that restrict matrilineality.

In terms of the legitimacy of children, in many cultures, no distinction is made between legitimate or illegitimate children on the basis of whether they were born within a marriage. Many women in the Caribbean region, for example, do not marry until later in life. Before that, a woman has sequential male partners with whom she bears children. None of her children are considered more or less "legitimate" than any other.

Other definitions of marriage focus on rights over the spouse's sexuality. But not all forms of marriage involve sexual relations; for example, the practice of woman-woman marriage exists among the Nuer of the Sudan and some other African groups (Evans-Pritchard 1951:108–109). In this type of marriage, a woman with economic means provides a brideprice to obtain a "wife," goes through the marriage rituals with her, and brings her into the residential compound just as a man would who married a woman. This wife contributes her productive labour to the household. The two women do not have a sexual relationship. Instead, the in-married woman will have sexual relations with a man. Her children will belong to the compound into which she married, however. Thus, this arrangement provides the adult woman's labour and her children's labour to the household compound.

Given the range of practices that can come under the heading of marriage, some anthropologists have given up trying to find a working definition that will fit all cases. Others have suggested an open checklist of features such as reproduction, sexual rights, raising children, or a ritual ceremony. Anthropologist Linda Stone has developed a definition that focuses on the kinship relationships formed upon marriage. This may be the most inclusive definition possible: Marriage involves an intimate relation between spouses and creates in-law kin relations (Stone 1998:183). This accounts for all possible combinations of number and sex of spouses and avoids the problem of confounding marriage with more casual relations.

Selecting a Spouse

All cultures have preferences about whom one should and should not marry or with whom one should or should not have sexual intercourse. Sometimes these preferences are informal and implicit and other times formal and explicit.

Two men exchange rings and vows in the Metropolitan Community Church of Toronto in January, 2001. They hope to have the first legally recognized same sex marriage in Canada.

Rules of Exclusion Some sort of **incest taboo**, or a rule prohibiting marriage or sexual intercourse between certain kinship relations, is one of the most basic and universal rules of exclusion.

In his writings of the 1940s, French anthropologist Claude Lévi-Strauss dealt with the question of why all cultures have kinship systems. In his classic ethnological study, *The Elementary Structures of Kinship* (1969 [1949]), he argues that incest avoidance motivated men to exchange women between families. This exchange, he says, is the foundation for social networks and social solidarity beyond the immediate group. Such networks allow for trade between areas with different resources and the possibility that peaceful relations will exist between bride-exchangers. He took bride exchange as the basis for distinguishing two types of systems: **restricted exchange systems**, in which women are exchanged only between two groups (A and B exchange with each other) and **generalized exchange systems**, in which exchange involves more than two groups and occurs in a more diffuse and delayed way (A gives to B, who gives to C, and then C gives to A). These two types of exchange determine how intensive or extensive a group's social network becomes. Restricted exchange systems build dense and tightly interwoven local networks. Generalized exchange systems create extensive and loose systems. Why should two such different systems exist? One hypothesis is that generalized exchange is an adaptation to risky economic contexts because it offers a wider security net of social relationships.

Western genetic research suggests an alternative theory about why there is a universal incest taboo: that larger breeding pools help reduce the frequency of certain genetically transmitted conditions. Both theories are functional, in that they attribute the universal existence of incest taboos to their adaptive contribution, although in two different ways. No one has resolved the question of why incest taboos exist.

The most basic and universal form of incest taboo is against marriage or sexual intercourse between fathers and their children, and mothers and their children. In most cultures, brother-sister marriage has also been forbidden. But there are exceptions. The most well-known example of the allowance of brother-sister marriage comes from Egypt at the time of the Roman Empire (Barnard and Good 1984:92). Census data from that era show that between 15 and 20 per cent of marriages were between full brothers and sisters, not just within a few royal families, as is popularly believed. In other cultures, such as the Nuer of Sudan, the incest taboo extends to the extended lineage, which may include hundreds of people. The question of cousins is dealt with in highly contrasting ways cross-culturally. Notably, incest taboos do not universally rule out marriage or sexual intercourse with cousins. In fact, some kinship systems promote cousin marriage, as discussed in the next section.

In addition to incest taboos, many other rules of exclusion exist, such as prohibiting marriage with people of certain religions, races, or ethnic groups. Such exclusionary rules are often stated in the inverse—as rules of preference for marriage within a particular religion, race, or ethnic group.

Preference Rules A variety of preference rules exist cross-culturally concerning whom one should marry. Rules of **endogamy** (or marriage within a particular group) stipulate that the spouse must be chosen from within a defined pool of people. In kin endogamy, certain relatives are preferred, often cousins. Two major forms of cousin marriage exist: between **parallel cousins** (children of either one's father's brother or one's mother's sister—the term *parallel* indicates that the gender of the linking siblings is the same) or between **cross-cousins** (children of either one's father's sister or one's mother's brother—the term *cross* indicates the different genders of the linking siblings). Parallel-cousin marriage is favoured by many Islamic groups, especially the sub-form called *patrilateral parallel-cousin marriage,* which indicates a tendency for cousin marriage in the direction of the father's line rather than the mother's. Hindus of southern India favour cross-cousin marriages, especially matrilateral cross-cousins (through the mother's line). But, while cousin marriage is the preferred form, it nonetheless constitutes a minority of all marriages in the region. A survey of 3527 couples in the city of Chennai (formerly called Madras) in South India showed that three-fourths of all marriages involved unrelated people, while one-fourth were between first cross-cousins (or

between uncle and niece, which is considered the same relationship as cross-cousin) (Ramesh, Srikumari, and Sukumar 1989). Westerners who are unfamiliar with cousin marriage systems may find them objectionable on the basis of the potential genetic disabilities from "close inbreeding." A study of thousands of such marriages in South India, however, revealed only a very small difference in rates of certain "birth defects" compared with cultures in which cousin marriage is not practised (Sundar Rao 1983).

Endogamy may also be based on location. Village endogamy is a basis of arranging marriages throughout the eastern Mediterranean among both Christians and Muslims. Village endogamy is the preferred pattern among Muslims throughout India and among Hindus of southern India. Hindus of northern India, in contrast, forbid village endogamy and consider it a form of incest. Instead, they practise village **exogamy** ("marriage out"). For them, a preferred spouse should live in a far-off village or town. Thus, marriage distance is greater in the north than the south, and brides are far less likely to maintain regular contact with their natal kin in the north. Many songs and folktales of North Indian women convey sadness about being separated from their natal families, a theme that may not make much sense in a situation of village endogamy, where the bride's parents are likely to be close by.

Status considerations often shape spouse selection. The rule of **hypergyny** requires the groom to be of higher status than the bride; in other words, the bride "marries up." Hypergyny is a strong rule in northern India, especially among upper-status groups. It is also implicitly followed among many people in North America, where females "at the top" have the hardest time finding an appropriate partner because there are so few options "above them." Women medical students are a prime population experiencing an increased marriage squeeze because of status hypergyny. The opposite is **hypogyny,** when the female "marries down." Status hypogyny is rare cross-culturally, as is age hypogyny, in which the groom is younger than the bride. Age hypogyny, though rare as a preferred pattern, is increasing in North America because of the "marriage squeeze" on women who would otherwise prefer a husband of equal age or somewhat older.

Physical features, such as ability, looks, and appearance are factors that may be explicitly or implicitly recognized, or both. Features such as facial beauty, skin colour, hair texture and length, height, and weight are

Males and females throughout much of Southeast Asia are approximately the same size, as is the case with this couple from Bali, Indonesia.

variously defined as important, depending on the culture. Invariably, however, "looks" tend to be more important for females. Marriage advertisements placed in newspapers in India (similar to the "personal ads" in Western newspapers) that describe an available bride often mention that her skin colour is "fair" or "wheatish" and may note that she is slender and tall—although she should not be too tall, that is, taller than a potential groom. Preference for having the groom be taller than the bride is more common in male-dominated contexts. Marriages where the spouses are similar in height are common in cultures where gender roles are relatively equal and where sexual *dimorphism* (differences in shape and size of the female body compared to the male body), is not marked, as in much of Southeast Asia.

Physical ability is another feature affecting marriage options. People with physical disabilities, particularly women, face constraints in marrying nondisabled partners (Sentumbwe 1995). Nayinda Sentumbwe, a blind researcher, conducted fieldwork with participants in education and rehabilitation programs for blind people in Uganda. He realized that all of the married blind women in his study had blind husbands, while the same was not true for the blind married men. In exploring the reason for this pattern, Sentumbwe considered Ugandan per-

ceptions of blind people and gender relations, especially the housewife role. Most Ugandans consider blindness to be the worst of all physical disabilities. In their perception, blindness decreases women's competence as wives and mothers and reduces their desirability as spouses. Ugandan housewives have many roles: mother, hostess, housekeeper, homestead-keeper, provider of meals, and provider of homegrown food, among others. It is important for men to have "competent" wives, and so blind men do not select blind women as partners. Instead, men often choose blind women as lovers. The relationship between lovers is private and does not involve social competence in the woman.

The importance of romantic love as a requirement for marriage is a matter of debate between sociobiologists and cultural constructionists (see Chapter 1). Sociobiologists argue that feelings of romantic love are universal among all humans because they play an adaptive role in uniting males and females in offspring care. Cultural constructionists, in contrast, argue that romantic love is far from universal, that it is an unusual, even "aberrant" factor influencing spouse selection (Little 1966, quoted in Barnard and Good 1984:94). In support of a cultural constructionist position, cultural materialists have examined differences in male and female economic roles to explain cross-cultural variations in an emphasis on romantic love. They say that romantic love is more likely to be an important factor in relationships in cultures where men contribute more to subsistence, and where women are therefore economically dependent on men. Sri Lankan young people in Toronto are reported to see love marriages as occurring between inexperienced or immature individuals. Arranged marriages "offered a tangible sense of security, family support and approval" (Morrison, Guruge, and Snarr 1999:151). Whatever the cause of romantic love, it is the norm for marriage in North America, South America, and Europe (Levine et al. 1995).

These debates have prompted cultural anthropologists to devote more research to how romantic love is defined and constructed cross-culturally and within different cultures. For example, Dorothy Holland and Margaret Eisenhart (1990) conducted a study of young American women just entering college from 1979 to 1981 and again in 1987 after they had graduated and begun their adult lives. Their research sites were two southern colleges in the United States, one predomi-

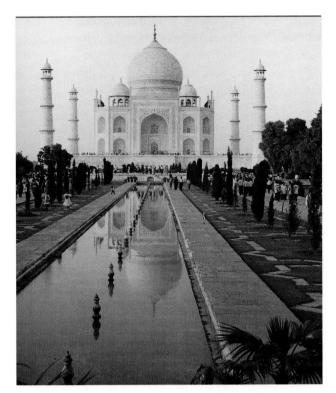

The Taj Mahal, located in Agra, North India, is a seventeenth century monument to love. It was built by the Mughal emperor Shah Jahan as a tomb for his favourite wife, Mumtaz Mahal, who died in childbirth in 1631.

viding the domestic context for their married life. African American women are socialized to be more economically autonomous, a tradition that stems from African traditions in which women earn and manage their own earnings.

Arranged marriages, not based initially on romantic love between the bride and groom, are formed instead as a link between the two families involved and considerations of what constitutes a "good match" between the families. Arranged marriages are common in many contemporary Middle Eastern, African, and Asian countries. Some theorists have claimed that arranged marriages are "traditional" while love marriages are "modern," and thus believe arranged marriages will disappear with modernity. However, Japan presents a case of a highly industrialized economy with a highly educated population in which arranged marriages constitute a substantial proportion of all marriages, about 25 to 30 per cent (Applbaum 1995). In earlier times, marriage partners would be found through personal networks, perhaps relying on an intermediary who knows both families. Now, in large cities such as Tokyo and Osaka, professional matchmakers have become important sources for finding marriage partners. One registers, pays a fee, and fills out forms about family background. The most common desirable characteristics in a spouse are the family's reputation and social standing, the absence of undesirable traits such as a case of divorce or mental illness in the family, and the potential spouse's education, income, and occupation.

Marriage Gifts

Most marriages are accompanied by some form of gift-giving of goods or services between the partners, members of their families, or friends. As Lévi-Strauss said long ago, exchange can be considered an essential aspect of marriage. In many societies, wedding prestations are the major economic transactions in a person's lifetime (Barnard and Good 1984:114). No one has been able to calculate how much the total flow of marriage prestations and the total cost of weddings is as a percentage of a given economic system, but it is likely to be significant in most contemporary cultures.

The major forms of marital exchanges cross-culturally are dowry and brideprice (Goody and Tambiah 1973). Dowry involves the transfer of goods, and sometimes

nantly attended by White Euro-Americans and the other by African Americans. They found a contrast between the women of the two colleges. The White women were much more firmly committed to notions of romantic love than the African American women. This pattern matched differences in career goals and expectations of future earning ability. White women were less likely to have strong and independent career goals and more likely to expect to be economically dependent on their spouse. The African American women expressed self-dependence and stronger career goals. Holland and Eisenhart suggest that the ideology of romantic love "derails" many young White women from competing with men in the job market. The theme of romantic love provides young women with a model of the heroic male provider as the ideal, with her role being one of attracting him and promoney, from the bride's side to the new conjugal unit for their use. Common throughout the northern Mediterranean, this "classic" form of dowry includes household goods such as furniture and cooking utensils and sometimes rights to a house. Dowry is the predominant form of marriage prestation in a broad region of Eurasia, from Western Europe through the northern Mediterranean and into China and India (Goody 1976). In northern India, what is called "dowry" is more appropriately termed "groomprice" since the goods and money pass not to the new couple, but rather to the groom's family (Billig 1992). In China during the Mao era, marriage gifts of any type were viewed as a sign of women's oppression and made illegal. Now, marriage gifts are becoming more common with the recent increase in consumerism (Whyte 1993).

Brideprice, or the transfer of goods or money from the groom's side to the bride's parents, is more common in horticultural and pastoral cultures, while dowry is associated with intensive agricultural societies. In cultures where dowry and brideprice are given, recent decades have brought an inflation in the required amounts, making it difficult in some cases for young people to marry. **Bride-service,** less common than brideprice, is still practised in some horticultural societies, especially in the Amazon. Bride-service involves the groom working for his father-in-law for a certain period of time before returning home with the bride. Bride-service is brideprice paid in labour rather than in goods. Many marriages involve prestations from both the bride's and groom's sides. For example, a typical pattern in Canada is for the groom's side to be responsible for the rehearsal dinner the night before the wedding, while the bride's side is responsible for everything else.

Weddings

Creating a marriage can be accomplished merely by the couple spending a night together or with an elaborate and costly wedding ceremony that takes place over several days. Weddings vary cross-culturally and intraculturally in terms of the accompanying feasts and festivities, which may involve special food and music, secular or religious ceremonies, variation in duration, and numerous costs. The degree of simplicity or elaboration of weddings can be explained to some extent by differences in production systems and a family's economic status within socially stratified contexts. In low-consumption, foraging societies, marriage receives little formal marking and little expenditure of effort, time, or money. Marjorie Shostak (1981) describes the simplicity of first marriages among the Ju/wasi foragers as studied in the 1970s:

> The marriage ceremony is quite modest, although negotiations and gift exchanges are typically begun long before the actual marriage takes place. A hut is built for the couple by members of both families, and is set apart from the rest of the village. As sunset approaches, friends bring the couple to the hut. The bride, head covered, is carried and laid down inside; the groom, walking, is led to the hut and sits beside the door. Coals from the fires of both families are brought to start the new fire in front of the marriage hut. The friends stay with them, singing, playing, and joking. The couple stay apart from each other, maintaining a respectful reserve, and do not join in the festivities. After everyone leaves, they spend their first night together in the hut. The next morning, oil is ceremonially rubbed on both of them—each by the other's mother. (130)

In the case of remarriage, the process is even simpler, although key elements are maintained. Nisa's description of her third marriage mentions the importance of kin in building the hut for the newly married couple and the new mother-in-law's ritual blessing (see the Voices box on page 209). In contrast, in socially stratified societies, substantial local cultural variation exists in weddings across class and ethnic groups. In Canada, this variation includes "common law marriage," an unmarked form that is achieved simply through the passage of time; secular weddings held in a court with minimal ritual; church weddings with or without much ritual and with or without expensive meals; and the fabulously expensive weddings of the very wealthy, followed by a costly honeymoon for the newlyweds. Whatever the cost, weddings in Canada are often expressions of distinct ethnic styles of celebration that are not always satisfied by commercial bridal services (see the Multiple Cultural Worlds box on page 211).

Forms of Marriage

Cultural anthropologists distinguish two basic forms of marriage based on the number of partners involved. **Monogamy,** the simplest, is marriage between two peo-

Nisa's Third Marriage

Among the Ju/wasi during the 1970s, most women stayed in one marriage for a long time. Nisa, in contrast, had five. Here she describes her marriage to her third husband, who is named Tashay. Tashay had seen Nisa and wanted to marry her. Although he was a stranger to her, the arrangements were made. Her description of the marriage emphasizes her feelings of *kua*, which means awe, fear, or respect, and which is associated with the intense emotion of this ritual event.

The day of the wedding everyone was there. All of Tashay's friends were sitting around, laughing and laughing. His younger brother said, "Tashay, you're too old. Get out of the way so I can marry her. Give her to me." And his nephew said, "Uncle, you're already too old. Now let me marry her." They were all sitting around, talking like that. They all wanted me.

I went to my mother's hut and sat there. I was wearing lots of beads and my hair was completely covered and full with ornaments.

That night there was another dance. We danced, and some people fell asleep and others kept dancing. In the early morning, Tashay and his relatives went back to their camp; we went to our huts to sleep. When morning was late in the sky, they came back. They stayed around and then his parents said, "Because we are only staying a short while—tomorrow, let's start building the marriage hut."

The next day they started. There were lots of people there—Tashay's mother, my mother, and my aunt worked on the hut; everyone else sat around, talking. Late in the day, the young men went and brought Tashay to the finished hut....

I was still at my mother's hut. I heard them tell two of my friends to go and

bring me to the hut. I thought, "Oohh... I'll run away." When they came for me, they couldn't find me. They said, "Where did Nisa go? Did she run away? It's getting dark. Doesn't she know that things may bite and kill her?" My father said, "Go tell Nisa that if this is what she's going to do, I'll hit her and she won't run away again. What made her want to run away, anyway?"

I was already far off in the bush. They came looking for me. I heard them calling, "Nisa... Nisa...." I sat down at the base of a tree. Then I heard [my friend] Nukha, "Nisa... Nisao... my friend... a hyena's out there... things will bite and kill you... come back... Nisa... Nisao."

When Nukha finally saw me, I started to run. She ran after me, chasing me, and finally caught me. She called out to others, "Hey! Nisa's here! Everyone come! Help me! Take Nisa, she's here!"

They came and brought me back. Then they laid me down inside the hut. I cried and cried. People told me, "A man is not something that kills you; he is someone who marries you, who becomes like your father or your older brother. He kills animals and gives you things to eat.... Why are you so afraid of your husband and what are you crying about?"

I listened and was quiet. Later, we went to sleep. Tashay lay down beside the opening of the hut, near the fire, and I lay down inside; he thought I might try and run away again. He covered himself with a blanket and slept.

While it was dark, I woke up. I sat up. I thought, "How am I going to jump over him? How can I get out and go to mother's hut to sleep beside her?" I looked at him sleeping. Then came other thoughts, other thoughts in the

middle of the night, "Eh... this person has just married me..." and I lay down again. But I kept thinking, "Why did people give me this man in marriage? The older people say he is a good person, yet...."

I lay there and didn't move. The rain came beating down. It fell steadily and kept falling. Finally, I slept. Much later dawn broke.

In the morning, Tashay got up and sat by the fire. I was so frightened I just lay there, waiting for him to leave. When he went to urinate, I went and sat down inside my mother's hut.

That day, all his relatives came to our new hut—his mother, his father, his brothers... everyone! They all came. They said, "Go tell Nisa she should come and her in-laws will put the marriage oil on her. Can you see her sitting over there? Why isn't she coming so we can put the oil on her in her new hut?

I refused to go. They kept calling for me until finally, my older brother said, "Uhn, uhn. Nisa, if you act like this, I'll hit you. Now get up and go over there. Sit over there so they can put the oil on you."

I still refused and just sat there. My older brother grabbed a switch from a nearby tree and started coming toward me. I got up. I was afraid. I followed him to where the others were sitting. Tashay's mother rubbed the oil on me and my aunt rubbed it on Tashay.

Then they left and it was just Tashay and me.

Source: Reprinted by permission of the publisher from *Nisa: The Life and Times of a !Kung Woman* by Marjorie Shostack, Cambridge, Mass.: Harvard University Press, 1981, pp. 153–155. Copyright 1981 by Marjorie Shostack.

ple—a male and female if the pair is heterosexual, or two people of the same gender in the case of a homosexual pair. Heterosexual monogamy is the most common form of marriage cross-culturally, and in many nations, it is the only form of marriage allowed by law. **Polygamy** refers to a marriage with multiple spouses, a pattern that is allowed by the majority of the world's cultures, even though the majority of people within such cultures may not practise plural marriage (Murdock 1965 [1949]:24). Two forms of polygamous marriage exist. The predominant pattern is **polygyny,** marriage of one husband with more than one wife. Within cultures that allow polygyny, the majority of unions nevertheless are monogamous. **Polyandry,** or marriage between one woman and more than one man, is rare. However, it has been practised among groups as diverse as the Kaingang of the Amazon, the Todas of southern India, and the Chukchee of Siberia. One region in which polyandry occurs over a large area includes Tibet and the high Himalayas of India and Nepal.

Anthropologists have asked why polygyny, marriage between one man and more than one woman simultaneously, exists in some cultures and not in others (White and Burton 1988). Evolutionary theorists of the nineteenth century suggested that polygyny constituted a middle stage. Engels's three stages, for example, went from *group marriage* (in which everyone was supposedly married to everyone else, a hypothetical situation unknown ethnographically for the past or the present), to polygyny, and then to monogamy. Biological determinists say that polygyny contributes to males' reproductive success by allowing them to maximize the spread of their genes in future generations. But neither the evolutionary nor sociobiological models offer insight into the cross-cultural variation in the distribution of polygyny. Economic theories have been proposed. One prominent economic hypothesis states that polygyny will be more likely in contexts where women's contribution to the economy is more important. Political and demographic factors have also been examined, especially the role of warfare in reducing the ratio of males to females, and the taking of female captives in warfare. Data for 142 societies show that one factor alone cannot explain the presence or absence of polygyny (White and Burton 1988). Instead, support for a set of interrelated views emerges:

- Polygyny fits with an expansionist economic strategy in homogeneous and high-quality environments.

- Polygyny is associated with warfare for plunder and/or female captives.

- Polygyny is associated with the presence of strongly bonded groups of males linked through ties between brothers.

- Polygyny is constrained in the context of plough agriculture or by high dependence on fishing.

Some support was found for the hypothesis about the effect of female contribution to subsistence, but not at such a strong level as for the above factors.

Change in Marriage

Marriage continues to be a major basis of forming kinship bonds cross-culturally. While the institution of marriage in general remains prominent, many of its specific details are changing. Almost everywhere, the age at first marriage is rising. This change is related to increased

A newly married husband and wife and their relatives in front of a church in Seoul, Republic of Korea.

Bridal Shows and Ethnicity

Toronto, reputed to be one of the most multicultural cities in the world, presents scenes for disparities between the variety of marriage practices in the region and the presumed practices of the local population. Some of these conflicts appeared at a recent Fall National Bridal Show in the city. A Trinidadian of East Indian origin thought this show could help her combine elements of ethnicity with a modern wedding, but found it was more for WASP brides: "I thought there would be saris or gold jewelry." Other brides-to-be were surprised at the scarcity of ethnic exhibitors: "I wanted to have a

Caribbean menu, but there's nothing that the caterers offer that's different… I was thinking of having a black cake [a traditional Caribbean wedding cake that resembles a rich fruit cake]. Even the cakes are bland, but they're hilarious-looking with real fountains with peach-coloured water and stuff pouring out of them."

Puzzled show organizers claimed the exhibitors cater to brides from all different cultural backgrounds. But this would involve making special requests, including gowns made from different fabrics or an ethnic menu. Visitors to the show felt exhibitors should have

carried cheongsam dresses or a menu with curried chicken with peas and rice, or gold and blue dashikis [African influenced wedding attire for grooms]. A visitor looked at a copy of Bride magazine, reading the etiquette guide for a proper marriage, "The groom takes the garter from your leg in front of the guests and tosses it behind him at all the single men." She laughs, "I don't think so."

Source: The Toronto Star, September 20, 1999.

emphasis on completing a certain number of years of education before marriage and rising aspirations about the potential spouse's economic status before contemplating marriage. Marriages between people of different nations and ethnicity are increasing, caused partly by increased rates of international migration (see Chapter 15). Migrants take with them many of their marriage and family practices. They also adapt to rules and practices in their area of destination. Pluralistic practices evolve, such as conducting two marriage ceremonies—one based on the "original" culture and the other conforming to norms in the place of destination.

Style changes in weddings abound. Globalization of Western-style "white weddings" promotes the adoption of many features that are familiar in the West: a white wedding gown for the bride, a many-layered wedding cake, and certain kinds of floral arrangements. What the bride and groom wear is an expression of both the bride's

and groom's personal identity and also the cultural identity of their family and larger social group. Clothing choice reflects adherence to "traditional" values, or may reject those in favour of more "modern" values. Euro-American trends are prominent worldwide (although pervasive, they are not accepted even in some parts of North America). See the Multiple Cultural Worlds box above. Throughout much of East and Southeast Asia, advertisements and upscale stores display the Western-style white wedding gown (but not so much in India, where white clothing for women signifies widowhood and is inauspicious). On the other hand, some resurgence of local "folk" styles is occurring in some contexts, such as in Morocco, where there is a trend for "modern" brides to wear a Berber costume (long robes and jewellery characteristic of the rural, mountain people) at one stage of the wedding ceremony.

Key Questions Revisited

How do cultures define kinship through descent?

Key differences in descent systems exist between unilineal systems, which are numerically predominant, and bilateral systems. Within unilineal systems, patrilineal systems differ from matrilineal systems in terms of property division, residence rules, and their implications for the status of males and females. The number of matrilineal kinship systems is declining in the face of Western influence, beginning with European colonial expansion in the 1500s.

How do cultures define kinship through sharing?

Kinship can also be created through acts of sharing and support. In cultures throughout much of Southeast Asia, women often breastfeed children of other women; this practice forms a kinship bond through the sharing of milk, in that all children who are breastfed by a woman are considered to be related. Some form of child transfers, from one primary caretaker to another, is probably a cross-cultural universal. In some societies, such as in Canada, legalized options for child transfers through adoption are common and even allow for the transfer of children from one nation to another. Ritualized sharing also creates kinship bonds as in the case of godparenthood.

How do cultures define kinship through marriage?

Marriage continues to be an important basis of kinship formation, even though it often results in divorce in many contexts. All cultures have rules of exclusion about which people should not be considered as a marriage partner, with some form of incest taboo found universally. All cultures likewise have preference rules stating which people would make the best choice as a marriage partner. Marriage preferences and arrangements reflect other aspects of the culture, for example, the relative importance of males or females in the economy.

Core Concepts

ambilineal descent, p. 199
avunculocal, p. 200
bilateral descent, p. 198
bride-service, p. 208
cross-cousins, p. 205
descent, p. 194
double descent, p. 198
endogamy, p. 205

exogamy, p. 205
extended families, p. 195
genealogy, p. 192
generalized exchange
   systems, p. 204
hypergyny, p. 205
hypogyny, p. 205
incest taboo, p. 204

kinship system, p. 190
kinship diagram, p. 192
marriage, p. 202
matrifocality, p. 199
matrilineal descent,
   p. 195
matrilocality, p. 203
monogamy, p. 208
neolocality, p. 200
parallel cousins, p. 205

patrilineal descent, p. 195
patrilocal, p. 196
polyandry, p. 210
polygamy, p. 210
polygyny, p. 210
primogeniture, p. 203
restricted exchange
   systems, p. 204
teknonyms, p. 197
unilineal descent, p. 194

Suggested Readings

John Borneman, *Belonging in the Two Berlins: Kin, State and Nation*. New York: Cambridge University Press, 1992. This book considers two levels of analysis: people's changing perceptions of the family and the government's policies related to the family.

Bonnie Fox, ed., *Family Bonds and Gender Divisions: Readings in the Sociology of the Family*. Toronto: Canadian Scholars Press, 1988. This book of readings published by a Canadian scholar includes many readings by anthropologists and articles on family and kinship of interest to Canadians.

Laurel Kendall, *Getting Married in Korea: Of Gender, Morality, and Modernity*. Berkeley: University of California, 1996. The ethnographic study examines preferences about desirable spouses, matchmaking, marriage ceremonies and their financing, and the effect of women's changing work roles on their marital aspirations.

Nancy Tapper, *Bartered Brides: Politics, Gender and Marriage in an Afghan Tribal Society*. New York: Cambridge University Press, 1991. Based on fieldwork before the Soviet invasion, this study examines marriage among the Maduzai, a tribal society of Turkistan. The book looks at how marriage relates to productive and reproductive aspects of society and the role it plays in managing political conflict and competition.

Margaret Trawick, *Notes on Love in a Tamil Family*. Berkeley: University of California Press, 1992. This reflexive ethnography takes a close look at the daily dynamics of kinship in one Tamil (South Indian) family. Special attention is given to sibling relationships, the role of older people, children's lives, and the way love and affection are played out in a particularly Tamil way.

Michael Young and Peter Willmott, *Family and Kinship in East London*. New York: Penguin Books, 1979. This classic study of kinship relationships among the working class of "Bethnal Green" gives particular attention to the importance of married women's continued close relationships with their mothers as maintained through residential proximity and visiting.

 Your *Cultural Anthropology*, Second Canadian Edition Media Edition CD-ROM contains many Web sites relevant to this chapter. Use it to explore the Web and to expand your knowledge of anthropology.

Domestic Groups

Some members of a bedu household in Yemen.

Key Questions

What is a household and what are major household forms?

What are some important economic and social features of households?

How are household patterns changing?

I *n casual conversation, North Americans might use the* *words family and household interchangeably to refer* *to people who live together. Social scientists have pro-* *posed a distinction between the two terms, both of which may* *refer to some sort of domestic group, or people who live to-* *gether. A* **family** *includes people who consider themselves re-* *lated through kinship (as described in Chapter 8—descent,* *marriage, or sharing). In North American English, the term* *family includes both "close" or "immediate" relatives and* *more "distant" relatives. One may live with and see some* *members of one's family every day, but others only once a* *year on a major holiday, or less. People who are considered* *close family relatives may be scattered in several different* *residences, including grandparents, aunts, uncles, and cousins;* *children of divorced parents, who live with one parent and* *visit the other; and children of divorced parents, who may* *live with different parents. The notion of the family as a clearly* *defined unit with firm boundaries thus often misrepresents* *the fluidity of this category (Lloyd 1995).*

In contrast to the term family, the term **household** refers to a domestic group that may or may not be re-lated by kinship and that share living space, including perhaps a kitchen and certain budgetary items such as food and rent. Most households around the world con-sist of family members who are related through kinship. An example of a non-kin household is a group of friends who live in the same apartment. A single person living alone is also a household.

This chapter discusses anthropological findings about a variety of domestic groupings, especially in terms of how households operate as economic units. It also con-siders the content of the relationships of household mem-bers and factors that lead to the breakup of domestic groups.

The Household: Variations on a Theme

In this section, we consider three major forms of house-holds and then examine the concept of household head-ship. The topic of female-headed households receives detailed attention as this pattern of headship is of con-siderable contemporary policy interest.

Household Forms

Household organization can be categorized into several types according to how many married adults are involved. Single-person households comprise only one member, living alone. A single-parent household comprises an adult with offspring. The **nuclear household** (which many people call the **nuclear family**) contains one adult couple (married or "partners"), with or without children. Complex households include a variety of household forms based on the presence of more than two married adults. Polygynous (multiple wives) and polyandrous (multiple husbands) households are one form of com-plex household in which one spouse has multiple part-ners. They may all live together in one residence or, as is the case in many African polygynous households, each wife has a separate residential unit within the overall household compound. **Extended households** contain more than one adult married couple. These couples may be related through the father-son line (making a patri-lineal extended household, such as the Lims of Taiwan who were mentioned in Chapter 8), the mother-daugh-ter line (making a matrilineal extended household), or through sisters or brothers (making a collateral extended household).

The precise cross-cultural distribution of these vari-ous types is not known. However, some broad general-izations can be offered. First, nuclear household units are found in all cultures (Murdock 1965 [1949]:2). The nuclear household as the exclusive household type is characteristic of about one-fourth of the world's cultures. Another one-fourth allows polygamous marriages. One-half of the cultures are characterized by the presence of extended households. The distribution of nuclear ver-sus complex household forms roughly corresponds with modes of production (refer to Figure 8.3 on page 194). The nuclear form is most characteristic of economies at the two extremes of the continuum: in foraging groups and in industrialized societies. As noted in Chapter 8, the greater prevalence of nuclear households in these two modes of production reflects the need for spatial mobility and flexibility in making a living. Polygynous or polyandrous households and extended households constitute a substantial proportion of households in hor-ticultural, pastoral, and nonindustrial agricultural economies. Throughout Asia—China, Japan, India—in much of Africa, and among First Nations people, some form of complex or extended households is both the ideal and frequently the reality.

In India, where extended households are the preferred form, the household may contain 50 or more members. Property provides the material base to support many people and, in turn, large land holdings require a large labour force to work the land. In northern India, more households own property, compared to southern and eastern India where rates of landlessness are higher. In addition to property differences, the unbalanced sex ratio in the North means there are more sons available to bring in wives and establish patrilineal extended households. Logically, then, patrilineal extended households are more common in the northern part of the country (Kolenda 1968).

Some anthropologists argue that the frequency of extended households will decline with industrialization and urbanization, which are considered key factors of modernity. This argument is based on an assumed European model of reduced numbers of extended farming households and increased numbers of nuclear households. Taking the nuclear household as a key marker of modernity, though, has its problems. First, historical evidence indicates that nuclear households characterized nonindustrial, premodern northwestern Europe (Goody 1996). So, the apparent transformation from extended households to nuclear households with modernity is not universally correct. Asian data clearly do not fit the model. In India, urban areas have a higher percentage of extended households than rural areas (Freed and Freed 1969). Further, data from India on literacy rates, often taken as an indicator of modernity and exposure to change, again show contradictory findings. A study in West Bengal state of eastern India found that extended household heads are more likely to be literate than nuclear household heads (Dasgupta, Weatherbie, and Mukhopadhaya 1993).

Moving from India to Japan, we again find that the extended household structure has endured within the context of an industrial and urban economy. The *ie,* or "stem household," has a long history in Japan (Skinner 1993) and is still important (Bachnik 1983). A variant of an extended household, a **stem household** contains two (and only two) married couples related through the males. Thus, only one son remains in the household, bringing in his wife, who is expected to perform the important role of caretaker for the husband's parents as they age. In

In China, the stem family household system is undergoing change as many people have one daughter and no son as a result of the One-Child Policy and generally lowered fertility.

Japan and in contemporary China, the patrilineal stem household is still a widely preferred form. Yet it is increasingly difficult to achieve since the rising aspirations of children often means that no child is willing to live with and care for the aging parents. In this context, parents sometimes exert considerable pressure on an adult child to come and live with them (Traphagan 2000). One compromise solution is for an adult child and his or her spouse to live near the parents but not with them.

These examples of the endurance of extended household formation in certain Asian contexts relate to the discussion, later in this chapter, of family businesses. It makes sense that extended households have a greater chance of survival when they function as "mini-corporations," with shared economic interests and a loyal set of managers and workers linked by kinship.

Household Headship

The question of who heads a household is often difficult to answer. This section reviews some of the approaches to this question and provides insights into how cross-cultural perceptions about **household headship** differ.

The "head" is the primary person (or people) in charge of supporting the household financially and making decisions. Cultural anthropologists realize that the concept of household head is an ethnocentric, Euro-American definition of one person who makes most of the money, controls most of the decision making, and was traditionally a man. European colonialism spread the concept of the male head of household around the world along with its male-biased legal system that vests household authority in the father.

The model of one male head has influenced the way official statistics are gathered and reported worldwide. The result is that if a household has a co-residing male and female, there will be a tendency to report the household as "male-headed," regardless of the actual internal dynamics. In Brazil, the official definition considers only a husband to be head of the household, regardless of whether he contributes to the household budget and is married to the woman. Thus, "[S]ingle, separated or widowed women who house and feed their children, grandchildren and elderly or handicapped parents are deprived of the title of head of the family. If they have a partner with them on the day when the census official arrives, he is considered to be the head of the family, whether or not he is the father of any of the children, contributes to the family income, or has been living there for years or only a few months" (de Athayde Figueiredo and Prado 1989:41). Similarly, according to official reports, 90 per cent of households in the Philippines are headed by males (Illo 1985). Anthropological research shows, however, that women play a prominent role in income generation and budgetary control, and both male and female domestic partners tend to share decision making. Thus, co-headship would be a more appropriate label for many households in the Philippines and elsewhere.

Many early anthropologists were also male-biased in their assessment of household headship. They overlooked household headship patterns that did not conform to their Eurocentric view of male headship. Beginning with the work of Nancie González, awareness of the prevalence and functioning of woman-headed households has increased. González was one of the first anthropologists to define and study matrifocality, a domestic pattern in which a female (or females) is the central, stable figure around whom other members cluster (1970:233). In matrifocal households, the mother is likely to be the primary, or only, income provider. The concept of matrifocality does not exclude the possibility that men may be part of the household. That is, a matrifocal household is under the control of a woman head who may or may not have a (male) partner.

There has been much public discussion in North America recently about partnerless women as household heads. Concern has arisen because the number of such households is increasing, and they are more likely to be poorer than households containing a married couple. What causes the formation of partnerless woman-headed households? A woman-headed household can come about if a partner existed at one time, but for some reason—such as separation, divorce, or death—is no longer part of the household, or a partner exists but is not co-resident because of long-term outmigration, imprisonment, or some other form of separate residence. (Most thinking about woman-headed households assumes a heterosexual relationship and thus does not account for woman-headed households formed by a single woman with children either adopted or conceived through artificial insemination, with or without a visiting woman partner.) Three theories are often proposed to account for the absence of a male spouse or partner.

- *Slavery:* The high frequency of woman-headed households among African Americans in the Western hemisphere is often said to be the heritage of slavery, which intentionally broke up conjugal ties. This theory has several problems. First, if slavery were the cause of woman-headed households, one would predict that all peoples who experienced slavery would have this household form. In Jamaica, which is populated mainly by descendants of African slaves, percentages of woman-headed households vary between rural and urban areas (Miller and Stone 1983). Yet both urban and rural people have the same heritage. In the United States, no generic "Black household" exists, just as there is no generic "White household": "Black Americans count for more than 10 million households, ranging from young adults in condominiums to suburban couples with two children and a swimming pool" (Hacker 1992:67). Second, historically in the United States, homes with two co-residing parents were the norm among Black Americans following the Civil War through the mid-twentieth century. This makes it difficult to describe woman-headed households today as a "legacy" of slavery. It is true that the slave system denied legal standing to adult pairings since owners did not want their slaves committed to lifetime relationships. Slaves were subject to sale, and wives and husbands, parents and children were separated. While such circumstances would seem to have led to a "breakup" of a conjugal (married) household tradition, it is now clear that the slaves themselves never accepted the arrangements imposed by the owners: "Once freed, blacks sought the durable unions they had been denied" (69). Third, in the United States, percentages of woman-headed households have increased in roughly the same proportion among Blacks and Whites. These parallels indicate that similar factors may underlie the changes for both populations. Last, the distribution of woman-headed households throughout the world is more widespread than the distribution of slavery. So, other factors must be involved in promoting the formation of this pattern.

- *Poverty:* Woman-headed households are said to be adaptations to poverty, because in many societies, the poor have a higher frequency of woman-headed households. If so, it is only one of many possible adaptations since not all low-income populations worldwide are characterized by high rates of woman-headed households. Within just the United States, significant ethnic differences exist: "Low-income Chinese, Japanese, and other Asiatic peoples generally have low frequencies of single-parent households, and many Mexican-American communities have a strong predominance of dual-parent families even though experiencing relatively low incomes and considerable unemployment" (Pelto, Roman, and Liriano 1982:40). As an explanatory factor, poverty needs to be considered along with attention to male and female income-earning capabilities, other resources available, and other support systems.

In the Caribbean region and throughout Latin America, the association between poverty and woman-headed households is strong. But beneath this seemingly negative association, some positive findings appear. In the Caribbean region, about one-third of all households are woman-headed, and most of the women have never been married (Massiah 1983). Instead, they have visiting unions (involving a steady sexual relationship, but the maintenance of separate residences). Many women who were interviewed as part of a study conducted in several of the islands commented that they sometimes expect and hope for financial support from their male partner or "baby father." Numerous others emphasized the value they place on freedom from a husband or permanent partner. One woman said, "Being single fits in with my independent thinking" (41).

Members of a matrifocal household in rural Jamaica: two sisters and their children.

Another commented on her visiting union: "I like freedom, so I'm keeping it like it is" (41).

In much of African-Caribbean culture, economic conditions dictate that men are not dependable sources of financial support. Women in low-income groups in the Caribbean and throughout much of Latin America have an advantage over males in earning money. Rural women earn income, for example, from gardening and marketing their produce. Urban women work in service occupations, small businesses, domestic service, and light industry. Cities offer more opportunities for such salaried employment than rural areas, and thus they attract greater numbers of female migrants. When men do get jobs, they are likely to be irregular or seasonal. On top of limited employment options, African-Caribbean men tend to withhold portions of their earnings for personal expenditures (Chant 1985).

In addition to income generation, women have an advantage over men in mobilizing supplementary household support from kin and friends. Thus, women in these contexts are less dependent on men's income than in places where they do not have access to such jobs and resources. In fact, having a nonearning male around the house who consumes and does not contribute constitutes a net economic loss. Thus, a woman-headed household can be viewed as a positive adaptation to economic and social circumstances (see the Critical Thinking box on page 220). The differences in male-female employment opportunities affect

Is a Father-Headed Household Best?

Much Western popular thought places the nuclear household, comprising a co-resident adult heterosexual couple and children, as "the best" type, and as "natural." Other forms, especially woman-headed households, are often viewed as "broken" versions of the nuclear household, and are said to be less adequate structures within which to raise children. Putting the "father" back into the household is an important policy goal in North America. Given the discussion on household headship, what can be said about the household debate?

women's preferences concerning location and household structure. In El Salvador, "a woman without a stable partner, regardless of her legal or religious marital status...generally preferred city to rural life; married women with working spouses like rural life" (Nieves 1979:139).

- *Unbalanced sex ratio:* Woman-headed households are said to occur in contexts of high male outmigration or in other demographic situations causing a shortage of males. The sheer availability of partners may put constraints on marriage. In Spanish Galicia, the local economy, inheritance rules, and household formation are related (Kelley 1991). This coastal region has a high percentage of households headed by unmarried women. In the village of Ezaro, for example, about one-fourth of all baptisms were of illegitimate children in the latter half of the nineteenth century. The proportion has declined in the twentieth century, but the Galician region still stands out from the rest of Spain in this respect. In Ezaro, households headed by unmarried mothers constitute over 10 per cent of the total. The general Mediterranean kinship system puts high value on marriage and male honour through control of the sexuality of female family members. Yet little or no stigma is attached to unwed motherhood in Galicia. Women household heads often gain honoured positions in their villages.

What accounts for this system? The answer lies in Galicia's high rates of male emigration. The scarcity of males promotes flexible attitudes towards unwed motherhood and other adaptive features not found elsewhere in the Mediterranean region. The women have important roles in production and property relations. In Ezaro, women are in charge of agricultural work. They inherit land and gain prestige and power from owning and managing agricultural land. Women's agricultural work is the basis of their reputation in the community: "Women's work is considered so critical to the prestige of the household in Ezaro that success at work is the single most important factor in the community's evaluation of a woman's character (and in her own self-evaluation). The good woman in Ezaro is the hardworking woman" (572). Her work is more important in this respect than her marital status.

Inheritance practices reflect the importance of women's agricultural work. The goal is to ensure continuity of the *casa*, the house, which includes both the physical structure and its members. Parents usually award one of their children with a *millora*, a larger share of the inheritance, making that child the principal heir. The rest is divided equally among siblings. Daughters are often chosen to receive the *millora*, and thus a single woman can become head of an estate. Her children ensure that the estate has continuity. In contrast, a man cannot become a household head and gain social status without being married.

The preceding theories about why woman-headed households exist can be labelled "compensatory theories." They suggest that a woman-headed household emerges as a default system when "something is wrong" or men are unavailable as spouses. This bias is based on the assumption that the heterosexual nuclear household is the "normal" pattern that occurs when everything is "okay." A cultural materialist view would say that a variety of household forms are expectable, depending on such factors as men's and women's economic roles, especially access to work, wages, and the distribution of productive resources such as property.

The Household as an Economic Unit

Households can be examined from a variety of perspectives: as economic units, political units, and social groups. This section discusses the economic workings of households. Three topics are addressed: work roles inside the household, households as businesses, and the financial impact of remittances (money that is sent) from nonresident members.

Gender, Labour, and Household Type

This section offers insights into how the gender division of labour in two different contexts is related to household roles and relationships. The first case is based on research in South Wales, U.K., where the "classic" nuclear household is still prevalent. The second is based on research among Tibetan peoples living in Nepal among whom polyandry is practised and households are, therefore, composed of several adult males all of whom are married to the same woman (Chapter 8).

The "Classic" Nuclear Household The "classic" Euro-American model of the nuclear household involves a division of labour in which only one spouse (the male) works in the wage economy and the other (the female) does unpaid work in the domestic domain, including child care. This pattern is common in North

America and Western Europe. An anthropological study in South Wales, U.K., addressed women's and men's perceptions of their contributions and value to the household (Murcott 1993 [1983]). In South Wales nuclear households, the husband works outside the home for wages while the wife remains in the home doing work that is unremunerated, including bearing and raising children, preparing meals, and cleaning. Welsh wives defined their domestic responsibility mainly in terms of their importance in providing "home cooking." Home cooking means preparation of a "cooked meal" of meat, potatoes, vegetables, and gravy: "[A] proper meal is a cooked dinner. This is one which women feel is necessary to their family's health, welfare, and, indeed, happiness. It is a meal to come home to, a meal which should figure two, three or four times in the week and especially on Sundays" (78). In contrast, the responsible husband goes out to work. At the end of his work day, he comes home for dinner. The responsible wife has prepared a cooked meal for him. As one woman commented: "When my husband comes home…there's nothing more he likes I think than coming in the door and smelling a nice meal cooking. I think it's awful when someone doesn't make the effort…. I think well if I was a man I'd think I'd get really fed up if my wife never bothered" (79). Cooking a proper

The woman on the lower right is part of a polyandrous marriage, which is common among Tibetan people. She is married to several brothers, two of whom stand behind her. The older man with the blue sash in the front row is her father-in-law.

meal is a more important task for a married woman than for a single person. Cultural evaluations of the "good wife" or the "good husband" tend to fit with the prevailing economy in South Wales where the wage job market is dominated by men.

The Polyandrous Household

How is the gender division of labour organized in households with multiple spouses? As noted in Chapter 8, polyandrous households are rare cross-culturally, but relatively common in some areas of Asia, especially in the Himalayan region. Among Tibetan peoples, fraternal polyandry, in which one wife has several husbands who are related as brothers, is the ideal form of marriage (Goldstein 1987). Research among Tibetan people who live in an area of Nepal near the border with Tibet reveals the following:

> Two, three, four or more brothers jointly take a wife, who leaves her home to come and live with them. Traditionally, marriage was arranged by parents, with children, particularly females, having little or no say. This is changing somewhat nowadays, but it is still unusual for children to marry without their parents' consent. Marriage ceremonies vary by income and region and range from all the brothers sitting together as grooms to only the eldest one formally doing so.… The eldest brother is usually dominant in terms of authority, that is, in managing the household, but all the brothers share the work and participate as sexual partners. Tibetan males and females do not find the sexual aspect of sharing a spouse the least bit unusual, repulsive, or scandalous, and the norm is for the wife to treat all the brothers equally. (39)

Tibetans say that they choose to marry polyandrously because of economic factors: It prevents division of land and animals, and helps everyone achieve a higher standard of living. Anthropological analysis reveals other economic benefits such as the more diverse and flexible male labour force than would be available in a monogamous household. The wife works in the fields and manages food processing and other household work. Of the husbands, one stays and works on the land, another may be away with the herds, and another may be involved in long-distance trade. In earlier times, before Tibet became controlled by China, its pattern of feudal serfdom required regular labour contributions from one male in each household. This posed yet another demand for male labour. In a monogamous system, this requirement would have negative effects on the household economy.

Polyandry thus provides a male labour "safety net" and helps to maximize economic advantage in an ecological context that requires diversification and flexibility.

Household Businesses

The subject of household businesses is important in anthropology and many other disciplines, including sociology, economics, business, and international development. Anthropologists have found fascinating material in their studies of family businesses in areas such as the division of labour and intergenerational conflict.

Household Businesses in Chinese Culture

In contemporary China, household businesses are regaining prominence, with the new economic policies that promote growth in the private sector. A study using nationwide survey data sought to assess what the role of women has been in the trend towards establishing new, nonagricultural businesses (Entwisle et al. 1995) (see the Multiple Cultural Worlds box). The sample covered about one-third of China's provinces and included 3764 households. Results show that the number of adults and the gender composition of the adults affect whether a household enterprise will be launched. The more adults there are, and the more adult men there are, the greater is the likelihood that the household will start a business: "Working-age men are almost three times as likely than women to work in the household business, and working-age women are more than twice as likely as men to work exclusively in agriculture.… Household businesses appear to be an opportunity for men, not for women" (47–48). Women's household roles in China have long been that of "filling in," by doing work that needed to be done while men pursue the "main" tasks. With the move towards privatization, agriculture is now secondary to business in importance. So women "fill in" while men move out of agriculture into business. However, this pattern may change if the private sector continues to grow and the number of shops increases because women often work in shops.

Farming Family Businesses in North America

In the United States and Canada, most household farms are either sold or liquidated after the retirement or death of their founders. This pattern exists in spite of the widespread preference of owners to pass

Chinese Household Businesses in Calcutta

Anthropological study of "overseas" Chinese households involved in the tanning industry in Calcutta, India, provides insights about the adjustments that Chinese migrants make within a new context (Oxfeld 1993). In India, Chinese migrants' success in the tanning business is largely due to the effective use of both male and female labour. The gender division of labour among Chinese migrants to India differs from that of Chinese people in Taiwan. Most notably, in rural Taiwanese household businesses, a clear division of labour between men and women is carefully maintained such that men and women do completely different tasks. Also, in Taiwan, a sharp distinction exists between the public and private domains, with men working outside the home and women working inside the home.

In Calcutta many Chinese households are involved in the tanning industry. In these households, some tasks are done only by men, but several other

During the ceremony that marks the opening of a new tannery of a Chinese household business in Calcutta, India, the male descendants of the owners carry red lanterns and walk in a procession to the new factory.

tasks involve contributions from both men and women. Both male and female household members perform sev-

eral tasks related to processing the leather. These shared tasks include mixing chemicals and packing the finished products. Both of these tasks are performed within the domestic domain.

Men, exclusively, perform the few tasks that involve interaction with unrelated males, such as buying rawhides. Rawhides are sold in two Muslim areas of the city where one rarely sees a woman in public. Buying rawhides also involves "hard-core bargaining" and sustained interaction with men, something from which women are excluded. Selling the finished leather is also men's work. It, too, involves interactions with other males in the public domain.

FOOD FOR THOUGHT

While the gender division of labour differs between Chinese households of Taiwan and Calcutta, what aspect of gender roles stays the same according to this description?

---

them on to their offspring. What factors promote successful succession? Most studies have looked at the relationships between fathers and sons, since they tend to be most involved in the day-to-day operation of businesses (Marotz-Baden and Mattheis 1994). The roles of daughters are often overlooked, but some interesting findings are emerging.

In two-generation farm households, daughters-in-law have higher stress levels than other adult members. A daughter-in-law's stress level will be high if she wants to be integrated into the business and perceives that she is not. Unresolved tensions between a dissatisfied daughter-in-law and the rest of the household, especially her mother-in-law, may have more serious consequences for intergenerational continuity of the business than tensions between father and son. The prevailing gender division of labour in North America designates men mainly

as the farm operators. Women are involved in bookkeeping, household organization, coordination of household and farm labour, and membership in community organizations. Transmission of the farm is usually through the male line. Because starting up a farm on one's own is costly, most young farmers or ranchers work with or for their parents. Marriage, then, means that a daughter-in-law moves from her natal home into that of her husband and his parents, which places the daughter-in-law in a vulnerable and stressful position. Role ambiguity for the daughter-in-law is closely related to the presence and power of her mother-in-law.

One might assume that over time, the daughter-in-law and mother-in-law relationship would strengthen with shared experiences and greater sharing of decision making. A study of 54 daughters-in-law in two-generational farm households in Montana showed, instead, that daughters-in-law thought their relationship with their mother-in-law had worsened over time, especially as more children were born. The daughters-in-law who perceived their relationships to be most strained also reported more stress and were less involved in decision making (Marotz-Baden and Mattheis 1994:133).

Remittances

Remittances or money that is sent to a household, usually by nonresident family members, constitute an important part of many household economies. Migrant labourers may leave home for a specific period of time or to earn a specific amount of money before returning. In other cases, migrants leave and do not return, but continue to send money back home. An important stream of the international flow of remittances comes from the Persian Gulf area, where men and women from many countries from Egypt to Bangladesh, Thailand, and the Philippines migrate to work; men work in the oil industry, and women work as domestic maids, nurses, and in other services.

A less well-known source of remittance income for some households is through sex work, or prostitution, of one or more of their members. Contribution to the household economy from sex work varies. In the United States, **family disaffiliation** (feeling alienated from one's family) is a frequent motivation for a woman to enter prostitution, especially among the Euro-American population (McCaghy and Hou 1994). These girls and women tend to come from divorced homes; they frequently have been victims of familial abuse and neglect; and they have a poor relationship with their parents. They use their earnings for self-support and do not frequently send money home. However, a study of African American sex workers in Milwaukee indicated that they often maintained contact with their families, and it is more likely that they would share their income from sex work with their families. In Asia, too, family disaffiliation is uncommon for female sex workers. Instead, kin support is a prominent motivation for doing sex work. In Thailand, few sex workers had broken ties with their families. Most visited their family once a year and sent regular remittances. In general, less stigma is attached to sex work if it is done for kin support, given the strong norms of family obligation in many Asian contexts.

Cambodian sex workers seek out customers in Phnom Penh. Cambodia is also a source of illegal transfer of sex workers into neighbouring Thailand.

Households as Social Units: Intrahousehold Dynamics

How do household members interact with each other? What are their emotional attachments, rights, and responsibilities? What are the power relationships between and among members of various categories such as spouses, siblings, and those of different generations?

Kinship systems define what the content of these relationships should be. In everyday life, people may conform more or less to the ideal, as was apparent in the description of problems between mothers-in-law and daughters-in-law in extended farming households of North America. The important dimension of how people may or may not diverge from ideal roles and relationships is, oddly, one that has been neglected for a long time by cultural anthropology and has only recently gained some attention.

Spouse/Partner Relationships

Anthropologists who study relationships between spouses and partners consider a range of topics: decision making, power relationships, the degree of attachment and commitment, duration of commitment, and the possibility of intimate relationships outside the primary relationship. This section presents findings on levels of emotional satisfaction between spouses and how they might relate to extramarital relationships.

A landmark sociological study of marriages in Tokyo in 1959 compared marital satisfaction of husbands and wives in love marriages and arranged marriages (Blood 1967). In all marriages, marital satisfaction declined over time, but differences between the two types emerged. The decline was greatest for wives in arranged marriages and least for husbands in arranged marriages. In love-match marriages, husbands' satisfaction dropped dramatically and a bit later than their wives' satisfaction, but both husbands and wives have nearly equal levels of satisfaction by the time they had been married nine years and more.

Sexual activity of couples can be both an indication of marital satisfaction and a cause of marital satisfaction. Anthropologists have not studied this topic much, but help from sociologists working with survey data is available. Analysis of reports of marital sex from a 1988 survey in the United States shows that frequency per month declines with duration of marriage, from an average of 12 times per month for people aged 19 to 24 years, to less than once a month for people 75 years of age and older (Call, Sprecher, and Schwartz 1995). Older married people have sex less frequently, as do those who report being less happy. Within each age category, sex is more frequent among three categories of people: those who are cohabiting but not married, those who had cohabited before marriage, and those who were in their second or later marriage. A more recent survey, conducted in 1992, revealed that the people who reported the highest levels of physical and emotional pleasure were those who, either married or cohabiting, were in relationships in which the spouse or partner had not had another sexual relationship in the past year (Laumann et al. 1994:364). Cross-cultural data are not available to show how these findings for the United States might compare to other settings.

Sibling Relationships

Sibling relationships are another understudied aspect of kinship dynamics. Suad Joseph (1994) provides an example of research on this topic in her study of a working-class neighbourhood of Beirut, Lebanon, prior to the civil war. She got to know several families well and became especially close to Hanna, the oldest son in one of these families. Hanna was an attractive young man, considered a good marriage choice, with friends across religious and ethnic groups. He seemed peace-loving and conscientious. Therefore, the author reports: "I was shocked...one sunny afternoon to hear Hanna shouting at his sister Flaur and slapping her across the face" (50). Aged 12, Flaur was the oldest daughter. "She seemed to have an opinion on most things, was never shy to speak her mind, and welcomed guests with boisterous laughter.... With a lively sense of humor and good-natured mischief about her, neighbors thought of her as a live wire" (50). Further consideration of the relationship between Hanna and Flaur indicated that Hanna played a fatherly role to Flaur. He would be especially irritated with her if she lingered on the street near their apartment building, gossiping with other girls: "He would forcibly escort her upstairs to their apartment, slap her, and demand that she behave with dignity" (51). Adult family members thought nothing was wrong and said that Flaur enjoyed her brother's aggressive attention. Flaur herself commented, "It doesn't even hurt when Hanna hits me" and that she hoped to have a husband like Hanna.

An interpretation of this common brother-sister relationship in Arab culture is that it is part of the socializing process that maintains and perpetuates patriarchal family relationships: "Hanna was teaching Flaur to accept male power in the name of love...loving his sister meant taking charge of her and that he could discipline her if his action was understood to be in her interest. Flaur was reinforced in learning that the love of a man could include that male's violent control and that to receive his love involved submission to control" (52). This close and unequal sibling relationship persists throughout life. Even after marriage, a brother maintains a position of responsibility towards his sister and her children, as does a married sister towards her brother and his children. This loyalty can lead to conflict between husband and wife

Love Hotels in Japan

To most of us, renting a hotel room by the hour means a drive to the edge of town, an embarrassed check-in, a stained and threadbare wall, and grunts from the next room. That formula wouldn't work in Japan, though, where privacy, decorum, and hygiene are all held at a premium. Yet the demand for hourly rooms is much higher in Japan, thanks in part to a more chauvinistic society that doesn't frown as heavily on philandering husbands as well as to a living-space shortage that drives even married couples to seek occasional trysts outside their cramped, thin-walled apartments.

But in Japan every problem seems to have a technological solution. The result in this case is the multibillion-dollar "love hotel" industry.

It's hard to miss some love hotels. They can be astoundingly gaudy affairs on the outside, often done up to vaguely resemble such out-of-place icons as cruise ships, wedding cakes, or the Statue of Liberty. Otherwise, love hotels are paradigms of discretion. You drive into a parking lot whose entrance is covered with long cloth fringes to foil prying eyes. Various types of pull-down or clip-on devices are available for covering up your license plate, lest a jealous spouse take to cruising the lot in search of your car.

The most impressive concession to privacy offered by many love hotels, however, is the ability to check in and out without interacting with any staff. Just inside the entrance to the hotel is an electronic screen that tells you the numbers of the rooms that are vacant. You then make your way to one of the rooms and gain entrance by inserting yen notes (typically about $30 an hour) into a computerized lock. The door flies open, and that room number disappears from the screen at the entrance.

High-tech touches inside the neat, if small and slightly garish, rooms can include wide-screen-video karaoke and a remote-controlled sound system that offers not only dozens of music chan-

nels but also noises such as gongs and crowing roosters (hey, whatever turns you on) and even the sounds you would hear in a train station (to be played as background when you phone your boss or spouse from the room to say you're going to be late).

When you leave, maids are electronically summoned by the computerized door lock to thoroughly clean and sanitize the room. One hour and five minutes after you first walked in, the room number is back up on the board.

Source: Michael P. Cronin, "The Love Hotel," *Inc. Technology* 17(4):116, 1995. Reprinted with permission, *Inc. magazine*, Technology Summer 1995 issue. Copyright 1995 by Goldhirsch Group, Inc., 38 Commercial Wharf, Boston, MA 02110.

FOOD FOR THOUGHT

What might be the connection between such hotels and marriage as it is practised in Japan?

as each vies for support and resources from their respective spouses in competition with siblings.

Domestic Violence

Domestic violence can occur between domestic partners, parents and children, and siblings. Violence between domestic partners, with males dominating as perpetrators and women as victims, seems to be found in almost all cultures, although in varying forms and frequencies (J. K. Brown 1992). A cross-cultural review of ethnographic evidence of wife beating revealed that wife beating is more common and more severe in societies where men control the wealth and less common and less severe where women's work groups are prominent (Levinson 1989). The presence of women's work groups appears to be related to a greater importance of women in production and matrifocal residence. Both factors provide women with the means to leave an abusive relationship. For example, among the Garifuna, an African-Indian people of Belize, Central America, incidents of spouse abuse occur, but they are infrequent and not extended (Kerns 1992). Women's solidarity in this matrifocal society to a large extent limits male violence against women.

Increased domestic violence worldwide throws into question the notion of the house as a refuge or place of security. In North America, for example, evidence exists for high and increasing rates of intrahousehold abuse of children (including sexual abuse), violence between spouses or partners, and abuse of aged family members. More cross-cultural research is needed to help policymakers understand the factors affecting the safety of individuals within households.

A shared bedroom in a battered woman's shelter, Tel Aviv, Israel. Many people wonder why abused women do not leave their abusers. Part of the answer lies in the unavailability and low quality of shelters throughout much of the world. Another factor is that a woman who leaves an abusive relationship is often in greater danger of serious injury (including death) than when she stays in the relationship.

Household Transformations

The composition and sheer existence of a particular household can change due to several factors including divorce, death, and possible remarriage. This section reviews some anthropological findings on these topics.

Divorce and Kinship Patterns

Divorce and separation, like marriage and other forms of long-term union, are cultural universals, even though they may be frowned on or forbidden. Marriages may break up for several reasons: Voluntary separation or death of one of the partners are the most common. Globally, distinct variations exist in the legality and propriety of divorce. Some religions, such as Roman Catholicism, prohibit divorce. In some cultures, such as Islamic societies, divorce is easier for a husband to obtain than for a wife. Important questions about marital dissolution include the causes for it, the reasons rates of divorce appear to be rising worldwide, and the implications for the welfare of children of divorced parents.

Why Do Divorce Rates Vary Cross-Culturally?

One hypothesis suggests that divorce rates will be lower in cultures with unilineal descent, where a large descent group has control over and interests in offspring (Barnard and Good 1984:119). Royal lineages, with their strong vested interests in maintaining the family line, are examples of groups especially unlikely to favour divorce, because divorce generally means losing control of offspring. When Princess Diana agreed to an uncontested divorce from Prince Charles in February 1996, she negotiated a lump sum payment estimated at £17 million. More importantly, she asked to continue to be involved in all decisions related to her children and remain in Kensington Palace. However, she was stripped of her title of honour, a poignant decision in light of her tragic death in August 1997.

How does this theory of a relation between kinship systems and divorce hold up in the face of evidence? In bilateral foraging societies, couples generally have a fluid way both of joining and then breaking up. The same is true for contemporary North America with its (more or less) bilateral system. Patrilineal kinship systems of Pakistan and northern India seem related to the low divorce rates there.

Are separation or divorce more characteristic of some kinds of unions than others? In North America, people in cohabiting relationships are more likely to split up than people who are formally married, and the same is likely to be true in other contexts as well (see the Voices box). In La Laja, Venezuela, a poor *barrio,* or neighbourhood in a city, three forms of marriage exist: church marriage, legal marriage, and common-law marriage through co-residence for a period of time (Peattie 1968:45). Church marriages are the least common form of marriage in La Laja. People say that they are expensive because of the costs for clothing and festivities required. Women in La Laja comment that a church marriage is bad because it permits no divorce: It is a contract with no escape clause in a society where separation often seems appropriate. Common-law marriages, the predominant form in La Laja, may be terminated by either party. For example, women said, "He left me for another woman." "He drank too much and I decided to spend the rest of my years in peace with my children" (46).

How durable are marriages with multiple spouses? Concerning the relationship between polygyny and divorce, a case study in Nigeria found that two-wife arrangements are the most stable, while unions with three or more wives have the highest rates of disruption (Gage-Brandon 1992).

Gender and Divorce Now we consider two examples of how gender roles affect an individual's ability to obtain a divorce and the nature of the settlement, including child custody. Both the situation in Islamic law and the challenges faced in Canada by lesbian mothers indicate how the law favours males.

Throughout most of the Islamic world, the law grants men easy access to divorce. Turkey is the only Islamic nation in which the law allows women and men equal access to divorce. Elsewhere, for Islamic women, divorce is difficult, expensive, and usually unsuccessful. Variations in the requirements for divorce under Islam exist according to different schools of law. The branch called *Maliki law* is the most liberal (Mir-Hosseini 1993). It provides three modes of divorce. The first and most common is separation by *khul'*, which is initiated by the husband. He secures his wife's consent and they come to an agreement about the compensation to be given to her. *Khul'* divorce does not require legal action.

The second type is the age-old form called *talaq* or "repudiation." This form is reserved for the husband,

---

Esmeralda Santiago, "When I Was Puerto Rican"

Esmeralda Santiago's story begins in Puerto Rico with her parents and seven siblings, but then takes her to New York City. At first bewildered by the differences she faced as well as the continuities—including the violent relationship between her parents—she won acceptance into New York City's High School of Performing Arts and then went on to Harvard University, where she graduated with highest honours. In the following passage, she describes what happened when her mother told her father she was leaving him to move with the children to New York.

"Tell them what?" She came out to the porch, hands on hips.

"That you're moving to New York." He didn't look at her, just spit the words out like phlegm into the night...

"How can you be so cruel" she said to Papi. "You know I have no choice..."

"I've given you a home. I'm not a rich man, but we've always had enough to eat."

"Do you consider that enough?" Her voice was tense and rising in pitch.

"I don't know what you want from me, Monín. I just don't know."

"I've lived with you for fourteen years. We have seven children together. You won't marry me. You won't leave me alone."

"Is that what you want? Marriage? What would that do? I've recognized them all. They all have my last name..."

They growled words that made no sense...I crouched against the wall and watched them injure each other without touching each other, hurling words that had the same effect as acid on metal. One by one Delsa, Norma, Héctor, Alicia, Edna, and Raymond came out on the porch, their eyes round as guavas, tears glistening on the tips of their lashes. (1993:206–207)

Source: Esmeralda Santiago, *When I Was Puerto Rican*. New York: Vintage Books, 1993.

FOOD FOR THOUGHT

This narrative comes from a particular Latino context. Does it seem culturally unique?

---

who simply says, "I divorce you" three times, with or without the knowledge or consent of the wife. The husband needs to get the *talaq* registered by two Notary Judges. Some limitations on *talaq* exist: A man cannot divorce a wife by *talaq* when he is intoxicated, in a fit of violence or anger, or when his wife is menstruating. The husband must pay a consolation gift whenever he repudiates his wife. The amount of compensation may be contested by the wife in court. It is not based on length of marriage, but more on the degree of harm to the wife, especially if the husband repudiated her on caprice; it is less if she is at fault or gave her consent. In Morocco, in 1987, 10 per cent of the 1898 divorce cases filed were initiated by men who sought to reduce the dues set by the Notary Judge when they registered their *talaq*.

The third way to obtain a divorce is *tatliq*, a form pursued by women. Grounds for divorce under *tatliq* include the husband's failure to provide maintenance, the husband having an incurable disease injurious to the wife (such as insanity or leprosy, but only if she was not aware of the condition before marriage), the husband's ill treatment of the wife, the husband's absence for a period of at least one year and its effect of causing the wife harm, and the husband's abandonment of marital relations resulting from his taking an oath of sexual abstinence (he is given a period of four months to break the oath). Divorce by *tatliq* requires extensive written proof, including medical certificates, bank statements, and reports by witnesses. Of 156 *tatliq* divorces recorded in two Moroccan cities, the husband's absence was nearly half of the total. Success rates for divorce by *tatliq* are low, with variation according to the grounds. Divorce on the grounds of harm has the lowest rate of acceptance, because it is so difficult to prove, given the demanding requirements for written testimony from witnesses and other documentation.

Lesbian mothers face many barriers in getting a fair divorce settlement from a former heterosexual marriage. Child custody is a key issue, as revealed by an ethnographic study conducted in California: "Of the formerly married heterosexual women I interviewed, 24 percent had either experienced an actual custody action or been threatened by one. The proportion of lesbian mothers who reported such experiences rose to 41 percent" (Lewin 1993:163). Judges tend to view lesbian mothers as unsuitable custodial parents because of their sexual orientation. In Canada, judges have adopted what might appear to be a more "reasonable" approach (Arnup 2000:203). Canadian courts argued that if the lesbian mothers were discreet about their lifestyles, they would be considered suitable mothers. However, as in the United States, Canadian lesbian mothers attempting to protect themselves from custody challenges from their former husbands often adopt an "appeasement strategy." They keep a low profile—abandoning claims to marital property and to child and spousal support, and compromising on issues such as visitation. One lesbian mother gave up her share in the marital house, saying "He never really brought it into the negotiations directly. But he would like call me and harass me, and by innuendo suggest that there were many issues that he could bring up if he wanted to.... So basically, I traded my equity in the house for that issue not being raised at that time" (Lewin 1993:170). These strategies have negative consequences, limiting contact between father and child and reducing parental discussion about the child.

Widow(er)hood

The position of a widow or widower carries altered responsibilities and rights. Women's position as widows is often marked symbolically. In some Mediterranean cultures, a widow must wear modest, simple, and black-coloured clothing, sometimes for the rest of her life. Her sexuality is supposed to be virtually dead. At the same time, her new "asexual" status allows her greater spatial freedom than before. She can go to public coffeehouses and taverns, something not done by women whose husbands are living.

Extreme restrictions on widows are recorded for parts of South Asia where social pressures on a widow strongly enforce self-denial and self-deprivation, especially among the propertied class. A widow should wear only a plain white sari, shave her head, eat little food, and live an asexual life. Many widows in India are abandoned, especially if they have no son to support them. They are considered polluting and inauspicious. In a similar fashion, in South Africa, widows experience symbolic and life-quality changes much more than do widowers:

> A widower is encouraged to take on the challenge of picking up the pieces and to face life again. He is reminded that he must be strong and swallow his pain. His body is not marked in any significant way except to have his head shaved, as is the custom in most African communities.

A widow of Madeira, Portugal, wearing the typical black, modest clothing required in some Mediterranean cultures as a sign of widowhood.

He also is required to wear a black button or arm band. The period of mourning for widowers is generally six months, compared to at least one year for widows.... The fear of the ritual danger embodied in widows is expressed in terms of "heat," "darkness," and "dirt."...Her body is marked in different communities by some or all of the following practices: shaving her head, smearing a mixture of herbs and ground charcoal on her body, wearing black clothes made from an inexpensive material, and covering her face with a black veil and her shoulders with a black shawl. A widow may express her liminal status in a variety of ways, [by] eating with her left hand, wearing clothes inside out, wearing one shoe, or eating out of a lid instead of a plate (Ramphele 1996:100).

Remarriage

Remarriage patterns are influenced by economic factors and gender-linked expectations that shape a person's de-

sirability as a partner. In North America, divorce frequently is followed by remarriage for both males and females, with a slight edge for men (Cornell 1989). In Japan, the tendency to remarry for males is significantly greater than for women. A marked age distribution in non-remarriage for women exists: "[W]hile divorced Japanese women, up to age 40, are already about 15% more likely to remain divorced than are their U.S. white female counterparts of the same age, after age 40 their situation grows rapidly more unfavorable for remarriage. In the subsequent decade it rises to 25% more divorced at age 45, 40% more at age 48, more than half again as many at age 50, and 65% more at age 51" (460). Older women's lower rates of remarriage are the result of age-hypergynous marriage and males' greater access to economic and political resources that increase their attractiveness as marriage partners in spite of their increasing age.

Social Change and Domestic Life

Changing economic opportunities in recent times have led to rapid change in household structures and dynamics. For example, employment of daughters in electronics factories in Malaysia has changed intrahousehold power structures (Ong 1987). The girls' mothers encourage them to take up factory work and urge them to contribute a proportion of their earnings to the household economy. This frees up daughters from their father's control (as is traditional among Malaysian Muslims), while giving greater control to the mother.

International migration is another major cause of change in family and household formations (see Chapter 15). Dramatic changes can occur in one generation when members of a farming household in, for example, Taiwan or India, migrate to England, France, Canada, or the United States. In their homeland, having many children makes economic sense, but it does not in their new destination. These migrants decide to have only one or two children and live in small, isolated nuclear households.

International migration creates new challenges for relationships between parents and children. The children often become strongly identified with the new culture and have little connection with their ancestral culture, and this pattern can be a source of anxiety for their parents. Often, values in the new culture conflict with those of the culture of origin, putting children in conflict with their parents over issues such as dating, dress, and career goals. In 1997, the people of Norway were confronted with a case of kidnapping of an 18-year-old Norwegian citizen named "Nadia," who was taken by her parents to Morocco and held captive there (Wikan 2000). The full story is a complicated one, but the core issues revolve around conflict between Moroccan family values and Norwegian ones. Nadia's parents felt that she should be under their control and that they had the right to arrange her marriage in Morocco, while Nadia held a Norwegian concept of personal autonomy. In the end, Nadia and her parents returned to Norway, where the courts granted that, for the sake of the family, the parents not be jailed on grounds of kidnapping their daughter. The case brought stigma to Nadia among the Muslim community of Norway, who viewed her as a traitor to her culture. She now lives at a secret address and avoids publicity. An anthropologist close to this case who served as an expert cultural witness during the trial of her parents reports that, in spite of her seclusion, she has offered help to other young women who have sought her out.

Cultural anthropologists and sociologists have valuable insights to offer policy-makers and concerned individuals about the current status of "the family" and future trends in family/household structure and dynamics in North America. In 1996, Canada registered its 10 millionth household, representing a more than doubling in number in less than 40 years (Statistics Canada 1999). During the same period, household size shrank from an average of 3.9 persons to 2.6 persons. In the United States the share headed by married couples declined from 74 per cent to 55 per cent. The current situation contains several seemingly contradictory patterns that were first noted in the early 1980s by two sociologists (Cherlin and Furstenberg 1992 [1983]): (1) the number of unmarried couples living together has more than tripled since 1970, and (2) one out of four children is not living with both parents. At current rates, half of all North American marriages begun in the 1980s will end in divorce.

What about domestic life in this new millennium? Basic outlines of the near future indicate the reduced economic dependence of women and the weakening of marriage in industrialized societies (Cherlin 1996:478–480). These changes, in turn, will lead to increased movement away from nuclear household living and increased diversity in household forms. At the beginning of the twenty-first century, three kinds of households are most common in North America: households composed of couples living in their first marriage, single-parent households, and households formed through remarriage (Cherlin and Furstenberg 1992 [1983]:3). A new fourth category is the **intergenerational household,** in which an "adult child" returns to live with his or her parents. About one in three unmarried adults between the ages of 25 and 55 share a home with their mother or father or both (*Psychology Today* 1995 [28]:16). Currently, in North America, adult offspring spend over two hours a day doing household chores, with daughters contributing about 17 hours a week and sons 14.4 hours. The daughters spend most of their time doing laundry, cooking, cleaning, and washing dishes, while sons are more involved in yard work and car care. Even so, the parents still do three-quarters of the housework.

Kinship and domestic arrangements are certainly not dull and static concepts. Just trying to keep up to date on their changing patterns in North America is a daunting task, not to mention the rest of the world.

What is a household and what are major household forms?

A household is a domestic group comprising people who may or may not be related by kinship and who share a living space and, often, budgetary responsibilities for the household. Nuclear households are defined as consisting of a mother and father and their children, but they can also be just a husband and wife without children. Nuclear households are found in all cultures, but are most clearly associated with industrial societies with their emphasis on neolocal residence upon marriage. Extended households include more than one nuclear household. Extended households are often both the ideal and the most common pattern in cultures where unilineal descent is practised and where either patrilocal or matrilocal residence upon marriage means that married children live with or near the parents of either the groom or bride. Stem households, which are especially common in East Asia, are a variant of extended households. In stem households, only one child, usually the first-born son, remains with the parents. Household headship can be either shared between two adult partners or can be borne by a single person as in woman-headed households.

What are some important economic and social features of households?

Households, depending on the context, are involved to varying degrees in production, consumption, and exchange. In nonindustrial societies, households often ful-fill all these functions. In industrial societies, they are more concerned with consumption and exchange since most production takes place outside the household. Intrahousehold dynamics, or social relationships among members of a household, involve interactions, predominantly between parents and children and among siblings. Research on intrahousehold dynamics has revealed that households are complex arenas of power conflicts as well as sharing, and security as well as occasional violence. Household breakup comes about through divorce, separation of cohabiting partners, or death of a spouse or partner.

How are household patterns changing?

The increasingly globally connected world in which we live has marked effects on household patterns. While marriage continues to be a prominent basis for nuclear and extended household formation, other options for household formation, such as cohabitation, continue to be important. Yet others are becoming more important in some contexts such as single-parent or single-person households. In contradiction to theories predicting the decline of the extended household with modernization, evidence suggests continuity of extended households in India and perhaps elsewhere. In Japan, however, maintaining the stem household structure has become more difficult due to children's increasing reluctance to live with their parents. The implications of changes in household forms and dynamics for the care of dependent members, especially children and the aged, is a key question of our times.

Core Concepts

Suggested Readings

Dorothy Ayers Counts, Judith K. Brown, and Jacquelyn C. Campbell, *Sanctions and Sanctuaries: Cultural Perspectives on the Beating of Wives.* Boulder, CO: Westview Press, 1992. This book includes 15 case studies plus an introductory overview and concluding comparative essay. One chapter considers the possible evolutionary origin of wife abuse. The wide range of cultural contexts studied include Australia, southern Africa, Papua New Guinea, India, Central America, the Middle East, and the Pacific.

Robert McC. Netting, Richard R. Wilk, and Eric J. Arnould, eds., *Households: Comparative and Historical Studies of the Domestic Group.* Berkeley: University of California Press, 1984. Several comparative chapters on topics such as changing forms and functions of the household and case studies of contemporary Thailand, Niger, Belize, and the United States, and historic analyses of the Baltic region and Sweden are included in this text.

Ellen Oxfeld, *Blood, Sweat, and Mahjong: Family and Enterprise in an Overseas Chinese Community.* Ithaca, NY: Cornell University Press, 1992. This ethnography addresses the Chinese immigrant community in Calcutta, India, and family involvement in the tanning industry; attention is given to the social history of the Hakka community, gender roles, and norms about family entrepreneurship.

Peter H. Stephenson, *The Hutterian People: Ritual and Rebirth in the Evolution of Communal Life.* Lanham, MD: University Press of America, 1991. This ethnography investigates how the Hutterites have maintained a vital and long-lived utopian religious community. Many of these people live in Canada's western provinces.

Debbie Taylor, *My Children, My God: A Journey to the World of Seven Single Mothers.* Berkeley: University of California Press, 1994. This narrative report by a journalist is based on interviews with seven single mothers in different countries: Uganda, Brazil, India, China, Australia, Egypt, and Scotland.

 Your *Cultural Anthropology,* Second Canadian Edition Media Edition CD-ROM contains many Web sites relevant to this chapter. Use it to explore the Web and to expand your knowledge of anthropology.

Chapter 10

Social Groups and Social Stratification

CHAPTER OUTLINE

A north Indian village carpenter seated in front of his house. The status position of carpenters is middling, neither as high and powerful as landholding elites or brahman priests, nor as low as those who deal with polluting materials such as animal hides or refuse.

Key Questions

What is the range of cross-cultural variation of social groups?

What is social stratification, and what are its effects on people?

What is civil society?

235

*C*anada's small population in a gigantic territory with two official languages "requires a greater use of the imagination…[demanding] of the citizenry a more open and active imagination, a more acute sensibility. It is not a situation for lazy minds and easy emotions" (Saul 1997:57). The United States, which the early nineteenth century French political philosopher Alexis de Tocqueville called a "nation of joiners," has been united around powerful and unifying symbols like the "stars and stripes." Some have questioned whether Canada has developed a similar sense of unity and it often seems the nation faces imminent dissolution. Yet, there is no question that for many Canadians, membership in social groups beyond the family is an important aspect of life. The question of what motivates people to join groups, what holds people together in groups, and how groups deal with leadership and participation have intrigued many scholars for centuries.

This chapter focuses primarily on non-kin groups and relates to the issue of cultural formation. At the end of Chapter 1, several factors related to the formation of local cultures were defined: class, race, ethnicity, gender, age, region, and institutions such as prisons or retirement homes. Thus far, we have looked at how these factors affect fieldwork, and how they vary in different economies and in different reproductive systems. This chapter looks again at these and other key factors of social differentiation in order to see how they affect group formation and the relationships between groups in terms of hierarchy and power. It first examines a variety of social groups and then considers the issue of inequalities between certain key social categories.

Social Groups

A **social group** is a cluster of people beyond the domestic unit who are usually related on grounds other than kinship, although kinship relationships may exist between people in the group. Two basic categories exist: the **primary group,** consisting of people who interact with each other and know each other personally, and the **secondary group,** consisting of people who identify with each other on some common ground but who may never meet with one another or interact with each other personally.

Members of all social groups have a sense of rights and responsibilities in relation to the group which, if not maintained, could mean loss of membership. Primary group membership involves more direct accountability about rights and responsibilities than secondary group membership because of its face-to-face characteristic. When discussing different kinds of groups, social scientists also draw a distinction between informal groups and formal groups (March and Taqqu 1986:5):

- Informal groups are smaller and less visible.
- Members of informal groups have close, face-to-face relationships with one another, while members of formal groups may or may not know each other.
- Organizational structure is less hierarchical in informal groups.
- Informal groups do not have legal recognition.

The array of social groups found around the world seems to defy theoretical formulations. Modes of economies do seem to affect the proliferation of social groups, with the greatest variety being found in agricultural and industrial societies (see Figure 10.1). One theory suggests that mobile populations, such as pastoralists, are less likely to develop enduring social groups beyond kin relationships. It may be true that foragers and pastoralists have less variety of social groups, but they are not completely without any social groupings. A prominent form of social group among foragers and pastoralists is an **age set,** which is a group of people close in age who go through certain rituals, such as circumcision, at the same time.

A related hypothesis is that settled and densely populated areas have more social groups as a way to organize society. Again, this may be generally true, but important variations and exceptions exist. Cross-culturally, both informal and formal groups appear to be more varied and active in Africa and Latin America than in South Asia (Uphoff and Esman 1984). In Bangladesh, a densely populated and agrarian country of South Asia, indigenous social groups are rare. The most prominent ties beyond the household are kinship-based: men's political linkages with their patrilineage (Miller and Khan 1986). In spite of the lack of indigenous social groups, however, Bangladesh has gained world renown for its success in forming local credit groups for grassroots development through an organization called the Grameen

FIGURE 10.1 Economies and Social Groups

FORAGING	HORTICULTURE	PASTORALISM	AGRICULTURE	INDUSTRIALISM (CAPITALIST)

Characteristics
Informal and primary
  Egalitarian structure
    Ties based on balanced exchange

Characteristics
Formal and secondary
  Recognized leadership
    Dues and fees

Ritual ties

Functions
Companionship

Functions
Special purposes
  Work, war, lobbying government

Types of Social Groups
Friendship

Friendship
Age-based work groups
Gender-based work groups

Types of Social Groups
Friendship
  Urban youth gangs
  Clubs, associations
Status Groups:
  Class, race, ethnicity, caste, age, gender
Institutional Groups:
  Prisons, retirement homes
Quasi-Political Groups:
  Human rights, environmental groups

Bank, which gives loans to poor people to help them start small enterprises.

In Bali, an island province of Indonesia, several formal and focused groups exist for specific purposes, including temple committees to provide for the costs of temple maintenance and collective rites; custom-law wards to cooperate in cremation ceremonies; neighbourhood groups to send food to the temple for the gods; and irrigation groups to provide water for the rice fields (Lansing 1995). Members of all households participate in several of these groups at the same time. The precise reasons why some cultures have strong and enduring social groups beyond kinship affiliations await further exploration and explanation from social scientists.

In the following sections, we will encounter a variety of social groups. We begin with the most face-to-face, primary groups of two or three people based on friendship and move to larger groups with explicit goals, such as countercultural groups and activist groups.

Friendship

Friendship fits in the category of a primary social group that is informal. One question that cultural anthropologists ask is whether friendship is a cultural universal. Unfortunately, at this point, insufficient cross-cultural research exists to answer the question definitively. Additionally, defining friendship cross-culturally is problematic. It is likely, however, that something like "friendship" (close ties between non-kin) is a cultural universal, although shaped in different degrees from culture to culture.

Social Characteristics of Friendship

Friends are chosen on a voluntary basis. Yet, the criteria of who qualifies as a friend may be culturally structured. For instance, gender segregation will limit cross-gender friendships and promote same-gender friendships. In Thailand, "friends until death" are friends who can be trusted with intimate knowledge of one's

Male and Female Friendships in Rural Spain

The prevailing gender division of labour and spatial gender segregation found in southern Spain shape differences in men's and women's friendship patterns (Uhl 1991). Women's lives are taken up mainly with unpaid household work within the domestic domain. Men's lives involve the two activities of work and leisure outside the house. This dichotomy is somewhat fluid, however, for women's domestic roles do take them into the public domain—markets, town hall, taking children to school—with some time for visiting friends.

Women often referred to their friends either with kin terms or as *vecina*, "neighbour," reflecting women's primary orientation to family and neighbourhood. For men, an important category of friend is an *amigo*, a friend with whom one casually interacts. This kind of casual friendship is the friendship of bars and leisure-time male camaraderie. It grows out of work, school, common sports and hobbies, and drinking together night after night. Women do not have such friendships. Men also are more likely than women to have *ami-gos(as) de trabajo*, friendships based on work activities. Differences between men and women also emerge in the category of "true friends," or *amigo(as) de la verdad* or *de confianza*. True friends are those with whom one shares secrets without fear of betrayal. Most men claimed to have many more true friends than the women had, reflecting their wider social networks.

motivations and desires (see the Multiple Cultural Worlds box above for another example). Another characteristic of friendship is that friends are supportive of each other, psychologically and sometimes materially. Support is mutual, shared back and forth in an expectable way. Friendship generally occurs between social equals. Anthropologist Thomas Dunk researched how a group of working-class men friends in Thunder Bay, Ontario, informally ensure that everyone contributes their fair share (as in balanced exchange, see Chapter 4). After a game of lob-ball (a form of softball) the men meet at a bar.

In the bar after the game, everyone takes turns buying rounds. If someone is short of money one evening, someone else or several other people stand him drinks. This "just happens"; one does not need to ask.... True friends, for these men, are people who give to each other without asking, and this extends beyond the walls of the bar after a game (Dunk 1991:92).

Friendships in Prison
Prisons, like colleges and universities, are social institutions with limited populations among whom relationships may develop. In the case of colleges and universities, people are there voluntarily and they have a good idea about how long they will be there. It makes sense to form enduring bonds with friends and classmates. In the context of prisons, people are not there voluntarily, and the formation of social ties is limited.

One factor that affects the formation of friendship in prisons is the duration of the sentence. A study that ex-plored this issue first had to deal with the difficulty of doing participant observation. A research team of two people included an "insider" and an "outsider" (Schmid and Jones 1993). The "insider" was an inmate serving a short-term sentence who did participant observation, conducted interviews, and kept a journal. The "outsider," a sociologist, met with him weekly to discuss findings (the sociologist also did the analysis). The inmate researcher was a male, and so this study deals only with male prisoners. Furthermore, since his was a short-term sentence, its findings concern the effects of short-term sentencing (of one or two years) on social relationships among inmates.

Three stages of short-term inmate adaptation are typical. In the first stage, inmates experience uncertainty and fear, based on their images of what life is like in prison. They avoid contact with other prisoners and guards as much as possible. The second stage involves the creation of a survival niche. The prisoner has selective interactions with other inmates and may develop a "partnership" with another inmate. Partners hang around together and watch out for each other. Maintaining a close tie with another inmate is difficult: "I think it would be almost impossible to carry on a relationship, a real close relationship, being here for two years or a year and a half. It's literally impossible. I think that the best thing to do is to just forget about it, and if the relationship can be picked up again once you get out, that's fine. And if it can't, you have to accept that" (453). In the third stage, the prisoner anticipates his eventual release, transfers to a minimum security area, increases contact with outside visitors, and begins the transition to the outside. In this stage, partners begin to detach from each other as one of the pair moves towards the outside world.

Friendship among the Urban Poor
Carol Stack's study of how friendship networks promote economic survival among low-income African Americans is a landmark contribution (1974). Her research was conducted in the late 1960s in "The Flats," the poorest section of a Black community in a Midwestern city. She found extensive networks of friends "supporting, reinforcing each other—devising schemes for self help, strategies for survival in a community of severe economic deprivation" (28). Close friends, in fact, are referred to by kin terms.

People in The Flats, especially women, maintain a set of friends through exchange: "swapping" goods (food, clothing) needed by someone at a particular time, sharing "child keeping," and giving or loaning food stamps and money. Such exchanges are part of a clearly understood pattern—gifts and favours go back and forth over time. Friends thus bound together are obligated to each another and can call on each other in time of need. In discussing the common practice of child keeping, Stack says:

> The exchange of children, and short-term fosterage, are common among female friends. Child-care arrangements among friends imply both rights and duties. Close friends frequently discipline each other's children verbally and physically in front of each other. In normal times, and in times of stress, close friends have a right to "ask" for one another's children. A woman visiting a friend and her children may say, "Let me keep your girl this week. She will have a fine time with me and my girls. She won't want to come back home to her mama." This kind of request among kin and friends is very hard to refuse. Temporary child-care services are also a means of obligating kin or friends for future needs. Women may ask to "keep" the child of a friend for no apparent reason. But they are, in fact, building up an investment for their future needs. (82)

In opposition to theories that suggest the breakdown of social relationships among the very poor, this research documents how poor people strategize and cope through social ties.

Clubs and Fraternities

Clubs and fraternities often define membership on some sense of shared identity. Thus, they may often, but not always, comprise people of the same ethnic heritage (such as the United Empire Loyalists in Canada), occupation or business, religion, or gender. Some groups appear to exist primarily to serve functions of sociability and psychological support rather than economic or political functions. Deeper analysis often shows that these groups do have economic and political roles.

Women's clubs in a lower-class neighbourhood in Paramaribo, Suriname, have multiple functions (Brana-Shute 1976). Many clubs exist, each with its own name, flag, and colour. The clubs raise funds to sponsor special events and support individual celebrations, meet financial needs, and send cards and flowers for funerals. All club members attend each other's birthday parties and death rites as a group. The clubs thus offer psychological support to the women, entertainment, and financial supports. A political aspect exists, too. Club members are often members of the same political party, and core groups of club members may attend political rallies and events together. These women constitute political interest groups that can influence political outcomes: "Interviews with politicians and party workers confirmed the existence of real pressure placed on them by women individually and in groups" (175). These clubs' activities, therefore, span the private and public domains.College fraternities and sororities are highly selective groups that serve a variety of explicit functions, such as entertainment and social service. They also form bonds between members that may help in securing jobs after graduation. Compared to sociologists, few anthropologists have studied the "Greek system" on American campuses. One exception is Peggy Sanday, who was inspired to study college fraternities after a gang rape of a woman student by several fraternity brothers at the campus where she teaches. In her book, *Fraternity Gang Rape: Sex, Brotherhood, and Privilege on Campus* (1990), she explores initiation rituals, the role of pornography, ritual dances, and heavy drinking at parties, and how they relate to a pattern of male bonding solidified by victimization and derision of women. Her interviews revealed the prevalence of gang rape, or a "train" in some, not all, fraternities. Fraternity party invitations may even hint at the possibility of a "train." Typically, the brothers seek out a "party girl"—a somewhat vulnerable young woman who may be especially seeking of acceptance or especially high on alcohol or other substances (her drinks may even have been "spiked"). They take her to one of the brother's rooms where she may or may not agree to have sex with one man—often she passes out. Then a "train" of men have sex with her. Rarely prosecuted, the male participants reinforce their sense of privilege, power, and unity with one another through this group ritual involving abuse of a female outsider.

Men's clubs in which strong male-male bonds are created and reinforced by the objectification and mistreatment of women are common, but not universal, cross-culturally. They are especially associated with cultures where male-male competitiveness is an important feature of society (Bird 1996) and in which warfare and group conflict are frequent. In many Amazonian groups, the men's house is fiercely guarded from being entered by women. If a woman were to trespass on male territory, she is subject to punishment by gang rape. One interpretation is that males have a high degree of anxiety about their identity as fierce warriors and as sexually potent males (Gregor 1982). Maintaining their identity as fierce males towards outsiders involves taking an aggressive position in relation to women of their own group. Parallels of "women-hating" men's clubs among women do not exist. College sororities are not mirror images of college fraternities. Women's groups and organizations, even if vo-

cally anti-male, do not involve physical abuse of males or ritualized forms of derision.

Countercultural Groups

Several kinds of groups are formed by people who seek consciously to resist conforming to the dominant cultural pattern, as in the "hippie" movement of the 1960s. This section considers examples of countercultural groups. One similarity among these groups is the importance of bonding through shared rituals.

Youth Gangs The term *gang* can refer to a variety of groups, such as one's friends, as in, "I think I'll invite the gang over for pizza" (Short 1996:325). The more specific term **youth gangs** refers to groups of young people, found mainly in urban areas, who are often considered a social problem by adults and law enforcement officials (Sanders 1994:5–15).

Youth gangs vary in terms of how formally they are organized. In contrast to friendships, gangs—like clubs and fraternities—often have formalized rituals of initiation for new members, a recognized leader, and symbolic markers of identity such as tattoos or special clothing. An example of an informal youth gang with no formal leadership hierarchy or initiation rituals are the "Masta Liu," found in Honiara, the capital city of the Solomon Islands (Jourdan 1995). The primary unifying feature of the male youth who become Masta Liu is the fact that they are unemployed. Most have migrated to the city from the countryside to escape what they consider an undesirable lifestyle there: working in the fields under control of their elders. Yet, as a group, they have developed a distinct lifestyle and identity:

> Drifting in and out of jobs, in and out of hope, they are very often on the verge of delinquency. Many of them have had some brush with the law…songs are being written about them, people talk about them…. The **liu** have become a significant segment of the urban population, not only because of their sheer numbers, but because of the influence they have on the development of the urban popular culture. Their life-style, the way they dress and talk, their taste in music and films, their outlook on life, all this gives a particular direction to social change in Honiara. (202)

Some *liu* live with extended kin in the city, others organize *liu*-only households. They spend their time wandering around town (*wakabaot*) in groups of up to 10: "They stop at every shop on their way, eager to look at the merchandise but afraid to be kicked out by the security guards; they check out all the cinemas only to dream in front of the preview posters…not even having the $2 bill that will allow them to get in; they gaze for hours on end, and without moving, at the electronic equipment displayed in the Chinese shops, without saying a word: one can read in their gaze the silent dreams they create" (210).

"Street gangs" are a more formal variety of youth gang. They generally have leaders and a hierarchy of membership roles and responsibilities. They are named and their members mark their identity with tattoos or "colours." While many street gangs are involved in violence, not all are. An anthropologist who did research among nearly 40 street gangs in New York, Los Angeles, and Boston learned much about why individuals join gangs, providing insights that contradict popular thinking on this subject (Jankowski 1991). One common stereotype is that young boys join gangs because they are from homes with no male authority figure with whom they could identify. This study showed that equal numbers of gang members were from homes with "intact" nuclear families as from families with an absent father (39).

Another common perception is that the gang replaces a missing feeling of "family" as a motive. This study, again,

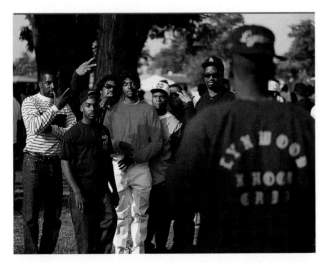

Members of two opposing youth gangs meet at a park in Los Angeles, California, in order to negotiate a truce.

showed that the same number of gang members reported having close family ties as those who didn't. So, then, what might be the reasons behind joining a male urban gang? It seems that a particular personality type characterized many gang members, a type that could be called a "defiant individualist." The defiant individualist type has five traits: intense competitiveness, mistrust or wariness, self-reliance, social isolation, and a strong survival instinct. Urban poverty possibly leads to the development of this kind of personality structure. It becomes a reasonable response to the economic blockades and uncertainty. The global spread of urban youth gangs would relate to global economic changes in urban employment. In many countries, the declining urban industrial base has created persistent poverty in inner-city communities (Short 1996:326). At the same time, aspirations for a better life have been promoted through schooling and the popular media. Urban gang members, in this view, are the victims of large structural forces beyond their control. Yet, research with gangs shows that they are not just passive victims of structural forces: Strong entrepreneurial interests motivate much gang activity. Many of these youths want to "get ahead," but social conditions channel their interests and skills into illegal pursuits rather than into legal pathways of material achievement.

Motorcycle Gangs Another "countercultural" group similar to the "street gangs" is the widespread North American (and growing global) phenomenon of outlaw motorcycle gangs. In the late 1940s young men who had served in the citizen armies of Canada and the United States formed clubs of motorcycle riders. Some of these developed into the "one percenters," the one per cent of motorcyclists who were troublemakers according to mainstream motorcycle enthusiasts. The "outlaw" clubs are characterized by wearing colours or club insignia which often include pictures of skulls or weapons meant to intimidate citizens and other gang members alike. The club member typically "chops" or modifies his "hog"(a Harley-Davidson motorcycle), and exhibits a loyalty to his brothers by helping defend a particular territory by physical force, if necessary.

Daniel R. Wolf (1991), an anthropologist who managed to become a member of one such club in Edmonton, describes how and why young working-class men find identity and satisfaction in the gang. Working-class employment does not provide the sense of self or meaning that may be available to other societal roles in industrial

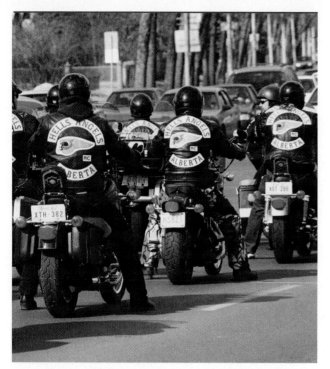

Members of the Hell Angels biker gang leave a chapel in Edmonton after the funeral of a brother who was killed in a motor vehicle accident.

Canada. Wolf argues that the motorcycle club provides these young alienated men with an identity and community they cannot find elsewhere (340). Riding in the wind, partying with brothers, and participating in sexual orgies with compliant women ("mamas") balance the constant threat of being hassled by the police and the dangers of physical injury both from citizens in "cages" (cars or trucks) running them off the roads and from fights with other gangs.

Body Modification Groups Of the many non-mainstream movements in North America, one includes people who have a sense of community strengthened through forms of body alteration. James Myers (1992) did research in California among people who feel they are a special group because of their interest in permanent body modification, especially genital piercing, branding, and cutting. His fieldwork involved six workshops organized especially for the San Francisco SM (sadomasochist) community by Powerhouse, a San Francisco Bay Area SM organization; the Fifth Annual Living in Leather Convention held in Portland, Oregon, in 1990;

and time in tattoo and piercing studios as well as talking with students and others in his home town who were involved in these forms of body modification. The study population included males and females, heterosexuals, gays, lesbians, bisexuals, and SMers. The single largest group was SM homosexuals and bisexuals. The study population was mainly White, and most had either attended or graduated from college.

Myers witnessed many modification sessions at workshops: Those seeking modification go up on stage and have their chosen procedure done by a well-known expert. Whatever the procedure, the volunteers evidence little pain (usually a sharp intake of breath at the moment the needle passes through or the brand touches skin). After that critical moment, the audience breathes an audible sigh of relief. The volunteer stands up, adjusts clothing, and members of the audience applaud. Myers interprets this public event as a kind of initiation ritual that binds the expert, the volunteer, and the group together. Pain has long been recognized as an important part of rites of passage, providing an edge to the ritual drama. The audience in this case witnesses and validates the experience and also becomes joined to the initiate through witnessing.

A prominent motivation for seeking permanent body modification was a desire to identify with a specific group of people, and the body marking is thus a sign of affiliation. As one informant said,

> It's not that we're sheep, getting pierced or cut just because everyone else is. I like to think it's because we're a very special group and we like doing something that sets us off from others…. You see all the guys at the bar and you know they are pierced and tattooed, and it gives you a good feeling to know that you're one of them…. Happiness is standing in line at a cafeteria and detecting that the straight-looking babe in front of you has her nipples pierced. I don't really care what her sexual orientation is, I can relate to her. (292)

Work Groups

Work groups are organized to perform specific tasks, although they also may have other functions including sociality and friendship among members. They are found in all modes of production, but they tend to be more prominent in pre-industrialized horticultural and agricultural

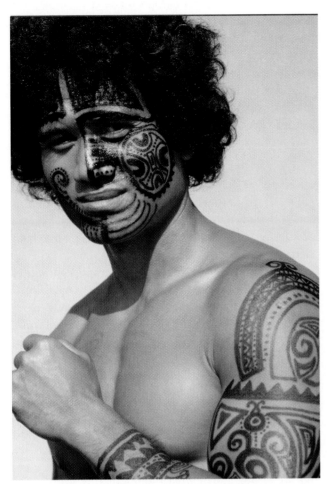

A Tahitian chief wears traditional tattoos that indicate his high status.

communities where land preparation, harvesting, or repair of irrigation canals requires large inputs of labour that exceed the capability of a single household unit. In her classic study of the Bemessi people of Cameroon, West Africa, Phyllis Kaberry (1952) describes a labour group system (called a *tzo*, translated as "working bee"):

> [A tzo] consists of women who are of about the same age and who are kin or friendly neighbors. For the preparation of corn beds there may be ten or twelve individuals; for weedings only three or four. About a week's notice is given and, once a woman has received help on her own plot, she is under an obligation to fulfill a similar duty to others on pain of being reported to the Fon (chief). The women usually work in pairs, chat, and urge each other on. Towards the end of the afternoon a small repast is

provided, which includes a little fish contributed by the husband. (56)

Youth work groups are common in African regions south of the Sahara, particularly in settled, crop-growing areas. Such work groups are often composed of one or more age sets. Among the Wolof of Gambia, the *ton*, or work group, is formed separately for boys and girls, and comprises several age sets (D. Ames 1959:224–237). The major responsibility of the youth groups is providing field labour. The group works one or more days in the village chief's fields for no remuneration. The group also maintains public paths and the public meeting area, constructs and maintains roads between villages, builds and repairs canals, combats brush fires, maintains the village mosque, and prevents animals from grazing where they aren't allowed (Leynaud 1961). Girls' groups exist, but in patrilocal contexts they are less durable because their marriage and relocation breaks ties with childhood companions (Hammond 1966:133). As adults, however, women in African cultures have many types of associations such as mothers' groups, savings groups, and work groups.

Irrigation organizations are formal groups devoted to maintaining irrigation canals and dealing with the tricky issue of distributing the water. Indigenous irrigation organizations are common around the world and have been the focus of much anthropological and sociological attention. These organizations are responsible for a highly valued good, and they tend to develop leadership and membership rules and roles. Given the fact that watershed systems are connected across large regions, irrigation organizations often provide a link between local groups. Allocating the water from the systems also requires careful administration. As is often the case, water is allocated proportionally according to landholdings (Coward 1976; 1979). But farmers who are downstream are more likely to be deprived of their fair share than farmers who are upstream and can divert more water to their fields. In order to deal with conflicts that arise from this built-in inequity in one area of the Philippines, subgroups of farmers formed to meet and discuss distribution problems.

Another administrative issue relates to corruption such as water theft, in which a particular farmer will tap off water out of turn (Price 1995). In one area of Egypt, water theft was more common as distance from the main canal increased. These farmers felt they were justified because they tended to get less water through the distribution system than farmers closer to the source.

Cooperatives

Cooperatives are a form of economic group, with two key features: surpluses are shared among the members, and decision making follows the democratic principle of one person, one vote (Estrin 1996). Agricultural and credit cooperatives are the most common forms of cooperatives worldwide, followed by consumer cooperatives. They bring together millions of people in a common cause.

Farmers' Cooperatives in Western India

In India's western state of Maharashtra, the sugar industry is largely owned and operated through farmer cooperatives (Attwood 1992). Most shareholders are small farmers, producing just one or two acres of sugar cane. Yet the sugar industry, owned and managed cooperatively, is huge, almost as large as the state's iron and steel industry. In contrast, in the northern states where sugar cane is grown, cooperatives are not prominent.

How and why are sugar cooperatives so successful in this region? The answer lies in the different pattern of social stratification. The rural social stratification system in Maharashtra is simpler than in northern India. In most villages, the Marathas are the dominant caste, but they constitute even more of a majority and they control even more village land than is typical of dominant castes. They also have stronger local ties with each other because their marital arrangements are locally centralized. Thus, they have a better basis for cooperating with each other in spite of class differences among themselves. Large farmers dominate the elected board of directors of the cooperatives. These "sugar barons" use their position to gain power in state politics. However, within the cooperatives, their power is held in check. They do not form cliques that exploit the cooperatives to the detriment of the less wealthy. In fact, large farmers cannot afford to alienate the small and middle farmers, for that would mean economic ruin for the cooperative and the loss of their own profits. The technology of sugar cane processing requires wide participation of the farmers. Mechanization involves investing in expensive heavy equipment. The machinery cannot be run at a profit unless it is used at full capacity during the crushing season. If small and middle farmers were displeased with their treatment, they might decide to pull out of the cooperative and put their cane into other uses. Then capacity would be underused and profits would fall. If the large farmers were to try to take advantage of the system, they would be "cutting their own throats." The success of cooperatives has much to do with the power balance between large farmers versus the middle and small farmers.

Craft Cooperatives in Panama

In Panama's east coastal region, Kuna women have long sewn beautiful *molas*, or cloth with appliquéd designs. This cloth is made for their own use as clothing (Tice 1995). Since the 1960s, *molas* have been important items for sale both on the world market and to tourists who come to Panama. Revenue from selling *molas* is now an important part of the household income of the Kuna. Some women continue to operate independently, buying their own cloth and thread and selling their *molas* either to an intermediary who exports them or in the local tourist market. But many other women have joined cooperatives that offer them greater economic security.

The cooperative buys cloth and thread in bulk and distributes it to the women. The women are paid almost the entire sale price for each *mola*, with only a small amount of the eventual sale prices being taken out for cooperative dues and administrative costs. Their earnings are steadier than what the fluctuating tourist season offers.

Beyond the initial economic reasons for joining the cooperative, other benefits include the use of the cooperative as a consumer's cooperative (buying rice and sugar in bulk for members), as a source of mutual strength and support, and as a basis for women's greater leadership skills and opportunities for political participation in the wider society.

Activist Groups

Activist groups worldwide are protesting political repression, violence, and human rights violations. Many such groups are initiated and organized by women. Even in cultures where they are primarily involved in the domestic domain, women often have a significant impact in the public domain, too. The CO-MADRES of El Salvador is an important social movement in Latin America (Stephen 1995). CO-MADRES is a Spanish abbreviation for an organization called, in English, the "Committee of Mothers and Relatives of Political Prisoners, Disappeared and Assassinated of El Salvador." It was founded in 1977 by a group of mothers in denunciation of the atrocities committed by the Salvadorean government and military. During the civil war that lasted from 1979 until 1992, a total of 80 000 people had died and 7000 more had disappeared, or one in every 100 Salvadoreans.

The initial group comprised nine mothers. A year later, it had grown to between 25 and 30, including some men. For two years, they had no office, but in time they secured a permanent space where they could set up files and an archive system. In 1979, they made their first international trip to secure wider recognition. This developed into a full-fledged and successful campaign for international solidarity in the

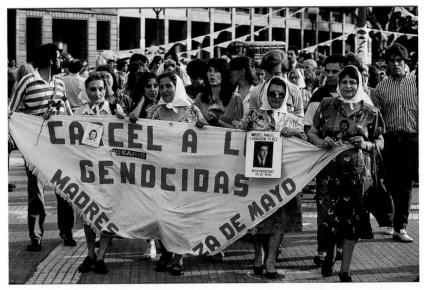

A march of the "Mothers of the Disappeared" in Argentina. This organization of women combines activism motivated by personal causes (the loss of one's child or children to political torture and death) and wider political concerns (state repressiveness in general).

1980s, with support in other Latin American countries, Europe, Australia, the United States, and Canada. The increased organization and visibility brought with it government repression. Their office was first bombed in 1980 and then four more times after that. In addition, a majority of the most active CO-MADRES have been detained, tortured, and raped. Forty-eight members of the CO-MADRES have been detained since 1977; five have been assassinated. Harassment and disappearances continued even after the signing of the Peace Accords in January 1992: "In February 1993, the son and the nephew of one of the founders of CO-MADRES were assassinated in Usulutan. This woman had already lived through the experience of her own detention, the detention and gang rape of her daughter, and the disappearance and assassination of other family members" (814).

In the 1990s, CO-MADRES focused on holding the state accountable for human rights violations during the civil war, as well as some new areas, such as providing better protection for political prisoners, seeking assurances of human rights protection in the future, working against domestic violence, educating women about political participation, and developing some economic proj-

ects to help women attain financial autonomy. They are part of a coalition of women's groups that worked on the 1994 political platform to secure better rights and conditions for women. The work of CO-MADRES, throughout its history, has incorporated elements of both the "personal" and the "political," concerns of mothers and family members for lost kin and for exposing and halting abuses of the state and military. The lesson learned from the case of CO-MADRES is that activist groups formed by women can be based on issues related to the domestic domain (murdered sons and other kin), but their activities can extend to the top of the public political hierarchy.

Other activist organizations formed around the problem of the marketing of infant formula in the developing countries and the subsequent decline in breastfeeding rates. In the 1970s activist groups in North America and Europe mobilized to expose how large multinational corporations were seeking markets for their infant formulas. Protest groups argued that selling breast milk substitutes to mothers who could not afford the cost of an adequate supply and who had limited access to clean water and fuel to sterilize bottles was causing a major health crisis, and they began consumer boycotts of companies such as Nestlé. This attention to unethical marketing practices ultimately forced debates resulting in the World Health Assembly passing the International Code on Marketing of Breast Milk Substitutes in 1981. Because of continuing flagrant violations of this code by several food and pharmaceutical corporations promoting infant formula, groups such as the International Baby Food Action Network (IBFAN) continue to monitor their compliance to the code. An umbrella organization, the World Alliance for Breastfeeding Action (WABA), formed by activists from various countries in 1991, continues to encourage the practice of breastfeeding through worldwide campaigns. For example, the Baby Friendly Hospital Initiative encourages health care providers to assist mothers to breastfeed immediately after birth, World Breastfeeding Week mobilizes grassroots support for breastfeeding, and Mother-Friendly Workplaces assists employed women to combine breastfeeding and employment (P. Van Esterik 1995:160).

The preceding two examples show how an external problem (such as state oppression or corporate greed) can motivate people to join together and work for change. Other groups, such as Alcoholics Anonymous (AA), are formed because of concerns about a personal problem which, through group support, can be solved. A comparative study of group dynamics in AA and two environmental activist groups in North Carolina revealed a common use of shared storytelling (Kitchell, Hannan, and Kempton 2000). Storytelling allows individual members to express their identity in the group and to find shared ground with other members. The stories also help motivate members to keep working on their cause, whether it is abstention from alcohol or political action. In AA, people's stories concerned their experiences with alcohol and coming to realize it as a problem in their lives. In the environmental groups, people's stories concerned their interactions with government and industry. The stories focus people, provide a base from which behavioural change is sought, and help teach other members how to move forward.

Social Stratification

Social stratification refers to hierarchical relationships between different groups—as if they were arranged in layers or "strata." Stratified groups may be unequal on a variety of measures, including material resources, power, human welfare, education, and symbolic attributes. People in groups in higher positions have privileges not experienced by those in lower groups, and they are likely to be interested in maintaining their privileged position. Social stratification emerged late in human history, most clearly with the emergence of agriculture. Now some form of social stratification is nearly universal.

Analysis of the categories—such as class, race, gender, and age—that form stratification systems reveals a crucial difference in the degree to which membership in a given category is an **ascribed position,** based on qualities of a person gained through birth, and those in which it is an **achieved position,** based on qualities of a person gained through action. Ascribed positions include one's race, ethnicity, gender, age, and physical ability. These factors are generally out of the control of the individual, although some scope for flexibility exists in gender through surgery and hormonal treatments and for certain kinds of physical conditions. Also, one can sometimes "pass" for being a member of another race or ethnic group. Age is an interesting ascribed category because an individual will pass through several different status levels associated with age. Achievement as a basis for group membership means that a person belongs on the basis of some valued attainment. Ascribed systems are thus more "closed" and achievement-based systems more "open" in terms of mobility within the system (either upward or downward). Some scholars of social status believe that increasing social complexity and modernization led to an increase in achievement-based positions and a decline in ascription-based positions.

In this section, we look at the way certain key social categories define group membership and varying relations of inequality among groups.

The Concept of Status Groups

Societies place people into categories—student, husband, child, retired person, political leader, or member of the Order of Canada—which are referred to as a person's **status** (position or standing in society) (C. Wolf 1996). Each status has an accompanying **role** (expected behaviour for someone of a particular status), with a "script" for how to behave, look, and talk. Some statuses have more prestige attached to them than others (the word *status* can be used to mean prestige, relative value, and worth). Groups, like individuals, have status, or standing in society. Noted German sociologist Max Weber called lower-status groups "disprivileged groups." These include, in different contexts and in different times, physically disabled people, people with certain illnesses such as leprosy or HIV/AIDS, Blacks, Jews, low-caste Indians, women, and others.

Within societies that have marked status positions, different status groups are marked by a particular lifestyle, including goods owned, leisure activities, and even linguistic styles. Higher status categories sometimes maintain group position by exclusionary practices in relation to lower status groups; for example, by group in-marriage and by socializing only within the group.

Class: Achieved Status

Social class refers to a person's or group's position in society defined primarily in economic terms. In many cultures, class is a key determining factor of one's status, while in others it is less important than, for example, one's birth into a certain family. However, even in societies in which class can determine status, they do not always match. A rich person may have become wealthy in disreputable ways and never gain high status in society. Both status and class groups are secondary groups, since one person is unlikely to know every other member of the group, especially in large-scale societies. In most instances, they are also informal groups since there are no recognized leaders or elected officials of the "urban elite" or the "working class." Subsegments of these large categories do organize themselves into formal groups, such as labour unions or exclusive clubs for the rich and famous. Class can be both ascribed and achieved since a person who is born rich has a greater than average chance of living an upper-class lifestyle. In "open" capitalist societies, the prevailing ideology is that mobility in the system is up to the individual. This view emphasizes the importance of human agency in the ability of an individual to overcome structural forces. Political economy theories, in contrast, argue that low-class position severely inhibits upward mobility because of the constraints and hardships of life in poverty.

The concept of class was especially important to the theories of Karl Marx. Situated within the context of Europe's industrial revolution and the growth of capitalism, Marx wrote that class differences, exploitation of the working class by the owners of capital, class con-sciousness among workers, and class conflict are forces of change that would eventually bring the downfall of capitalism.

In contrast to Marx's approach, French sociologist Émile Durkheim viewed social differences (including class) as the basis for social solidarity (1966 [1895]). He distinguished two major forms of societal cohesion: **mechanical solidarity,** which exists when groups that are similar join together, and **organic solidarity,** which prevails when groups with different abilities and resources are linked together in complementary fashion. Mechanical solidarity creates less enduring relationships because it involves little mutual need. Organic solidarity builds on need and creates stronger bonds. Durkheim placed these two concepts in an evolutionary framework, saying that in pre-industrial times, the division of labour was only minimally specialized: Everyone did what everyone else did. With increasing social complexity and economic specialization, organic solidarity developed.

Race, Ethnicity, and Caste: Ascribed Status

Three ascribed systems of social stratification are based on divisions of people into large, unequally ranked groups on the basis of race, ethnicity, and **caste** (a ranked group, determined by birth, often linked to a particular occupation and to South Asian cultures). Like status and class groups, these three types of groups are also secondary social groups, since no one can have a personal relationship with all other members of the entire group. Some social scientists emphasize the differences among these three systems of social stratification, while others focus on similarities. Gerald Berreman (1979 [1975]) emphasizes similarities in systems of social inequality:

Racism and casteism are indistinguishable in the annals of man's inhumanity to man, and sexism is closely allied to them as man's inhumanity to woman. All are invidious distinctions imposed unalterably at birth upon whole categories of people to justify the unequal social distribution of power, livelihood, security, privilege, esteem, freedom—in short, life chances. Where distinctions of this type are employed, they affect people and the events which people generate in surprisingly similar ways despite the different historical and cultural conditions in which they occur. (213)

In all hierarchical systems, powerful people and groups seek to maintain dominance. Those in power face an "organizational challenge" of how to maintain their position (Harris 1971, quoted in Mencher 1974:469). There are two ways to meet this challenge: (1) through institutions that control the content of ideology, and (2) through institutions that physically suppress the subversive. The following sections on race, ethnicity, and caste provide insights about how both ideological and physical control maintain systems of inequality.

Race Racial stratification results from the unequal meeting of two formerly separate groups through colonization, slavery, and other large-group movements (Sanjek 1994). Europe's "age of discovery," beginning in the 1500s, ushered in a new era of global contact. In contrast, in relatively homogeneous cultures, ethnicity is a more important distinction than race. In contemporary Nigeria, for example, the population is relatively homogeneous, and ethnicity is the more salient term there (Jinadu 1994). A similar situation prevails in Rwanda and other African states.

A key feature of racial thinking is its insistence that behavioural differences among peoples are "natural," inborn, or biologically caused (in this, it resembles sexism, ageism, and casteism). Throughout the history of racial categorizations in the West, such features as head size, head shape, and brain size have been accepted as the reasons for behavioural differences. Franz Boas contributed to de-linking supposed racial attributes from behaviour. He showed that people with the same head size but from different cultures behaved differently, and people with different head sizes within the same cultures behaved similarly. For Boas and his followers, culture, not biology, is the key explanation for behaviour. Thus, race is not a biological reality; there is no way to divide the human population into races on the basis of certain biological features. Yet, "social race" exists and continues to be a basis of social stratification. In spite of some progress in reducing racism in North America in the twentieth century, racial discrimination persists. One way of understanding this persistence is to see racial discrimination as linked to class formation, rather than separate from it (Brodkin 2000). In this view, racial stereotyping and discrimination functions to maintain people in less desirable jobs, or unemployed, as necessary aspects of advanced industrial capitalism, which depends on a certain number of low-paid workers and even a certain amount of unemployment.

Racial classifications in the Caribbean and Latin America are especially complicated systems of status classification. This complexity results from the variety of contact over the centuries between peoples from Europe, Africa, Asia, and indigenous populations. Skin tone is one basis of racial classification, but it is mixed with other physical features and economic status as well. In Haiti, for example:

> [S]kin texture and depth of skin tone, hair color and appearance, and facial features also figure in any categorization...color categories embrace characteristics that go far beyond the perceived phenotype into the field of social relations. These can include income, social origin, level of formal education, customary behaviour, ties of kinship or marriage...and different combinations of these social traits can move a person from one category to a more or less proximate one. (Trouillot 1994:148–149)

Thus, two people of the same "colour" can be classed in different categories because of other biological and social factors.

An extreme example of racial stratification was the South African policy of apartheid, legally sanctioned segregation between dominant Whites and non-Whites. White dominance in South Africa began in the early 1800s with White migration and settlement. In the 1830s, slavery was abolished. At the same time, increasingly racist thinking developed among Whites (Johnson 1994:25). Racist images, including visions of Africans as lazy, uncontrolled, and libidinous, served as the rationale for colonialist domination in place of outright slavery. In spite of years of African resistance to White domination, the Whites succeeded in maintaining and increasing their control for nearly two centuries. In South Africa, Blacks constitute 90 per cent of the population, a numerical majority dominated through strict apartheid by the White minority until only recently. Every aspect of life for the majority of Africans was far worse than for the Whites. Every measure of life quality—infant mortality, longevity, education—showed great disparity between the Whites and the Africans. In addition to physical deprivation, the Africans experienced psychological suffering through constant insecurity about raids from the police and other forms of violence (see the Voices box on page 249).

Mark Mathabane, "Growing Up Under Apartheid"

I am always asked to explain what it felt like to grow up black under South Africa's system of legalized racism known as apartheid, and how I escaped from it and ended up in America…. The last thing I ever dreamed of when I was daily battling for survival and for an identity other than of inferiority and fourth-class citizen, which apartheid foisted on me, was that someday I would attend an American college, edit its newspaper, graduate with honors, practise journalism and write a book.

How could I have dreamed of all this when I was born of illiterate parents who could not afford to pay my way through school, let alone pay the rent for our shack and put enough food on the table; when black people in Alexandra lived under constant police terror and the threat of deportation to impoverished tribal reserves; when at ten I contemplated suicide because I found the burden of living in a ghetto, poverty-stricken and without hope, too heavy to shoulder; when in 1976 I got deeply involved in the Soweto protests in which hundreds of black students were killed by the police, and thousands fled the country to escape imprisonment and torture?…

Much has been written and spoken about the politics of apartheid: the forced removals of black communities from their ancestral lands, the Influx Control and Pass laws that mandate where blacks can live, work, raise families, be buried; the migrant labour system that forces black men to live away from their families eleven months out of a year; the breaking up of black families in the ghettos as the authorities seek to create a so-called white South Africa;

the brutal suppression of the black majority as it agitates for equal rights. But what does it all mean in human terms?

When I was growing up in Alexandra it meant hate, bitterness, hunger, pain, terror, violence, fear, dashed hopes and dreams…. In the ghettoes black children fight for survival from the moment they are born. They take to hating and fearing the police, soldiers and authorities as a baby takes to its mother's breast.

In my childhood these enforcers of white prerogatives and whims represented a sinister force capable of crushing me at will; of making my parents flee in the dead of night to escape arrest under the Pass laws; of marching them naked out of bed because they did not have the permit allowing them to live as husband and wife under the same roof. They turned my father—by repeatedly arresting him and denying him the right to earn a living in a way that gave him dignity—into such a bitter man that, as he fiercely but in vain resisted the emasculation, he hurt those he loved the most.

The movies, with their lurid descriptions of white violence, reinforced this image of white power and terror. Often the products of abject poverty and broken homes, many black children, for whom education is inferior and not compulsory, have been derailed by movies into the dead-end life of crime and violence. It is no wonder that black ghettos have one of the highest murder rates in the world, and South African prisons are among the most packed. It was purely by accident that I did not end up a *tsotsi* (thug, murderer, mugger, gangster)…. The turning point came when one day in my eleventh year I accompanied my

grandmother to her gardening job and met a white family that did not fit the stereotypes I had grown up with. Most blacks, exposed daily to virulent racism and dehumanized and embittered by it, do not believe that such whites exist. From this family I started receiving "illegal books" like *Treasure Island* and *David Copperfield*, which revealed a different reality…. At thirteen I stumbled across tennis, a sport so "white" most blacks thought I was mad for thinking I could excel in it…. Through tennis I learned the important lesson that South Africa's 4.5 million whites are not all racists. As I grew older, and got to understand them more—their fears, longings, hopes, ignorance and mistaken beliefs, and mine—this lesson became the conviction that whites are in some ways victims of apartheid, too, and that it is the system, and not they, that has to be destroyed; just as it was Hitler's regime that had to be extirpated, not the German people. Such an attitude helped me survive the nightmare into which my life was plunged by the Soweto protests of 1976. A tennis scholarship to an American college, arranged by professional tennis player Stan Smith, in 1978, became my passport to freedom.

Source: Reprinted with the permission of Simon & Schuster from *Kaffir Boy* by Mark Mathabane, pp. ix-x. Copyright © 1986 by Mark Mathabane.

FOOD FOR THOUGHT

Do you know of any other people who have escaped from extremely difficult circumstances in which race, ethnicity, age, or gender was a factor limiting their life chances?

Since the end of apartheid in South Africa in 1994, many social changes have taken place. One study describes the early stages of the dismantling of apartheid in the city of Umtata, the capital of Transkei (Johnson 1994). Before the end of apartheid, Umtata "was like other South African towns: all apartheid laws were in full force; public and private facilities were completely segregated; only whites could vote or serve in the town government; whites owned all the major economic assets" (viii). When the change came, Umtata's dominant

Whites bitterly resisted at first. They did not want to lose their privileges, and they feared reprisals by the Africans. These things did not happen, however. The initial stages of transition brought "neoapartheid," in which White privilege was not seriously threatened. Then members of the dominant group began to welcome the less tense, "nonracial" atmosphere.

In contrast to the explicitly racist discrimination of South African apartheid, racism exists within contexts where no public discourse about race or racism is found, where instead there is silence about it (Sheriff 2000). In such a context, the silence works to allow racial discrimination to continue in ways that are as effective as a clearly stated policy such as apartheid, or perhaps even more so since it is more difficult to critique and dismantle an institution whose existence is denied. As Canadian anthropologist Stanley Barrett says:

> Racism has been endemic in Canada. It has stretched from the early slavery at the nation's dawn down through the Fascist phase prior to the Second World War to the Paki-bashing of recent years. It has reached from the Pacific to the Atlantic, taking different forms according to the local ethnic composition, targeting Asians in Vancouver, blacks in Nova Scotia, and Jews everywhere. It has been represented in corporate and government boards and among manual labourers at construction sites. And it has appeared both visibly in the form of violent attacks and covertly in the form of variations in wages and employment opportunities based on racial criteria. Many observers might want to argue that what racism does exist in Canada has simply been the sad product of deviant individuals, or a temporary problem brought on by unemployment or some other crisis. Yet the degree, scope, and persistence of the phenomenon lead to a single conclusion; racism in Canada has been institutionalized…racism that is intrinsic to the structures of society. It may be overt or covert, expressed formally in the laws of the land, or less visibly in patterns of employment and the content of school textbooks…. What is significant about institutional racism, whether open (the reservation system for Native peoples) or hidden (ordinary white Canadians are more cautious about appearing racist), is not only that differential advantage along racial lines is embedded in society itself, but also that it perpetuates itself over time, for that is the nature of the institutional framework: independent of individual volition, relatively unconscious and unmotivated, it reproduces itself…in-

stitutional racism is almost synonymous with "the way things are. (Barrett 1987:307–308)

Ethnicity Ethnicity includes a shared sense of identity on some grounds and a set of relations to other groups (Comaroff 1987). Identity is formed sometimes on the basis of a perception of shared history, territory, language, or religion. As such, ethnicity can be a basis for claiming entitlements to resources such as land or artifacts, and a perceived basis for defending or regaining those resources.

States are interested in managing ethnicity to the extent that it does not threaten security. China has one of the most formalized systems for monitoring its many ethnic groups, and it has an official policy on ethnic minorities, meaning the non-Han groups (Wu 1990). The government lists a total of 54 groups other than the Han majority, which constitutes about 94 per cent of the total. The other 6 per cent of the population is made up of the 54 groups, about 67 million people. The non-Han minorities occupy about 60 per cent of China's land mass and are located in border or "frontier" areas such as Tibet, Yunnan, Xinjiang, and Inner Mongolia. Basic criteria for defining an ethnic group include language, territory, economy, and "psychological disposition." The Chinese government establishes strict definitions of group membership and group characteristics, including setting standards for ethnic costumes and dances. The Chinese treatment of the Tibetan people is especially severe and can be considered an attempt at ethnocide or annihilation of the culture of an ethnic group by a dominant group. The Tibetans continue to resist the loss of their culture and absorption into the Han mainstream. The government's treatment of Tibetan traditional medicine over the past several decades illustrates how the Han majority uses certain aspects of minority cultures (see the Critical Thinking box).

People of one ethnic group who move from one place to another are at risk of exclusionary treatment from the local residents at their new location. Rom, or gypsies, are a **diaspora population** (dispersed group living outside their original homeland) scattered throughout Europe and North America. Their history is one of mobility and marginality since they first left India around 1000 CE (Fonseca 1995). Everywhere they live, they are marginalized and looked down on by the settled populations. Traditional Rom lifestyle is one of movement, with temporary camps of their wagons often appearing overnight

The Chinese Takeover of Tibetan Medicine

In 1951, Tibet became part of China, and the Chinese government undertook measures to bring about the social and economic transformation of what was formerly a decentralized, Buddhist feudal regime. This transformation has brought increasing ethnic conflict between Tibetans and Han Chinese, including demonstrations by Tibetans and crackdowns from the government. Traditional Tibetan medicine has become part of the Chinese-Tibetan conflicts because of its culturally significant and religiously important position in Tibetan society (Janes 1995:7).

Several policy swings of the Chinese state towards Tibetan traditional medicine occurred in the second half of the twentieth century: Between 1951 and 1962, it was tolerated but largely ignored; by 1962, it was officially included as a component of the public health system and given funds for clinical opera-

tions and training programs; in 1966, it was delegitimized; in 1978, it was near extinction; and in 1985, it re-emerged as a legitimate sector of the government health bureaucracy, having a major role in providing primary health care in the Tibetan region, with a substantial operating budget and over 1200 physicians.

Linkage with a centralized medical system substantially transformed traditional Tibetan medicine. The training of physicians is one area of major change. Previously based on a model of apprenticeship training, it is now Westernized and involves several years of classroom-based, lecture-oriented learning followed by an internship. At Tibet University, only half of all formal lecture-based instruction is concerned with traditional Tibetan medicine. Curriculum changes have reduced the integrity of Tibetan medicine: It has been separated from its Buddhist content, and parts of

it have been merged with a biomedical approach. While one might say that overall, traditional Tibetan medicine has been "revived" in China, stronger evidence supports the argument that the state has co-opted it and transformed it for its own purposes.

CRITICAL THINKING QUESTIONS

How could the Chinese government justify the suppression of Tibetan traditional medicine?

Why do you think the Chinese government eventually revived Tibetan traditional medicine?

Which form of medicine dominates Chinese government health planning and policy—biomedical or traditional medicine? Can you suggest why?

---

on the outskirts of a town. For decades, European governments have tried to force the Rom to settle down. In addition, Rom migration to cities in Eastern Europe is increasing because of the recent economic crisis, unemployment, and declining standard of living. In cities, high-status groups reside in areas segregated from others (Ladányi 1993). Low-status people must live where no one else wants to reside. In Budapest, Hungary, the Rom minority is the most disadvantaged ethnic group. Not all Rom in Budapest are poor, though. Some 1 per cent has gained wealth, and they live in high-status neighbourhoods. However, the vast majority live in substandard housing, usually in areas where low-income Hungarians reside, in the slum inner areas of Pest. Since the fall of state socialism, discrimination against Roms has increased. Rom houses have been torched, and their children have been harassed while going to school.

A less difficult but still not easy adjustment is being experienced by Indo-Canadians (immigrants from India

to Canada). Research among a sample of nearly 300 Indo-Canadians in Vancouver, British Columbia, revealed that about half of all the respondents reported experiencing some form of discrimination in the recent past (Nodwell and Guppy 1992). The percentage was higher among men (54 per cent) than among women (45 per cent). The higher level for men was consistent across the four categories: verbal abuse, property damage, workplace discrimination, and physical harm. Verbal abuse was the most frequent form of discrimination, reported by 40 per cent of both men and women. Indo-Canadians of the Sikh faith who were born in India say that they experience the highest levels of discrimination in Canada. Apparently, however, their actual experience of discrimination is not greater than for other Indo-Canadians. The difference is that Sikhs who were born in India are more sensitive to discrimination than others. Sikhism, as taught and practised in India, supports a strong sense of honour, which should be protected and, if wronged, avenged.

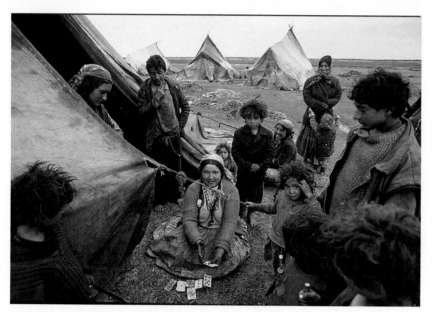

A Rom encampment in Romania's Transylvania region. Not all European Rom are poor, however. Some urban Rom have become wealthy.

This study helps explain differences in perception of discrimination among ethnic migrants. It does not explain why such high levels of discriminatory treatment exist in a nation committed to ethnic tolerance.

Caste The caste system is a form of social stratification found in its clearest form in India, among its Hindu population, and in other areas of Hindu culture such as Nepal, Sri Lanka, and Fiji. It is particularly associated with Hindu peoples because ancient Hindu scriptures are taken as the foundational sources for defining the major social categories called *varnas* (a Sanskrit word meaning "colour," or "shade"). The four varnas are: the brahmans who were priests; the *kshatriya*, or warriors; the *vaishya*, or merchants; and the *shudras*, or labourers. Of these, men of the first three *varnas* could go through a ritual ceremony of "rebirth" and thereafter wear a sacred thread. These three categories are referred to as "twice-born," and their status is higher than that of the *shudra varna*. Beneath the four varna groups were people considered so low that they were outside the caste system itself (hence, the word *outcast*). Throughout history, these people have been referred to by many names in Indian languages and by the English term *untouchable*. Mahatma

Gandhi, himself a member of an upper caste, renamed them *harijans* (or "children of god") as part of his attempt to raise their status into that of the level above them. Currently, members of this category have adopted the term **dalit** (meaning "oppressed" or "ground down") as their favoured name.

Each of the four *varnas* and the *dalit* category contains many locally named groups called *castes* or, more appropriately, *jatis*. The term *caste* is a Portuguese word meaning "breed" or "type" and was first used by Portuguese colonialists in the fifteenth century to refer to the closed social groups they encountered (Cohn 1971:125). *Jati* means "birth group," and conveys the meaning that a Hindu is born into his or her group. It is an ascribed status and cannot be changed under normal conditions. Just as the four *varnas* are ranked with each other, so are all the *jatis* within them. For example, the category of brahmans "may be subdivided into priestly and non-priestly subgroups, the priestly Brahmans into Household-priests, Temple-priests and Funeral-priests; the Household-priests into two or more endogamous circles; and each circle into its component clans and lineages non-priestly Brahmans are superior in relation to priestly ones, and Household-priests in relation to Funeral-priests" (Parry 1966:77).

Status levels also exist among *dalits*. In western Nepal, artisans such as basket-weavers and ironsmiths are the highest tier (M. Cameron 1995). They do not touch any of the people beneath them. The second tier includes leatherworkers and tailors. The bottom tier comprises people who are "untouchable" to all other groups including other *dalits* because their work is extremely polluting according to Hindu rules: musicians (some of their instruments are made of leather and they perform in public) and sex workers.

Indian anthropologist M. N. Srinivas (1959) contributed the concept of the **dominant caste** to refer to the tendency for one caste in any particular village to control most of the land and, often, to be numerically

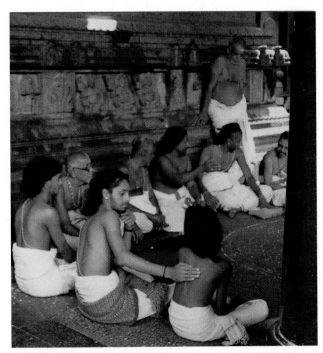

Only a special category of brahman priests can officiate at the Chidambaram temple in south India. Here, members of an age-mixed group of priests sit for a moment's relaxation.

preponderant as well. Although brahmans are at the top of the social hierarchy in terms of ritual purity, they are not always the dominant caste. Throughout northern India, it is common for *jatis* of the *kshatriya varna* to be the dominant village group. This is the case in Pahansu village, where a group called the Gujars is dominant (Raheja 1988). The Gujars constitute the numerical majority, and they control most of the land (see Table 10.1 below). Moreover, they dominate in the **jajmani system,** a patron-provider system in which landholding patrons (*jajmans*) are linked through exchanges of food for services with brahman priests, artisans (blacksmiths, potters), agricultural labourers, and other workers such as sweepers (Kolenda 1978:46–54). In Pahansu, Gujars have power and status as the major patrons, supporting many different service providers who are thus beholden to them.

Some anthropologists have described the jajmani service system as one of mutual interdependence (organic solidarity, to use Durkheim's term), which provides security for the less well-off. Joan Mencher (1974) and others argue that the system benefits those at the top to the detriment of those at the bottom. Mencher has done fieldwork among low-caste people. This perspective, from "the bottom up," views the patron-service system

TABLE 10.1 Caste Ranking in Pahansu Village, North India

CASTE NAME	TRADITIONAL OCCUPATION	NUMBER OF HOUSEHOLDS	OCCUPATION IN PAHANSU
Gujar	agriculturalist	210	owner cultivator
Brahman	priest	8	priest, postman
Baniya	merchant	3	shopkeeper
Sunar	goldsmith	2	silversmith, sugar cane press operator
Dhiman (Barhai)	carpenter	1	carpenter
Kumhar	potter	3	potter, tailor
Nai	barber	3	barber, postman
Dhobi	washerman	2	washerman
Gadariya	shepherd	4	agricultural labourer, weaver
Jhivar	water-carrier	20	agricultural labourer, basket-weaver
Luhar	ironsmith	2	blacksmith
Teli	oil-presser	2	beggar, cotton-carder, agricultural labourer
Maniharan	bangle-seller	1	bangle-seller
Camar	leatherworker	100	agricultural labourer
Bhangi	sweeper	17	sweeper, midwife

Source: Adapted from Raheja 1988:19.

and the entire caste system as one of exploitation by those at the top. Mencher says that the benign interpretation is based on research conducted among the upper castes who present this view. A more comprehensive look reveals that while both patrons and clients have rights and responsibilities, the relationship is not equal. Patrons have more power. Dissatisfied patrons can dismiss service providers, refuse them loans, or not pay them. Service providers who are dissatisfied with the treatment they receive from their patrons have little recourse. Male patrons often demand sexual privileges from low-caste females from service-providing households.

Whatever one's perspective on whether the jajmani system is exploitative or supportive, it is clear that, throughout South Asia, it has declined in recent decades. Industrial manufacturing and marketing are the main factors leading to these changes. They have created less need for some service providers, especially craftspersons such as tailors, potters, and weavers. With less need for their skills in the countryside, many former service providers have left the villages to work in urban areas. This trend has been noted since the 1950s and 1960s (Elder 1970). The tie that remains the strongest is between patrons and their brahman priests, whose ritual services cannot be replaced by machines.

The caste system involves several mechanisms that maintain it: marriage rules, spatial segregation, and ritual. These operate in addition to the basic material constraints that prevent low-caste people from obtaining property and skilled jobs—control of land markets and control of educational opportunities by dominant groups. Marriage rules strictly enforce *jati* endogamy. Marriage outside one's *jati*, especially in rural areas and particularly between a higher-caste female and lower-caste male, is cause for serious, even lethal, punishment by caste elders and other local power-holders. Indian newspapers frequently carry accounts of local action taken to punish offenders who may be beaten to death or stoned. Sometimes the female's life is spared, but she may be branded, have her head shaved, and be subject to social scorn. Among urban educated elites, a trend to allow inter-*jati* marriages is perceptible, but such marriages are still not preferred.

Spatial segregation functions to maintain the privileged preserve of the upper castes and to continually remind the lower castes of their marginal status. In many rural contexts, the *dalits* live in a completely separate cluster; in other cases, they have their own neighbourhood sections into which no upper-caste person will venture. Ritual rules and practices also serve to maintain dominance. The rich upper-caste leaders sponsor important annual festivals, thereby regularly restating their claim to public prominence (Mines 1994).

Social mobility within the caste system has traditionally been limited, but instances have been documented of group "up-casting." Several strategies exist, including gaining wealth, affiliation, or merger with a somewhat higher *jati*, education, migration, and political activism (Kolenda 1978). A group that attempts to gain higher *jati* status takes on the behaviour and dress of twice-born *jatis*. These include men's wearing the sacred thread, vegetarianism, non-remarriage of widows, seclusion of women from the public domain, and the giving of larger dowries for the marriage of a daughter. Some *dalits* have opted out of the caste system by converting to Christianity or Buddhism. Others are becoming politically organized through the Dalit Panthers, a social movement seeking greater power and improved economic status for *dalits* (Omvedt 1995).

Discrimination on the basis of caste was made illegal by the Indian constitution of 1949, but constitutional decree did not bring an end to these deeply structured inequalities. The government of India has instituted policies to promote the social and economic advancement of *dalits*, such as reserving places for them in medical schools, seats in the government, and public sector jobs. This "affirmative action" plan has infuriated many of the upper castes, especially brahmans who feel most threatened. Is the caste system on the decline? Surely, aspects of it are changing. Especially in large cities, people of different *jatis* can "pass" and participate more equally in public life—if they have the economic means to do so.

Civil Society: Between Groups and Government

The concept of **civil society** refers to the social domain of diverse interest groups that function outside the government to organize economic and other aspects of life. It has a long history in Western philosophy, with many different definitions proposed by thinkers such as John Locke, Thomas Paine, Adam Smith, and Karl Marx

(Kumar 1996:89). According to the German philosopher Georg Wilhelm Friedrich Hegel, civil society encompasses the social groups and institutions between the individual and the state. Italian social theorist Antonio Gramsci wrote that there are two basic types of civic institutions: those that support the state such as the church and schools, and those that oppose state power such as trade unions, social protest groups, citizens' rights groups, and counterculture groups.

Among other issues in post-socialist states, concern about the environment has prompted the emergence of many non-governmental organizations (NGOs). In Poland, youth activism related to the environment grew in strength in the late 1980s (Glínski 1994:145). This was the first generation to come after Stalin that did not experience martial law, so they had less fear of organizing than their parents. Furthermore, the government's policy of limited liberalization involved concessions to social groups and the interests they expressed. The mass media now have greater freedom of expression. Many of the ecological groups drew on countercultural values (values in opposition to the dominant culture) of the 1960s and 1970s: "This was evident in their quest for alternative values, their distance from the political system, and their gentle, if ironic, form of communicating with the surrounding world. The counterculture orientation also encouraged the nonviolent posture adopted by the Polish youth environmental groups in the 1980s as well as the relative moderation of programs and activities" (146–147).

Polish "green organizations" are distanced from the government. This distance is related to several factors. First, the government itself has not incorporated environmental concerns into its agenda. Furthermore, political elites actively sought to marginalize youth and countercultural groups: "There was no dialogue between the government and environmentalists over controversial questions. On the contrary, old bureaucratic methods were employed: police units were dispatched against young people protesting the construction of a nuclear power plant in Zarnowiec (1989) and a dam at Czorsztyn (1990, 1991, 1992)" (151). All of this increased the youths' sense of alienation from political institutions. In the local elections of 1990, youth group participation was sporadic, and few members of ecology groups were elected to local bodies. The first fully democratic parliamentary election in 1991 did not seek to involve the youth ecological movement. On the other hand, "artificially green" political parties developed, using ecological names and slogans to win parliamentary seats, but chose candidates from outside the environmental movement. The activists saw through these ploys and did not support such ecological "pseudo-parties." As of the early 1990s, some preliminary movement towards dialogue with the Ministry of Environmental Protection had occurred, and the Ministry established a special office for contact with youth groups and held monthly meetings with them. The youth groups evolved into a second stage: They built effective, professional NGOs. Several foundations and ecological groups began to seek financial support for their activities, often from foreign sources. They have made efforts to coordinate the activities of different groups and organizations. Most youth ecological groups have participated actively in all of these processes.

International interest in the notion of civil society has increased recently, given the changes in government structure in many post-socialist states. There is now potential for growth of civil society in these transforming states, but the way civil institutions will emerge and develop is still unfolding.

What is the range of cross-cultural variation of social groups?

Groups can be classified in terms of whether all members have face-to-face interaction with one another, whether membership is based on ascription or achievement, and how formal the group's organization and leadership structure is. Thus, groups extend from the most informal, face-to-face groups, such as those based on friendship, to groups that have formal membership requirements and whose members are widely dispersed and never meet each other. All groups have some criteria for membership, often based on a perceived notion of similarity. Many groups require some sort of initiation of new members which, in some cases, involves dangerous or frightening activities that serve to bond members to one another through a shared experience of helplessness.

What is social stratification, and what are its effects on people?

Social stratification is a concept based on the fact that people are, first, formed in groups. It refers to hierarchi-cal relationships between and among different groups. Stratified intergroup relations are commonly based on categories such as class, race, ethnicity, gender, age, and ability. The degree of social inequality among different status groups is highly marked in agricultural and industrial societies, whereas status inequalities are not characteristic of foraging societies and are not significant in most pastoral and horticultural societies. India's caste-based system is an important example of a rigid structure of social inequality based on a person's birth group.

What is civil society?

An area of group organization that lies midway between social groups discussed in this chapter and government (to be discussed in the following chapter) is that of civil society, or groups that serve political and economic functions in a quasi-governmental way. General interest in civil society is relatively recent and so, also, is anthropological research on such groups. However, recent years have brought an increase in anthropological research on NGOs.

Core Concepts

achieved position, p. 246
age set, p. 236
ascribed position, p. 246
caste, p. 247
civil society, p. 254

cooperatives, p. 244
dalit, p. 252
diaspora population, p. 250
dominant caste, p. 252

jajmani system, p. 253
mechanical solidarity, p. 247
organic solidarity, p. 247
primary group, p. 236
role, p. 246
secondary group, p. 236

social group, p. 236
social stratification, p. 246
status, p. 246
youth gangs, p. 240

Suggested Readings

Gerald Berreman, *Caste and Other Inequities: Essays on Inequality*. Delhi: Folklore Institute, 1979. These 18 essays on caste and social inequality in India were written over a period of 20 years. Topics include caste and economy, caste ranking, caste and social interaction, and a comparison of caste with race in the United States.

Steven Gregory and Roger Sanjek, eds., *Race*. New Brunswick, NJ: Rutgers University Press, 1994. The editors each provide a useful introductory chapter. Seventeen other contributions cover aspects of racism in the United States and the Caribbean, how race articulates with other inequalities, and racism in higher education and anthropology.

Martín Sánchez Jankowski, *Islands in the Street: Gangs and American Urban Society*. Berkeley: University of California Press, 1991. This book includes attention to theories about street gang life, comparisons of different ethnic patterns of gang behaviour in three cities in the United States, and variations in why youths join street gangs.

Kathryn March and Rachelle Taqqu, *Women's Informal Associations in Developing Countries: Catalysts for Change?* Boulder: Westview Press, 1986. This book provides an overview of various types of women's informal organizations and an assessment of their positive role in women's lives in developing countries. It also includes attention to credit, labour, ritual, and religious associations.

Jerome Rousseau, *Central Borneo: Ethnic Identity and Social Life in a Stratified Society*. Oxford: Clarendon Press, 1990. Based on fieldwork and archival material, this book outlines the social organization, kinship patterns, and interregional links among the peoples of central Borneo.

Karin Tice, *Kuna Crafts, Gender, and the Global Economy*. Austin: University of Texas Press, 1995. This ethnographic study looks at how the tourist market has affected women's production of molas in Panama and how women have organized into cooperatives in order to improve their situation.

 Your *Cultural Anthropology*, Second Canadian Edition Media Edition CD-ROM contains many Web sites relevant to this chapter. Use it to explore the Web and to expand your knowledge of anthropology.

Chapter 11

Politics, Conflict, and Social Order

Supporters of independence for East Timor celebrate on the streets of Dili as Indonesian soldiers leave the capital in September 1999.

Key Questions

What do political and legal anthropology cover?

What are the major cross-cultural forms of political organization and social order?

What are cross-cultural patterns of social conflict?

259

*O*n September 11, 2001, the twin towers of the World Trade Center in lower Manhattan, New York City, were destroyed by two highjacked airliners. Over the course of 2002, many of the leaders of Canada's political parties resigned or announced their retirement. These seemingly disparate events are cultural happenings related to public power and politics. Political anthropology, a subfield of cultural anthropology, addresses the area of human behaviour and thought related to power: who has it and who doesn't; degrees of power; the bases of power; abuses of power; relationships between political and religious power; political organization and government; social conflict and social control; and morality and law. The subfield of legal anthropology focuses on the issues of order and conflict. Anthropologists in all four fields address political and legal topics. Archaeologists study the evolution of centralized forms of political organization and the physical manifestations of power in monumental architecture, housing, and material possessions. Primatologists do research on dominance relationships, coalitions, and aggression among nonhuman primates. Linguistic anthropologists analyze power differences in interpersonal speech, the media, political propaganda, and more.

Political Anthropology

When cultural anthropologists consider the concept of politics, they tend to take a broader view than a political scientist because their cross-cultural data indicate that many kinds of behaviour and thought are political in addition to formal party politics, voting, and government. Cultural anthropologists offer important examples of political systems that might not look like political systems at all to people who have grown up in large states. This section explores basic political concepts from an anthropological perspective and raises the question of whether political systems are universal to all cultures.

British anthropologists, especially Bronislaw Malinowski and A. R. Radcliffe-Brown, long dominated theory-making in political anthropology. Their approach, referred to as *functionalism*, emphasized how institutions such as political organization and law promote social cohesion. Later, the students of these two teachers developed divergent theories. For example, in the late 1960s, some scholars began to look at aspects of political organization that pull societies apart. The new focus on disputes and conflict prompted anthropologists to gather infor-

mation on dispute "cases" and to analyze the actors involved in a particular conflict through "processual analysis."

The processual approach to local politics has been countered by a swing towards a more macro view (Vincent 1996), which examines politics, no matter how local, within a global context (Asad 1973). This global perspective has prompted many studies of colonialism and neocolonialism in political anthropology and historical anthropology. Ann Stoler's book, *Capitalism and Confrontation in Sumatra's Plantation Belt, 1870–1979* (1985), on the history and cultural impact of Dutch colonialism in Indonesia, is a classic study in this genre. In the 1980s, the experiences of *subaltern* peoples (those subordinated by colonialism) and subaltern movements in former colonized regions attracted research attention, particularly from native anthropologists of decolonizing countries. The history of political anthropology in the twentieth century illustrates the theoretical tensions between the actor-as-agent approach (processual approach) and the structural, political economy perspective that sees actors as constrained in their choices by larger forces.

Politics: The Use of Power, Authority, and Influence

Politics refers to a culturally defined conflict over use of power whether in the public arena or within families and domestic groups. **Power** "is the capacity to take...action in the face of resistance...[and] to pursue one's will effectively, if necessary, by imposing it on others" (M. Smith 1966:3). Power means the ability to bring about desired results, often through the possession or use of force. Closely related to power are authority and influence. **Authority** implies "the right to take certain forms of action" (3). It is usually based on a person's achieved or ascribed status, moral reputation, or other basis for respect. **Influence** is another way of achieving a desired end, through exerting social or moral pressure, not force, on someone or some group. Compared to authority, influence may be reinforced by social position and status, but it may also be exerted from a low-status and marginal position. All three terms are relational. A person's power, authority, or influence exists in relation to others. Power implies the greatest likelihood of a coercive and hierarchical relationship, and authority and influence offer the most scope for consensual, cooperative decision making. Power, authority, and influence are all related to politics, with power being the strongest basis for action and decision making.

Politics: A Cultural Universal?

Is politics a human universal? Some anthropologists would say "No." They point to instances of cultures with scarcely any institutions that can be called political, with no durable ranking systems and very little aggression. Foraging lifestyles, as a model for early human evolution, suggest that nonhierarchical social systems characterized human life for 90 per cent of its existence. Only with the emergence of private property, surpluses, and other changes did ranking systems, government, formal law, and organized group aggression emerge. Also, studies show how dominance-seeking and aggression are learned behaviours, emphasized in some cultures and among some segments of the population such as the military, and de-emphasized among others such as religious leaders, healers, and child care providers. Being a good politician or a Major-General is a matter of socialization (see the Multiple Cultural Worlds box below). Other anthropologists argue that, despite a wide range of variation, politics is a human universal. Every society is organized to some degree by kinship relationships, and many anthropologists would not draw a clear boundary between how kinship organizes power and political organization organizes power.

MULTIPLE CULTURAL WORLDS

Socialization of Women Politicians in Korea

Parental attitudes affect children's involvement in public political roles. Chunghee Sarah Soh's (1993) research in the Republic of Korea reveals how variation in paternal roles affects daughters' political leadership roles. Korean women members of the National Assembly can be divided into two categories: elected members (active seekers) versus appointed members (passive recipients). Korea is a strongly patrilineal and male-dominated society, so women political leaders represent "a notable deviance from the usual gender-role expectations" (54). This "deviance" is not stigmatized in Korean culture; rather, it is admired within the category of *yŏgŏl*. A *yŏgŏl* is a woman with "manly" accomplishments. Her personality traits include extraordinary bravery, strength, integrity, generosity, and charisma. Physically, a *yŏgŏl* is likely to be taller, larger, and stronger than most women, and to have a stronger voice than other women. Why do some girls grow up to be a *yŏgŏl*?

Analysis of the life histories of elected and appointed women legislators offers clues about differences in their socialization. Elected women legislators were likely to have had atypical paternal experiences of two types: either an absent father, or an atypically nurturant father. Both of these experiences facilitated a girl's socialization into *yŏgŏl* qualities, or, in the words of Soh, into developing an androgynous personality combining traits of both masculinity and femininity. In contrast, the presence of a "typical" father results in a girl developing a more "traditional" female personality that is submissive and passive.

One intriguing question that follows from Soh's findings is: What explains the socialization of different types of fathers—those who help daughters develop leadership qualities and those who socialize daughters for passivity?

Representative Kim Ok-son greets some of her constituents who are members of a local Confucian club in Seoul, Republic of Korea. She is wearing a men's style suit and has a masculine haircut.

FOOD FOR THOUGHT

In your experience, what socialization factors might influence boys or girls to become politicians?

Political Organization and Leadership

Political organization refers to groups that exist for purposes of public decision making and leadership, maintaining social cohesion and order, protecting group rights, and ensuring safety from external threats. Power relationships situated in private, within the family, for example, may be considered "political" and may be related to wider political realities, but they are not considered forms of political organization. Political organizations have several features that overlap with the groups and organizations discussed in the previous chapter:

- *Recruitment principles:* Criteria for determining admission to the unit.

- *Perpetuity:* Assumption that the group will continue to exist indefinitely.

- *Identity markers:* Particular characteristics that distinguish it from others, such as costume, membership card, or title.

- *Internal organization:* An orderly arrangement of members in relation to each other.

- *Procedures:* Prescribed rules and practices for behaviour of group members.

- *Autonomy:* Ability to regulate its own affairs. (Tiffany 1979:71–72)

Cultural anthropologists cluster the many forms of political organization that occur cross-culturally into four major types (see Figure 11.1 below). The four types of political organization correspond, generally, to the major economic forms (see Chapter 3). Recall that the categories of economies represent a continuum, suggesting that there is overlap between the different types rather than neatly drawn boundaries; this overlap exists between types of political organization as well.

Bands

Anthropologists use the term **band** to refer to the political organization of foraging groups. Since foraging has been the predominant mode of production for almost all of human history, the band has been the most longstanding form of political organization. A band com-

---

FIGURE 11.1   Economies and Political Organization

FORAGING	HORTICULTURE	PASTORALISM	AGRICULTURE	INDUSTRIALISM (CAPITALIST)
Political Organization				*Political Organization*
Band	Tribe	Chiefdom	Confederacy	State State
Leadership				*Leadership*
Band leader	Headman/headwoman Big-man Big-woman	Chief Paramount chief		King/queen/president prime minister/emperor
Social Change				
	More surpluses of resources and wealth			
	Increased population density and residential centralization			
	More social inequality/ranking			
	Less reliance on kinship relations as the basis of political structures			
	Increased internal and external social conflict			
	Increased power and responsibility of leaders			
	Increased burdens on the population to support political organization			

prises a small group of households, between 20 and a few hundred people at most, who are related through kinship. These units come together at certain times of the year, depending on their foraging patterns and ritual schedule.

Band membership is flexible: If a person has a serious disagreement with another person or a spouse, one option is to leave that band and join another. Leadership is also informal in most cases, with no one person being named as a permanent leader for the whole group at all times. Depending on the events at hand, such as organizing the group to relocate or to send people out to hunt, a particular person may come to the fore as a leader for that time. That person's advice and knowledge about the task may be especially respected.

There is no social stratification between leaders and followers. Anthropologists refer to a band leader as a "first among equals." Leadership is informal and is based on the sheer quality of the individual's advice and personality. If a person gives bad advice, people will not continue to listen. Band leaders have limited authority or influence, but no power. They cannot enforce their opinions. Social levelling mechanisms prevent anyone from accumulating much authority or influence, since strong values of self-effacement prevail over self-aggrandizement. Political activity in bands involves mainly decision making about migration, food distribution, and interpersonal conflict resolution. External conflict between groups is rare since territories of different bands are widely separated and the population density is low.

The band level of organization barely qualifies as a form of political organization since groups are flexible, leadership ephemeral, and there are no signs or emblems of political affiliation. In fact, many anthropologists would say that "real" politics did not exist in undisturbed band societies such as the Ju/wasi of southern Africa, the Inuit of northern Canada and Alaska, and the Andaman Islanders of India.

Tribes

A tribe is a more complex form of political organization than the band. Typically associated with horticulture and pastoralism, tribal organization developed only about 12 000 years ago with the advent of these modes of production. A **tribe** is a political group that comprises several bands or lineage groups, each with similar language

and lifestyle and occupying a distinct territory. These groups may be connected through a **clan** structure in which most people claim descent from a common ancestor, although they may be unable to trace the exact relationship. Kinship, as in the band, is the primary basis of membership. Tribes contain from a hundred to several thousand people. They are found in the Middle East, South Asia, Southeast Asia, the Pacific, Africa, and among First Nations people in North America.

In terms of group leadership, a tribal headman (most are male) is a more formal and effective leader than a band leader. Key qualifications for this position are being hardworking and generous, and possessing good personal skills. A headman is a political leader on a part-time basis only. Like all other group members, he is primarily involved in production. Yet, this role is more demanding than being a band leader. Depending on the mode of production, a headman will be in charge of determining the times for hunting, moving herds, and planting and harvesting, and setting the time for seasonal feasts and celebrations. Internal and external conflict resolution is also his responsibility. A headman relies mainly on authority and persuasion rather than power. These strategies are effective because tribal members are all kin and have a certain loyalty to each other. Furthermore, exerting force on kinspersons is generally avoided.

Recent ethnohistorical research argues that the Ojibway of northwestern Ontario, who were previously thought to have lived in small, mutually hostile bands, participated in a tribal-wide organization called the Grand Council that involved ranked male leaders including a grand chief, civil chiefs, war chiefs, and others. Abundant resources, especially wild rice and sturgeon, allowed the Rainy River Ojibway in the mid-nineteenth century to control access to their territory. Seasonal gatherings in large groupings at maple groves (to tap for maple sugar), fishing stations, berry patches, garden sites (growing potatoes and corn), and rice fields were "the foundation for tribal government and Ojibwa military power"(Lovisek, Holzkamm, and Waisberg 1997:138). Colonial officials had to abide by the Grand Council's rules when moving through the territory, and Ojibway religious leaders were successful in resisting Christian missionizing for a time.

Among horticulturalists of the Amazonian rain forest, tribal organization is the dominant political pattern. Each local tribal unit, which is itself a lineage, has a headman (or perhaps two or three). Each tribal group is au-

Chief Paul Payakan, leader of the Kayapo, a group of indigenous people living in the rain forest of the Brazilian Amazon. Payakan was instrumental in mobilizing widespread political resistance in the region against the construction of a hydroelectric dam.

tonomous, but recently many have united temporarily into larger groups, in reaction to threats to their environment and lifestyle from outside forces.

Pastoralist tribal formations are often linked into a confederacy, with local units or segments each maintaining substantial autonomy. The local segments meet together rarely, usually at an annual festival. In case of an external threat, the confederacy gathers together. Once the threat is removed, local units resume their autonomy. The overall equality and autonomy of each unit in relation to the others, along with their ability to unite and then disunite, is referred to as a **segmentary model** of political organization (a pattern of smaller units within larger units that can unite and separate depending on external threats).

Big-Man Leadership

The **big-man system** is a form of political organization in which key individuals de-

vote much of their efforts to developing a political following through a system of redistribution based on personal ties and grand feasts (as mentioned in Chapter 4). Anthropological research in Melanesia, a large region in the South Pacific, established the big-man type of politics, and most references to it are from this region (Sahlins 1963; A. Strathern 1971). Nevertheless, personalistic, favour-based political groupings are found elsewhere.

Compared to a tribal headman, a big-man has an expanded following that includes people in several villages. A big-man tends to have greater wealth than his followers, although people continue to expect him to be generous. The core supporters of a big-man tend to be kin, with extended networks including non-kin. A big-man has heavy responsibilities in regulating both internal affairs—cultivation—and external affairs—intergroup feasts, exchanges of goods, and war. In some instances, a big-man is assisted in carrying out his responsibilities by a group of other respected men. These councils include people from the big-man's different constituencies.

Big-man political organization is common in Papua New Guinea. In several tribes in the Mount Hagen region of the New Guinea Highlands, an aspiring big-man develops a leadership position through making *moka* (A. Strathern 1971). Making *moka* involves exchanging gifts and favours with individuals and sponsoring large feasts where further gift-giving occurs. A crucial factor in bigmanship in the Mount Hagen area is having at least one wife. An aspiring big-man urges his wives to work harder than ordinary women in order to grow more food to feed more pigs. (Pigs are an important measure of a man's status and worth.) The role of the wife is so important that a man whose parents died when he was young is at an extreme disadvantage. He has impaired chances of getting a wife or wives since he lacks financial support from his parents for the necessary bridewealth.

Using his own wife's (or wives') production as an exchange base, the aspiring big-man begins to extend his *moka* relationships, first with kin and then beyond. By giving goods to people, he gains prestige over them. The recipient, later, will make a return gift of somewhat greater value: "One of the most striking features of the moka is the basic rule that to make moka one must give more than one has received. It is strictly the increment that entitles a man to say he has made moka" (A. Strathern 1971:216). The exchanges continue to go back and forth, over the years. The more one gives, and the more people

Throughout much of the South Pacific, big-man politics has long involved the demonstration of generosity on the part of the leaders, who are expected to be able to mobilize resources for impressive feasts such as this one on Tanna Island.

in one's exchange network, the greater prestige the big-man develops. Degrees of big-manship exist throughout the Pacific region. In the Mount Hagen region, there are "minor big-men" and a "major big-men." One well-known big-man of the Kawelka tribe, Ongka, worked for years to make a grand *moka,* which is documented in the film *Ongka's Big Moka.*

Chiefdoms

A **chiefdom** is a political grouping of permanently allied tribes and villages under one recognized leader. Compared to most tribes, chiefdoms have larger populations, often numbering in the thousands, and are more centralized and socially complex. Heritable systems of social ranking and economic stratification are found in chiefdoms (Earle 1991), with social divisions existing between the chiefly lineage or lineages and non-chiefly groups. Chiefs and their descendants are considered to be superior to commoners, and intermarriage between the two strata is forbidden. Chiefs are expected to be generous, but they may have a more luxurious lifestyle than the rest of the people; they are not simply "first among equals." The chiefship is an "office" that must be filled at all times. When a chief dies or retires, he or she must be replaced. In contrast, the death of a band leader or big-man does not require that someone else be chosen as a replace-ment. A chief has more responsibilities than a band or tribal leader. He or she regulates production and redistribution, solves internal conflicts, and plans and leads raids and warring expeditions. Criteria for becoming a chief are more clearly defined. Besides ascribed criteria (birth in a chiefly lineage, or being the first son or daughter of the chief), achievement is still important. Achievement is measured in terms of personal leadership skills, charisma, and accumulated wealth. Chiefdoms have existed in many places, including the Ashanti of West Africa and the Cahokia chiefdom in the area of present-day St. Louis, Missouri.

Anthropologists and archaeologists are interested in how and why chiefdom systems evolved as an intermediary unit between tribes and states, and what the political implications of this evolution are (Earle 1991). Several political strategies support the expansion of power in chiefdoms: controlling more internal and external wealth and distributing feasting and gift exchanges that create debt ties; improving local production systems; applying force internally; forging stronger and wider external ties; and controlling ideological legitimacy. Research on many chiefdoms historically and in contemporary times shows that depending on local conditions, different strategies were employed. Internal control of irrigation systems was the most important factor in the emergence of chiefdoms in prehistoric southeastern Spain, while control of external trade was more important in the prehistoric Aegean region (Gilman 1991).

Gender and Leadership Much evidence about leadership patterns in chiefdoms comes from historical examples. Prominent chiefs—men and women—are documented in colonial archives and missionary records. Many historic examples of women chiefs and women rulers come from West Africa, including the Queen Mother of the Ashanti of Ghana and of the Edo of Nigeria (Awe 1977). Oral histories and archival records show that Yoruba women had the institution of the *iyalode,* or chief of the women. The *iyalode* was the women's political spokesperson in the "council of kingmakers," the highest level of government. She was a chief in her own right, with chiefly insignia, including a necklace of special beads, a wide-brimmed straw hat, a shawl, personal servants, special drummers, and bell ringers. She had her own council of subordinate chiefs. The position of *iyalode* was completely based on achievement. The most important qualifications were a woman's proven ability as a leader, economic resources to maintain her new status as chief, and popularity. Tasks included dispute settlement in her court and meeting with women to formulate the women's stand on such policy issues as the declaration of war and the opening of new markets. Although she represented all women in the group and had massive support, she was outnumbered at the council of kingmakers because she was the only female and the only representative of half of the population.

Why do women play greater political roles in some chiefdoms than others? The most successful answers point to women's economic roles as the primary basis for political power, as among the Iroquois and many African horticultural societies. In contrast, the dominant economic role of men in Native American groups of the prairies, following the introduction of the horse by the Spanish and the increased importance of buffalo hunting by men, supported male-dominated political leadership in such groups as the Cheyenne.

A marked change in leadership patterns among chiefdoms in the past few hundred years has been the decline of women's political status in many groups, mainly because of European and North American colonial and missionary influences (Etienne and Leacock 1980). For example, the British colonialists redefined the institution of *iyalode* in Nigeria. Now "she is no longer a member of any of the important councils of government. Even the market, and therefore the market women, have been removed from her jurisdiction, and have been placed under the control of the new local government councils in each town" (146). Ethnohistorical research on chiefdoms in Hawaii provides a similar view of formerly powerful women chiefs (Linnekan 1990). Following Captain Cook's arrival in 1778, a Western-model monarchy was established. By the time the United States annexed the islands in 1898, indigenous Hawaiian leaders had been displaced from prominent economic and political roles by Westerners.

Confederacies

An expanded version of the chiefdom occurs when several chiefdoms are joined in a confederacy, headed by a chief of chiefs, "big chief," or paramount chief. Many prominent confederacies have existed: in Hawaii in the late 1700s and in North America, including the Iroquois league of five nations that stretched across New York state, the Cherokee of Tennessee, the Algonquins who dominated the Chesapeake region in present-day Virginia and Maryland, and the Huron of southern Ontario. The Huron confederacy, called *wendat*, included five distinct groups living in the region around Lake Simcoe, Georgian Bay, and Lake Huron in southern Ontario. In the Huron confederacy, each village had a chief and there were regional and confederacy councils that brought together chiefs from all the villages. Chiefs of principal villages were the heads of councils. The confederacy council met at least once a year and decided issues of war and peace. Special pools of goods were built up as a public treasury and were administered by chiefs for long-distance trade (Trigger 1969; 1976).

States

A **state** is a centralized political unit encompassing many communities and possessing coercive power. The earliest evidence of the state form of political organization comes from Mesopotamia, China, India, and Egypt, perhaps as early as 4000 BCE. States emerged in these several locations with the development of intensive agriculture, increased surpluses, and increased population density. The state is now the form of political organization in which all people live. Band organizations, tribes, and chiefdoms still exist, but they are incorporated, to a greater or lesser degree, within state structures.

Origins of the State Many scholars have proposed theories of why the state evolved (Trigger 1996). Marxist theory says that the state emerged to maintain ruling-class dominance. Demographic theory posits that population density drove the need for central mechanisms for social control. Economic theory argues that the state emerged in response to the increased surpluses of food production in the neolithic era, which produced sufficient wealth to support a permanent ruling class. Political theory says that the state arose as a necessary arbiter as competition increased for arable land and access to food surpluses. Rather than emphasizing a single causal factor, most scholars now incorporate multiple causes in their theories. Another development is that scholars have moved from the "why" question to the "how" question (Trigger 1996). New areas of inquiry include the state's increased bases for central power, such as finances and information management.

Powers of the State

The state and its leaders have much more power and responsibility than leaders of other categories of political organization:

- *States define citizenship and its rights and responsibilities.* In complex nations, since early times, not all residents were granted equal rights as citizens.

- *States monopolize the use of force and the maintenance of law and order.* Internally, the state controls the population through laws, courts, and the police. Externally, the state uses force to defend the nation's borders and offensively to extend territory.

- *States maintain standing armies and police* (as opposed to part-time forces).

- *States keep track of their citizens in terms of number, age, gender, location, and wealth through census systems that are regularly updated.* A census allows the state to maintain formal taxation systems, military recruitment, and policy planning such as population settlement, immigration quotas, and social benefits such as old-age pensions.

- *States have the power to extract resources from citizens through taxation.* All political organizations are supported by contributions of the members, but variations occur in the rate of contributions expected, the form in which they are paid, and the return that members get in terms of services. Public finance in states is based on formal taxation that takes many forms. **In-kind taxation** is a system of mandatory, non-cash contributions to the state. For example, the Inca state used the *corvee*, a labour tax, to finance public works such as roads and monuments and to provide agricultural labour on state lands. Cash taxes, such as the income tax that takes a percentage of wages, emerged only in the past few hundred years.

- *States manipulate information.* Control of information to protect the state and its leaders can be done directly through censorship, restricting public access to certain information, and promoting favourable images through propaganda; it can be done indirectly through pressure on journalists and television networks to present information in certain ways.

Gender and Leadership

Most states are hierarchical and patriarchal, excluding members of lower classes and women from equal participation. Some contemporary states are less male-dominated than others, but none are female-dominated. One view of gender inequality in states suggests that increasing male dominance with the evolution of the state is based on male control of the technology of production and warfare (Harris 1993). Women in most cultures have been excluded from these areas of power, and they have not been able to reverse or equalize these longstanding power relationships except in states that are relatively peaceful, such as Finland, Norway, Sweden, and Denmark.

Strongly patriarchal contemporary states preserve male dominance through ideologies that restrict women's political power, such as *purdah* (female seclusion and segregation from the public world), as practised in much of the Muslim Middle East, Pakistan, and North India. In China, scientific beliefs that categorize women as less strong and dependable than men have long been used to rationalize the exclusion of women from politics (Dikötter 1998).

A handful of contemporary states have or have recently had women as prime ministers or presidents. Such powerful women include Indira Gandhi in India, Golda Meir in Israel, Margaret Thatcher in the United Kingdom, and Benazir Bhutto in Pakistan. Female heads of state in Latin America and Asia are often related by kinship (as wife or daughter) to former heads of state. Indira Gandhi, for example, was the daughter of the popular first prime minister of independent India, Jawaharlal Nehru (she is not related to Mahatma Gandhi). It is unclear as to how much these women's leadership positions can be explained by their inheriting the role or through the political socialization they may have received, directly or indirectly, as a result of being born into political families. Canada has many well-known political families in which males are prominent. Rarely do wives step into a husband's position, although many have wielded indirect political power (for example Mila Mulroney). Political daughters also exist. Sheila Copps, a minister in the Chrétien government, is the daughter of a respected politician who was mayor of Hamilton, Ontario, for many years.

Symbols of State Power

Religious beliefs and symbols are often closely tied to the power of state leadership: The ruler may be considered to be a deity or part deity, or a high priest of the state religion, or may be closely linked with the high priest who serves as adviser. Architecture and urban planning remind the populace of the greatness of the state. In pre-Columbian Mexico, the central plaza of city-states, such as Tenochtitlán (founded in 1345), was symbolically equivalent to the centre of the cosmos and thus the locale of greatest significance (Low 1995). The most important temples and the residence of the head of state were located surrounding the plaza. Other houses and structures, in decreasing order of status, were located on avenues in decreasing proximity to the centre. The grandness and individual character of the leader's residence indicate power, as do monuments—especially tombs to past leaders or heroes or heroines. Egypt's pyramids, China's Great Wall, and India's Taj Mahal are a few of the world's great architectural reminders of state power.

In democratic states where leaders are elected by popular vote and in socialist states where political rhetoric emphasizes social equality, expense and elegance are "toned down" in some ways by the adoption of more egalitarian ways of dress (even though in private, these leaders may live relatively opulent lives in terms of housing, food, and entertainment). The earlier practice of all Chinese leaders wearing a "Mao jacket," regardless of their rank, was a symbolic statement of their anti-hierarchical philosophy.

Local Power and Politics in Democratic States

The degree to which the state influences the lives of its citizens varies. So-called totalitarian states have the most direct control of local politics. In most other systems, local politics and local government are granted some degree of power. In highly centralized states, the central government controls public finance and legal institutions, leaving little power or autonomy in these matters to local governments. In decentralized systems, local governments are granted some forms of revenue generation (taxation) and the responsibility of providing certain services. Local politics continue to exist within state systems, with their strength and autonomy dependent on how centralized the state apparatus is.

In Japan, relatively egalitarian systems of local power structures exist in villages and hamlets. Families subtly vie for status and leadership roles through gift-giving, as is common in local politics worldwide (R. Marshall 1985). Egalitarianism prevails as a community value, but people strive to be "more than equal" by making public donations to the *buraku*, or hamlet. The custom of "giving a gift to the community" is a way that hamlet families can improve their positions in the local ranking system. In one hamlet, all 35 households recently gave gifts to the community on specified occasions: the forty-second birthday of male family members, the sixty-first birthday of male family members, the seventy-seventh birthday of male family members, the marriage of male family members, the marriage of female family members whose husband will be the household successor, the birth of the household head or successor couple's first child, and the construction of a new house. These occasions for public gift-giving always include an invitation to a meal for members of all hamlet households:

> *About a month before the meal is scheduled, the donor household notifies the hamlet head of its intentions and places with him the cash portion of its gift, from which provisions for the meal will be purchased.... The donor family and the hamlet head agree on a suitable date and*

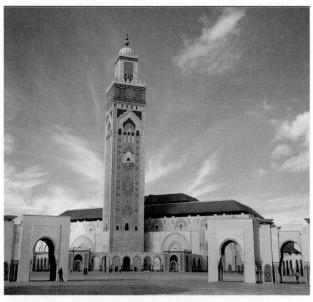

This expansive, and expensive, mosque in Casablanca was constructed by and named after the late King Hassan II. It was a clear statement of his presence and power in Morocco.

time for the meal, usually a Sunday afternoon as a prelude to a general meeting of the hamlet as council for the discussion of hamlet affairs.... When the hamlet members are all seated in the hamlet hall and the meal has been placed before them...the hamlet head holds up the decorated envelope in which he received the cash gift and reads from it the donor household's name, the amount of the gift, and the nature of the occasion. During the meal the envelope is circulated from hand to hand around the tables and examined without comment as it travels around the hall. (169)

Since the 1960s, it has also become common to give an item that is useful for the hamlet, such as a set of fluorescent light fixtures for the hamlet hall, folding tables, space heaters, and vacuum cleaners.

Local politics within a democratic framework reveal another type of gift-giving and exchange in the interest of maintaining or gaining power. Here we see people in elected positions of power giving favours in expectation of political loyalty in return. In these cases, various **factions** vie with each other. A faction, a more formalized aspect of local politics, is a politically oriented conflict group whose members are mobilized and maintained by a leader to whom the main ties of loyalty and affiliation are lateral—from leader to follower—rather than horizontal between members (Brumfiel 1994b). Factions tend to be personalistic, transitory, lacking formal rules and meeting times, and lacking formal succession. Factional politics is not redistributive, however. It often leads to conflict and unequal resource distribution.

Change in Political Systems

In the early days of political anthropology, researchers examined the varieties of political organization and leadership and created categories such as bands, tribes, chiefdoms, and states. Contemporary political anthropologists are more interested in political dynamics and change, especially in how the pre-eminent political form, the state, affects local people's lives. This section covers selected topics in the anthropological study of political change.

A political rally of indigenous people in Bolivia.

Emergent Nations and Fractured States

It is not easy to explain clearly what a nation is and what the relationship of this concept is to the state since many different definitions exist for a "nation" and some of them overlap with definitions given for a "state" (Maybury-Lewis 1997:125–132). Furthermore, popular usage often uses the two terms interchangeably. One basic definition says that a **nation** is a group of people who share a language, culture, territorial base, political organization, and history (Clay 1990). In this sense, a nation is culturally homogeneous, and thus, Canada would not be considered a nation but rather a unit composed of many nations. Referring to "national policy" as something that relates to the unit as a whole is then a misnomer. Yet another related term is the *nation-state,* which some people say refers to a state that comprises only one nation, while others think it refers to states that comprise many nations.

Depending on their resources and power, nations may constitute a political threat to states. Anyone reading this book can easily think of several examples from historic and contemporary times. In response to this (real or perceived) threat, states seek to create and maintain a sense of unified identity. Political scientist Benedict Anderson, in his widely read book *Imagined Communities* (1991 [1983]), writes about the efforts that state-builders employ to create a sense of belonging and commitment—"imagined community"—among diverse peoples. Strategies for building state identity among the many nations within a state include the imposition of one language as "the" national language; the construction of monuments and museums; and the creation of songs, poetry, and other media-relayed messages about the "motherland." Anderson points, for example, to the construction of tombs of "Unknown Soldiers" as major unifying symbols: "The public ceremonial reverence accorded these monuments, precisely because they are deliberately empty or no one knows who lies inside them, has no true precedents in earlier times" (9).

World peace increasingly involves intrastate and cross-state ethnic politics and conflict. The Tibetans, the Chechens, the Kayapo, the Eritreans (whose war of liberation ended in 1993), the Palestinians, the Sikhs of northwestern India, the Kurds of Turkey and Iraq, and the Assamese of eastern India…the list goes on…are all groups building their own solidarities and political momentums. Attempts by nationalistic states to force homogenization of these and other ethnic groups will prompt resistance of varying degrees from those who wish to retain autonomy. Cultural anthropologists are becoming more involved in studying both local and global aspects of ethnic relations. Their data can contribute to the realm of "peace and conflict" studies and policy through providing case studies and theories based on comparative analysis.

Globalization and Politics

Since the seventeenth century, the world's nations have been increasingly linked in a hierarchical structure. This structure of power relations is largely regulated through international trade. In the seventeenth century, Holland was the one core nation, dominating world trade. It was then surpassed by England and France, which remained the two most powerful nations up to around 1900. In the early part of the twentieth century, challenges for world dominance were made by the United States and

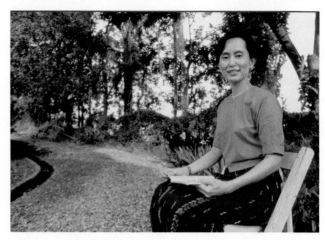

Aung San Suu Kyi is the leader of the Burmese democracy and human rights movement. The daughter of Burma's assassinated national hero, Aung San, she was under house arrest from 1989 to 1995. She was awarded the Nobel Peace Prize, making her the eighth woman to receive the award.

later by Germany and Japan. The outcome of World War II placed the United States as leader of the "core." Greater complexities in world-systems theory now allow for an additional category of semiperiphery states, intermediary between the core and the periphery.

Cultural anthropology's traditional strength has been the study of small, bounded local groups, so anthropologists have had relatively little to say about international affairs. Now, more anthropologists have enlarged their focus to include the international level, studying both how global changes affect local politics and how local politics affect international affairs. Worldwide communication networks facilitate global politics. Ethnic politics, although locally initiated, increasingly has international repercussions. Migrant populations promote interconnected interests across state boundaries.

The Anthropology of Order and Conflict

Socially agreed-upon ways of behaving shape people's everyday life in countless ways. We wait for our turn to get on a bus rather than pushing to the head of the line, and we pay for a sandwich at the deli instead of stealing it. Anthropologists in all four fields have devoted attention to the subjects of social order and social conflict. Historical archaeologists, studying cultures that had writing, have traced the development of written law through time. Other archaeologists have examined artifacts such as weapons, remains of forts, and the waxing and waning of political centres in order to understand group conflict in the past. Many primatologists study nonhuman primate patterns of cooperation, coalitions, and conflict. Linguistic anthropologists have done research on social conflict related to national language policies and on how communication patterns within the courtroom influence outcomes. Legal anthropology is the subfield within cultural anthropology that is most directly concerned with the study of social control and social conflict.

Over the course of the twentieth century, the direction of legal anthropology has headed away from its original foundations in functionalism (the way a particular practice or belief contributed to social cohesion) towards a view that focuses on internal divisiveness. Helping to launch the subfield through his classic book *Crime and Custom in Savage Society* (1962 [1926]), functionalist Malinowski wrote that in the Trobriand Islands, social ties themselves promoted mutual social obligation and harmony. No separate legal institutions existed throughout Melanesia; instead, law was embedded in social life. Thus, he made the important contribution that social relationships can perform the same functions as formal laws and courts.

Later, in the mid-twentieth century, Max Gluckman (1955; 1963) diverged from functionalism in studying disputes and conflict. His research in central African villages revealed how the court systems resolved conflict. Much early research on indigenous law and legal processes, including Gluckman's, was commissioned by colonial administrations. The colonialists wanted to learn about local customs in order to rule over the colonized peoples more effectively. This early work was mainly concerned with documenting how different cultures defined law, justice, and punishment.

By the 1960s, another new turn was established with the study of law in action. This transition brought an emphasis on collecting ethnographic data on the dispute event and the chain of events that followed it. June Starr's book, *Dispute and Settlement in Rural Turkey* (1978), ex-emplifies this approach of extended case analysis. Her book is built around 32 dispute cases, including two boys fighting at a wedding, a man's dog killing a chicken, the lighthouse keeper's wife taking a lover, and a dispute among siblings about dividing the family land. In examining each case, Starr provides information on the social relationships of the disputants, the cultural significance of the dispute, Turkish law in relation to the offence (for example, Turkish law says that it is a criminal offence to shoot a gun at a wedding), forms of resolution, and why particular resolutions emerged compared to others. This approach highlights rules of law and order, but situates them in the cultural context for interpretation.

Several new directions have emerged in legal anthropology: the study of legal discourse, especially in courtroom settings, law and transnational processes in colonial and post-colonial settings, **critical legal anthropology** (an approach that examines how the law and judicial systems serve to maintain and expand the dominant power interests rather than protecting those who are marginal and less powerful), and law and human rights in cross-cultural perspective (Merry 1992). Research in critical legal studies is discussed in Social Inequality and the Law, on page 275.

Systems of Social Control

The concept of social control has several meanings depending on one's theoretical perspective. A generally accepted definition in anthropology is that **social control** is "the processes which help produce and maintain orderly social life" (Garland 1996:781). Scholars of the more critical bent would emphasize the negative aspects of social control systems as supporting hierarchy and domination, either directly or indirectly. Underlying both views are two premises:

- Social control systems exist to ensure a certain degree of social conformity to agreed-upon rules.

- Some people in all cultures may violate the rules and resist conformity (what sociologists refer to as "deviant behaviour").

Social control systems include internalized social controls that exist through socialization for proper behaviour, education, and peer pressure, and formal systems of codified rules about proper behaviour and punishments for deviation. The Amish and Mennonites, Christian immigrant groups from Europe, rely on internalized social controls more than most cultural groups in the United States and Canada. These groups have no police force or legal system; the way social order is maintained is through religious teaching and group pressure. If a member veers from correct behaviour, punishment such as ostracism ("shunning") may be applied.

Norms and Laws

Cultural anthropologists distinguish two major instruments of social control: norms and laws. **Norms** are generally agreed-upon standards for how people should behave. All societies have norms. They are usually unwritten and learned unconsciously through socialization. Norms include, for example, the expectation that children should follow their parents' advice, that people standing in line should be orderly and not try to "jump" the line, and that an individual should accept an offer of a handshake (in cultures where handshakes are the usual greeting) when meeting someone for the first time. In rural Bali, etiquette dictates certain greeting forms between people of different status: "[P]ersons of higher status and power are shown very marked respect: they are greeted submissively and treated obsequiously; if seated, then others moving past them crouch…so as not to loom above them" (Barth 1993:114). Enforcement of norms tends to be informal; for example, a violation may simply be considered rude and the violator avoided in the future. In others, punishment may be involved, such as asking someone who is disruptive in a meeting to leave.

The categories of norm and law form a continuum in terms of how explicitly they are stated and how strongly they are enforced. A **law** is a binding rule created through enactment or custom that defines right and reasonable behaviour. Laws are enforceable by threat of punishment. Systems of law are more common and more elaborate in state-level societies, but many nonstate societies have formalized laws. Often the legitimacy and force of law are based on religion. For example, Australian Aborigines believe that law came to humans during the "Dreamtime," a time in the mythological past when the ancestors created the Aboriginal world. Contemporary Islamic states explicitly link law and religion. Secular Western states consider their laws to be religiously neutral, but in fact, much Western legal practice is heavily influenced by Judeo-Christian beliefs. Critiques of law versus norms have focused on how, in some instances, laws are less morally sound than norms.

Social Control in Small-Scale Societies

Anthropologists distinguish small-scale societies and large-scale societies in terms of prevalent forms of conflict resolution, social order, and punishment of offences. Formal laws are rare among foraging groups, although Inuit and Australian Aborigines are notable for their more formalized, although unwritten, law systems. Because bands are small, close-knit groups, disputes tend to be handled at the interpersonal level through discussion or one-on-one fights. The group may act together to punish an offender through shaming and ridicule. Emphasis is on maintaining social order and restoring social equilibrium, not hurtfully punishing an offender. Ostracizing an offending member (forcing the person to leave the group) is a common means of formal punishment. Capital punishment has been documented, but is rare. For example, in some Australian Aboriginal societies, a law restricts access to religious rituals and paraphernalia to men who have gone through a ritual initiation. If an initiated man shared secrets with an uninitiated man, the elders would delegate one of their group to kill the offender. In such instances, the elders act like a court.

In nonstate societies, punishment is often legitimized through belief in supernatural forces and their ability to affect people. Among the highland horticulturalists of the Indonesian island of Sumba, one of the greatest offences is to fail to keep a promise (Kuipers 1990). Breaking a promise will bring on "supernatural assault" by the ancestors of those who have been offended by the person's misbehaviour. The punishment may come in the form of damage to crops, illness or death of a relative, destruction of the offender's house, or having clothing catch on fire. When such a disaster occurs, the only choice is to sponsor a ritual that will appease the ancestors.

Conflict resolution among horticulturalists relies on many of the same methods as among foragers, notably public shaming and ridicule. In the Trobriands of the early twentieth century, Malinowski (1961 [1926]) reports

The rare quarrels which occur at times take the form of an exchange of public expostulation (yakala) in which the two parties assisted by friends and relatives meet, harangue one another, hurl and hurl back recriminations. Such litigation allows people to give vent to their feelings and shows the trend of public opinion, and thus it may be of assistance in settling disputes. Sometimes it seems, however, to harden the parties. In no case is there any definite sentence pronounced by a third party, and agreement is but seldom reached then and there. (60)

Village *fission* (breaking up) and ostracism are other common mechanisms for dealing with unresolvable conflict. The overall goal in dealing with conflict in small-scale societies is to return the group to harmony.

Social Control in States

In societies that are more densely populated, more socially stratified, and have more wealth, increased stresses form around the distribution of surplus, inheritance, and rights to land. In addition, increased social scale means that not everyone knows everyone else, and face-to-face accountability may exist only in local neighbourhoods.

Specialization As with all aspects of the division of labour, the specialization of tasks related to law and order—police, judges, lawyers—increases with the emergence of state organization. In pre-state societies, it is often society at large that determines right from wrong and punishes offenders, or the elders may have special authority and be called on for advice. In tribal societies, special advisers, such as the so-called "leopard-skin chief" of the Nuer of Sudan, have had a role in decision making about crime and punishment. However, full-time professionals, such as judges and lawyers, emerged with the state. These professionals often come from powerful or elite social groups, a fact that perpetuates elite biases in the justice process itself. In North America, the legal profession is committed to opposing discrimination on the basis of gender and race, but it is nonetheless characterized by a lack of representation of women and minorities. Minority women, who face a double bind, are especially underrepresented (Chanen 1995:105). **Policing** includes processes of surveillance and the threat of punishment related to maintaining social order (Reiner 1996). Police are the specific organization and personnel who discover, report, and investigate crimes. As a specialized group, police exist mainly in complex state societies.

A "leopard-skin chief" among the cattle-herding Nuer of the Sudan acted as an intermediary between people and groups in conflict, including instances of murder. His power, however, is limited to negotiation and the ability to threaten punishment through supernatural means.

Trials and Courts In societies where misdoing and punishment are defined by spirits and ancestors, a person's guilt is evidenced simply by the fact that misfortune has befallen him or her. If a person's crops were damaged by lightning, then that person must have done something wrong. In other instances, guilt may be determined through **trial by ordeal,** a form of trial in which the accused person is put through some kind of test that is often painful. In this case, the guilty person will be required to place a hand in boiling oil, for example, or to have a part of their body touched by a red-hot knife. Being burned is a sign of guilt, while not being burned means the suspect is innocent. The court system, with lawyers, judge, and jury, is used in many contemporary societies, although there is variation in how cases are presented and juries constituted. The goal of contemporary court trials is to ensure both justice and fairness. Analysis of actual courtroom dynamics and patterns of decision making in North America and elsewhere, however, reveals serious problems in achieving these goals.

Punishment As one commentator says, "Punishment is an intended evil" (Christie 1996:708). It involves doing something unpleasant to someone who has committed an offence. Studies of punishment have considered such questions as the bases or reasons for punishment, forms of punishment, effects of various forms of punishment, and the relationship between types of societies and levels of punishment. Some theories argue that the degree of punishment should match the crime; others say the punishment should be a means of getting people to obey the law in the first place and thus should be a deterrent. Little solid knowledge exists about the effectiveness of different forms of punishment, for example, between prison sentences of one versus two years, or long-term imprisonment versus the death penalty as crime deterrents. One result is clear: People who are imprisoned are stigmatized by it, become more marginalized, and therefore have an increased likelihood of committing further crimes.

The prison, as a place where people are forcibly detained as a form of punishment, has a long history. The dungeons and "keeps" of old forts and castles all over the world are vivid evidence of the power of some people to detain and inflict suffering on others (Millett 1994). In general, however, such prisoners were not detained for long periods—they were tried and punished and their cell emptied. Long-term detention of prisoners did not become common until the seventeenth century in Europe (Foucault 1977). The first penitentiary in the United States was built in Philadelphia in the late 1700s (Sharff 1995), and the first in Canada in Kingston in 1835. Cross-nationally and through history, percentages of imprisoned people vary widely. The United States and Russia have high percentages compared to other contemporary Western countries: 550 and 470 prisoners per 100 000 inhabitants, respectively. The British Isles rate is about 100, Canada about 111, while the Scandinavian countries have among the lowest rates, at under 60. In the United States, the prison population has tripled over the past 100 years, in spite of fairly even levels of crime. In Canada, the prison populations in both federal and

The interior scene of the Cellular Jail in India's Andaman Islands, which was so named because all prisoners had single cells, arranged in long rows, in order to prevent them from any social interaction and possible collusion to escape or rebel.

provincial jurisdictions dropped in the 1990s and have never attained the levels of incarceration observed in the United States.

The death penalty (capital punishment) is rare in pre-state societies because condemning someone to death requires a high degree of power. A comparison of capital punishment in the contemporary United States with human sacrifice among the Aztecs of Mexico of the sixteenth century reveals striking similarities (Purdum and Paredes 1989). Both systems involve the death of mainly able-bodied males who are in one way or another socially marginal. In the United States, most people who are executed are non-White, have killed Whites, are poor, and have few social ties. Aztec sacrificial victims were mainly male war captives from neighbouring states, but

Aztec children were also sometimes sacrificed. The deaths in both contexts have a political message: They communicate a message of the state's power and strength to the general populace, which is why they are highly ritualized and well publicized as events.

Social Inequality and the Law

Scholars working in the area of critical legal anthropology have examined discrimination against indigenous people, women, and minorities in various judicial systems around the world. While one could draw examples from many countries about how racial biases and discrimination affect legal processes, the example here comes from Canada.

First Nations peoples in Canada make up 3 per cent of the total population, but account for 12 per cent of federal prison admissions and 20 per cent of provincial prison admissions (Ponting and Kiely 1997). Practices in the justice system in Canada result in lawyers spending less time with First Nations clients than with other clients. Accused First Nations peoples are more likely to be denied bail, and First Nations defendants are more than twice as likely to be incarcerated. In Manitoba, typical of western Canada, more than half of all inmates are from First Nations (155).

Change in Legal Systems

As with other cultural domains, law-and-order systems change over time. European colonialism since the seventeenth century has had major impacts on indigenous systems. On the other hand, law is often viewed as an instrument of social change. This section looks briefly at these two aspects of change.

European Colonialism and Indigenous Systems
Colonial governments, to varying degrees, attempted to learn about and rule their subject populations through what they termed "customary law" (Merry 1992). By seeking to codify customary law, colonial governments created fixed rules where former flexibility and local variation had existed. Leopold Pospisil (1979) reports on how his research on one Kapauku group's traditional law in New Guinea was erroneously co-opted by the Dutch for use throughout the entire Kapauku population:

The colonial administrator was often called upon to adjudicate a great variety of civil cases.... How did the Dutch officer in his new role as dispenser of civil justice discover what tribal law was? I was astounded to see my book Kapauku Papuans and Their Law *(1958) being used by the administration official as a legal codex—as the "authorized version" of Kapauku law. Although I was amused, this was certainly not the reaction of all the Kapauku. As a matter of fact, my book was very unpopular with some of them for an obvious reason. My work dealt only with the legal system of the Ijaaj-Pigome confederacy of the southern part of the Kamu Valley, which differed from every other confederacy's legal system. By applying the Ijaaj-Pigome legal system to the whole of Kapauku society, the Dutch officer had invested the system with a status it had never previously held. The only amused people were my Ijaaj-Pigome friends, who joked about it or even poked fun at the other Kapauku. One of them, tongue in cheek, even mockingly threatened the others: "If you fellows don't behave we shall make our American big man write another and even tougher book." In an effort to undo the injustice, I explained the problem to the officer. He was surprised and admitted that he thought the opposition to his ruling was due to the stubborn nature of some of the litigants. (132)*

Often the colonialists overrode customary law and imposed their own laws. Homicide, marriage, land rights, and indigenous religion were frequent areas of European imposition. Colonial governments everywhere banned headhunting and blood feuds. Among the Nuer of Sudan, British legal interventions resulted in substantial confusion among the Nuer about the issue of blood feuds (Hutchinson 1996). Nuer practices involved either the taking of a life in repayment for a previous homicide, or negotiated payments in cattle depending on the relations between the victim and the assailant, what type of weapon was used, and a consideration of current rates of bridewealth as an index of value. In contrast, the British determined a fixed (non-negotiable) amount of indemnity. They imprisoned people for committing a vengeful murder. From the Nuer point of view, these changes were incomprehensible. They interpreted being put in prison as a way of protecting the person from a reprisal attack.

Any socially plural society will have the option of multiple legal solutions. Colonial imposition of European legal systems onto indigenous systems added another layer, and one that had pre-eminent power over others.

Legal pluralism refers to a situation in which more than one kind of legal process might be applied to identical cases (Rouland 1994:50). For example, should a case of murder in the Sudan be tried according to indigenous Sudanese principles or European ones? Post-colonial nations are now in the process of attempting to reform their legal systems and develop more unified codes (Merry 1992:363).

Studying Conflict and Violence

No doubt it is safer and perhaps easier to study peaceful communities than violent ones. Special challenges facing anthropologists doing fieldwork in violent contexts include shock and bewilderment, how to deal with rumours, how to respond to unpredicted and accidental happenings, and requests from the people involved for help or even complicity (Robben and Nordstrom 1995:13–20). These themes appear in the account by Indian anthropologist Veena Das (1984), who worked with victims of the Delhi riots that erupted after the assassination of prime minister Indira Gandhi. Das, some colleagues, and other concerned citizens, became involved in research and public service after the riots subsided. She describes the context:

> Following the assassination of the Indian Prime-Minister, Indira Gandhi, in Delhi on 31 October 1984, there was widespread violence against the Sikhs for three days.... By 3 November, it became clear to civil-rights groups, university teachers and students, retired bureaucrats, journalists, and other concerned citizens, that they had to take the major responsibility for establishing relief camps, procuring food and medicines, and collecting information about the number of people dead or missing.... It was in this context that my colleagues and I decided to enquire into the pattern of riots by going into the affected localities rather than restricting ourselves to relief camps. (4)

In the most afflicted locality, over 200 people were killed. The researchers were met with urgent requests by the victimized residents that the details of their suffering be made known: "One man, whose two sons had been killed, offered to raise 50 rupees later if we could have an account of their suffering published in a news-paper" (5). The writings of the academics received criticism from others that they would lead to vengeance and continued ethnic conflict. Das responds by saying that anthropologists have the responsibility to express "the ethnographic voice" and all its details, even if they seem "gory" or "trivial." She points to another lesson that emerges from doing research in a time of violent crisis compared to "reasonable normality":

> If one is working among victims of a collective tragedy, one's movements are naturally determined by the sole criterion of the needs of the people. Procuring rations, arranging for medical help, filling forms and establishing liaisons with police officers and administrators—these are the activities that define the trajectory of one's existence...society seems to take control of the researcher, who simply has to lend himself or herself to become the anonymous space on which the hitherto suppressed knowledge of society inscribes itself. (5–6)

Social Conflict and Violence

All systems of social control have to deal with the fact that conflict and violence may occur. This section turns to a consideration of the varieties of social conflict as studied by cultural anthropologists.

Types of Social Conflict

Feuding **Feuding,** or long-term, retributive violence that may be lethal between families, groups of families, or tribes, is probably the most universal form of intergroup aggression. Its practice is motivated by a concept of revenge that leads to the pattern of long-term, back-and-forth violence between two groups. Feuding has long had an important role among the horticultural Ilongot people of the Philippine highlands (Rosaldo 1980). From 1883 to 1974, Ilongot feuds were structured around headhunting as the redress for an insult or offence. Manhood was defined by the taking of a first head, and fathers were responsible for transferring the elaborate knowledge of headhunting to their sons. In 1972, the government banned headhunting and attempted to stop the Ilongot from practising shifting cultivation. The repercussion of these changes has been devastating:

Ilongots perceive that the social fabric has been torn asunder. To give up dry rice horticulture and take up wet rice agriculture, for instance, is to surrender Ilongot ethnic identity for that of a Philippine lowlander.… In 1972, martial law brought the painful rupture in the transmission from father to son of the elaborate techniques of headhunting, and the Ilongots, by the time we were again living among them two years later, sometimes said they no longer were Ilongots. (60)

Ethnic Conflict Ethnic pluralism is a characteristic of most states in the world today. Ethnic conflict and grievances may result from an ethnic group's attempt to gain more autonomy or more equitable treatment (Esman 1996). It may also be caused by a dominant group's actions to subordinate, oppress, or eliminate an ethnic group by genocide or ethnocide. In the past few decades, political violence has increasingly been enacted within states rather than between states and constitutes the majority of "the 120-odd shooting wars in the world today" (Clay 1990). Political analysts and journalists often cite ethnicity, language, and religion as the causes of certain conflicts. Ethnic identities give people an ideological sense of commitment to a cause, but one must always look beneath these labels to see if deeper issues exist.

Such deeper causes may include claims to land, water, ports, and other material resources.

The vast region of Central Asia is populated by many ethnic groups, none of whom has a pristine indigenous claim to the land. Yet, in Central Asia, every dispute appears on the surface to have an ethnic basis: "Russians and Ukrainians versus Kazakhs over land rights and jobs in Kazakhstan, Uzbeks versus Tajiks over the status of Samarkhand and Bukhara, conflict between Kirghiz and Uzbeks in Kyrghyzstan, and riots between Caucasian Turks and Uzbeks in the Fergana Valley of Uzbekistan" (Clay 1990:48).

Attributing all such problems to ethnic differences overlooks the fact that the concept of a functioning plural society is more firmly entrenched in the Central Asian states than anywhere else in the former Soviet Union. In contrast to the Baltic states, the Central Asian nations have granted citizenship to all inhabitants. This acceptance of diversity follows an old pattern: Different ethnic groups fit different economic slots. This could be called a *segmentational model*, in which different groups control significant resources and institutions, contrasted with a *stratificational model*, in which one group dominates others (Esman 1996). A more illuminating way of analyzing the basis of conflict in Central Asia is to consider the

Ethnicity and Genocide in Rwanda

The media has depicted genocide in Rwanda in the 1991–1993 and 1994 periods in terms of ethnic conflicts characterized by attacks of the peasant Hutu on the Tutsi elite. In fact, the situation is more complicated than this simple picture suggests (Jefremovas 1997). The pre-colonial Rwandan state saw the kings destroying the power of lineage organizations and developing feudal relations between peasants and their lords. The elite were mostly Tutsi but both ethnic groups, Hutu and Tutsi, were represented among the elite and the poor peasantry. When the Belgians took control in 1912, they introduced racist theories that viewed the Tutsi as a superior type of person who ruled by natural right. They used this ideology in order to replace the king with their own recruit. In addition, the Belgian colonialists were obliged to purge the Rwandan elite of Hutu lords because of this racist analysis. In the post-colonial state, a party representing the Hutu took power partly in response to this colonial racist ideology. The killings that occurred in the early 1990s were not based on "ethnic violence" or "ancient hatreds," but rather were cold-blooded political murders "ruthlessly orchestrated by a morally bankrupt elite" (102). The new government of Rwanda now argues that Tutsi and Hutu were never ethnic groups, but rather, Tutsi were rich people, and Hutu, poor. As Jefremovas points out, this again simplifies the real situation where these categories continue to "have power and mean real discrimination" (102).

division between centres and hinterlands and their different access to crucial resources. Uzbekistan has most of the cities and irrigated farmland, but small states like Kyrghyzstan and Tajikistan control most of the water. Turkmenistan has vast oil and gas riches. "No ethnic catalyst would be needed to provoke conflict in such situations; simple need or greed would more than suffice" (51).

Ethnic conflicts are waged in many different ways, from the cruelest and most gruesome killings and rapes (see the Multiple Cultural Worlds box) to various forms of power jockeying. An example of the latter type of conflict concerns whether Muslim girl students may wear head scarves in school in France. The Israeli-Palestinian situation encompasses many forms of conflict. For example, in Israel, land that appears to be unused is said to belong to the state (M. N. Cohen 1993). Palestinians who live in areas near the expanding municipal border of Jerusalem attempt to prevent further encroachment by planting olive trees (their symbol) on the land, thus claiming the land as theirs. In turn, the Israelis have programs for planting pine trees around Jerusalem as part of the mayor's "green-belt" plan, a strategy that claims the land as Israeli.

Revolution
A **revolution** is a "political crisis propelled by illegal and usually violent actions by subordinate groups which threatens to change the political institutions or social structure of a society" (Goldstone 1996:740). Revolutions are sometimes called "wars," but they receive separate consideration here as within-state conflicts that are considered illegal by the state. Revolutions have occurred in a range of societies, including pre-industrial monarchies, post-colonial developing countries, and totalitarian states. Scholars who have compared revolutions in modern times—England 1640, France 1789, Mexico 1910, China 1911, Russia 1917, Iran 1979—say that interrelated factors, such as a military or fiscal crisis and a weak state military machine, may begin a revolution. The process of revolutions varies in terms of the degree of popular participation, roles of radicals and moderates, and leadership.

Theorists also argue about the different role of rural versus urban sectors in fomenting revolution. Many revolutions occurred in mainly agrarian countries and were propelled by rural participants, not urban radicalism (Skocpol 1979; E. Wolf 1969). Such agrarian-based revolutions include the French, Russian, and Chinese revo-

lutions. A rural-based movement also characterizes many national liberation movements against colonial powers such as French Indochina, Guinea-Bissau, Mozambique, and Angola (Gugler 1988). Algeria was a somewhat more urbanized country, but it was still about two-thirds rural in 1962 when the French finally made peace there. In all of these cases, the colonial power was challenged by a rural-based guerrilla movement that controlled crop production, processing, and transport and thus could strike at the heart of the colonial political economy.

On the other hand, some revolutions have been essentially urban in character, including those in Bolivia, Iran, and Nicaragua. The case of Cuba is mixed since rural-based guerrillas played a prominent role, and the cities provided crucial support for the guerrillas. The importance of cities in these revolutions is related to the fact that the countries were highly urbanized. Thus, revolutionary potential exists where resources are controlled and where the bulk of the population is located. Given the rapid urban growth and limited resources in developing countries, it is possible that the world may be entering "the age of urban revolutions" (Gugler 1988).

Warfare
Several definitions of war have been proposed (Reyna 1994). Is it open and declared conflict between two political units? This definition would rule out, for example, the America-Vietnam War because it was undeclared. Is it simply organized aggression? This definition is too broad since not all organized violence can be considered warfare. Perhaps the best definition is that **war** is "organized, purposeful group action, directed against another group...involving the actual or potential application of lethal force" (Ferguson 1994, quoted in Reyna 1994:30). A critical point is that lethal force during war is legal if it is conducted according to the rules of battle (see the Critical Thinking box on page 280).

Cultural variation exists in the frequency and seriousness of wars. Intergroup conflicts between different bands of foragers are relatively rare. More often, they involve conflicts between individuals belonging to different groups, not group conflicts per se. Conflicts are usually fought out person-to-person, either with words or fists. The informal, nonhierarchical political organization among bands is not conducive to waging armed conflict. Bands do not have specialized military forces or leaders.

Archaeological evidence indicates that warfare emerged and intensified during the neolithic era. Plant and animal domestication required more extensive land use, and it was accompanied by increased population densities. The combined economic and demographic pressures put more and larger groups in more direct and more intense competition with each other. Tribal leadership patterns facilitate mobilization of warrior groups for raids, but not all tribes have equal levels of warfare.

Many chiefdoms are characterized by relatively high rates of warfare and casualty rates. They have increased capacity for war in terms of personnel and surplus foods to support long-range expeditions. In many chiefdoms, the chief could call on his or her retainers as a specialized fighting force as well as general members of society. Chiefs and paramount chiefs could be organized into more effective command structures (Reyna 1994:44–45). These levels of aggregation and potential for more extensive and massive campaigns continued to expand as chiefdoms and confederacies evolved into state-level organizations. In states, standing armies and complex military hierarchies are supported by the increased material resources under the control of leaders through taxation and other forms of revenue generation. Greater state power allows for more powerful and effective military structures, which in turn increase the state's power; thus, a mutually reinforcing relationship emerges between the military and the state.

Examining the causes of war between states has occupied scholars in many fields for centuries. Some experts point to common, underlying causes, such as attempts to extend boundaries, secure more resources, ensure markets, support political and economic allies, and resist aggression from other states. Others point to humanitarian concerns that prompt participation in "good wars," to defend values such as freedom or to protect human rights as defined in one nation and being violated in another. Experts also study the immediate causes of the war—the catalyst—such as the assassination of Archduke Ferdinand in sparking World War I.

Thomas Barfield (1994b) compared wars in Afghanistan since the seventeenth century. Warfare increasingly became a way for kings to justify their power in terms of the necessity to maintain independence from outside forces such as the British and Czarist Russia (Barfield 1994b). The last king was murdered in a coup in 1978. When the then Soviet Union invaded in 1979, there was no centralized ruling group to meet it. The Soviet Union deposed the ruling faction and replaced it with one of their own and "then engaged in a wholesale war against the population. Three million Afghans fled to Pakistan and Iran, over one million were killed, millions of others were displaced internally" (7). Yet, in spite of having no central command, divided by ethnic and sectarian differences, and outmatched in equipment by Soviet forces, a war of resistance eventually wore down the Soviets, who withdrew in 1989. Subsequently, in 2001 and 2002, the United States with its allies deposed another Afghan government, the Taliban, in the aftermath of the destruction of the World Trade Center towers in New York City.

The case of Afghanistan suggests that war was a more effective tool of domination in the premodern period when war settled matters more definitively. "The number of troops needed after a conquest were relatively few because they were not expected to have to put down continual internal revolts, but to defend the new conquest from rival outsiders" (7). Success in the Soviet Union's attempt to hold Afghanistan would have required more extensive involvement and commitment, including introduction of a new political ideology or economic structure that would win the population over, population transfer to remove opposition, and immigration of allies into the area. Barfield notes that in contemporary times, "winning battles or wars becomes only the first stage in a much more complicated process with no guarantees of ultimate success" (10). His findings thus point us in new directions of research and analysis concerning state-to-state conflict.

Nonviolent Conflict Mohandas K. Gandhi was one of the greatest designers of strategies for bringing about peaceful political change. Born in India, he was married at the age of 12, and then began to study law in London when he was 19 years old (Caplan 1987). After his studies, he went to South Africa, where he worked as a lawyer, serving the Indian community. He became active in organizing the Indians to protest racial injustices. In South Africa, he evolved his primary method of civil disobedience through nonviolent resistance. The two basic tenets of Gandhi's approach are the Hindu ethic of *ahimsa* (nonviolence) and the concept of *satyagraha* (truth force). In 1915, he returned to India, joined the nationalist struggle against British colonialism, and put into action his model of civil disobedience through nonviolent resistance, public fasting, and strikes, characterized in Gandhian politics by mass prayer and fasting.

Warfare between Europeans and First Nations Peoples

In the seventeenth and eighteenth centuries in northeastern North America, several incidents of warfare occurred between the advancing European colonials or frontiersmen and groups of First Nations peoples. Warfare is a cultural phenomenon no less influenced by rules of behaviour than other cultural events. At the time of this particular conflict, Europeans had codes of behaviour during warfare different from those of the First Nations people.

Thomas Abler, an anthropologist at the University of Waterloo, compares First Nations incidents of scalping, torture, and cannibalism to the European incidents of rape during warfare (1992). He argues that many groups of First Nations people in warfare took scalps from dead enemies and displayed them on return to camp. Europeans interpreted this behaviour as deviant or strange, although it was common practice in Europe at the time to display heads of enemies on pikes or poles. Abler notes that by the end of the seventeenth century, European frontiersmen were taking and displaying native scalps, and European colonial governments were paying for them. For First Nations peoples, scalps played important roles in ritual events after the battle. To participate in colonial payment schemes, they divided a scalp in two, one part for the cash reward, the second for ritual events.

The other feature of warfare that disturbed Europeans was the torture and cannibalism of captives in war performed by First Nations peoples throughout the northeast. Of course, Europeans tortured captives, but this was done to exact confessions and as part of an execution process. Moreover, in Europe it was done by professionals in front of spectators as a form of entertainment. In the First Nations groups, all members of a community participated in the torture, which could last all night until the captive died. Then the body was typically dismembered and parts of it were eaten perhaps to obtain the essence of the enemy's power.

Not found in First Nations groups but common among Europeans at war was the practice of raping women. Abler gives evidence that many Europeans, both men and women, reported that captive women were never raped by First Nations warriors, although European men regularly raped First Nations women who were captured in war. While the Europeans adopted scalping, they did not adopt cannibalism, while First Nations in the northeast never adopted rape in warfare. "The failure of such practices to cross cultural boundaries allows each side to view the actions of the other with horror and to classify enemy behaviour as barbaric" (15).

CRITICAL THINKING QUESTIONS

Looking at warfare from a critical thinking perspective, consider what aspects of warfare are universal.

How do societies try to put limits on the excesses of war? How successful do you think these attempts are?

How would a cultural anthropologist study contemporary warfare?

Celibacy is another key feature of Gandhian philosophy because avoiding sex helps maintain one's inner strength and purity. Regardless of whether one agrees with Gandhi's approach to food and sex, it is clear that the methods he developed of nonviolent civil disobedience have had a profound impact on the world. Martin Luther King, Jr., and his followers adopted many of Gandhi's tactics during the Civil Rights Movement in the United States, as did members of the Peace Movement of the 1960s and 1970s in the United States and the Environmental Movement of the 1990s in North America.

Political scientist James Scott (1985) used the phrase "weapons of the weak" as the title of his book on rural people's resistance to domination by landlords and government through tactics other than outright rebellion or revolution. Most subordinate classes throughout history have not had the "luxury" of open, organized political activity because of its danger. Instead, people have had to resort to ways of living with or "working" the system. Everyday forms of resistance include "foot dragging," desertion, false compliance, feigned ignorance, and slander, as well as more aggressive acts such as theft, arson,

Mahatma Ghandi (left), leader of the Indian movement for freedom from British colonial control, on his famous "Salt March" of 1930, in which he led a procession to the sea to collect salt in defiance of British law. He is accompanied by Sarojini Naidu, a noted freedom fighter.

and sabotage. Many contemporary anthropologists have followed Scott's lead and contributed groundbreaking studies of everyday resistance.

Maintaining World Order

Computer-operated war missiles, e-mail, faxes, satellite television, and jet flights mean that the world's nations are more closely connected and able to influence each other's fate than ever before. Modern weaponry means that such influences can be even more lethal. In the face of these geopolitical realities, politicians, academics, and the pub-

lic ponder the possibilities for world peace. Anthropological research on peaceful, local-level societies shows that humans are capable of living together in peace. The question is: Can people living in larger groups that are globally connected also live in peace? Numerous attempts have been made, over time, to create institutions to promote world peace, of which the United Nations is the most established and respected. One of the United Nation's significant accomplishments was the creation of a world court, the International Court of Justice, which is located at the Hague in Holland (Nader 1995). In 1946, two-thirds of the Court's judges were American or Western European. Now the Court has many judges from developing countries and more sympathy for such nations. Despite this more balanced representation from a wide range of countries, there has been a decline in use of the International Court of Justice and an increased use of international negotiating teams for resolving disputes between nations. Laura Nader analyzed this decline and found that it follows a trend in the United States beginning in the 1970s to promote "alternate dispute resolution" (ADR). The goal was to move more cases out of the courts and to privatize dispute resolution. In principle, ADR seems a more peaceful and more dignified option. Deeper analysis of actual cases and their resolution shows, however, that this bilateral process tends to favour the stronger party. Nader looked at several cases of international river disputes. In each example, adjudication (formal decree by a judge) would have resulted in a better deal for the weaker party than bilateral negotiation did. Overall, less powerful nations are being negatively affected by the trend to move away from using the International Court of Justice.

Is it possible that cultural anthropologists have the capacity to be involved in peace-keeping organizations? Robert Carneiro (1994) has a pessimistic response. During the long history of human political evolution from bands to states, Carneiro says that warfare has been the major means by which political units enlarged their power and domain. Foreseeing no logical end to this process, he predicts that war will follow war until superstates become ever larger and one megastate is the final result. He also considers the United Nations powerless in dealing with the principal obstacle to world peace, which is national sovereignty interests.

If the belief exists that war is inevitable, that leaves little room for hope that anthropological knowledge might be applied to peace-making efforts. Despite Carneiro's views, cultural anthropologists have shown that war is not a cultural universal, and that different cultures have ways of solving disputes without resorting to killing. The cultural anthropological perspective of critical cultural relativism (review this concept, Chapter 1) can provide useful background on issues of conflict and prompt a deeper dialogue between parties.

One positive point emerges with regard to the possibility of world peace. The United Nations does provide an arena for airing disputes. A more optimistic view suggests that international peace organizations play a major role in providing analysis of the interrelationships among world problems and helping others see the causes of violence (Vickers 1993:132). In addition, some people see hope for local and global peacemaking through nongovernmental organizations (NGOs) and local grassroots initiatives that seek to bridge group interests, such as the Joint Palestinian/Israeli Women's Coordinating Committee.

What do political and legal anthropology cover?

Political anthropology is the study of power relationships in the public domain and how they vary and change cross-culturally. Political anthropologists study the concept of power, as well as related concepts such as authority and influence. They have discovered differences and similarities between politics and political organization in small-scale societies and large-scale societies as they looked at issues such as leadership roles and responsibilities, the social distribution of power, and the emergence of the state. Legal anthropology encompasses the study of cultural variation in social order and social conflict. Legal anthropologists are increasingly examining how legal systems change. Global colonialism and contemporary globalization have changed indigenous systems of social control and law, often resulting in legal pluralism.

ferent villages. Chiefdoms may include several thousand people. Rank is inherited and social divisions exist between the chiefly lineage or lineages and non-chiefly groups. A state is a centralized political unit encompassing many communities and possessing coercive power. A wide variety of types of legal specialists is more frequently associated with the state than with small-scale societies in which social shaming and shunning are common methods of punishment. States arose in several locations with the emergence of intensive agriculture, increased surpluses, and increased population density. Most states are hierarchical and patriarchal. In states, imprisonment and capital punishment may exist, reflecting the greater power of the state. Strategies for building nationalism include imposition of one language as "the" national language, monuments, museums, songs, poetry, and other media-relayed messages about the "motherland." Ethnic/national politics have emerged within and across states as groups compete for either increased rights within the state or autonomy from it.

What are the major cross-cultural forms of political organization and social order?

Patterns of political organization and leadership vary according to mode of production and global economic relationships. Foragers have a minimal form of leadership and political organization in the band. Band membership is flexible. If a band member has a serious disagreement with another person or a spouse, one option is to leave that band and join another. Social control in small-scale societies seeks to restore order more than to punish offenders. Leadership in bands is informal. A tribe is a more formal type of political organization than the band. A tribe comprises several bands or lineage groups, with a headman or headwoman as leader. Bigman political systems are an expanded form of tribe, with leaders having influence over people in several dif-

What are cross-cultural patterns of social conflict?

Cross-cultural data on levels and forms of conflict and violence indicate that high levels of lethal violence are not universal and are more associated with the state than earlier forms of political organization. Social conflict ranges from face-to-face conflicts, as among neighbours or domestic partners, to larger group conflicts between ethnic groups and states. Solutions that would be effective at the interpersonal level are often not applicable to large-scale, impersonalized conflict. Cultural anthropologists are turning their attention to studying global conflict and peace-keeping solutions. Key issues involve the role of cultural knowledge in dispute resolution and how international or local organizations can help achieve or maintain peace.

Core Concepts

authority, p. 260
band, p. 262
big-man system, p. 264
chiefdom, p. 265
clan, p. 263

critical legal anthropology, p. 271
factions, p. 269
feuding, p. 276
influence, p. 260
in-kind taxation, p. 267

law, p. 272
legal pluralism, p. 276
nation, p. 269
norms, p. 272
policing, p. 273
political organization, p. 262
politics, p. 260

power, p. 260
revolution, p. 278
segmentary model, p. 264
social control, p. 271
state, p. 266
trial by ordeal, p. 273
tribe, p. 263
war, p. 278

Suggested Readings

Mona Etienne and Eleanor Leacock, eds., *Women and Colonization: Anthropological Perspectives*. New York: Praeger, 1980. This classic collection examines the impact of Western colonialism and missionary intervention on women of several indigenous groups of North America, South America, Africa, and the Pacific.

Thomas Gregor, ed., *A Natural History of Peace*. Nashville: University of Tennessee Press, 1996. This book contains essays on "What is Peace," reconciliation among non human primates, the psychological bases of violent and caring societies, community-level studies on Amazonia and Native America, and issues of peace and violence between states.

Phillip Gulliver, *Disputes and Negotiations: A Cross-Cultural Perspective*. New York: Academic Press, 1979. This classic analysis shows how the issues and behaviour surrounding negotiation are similar in cultures that differ widely in values, rules, and cultural assumptions.

Carolyn Nordstrom and Antonius C. G. M. Robben, eds., *Fieldwork under Fire: Contemporary Studies of Violence and Survival*. Berkeley: University of California Press, 1995. After an introductory chapter that discusses general themes, several examples of fieldwork experiences in dangerous situations including Palestine, China, Sri Lanka, United States, Croatia, Guatemala, and Ireland are given.

Dan Rabinowitz, *Overlooking Nazareth: The Politics of Exclusion in Galilee*. New York: Cambridge University Press, 1997. This book presents an ethnographic study of Palestinian citizens in an Israeli new town. It examines specific situations of conflict and cooperation and provides wider theoretical insights about nationalism and ethnicity. Biographical accounts of three Palestinians—a medical doctor, a basketball coach, and a local politician—are included.

Bruce G. Trigger, *The Huron: Farmers of the North*. New York: Holt, Rinehart and Winston, 1969. This fascinating monograph combines archaeological, historical, linguistic, and ethnographic evidence on the Huron of southern Ontario.

Joan Vincent, *Anthropology and Politics: Visions, Traditions, and Trends*. Tucson: The University of Arizona Press, 1990. This text presents a definitive history of the emergence of political anthropology, with a detailed presentation of theories and findings through the late 1980s.

 Your *Cultural Anthropology,* Second Canadian Edition Media Edition CD-ROM contains many Web sites relevant to this chapter. Use it to explore the Web and to expand your knowledge of anthropology.

Chapter 12

Religion

CHAPTER OUTLINE

A Catholic procession during Easter week in Guatemala.

Key Questions

What is religion and what are the basic features of religions cross-culturally?

How do world religions reflect globalization and localization?

What are some important aspects of religious change in contemporary times?

When studying the religious life of people of rural northern Greece, anthropologist Loring Danforth observed rituals in which participants walk across several yards of burning coals (1989). They do not get burned, they say, because their faith and a saint protect them. Upon his return to the United States, Danforth met an American who regularly walks on fire as part of his New Age faith and also organizes training workshops for people who want to learn how to fire-walk. Danforth himself fire-walked in a ceremony in rural Maine. While not every anthropologist who studies religion undertakes such challenges during fieldwork, they all do share an interest in enduring questions about humanity's understanding of the supernatural realm and relationships with it, such as: Why do some religions have many gods and others just one? Why do some religions advocate animal sacrifice? Why do some religions give greater room for women's participation? How do different religions respond to changing conditions in the political economy?

Religion has been a cornerstone topic in cultural anthropology since its beginning. Over these many decades, a rich collection of material has accumulated. Early attention was focused on religions of nonstate societies. More recently, anthropologists devoted attention to the major religions of state-level societies. With increasing globalization and population movements, religious traditions are also moving and changing as they adapt to new cultural contexts.

What Is Religion?

Since the earliest days of anthropology, various definitions of religion have appeared. One of the simplest, offered by E. B. Tylor in the late 1800s, is that religion is the belief in spirits. The definition favoured by a cultural materialist approach is that **religion** is both beliefs and actions related to supernatural beings and forces (what Tylor referred to as "spirits"). In defining religion so that it fits the cross-cultural material, anthropologists avoid a narrow definition that says religion is the belief in a supreme deity. In many religions, no concept of a supreme deity exists, while others have multiple deities. Religion is related to but not the same as a people's **world view**, or way of understanding how the world came to be, its design, and their place in it. World view is a broader concept and does not include the criterion of concern with

a supernatural realm. An atheist has a world view, but not a religious one.

Magic versus Religion

In the late 1800s, Tylor wrote that magic, religion, and science are alike in that they are different ways people have tried to explain the physical world and events in it. For Tylor, the three systems were contradictory and incompatible. Tylor thought that magical laws were false and scientific laws were true, and that religion is based on the false assumption that the world operates under the control of supernaturals. James Frazer followed many of Tylor's ideas. He defined **magic** as the attempt to compel supernatural forces and beings to act in certain ways, in contrast to religion, which is the attempt to please supernatural forces or beings. After reviewing many practices cross-culturally that he considered to be magical, Frazer deduced two general principles of magic that correspond to two major categories of magic. First is the "law of similarity," the basis of what he called "imitative magic." It is founded on the assumption that if person or item X is like person or item Y, then actions done to person or item X will affect person or item Y. The most well-known example is a voodoo doll. By sticking pins into doll X that represents person Y, then person Y will experience pain or suffering. The second is the "law of contagion," which is the basis for "contagious magic." The law of contagion says that persons or things once in contact with a person can still have an effect on that person. Common items for working contagious magic are a person's hair trimmings; nail clippings; teeth; spit or blood or fecal matter left carelessly beside a pathway; or the placenta of a baby. In cultures where contagious magic is practised, people are careful about disposing of their personal wastes so that no one else can get hold of them.

Early scholars of religion supported an evolutionary model, with magic as the predecessor of religion. They evaluated magic as less spiritual and ethical than religion and therefore more "primitive." They assumed that, in time, magic would be completely replaced by the "higher" system of religion, and then ultimately by science as the most rational way of thinking. They would be surprised to see the widespread presence of magic in the modern world as evidenced, for example, by a recent ethnographic study of magic and witchcraft in contemporary London (Luhrmann 1989). In fact, magic exists in all cultures. In different situations, people turn to magic, religion, or science. For example, magic is prominent in sports (Gmelch 1997 [1971]). Professional baseball players repeat actions or use charms (including a special shirt or hat) to help them win on the assumption that if it worked before, it may work again. They are following Tylor's law of contagion. Such magical thinking is most common in contexts where uncertainty is greatest. In baseball, pitching and hitting involve more uncertainty than fielding, and pitchers and hitters are more likely to use magic. Besides sports, magical practices are prominent in farming, fishing, the military, and love. Thus, we can no longer accept an evolutionary model by which religion has replaced magic, since magic is still widely practised. In a similar fashion, one cannot argue that science has replaced religion.

Theories of the Origin of Religion

Why did religion come into being? The universal existence of some form of religion has prompted many theorists to adopt a functionalist approach. According to this view, religion provides ways of explaining and coping with universal "imponderables of life" such as birth, illness, misfortune, and death.

Tylor's theory, as proposed in his book *Primitive Culture* (1871), was based on his assumption that early people had a need for explanation, especially for the difference between the living and the dead. They therefore developed the concept of a soul that exists in all living things and departs from the body after death. Tylor named this way of thinking **animism,** the belief in souls or "doubles." Eventually, Tylor speculated, the concept of the soul became personified until, later, human-like deities were conceived. For Tylor, religion evolved from animism to **polytheism** (the belief in many deities) to **monotheism** (the belief in one supreme deity). According to Tylor's definition of animism, beliefs in this category have not become extinct. They still exist in beliefs about angels and visitations of the dead and the New Age religious use of crystals (Stringer 1999). In contrast to Tylor, Frazer suggested that religion developed out of the failure of magic. Neither scholar suggested a place or time period during which these developments may have occurred, and both based their theories on speculation rather than archaeological or other empirical data.

Later, Émile Durkheim offered a functional explanation for how and why religion emerged in his book *The Elementary Forms of the Religious Life* (1966 [1895]). He reviewed ethnographic data on "primitive" religions cross-culturally and was struck by their social aspects: Durkheim speculated that early humans realized, through clan gatherings, that contact with one another made them feel uplifted and powerful. This positive feeling, arising from social solidarity, became attached to the clan totem, an emblem of their group that became the first of many future objects of worship. Religion therefore originated to serve society by giving it cohesion through shared symbols and group rituals.

Durkheim's focus on social solidarity represents a functional approach to religion in which religious beliefs and practices are interpreted as serving roles other than purely religious ones. Malinowski documented its psychological functions, writing about how rituals help reduce anxiety and uncertainty. Marx, taking a class conflict approach rather than a functional one, emphasized religion's political and economic role in being an "opium of the people" and supporting oppressive power structures. By this phrase, Marx meant that religion provides a superficial form of comfort to the poor, masking the harsh realities of class inequality and thereby preventing uprisings of the poor against the rich.

A third major theoretical theme, "symbolic analysis," informs Freud's theory of the role of the unconscious. Many anthropologists agree with Freud that religion is a "projective system" that expresses people's unconscious thoughts, wishes, and worries. Anthropologists have also applied Freudian analysis of symbols and their underlying or hidden meanings in dreams to the analysis of myths.

A fourth major theoretical theme, which can be seen to combine Durkheimian functionalism with symbolic analysis, comes from Clifford Geertz (1966), who proposed in his early writings that religions are primarily systems of meaning. In this view, religion offers a conception of reality, "a model of life," and a pattern for how to live, a "model for life."

Varieties of Religious Beliefs

Religions comprise beliefs and behaviour. Scholars of religion generally address belief systems first since they appear to inform patterns of religious behaviour. Religious beliefs tend to be shared by a group, sometimes by very large numbers of people. Through the centuries, people have found ways to give their beliefs permanence. Elders teach children the group's songs and tales, artists paint the stories on rocks and walls, and sculptors create images in wood and stone that depict aspects of religious belief.

In this section, we consider cross-cultural variation in religious beliefs. We discuss major forms in which religious beliefs are transmitted from one generation to the next. We then review a range of beliefs about supernatural beings.

How Beliefs Are Expressed

Beliefs are expressed and transferred over the generations in two main formats: **myth**, narrative stories about supernatural forces or beings, and **doctrine**, direct and formalized statements about religious beliefs.

Myth A myth is a narrative that has a plot with a beginning, middle, and end. The plot may involve recurrent motifs, the smallest units of narrative. Myths convey messages about the supernaturals indirectly, through the medium of the story itself, rather than by using logic or formal argument. Greek and Roman myths, such as the stories of Zeus, Athena, Orpheus, and Persephone, are world-famous. Some people would say that the Bible is a collection of mythology; others would object to that categorization as it suggests that the stories are not "real" or "sacred."

Myths are distinguished from folktales, which are largely secular stories, although borderline cases exist. For example, some people would classify "Cinderella" as a folktale, while others would quickly point out that the fairy godmother is not an ordinary human and so "Cinderella" should be considered a myth. These arguments are more entertaining than important.

In earliest times, myths were part of people's oral tradition. Only with the emergence of writing were these stories recorded, and then only if they were of great importance, perhaps part of a royal or priestly tradition. Many of the world's myths, especially their local variants, are still unwritten.

Anthropologists have asked why myths exist. The functionalist explanation is that myths help to maintain the society itself. Malinowski says that a myth is a "charter" for society in that it expresses core beliefs and teaches morality. French anthropologist Claude Lévi-Strauss,

probably the most famous mythologist, says that myths are tribal peoples' form of philosophy, their way of explaining the world. The philosophical message does not lie on the surface of the myths. It is embedded in their underlying structure and the symbolism of key characters and events. Human beings, he says, think in terms of binary classification. He finds binary oppositions as the basic structure of all myths—for example nature versus culture, life versus death, raw versus cooked food, wild versus tame animals, and incest versus exogamy. Such oppositions are philosophically uncomfortable for people to face—for example, the fact that life cannot exist without death. Myths help people deal with the deep puzzles and discomforts of life by presenting the oppositions along with a third position that mediates between the two extremes and provides a solution. For example, many Pueblo Indian myths juxtapose grass-eating animals (vegetarians) with predators (carnivores). The mediating third character is the raven, who is a carnivore but, unlike other creatures, does not have to kill to eat meat because it is a scavenger.

Epics tend to be longer than myths and focus more on heroic traditions. Many epics are firmly associated with particular ethnic groups or nations, such as the *Odyssey* and the *Iliad* of Greece. Less well-known in North America are India's two great Hindu epics, the *Mahabharata* and the *Ramayana*. Iceland's *eddas* of the thirteenth century are grouped into two categories: mythic (dealing with gods) and heroic (dealing with humans).

Doctrine Doctrine, the other major form in which beliefs are expressed, explicitly defines the supernaturals—who they are, what they do, and how to relate to them through religious practice; the world and how it came to be; and people's roles in relation to the supernaturals and to other humans. Doctrine, which is written and formal, is close to law in some respects because it makes direct links between incorrect beliefs and behaviours and the punishments for each. Many religious scriptures incorporate both myth and doctrine.

Doctrine is more common in institutionalized, large-scale religions than with localized, small-scale "folk" religions. Thus, the major world religions discussed later in this chapter all have established doctrine to which followers should adhere. Doctrine, however, can and does change (J. Bowen 1998:38–40). Over the centuries, various popes have pronounced new doctrine for the Catholic church. A papal declaration of 1854, given with

A stone sculpture at Mamallapuram, South India, dating from the eighth to ninth centuries, depicts the impending triumph of the goddess Durga (riding the lion, on the left) over the bull-headed demon. The story of her creation by the gods and her ultimate saving of the world through the killing of the demon has inspired countless works of art in India.

ture believe in their existence. Supernaturals range from impersonal forces to those that look just like humans. Supernaturals can be supreme and all-powerful creators or smaller-scale, annoying spirits that take up residence in people through "possession."

Animatism refers to belief systems in which the supernatural is conceived of as an impersonal power. A well-known example is *mana*, a concept widespread throughout the Melanesian region of the South Pacific. Mana is a force outside nature that works automatically; it is neither spirit nor deity. It manifests itself in objects and people and is associated with personal status and power since some people accumulate more of it than others. Some supernaturals are **zoomorphic** (deities that appear in the shape, or partial shape, of animals). No satisfactory theory has appeared to explain why some religions develop zoomorphic deities, and for what purposes, and why others do not. Religions of classical Greece and Rome, and ancient and contemporary Hinduism are especially rich in zoomorphic supernaturals.

Anthropomorphic supernaturals (deities in the form of humans) are common, but not universal. Allah, the supreme deity of Islam, is not anthropomorphized and can be represented only in the form of writing the name Allah. The human tendency to perceive of supernaturals in their own form was noted 2500 years ago by the Greek philosopher Xenophanes (who lived sometime between 570 and 470 BCE). He said: "If cattle and horses, or lions, had hands, or were able to draw with their feet and produce the worlds which men do, horses would draw the forms of gods like horses, and cattle like cattle, and they would make the gods' bodies the same shape as their own" (*Fragments* 15). But why some religions do and others do not have anthropomorphic deities is another question that is impossible to answer. Such deities are more common in sedentary societies than among foragers.

the intent of reinvigorating European Catholicism, gave authenticity to the concept of the Immaculate Conception, an idea with substantial popular support.

Muslim doctrine is expressed in the Qur'an, the basic holy text of the Islamic faith that consists of revelations made to the prophet Muhammed in the seventh century, and the *hadith*, collections of Muhammed's statements and deeds (J. Bowen 1998:38). In Kuala Lumpur, Malaysia, a small group of highly educated women called the Sisters in Islam regularly debate with members of the local *ulama* (male religious authorities who are responsible for interpreting Islamic doctrine especially concerning families, education, and commercial affairs) (Ong 1995). In recent years, the debates have concerned such issues as polygamy, divorce, women's work roles, and women's clothing.

Beliefs about Supernatural Forces and Beings

In all cultures, some concept of otherworldly beings or forces exists, even though not all members of the cul-

Anthropomorphic supernaturals, like humans, can be moved by praise, flattery, and gifts. They can be tricked. They have emotions: They get irked if neglected, they can be loving and caring, or they can be distant and unresponsive. Most anthropomorphic supernaturals are adults. Few are very old or very young. Humans and supernaturals have similar marital and sexual patterns. Divine marriages tend to be heterosexual. In societies where polygyny occurs, male gods also have multiple wives. Deities have sexual intercourse, within marriage and sometimes extramaritally. Gods of the Greek and Roman pantheon, the entire collection of deities, often descended to earth and kidnapped and raped human women. So far, however, legal divorce has not occurred among supernaturals, although separations have. While many supernaturals have children, grandchildren are not prominent.

In pantheons, a division of labour exists by which certain supernaturals are responsible for particular domains. This greater specialization among the supernaturals reflects the greater specialization in human society. There may be a deity of forests, rivers, the sky, wind and rain, agriculture, childbirth, disease, warfare, and marital happiness. Some gods are more effective for material wealth and others for academic success. The supernaturals have political roles and hierarchies. High gods, like Jupiter and Juno of classical Roman religion, are distant from humans and hard to contact. The more approachable deities are below them on the hierarchy. Next, one finds a miscellaneous collectivity of spirits, good and bad, often unnamed and uncounted, in the lowest tier. This discussion clearly applies to polytheistic religions, but it is also relevant to monotheistic religions, such as Islam and Catholicism, that incorporate lesser supernaturals such as saints (See the Multiple Cultural Worlds box).

Deceased ancestors can also be supernaturals. In some religions, spirits of the dead can be prayed to for help, and in turn they may require respect and honour from the living (J. Smith 1995:46). Many African, Asian, and First Nations religions have a cult of the ancestors, as did religions of ancient Mesopotamia, Greece, and Rome. In contemporary Japan, ancestor veneration is the principal religious activity of many families. Three national holidays recognize the importance of the ancestors: the annual summer visit of the dead to their home and the visits by the living to graves during the two equinoxes.

MULTIPLE CULTURAL WORLDS

The Blessed Kateri Tekakwitha: A "Saint" for All First Nations Peoples

Kateri Tekakwitha was a Mohawk First Nations woman born in upstate New York in 1656. She was converted to Christianity by the French Jesuit missionaries in 1676 at the age of 20 and moved to the Jesuit mission at Kahnawake near Montreal. Under the influence of the Jesuits, Kateri took a vow of virginity and practised extreme austerities such as flagellations, branding, exposure, and fasting (Holmes 2001:89). She died after only two years at the mission, but her piety was celebrated by the Jesuits who reported she died calling out "Jesus! Mary! I love you!" Pope John Paul II beatified her in 1980. Many First Nations people hoped the Pope would canonize her on his visit to Toronto in 2002, but this did not happen.

Her devotees are found among many First Nations converts to Roman Catholicism all over North America. Holmes reports that knowledge about her reached the Navajo and Pueblo of the Southwest United States in the 1930s. For these people, Kateri represents hope for unity among all First Nations people in North America. One Pueblo person reported that Kateri's deathbed words were "You must gather people from all different places and start having conferences." Another claimed she said "The Catholic way and the Native American way can just build [together]" (96). Kateri has come to represent unity between the "Indian" way and the "Catholic" way and, moreover, unity among "her" people, that is, all the First Nations people of North America (94). For many of "her" people, she is already a saint.

FOOD FOR THOUGHT

Can you think of another important religious figure that unites a particular group of people?

Andy Fernando, "The First Salmon Ceremony"

Andy Fernando is the former chairman of the Upper Skagit Tribal Community in the state of Washington. The following description of the First Salmon ceremony originally appeared in an essay he wrote as an introduction to a book about Northwest Coast Indian fishing rights.

During the long winter months, Indian families mostly remained indoors in their great cedar longhouses…Fresh food, particularly their staple diet of salmon, was scarce…But in those spring months king salmon would return to the river…The entire village would gather together and appoint fishermen to each catch one salmon—no more.

In fine regalia, accompanied by a fanfare of deerskin drum and special village songs, the first salmon caught would be carried from the riverbank…A village leader, or shaman, would carefully clean and save the salmon's entrails, then carve away the meat until a carcass of head, bones, and tail was left, still connected. The entrails would be placed in the skeleton, and the framework of bones…laid on a mat of fresh, spring-green ferns. Meanwhile, the villagers would have raised a fire…When the salmon was cooked, everyone would gather to eat…In the end, the headmen would lift the fern mat cradling the remains of the

salmon, and, followed by the villagers, walk to the riverbank…Placing the fern mat on the water, with the salmon's head pointed downstream, the headman would release the mat to float on the river toward the sea.

Source: Andy Fernando, in *Native Heritage: Personal Accounts by American Indians 1790 to the Present*, Arlene Hirschfelder, ed. New York: MacMillan,1995, pp. 222–224.

FOOD FOR THOUGHT

What is a seasonal ritual that is important to a religion in your cultural experience? What happens at the ritual?

Important ancestors sometimes evolved into deities with wide popularity.

Beliefs in Action: Ritual Practices

Ritual refers to patterned forms of behaviour. Religious rituals have to do with the supernatural realm. Many rituals are the enactment of beliefs expressed in myth and doctrine, such as the Christian ritual of communion. There are also secular rituals such as a sorority or fraternity initiation or a common-law wedding, all patterned forms of behaviour with no connection to the supernatural realm. It is not always easy to distinguish a religious ritual from a secular ritual. Consider the holiday of Thanksgiving, which originated as a sacred meal, with its primary purpose to give thanks to God for the first fruits of the harvest. Today, its original Christian meaning is not maintained by everyone who celebrates this holiday with a special meal of a roasted turkey.

Anthropologists and scholars of religion have categorized rituals in many ways. One division is based on how regularly the ritual is performed. Regularly performed rituals are called *periodic rituals*. Many periodic rit-

uals are performed annually to mark a seasonal event like planting or harvesting, or to commemorate some important event. For example, an important periodic ritual in Buddhism, Visakha Puja, or Buddha's Day, commemorates the birth, enlightenment, and death of the Buddha (all on one day!). On this day, Buddhists gather at monasteries, hear sermons about the Buddha, and perform rituals such as pouring water over images of the Buddha. Calendrical events such as the shortest or longest day of the year, or the new moon or full moon, often shape ritual cycles. Nonperiodic rituals, in contrast, occur irregularly, at unpredictable times, in response to unscheduled events such as a drought or flood, or to events in a person's life, such as illness, infertility, birth, marriage, or death.

Life-Cycle Rituals

Belgian anthropologist Arnold van Gennep (1960 [1908]) first proposed the category of life-cycle rituals in 1908. **Life-cycle rituals,** or rites of passage, mark a change in status from one life stage to another of an individual or group. Victor Turner's (1969) fieldwork among the Ndembu, horticulturalists of Zambia, provided insights about the phases of life-cycle rituals. Among the Ndembu, and cross-culturally, life-cycle rituals have three phases:

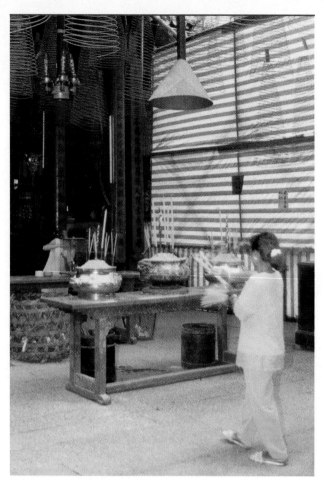

A woman praying at a Buddhist pagoda in Ho Chi Minh City, Vietnam, is dwarfed by spiralled hanging incense. The temple is dedicated to Me Sanh, a fertility goddess. Both men and women, but especially women, come here to pray for children.

son for the new status. Reintegration, the last stage, occurs when the initiate emerges and is welcomed by the community in the new status.

How can we explain variations in the occurrence and amplification of such rituals? Here is an example of explanation related to the mode of reproduction. Ritual marking of a baby's entry into society as a human is a common practice, but it varies in terms of how soon after birth the ceremony is done. Where infant mortality rates are high, the ceremony tends to be done late, when the baby is a year old or older. Until the ceremony has been performed, the baby is not named and is not considered "human." This timing may be a way of ensuring that the baby has gotten through the most dangerous period and is likely to survive.

Differences in the distribution of puberty rituals for boys and girls have been interpreted as reflecting the

An Apache girl's puberty ceremony. Cross-cultural research indicates that the celebration of girls' puberty is more likely to occur in cultures in which adult women have valued productive and reproductive roles.

separation, transition, and reintegration. In the first phase, the initiate (the person undergoing the ritual) is separated physically, socially, or symbolically from normal life. Special dress may mark the separation; for example, a long white gown for a baby that is to be baptized in a church. In many cultures of the Amazon and in East and West Africa, adolescents are secluded for several years in separate huts or areas away from the village. The transition phase, or the "liminal phase," is the time when the person is no longer in their previous status, but is not yet a member of the next stage. Liminality often involves the learning of specialized skills that will equip the per-value and status of males and females within society. Most societies have some form of puberty ceremony for boys, but puberty ceremonies for girls are less common. A cross-cultural analysis found that this difference is related to the mode of production and gender division of labour (J. K. Brown 1978). In societies where female labour is important and valued, girls have elaborate (and sometimes painful) puberty rites. Where their labour is not important, menarche is unmarked and there is no puberty ceremony. Female puberty rites function to socialize the female labour force. Girls going through initiations often receive training related to their expected adult economic roles. For example, among the Bembe of southern Africa, a girl learns to distinguish 30 or 40 different kinds of mushrooms and to know which ones are edible and which are poisonous.

Pilgrimage

Pilgrimage is round-trip travel to a sacred place or places for purposes of religious devotion or ritual. Prominent pilgrimage places are Varanasi in India (formerly called Banaras) for Hindus; Mecca in Saudi Arabia for Muslims; Bodh Gaya in India for Buddhists; Jerusalem in Israel for Jews, Christians, and Muslims; and Lourdes in France for Christians. Pilgrimage often involves hardship, with the implication that the more suffering that is involved, the more merit the pilgrim accumulates. Compared to a weekly trip to church or synagogue, pilgrimage removes a person further from everyday life, is more demanding, and is therefore potentially more transformative.

Victor Turner (1974) has applied his three sequences of life-cycle rituals to pilgrimage as well: the pilgrim first separates from everyday life, then enters the liminal stage during the actual pilgrimage, and finally returns to be reintegrated into society in a transformed state. Indeed, in many pilgrimage traditions, a person who has done certain pilgrimages gains enhanced public status, for example, the status of *haji* (someone who has done the *haj*, or pilgrimage to Mecca) in the Islamic faith.

Connections between myth and pilgrimage are strong. For example, in the Hindu goddess tradition, the story of Sati is the basis for the sanctity of four major and forty-six minor pilgrimage sites in India (Bhardwaj 1973). Because of an argument with her father over whether or not her husband Shiva was welcome at a big sacrifice her family was holding, the unhappy Sati committed suicide. When Shiva heard about her death, he was dis-

traught. He picked up her body and carried it over his shoulder as he wandered across India, grieving. Along the way, parts of her body fell to the ground. The places where they dropped became holy. Some of these include her tongue at Jwala Mukhi and her throat at Vaishno Devi, both in the Himalayas, and her genitals in the eastern state of Assam.

Pilgrimage, especially in India, may involve bathing in a sacred river or in a pond near a temple, or even in the ocean (A. Gold 1988). Flowing water is believed to have great powers of purification in the Hindu tradition. Many of India's most famous pilgrimage sites are located on rivers, such as Varanasi (Banaras), the most prominent place of Hindu pilgrimage, which is located on the Ganges River.

Rituals of Reversal

Some rituals involve an element of reversal, in which normal social roles and order are temporarily inverted. Scholars say these rituals allow for social "steam" to be let off temporarily and they also may provide a reminder about the propriety of normal, everyday roles and practices to which people must inevitably return once the ritual is over.

These rituals, called **rituals of reversal,** are common cross-culturally, with one of the most well-known in the West being carnival. Carnival is celebrated throughout the northern Mediterranean region, North and South America, and the Caribbean. It is a period of riotous celebration before the Christian fast of Lent (Counihan 1985). Carnival begins at different times in different places, but always ends at the same time on Mardi Gras (or Shrove Tuesday), the day before Lent begins. The word *carnival* is derived from Latin and means "flesh farewell," referring to Lent. In Bosa, a town in Sardinia, Italy, carnival involves several aspects of social role reversal and relaxing of usual social norms: "The discotheques extend their hours, and mothers allow their daughters to attend more often and longer than at other times of the year. Men and women play sexually, fondling and flirting with each other in the discotheques and masquerades that are totally illicit at other times of the year" (14). Carnival in Bosa has three major phases. The first is impromptu street theatre and masquerades that take place over several weeks, usually on Sundays. The theatrical skits are social critiques of current events and local

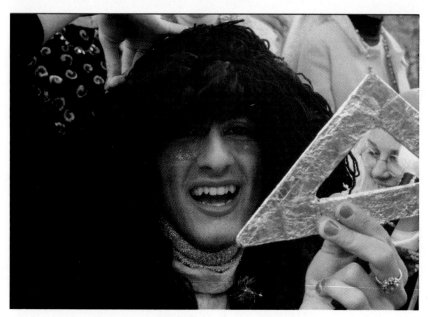

A young Bosan man dressed as an over-sexualized woman, one of the most common costumes in the carnival street-theatre masquerades in the Sardinian town of Bosa.

chant the word "Giolzi." They storm at people, pretending to search their bodies for *Giolzi* and then say "Got it!" It is not clear what *Giolzi* is, but whatever it is, it represents something that makes everyone happy. How does an anthropologist interpret these events? Carnival allows people to act out roles that are normally closed off to them, for a short time, before they have to go back to their normal positions. It also provides a time in which everyone has fun for a while. In this way, rituals of reversal can be seen to function as mechanisms of maintaining social order: After the allotted days of revelry, everyone returns to their original places for another year.

happenings. The masquerades mainly involve men dressing up as exaggerated women:

> *Young boys thrust their padded breasts forward with their hands while brassily hiking up their skirts to reveal their thighs.… A youth stuffs his shirt front with melons and holds them proudly out.… The high school gym teacher dresses as a nun and lifts up his habit to reveal suggestive red underwear. Two men wearing nothing but bikinis, wigs, and high heels feign a stripper's dance on a table top. (15)*

The second phase occurs during the morning of Mardi Gras when hundreds of Bosans, mostly men, dress in black like widows and flood the streets. They accost passersby, shaking in their faces dolls and other objects that are maimed in some way or bloodied. They shriek at the top of their lungs as if mourning, and they say, "Give us milk, milk for our babies.… They are dying, they are neglected, their mothers have been gallivanting since St. Anthony's Day and have abandoned their poor children" (16). The third phase, called *Giolzi,* takes place during the evening. Men and women dress in white, wearing sheets for cloaks and pillow cases for hoods. They blacken their faces. Rushing into the street, they hold hands and

Sacrifice

Many rituals involve some form of **sacrifice,** or offering of something for transference to the supernaturals. Sacrifice has a long history throughout the world and may be one of the oldest forms of ritual. It may involve the killing and offering of animals, or humans (offerings may be of a whole person, parts of a person's body, or blood), and the offering of vegetables, fruits, grains, flowers, or other products. One anthropologist has suggested that flowers are symbolic replacements for former animal sacrifices (Goody 1993).

Throughout the Aztec region of Mesoamerica, sacrifice (not just human sacrifice) has long been practised. State-level sacrifices were performed by trained priests, ostensibly to "feed" the gods on behalf of the welfare of the state. Apparently the gods were fond of human blood—as well as other items such as quails, crocodiles, jaguars, ducks, salamanders, and cakes made from the amaranth plant—because one of the most widely offered items for important events like a coronation or naming newborn babies was a limited amount of ritually induced bleeding. Symbolic anthropologists would accept the religious logic involved in pleasing the gods as a sufficient explanation for blood sacrifice. Cultural materialists would be inclined to propose an ecological explanation for the practice (see the Critical Thinking box on page 297).

Why Did the Aztecs Practise Human Sacrifice and Cannibalism?

Evidence of state-sponsored human sacrifice and cannibalism of the victims among the Aztecs of Mexico comes from accounts written by the Spanish conquistadors (Harris 1977; 1989; Sanday 1986). The Aztec gods required human sacrifice—they "ate" human hearts and "drank" human blood. Most of the victims were prisoners of war, but many others were slaves, and sometimes young men and women, and even children.

The victims were marched up the steep steps of the pyramid, held lying on their backs over a stone altar, and slit open in the chest by a priest, who wrenched out the heart (said to be still beating), which was then burned in offering to the gods. The body was rolled down the other side of the temple, where it was retrieved by butchers and prepared for cooking. The skull was returned to the temple area to be put on display racks. Although no one knows for sure how many victims were sacrificed over all, estimates are in the hundreds of thousands. At a single site, a chronicler reported that the display racks contained more than 100 000 skulls (Harris 1977:106). At one especially grand event, victims were arranged in four lines, each two miles long. Priests worked for four days to complete the sacrifices.

Human sacrifice and cannibalism of any scale might seem to invite the question "Why?" Certainly one must ask "why" about sacrifice and cannibalism as practised on the grand scale of the Aztecs. Of the many attempted explanations, two perspectives are compared here: an etic view and an emic view.

Michael Harner (1977) and Marvin Harris (1977; 1989) propose an etic explanation based on references to factors in the regional ecology and the politics of Aztec expansionism. The region of the Aztec empire lacked sufficient amounts of animal sources of protein to satisfy its growing population. While the ruling classes managed to maintain their supply of delicacies such as dog, turkey, duck, deer, rabbit, and fish, little was available for the poor. Yet the rulers needed to support and retain the loyalty of their army in order to protect and expand the empire's boundaries, and they needed to keep the masses happy. Providing the gods with human hearts and blood was a powerful statement of the empire's strength. It had the additional benefit of yielding huge amounts of meat for soldiers and commoners. Such "cannibal redistribution" could be manipulated by the state to reward particular groups and to compensate for periodic shortages in the agricultural cycle.

Peggy Sanday (1986) rejects the etic perspective and provides an emic one based on texts describing the Aztec people's own rationale and motives. Sacrifice and cannibalism, she says, followed religious logic and symbolism and were practised to satisfy the gods' hunger, not human hunger. Aztec religion says that the gods require certain sacrifices in order for the universe to continue to operate. Human flesh was not consumed as an "ordinary meal," but as part of a religious identification with the gods, just as people would wear the skins of sacrificed victims in order to participate in their sacredness. Sanday says that the etic explanation, in focusing on the "business" aspects of Aztec sacrifice and cannibalism, has missed the tradition's religious meaning for the Aztecs.

CRITICAL THINKING QUESTIONS

How do the etic and emic interpretations differ in the data they use?

Which theory do you find more convincing, and why?

Is there any other way to explain Aztec human sacrifice and cannibalism?

Religious Specialists

Not all rituals require the presence of a religious specialist, or someone with special and detailed training, but all require some level of knowledge on the part of the performer(s) about how to do them correctly. Even the daily, household veneration of an ancestor requires some knowledge gained through informal learning. At the other extreme, many rituals cannot be done without a highly trained specialist.

Shamans and Priests

General features of the categories of shaman and priest illustrate some key differences between these two types of specialists (as with all types, many specialists fit somewhere in between). Shamans or shamankas (the female form with the -ka ending derives from the original

Siberian usage) are part-time religious specialists who gain their status through direct relationships with the supernaturals, often by being "called." A potential shaman may be recognized by special signs, such as the ability to go into a trance. Anyone who demonstrates shamanic abilities can become a shaman; in other words, this is an openly available role. Shamans are more associated with pre-state societies, yet in many ways, faith healers and evangelists in North America could be considered to fit in this category. One of the most important functions of shamanic religious specialists is in healing, usually upon request from an afflicted individual, as described in Chapter 7 on medical anthropology.

In states, the more complex occupational specialization in religion means that there is a wider variety of types of specialists, especially what anthropologists refer to as "priests" (not the same as the specific modern role of the Catholic priest), and the development of religious hierarchies and power structures. The terms **priest** and **priestess** refer to a category of full-time religious specialists whose positions are based mainly on abilities gained through formal training. A priest may receive a divine call, but more often the role is hereditary, passed on through priestly lineages. In terms of ritual performance, shamans are more involved with nonperiodic rituals. Priests perform a wider range of rituals, including periodic state rituals. In contrast to shamans, who rarely have much secular power, priests and priestly lineages often do.

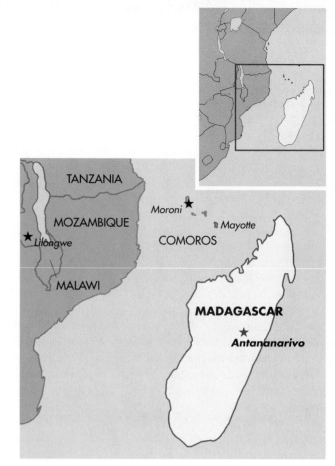

Other Specialists

Certain other specialized roles are widely found. Diviners are specialists who are able to discover the will and wishes of the supernaturals through techniques such as reading animal entrails. Palm readers and tarot card readers fit into the category of diviners. Prophets are specialists who convey divine revelations usually gained through visions or dreams. They often possess charisma (a specially attractive and powerful personality) and may be able to perform miracles. Prophets have founded new religions, some long-lasting and others short-lived. Witches use psychic powers and affect people through emotion and thought. Mainstream society often condemns witchcraft as negative. Some scholars of ancient and contemporary witchcraft differentiate between positive forms that involve healing and negative forms that seek to harm people.

Even in cases where witchcraft or sorcery is interpreted as negative, the intent or result is not always that clear. Michael Lambek, in a study of a community on Mayotte Island off the east coast of Africa, discussed the implications of interpreting a death being caused by sorcery (1993). A woman was suspected of stealing another woman's bracelet. In retaliation, the victim and her husband declared they would curse the thief if the bracelet was not returned. The bracelet was not returned and some time later the suspected thief died. Lambek notes that not all people in the community agreed with the idea that the curse caused the death. Moreover, this particular version of events developed years after the woman's death (388). Also, many in the community were not concerned with identifying the source of the sorcery for purposes of revenge. No one could be sure of the effects of such accusations (264).

World Religions

The term **world religions** was coined in the nineteenth century to refer to religions with many followers that crossed national borders and had a few other specific features, such as a concern with salvation (the belief that human beings require deliverance from an imperfect world). At first, the term referred only to Christianity, Islam, and Buddhism. It was later expanded to include Judaism, Hinduism, Confucianism, Taoism, and Shintoism. The category of world religions is even less appropriate now because many more religions cross national boundaries and therefore have "world" reach. Nonetheless, since college religion courses teach entire semesters of material on these "world religions," this chapter provides an anthropological perspective on five of them.

Cultural anthropologists emphasize that no world religion exists as a single monolithic entity, but rather each is composed of many variants such as regional and class variations, as well as doctrinal differences between reformist and fundamentalist interpretations. The five religions considered here are presented roughly in order of their age, although no one can say for sure whether Judaism or Hinduism predates the other. These five religions are discussed in terms of their general history, distribution, and teachings. Then examples are given of how they vary in different contexts to show how the same texts and teachings are localized.

Hinduism

Over 650 million people in the world are Hindus (Hiltebeitel 1995). The majority live in India, where Hinduism accounts for about 80 per cent of the population. The other 20 million, the Hindu diaspora, live in the United States, the United Kingdom, Canada, Malaysia, Fiji, Trinidad, Guyana, and Hong Kong. A Hindu is typically born a Hindu, and Hinduism does not actively seek converts. The four Vedas, composed in Sanskrit in northern India between 1200 and 900 BCE, are the core texts of Hinduism. Many other scholarly texts and popular myths and epics, especially the Mahabharata (the story of a war between two lineages, the Pandavas and the Kauravas) and the Ramayana (the story of king Rama and his wife Sita), also serve as unifying scriptures.

Throughout India, a multiplicity of local traditions exist, some of which carry forward elements from pre-Vedic times. Thus, Hinduism incorporates a diversity of ways to be a Hindu. It offers a rich polytheism and at the same time a philosophical tradition that reduces the multiplicity of deities into oneness. Deities range from simple stones (in Hinduism, stones can be gods) placed at the foot of a tree to elegantly carved and painted icons of gods such as Shiva, Vishnu, and the goddess Durga. Everyday worship of a deity involves lighting a lamp in front of the god, chanting hymns and mantras (sacred phrases), and taking *darshan* (sight of) the deity (Eck 1985). These acts bring blessings to the worshipper.

While certain standard features of Hinduism exist as noted above, acceptance of key texts and worship of important, well-known deities, many localized versions of Hinduism throughout India involve the worship of deities and practice of rituals unknown elsewhere. For example, fire-walking is an important part of goddess worship in southern and eastern India (J. Freeman 1981; Hiltebeitel 1988) and among some Hindu groups living outside India, notably Fiji (C. Brown 1984). Besides regional variations, caste differences in beliefs and practices even within the same area or village are marked. Lower-caste deities prefer offerings of meat sacrifices and alcohol, while upper-caste deities prefer offerings of flowers, rice, and fruit. Temple structures range from magnificent buildings to a simple canopy placed over the deity for shade. Yet the "unity in diversity" of Hinduism has long been recognized as real, mainly because of the shared acceptance of elements of Vedic thought.

Hindu Women and Karma in Great Britain

One of Hinduism's key concepts is that of *karma,* translated as destiny or fate. A person's karma is determined at birth on the basis of his or her previous life and how it was conducted. The karma concept has prompted many outsiders to judge Hindus as fatalistic, that is, lacking a sense of agency. But anthropological research on how people actually think about karma in their everyday lives reveals much individual variation from fatalism to a strong sense of being in charge of one's destiny. One study looked at women's perceptions of karma among Hindus living in Britain (Knott 1996). Some Hindu women are fatalistic in their attitudes and behaviour, while others are not. One woman who had a strongly fatalistic view of karma said:

[W]hen a baby's born...we have a ritual on the sixth day. That's when you name the baby, you know. And on that day, we believe the goddess comes and writes your future...we leave a blank white paper and a pen and we just leave it [overnight], and a pair of brand new clothes.... So I believe that my future—whatever happens—is what she has written for me. That tells me [that] I have to do what I can do, and if I have a mishap in between I have to accept that. (24)

Yet another woman said that her sufferings were caused by the irresponsibility of her father and the "bad husband" to whom she had been married. She challenged her karma and left her husband: "I could not accept the karma of being with Nirmal [her husband]. If I had done so, what would have become of my children?" (25). Since Hindu women's karma dictates being married and having children, leaving one's husband is a major act of resistance. For some young women informants, questioning the role of karma was the same as questioning their parents' authority. Such intergenerational conflicts create feelings of ambiguity and confusion.

Options for women seeking support for their struggle to sort out their roles can be either religious (praying more and fasting) or secular (seeking the advice of a psychological counsellor or social worker). Some Hindu women in Britain have themselves become counsellors and help support other women's independence and self-confidence. This work involves clear subversion of the traditional rules of karma for women.

Buddhism

Buddhism originated in a founding figure, Siddhartha Gautama (*c.* 566–486 BCE), revered as the Buddha or Awakened One (Eckel 1995:135). It began in northern India, where the Buddha grew up. From there, it spread throughout the subcontinent, into Inner Asia and China, to Sri Lanka and on to Southeast Asia. In the past 200 years, Buddhism has spread to Europe and North America. Buddhism's popularity subsequently faded in India, and Buddhists now constitute less than 1 per cent of India's population. Its global spread is matched by a great diversity of doctrine and practice, to the extent that it is difficult to point to a single essential feature (for example, no single text is accepted as authoritative for all forms of Buddhism), other than the importance of Gautama Buddha. Many Buddhists worship the Buddha

as a deity, while others do not—they honour his teachings and follow the pathway he suggested for reaching nirvana, or release from worldly life.

Buddhism first arose as a protest against certain features of Hinduism, especially caste inequality, yet it retained and revised several Hindu concepts such as karma. In Buddhism, everyone has the potential for achieving nirvana (enlightenment and the overcoming of human suffering in this life), the goal of Buddhism. Good deeds are one way to achieve a better rebirth with each incarnation until, finally, release from *samsara* (the cycle of birth, reincarnation, death, and so on) is achieved. Compassion towards others, including animals, is a key virtue. Branches of Buddhism have different texts that they consider their canon. The major division is between the Theravada Buddhism practised in Southeast Asia and the Mahayana Buddhism of Tibet, China, Taiwan, Korea, and Japan. Buddhism is associated with a strong tradition of monasticism through which monks and nuns renounce the everyday world and spend their lives meditating and doing good works. Buddhists have many and varied annual festivals and rituals. Some events bring pilgrims from around the world to India—to Sarnath, where the Buddha gave his first teaching, and Gaya, where he gained enlightenment.

Buddhism gained an established footing in Japan in the eighth century. The city of Nara was an important early centre of Buddhism. Here, the emperor sponsored the casting of a huge bronze statue of the Buddha, housed in the Todaiji, the "Great Eastern Temple."

Buddhism and Indigenous Spirits in Burma

One theory says that wherever Buddhism exists outside India, it is never the exclusive religion of the devotees because it arrived to find established religions already in place (Spiro 1967). In any particular context, Buddhism and the local traditions may have blended (such blending is called religious **syncretism**), both may coexist in a pluralistic fashion, or Buddhism may have taken a major role and incorporated the indigenous traditions. The situation in Burma (Myanmar) fits in the second category. Indigenous Burmese beliefs remained strong because they offer a more satisfying way of explaining and dealing with everyday problems. According to Burmese Buddhism, a person's karma is a result of action in previous lives and determines his or her present condition. If something bad happens, it's because of karma and the person can do little but suffer through it. Burmese supernaturalism, on the other hand, says that the bad thing happened because of the actions of capricious spirits called *nats*. Ritual actions can combat the influence of *nats*. In other words, *nats* can be dealt with, karma cannot.

Buddhism, however, became an important cultural force and the key basis for social integration in Burma. One village, for example, had three Buddhist monasteries, with four resident Buddhist monks and several temporary monks. Every male child was ordained as a temporary member of the monastic order. Almost every villager observed Buddhist holy days. While Buddhism is held to be the supreme truth, spirits are called upon when it comes to dealing with everyday problems such as a toothache or a monetary loss.

Buddhism and Religious Roles for Women

In Theravada Buddhism there are limited religious roles for women. However, women in many parts of Southeast Asia have created roles for the pursuit of a religious path. One possible route in Thailand is to begin wearing white robes, following the eight precepts or Buddhist commandments (which forbid taking life, stealing, lying, and taking intoxicants, among others) and living in a monastic establishment. In urban Thailand there are several such centres for "women in white." A growing trend is for young women who are dissatisfied with the demands of village life to go to the city and take up the white robe, spending their days in meditation and religious study (P. Van Esterik 2000). Another possibility for women is to intensify religious activity, especially meditation, while continuing their normal everyday activities. A very few of these women become meditation teachers educating their followers, both lay and monastic, in the intricacies of Buddhist thought and the techniques of meditation that can eventually lead to nirvana (J. Van Esterik 1996).

Judaism

Contemporary varieties of Judaism range from conservative Hasidism to Reform Judaism, which emerged in the early 1800s. One difference between these two perspectives concerns the question of who is Jewish. Jewish law traditionally defined a Jewish person as someone born of a Jewish mother. In contrast, Reform Judaism recognizes as Jewish the offspring of a Jewish father and non-Jewish mother. Followers of Judaism share in the belief in the Torah (the Five Books of Moses, or Pentateuch) as the revelation of God's truth through Israel, a term for the "holy people" (Neusner 1995:598–607). The Torah explains the relationship between the supernatural and human realms and guides people in how to carry out the world view through appropriate actions. A key feature of all forms of Judaism is the identification of what is wrong with the present and how to escape, overcome, or survive that situation. Jewish life is symbolically interpreted as a tension between exile and return, given its foundational myth in the exile of the Jews from Israel and their period of slavery in Egypt.

Judaism is monotheistic, teaching that God is one, unique, and all-powerful. Humans have a moral duty to follow Jewish law, to protect and preserve life and health, and to follow certain duties, such as observing the Sabbath. The high regard for human life is reflected in the general opposition to abortion within Jewish law and opposition to the death penalty. Words, both spoken and written, have high importance in Judaism: There is an emphasis on truth-telling in life and the use of established literary formulas at precise times during worship. These formulas are encoded in a *sidur*, or prayer book. Dietary patterns also distinguish Judaism from other religions; for example, rules of kosher eating forbid the mixing of milk and milk products with meat.

Who's Who at the Kotel

The most sacred place to all Jews is the *kotel*, or Western Wall in Jerusalem. Since the 1967 war, which brought Jerusalem under Israeli rule, the *kotel* can be considered the most important religious shrine and pilgrimage site of Israel. The *kotel* is located at one edge of the Temple Mount (or Haram Sharif), an area sacred to Jews, Muslims, and Christians. According to Jewish scriptures, God asked Abraham to sacrifice his son Isaac on this hill. Later, King Solomon built the First Temple here in the middle of the tenth century BCE. It was destroyed by Nebuchadnessar in 587 BCE, when the Jews were led into captivity in Babylon. Around 500 BCE, King Herod built the Second Temple on the same site. The *kotel* is a remnant of the Second Temple. Jews of all varieties and non-Jews come to the *kotel* in vast numbers from around the world. The *kotel* plaza is open to everyone, pilgrims and tourists. The wall is made of massive rectangular stones weighing between two and eight tonnes each. At its base is a synagogue area, partitioned into men's and women's sections.

The *kotel* (or Western Wall) in Jerusalem is a sacred place of pilgrimage especially for Jews. Males pray at a section marked off on the left while women keep to the area on the right. Both men and women should cover their heads, and women should take care when leaving the wall area to keep their faces towards it and avoid turning their backsides to it.

An ethnographic study of what goes on at the *kotel* reveals how this single site brings together a variety of Jewish worshippers and more secular visitors. There is great diversity among the visitors, evident in the various styles of dress and gesture:

> *The Hasid…with a fur shtreimel on his head may enter the synagogue area alongside a man in shorts who utilizes a cardboard skullcap available for "secular" visitors. American youngsters in jeans may ponder Israeli soldiers of their own age, dressed in uniform, and wonder what their lot might have been if they were born in another country. Women from Yemen, wearing embroidered trousers under their dresses, edge close to the Wall as do women accoutred in contemporary styles whose religiosity may have been filtered through a modern education.… The North African-born Israeli, uttering a personal prayer with his forehead against the Wall becomes an object of comment for a European tourist. Pious women, with their heads covered for modesty, instruct their children in the decorum appropriate to the prayer situation. People from many parts of the country, nay the world, meet unexpectedly. (Storper-Perez and Goldberg 1994:321)*

In spite of plaques that state the prohibition against begging, there are beggars who offer to "sell a blessing" to visitors. They may remind visitors that it was the poor who built the wall in the first place. Another category of people is young Jewish men in search of prospective "born again" Jews who "hang around" looking for a "hit" (in their words). Most of the hits are young Americans who are urged to take their Jewishness more seriously and, if male, to be sure to marry a Jewish woman. Other regulars are Hebrew-speaking men who are available to organize a prayer service. One of the most frequent forms of religious expression at the *kotel* is the insertion of written prayers into the crevices of the wall.

The social heterogeneity of the Jewish people is thus brought together in a single space, creating some sense of what Victor Turner (1969) called *communitas*, a sense of collective unity out of individual diversity.

Passover in Kerala The Jews of the Kochi area (formerly called Cochin) of Kerala, South India, have lived there for about 1000 years (Katz and Goldberg 1989). The Maharaja of Kochi had good relations with and respect for the Jewish people, who were mainly merchants. He relied on them for external trade and contacts. In recognition of this, he allowed a synagogue, which is still standing, to be built next to his palace. Syncretism is apparent in Kochi Jew lifestyle, social structure, and rituals. Crucial aspects of Judaism are retained, along with adoption of many aspects of Hindu practices. Three aspects of syncretism with Hinduism are apparent in Passover, one of the most important annual rituals of the Jewish faith. First, compared to the typically joyous Western/European Passover celebration, the Kochi version has adopted a tone of austerity and is called "the fasting feast." Kochi Passover, secondly, allows no roles for children who, at a traditional *Seder* (ritual meal) usually ask four questions as a starting-point of the narrative. The Kochi Jews chant the questions in unison. This change relates to the fact that in Hinduism, children do not have solo roles in rituals. Third, a Kochi Seder stresses purity even more than standard Jewish requirements. Standard rules about maintaining the purity of kosher wine usually mean that no gentile (non-Jew) should touch it. But Kochi Jews say that if the shelf or table on which the wine sits is touched by a gentile, the wine is impure. This extra level of "contagion" is influenced by Hindu concepts of pollution.

A celebration of the Christian holy day of Palm Sunday in Port-au-Prince, Haiti. European colonialism brought thousands of Africans as slaves to the "New World," and it also exported Christianity through missionary efforts. Many forms of Christianity are now firmly entrenched in the Caribbean region as well as in Central and South America.

Christianity

Christianity has many ties with Judaism, from which it sprang, especially in terms of the Biblical teachings of a coming saviour, or messiah. It began in Palestine and the eastern Mediterranean in the second quarter of the first century (Cunningham 1995:240–253). Most of the early believers were Jews, who took up the belief in Jesus Christ as the "messiah" (annointed one) who came to earth in fulfillment of prophesies contained in the Hebrew scriptures. Today, Christianity is the largest of the world's religions with about 1.5 billion adherents, or nearly one-third of the world's population. It is the majority religion of Australia, New Zealand, the Philippines, Papua New Guinea, most countries of Europe, and North and South America, and about a dozen southern African countries. Christianity is a minority religion throughout Asia, but Asian Christians constitute 16 per cent of the world's total Christians and are thus a significant population.

Christians accept the Bible (Old and New Testaments) as containing the basic teachings, the belief that a supreme God sent his son to earth as a sacrifice for the welfare of humanity, and the importance of Jesus as the model to follow for moral guidance. The three largest branches of Christianity are Roman Catholic, Protestant, and Eastern Orthodox. Within each of these branches, various denominations exist. Christianity has existed the longest in the Near East and Mediterranean regions. In contemporary times, the greatest growth in Christianity is occurring in sub-Saharan Africa, parts of India, and Indonesia. It is currently experiencing a resurgence in Eastern Europe.

Protestantism among White Appalachians

Studies of variants of Protestantism in Appalachia describe local traditions that outsiders who are accustomed to standard, urban versions may view as "deviant." For example, churches in rural West Virginia and North Carolina, called Old Regulars, emphasize in their worship three obligatory rituals: foot washing, communion (a ritual commemorating the "Last Supper" that Jesus had with his disciples), and baptism (Dorgan 1989). The foot washing ceremony occurs once a year in conjunction with communion, usually as an extension of the Sunday service. An elder is called to the front of the church, and he "introduces" the service. He preaches for about 10 to 20 minutes, and then there is a round of handshaking and embracing. Two deaconesses come forward to "prepare the table" by uncovering the sacramental elements placed there earlier under a white tablecloth (unleavened bread, serving plates for the bread, cups for the wine, a decanter or quart jar or two of wine). The deacons come forward to prepare the bread by breaking it into small pieces while the moderator pours the wine into the cups. By now, the men and women have formed separate groups as the deacons serve the bread and wine (a few groups have allowed deaconesses to serve the women's side; this issue has caused conflicts and splits among traditional groups). After the deacons serve each other, it is time for the foot washing. The moderator may begin this part of the service by quoting from the New Testament (the book of John, chapter 13, verse 4): "He riseth from supper, and laid aside his garments; and he took a towel and girded himself." While speaking these lines, he removes his coat and then ties a long towel around his waist. He takes a basin from the piles of basins by the communion table and puts water in it, selects a senior elder and removes his shoes and socks, then washes his feet slowly and attentively. Other members come forward and take towels and basins. Soon "the church is filled with crying, shouting, and praising as these highly poignant exchanges unleash a flood of emotions. A fellowship that may have remained very solemn during the communion will now participate in a myriad of intense expressions of religious enthusiasm and literally scores of high-pathos scenes will be played out" (106). Participants take turns washing and being washed. A functional interpretation of the ritual of foot washing is that it helps maintain interpersonal harmony in small religious communities.

Another feature of worship in some small, Protestant subdenominations in West Virginia involves the handling of poisonous snakes. This practice also finds legitimation in the New Testament (Daugherty 1997 [1976]). According to a passage in Mark (16:15–18): "In my name shall they cast out devils; they shall speak with new tongues; they shall take up serpents; and if they drink any deadly thing, it shall not hurt them; they shall lay hands on the sick, and they shall recover." Members of "Holiness-type" churches believe that the handling of poisonous snakes is the supreme act of devotion to God.

They are Biblical literalists and have chosen serpent-handling as their way of celebrating life, death, and resurrection, and proving that only Jesus has the power to deliver them from death. During their services, the Holy Ghost (not the Holy Spirit) enables them to pick up serpents, speak in tongues, testify to the Lord's greatness, and drink strychnine or lye. Most serpent handlers have been bitten many times, but few have died. One interpretation says that the risks of handling poisonous rattlesnakes and copperheads mirrors the risks of the environment. The people are poor, with high rates of unemployment and few prospects for improvement. Are these people psychologically troubled? Apparently not. Psychological tests indicate they are more emotionally healthy than members of mainline Protestant churches.

The Last Supper in Fiji Among Christians in Fiji, the image of the "Last Supper" is a dominant motif (Toren 1988). This scene, depicted on tapestry hangings, adorns most churches and many houses. People say, "Christ is the head of this household, he eats with us and overhears us" (697). The image's popularity is the result of its fit with Fijian notions of commensality (communal eating) and kava drinking. Seating rules at such events place the highest-status people, such as the chief, and others close to him, at the "above" side of the room, away from the entrance. Others sit at the "lower" end, facing the highly ranked people. Intermediate positions are located on either side of the person of honour, in ranked order. Da Vinci's rendition of the Last Supper places Jesus Christ in the position of a chief, with the disciples in an ordered arrangement around him. "The image of an ordered and stratified society exemplified in people's positions relative to one another around the kava bowl is encountered virtually everyday in the village" (706). The disciples and the viewers "face" the chief and eat and drink together, as is appropriate in Fijian society.

Syncretism happens when features of two cultures match each other in some way. Many situations of non-fit can also be provided. Christian missionaries have had difficulty translating the Bible into indigenous languages because of lack of matching words or concepts, and because of differing kinship and social structures. Some Amazonian groups, for example, have no word that fits the Christian concept of "Heaven" (Everett 1995, personal communication). In other cases, matrilineal peoples have found it difficult to understand the significance of the Christian construct of "God the father."

Islam

Islam is based on the teachings of the prophet Muhammed (570–632 CE), and is thus the youngest of the world religions (R. Martin 1995:498–513). The Arabic word *Islam* means "submission" to the will of the one god, Allah, through which peace will be achieved. Islam also implies acceptance of Muhammed as the last and final messenger of God, "the seal of the prophets." Muslim majority nations are located in northern Africa; the Middle East, including Afghanistan, Pakistan, and Bangladesh in South Asia; and several nations in Central Asia and Southeast Asia. In fact, the majority of the world's Muslims (60 per cent) live either in South Asia or Southeast Asia. While Islam originally flourished among pastoral nomads, only 2 per cent of its adherents now are in that category.

A common and inaccurate stereotype of Islam among many non-Muslims is that, wherever it exists, it is the same. This erroneously monolithic model tends to be based on some imagined version of Arab Islam as practised in Saudi Arabia. In recent years, features of Arab-defined Islam are spreading globally, specifically guidelines about dress such as head-veiling for women and long robes for men (Nagata 1984). Yet not everyone in global Islamic cultures accepts these rules. In Malaysia, young people seem more willing to become part of the *dakwah* movement (call to faith), while their parents are more likely to be skeptical of the new practices and seek to have their children "deprogrammed" by a religious practitioner they trust. A comparison of Islam in highland Sumatra, Indonesia, and Morocco in North Africa reveals culturally constructed differences (J. Bowen 1992). The annual Feast of Sacrifice is celebrated by Muslims around the world. It commemorates God's sparing of Abraham's son Ishmael (Isaac in Christian and Jewish traditions). It takes place everywhere on the tenth of the last month of the year, also called Pilgrimage Month. The ritual reminds Muslims of their global unity within the Islamic faith. One aspect of this event in Morocco involves the king publicly plunging a dagger into a ram's throat, a re-enactment of Muhammad's performance of the sacrifice on the same day in the seventh century. Each male head of a household follows the pattern and sacrifices a ram. Size and virility of the ram are a measure of the man's power and virility. Other men of the household stand to witness the sacrifice, while women and children are absent or in the background. After the ram is killed, they come forward and dab its blood on their faces. In some villages, women play a more prominent role before the sacrifice by daubing the ram with henna (red dye), thus sanctifying it, and using its blood afterwards in rituals to protect the household. These national and household rituals are highly symbolic of male power in the public and private domains—the power of the monarchy and the power of patriarchy. Is this the standard, universal way of celebrating the Feast of Sacrifice?

The degree of local adaption to Moroccan culture becomes clear when compared with the ritual's enactment in Sumatra, which has a less patriarchal culture and a political structure that does not emphasize monarchy. In Isak, a traditionalist Muslim village, people have been Muslims since the seventeenth century. They sacrifice all kinds of animals, including chickens, ducks, sheep, goats, and water buffalo. As long as the throat is cut and the meat is eaten, it satisfies the demands of God. Before cutting the victim's throat, the sacrificer dedicates it to one or more relatives. In contrast to Morocco, most sacrifices receive little notice and are done mainly in the back of the house with little fanfare. Both women and men of the household refer to it as "their" sacrifice, and there are no signs of male dominance. Women may sponsor a sacrifice, as did one wealthy woman trader who sacrificed a buffalo (the actual cutting, however, is done by a man). The Moroccan ritual emphasizes fathers and sons. The Isak ritual includes attention to a wider range of kin on both the husband's and wife's side, daughters as well as sons, and dead relatives, too. In the Indonesian context, no centralized dynastic meanings are given to the ritual. The differences are not because Moroccans know the scriptures better than Sumatrans. The Isak area has many Islamic scholars who consult the scriptures and discuss issues. Rather, the cultural context into which the same scriptural tradition is placed shapes it to local interests and needs.

African Religions

The distinction between the world religions and "local religions" is blurry because many local religions are now practised by people who have migrated to other nations. This is true for African religions, many of which spread outside Africa through the enforced movements of people as slaves, and for other religions such as

Confucianism, which have been diffused by voluntary migration. This section attempts to summarize some key features of African religions and then provides an example of a new religion with African roots, Ras Tafari.

Features of African Religions

As of 1994, Africa's total population comprised 341 million Christians, 285 million Muslims, and about 70 million practising indigenous religions (J. Smith 1995:15–16). With its diverse geography, cultural variation, and history, Africa encompasses a wide range of indigenous religions. Some common, but not universal, features of indigenous African religions include the following:

- myths about a rupture that once occurred between the creator deity and humans;
- a pantheon that includes a high god and many secondary supernaturals ranging from powerful gods to lesser spirits;
- elaborate initiation rituals;
- rituals involving animal sacrifices and other offerings, meals, and dances;
- altars within shrines as focal places where humans and deities meet; and
- close links between healing and divination.

A sacred altar in a local African religion in Togo, West Africa.

While these general features are fairly constant, African indigenous religions are rethought and reshaped with variable results (Gable 1995). Furthermore, as African religions have moved around the world to new locations with the movement of African peoples, they have been adapted in various ways to their new contexts, as discussed in the following section on the Ras Tafari religion.

Ras Tafari

Also called Rastafarianism, Ras Tafari is a relatively new religion—it was first enunciated in the 1930s—of the Caribbean, North America, and Europe. Numbers of Rastafarians are unknown because they refuse to be counted (J. Smith 1995:23). Ras Tafari is an unorthodox, protest religion that shares few of the features of African religions mentioned above. Ras Tafari traces its history to several preachers of the early twentieth century who taught that Ras ("Prince") Tafari, then the Ethiopian Emperor Haile Selassie I, was the "Lion of Judah" who would lead Blacks to the African promised land. Rastafarianism does not have an organized set of doctrines, and there are no written texts or enforced orthodoxy. However, Yawney and Homiak report that a Ras Tafari assembly in 1983 declared that one group in the movement, the House of Nyahbinghi, be accepted as the foundational Ras Tafari orthodoxy (2001:256). This orthodoxy includes such shared beliefs of the many diffuse groups that Ethiopia is Zion, or heaven on earth, and Emperor Haile Selassie I of Ethiopia is a living god, and that all African people are one and have the right of return to Africa. Since the death of Haile Selassie in 1975, a greater emphasis has been placed on pan-African unity and Black power, and less on Ethiopia. Rastafarianism is particularly strong in Jamaica where it first emerged. It is associated with reggae music, dreadlocks, and *ganja* (marijuana) smoking. Variations within the Rastafarian movement in Jamaica range from beliefs that one must fight oppression to the position that living a peaceful life brings victory against evil.

Directions of Change

All religions have established mythologies and doctrines that provide a certain degree of continuity and, often, conservativism in religious beliefs and practices. Yet, nowhere are religions frozen and unchanging. Cultural anthropologists have traced the resurgence of religions that seemed to have been headed towards extinction through colonial forces, and they have documented the emergence of seemingly new religions. Likewise, they are observing the contemporary struggle of once-suppressed religions in socialist states to find a new position in the post-socialist world. Religious icons, once a prominent part of Russian Orthodox churches, were removed and placed in museums. Now, the churches want them back. Indigenous people's beliefs about the sacredness of their land are an important part of their attempts to protect their territory from encroachment and development by outside commercial interests. The world of religious change offers these examples, and far more, as windows into wider cultural change.

Men march with bamboo sticks representing guns as part of a cargo cult on Tanna Island in the South Pacific. This procession imitates that of foreign soldiers and is intended to help bring the arrival of "goods" associated with the foreign presence.

Revitalization Movements

Revitalization movements are organized movements that seek to construct a more satisfying culture, either through re-establishing all or parts of a religion that has been threatened by outside forces or by adopting new practices and beliefs. Such movements often arise in the context of rapid cultural change and appear to represent a way for people to try to make sense of their changing world and their place in it. One such movement that emerged as a response of First Nations to the invasion of their land by Europeans and Euro-Americans was the Ghost Dance movement (J. Smith 1995:385). In the early 1870s, a shaman of the Paiute tribe named Wodziwob declared that the world would soon be destroyed and then renewed: First Nations peoples, plants, and animals would come back to life. He instructed people to perform a circle dance at night to encourage the spirits to bring this renewal. This movement spread to other tribes in California, Oregon, and Idaho, but ended when the prophet died and his prophecy was unfulfilled. A similar movement emerged in 1890, led by another Paiute prophet, Wovoka, who had a vision during a total eclipse. His message was the same: destruction, renewal, and the need to perform circle dances in anticipation of the impending event. The dance spread widely and with differing effects. Among the Pawnee, it provided the basis for a cultural revival of old ceremonies that had fallen into disuse. The Sioux altered Wovoka's message and adopted a more overtly hostile stance towards the United States government and White people. Newspapers began to carry stories about the "messiah craze," referring to Wovoka. Ultimately, the government took action against the Sioux, killing Chief Sitting Bull and Chief Big Foot and about 300 Sioux at Wounded Knee. In the 1970s, the Ghost Dance was revived by the American Indian Movement, an activist organization seeking to improve First Nations rights.

Cargo cults are a variety of revitalization movements that sprang up in much of Melanesia (including Papua New Guinea and Fiji) and in New Zealand among the indigenous Maori peoples, in response to Western influences. Most prominent in the first half of the nineteenth century, they are characterized by their emphasis on the acquisition of Western trade goods, or "cargo" in local terms. Typically, a prophetic leader emerges with a vision of how the cargo will arrive. In one instance, the leader predicted that a ship would come, bringing not only cargo, but also the dead ancestors. Followers set up tables for the expected guests, complete with flower arrangements. Later, after World War II and the islanders' experiences of aircraft arrivals bringing cargo, the mode of arrival changed to planes. Once again, people would wait expectantly for the arrival of the plane. The cargo cults emerged as a response to the disrupting effects of new goods being suddenly introduced into indigenous settings. The outsiders imposed a new form of exchange system that emphasized the importance of Western goods and denied the importance of indigenous valuables, such as shells and pigs. This transformation undermined traditional patterns of status-gaining through the exchange of indigenous goods. Cargo cult leaders sought help, in the only way they knew, in obtaining Western goods so they could gain social status in the new system.

Contested Sacred Sites

Religious conflict often becomes focused on sacred sites. One place of recurrent conflict is Jerusalem, where many religions and sects within religions compete for control of sacred terrain. Three major religions claim they have primary rights: Islam, Judaism, and Christianity. Among the Christians, several different sects vie for control of the Church of the Holy Sepulchre. In India, frequent conflicts occur between Hindus and Muslims over sacred sites. Hindus claim that Muslim mosques have been built on sites sacred to Hindus. On some occasions, the Hindus have proceeded to tear down the mosques. In the United States, White racists burned several African American churches in the south during 1977. Conflicts also occur between religious and secular interests. In the Middle East, some Jewish leaders in Israel resist archaeological research because the ancient Jewish burial places should remain undisturbed. The same situation exists for First Nations peoples, whose burial grounds have often been destroyed for the sake of urban development in North America. Around the world, large-scale development projects such as dams and mines have destroyed indigenous sacred areas, and resistance to such destruction is growing (see the Multiple Cultural Worlds box).

Religious Freedom as a Human Right

According to a United Nations Declaration, freedom from religious persecution is supposed to be a universal human right. Violations of this right by nations and by competing religions are common. Sometimes people who are

MULTIPLE CULTURAL WORLDS

The Loss of the Place Where Happiness Dwells

The Place Where Happiness Dwells was a summer meeting ground for the Dunne-za/Cree of the North River region of British Columbia. These hunting and gathering peoples spent part of the summer round of activities, including important religious ceremonies, on a piece of land that was special to them, the land where happiness dwells. This land was sold in 1945 to the Department of Indian Affairs at the instigation of the Indian agent. Many years later in 1987, a suit to take back the land was initiated by the band arguing that the land could not be alienated from the Dunne-za/Cree because of responsibilities accepted by the government in an 1899 treaty with the band (Riddington 1990:186ff). Anthropologist Hugh Brody testified on behalf of the Dunne-za/Cree as an expert witness. He tried to convey to the court how decisions were made in a hunting and gathering group where there is no leader, and how important a summer gathering place is for people who travel in smaller groups hunting and trapping elsewhere in the other seasons. Unfortunately, the judge never accepted this picture of the band. Nor did he accept the testimony of the elders. The elders were frustrated by the cross-examination style of government lawyers who seemed to doubt the veracity of their testimony. The judge decided against the Dunne-za/Cree mainly because the land was now valuable due to the discovery of oil and gas deposits. The judge thought the band wanted the property returned because of this value, without considering the fact that they had suffered a significant cultural loss.

FOOD FOR THOUGHT

Why is a piece of land so important for getting a hunting and gathering group together?

being persecuted on religious grounds can seek and obtain sanctuary in other places or nations. Thousands of Tibetan Buddhist refugees, including their leader the Dalai Lama, fled Tibet after it was taken over by the Chinese. Several Tibetan communities have been established in exile in India, the United States, and Canada, where the Tibetan people attempt to keep their religion, language, and heritage alive.

Currently, a resurgence of interest in studying religion is occurring among cultural anthropologists in North America, after several decades of relative neglect. Some of this new interest, it is hoped, will be directed at the issue of religious freedom, human rights, and the implications for human welfare in this changing world.

Key Questions Revisited

What is religion and what are the basic features of religions cross-culturally?

Early cultural anthropologists defined religion in contrast to magic and suggested that religion was a more evolved form of thinking about the supernatural realm. They collected information on religions of non-Western cultures and constructed theories about the origin and functions of religion. Since then, ethnographers have described the basic features of religious systems and documented a rich variety of beliefs, many forms of ritual behaviour, and different types of religious specialists. Beliefs are expressed either in myth or doctrine, and they often are concerned with defining the roles and characteristics of supernatural beings and how humans should relate to them. Rituals, or the action side of beliefs, include life-cycle rituals, pilgrimages, cleansing rituals, rituals of reversal, and sacrifice. In some sense, all rituals are transformative for the participants. Many rituals, but not all, require the participation of a trained religious specialist such as a shaman/shamanka or priest/priestess. Religious specialist roles are fewer, less formalized, and carry less secular power and status in nonstate societies. In states, religious specialists are often organized into hierarchies, and many specialists gain substantial secular power.

How do world religions reflect globalization and localization?

The five world religions are based on a coherent and widely agreed-upon set of teachings, but as members of these religions move around the globe, the religious beliefs and practices are contextualized into localized variants. When a new religion moves into a culture, it may be blended with indigenous systems (syncretism), coexist with indigenous religions in a pluralistic fashion, or may take over and obliterate the original beliefs.

What are some important aspects of religious change in contemporary times?

Cultural anthropologists have documented and sought to explain why and how religious change occurs. Religious movements of the past two centuries have often been prompted by colonialism and other forms of social contact. In some instances, indigenous religious leaders and cults arise in the attempt to resist unwanted outside forces of change; in other instances, they arise as ways of incorporating new ideas and values from the outside.

Core Concepts

animatism, p. 291
animism, p. 289
anthropomorphic, p. 291
cargo cults, p. 307
doctrine, p. 290

life-cycle rituals, p. 293
magic, p. 288
monotheism, p. 289
myth, p. 290

polytheism, p. 289
priest/priestess, p. 298
religion, p. 288
revitalization movements, p. 307
ritual, p. 293

rituals of reversal, p. 295
sacrifice, p.296
syncretism, p. 301
world religions, p. 299
world view, p. 288
zoomorphic, p. 291

Suggested Readings

Diane Bell, *Ngarrindjeri Wurruwarrin: A World That Is, Was, and Will Be*. North Melbourne, Australia: Spinifex Press, 1998. This is an ethnography about Australian Aboriginal struggles to protect their sacred land from encroachment by developers, with attention to the people's own voices, the perspective of the Australian government, the media, and even disputes among anthropologists about what constitutes truth and validity.

Thomas D. Blakely, Walter E. A. van Beek, and Dennis L. Thompson, *Religion in Africa: Experience and Expression*. Portsmouth, NH: Heinemann, 1994. This book contains an introductory overview and 20 chapters on topics including the impact of Islam and Christianity on African religious systems, women's spirit cults, myth and epic, and new religious movements.

Karen McCarthy Brown, *Mama Lola: A Vodou Priestess in Brooklyn*. Berkeley: University of California Press, 1991. The life story of Mama Lola, a Vodou practitioner, is set within an ethnographic study of a Haitian community in New York.

Klara Bonsack Kelley and Harris Francis, *Navajo Sacred Places*. Bloomington: Indiana University Press, 1994. The authors report on the results of a research project to learn about Navajo cultural resources, especially sacred sites, and the stories associated with them in order to help protect these places.

Gregory Forth, *Beneath the Volcano: Religion, Cosmology and Spirit Classification Among the Nage of Eastern Indonesia*. Leiden: KITLV Press, 1998. This ethnography focuses on Nage ideas about spirits and how these influence ritual practice and relations with humans. This is an important addition to scholarship; it examines the religion of a people not previously investigated in the anthropological literature.

Michael Lambek, *Knowledge and Practice in Mayotte: Local Discourses of Islam, Sorcery, and Spirit Possession*. Toronto: University of Toronto Press, 1993. This reflexive study of religious practice among an Islamic people on an island off the east coast of Africa probes the meanings of sorcery and spirit possession.

Anna S. Meigs, *Food, Sex, and Pollution: A New Guinea Religion*. New Brunswick, NJ: Rutgers University Press, 1984. This book provides an analysis of taboos surrounding food, sex, and vital bodily essences among the Hua people of Papua New Guinea.

Fatima Mernissi, *Beyond the Veil: Male-Female Dynamics in Modern Muslim Society*. Bloomington: Indiana University Press, revised edition, 1987. The author considers how Islam perceives of female sexuality and seeks to regulate it on behalf of the social order. This edition contains a new chapter on Muslim women and fundamentalism.

 Your *Cultural Anthropology*, Second Canadian Edition Media Edition CD-ROM contains many Web sites relevant to this chapter. Use it to explore the Web and to expand your knowledge of anthropology.

Chapter 13

Communication

CHAPTER OUTLINE

Aini (Akha) women, members of one of China's many minority groups, converse with each other, in Yunnan province.

Key Questions

What aspects of communication do linguistic anthropologists study?

How do culture, society, and communication interact?

What are some important factors affecting language change?

*M*any animals and insects such as chimpanzees, lions, and bees have sophisticated ways of communicating about where food is available or warning about an impending danger. People are in almost constant communication with other people, supernaturals, and pets or other domesticated animals. **Communication** *refers to the conveying of meaningful messages from one person or animal or insect to another. Means of communication among humans include eye contact, body posture, position and movements of limbs, and language.* **Language** *refers to a form of communication that is a systematic set of arbitrary symbols shared among a group and passed on from generation to generation. It may be spoken, signed, or written.*

This chapter discusses culture and communication, drawing on work in linguistic anthropology, one of general anthropology's four fields. It discusses characteristics of human language that set it apart from communication among other animals and considers what we know about the origins of languages. Then the role of language in our multicultural worlds is explored, including how language relates to thought in general, different styles and patterns of languages used by different groups of people, and the growing importance of communication via the mass media.

Linguistic Anthropology

Linguistic anthropology is devoted to the study of communication, mainly, but not exclusively, among humans. Some of the earliest research in linguistics was carried out by Franz Boas; he recorded many of the languages, myths, and rituals of First Nations groups, particularly those on the Northwest Coast and in the Canadian Arctic. Another force driving the development of linguistic anthropology was the discovery through cross-cultural fieldwork that many existing non-Western languages had never been written down. Study of non-Western languages revealed a wide range of different phonetic systems (pronunciation of various sounds) and exposed the inadequacy of Western alphabets to represent such sounds. This gap prompted the development of the International Phonetic Alphabet, which contains symbols to represent all known sounds, such as the symbol "!" to indicate a click sound common in southern African languages.

More recently, linguistic anthropologists have begun to explore new areas of research, including the relationship between nationalism and language, the role of language in the mass media, and language politics. Many anthropologists are designing practical applications of research findings to promote improved language learning among school children, migrants, and refugee populations. Applied linguistic anthropologists work on projects such as modifying standardized tests to reduce bias against children from varied cultural backgrounds.

Connections with Other Fields

From the above description, it is clear that cultural anthropology and linguistic anthropology have similar and overlapping interests. This is true for all of anthropology's subfields. For example, archaeologists work closely with linguists in searching for the origins, spread, and changes in language and deciphering ancient languages, thereby shedding light on human history. Some early forms of writing continue to defy translation, such as the script used in the Mohenjo-daro civilization of present-day Pakistan that is dated around 3500 BCE.

Some physical anthropologists and human geneticists use linguistic data to complement their attempts to trace genetic relationships of populations throughout history (Cavalli-Sforza, Menozzi, and Piazza 1994). Communication among nonhuman primates is also of great interest to physical anthropologists. Attempts to teach chimpanzees to talk have been largely unsuccessful. Chimpanzees lack adequate motor control over the anatomical parts crucial for the formation of many human sounds.

Some success has been achieved in teaching nonhuman primates to understand and use arbitrary symbols. Symbolic understanding has long been held to constitute a major dividing line between communication abilities of nonhuman primates and human language. In 1966, a female chimpanzee named Washoe began learning how to use American Sign Language (ASL). She acquired the use of 160 signs in about five years, and she was able to use them to generate novel combinations. Another chimp, Sarah, learned abstract principles such as choosing a red chip when asked the question "what is an apple the same as?" Signing chimpanzees can pass sign language on to their offspring. So far, competence levels have been at about that of a three-year-old child. Studying these rudimentary signing systems may shed light on the early stages of human communication.

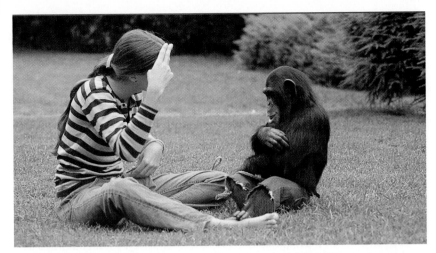

Chimpanzees have demonstrated a remarkable ability to learn aspects of human language. Here, trainer Joyce Butler signs "Nim" and Nim signs "Me."

Fieldwork Challenges

Research in linguistic anthropology shares basic methods with cultural anthropology, but its more specialized areas have unique approaches to data gathering and analysis. The study of language **pragmatics,** or language in use, relies on tape recordings or video recordings of people and events. The tapes are then analyzed qualitatively or quantitatively. Video recordings, for example, may be subjected to a detailed "frame analysis" that can pinpoint when communication breaks down or misunderstandings occur.

Linguistic anthropologists argue that the analysis of recorded data is best done when situated within broader knowledge about the culture. This approach derives from Malinowski's view that communication is "embedded" in its social context and that it must therefore be studied in relation to that context. An example of such a contextualized approach is a study of speech in Western Samoa that gathered many hours of tape-recorded speech along with long-term participant observation in the area (Duranti 1994). Analysis of the transcriptions of the recorded talk revealed two major findings about how speech is related to social status as used in village council meetings. First, turn-taking patterns reflected and restated people's power positions in the group. Second, people used particular grammatical forms and word choices that indirectly either praised or blamed others,

thus shaping and reaffirming people's moral roles and status relations. Nonlinguistic data that assisted in forming these interpretations included observation of seating arrangements and the order of the distribution of *kava* (a ritually shared intoxicating beverage). The findings about the role of language in creating and maintaining social and moral order contribute to a richer understanding of the wider social context of status formation in Samoa.

Most anthropologists face the challenge of translation. One has to understand more about a language than just vocabulary in order to provide a reliable and meaningful translation. An anthropologist once translated a song that occurred at the end of a play in Zaire (Fabian 1995). The play was presented in the Swahili language, so he assumed that the final song was, too. Thus, he assumed that the repeated use of the word *tutubawina,* a Swahili word, indicated that it was a fighting song. But a Swahili speaker assisting the anthropologist said, no, it was a soccer song. The puzzled anthropologist only later learned, by writing to the theatre performers, that the word *tutubawina* as used in this song was not a Swahili word. From a different language, it indicates a marching song.

Linguistic anthropologists who seek to study ordinary language use all face the problem of the **observer's paradox** (the impossibility of doing research on "natural" communication events without affecting the "naturalness" sought) (McMahon 1994:234). The mere presence of the anthropologist with a tape recorder tends to make the speaker concentrate on speaking "correctly" and more formally. Several options exist for dealing with the paradox: recording informants in a group, observing and recording speech outside an interview situation, or using structured interviews in which the informant is asked to perform various speech tasks at varying levels of formality. In this last technique, the informant is first asked to read a word list and a short passage. The next stage is a question-and-answer session. Last, the interviewer encourages the informant, who may be more relaxed by now, to produce informal conversational speech by asking about childhood rhymes and sayings, encouraging diversions to get the informant to talk for longer periods, and posing questions that are likely to prompt an emotional response. Another strategy is to use "role plays" in which informants are asked to act out a particular scene, such as arguing about something. Data from such semi-structured techniques can be compared with the more casual styles of "natural" speech to assess the possible bias created.

Human Verbal Language

Most anthropologists agree that nonhuman primates share some abilities with humans to communicate through sounds and movements, and that some can be trained to recognize and use arbitrary symbols that humans use. Whatever progress will be made in teaching nonhuman primates aspects of sign language, it is unlikely that they could ever develop the range of linguistic ability that humans possess because human verbal language depends on the richness of arbitrary symbols.

This section describes the key characteristics of human language and provides a brief introduction to some of the formal properties of language.

Key Characteristics: Productivity and Displacement

Human language is said to have infinite **productivity,** or the ability to communicate many messages efficiently. In contrast, consider gibbon communication in the wild. Gibbons have nine calls that convey useful messages such as "follow me," "I am angry," "here is food," "danger," and "I am hurt." If a gibbon wants to communicate particular intensity in, say, the danger at hand, the only option is to repeat the "danger" call several times and at different volumes: "danger," "*danger*," "DANGER," and so on. This variation allows some productivity, but with greater degrees of danger, the system of communication becomes increasingly inefficient. By the time 20 danger calls have been given, it may be too late. In comparison, human language's capacity for productivity makes it extremely efficient. Different levels of danger can be conveyed in these ways:

"I see a movement over there."

"I see a leopard there."

"A leopard—help!"

"Help!"

Human language also uses the feature of **displacement,** which allows people to talk about displaced domains—events in the past and future—as well as the immediate present. According to current thinking, displacement is not a prominent feature of nonhuman primate communication. A wild chimpanzee is unlikely to be able to communicate the message "Danger: there may be a leopard coming here tonight." Instead, it communicates mainly what is experienced in the present. Even if nonhuman primates can learn to use displacement, it is still true that its use among humans is far more prevalent. Among humans, the majority of language use relates to displaced domains, including reference to people and events that may never exist at all, as in fantasy and fiction.

Formal Properties of Language

Besides the above general characteristics, human language can be analyzed in terms of its formal properties: sounds, vocabulary, and grammar, features that lie within formal linguistics (Agar 1994). Learning a new language usually involves learning different sets of sounds. The sounds that make a difference for meaning in a language are called **phonemes.**

Anthropologist Diamond Jenness, who learned several First Nations languages, considered the Algonquian languages the most musical because of their richness of vowel sounds, avoidance of harsh consonants, and use of whispered syllables. He found the Salish languages very harsh because of consonant clusters that English speakers find hard to pronounce, and found the Athapascan languages the most difficult to learn (J. Price 1979:23). Similarly, Sharon Hutchinson (1996) was attracted to the rich, melodic qualities of the Nuer language, but found it difficult to hear and control the heavy aspiration (audible release of breath). These subjective judgments about other languages reflect our experience using different phonemes.

A native English speaker trying to learn the North Indian language called Hindi is challenged to learn to produce and recognize several new sounds. For example, four different *d* sounds exist. None are the same as an English *d*, which is usually pronounced with the tongue

FIGURE 13.1   Dental and Retroflex Tongue Positions

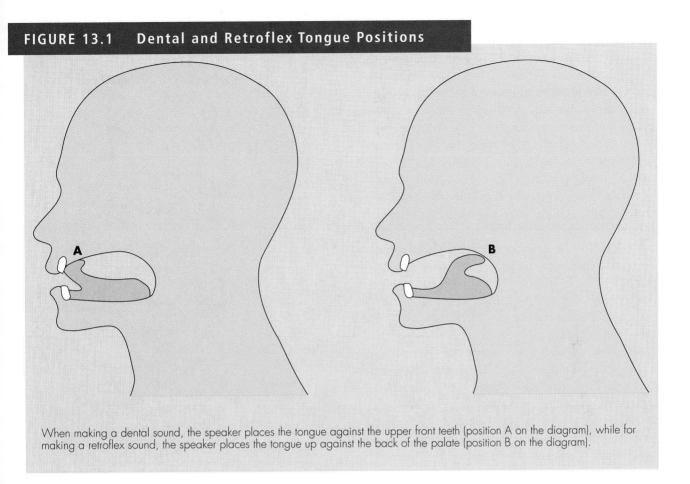

When making a dental sound, the speaker places the tongue against the upper front teeth (position A on the diagram), while for making a retroflex sound, the speaker places the tongue up against the back of the palate (position B on the diagram).

placed on the ridge behind the upper front teeth (try it). One *d* in Hindi, which linguists refer to as a "dental" sound (see Figure 13.1), is pronounced with the tongue pressed firmly behind the upper front teeth (try it). Next is a dental *d* that is also aspirated (pronounced "with air"); making this sound involves the tongue being in the same position and a puff of air expelled during pronunciation (try it, and try the regular dental *d* again with no puff of air at all). Next is what is referred to as a "retroflex sound," accomplished by flipping the tongue back to the central dome of the roof of the mouth (try it, with no puff of air). Finally, there is the aspirated retroflex *d* with the tongue again in the centre of the roof of the mouth and a puff of air. Once you can do this, try the whole series again with a *t*, because Hindi follows the same pattern with this letter as with the letter *d*. Several other sounds in Hindi require careful use of aspiration and placement of the tongue for communicating the right word. A puff of air at the wrong time can produce a serious error, for example, saying the word for "breast" when you want to say the word for "letter."

Grammar refers to the rules for combining sounds into sequences that carry meaning. All languages have grammars, although they vary in form. Even within the languages of contemporary Europe, German is characterized by its placement of the verb at the end of the sentence (try to compose an English sentence with the verb at the end). Phonemes, vocabulary, and grammar are the formal building blocks of language.

Language Origins and History

When did language capacity evolve, and what were the first human languages like? Did grunts and exclamations evolve into words and sentences? Did early humans attempt to imitate the sounds of nature? How did people decide to put together a set of arbitrary symbols with meanings that everyone would accept? No one knows, nor will we ever know, how language started in the first place. The prevailing view is that early humans began to develop language around 50 000 years ago, using calls, body postures, and gestures. Human **paralanguage** (a category that includes all forms of nonverbal communication such as body posture, voice tone, touch, smells, and eye and facial movements) is thus considered the earliest aspect of human language.

No contemporary human language can be considered a "primitive" model of early human language. That would defy the principle of **linguistic relativism,** which says that all languages have passed through thousands of years of change, and all are equally successful forms of communication. Languages differ in their structure and in the meaning they attribute to various concepts (or "semantics"), but all are equally capable of conveying subtle meanings and complex thoughts. There is no such thing as a "simple" language—one that is easy to learn because it is less complex than others. Early scholars of comparative linguistics were sometimes misled by ethnocentric assumptions that language structures of European languages were normative and that languages that did not have the same structure were somehow deficient. Chinese was thus considered to be "primitive" on these grounds, as were many First Nations languages. Now we know that different languages have complexity in different areas—sometimes verb forms, sometimes noun forms.

Writing Systems

Gesture and speech have no way of being recorded in the archaeological record. Attempts to trace the beginnings of language are thus limited to working with the data we do have, which is records of written language. Evidence of the earliest written languages comes from Mesopotamia, Egypt, and China (Postgate, Wang, and Wilkinson 1995). Some scholars say that symbols found on pottery in China dated at 5000 to 4000 BCE should be counted as the earliest writing. At question here is the definition of a writing system: Does the presence of symbolic markings on pots constitute a "writing system" or not? Most scholars say that a symbolic mark that could refer to a clan name is not necessarily evidence of a writing system that involves the use of words in relation to each other in a systematic way. A similarity of forms in all early writing systems is the use of **logographs** (symbols that convey meaning through a form or picture that resembles what is being referred to). Over time, some logographs were kept with their origi-

FIGURE 13.2 Chinese Writing Styles

Source: Courtesy of Molly Spitzer Frost.

nal meaning, others were kept but given more abstract meaning, and other non-logographic symbols were added (see Figure 13.2).

The emergence of writing is associated with the political development of the state. Some scholars take writing as a key diagnostic feature that distinguishes the state from earlier political forms because record keeping was an essential task of the state. The Inca state is one exception to this generalization; it used *quipu,* or cords of knotted strings of different colours, for keeping accounts and recording events. Two interpretations of early writing systems exist. One says that the primary use of early writing was ceremonial because of the prevalence of early writing on tombs, bone inscriptions, or temple carvings. The other says that the primary function of early writing was utilitarian, for government record keeping and trade. The archaeological record is naturally biased towards durable substances. This bias favours the amount of ceremonial writing preserved because durable substances such as stone would have been more likely to be

Quipu, or knotted strings, was the basis of state-level accounting in the Incan empire. The knots conveyed substantial information for those who could interpret their meaning.

used for ceremonial writing since it was intended to last. Utilitarian writing would more likely have been done on perishable materials since people would be less concerned with permanence—somewhat like the way we treat shopping lists. Thus, perhaps much more utilitarian writing existed than has been preserved.

Historical Linguistics

Historical linguistics is the study of language change through history using formal methods that compare shifts over time and across space in formal aspects of language such as **phonetics** (the study of the production of speech sounds), grammar, and semantics. This approach originated in the eighteenth century with a discovery made by Sir William Jones, a British colonial administrator working in India. During his spare time in India, he studied Sanskrit, the ancient language of India. He was the first to notice strong similarities between Sanskrit, Greek, and Latin in vocabulary and grammar. For example, the Sanskrit word for "father" is *pitr*, in Greek it is *patér*, and in Latin, *pater*. This was an astounding discovery for the time, given the prevailing European mentality that placed its cultural heritage firmly in the classical Greco-Roman world and depicted the "Orient" as completely separate from Europe (Bernal 1987).

Following Jones's discovery, other scholars began comparing lists of words and grammatical forms in different languages; for example, French: *père*, German:

Vater, Italian: *padre*, Old English: *faeder*, Old Norse: *fadhir*, Swedish: *far*. With these lists, scholars could also determine degrees of closeness and distance in their relationships, for example, that German and English are closer to each other, and French and Spanish are closer to each other. Later scholars contributed the concept of "language families," or clusters of related languages. Nineteenth century linguists attempted to reconstruct ancient ancestral languages. Comparison of contemporary and historic Eurasian languages and shifts in sound, vocabulary, and meaning yielded a model of a hypothetical early parent language called Proto-Indo-European (PIE). For example, the hypothetical PIE term for "father" is p#ter (the "#" symbol is pronounced like the *u* in "mutter"). The PIE homeland has not been located and may never be, since PIE speakers were probably pastoralists whose lifestyle left few remains in the archaeological record. Linguistic evidence suggests that the PIE homeland was located somewhere in Eurasia, perhaps in or near Turkey. The PIE language is dated as existing by 4000 BCE or earlier. Dating is based on the evidence of linguistic divergence. From its area of origin, PIE speakers subsequently spread out in waves towards Europe, Central Asia, eastern Asia, and South Asia. The farther they moved from the PIE centre in terms of time and space, the more their language diverged from original PIE.

Language, Thought, and Society

This section presents material that demonstrates the relationships between language, thought, and society. First, we discuss two theoretical approaches to these relationships. Then, we look in greater depth at how different "levels" of language are also related to thought and society.

The Ethnography of Speaking

During the twentieth century, two major theoretical perspectives were influential in defining the relationship between language, thought, and society. The first argues that language determines culture; the second reverses the causality, arguing that culture determines language.

They are presented here as alternative models, but careful reading of all the writings of each founder and subsequent research would reveal that the contrasts are not really this simple (Hill and Mannheim 1992). Nonetheless, the "extreme" forms have persisted in the literature over several decades.

The Sapir-Whorf Hypothesis Edward Sapir and Benjamin Whorf formulated an influential model, called the **Sapir-Whorf hypothesis,** which claims that language determines culture, or in its weaker version, that language influences people's perceptions of the world around them (Valentine 1995). For example, if a language has no word for what in English is called *snow,* then a person who has been brought up in that language cannot think of *snow* as it is meant in English. Whorf first began developing this theory through study of different languages' vocabulary and grammar. He was so struck by the differences that he is often attributed with saying that people who speak different languages inhabit "different worlds." This catchy phrase became the basis for what is called **linguistic determinism,** which states that language determines consciousness of the world and behaviour. Extreme linguistic determinism implies that the frames and definitions of a person's primary language are so strong that it is impossible to fully learn another language or understand another culture (Agar 1994:67).

Sociolinguistics Scholars working in the related area of **sociolinguistics** argue that culture, society, and a person's social position determine the content and form of language. Linguists and anthropologists researched the reasons for linguistic variation within a speech community. William Labov's (1966) research of the 1960s established this approach. He conducted several famous studies of the use of particular speech sounds among people of different classes in New York City, hypothesizing that class differences would be reflected in the pronunciation of certain sounds in words. Class difference is not the only social factor affecting language use. For instance, researchers who study Montreal French (e.g., Sankoff and Laberge 1978) found that people's language use correlates with the linguistic demands of their job: people employed as lawyers, teachers, and receptionists tend to use more standard or prestigious speech variants than do those whose jobs require less public use of language, such as laboratory technicians, mechanics, and computer programmers. This variation cuts across class;

for example a receptionist, whose job ranks lower than that of a laboratory technician, feels more pressure to use standard language.

Lisa Valentine (1995) conducted a sociolinguistic study of the discourse or language-in-use of the Severn Ojibwe people of northern Ontario, demonstrating how new speech forms are shaped by the liturgy and music of the Anglican Church, and the newspapers, radio, and television services provided by the Native Communications Society in the small, isolated community where everyone speaks Severn Ojibwe.

Focal vocabulary is a topic that links the Sapir-Whorf hypothesis to sociolinguistics. **Focal vocabularies** are clusters of words that refer to important features of a particular culture. Studying focal vocabularies can contribute to understanding how language is both a thought-world (according to the Sapir-Whorf hypothesis) and a cultural construction responsive to a particular social context. Studying a culture's focal vocabularies provides useful comparative insights. For example, Inuktitut has a more amplified focal vocabulary related to cold weather precipitation, as do English speakers who are avid skiers; Arabic has many words for camels; and a horse breeder has a more elaborate focal vocabulary for kinds of horses.

Language Socialization **Language socialization,** or language learning through everyday interactions, is another area that links the two models described in this section. Language socialization includes two processes: socialization to *use* language and socialization *through* language (Ochs 1990:287). The first part of the definition refers to language acquisition, how children learn to be native speakers. Language acquisition concerns people in many fields, especially psychology and education. Anthropological study of language acquisition adds an important comparative element, showing how children acquire aspects of language such as storytelling, for example.

Language is also an important part of socializing children into a culture. Research shows again that culture shapes the content and process of such socialization. Language has the characteristic of **indexicality;** that is, certain linguistic features "index," or point to, the identities, actions, or feelings of the speaker and convey important social information. For example, two ways of making requests exist in Samoan (Ochs 1990). One, the imperative "Give it to me," uses the neutral form of "me" (*Mai ia te a'u*) and sets the meaning of the construction as a demand. The second uses the sympathy-marked form of "me" (*Mai taita*) and indexes that the speaker is begging. How do children gain knowledge of indexes? The answer lies in their participation in recurrent communicative events. In contrast to formal language learning in school, learning indexicality is indirect and unconscious.

Multiple Levels of Language

A characteristic of contemporary language use is the proliferation of people who speak more than one language. Some of this change is the result of colonialism and, now, increased migration related to economic globalization. Another characteristic is the existence of intralanguage variation in such matters as word choice, intonation, and even grammar, which is tied to social differences of the users.

Bilingualism Global culture contact since the era of colonial expansion beginning in 1500 has meant that people have been increasingly exposed to more than one language. One result is that more people are bilingual. **Bilingualism** simply refers to the capacity to speak two languages. A true bilingual has "native speaking abilities" in two languages. Bilingualism is often the result of migration from one language area to another.

Many world populations are bilingual because their country was colonized and a second language was introduced. As the result of the close proximity and high exposure to many languages, Europeans often grow up learning more than one language. Europeans also developed Esperanto, an artificial language intended to reduce barriers between people speaking different languages; it is evidently gaining popularity among Internet users. However, it has not replaced bilingualism and multilingualism.

Linguistic pluralism, the tolerance for linguistic diversity, is an important policy issue in Canada. The British North America Act of 1867, the Canadian Constitution, and the Official Languages Act of 1969 guarantee the equality of English and French as part of the national identity of Canada. Efforts of the federal government to promote bilingualism and of the current Quebec government to promote a unilingual French society are complicated by political opposition to Quebec separation, and the cost of maintaining bilingual policies and programs across Canada.

Bilingualism in Canada requires signs in both official languages.

Bilingualism confers substantial advantages to people, giving them access to an alternative way of viewing the world and in some cases economic advantages. However, in a study conducted in the 1960s, monolingual French speakers in Quebec were found to have the lowest income, monolingual English speakers, the highest income, and bilingual speakers intermediate incomes (Dorais 1979:165). Studies of the effects of differing degrees of bilingualism on the problem-solving abilities of children in the third grade suggested that bilingual children had higher levels of control of attention when solving linguistic problems than monolingual children, and used the higher levels of control in more generalized situations (Bialystok and Majumder 1998).

Dialects A **dialect** is a way of speaking in a particular place, or, more precisely, a subordinate variety of a language arising from local circumstances (R. Williams 1983:105). Thus, there is standard English and there are dialects of English. For example, the British singing group the Beatles originated in the city of Liverpool, known for its distinct dialect called "Scouse." Cockney, spoken in London, is another prominent dialect. Speakers of both dialects would be able to understand each other, but with some difficulty.

Standard forms of a language will have the stamp of authority of the nation and will be taught using standardized textbooks. Dialects may appear in literature or films as a way of adding "local colour." It is often difficult for dialect speakers to avoid being considered somehow second class because they do not speak the standard language. Dialectical differences become a subject of debate in Canada particularly when they result in discrimination.

In the spirit of nationalistic pride in the 1970s, many writers in Quebec chose to write in *joual,* a form of French that incorporates many idiomatic expressions, anglicisms, and blasphemy. Some have argued, however, that *joual* is not the predominant dialect of Quebec French, but of working-class francophones of Montreal. The dialectical difference between *joual,* Montrealais, and Parisian French reflect differences in identity with implications beyond language.

Newfoundland dialects are of great interest to linguists and folklorists. Studies of the regional dialects of one of the oldest overseas communities in the English-speaking world reflect features characteristic of their source dialects from the English West Country, including Dorset and Devon, and southeast Ireland. From the early seventeenth century, small enclaves of seasonal voyagers and settlers inhabited the bays and developed unique vocabularies; for example, classifications of water bodies by type of ocean floor, and names for seals at every stage of development, significant for coastal fishing and sealing (Story, Kirwin, and Widdowson 1982).

Language Codes Within a single language, particular subcultures are likely to have distinctive **codes,** or ways of speaking that may include marked vocabulary, grammar, and intonation depending on age, gender, occupation, class, region, and family role of the speaker and listener. Most people know more than one code and are able to **code-switch,** or move from one code to another as needed. For example, consider how you talk to your college friends when you are in a group, compared to how you might speak to a physician or potential employer. Code-switching can be an intentional strategy used to further the interests of the speaker. Generally, code-switching follows status lines, with a dominant language or code being used to make a statement of power or authority (see the Multiple Cultural Worlds box). In the

MULTIPLE CULTURAL WORLDS

Code-Switching in Martinique

Martinique is an overseas department of France located in the eastern Caribbean. Martinicans are officially French citizens. As part of his ethnographic fieldwork in Martinique, David Murray (2002) had to learn to code-switch between Creole and French; learning to code-switch also socialized him into how the ambiguities of gender, race, and class are performed linguistically.

In Martinique, Creole and French have coexisted for centuries. French is generally the language of authority, prestige, legitimacy, and official discourse, and it is used for media and schooling. Creole is the language of subversion, marginality, and emotion. Locals know how to code-switch be-

tween French and Creole to reinforce gender distinctions, disrupt normative conduct, and mark outsiders from insiders. For example, while men switch freely between Creole and French, women are not encouraged to speak Creole, as it is considered vulgar. However, some men speak French exclusively, and women vendors usually speak Creole to each other in the female-dominated space of the market (39).

Murray's ethnography explores the local complexities of identity formation made visible through language use. While French is considered necessary for economic reasons in a global economy, it reflects Martinique's colonial past. But Creole has not emerged as a

symbol of Martinique separatism or identity. Both languages are central in public life.

As Martinique explores the politics of separation from and unity with a colonizing nation state, Quebec has emerged as a utopian destination of possible escape from the confines of the island. It is idealized as a French-speaking zone of racial and sexual freedom where people are friendlier and more tolerant than the French, a place like Martinique that has a shared colonial history with France. Thus, as Murray learned, the effects of colonialism are implicated in code-switching and language use in interesting and unpredictable ways (150).

Cultural Cueing in the Medical Interview

Subtle differences in linguistic patterns between speakers of different languages or dialects can lead to serious miscommunication. For example, health care providers who speak standard English often misinterpret messages conveyed to them by speakers of other languages and dialects. Linguistic cues are words or phrases that preface a remark to give the speaker's attitude towards what is being said, especially the degree of confidence in it. Standard English includes cues such as "maybe" and "in my opinion."

Health care providers who speak standard English often misinterpret messages conveyed to them by speakers of Mohawk English (Woolfson et al. 1995). Three functions of cueing in Mohawk English indicate the speaker's unwillingness or inability to verify the certainty of a statement; respect for the listener; or the view of Mohawk religion that health is in the hands of the creator and any statement about health must acknowledge human limitations. The many cues may appear to health care practitioners as indecisiveness or non-cooperation. These interpretations are incorrect, given the rules that the speakers are following about the validity of statements, humility, and religious belief.

Cultural interpreters may be brought in when patients and healers have different cultural backgrounds. For example, Cree and Ojibway interpreters assisted in obtaining informed consent from First Nations patients in Winnipeg hospitals. As in the Mohawk example, health professionals considered that these patients had limited ability to make informed consent decisions. Interpreters had to do more than provide accurate translations: They had to act as advocates during medical interviews (Kaufert and O'Neil 1990).

FOOD FOR THOUGHT

Have you ever thought that you were miscueing in some context? Was it related to cultural differences between you and the person you were speaking with?

decolonizing nations, people may wish to make a statement of resistance to the colonial powers by avoiding complete switching to the colonial language, but instead using **code-mixing.** In code-mixing, the speaker starts in the native language and then introduces strands of the colonial language (Myers-Scotton 1993:122).

Gender codes, or socially prescribed ways of speaking like a female or like a male, are common in most languages. In North America, women are widely regarded as being cooperative speakers, men as competitive speakers; women as indirect speakers, and men as direct speakers (Tannen 1990). However, cross-linguistic research has shown that such generalizations are suspect: for example, research on Malagasy culture has shown indirect speech to be associated with males and direct speech to be associated with females, the opposite of the pattern often claimed to be universal (Keenan 1974). Further, linguistic research conducted in North America shows that women and men vary their speech according to the particular context of the interaction, the degree of formality of the situation, the speaker's interlocutor, and so on, as we just mentioned: Uniform use of stereotypically male or female speech probably exists only in parody, such as in situation comedies or in drag performances.

As for the idea that women are more cooperative speakers, researchers make the case that both women's and men's speech, if studied carefully and in sufficient detail, bears features of both cooperative and competitive talk (D. Cameron 1997). This does not mean that the stereotype of what it means to "talk like a lady" (Lakoff 1973) does not exert an influence on the speech of girls and women, or that boys and men are not encouraged to conform to particular speech patterns.

Consider the power of male silence in North American culture. Girls and women who talk "too much" or too assertively may be judged aggressive or unfeminine; boys and men who display dynamic intonational patterns typically associated with North American English female speech may be judged effeminate. In reality, males and females make strategic use of speech features associated with "femininity" and "masculinity" within a culture, but gender stereotypes of language use are but one influence on males' and females' communicative behaviour.

Gender codes in spoken Japanese also reflect and reinforce gender differences and hierarchies (Shibamoto 1987). Certain words and sentence structures convey femininity, humbleness, and politeness. A common contrast between male and female speech is the attachment of the honorific prefix *o-* to nouns by females. This addition gives female speech a more refined and polite tone. Polite forms of speech, cross-culturally, are more associated with female gender codes than male gender codes. This gender difference carries over into related areas of speech. For example, a study of apologizing carried out on the Pacific Island of Vanuatu found that women apologize more frequently than men (Meyerhoff 1999).

Discourse, Identity, and Power

Some sociolinguists study **discourse** (language in use) in particular domains to reveal power dynamics, how people of different groups convey meaning, and how miscommunication occurs. Discourse styles and content provide clues about a person's social background, age, gender, and status. Consider what cultural information can be gleaned simply from the following bit of a conversation:

"So, like, you know, Ramadan?"

"Yeah."

"So I'm like talking to X, you know, and like she goes, 'Hey Ramadan starts next week.'"

"And I'm like, what do you say, Happy Ramadan, Merry Ramadan?" (Agar 1994:95)

If you thought that the speakers were college students, you were correct. They were young women who were probably born in North America, native English speakers likely to be White, and non-Muslim. Anthropologists have studied such conversations in varied contexts to learn how people learn culturally appropriate discourse styles, from cursing someone out to telephone conversations to political speeches. The following examples illustrate how discourse is related to identity and power relationships in two domains: children's arguments and teenage girls' everyday talk.

Children's dispute styles in different cultures reveal how argumentation is learned and how power dynamics are played out. Comparative research on children's disputes shows that argument style is culturally learned. For example, among Hindi-speaking Indian children of Fiji, overlapping is the norm, with little regard for strict turn-taking (Lein and Brenneis 1978). Other work on turn-taking versus overlapping styles indicates that offended feelings can arise when turn-takers try to con-verse with overlappers. The turn-taker feels that the overlapper is rude, and the overlapper feels that the turn-taker is distant and unengaged.

A study of how North American children argue identified stylistic strategies that include use of volume, speed, and stress and intonation (Brenneis and Lein 1977). Elevated volume was prominent, although sometimes an echo pattern of a soft statement followed by a soft response would occur. Acceleration of speed was common among older children, and less so among younger children. Strict adherence to turn-taking was followed, with no overlapping. Stress and intonation are used in rhythmical patterns, sometimes with a demand for rhyming echoes as in:

You're *skinny.*

You're *slimmy.*

You're *scrawny.*

You're...*I don't know.*

Many of the children's arguments involved insults and counter-insults. The voices of children in a downtown Toronto after-school program echo similar patterns:

As we sat together on the mat, Katie, Nadine and I discussed our favourite songs. The girls named popular songs that they had heard on the radio. Suddenly, the conver-

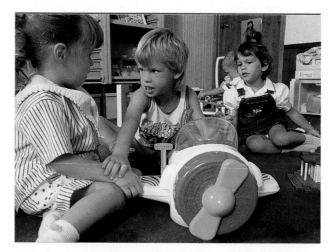

Preschool children already know much about gender roles and strategies. A boy (centre) seeks to dominate a girl in the play area of a child care centre.

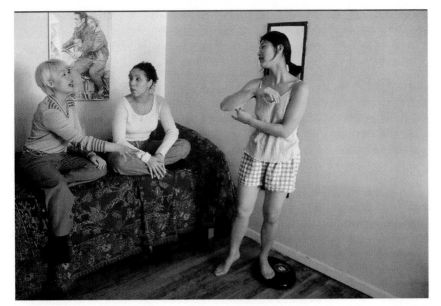

In North America, many teenage girls discuss body weight. The girl on the scale is pointing out the fat under her arm.

sation shifted from music to focusing on other events in their lives. As we spoke, a boy named Julio wandered in. The girls immediately yelled at him to get out: "boys aren't allowed." Then they proceeded to compare the body sizes of several children. "Fat Amanda" occupied the conversation for the next few minutes. "Fat Amanda," Nadine chanted "Oh she's smelly too. She stunk up the whole laundry room. When my mother went down there, she had to plug her nose." (Caputo 2001:183)

The above comments about body appearance by eight- and nine-year-old girls anticipate the concern with body weight of older Euro-American adolescent girls (Nichter and Vuckovic 1994). A study of 253 girls in the eighth and ninth grades in two urban high schools reveals the contexts and meanings of "fat talk." Fat talk usually starts with a girl commenting, "I'm so fat." The immediate response from her friends is, "No, you're not." Girls in the study say that fat talk occurs frequently throughout the day. The following representative conversation between two 14-year-olds was recorded during a focus-group discussion:

Jessica: I'm so fat.

Toni: Shut up, Jessica. You're not fat—you know how it makes you really mad when Brenda says she's fat?

Jessica: Yeah.

Toni: It makes me really mad when you say that cuz it's not true.

Jessica: Yeah, it is.

Toni: Don't say that you're fat. (112)

Girls who use fat talk are typically not overweight and are not dieting. The weight of the girls in the study was within "normal" range, and none suffered from a serious eating disorder. Fat talk sometimes functions as a call for positive reinforcement from friends that the initiator is an accepted group member. In other cases, it occurs at the beginning of a meal, "especially before eating a calorie-laden food or enjoying a buffet-style meal where an individual is faced with making public food choices" (115). In this context, fat talk is interpreted as functioning to absolve the girl from guilt feelings and to give her a feeling that she is in control of the situation.

Human Paralanguage

Human communication involves a range of nonverbal forms, including tone of voice, silence, and the full gamut of body language from posture to dress to eye movements. Referred to collectively as paralanguage, these ways of communication follow patterns and rules just like verbal language. Like verbal language, they are learned—often unconsciously—and, without learning, one will be likely to experience communication errors, sometimes funny and sometimes serious. Like verbal language, they vary cross-culturally and intraculturally.

Silence

The use of silence can be an effective form of communication, but its messages and implications differ cross-culturally. In Siberian households, the lowest status person is the in-marrying daughter, and she tends to speak very little (Humphrey 1978). However, silence does not always indicate powerlessness. In North American courts, comparison of speaking frequency between the judge, jury, and lawyers shows that lawyers, who have the least power, speak most, while the silent jury holds the most power (Lakoff 1990:97–99). While some First Nations groups value oratory, others value silence. For example, the Kaska of northern British Columbia and the Yukon did not value verbal fluency or use baby talk, and they used silence as a response to pain or frustration. Knowing how and when to keep silent was highly valued (Darnell 1970). Many outsiders, including social workers, have misinterpreted this as either reflecting the Kaskan sense of dignity, or, more insultingly, a lack of emotion or intelligence.

How wrong and ethnocentric such judgments are is clearly revealed by a study of silence among the Western Apache of Arizona (Basso 1972 [1970]). The Western Apache use silence in four contexts. First, when meeting a stranger, someone who cannot be identified, especially at fairs, rodeos, or other public events, it is considered bad manners to speak right away. That would indicate interest in something like money, or work, or transportation, which are possible reasons for exhibiting such bad manners. Second, silence is important in the early stages of courting. Sitting in silence and holding hands for several hours is appropriate. Speaking "too soon" would indicate sexual willingness or interest. That would be immodest. Third, when children come home after a long absence at boarding school, parents and children should meet each other with silence for about 15 minutes rather than rushing into a flurry of greetings. It may be two or three days before sustained conversations are initiated. Last, a person should be silent when "getting cussed out," especially at drinking parties. An underlying similarity of all these contexts is the uncertainty, ambiguity, and unpredictability of the social relationships. Rather than chattering to "break the ice," the Apache response is silence. The difference between the Apache style and the Euro-American emphasis on quick and continuous verbal interactions in most contexts can cause cross-cultural misunderstandings. Outsiders, for example, have misinterpreted Apache parents' silent greeting of their returning children as bad parenting or as a sign of child neglect.

Kinesics

Kinesics refers to the study of communication that occurs through body movements, positions, facial expressions,

Nonverbal communication in Japanese culture is especially marked by the frequent use of bowing. Two Japanese businessmen meet each other, bow, and exchange business cards.

and spatial behaviour. Just like verbal language, nonverbal language has rules for correct usage, possibilities for code-switching, and cross-cultural variation. Serious misunderstandings of body language can easily happen because, like verbal language and international forms of sign language, it is based on arbitrary symbols. Different cultures may emphasize different "channels" more than others: Some are more touch-oriented than others, for example, or use facial expressions more. Eye contact is something valued in Euro-American conversations, but in many Asian contexts, direct eye contact could be considered rude or possibly also a sexual invitation. Nonverbal communication is important in indexing social relationships, especially dominance and accommodation, or positive versus negative feelings.

Dress and Appearance

Manipulation of the body is a way of sending messages. Marks on the body, clothing, and hair styles convey a range of messages about age, gender, sexual interest or availability, profession, wealth, and emotions. In North America, gender differentiation begins in the hospital nursery with the colour coding of blue for boys and pink for girls. In Japan, the kimono carries an elaborate system for coding gender, life-cycle stage, and formality of the occasion (see Figure 13.3):

> *Ceremonial kimonos worn by unmarried women stand out by virtue of their sleeves, vivid colors, and busy designs. Kimono length of sleeve refers to a dimension that Western clothing lacks. For us, long or short sleeves mean the total length of the tube of sleeve material. For kimono the dimension is standardized just above the wrist bone; the "depth" of the bag of the sleeve is the important, variable part. Miss's ceremonial kimono takes its name, furisode, from its deep fluttering sleeves. In full-blown furisode, sleeves reach to the ankles. There are also ko- (little) and chu- (mid) versions of furisode, reflecting lesser degrees of formality.... The cultural dimension of social responsibility varies in inverse proportion to the depth of one's kimono sleeve—the more responsibility (adult males), the shorter the sleeve. (Dalby 1993:195–196)*

Messages conveyed through hair (McCracken 1996) or dress, like other linguistic cues, have the property of arbitrariness. Consider the different meaning of veiling in Egypt and Kuwait. The veiling of Kuwaiti women is a nationalist message that distinguishes wealthy, leisured, and honourable Kuwaiti women from poor, labouring, immigrant women workers. Consider, in contrast, the practice and meaning of veiling in Egypt, a comparatively "moderate" nation in terms of Muslim values. In 1962, women gained the right to vote and they increasingly entered the work force. Recent economic decline, however, has put pressure on women to retreat to the domestic domain. The new veiling movement in Egypt emerged in the late 1970s as the economy declined (MacLeod 1992). Egyptian women who are veiling, like Kuwaiti women, have adopted the head scarf rather than full traditional veiling. But the new veiling in Egypt is done mainly by women from the lower and middle economic levels, where it has been adopted as a way for working-class women to accommodate to pressures from Islamic fundamentalism to veil, while preserving their right to keep working outside the home. The scarf says, "I am a good Muslim and a good wife/daughter."

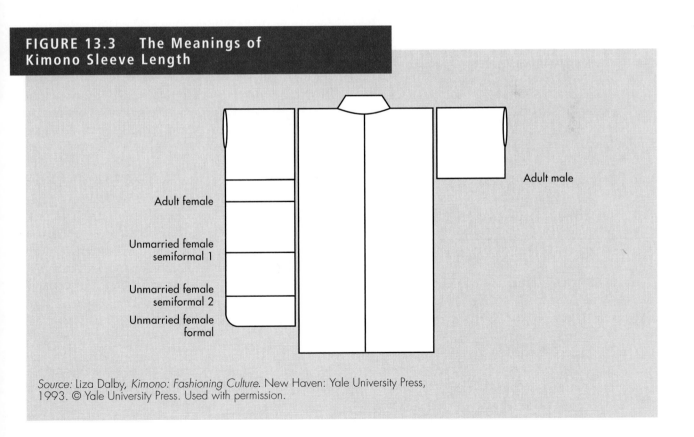

FIGURE 13.3   The Meanings of Kimono Sleeve Length

Adult male

Adult female

Unmarried female semiformal 1

Unmarried female semiformal 2

Unmarried female formal

Source: Liza Dalby, *Kimono: Fashioning Culture.* New Haven: Yale University Press, 1993. © Yale University Press. Used with permission.

Mass Media

Mass media refers to communication via electronic media such as radio, television, film, and recorded music, or the print media of newspapers, magazines, and popular literature. In the 1960s, long before media anthropology became popular, Marshall McLuhan, the University of Toronto English professor who became the chief theorist and prophet of mass communications, examined how new technologies created new environments for communication (1964). He predicted the importance of the media using phrases such as the "global village" and "the medium is the message/massage." Media anthropologists study the media process, content, audience response, and social effects of media presentations. Media anthropology seeks to bring together the interests and goals of both anthropology and the media by promoting a contextualized view. In journalism, for example, media anthropology promotes going beyond the reporting of crises and other events to presenting a more holistic, contextualized story. Another applied goal is to disseminate more of anthropology's findings to the general public via radio, television, print journalism, magazines, and the Internet. An anthropological critique of mass media asks to what degree access to its messages are mind-opening and liberating or propagandizing and controlling, and whose interests the media are serving.

The Media Process

Anthropologist Mark Pedelty has devoted attention to the media process (meaning the study of who creates media messages and how they are disseminated) in his book *War Stories* (1995) in which he examines the culture of war correspondents in El Salvador. He finds that their culture is highly charged with violence and terror: "War correspondents have a unique relationship to terror, however, a hybrid condition that combines voyeurism and direct participation.... They need terror to realize themselves in both a professional and spiritual sense, to achieve and maintain their culture identity as 'war correspondents'" (2). Pedelty researched a range of topics, including status differences between regular staff correspondents and "stringers" (freelancers who sell their stories where they can), events such as press conferences, the way reporters track down stories, news censorship, cultural differences in attachment to the ideal of objective reporting, and war correspondents' mental health (they tend to have frequent bad dreams and burnout). He probes the psychological ambivalence of war correspondents who are often accused of making a living from war and violence and who become dependent on the continuation of war for their livelihood. Even the Salvadoran correspondents, whose country was being racked by violence, worried that the end of the war would also mean the end of their ability to support their families. Pedelty also addresses media censorship, direct and indirect, and how it affects what stories readers receive and the way events are described. In the early period of his fieldwork, he talked with an experienced European reporter about how she alters her story depending on which newspaper she is writing for. She showed him computer printouts of two reports she had recently written about the same event, one for a European news institution and the other for a U.S. newspaper. The two reports were different in the use and order of "facts" presented and in the use of quotations.

Nationalist media bias is clear in reports of sporting events. Canadian Donovan Bailey from Oakville, Ontario, won the 100-metre final at the 1996 summer Olympics in Atlanta. In the history of the modern Olympics, whoever won the 100-metre race was considered the "world's fastest man." However, the American press claimed that the title should go to American sprinter Michael Johnson on the basis of his record-breaking performance in the 200-metre race. Bailey complained that he did not get the respect he deserved from the American media because he was Canadian. The American magazine *Sports Illustrated* responded by calling Bailey a "whiner." To determine who was the "world's fastest man," Bailey and Johnson ran a 150-metre race at the SkyDome in Toronto on June 1, 1997. Johnson quit midway through the race, complaining of a strained quadriceps muscle, with Bailey well out in front. Not surprisingly, the event was reported very differently in the American and Canadian media. In addition to nationalist bias, racial bias is also evident in news reporting (see the Critical Thinking box).

Television Studies

Ethnographic studies of television began in the 1980s. Along with related research done by scholars in English, comparative media studies, and communication studies, a substantial body of material is being amassed that situates television within its social context. A major question is how television both determines culture and reflects culture. The basic theoretical tension between structure and agency is of key importance in this area. Most anthropological and related studies of television treat television shows as "texts" that can be approached through analysis of content, dominant symbols, and plot, just as one would analyze a novel or play.

Ethnographic research within a Japanese television station provided one anthropologist with insights into the social organization of the workplace and how it mirrors the messages put forth through television programming (Painter 1996). The primary audience for Japanese television is the category of *shufu*, housewives. A Japanese television network classified housewives into six categories, ranging from the strongly self-assertive "almighty housewife" to the "tranquil and prudent" housewife. A popular form of programming for housewives is the *homu dorama*, the "home drama" or domestic serial. These serials consistently represent traditional values such as filial piety and the proper role of the daughter-in-law in regard to her mother-in-law. Caring for the aged has become a prominent theme that supplies the central tension for many situations in which women have to sort out their relationships with each other.

In contrast, television representations of men emphasize their negotiation of social hierarchies within the workplace and other public organizations. While the dominant mode of representation puts women in traditional domestic roles, many women in contemporary Japan are rejecting such shows. In response, producers are experimenting with new sorts of dramas in which women are shown as active workers and aggressive lovers—anything but domesticated housewives. One such show is a 10-part serial aired in 1992 called *Selfish Women*. The story concerns three women: an aggressive single businesswoman who faces discrimination at work, a young mother who is raising her daughter alone while her photographer husband lives with another woman, and an ex-housewife who divorced her husband because she found home life empty and unrewarding. There are several male characters, but except perhaps for one, they are depicted as less interesting than the women. The show's title is ironic. In Japan, women who assert themselves are often labelled "selfish" by men. The lead women in the drama use the term in a positive way to encourage

each other:…"Let's become even more selfish!"…Painter (1996) comments that, "though dramas like *Selfish Women* are perhaps not revolutionary, they are indicative of the fact that telerepresentations of gender in Japan are changing, at least in some areas" (69).

In Canada, the Canadian Broadcasting Corporation (CBC), a Crown corporation, was created in 1936 to enhance Canadians' sense of national identity through its emphasis on Canadian content, and to give Canadians an alternative to American programming.

Language and Social Change

Languages change constantly, sometimes slowly and in small ways, other times rapidly and dramatically. Most of us are scarcely conscious of such changes. Colonialism was a major force of change. Not only did colonial powers declare their own language as the language of government, business, and higher education, but often direct steps were taken to suppress indigenous languages and literatures (see the Voices box on page 331).

A **pidgin** is a contact language that emerges when different cultures with different languages come to live in close proximity and therefore need to communicate (McMahon 1994:253). Pidgins are generally limited to highly functional domains, such as trade, since that is what they were developed for. A pidgin therefore is no one's first language. Many pidgins of the Western hemisphere developed out of slavery, where owners needed to communicate with their slaves. A pidgin is always learned as a second language. Tok Pisin, the pidgin language of Papua New Guinea, consists of a mixture of many languages, some English, Samoan, Chinese, and Malayan. Tok Pisin has been declared one of the national languages of Papua New Guinea, where it is transforming into a **creole**, or a language descended from pidgin with its own native speakers and involving linguistic expansion and elaboration. About 200 pidgin and creole languages exist today, mainly in West Africa, the Caribbean, and the South Pacific.

National policies of cultural assimilation of minorities have also led to the extinction of many ethnic languages. One motivation for the establishment of residential

Bias in News Reporting

Francis Henry and Carol Tator (2002) researched how mainstream Canadian media construct a view of Canadian society that silences, erases, or marginalizes a significant proportion of this country's population (226). They argue that mainstream media representations define dominant discourses (ways of talking about a topic). The way the media interpret events influences the way readers think about events, creating an ideological climate that seems natural, but in fact contains unchallenged assumptions about the world (26). As this study shows, images disseminated by the mainstream media of immigrants and First Nations peoples are not the images these groups would present of themselves, and these images often reinforce negative stereotypes.

The authors document how the selection of news stories raises the public's anxiety about crime, keeps sensational stories in the news, over-reports crimes allegedly committed by people of colour—especially young Black males—and describes such crimes with emotional hyperbole. They analyzed the news reports about the murder in Toronto of a young White woman by several Black Jamaican men in the Just Desserts Café in Toronto in 1994 to re-

veal how the use of phrases such as "urban terrorism," "slaughter," "drug-crazed," and "gun-toting barbarians" helped create a moral panic about the need for law and order (202). By selection of stories, editorials, and specific rhetorical strategies, the mainstream media produce discourse that constructs immigrants as prone to criminality. News reports about Jamaicans and Vietnamese, for example, emphasized crime, immigration, and social problems. In an analysis of news stories from 1994–1997 on Jamaicans in Canada, 45 per cent of the stories fell into the categories of sports or entertainment (Henry and Tator 2002:167). Coverage of First Nations peoples in several newspapers represented them as pathetic victims, angry warriors, or noble environmentalists, stereotypes that could result in misunderstanding.

The problem, according to Henry and Tator, is lack of reflexivity and critical self-awareness among journalists who work for the mainstream media, few of whom are visible minorities, with the result that few oppositional and counter discourses are articulated in the mainstream media. But resistance to media stereotyping is growing. Recently, the Canadian Tamil community launched a

lawsuit against the *National Post* for targeting its community and for labelling Tamils as "terrorists" and "criminals." The Canadian Islamic Congress continuously monitors the media for bias in the coverage of Islam—a particularly important task following the events of September 11, 2001. Ethnic presses also have a critical role to play by challenging familiar stereotypes and providing the social, cultural, historical, and political context missing from the mainstream press (239).

CRITICAL THINKING QUESTIONS

Can you identify any differences in content or approach in two versions of the same story presented in different daily newspapers published on the same day?

Do the stories reveal any bias on the basis of gender or race?

Is there any difference in the way the same story is covered in the ethnic press and alternative press?

Can you identify any dominant discourses that might have influenced the selection of articles and the content of editorials in the mainstream, ethnic, and alternative presses?

schools for First Nations children was to eradicate Aboriginal languages. For example, residential schools were run in British Columbia from 1880, and lasted into the 1960s. Conditions were harsh; punishment was most severe for using Aboriginal languages (Tennant 1990:78). Yet Aboriginal languages in Canada were not obliterated. Of those who identify an Aboriginal language as their first language, 43 per cent speak Cree, 14 per cent speak Inuktitut, 13 per cent speak Ojibwa, 3 per cent speak Athabaskan, and 1 per cent speak Sioux; but the average age of the speakers is over 40 (Frideres 1998:136).

There are policies in place to revive and maintain these languages. While Inuit residential schooling used to be English or French based, Grades 1 to 3 are now taught in Inuktitut, even for non-Inuit children (Frideres 1998:400). Native-as-a-Second-Language (NSL) programs in Ontario aim to develop literacy and encourage the functional use of Aboriginal languages. Teacher training programs for Cree, Delaware, and Ojibway are taught in Thunder Bay; Cayuga, Oneida, and Mohawk are taught in St. Catharines (King 1998:410).

Because language is such a vital part of culture, language rights and political rights are closely intertwined. One of the most complex examples of language politics and identity concerns the relation between French and English in Canada. Many of the language policies of Quebec, such as Bill 101, reflect the fear that without protection, the French language in Quebec will be contaminated by English, become corrupted and degenerate, with a resulting loss in cultural identity. Others argue that only in a bilingual Canada will French be protected, and that separation would result in a loss of French language in anglophone North America, particularly in the era of NAFTA.

Ngũgĩ wa Thiong'o, "On Decolonizing the Mind"

VOICES

I was born into a large peasant family: father, four wives and about twenty-eight children.... We spoke Gĩkũyũ in and outside the home. I can vividly recall those evenings of story-telling around the fireside.... Our appreciation of the suggestive magical power of language was reinforced by the games we played with words through riddles, proverbs, transpositions of syllables, or through nonsensical but musically arranged words....

And then I went to school.... English became the language of my formal education. In Kenya, English became more than a language: it was the language...one of the most humiliating experiences was to be caught speaking Gĩkũyũ in the vicinity of the school. The culprit was given corporal punishment—three to five strokes of the cane on bare buttocks—or was made to carry a metal plate around the neck with inscriptions such as I AM STUPID or I AM A DONKEY. Sometimes the culprits were fined money they could hardly afford.... The attitude to English was the exact opposite: any achievement in spoken or written English was highly rewarded; prizes, prestige, applause....

So what was the colonial imposition of a foreign language doing to us children? The real aim of colonialism was to control the people's wealth.... But its most important area of domination was the mental universe of the colonised.... The images of this world and his place in it implanted in a child take years to eradicate, if they ever can be.

Source: Stuart Hirschberg, ed., *One World, Many Cultures*, pp. 402–409.

Key Questions Revisited

What aspects of communication do linguistic anthropologists study?

While anthropologists in all four fields address the topic of communication, linguistic anthropologists have the deepest interest in human communication as it relates to culture. The earliest linguistic anthropologists, who established linguistics as a field of anthropology in the late eighteenth century, documented disappearing Native American languages. Contemporary linguistic anthropologists are more likely to be engaged in studying the formal properties of language, historical linguistics, the relationship between social context and communication (more broadly including the role of the media), and how communication systems are changing.

How do culture, society, and communication interact?

Linguistic anthropologists have theorized and studied how communication shapes culture and how culture shapes communication. One prominent theory, the Sapir-Whorf hypothesis, gives primacy to a person's language in determining how that person thinks and behaves. An alternative view, from sociolinguistics, reverses the arrow of causality and says that a person's culture shapes the person's language. Research on human communication patterns cross-culturally and within cultures provides substantial evidence for the latter view. Paralanguage, or nonverbal forms of communication, is another prominent aspect of human communication. Like verbal language, paralanguage or kinesics can lead to misunderstanding when cultural cues are misread. The use of silence, body posture, dress, and adornment all convey culturally meaningful messages. Research on the media process offers insights into how and why particular messages are chosen and produced for mass consumption.

What are some important factors affecting language change?

Often, large structural forces, such as colonialism and now globalization, have promoted the spread of particular forms of communication, the decline of others, and in many cases a situation of linguistic pluralism. Studies indicate that people in local cultures react to outside forces of change in a variety of ways, sometimes by attempting to resist adoption of a new language, other times incorporating and localizing aspects of the new language. Most anthropologists support linguistic pluralism as reflecting and supporting cultural pluralism.

Core Concepts

Suggested Readings

John Edwards, *Language in Canada*. Cambridge: Cambridge University Press, 1998. This book examines bilingualism, multiculturalism, Aboriginal languages, and language issues in every province of Canada.

Joy Hendry, *Wrapping Culture: Politeness, Presentation and Power in Japan and Other Societies*. New York: Oxford University Press, 1993. This book explores the pervasive idiom and practice of "wrapping" in Japanese culture, including verbal language, gift-giving, and dress. In verbal language, wrapping involves the use of various forms of respect, indicating social levels of the speakers, and the use of linguistic forms of beautification, which have the effect of adornment.

Robin Toimach Lakoff, *Talking Power: The Politics of Language in Our Lives*. New York: Basic Books, 1990. Lakoff explores strategies of communication and language power-plays in English in the United States, providing examples from courtrooms, classrooms, summit talks, and joke-telling.

William L. Leap, *Word's Out: Gay Men's English*. Minneapolis: University of Minnesota Press, 1996. Fieldwork among gay men in the Washington, D.C., area produced this ethnography that addresses gay men's speech as a cooperative mode of discourse, bathroom graffiti, and discourse about HIV/AIDS.

Catherine A. Lutz and Jane L. Collins, *Reading National Geographic*. Chicago: University of Chicago Press, 1993. This study presents the way *National Geographic's* editors, photographers, and designers select text and images of Third World cultures and how middle-class American readers interpret the material.

Susan U. Philips, Susan Steele, and Christine Tanz, *Language, Gender and Sex in Comparative Perspective*. New York: Cambridge University Press, 1987. An introductory essay, followed by 11 chapters, explores women's and men's speech in Japan, Western Samoa, and Mexico; children's speech in American preschools and in Papua New Guinea; and sex differences in how the brain is related to speech.

William A. Smalley, *Linguistic Diversity and National Unity: Language Ecology in Thailand*. Chicago: University of Chicago Press, 1994. This book describes levels of linguistic variation in Thailand, paying attention to standard Thai in relation to regional languages and local dialects. Also, the book provides a detailed analysis of changes in sounds and vocabulary as part of wider processes of social change such as migration and urbanization.

Lisa Philips Valentine, *Making It Their Own: Ojibwe Communicative Practices*. Toronto: University of Toronto Press, 1995. This ethnographic study examines a variety of speech events in a small community of Ojibwe people in northern Ontario, Canada. It includes attention to speech variations among speakers, code-switching, and multilingualism as well as connections between spoken language and church music.

Your *Cultural Anthropology*, Second Canadian Edition Media Edition CD-ROM contains many Web sites relevant to this chapter. Use it to explore the Web and to expand your knowledge of anthropology.

Chapter 14

Expressive Culture

CHAPTER OUTLINE

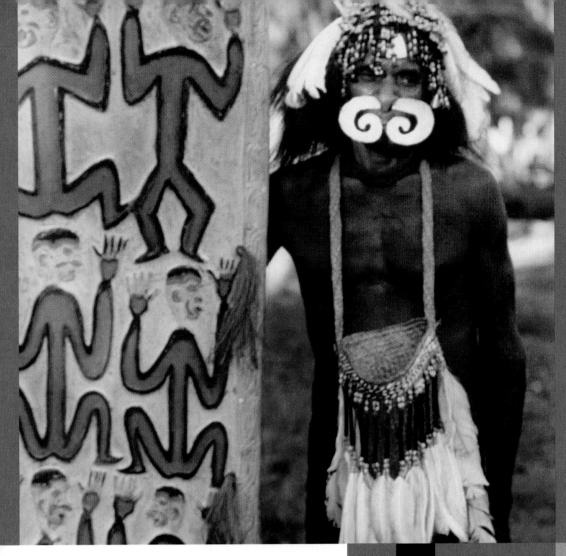

A carver of the Asmat culture in Northern Papua, New Guinea, with a shield he carved.

Key Questions

What is art and how does cultural anthropology study it?

What do play and leisure activities tell us about culture?

How is expressive culture changing in contemporary times?

*I*n the year 2004, the Louvre in Paris, one of the most well-known art museums in the world, will open a huge new museum in the shadow of the Eiffel Tower that will display so-called tribal art of Africa, Asia, the South Pacific, and the Americas (Corbey 2000). This project reflects the interest of France's President Jacques Chirac in non-Western art. It also reflects a new appreciation for the role of cultural anthropologists in helping museums to provide cultural context for objects that are displayed since Maurice Godelier, a specialist on New Guinea, is closely involved in planning the new exhibits. This effort crystalizes many of the questions raised in this chapter including: What is to be considered art worthy of display in a museum, and how should it be displayed?

In this chapter, we consider a vast area of human behaviour and thought called *expressive culture,* which is learned and patterned ways of creative endeavour that include art, leisure, and play (definitions of these terms are provided in the relevant sections below). We start with a discussion of what the anthropology of art encompasses and some theoretical perspectives on cross-cultural art. Examples of art discussed are sculpture, music, theatre, architecture, and interior design. The following section reviews findings from the field of museum studies in which scholars are seeking appropriate ways of representing culture in a museum context. We then turn to a cross-cultural look at play and leisure activities. Last, we consider directions of change in expressive culture.

What Is Art?

Are ancient rock carvings art? Is subway graffiti art? An embroidered robe? A painting of a can of Campbell's soup? Philosophers, art critics, anthropologists, and art lovers have all struggled with the question of what art is. The question of how to define art involves more than mere word games. The way art is defined affects the manner in which a person classifies, values, and treats artistic creations and those who create art. Anthropologists propose broad definitions of art to take into account emic definitions cross-culturally. One definition says that **art** is the application of imagination, skill, and style to matter, movement, and sound that goes beyond the purely practical (Nanda 1994:383). The anthropological study of art considers both the process and the products of such human skill, the variation in art and its preferred forms

cross-culturally, and the way culture constructs and changes artistic traditions. The skill that is involved is defined and recognized as such in a particular culture. Such culturally judged skill can be applied to any number of substances and activities and can be considered art: for example, a beautifully presented meal, a well-told story or joke, or a perfectly formed basket. In this sense, art is a human universal, and no culture can be said to lack artistic activity.

Art is often classified by eras, such as paleolithic or modern art. Other categories are based on medium of expression: for example, graphic or plastic arts (painting, drawing, sculpture, weaving, basketry, and architecture); the decorative arts (interior design, landscaping, gardening, costume design, and body adornment such as hairstyling, tattooing, and body painting); performance arts (music, dance, and theatre); and verbal arts (poetry, writing, rhetoric, storytelling, and joke telling).

A long-standing distinction in English exists between "fine art" and "folk art." The distinctions are based on a Western-centric judgment that defines **fine art** as rare, expensive art produced by artists usually trained in the Western classical tradition. This is the kind of art that is included in college courses called "Fine Art." The implication is that all other art is less than fine and more appropriately called folk art, or "ethnic art" or "primitive art" or "crafts." Western fine art are has the following characteristics: It is created by a formally schooled artist, the product is made for the market (for sale or on commission), the product is clearly associated with a particular artist, the product's uniqueness is valued, and the product is not primarily utilitarian but is rather "art for art's sake." In contrast, all the rest of the world's art that is non-Western and nonclassical—referred to as **folk art**—is supposedly characterized by the opposite features: It is created by an artist who has not received formal training, it is not produced for the market, the artist is anonymous and does not sign or individually claim the product, and it is made primarily for use in food storage and preparation, ritual, or war. The categories of folk and fine art prompt further thinking as to their adequacy.

Just as all cultures have art, all cultures have a sense of what makes something art versus non-art. The term *esthetics* refers to agreed-upon notions of quality (R. Thompson 1971:374). Before anthropologists proved otherwise, Western art experts considered that esthetics did not exist or was poorly developed elsewhere. We now know that established criteria for artistic quality exist everywhere regardless of whether they are written down and formalized. Franz Boas, from his wide review of many forms of art in pre-state societies, deduced principles that he claimed were universal for these cultures, especially symmetry, rhythmic repetition, and naturalism (Jonaitis 1995:37). These principles do apply in many cases, but they are not as universal as Boas thought they were.

Ethno-esthetics consider local variations in esthetic criteria. The set of standards concerning wood carving in West Africa illustrates the importance of considering cultural variation (R. Thompson 1971). Among the Yoruba of Nigeria, esthetic guidelines include the following:

- Figures should be depicted midway between complete abstraction and complete realism so that they resemble "somebody," but no one in particular (portraiture in the Western sense is considered dangerous).

- Humans should be depicted at their optimal physical peak, not in infancy or old age.

- There should be clarity of line and form.

- The sculpture should have the quality of luminosity achieved through a polished surface, the play of incisions, and shadows.

- The piece should exhibit symmetry.

A few anthropological studies have also documented intracultural differences in esthetic standards. For example, one anthropologist showed computer-generated graphics to the Shipibo Indians of the Peruvian Amazon and learned that men liked the abstract designs, while the women thought they were ugly (Roe in Anderson and Field 1993:257). If you are wondering why this difference would exist, consider the interpretation of the anthropologist: Shipibo men are the shamans and take hallucinogenic drugs that may give them familiarity with more "psychedelic" images.

Yoruba wood carving is done according to esthetic principles that require clarity of line and form, a polished surface that creates a play of light and shadows, symmetry, and the depiction of human figures that are neither completely abstract nor completely realistic and that are shown as adults and never very young or very old.

Studying Art in Society

The anthropological study of art seeks to understand more than just the products of art, but also who makes it and why, its role in society, and its wider social meanings. Franz Boas was the first anthropologist to emphasize the importance of studying the artist in society. A significant thread in general anthropology's theoretical history—functionalism—also dominated work of the early twentieth century on art. Anthropologists wrote about how paintings, dance, theatre, and songs serve to socialize children into the culture; provide a sense of social identity and group boundaries; and promote healing. Art may legitimize political leaders and enhance efforts in war through magical decorations on shields and weapons. Art may serve as a form of social control, as in African masks worn by dancers who represent deities visiting humans to remind them of the moral order. Art, like language, can be a catalyst for political resistance or grounds for ethnic solidarity in the face of the state.

With its breadth of topical interest, the anthropology of art relies on a range of methods in data gathering and analysis. For some research projects, participant observation provides most of the necessary data. In others, participant observation is complemented by collecting and analyzing oral or written material such as video and tape recordings. Some anthropologists have become apprentices in a certain artistic tradition. For example, in undertaking one of the earliest studies of Native American potters of the Southwest, Ruth Bunzel (1972 [1929])

CRITICAL THINKING

Navajo Textiles: Back to the Rez

The blankets and rugs woven by thousands of Navajo women living in the Southwest United States are highly desired by North American art collectors. Pre-1940 textiles typically sell for thousands of dollars at international auctions and galleries. Anthropologist/weaver Kathy M'Closkey of the University of Windsor spoke at a conference about the difficulties faced by contemporary Navajo weavers unable to receive adequate compensation for their rugs. The investment potential of historic weaving diminished the demand for contemporary textiles. However, the recent popularity of the southwest look in fashion and home furnishings created a demand for Navajo-like patterns. Entrepreneurs appropriated the designs using illustrations of historic textiles as models for copyweaving, or knockoffs, made in Mexico and other countries. Navajo patterns remain unprotected by copyright, as the designs have been part of the public domain for decades.

After hearing M'Closkey's presentation, a conference participant donated the century-old Navajo blanket pictured here to the Navajo Nation Museum and Cultural Center in Window Rock, Arizona. He found it in his mother's cedar chest, where she had carefully stored it away after purchasing it in Arizona during the 1920s. Navajo weavers were thrilled with the gift, as they seldom see the old textiles. Their ancestors had to exchange textiles for groceries at reservation trading posts in order to survive. Averaging two cents per hour in credit, Navajo women's weaving was treated as raw wool by the traders, ignoring the hours of work Navajo women put into creating the rugs.

Well-known American abstract artists collected historic Navajo textiles for more than 50 years. Several artists were greatly influenced by Navajo blanket weavers' use of colour and design. The first international touring exhibition of historic Navajo blankets (1972–1974) featured many examples from the collections of famous artists. Almost immediately the demand for the rare textiles escalated, culminating in a $522 000 sale of a historic Navajo blanket at Sotheby's in 1989. Formerly referred to as "craft," these old blankets are now revered as "art" (M'Closkey 1994). The blanket shown could have been sold as art on the auction block; instead, it went back home.

Anthropologist/weaver Kathy M'Closkey displays a century-old Navajo blanket.

CRITICAL THINKING QUESTIONS

Since many languages lack a term that translates as art, how can art be defined cross-culturally?

Why are textiles and weavings more likely to be exhibited in museums rather than art galleries?

How useful are the categories of fine art, folk art, and craft for anthropologists studying artistic production? What other categories can you suggest?

learned how to make pottery and thereby gained important data on what the potters thought constituted good designs. Kathy M'Closkey's (1996) experience as a weaver facilitated her research on Navajo rugs (see the Critical Thinking box on page 338).

In contrast, anthropologists who study past traditions, such as paleolithic art, cannot do participant observation or talk to the artists. They have to rely on indirect interpretation of silent symbols, shapes, colours, and contexts. Ethno-archaeology helps in this endeavour by providing clues about the past from the present. One example of this is a recent interpretation of the "Venus" figurines, the first human images from the European Upper Paleolithic period between 27 000 and 21 000 BCE (McDermott 1996). Little is known about why these palm-sized statuettes were made or who made them. Stylistically, each figurine has large breasts, abdomen, and buttocks, and small head, arms, and legs. Past interpretations of this characteristic shape have seen it as an intentional distortion to emphasize sexuality and fertility. A new theory proposes that women, especially pregnant women, sculpted these figurines as self-representations. A woman who used herself as a model would have a view of her body very much like that of the figurines (McCoid and McDermott 1996).

A new theory about the Venus figurines claims that they were self-portraits, crafted by women. A photograph of a pregnant woman looking down at herself presents a shape very much like that of the Venus figurines—but the shape is actual, not a distortion.

A top-down view of the "Venus" figurine, one of the first human images known. These small statues have often been interpreted as fertility goddesses on the basis of the large breasts, abdomen, and buttocks, and small head, arms, and legs. These features are said to be intentional distortions of the artist done to emphasize fertility.

This section presents findings in two important areas of the anthropological study of art: first, the artist, and then how art, gender, ethnicity, and power are related.

Focus on the Artist

In the early twentieth century, Boas urged his students to go beyond the study of the products of artistic endeavour and study the artists. The special role of the anthropologist is to add to the understanding of art by studying the process of creating art both within its social context and from the artist's perspective. Ruth Bunzel's (1972 [1929]) study of Pueblo potters is an example of this tradition. She paid attention to the variety of pot shapes and motifs employed and also interviewed individual potters about their personal design choices. One Zuni potter commented, "I always know the whole design before I start to paint" (49).

The social status of artists varies widely. Artists may be revered and wealthy as individuals or groups, or stigmatized and economically marginal. In ancient Mexico, gold workers were a highly respected group. In First Nations groups of the Pacific Northwest Coast, male carvers and painters had to be initiated into a secret society, and they had higher status than other men. Often a gender division of artistic involvement exists. Among the Navajo, men do silversmithing, while women weave. In the Caribbean, women of African descent are noted for their carvings of calabashes (large gourds). Artists and performers often live outside the boundaries of mainstream society or challenge social boundaries.

In Morocco, a *shikha* is a female performer who sings and dances at festivities, including rites-of-passage ceremonies such as birth, circumcision, and marriage (Kapchan 1994). *Shikhat* (the plural ends with a *t*) usually appear in a group of three or four with accompanying musicians. Their performance involves suggestive songs and body movements, including reaching a state of near-possession when they loosen their hair buns. With their long hair waving, they "lift the belt," a special technique accomplished through an undulating movement that rolls the abdomen up to the waist. Their entertainment at these mixed-gender events creates a lively atmosphere as they dance, sing, and draw participants into dancing with them: "[S]hikhat dominate and dictate the emotional tenor of celebrations. Through the provocative movements and loud singing of the shikhat, the audience is drawn up and into a collective state of celebration, their bodies literally pulled into the dance" (93).

In their private lives, *shikhat* are on the social fringes, leading lives as single women who transgress rules for proper females. They own property, drink alcohol, smoke cigarettes, and may have several lovers. Most of the *shikhat* have been rejected by their natal families, and they live alone or in groups. Middle- and upper-class women consider them vulgar and generally distance themselves from them. *Shikhat* who become successful, widening their performance spheres to larger towns and cities, manage to save money and become landowners and gain economic status. The modern mass media is contributing to an increased status of *shikhat* as performers. Video cassette recordings of *shikhat* music are popular, and the Moroccan term *mughanniyya* (singer) is being used to refer to them, implying more status. State-produced television broadcasts carry performances of regional *shikhat* groups as a way of presenting the diverse cultures of the nation. All of these forces are leading to a re-evaluation of the social standing of performers of this ancient art form.

As with other occupations, artists are more specialized in state-level societies. In foraging groups, some people may be singled out as especially good singers, storytellers, or carvers. Generally, however, among foragers, artistic activity is open to all, and artistic products are shared equally by all. With increasing social complexity and a market for art, specialized training is required to produce certain kinds of art and the products are sought after by those who can afford them. Class differences in artistic styles and preferences emerge along with the increasingly complex division of labour.

Ethnicity, Gender, and Power

Art forms and styles, like languages, are often associated with particular ethnic groups' identity and sense of pride. For example, the Berbers of highland Morocco are associated with carpets, the Navajo with woven blankets, and the Inuit with stone carving.

Cultural anthropologists provide many examples of linkages between various dimensions (ethnicity, gender, race) and power issues. In some instances, more powerful groups appropriate the art forms of less powerful groups. In others, forms of art are said to be expressive of resistance. One anthropological study reveals how political interests affect "ownership" of ethnic artistic expression (see the Multiple Cultural Worlds box on page 341). A study of a form of popular performance art in a Florida town, male strip dancing, shows how societal power relations between men and women are reinforced in this form of leisure activity (Margolis and Arnold 1993). Advertisements in the media tell women that seeing a male strip dancer is "their chance," "their night out." Going to a male strip show is thus presumably a time of reversal of traditional gender roles in which men are dominant and women submissive. The researchers asked if gender roles are reversed in a male stripper bar, and their answer was "no." Women customers are treated like juveniles, controlled by the manager who tells them how to tip as they stand in line waiting for the show to open, and symbolically humbled in relation to the dancers, who take on the role of lion-tamers, for example. The "dive-bomb" is further evidence that the women are not in charge. The dive-bomb is a particular form of tipping the dancer. The woman customer gets on her hands and knees and tucks a bill held between her teeth into the dancer's G-string.

Not all forms of popular performance are mechanisms of social control and hierarchy maintenance, how-

Invisible Hands Crafting Israeli Souvenirs

Maskit, an upscale national emporium perceived as "an ambassador of Israel" sells arts and crafts souvenirs to tourists (Shenhav-Keller 1993:183). Ethnographic study shows how the sellers "put Israeli society on display via its souvenirs." It also reveals how certain artists and craftspeople are selectively rendered invisible. The tourist artifact, or souvenir, can be analyzed like a "text" that contains social messages. Looking at souvenirs this way reveals what both marketeers and tourists choose to "preserve, value, and exchange" (Clifford 1988:221). Shelly Shenhav-Keller (1993) conducted participant observation in the original Maskit store in Tel Aviv and interviewed Jewish Israeli, Arab Israeli, and Palestinian artists and artisans whose crafts were sold there.

In the Maskit stores, three central themes in Israeli society are expressed in the choice and presentation of sou-venirs: Israel's attitudes towards its ancient and recent past, its view of its religion and culture, and its approach to Arab Israelis and Palestinians. The original Maskit shop sold fashion (women's clothing, wedding gowns, and dresses with three different styles of Arab embroidery), jewellery, ritual items (candlesticks, goblets, incense burners, prayer books), books, children's clothing and toys, embroidered items, carpets, ceramics, glassware, and copperware.

Over the years, changes have occurred in who is producing the art sold in Maskit. Many of the original Jewish Israeli artists have aged and their descendants have not taken up the craft. This is most marked in Yemenite embroidery and silversmithing; now, Arab embroidery is sought as a replacement. After the 1967 Six-Day War, Arab Israeli and Palestinian craftsmanship became increasingly available with the incorporation of new areas within Israel, including the Occupied Territories. Most of the Arabs who were absorbed into the souvenir industry became hired labourers in factories and workshops owned by Maskit or by Israeli artisans who sold their works to Maskit. Yet Maskit provides no information about the role of Israeli Arabs or Palestinians. The carpets, for example, are presented as handwoven Israeli carpets even though Arab Israelis wove them.

FOOD FOR THOUGHT

Do you know of another example in which something attributed to one ethnic group or culture is actually produced by people not part of that group? Or do you think the Maskit use of Arab craftsmen to make "Israeli" souvenirs is unique?

---

ever. In North America, for example, urban Black youths' musical performance through rap music can be seen as a form of protest. Hip-hop artists protest economic oppression, the danger of drugs, and men's disrespect for women through their lyrics and performances.

Performance Arts

The performance arts include mainly music, dance, and theatre. **Ethnomusicology,** an established subfield, examines musical traditions cross-culturally. Ethnomusicologists study a range of topics including the form of the music itself, the social position of musicians, how music interacts with other domains of culture, and change in musical traditions. This section provides a case study of the parallels between musical patterns and the gender division of labour in a foraging group in Malaysia. We next turn to an example of how anthropologists study theatre and, in this case, see how theatre and religion fit together.

Music and Gender: Balance Among the Temiar

An important topic for ethnomusicologists is gender differences in access to performance roles in music (for readers interested in approaching this topic as a research question, see Table 14.1). For example, among the Temiar, a group of Orang Asli forager-hunters of highland Malaysia, musical traditions emphasize balance and complementarity between males and females (Roseman 1987). Kinship and marriage rules are relatively flexible and open. Temiar marriages are not arranged, but are based on the mutual desires of each spouse. Marriage may be either village endogamous or exogamous. Descent is bilateral, and marital residence follows no particular rule following a period of bride service. Marriages often end in separation, with the usual pattern for everyone being serial monogamy. Men, however, have a certain edge over women in political and ritual spheres. Men dominate as headmen and as spirit mediums who sing the songs that energize the spirits (although historical records indicate that women have been spirit mediums in the past). In most performances, individual male singers are the nodes through which the songs of spirit-guides enter the community, but women's performance role is significant. For example, the delegation of gender roles as male initial singer and female chorus is sometimes varied when the female chorus itself transforms into a self-contained initiator-respondent unit. One woman sings, and the others respond chorally. Overall, the male spirit medium role is not necessarily of higher priority or status. The leader/chorus distinction establishes "temporal" priority, but overall gender distinctions are blurred through substantial overlap between phrases and through repetition. The performance is one of intergender, community participation with integrated male and female complementary roles as in Temiar society in general.

Dance ethnologist Sarala Dandekar in Odissi costume represents the dancer/goddess of classical Indian dance.

Table 14.1   Ethnographic Questions about Gender and Music

If you were doing an ethnographic study of gender roles in musical performance, the following questions would be useful in starting the inquiry. But they would not exhaust the topic. Can you think of questions that should be added to the list?

1. Are men and women equally encouraged to use certain instruments and repertoires?
2. Is musical training available to all?
3. Do male and female repertoires overlap, where, and for what reasons?
4. Are the performances of men and women public, private, or both? Are women and men allowed to perform together? In what circumstances?
5. Do members of the culture give equal value to the performances of men and women? On what criteria are these evaluations based, and are they the same for men and women performers?

Source: Robertson 1987.

Theatre and Myth: Ritual Dance-Drama in India and Canada

Theatre is a "form of enactment," related to other forms such as dance, music, parades, competitive games and sports, and verbal art (Beeman 1993). These forms seek to entertain through conscious forms of acting, movement, and words. One theatrical tradition that offers an exuberant blend of mythology, acting, and music is Kathakali ritual dance-drama of southern India (Zarrilli 1990). Stylized hand gestures, elaborate makeup, and costumes contribute to the attraction of these dramas, which dramatize India's great Hindu epics, especially the Ramayana and the Mahabharata.

Costumes and makeup transform the actor into one of several well-known characters from Indian mythology. The audience can easily recognize the basic character types at their first entrance by "reading" the costuming and makeup. Six basic makeup types exist to depict characters ranging from the most refined to the most vulgar, going along a continuum. Characters such as kings and heroes have green facial makeup, reflecting their high degree of refinement and moral uprightness. The most vulgar characters are associated with black facial makeup and occasionally black beards.

The teaching and performance of Hindu dance-dramas in Canadian cities offer opportunities to observe processes of cultural change and adaptation. First-generation South Asian immigrants to Canada introduced Kathakali and other classical forms to immigrant and non-immigrant audiences, creating an appreciation for Indian dance-drama. Second-generation Indo-Canadian dancers recognize the need to preserve the integrity of the classical repertoire, but also use dance as a means of personal expression and seek opportunities for collaborative multicultural dance exchanges. "The Rebel Goddess," an experimental work performed in Toronto in 1999, draws attention to the crisis of the creative spirit of the dancer trapped within the elaborate rules of the classical Indian dance.

Architecture and Decorative Arts

Like other forms of art, architecture is interwoven with other aspects of culture. Architecture may reflect and protect social rank and class differences as well as gender, age, and ethnic differences. Decorative arts—including interior decoration of homes and buildings, and external design features such as gardens—reflect people's social position and also stand as statements of their status and "taste." Local cultures have long defined preferred standards in these areas of expression, but global influences from the West as well as from Japan and, increasingly, non-Western cultures, have been adopted and adapted by other traditions.

Architecture and Interior Decoration

Foragers, being nomadic, build dwellings as needed, and then abandon them. Owning little and having few surpluses means that permanent storage structures are not needed. The construction of dwellings does not require the efforts of groups larger than the family unit. Foragers' dwellings are an image of the family and not of the wider society. The dwellings' positioning in relation to each other reflects the relations between families. More elaborate shelters and greater social cohesiveness in planning occur as foraging is combined with horticulture, as in the semi-permanent settlements in the Amazon rain forest. People live in the settlement part of the year, but break up into smaller groups that spread out into a larger area for foraging. Important decisions concern location of the site in terms of weather, availability of drinking water, and defensibility. The central plaza must be elevated for drainage, and drainage channels must be dug around the hearths. The overall plan is circular. In some groups, separate shelters are built for extended family groups; in others, they are joined into a continuous circle with connected roofs. In some cases, the headman has a separate and larger shelter.

Pastoralists have designed ingenious portable structures such as the teepee and yert. The teepee is a conical tent made with a framework of four wooden poles tied at the top with thongs, to which are joined other poles to complete the cone; this frame is then covered with buffalo hide. A yert is also a circular, portable dwelling, but its roof is flatter than that of a teepee. The covering is made of cloth. This extremely lightweight structure is easy to set up, take down, and transport, and is highly adaptable to all weather conditions. Encampments often involved the arrangement of the teepees or yerts in several concentric circles, with social status as the structuring principle placing the council of chiefs and the head chief in the centre.

In settled agricultural communities where permanent housing is the norm, decoration is more likely to be found in homes. Wall paintings, sculptures, and other features may distinguish the homes of more wealthy individuals. The great wooden houses with their painted facades and carved totem poles made by First Nations communities on the Northwest Coast of North America reflected the stability of their resource base and the high value placed on displaying rank. With the development of the state, around 4000 BCE, urban areas grew larger and showed the effects of centralized planning and power (for example, in grid-style street planning rather than haphazard street placement). The symbolic demonstration of the power, grandeur, and identity of states was—and still is—expressed architecturally through the construction of impressive monuments: temples, administrative buildings, memorials, and museums.

Universities also exhibit their own unique use of space, from the ivy-covered walls of Canada's oldest universities to the modern suburban high-rise campuses. York University's Anthropology Department is housed in Vari Hall, a new building whose open rotunda space has become a focal point for a university lacking ivy-covered walls and a central quadrangle. The space has been used for university ceremonies and has become a symbol of the university. However, the round, light three-story space is also used by students for studying, sleeping, talking, cuddling, and watching others from the higher floors. It has become a contested space as it has also been appropriated for student and faculty protests (Rodman, Hawkins, and Teramura 1998).

Studying the way people design and decorate the interior of buildings and homes links cultural anthropologists with people working in other professions and disciplines, including interior design, advertising, and consumer studies. One study of interior decoration in Japan used as data the contents of home decorating magazines and observations within homes to see what decorative choices people made (Rosenberger 1992). A recurrent thread was the way certain aspects of Western decorating styles were incorporated and localized (given a particularly Japanese flavour). Home decorating magazines target middle- and upper-class housewives who seek to identify their status through new consumption styles. A general trend was the abandonment of three key features of traditional Japanese design: *tatami, shoji,* and *fusuma. Tatami* are 5-cm-thick mats, about 1 metre by 2 metres. *Shoji* are the sliding screen doors of *tatami* rooms, one covered with glass and the other with translucent rice paper often printed with a design of leaves or waves. *Fusuma* are sliding wall panels made of thick paper; they are removable so that rooms can be enlarged for gatherings. The *tatami* room usually contains a low table with pillows for seating on the floor. A special alcove may contain a flower arrangement, ancestors' pictures,

and a Buddhist altar. Futons are stored in closets around the edges and brought out at night for sleeping.

In seeking to distance themselves from the old style, the Japanese have made several changes, including giving the kitchen a more central location and displaying objects such as furniture, VCRs, and stereos. According to Rosenberger, these changing surfaces accompany deeper social changes involving new aspirations about marriage and family relationships. The home decorating magazines promote the idea that the new style brings with it happier children with better grades, and closer husband-wife ties. Tensions exist, however, between these ideals and the realities of middle- and upper-class life in Japan. Women feel compelled to work either part time or full time to be able to contribute to satisfying their new consumer needs. Simultaneously, Japanese women are discouraged from pursuing careers and are urged to devote more time to domestic pursuits, including home decorating and child care in order to provide the kind of life portrayed in the magazines. Furthermore, the Western-style, happy nuclear family image contains no plan for the aged. The wealthiest Japanese families manage to satisfy both individualistic desires and filial duties because they can afford a large house in which they dedicate a separate floor for the husband's parents, complete with traditional *tatami* mats. Less wealthy people have a more difficult time dealing with this complex and conflicting set of values.

Gardens and Flowers

Gardens for use, especially for food production, can be differentiated from gardens dedicated to decoration and beauty. Not all cultures have developed the concept of the decorative garden. Inuit peoples cannot construct gardens in the snow. Purely nomadic peoples have no gardens since they are on the move. The decorative garden seems to be a product of state-level societies, especially in the Middle East, Europe, and Asia (Goody 1993). Variation exists in what is considered to be the appropriate contents, design, and purpose of a garden. A Japanese garden may contain no blooming flowers, focusing instead on the shape and placement of trees, shrubs, stones, and bodies of water (Moynihan 1979). Elite Muslim culture, with its core in the Middle East, has long been associated with formal decorative gardens. A garden, enclosed with four walls, is symbolically equivalent to the concept of "paradise." The Islamic garden pattern involves a square design with symmetrical layout, fountains, waterways, straight pathways, all enclosed within walls through which symmetrically placed entrances allow access. Islamic gardens were often used to surround the tombs of prominent people, with the usual plan placing the tomb in the centre of the garden. India's Taj Mahal, built by Muslim Emperor Shah Jahan, follows this pattern, with one modification in the landscaping: The tomb was placed at one edge of the garden rather than in the centre. The result is a dramatic stretch of fountains and flowers leading up to the monument from the main gate.

The contents of a garden, like a fancy dinner menu with all its special ingredients or a personal collection of souvenirs from around the world with all their memories and meanings, makes a statement about its owner's identity and status. For example, in Europe during the heyday of colonialism, imperial gardens contained specimens from remote corners of the globe, collected through scientific expeditions. Such gardens are created through the intentional collection and placement of otherwise diverse plants in one place.

Cut flowers are now important economic products, as they provide income for gardeners throughout the world. They are also exchange items. In France, women receive flowers from men more than any other kind of gift (Goody 1993:316). In much of the world, "special occasions" require gifts of flowers. In the West, as well as in East Asia, funerals are times for special displays of flowers. Ritual offerings to the deities in Hinduism may be single flowers or flowers such as marigolds woven into a chain or necklace. Individual flowers also acquire local meanings, as in Canada, where poppies are associated with Remembrance Day (commemorating the world wars), and daffodils with the Canadian Cancer Society. Flowers are often important as motifs in Western and Asian secular and sacred art, although less so in African art. In his comparative study of the use of flowers in ritual and art, Jack Goody (1993) tried to understand the relative absence of flowers in the religion and graphic arts of Africa (except for Islamicized cultures of Africa where flowers are prominent). Some possible answers include ecological and economic factors. Eurasia possesses a greater variety of blooming plants than Africa. African gardens produce food not flowers. In many African kingdoms, luxury goods included fabrics of various design, gold ornaments, and wooden carvings rather than flowers.

The Anthropology of Museums

In this section we consider the concept of the museum and the debates about the role of museums in exhibiting and representing culture. Museum anthropology developed in the 1980s, and includes both anthropologists who work in museums helping to prepare exhibits and anthropologists who study museums—what they choose to display and how they display it—as important sites of culture itself (M. Ames 1992; A. Jones 1993; Stocking 1985).

What Is a Museum?

A museum is an institution that collects, preserves, interprets, and displays objects on a regular basis (Kahn 1995:324). Its purpose may be esthetic or educational. Museums have played and continue to play a key role in Canadian anthropology. The term comes originally from a Greek word referring to a place for the muses to congregate, where one would have philosophical discussions or see artistic performances. In Europe, the concept of the museum developed into a place where art objects were housed and displayed. Ethnographic and science museums came later, inspired by Europe's emerging interests in exploration in the 1500s and the accompanying scientific urge to gather specimens from around the world and classify them into an evolutionary history.

The concept of the museum and its several forms has now diffused to most parts of the world. Contemporary versions include children's museums, heritage parks, and local museums. The Saputik ("The Weir") Museum in Puvirnituq, Quebec, is an example of a community museum created by an Inuit elder. Aptly named, "The Weir" is a place to catch and hold personal objects before they pass out to sea to be lost forever (Graburn 1998). The Canadian Museum of Civilization and many other museums have shifted from an exclusively object-oriented approach to one that stresses cultural performances and interactive media experiences using new information and communication technologies (McDonald and Alsford 1989).

Exhibiting Racism

"Into the Heart of Africa" was the Royal Ontario Museum's (ROM) most controversial exhibit. From November 1989 until its premature closing in August 1990, the temporary exhibition displayed photographs and objects such as masks, jewellery, and sculptures collected between 1870 and 1925 by Canadian missionaries to Africa, soldiers serving in the British Army, and explorers. These artifacts were not presented to the public as a traditional museum exhibit. Canadian anthropologist Jeanne Cannizzo designed the exhibit to encourage audiences to actively engage with and interpret the displays rather than passively observe them. As an example of reflexive museology, viewers were expected to critique British colonial ideology and the complicity of Canadians in sustaining it. For example, Cannizzo highlighted racist colonial language by using such phrases as the "unknown continent" and "barbarous customs" in the explanatory panels of the exhibits. She placed these terms in quotation marks to encourage viewers to challenge and critique their use.

Unfortunately, many visitors to the ROM did not recognize the reflexive and ironic nature of the exhibits. Instead, they thought the exhibit glorified Imperialism and was racist in its portrayal of Africans. In March 1990, a group called the Coalition for the Truth about Africa (CFTA) began weekly protests outside the ROM. The CFTA and others challenged the authority of the ROM to represent Africa, and criticized the ROM's failure to consult Black community members about the exhibit.

While the media portrayed the controversy as a conflict between the ROM and the CFTA, Shelley Butler's ethnographic analysis of the exhibit (1999) reveals the many differing views and understandings of both the exhibit and the controversy. The ROM was accused by the CFTA of being elitist and only representing the interests of a small portion of Toronto's population. Nevertheless, the exhibit provided a forum for highlighting contemporary issues of racism in Canada and the authority of the museum to represent the "truth" about other peoples, cultures, and objects (Butler 1999).

The "Politics" of Exhibits

Museum anthropologists are now at the forefront of serious debates about who gets to represent whom, the ownership of particular objects, and the public service role of museums. The political aspects of museums have always existed, but now they are part of explicit discussion (see the Multiple Cultural Worlds box). A major area of debate is whether objects from non-Western cultures should be exhibited, like Western art objects, with little or no ethnographic context (Clifford 1988; Watson 1997). Most anthropologists would support the need for context, not just for non-Western objects, but for all objects on display. But the important point that all forms of expressive culture are context-bound and can be better understood and appreciated within their social context is unfortunately a rare view among Western art historians and critics (Best 1986). For example, the museum label of Andy Warhol's hyperrealistic painting of a can of Campbell's soup should include information on the social context in which such art was produced and some background on the artist.

Debates also exist about who should have control of objects in museums that may have been claimed through colonial and neocolonial domination. The issue of **repatriation,** or returning objects to their original homes, is a matter of international and national concern. The complexity of this process can be seen in the repatriation of objects confiscated by the Canadian government in 1922 following a large "illegal" potlatch held in Alert Bay, British Columbia. The local Indian Agent alerted the RCMP about the potlatch, and authorities confiscated over 450 ritual items such as coppers, masks, rattles, headdresses, blankets, and boxes, paying their owners a small price for them. The regalia ended up in major Canadian and American museums. The Canadian Museum of Civilization and the Royal Ontario Museum (ROM) agreed to return their collections not to individual families, but to two local museums that would be built to preserve and display the items. The Kwagiulth Museum and Cultural Centre on Quadra Island (opened in 1979) and the U'mista Cultural Centre in Alert Bay, Cormorant Island (opened in 1980), stress the family ownership of the items, and the local histories of the objects. The

U'mista Cultural Centre displays large white cards with texts and quotations about the confiscation of the regalia that has been repatriated. In contrast, the University of British Columbia Museum of Anthropology provides brief labels with a small drawing of the object in its original setting (Clifford 1997; D. Cole 1985).

In 1999, four intricate wampum belts over 500 years old were given back by museum officials to an assembly of Iroquois chiefs at a ceremony at the Six Nations Grand River Territory near Brantford. They had been stored in the ROM since 1922, when they had been given to the museum by a Mohawk woman for safekeeping. The belts were repatriated after the Six Nations reserve approached the museum to return the wampum records. They received similar ones from other museums around North America. Wampum served as a record of laws, treaties, and promises, and it helps the Iroquois remember their oral history. One member of the reserve commented: "The last person we had who could recite the entire Great Law passed away…Getting the wampum back may help stop the erosion" (*Toronto Star*, November 12, 1999).

In the United States and Canada, many Aboriginal groups are lobbying successfully for the return of ancestral bones, grave goods, and potlatch goods. In 1990, the United States passed the Native American Graves Protection and Repatriation Act (NAGRPA), opting for legislation requiring inventories of archaeological and ethnographic holdings. Tensions between museums and First Nations peoples in Canada came to a head over "The Spirit Sings" exhibit developed by the Glenbow Museum to celebrate the 1988 Calgary Winter Olympics. The Lubicon Cree of northern Alberta called for an international boycott of the exhibit because they were engaged in a land claim dispute with the provincial and federal governments, and the exhibit was sponsored by Shell Oil, the company drilling on the land they claimed. The confrontation resulted in the formation of a Task Force on Museums and First Peoples in 1989, under the joint sponsorship of the Assembly of First Nations and the Canadian Museums Association. The task force, which included Native and non-Native members, opted to develop a cooperative model of equal partnerships guided by moral, ethical, and professional responsibilities, rather than by legislation such as NAGRPA. The task force developed principles to serve as a basis for recommendations, including acknowledging that both museums and First Nations peoples share a mutual interest in the cultures and histories of Aboriginal peoples; that museums should recognize the authority of First Nations peoples to speak for themselves and that First Nations peoples should recognize the professional knowledge of museum academics; and that both should work together as equal partners to meet their differing needs and interests (Nicks 1992).

Other parts of the world face different repatriation problems. The breakup of the Soviet Union prompted claims from several independent states that wish to retrieve artistic property that originated in their locale but was taken to Soviet national museums in Moscow and St. Petersburg. For example, Central Asian republics lost medieval carpets to Moscow and St. Petersburg museums; there are Georgian arms in the Armory of the Moscow Kremlin; and Ukrainians seek the return of objects of historical interest, such as the ceremonial staff of their national hero, the *hetman* (headman) Mazepa, who fought for Ukrainian independence against Peter the Great (Akinsha 1992a). In all, Ukraine is demanding the return of about 2 million art objects that originated in Ukrainian territory and are currently housed in Russian museums (Akinsha 1992b). Many of these objects are the pride of Russian museums, such as the Hermitage in St. Petersburg, which now faces the loss of many key objects.

Another dimension of dispute about art in Russia concerns the state and the church. The Soviet state put many icons and other religious objects in museums and turned churches into museums. Now the Russian Orthodox Church is campaigning for the return of church property. Churches are demanding that "all sacred objects of the church, all church buildings, and masterpieces of church art that were confiscated by the state after 1917 must be returned without exception to the ownership of the Russian Orthodox Church" (Akinsha 1992a:102). Art historians and museum officials protest that the churches have neither the resources nor the experience to care for these treasures. On the other hand, there are threats of theft and violence from those who wish to return the icons to churches and monasteries. In response, some museums have removed certain pieces from display. Also, a number of museums have posted on their Web sites artworks whose ownership prior to and during World War II cannot be certified, in the hopes of returning artwork stolen from the Jewish people by the Nazis.

Play and Leisure

This section turns to another area of expressive culture: what people do "for fun." It is impossible to draw clear lines between the concepts of play, leisure, art, and performance, however, since they often overlap. For example, a person could paint watercolours in her leisure time, yet simultaneously be creating a work of art. In most cases, though, play and leisure can be distinguished from other activities by the fact that they have no direct, utilitarian purpose for the participant.

In the 1930s, Dutch historian Johan Huizinga offered some features of play: It is unnecessary and thus free action; it is outside of ordinary life; it is closed and limited in terms of time; it has rules for its execution; and it contains an element of tension and chance (as summarized in Hutter 1996).

Leisure activities often overlap with play, but many leisure activities, such as reading or lying on a beach, would not be considered play because they lack rules, tension, or change. Often, the same activity, depending on the context, could be considered work instead of play. For example, gardening as a hobby would be classified as a leisure activity, even though weeding, pruning, and watering are the same activities that could be considered work for someone else. Playing a game with a child might be considered recreational, but if one has been hired as the child's babysitter, then it is work. Professional sports is an area where the line between play and work breaks down completely since the "players" are paid to "play." Further, while play and leisure may be pursued from a nonutilitarian perspective, they are often surrounded by a wider context of commercial and political interests. For example, nonprofessional athletes competing in the Olympic games are part of a wider set of powerful interests, from advertisers to host cities to athletic equipment companies.

Play and leisure activities include varieties of games such as sports, hobbies, and recreational travel. Cultural anthropologists study play and leisure within their cultural contexts and as part of social systems. They ask, for example, why do some activities involve teams rather than individuals; what are the social roles and status of people involved in particular activities; what are the "goals" of the activities and how are they achieved; how much danger or violence is involved in the activities; how are certain activities related to group identity; and how do activities link or separate different groups within or between societies or nations.

Games and Sports as Cultural Microcosm

Games and sports, like religious rituals and festivals, can be interpreted as reflections of broader social relationships and cultural ideals. In Geertz's terms, they are both "models of" a culture, depicting in miniature, key ideals, and "models for" a culture, through socializing people into certain values and ideals. American football can be seen as a model for corporate culture in that it relies on a clear hierarchy with leadership vested in one key person (the quarterback), and the major goal is to expand territorially by taking over areas from the competition. Canadian football carries less mythic value as a symbol of national identity, as it is more of a historical compromise between British rugby and American football. In spite of the importance of the Grey Cup, it is hockey that inspires a shared national identity.

Hockey in Canada, both casual street hockey and professional sport spectacle, has deeply rooted meanings linked to images of national character and identity (Gruneau and Whitson 1993). Hockey is part of the collective memory of many English and French Canadian men who grew up in towns with community hockey leagues. The organized, rule-governed professional game emerged in Montreal in the 1870s, as an event with spectators. In 1892, Canada's Governor General Lord Stanley donated a trophy cup to recognize the Dominion's best hockey team. By 1917, the National Hockey League (NHL) had added American franchises, as Canada's national winter pastime became a continental business, fuelling fears that the NHL would no longer be Canadian, and that it would be taken over by American business interests. By the 1930s, radio broadcasts of *Hockey Night in Canada* could be heard across the country and became a national symbol in spite of American money, influence, and teams in the NHL. Later, television provided the same unifying national entertainment.

Hockey continues to be part of a collective representation of what it means to be Canadian—a representation that ignores differences of race, ethnicity, class, and gender in participation, as if hockey emerged as a natural adaptation to ice and cold winters. Yet the game has deep roots in both rural and urban communities. Games between the Toronto Maple Leafs and the Montreal Canadiens dramatized the rivalry between the two solitudes, much as other NHL games bring out fears of selling out to American interests and losing a piece of distinctive national culture. Canada's 1972 win over the Soviet hockey team is still celebrated as a reflection of national identity and national character (Gruneau and Whitson 1993).

Sports and Spirituality: Male Wrestling in India

In many non-Western settings, sports are closely tied with aspects of religion and spirituality. Asian martial arts, for example, require forms of concentration much like meditation, leading to spiritual self-control. Male wrestling in India, a popular form of entertainment at rural fairs and other public events, also involves a strong link with spiritual development and asceticism (Alter 1992). A wrestler's daily routine is one of self-discipline. Every act—defecation, bathing, comportment, devotion—is integrated into a daily regimen of discipline. Wrestlers come to the *akhara* (equivalent to a gymnasium) early in the morning for practice under the supervision of a guru or other senior *akhara* member. They practise moves with different partners for two to three hours. In the early evening, they return for more exercise, which consists of two primary exercises. In all, a strong young wrestler will do around 2000 push-ups and 1000 deep kneebends a day in sets of 50 to 100.

The wrestler's diet is prescribed by the wrestling way of life. Wrestlers are mainly vegetarian and avoid alcohol and tobacco, although they do consume *bhang*, a beverage made of blended milk, spices, almonds, and concentrated marijuana. In addition to regular meals, wrestlers consume large quantities of milk, *ghee* (clarified butter), and almonds. These substances are considered sources of strength as they help to build up the body's semen, according to traditional dietary principles.

Several features about the wrestler's life are similar to those of a Hindu *sannyasi*, or holy man who renounces life in the normal world. The aspiring *sannyasi* studies under a guru and learns to follow a strict routine of discipline and meditation called *yoga*, and has a restricted diet to achieve control of the body and its life force. Both wrestler and *sannyasi* as chosen life roles focus on discipline as a way of achieving a controlled self. Indian wrestling does not involve the stereotype of the "dull-witted sportsman" as it does in North America; rather, the image is of perfected physical and moral health.

Play, Pleasure, and Pain

Many leisure activities fit in a border area between pleasure and pain, since they may involve physical discomfort as well. Serious injuries may result from mountain climbing, horseback riding, or playing touch football in the backyard. Hockey, both recreational and professional, has increasingly in-

Indian wrestlers in the village of Sonepur. These wrestlers follow a rigorous regimen of dietary restrictions and exercise in order to keep their bodies and minds under control. Like Hindu ascetics, they seek to build up and maintain their inner strength through such practices.

corporated violence in what is undeniably a forceful, physical game. A more intentionally dangerous category of sports is **blood sports,** competition that explicitly seeks to bring about a flow of blood or even death, either between human contestants or with animal competitors, or in animal targets of human hunting (Donlon 1990). In North America and Europe, professional boxing is an example of a highly popular blood sport that has not been analyzed yet by anthropologists. Cultural anthropologists have looked more at the use of animals in blood sports such as cockfights and bullfights. Interpretations of these sports range from seeing them as forms of sadistic pleasure or vicarious self-validation (usually of males) through the triumph of their representative pit bull or fighting cock, or as the triumph of culture over nature in the symbolism of bullfighting.

Even the seemingly pleasurable experience of a Turkish-style bath can involve discomfort and pain. One phase of the process involves scrubbing the skin roughly several times with either a rough natural sponge, a pumice stone, or a piece of cork wood wrapped in cloth (Staats 1994). The scrubbing removes layers of dead skin and "opens the pores" so that the skin will be beautiful. In Turkey, an option for men is a massage that can be quite violent, involving deep probes of leg muscles, cracking of the back, and being walked on by the (often hefty) masseur. In Ukraine, being struck repeatedly on one's bare skin with birch branches is the final stage of the bath. However, violent scrubbing, scraping, and even beating of the skin, combined with radical temperature changes in the water, are combined with valued social experiences at the bathhouse (see the Voices box).

Leisure Travel

Anthropologists who study leisure travel, or tourism, have often commented that their work is taken less seriously than it should be because of the perspective that they are just "hanging out" at the beach or at five-star hotels. Anthropological research on tourism and its impact is an important subject. Tourism is now one of the major economic forces in the world; it is growing, and it has dramatic effects on people and places in tourist destination areas. Expenditure of money, time, and effort for nonessential travel is nothing new. In the past, pilgrimage to religious sites has been a major preoccupation of many people (see Chapter 12). A large percentage

of worldwide tourism involves individuals from the industrialized nations of Europe, North America, and Japan travelling to the less industrialized nations. Ethnic tourism, cultural tourism, and off-the-beaten-path tourism are attracting increasing numbers of travellers.

These new kinds of tourism are often marketed as providing a view of "authentic" cultures. Images of indigenous people as the "Other" figure prominently in travel brochures and advertisements. Tourist promotional literature often presents a "myth" of other peoples and places (Silver 1993:304) and offers travel as a form of escape to a mythical land of wonder. The travel industry promotes images that are likely to be verified during travel—people want to see what the brochures show. For example, tourist promotional literature presents the Kenyan safari as a particular kind of imaginative representation of the wild (Little 1991). In fact, research on Western travel literature shows that, from the time of the earliest explorers to the present, it has been full of "primitivist" images about indigenous peoples (Pratt 1992). They are portrayed as having static or "stone age" traditions and remaining largely unchanged by the forces of Western colonialism, nationalism, economic development, and tourism itself (Bruner 1991). Tourists often seek the culture that the tourist industry defines rather than gaining a genuine, more complicated, and perhaps less photogenic version of a culture (K. Adams 1984). For the traveller, obtaining these desired cultural images through mass tourism involves packaging the "primitive" with the "modern" because most tourists want comfort and convenience along with their "authentic experience." Thus, advertisements may minimize the foreignness of the host country noting, for example, that English is spoken, that the destination is remote yet accessible. Primitivist imagery attracts tourists, while a dash of similarity offers enough of the comforts of home to make it all acceptable. For example, "The Melanesian Discoverer" is a ship that cruises the Sepik River in Papua New Guinea, providing a way for affluent tourists to see the "primitive" while travelling in luxury.

So far, the anthropology of tourism has focused most of its attention on the impact of global and local tourism on indigenous peoples and places. Such impact studies are important in exposing the degree to which tourism helps or harms local people. For example, the formation of Amboseli National Park in Kenya affected the access of the Maasai to strategic water resources for their herds

Fatima Mernissi, "Childhood Tales of the Hammam"

Sociologist Fatima Mernissi (1995) grew up in a harem (pronounced "hareem"), the part of the household reserved for women and children, in Fez, a traditional Islamic city of Morocco. A trip to the *hammam* (bath house) was an occasion when those living in the harem could leave their secluded quarters for several hours. Before going to the *hammam*, the women would devote many hours to a first stage—preparing clay and other solutions for facial masks and putting *henna* (a reddish-orange dye used as a cosmetic and for hair colouring and conditioning) in their hair, all of which would be rinsed off in the *hammam*. Male and female children go with their mothers to the female *hammam* until boys are about 10, when they then start to go with the men to their separate *hammam*.

The hammam *that we went to in order to bathe and wash off our beauty treatments was all white marble walls and floors, with a lot of glass in the ceilings to keep the light flowing in. The combination of ivory light, mist, and nude adults and children running around made the hammam seem like a steamy-hot, exotic island that had somehow become adrift in the middle of the disciplined Medina. Indeed, the hammam would have been paradise, if it had not been for its third chamber.*

The first chamber of the hammam *was steamy, yes, but nothing exceptional, and we passed through it quickly, using it mainly as a way to get used to the steamy heat. The second chamber was a delight, with just enough steam to blur the world around us into a sort of extraterrestrial place, but not enough to make breathing difficult. In that second chamber, women would get into a cleansing frenzy, sloughing off dead skin with mhecca, or round pieces of cork wrapped up in hand-crocheted woolen covers.*

To wash out the henna and the oils, the women used ghassoul, *a miraculous clay shampoo and lotion which made your hair and skin feel incredibly smooth. "The ghassoul is what transforms your skin into silk," claimed Aunt Habiba. "That's what makes you feel like an ancient goddess when you step out of the hammam."…*

Ghassoul *was used in the second chamber of the hammam as a shampoo, and in the third and hottest chamber, where the most compulsive cleansing took place, as a smoothing and cleansing cream. Samir and I hated that third room, and even called it the torture chamber, because it was there that the grownups insisted on "seriously" taking care of us children. In the first two chambers of the hammam, the mothers would forget about their offspring, so involved were they with their beauty treatments. But in the third chamber, just before undertaking their own purification rituals, the mothers felt guilty about neglecting us, and tried to make up for it by turning our last moments in the hammam into a nightmare. It was then and there that everything suddenly went wrong, and we started sliding from one misfortunate experience to the next.*

First of all, the mothers filled buckets of cold and hot water directly from the fountains, and poured it over our heads before testing it properly first. And they never succeeded in getting the right temperature. The water was either scaldingly hot or ice cold, never anything in between…. Some would manage to escape from their mother's grip for a moment, but since the marble floor was slippery with water and clay, and the room so crowded, they never got away for very long. Some would try to avoid going in the third chamber in the first place, but in that case, which was often what happened to me, they would just be picked up by their feet and forced in, despite their shrill screams.

Those were the few terrible moments that practically erased the whole delightful effect of the hammam session. (234–238)

Source: Fatima Mernissi, *Dreams of Trespass* (pages 234–238). Text © 1994 Fatima Mernissi. Reprinted by permission of Addison-Wesley Longman, Inc.

FOOD FOR THOUGHT

Have you participated in any leisure activities that cross the line between pleasure and pain? Why do you think people participate in such activities?

(Honadle 1985, as summarized in Drake 1991). The project staff promised certain benefits to the Maasai if they stayed off the reserve, but many of those benefits (including shares of the revenues from the park) never materialized. In contrast, local people in Costa Rica were included in the early planning stages of the Guanacaste

The Hula Renaissance

Beginning in the early 1970s, the "Hawaiian Renaissance" grew out of political protest; specifically, Hawaiian youth spoke out against encroaching development from the outside that was displacing the indigenous people from their own land and resources (Stillman 1996). Hula and other practices such as canoe paddling and the Hawaiian language were the focus of revival.

Over the past two decades, hula schools have proliferated and hula competitions between many islands have become widely attended events. Since 1992, hula competitions have reached a level of international dissemination, with the first World Invitational Hula Festival held in Honolulu. This event is less popular, however, with indigenous Hawaiians since they feel that international competitors are not of comparable quality.

The hula competitions have helped ensure the continued survival of this ancient art form. The format of competitions, however, has brought changes to the older styles in performance style and presentation. Timing is one crucial factor. Most competitions deduct points if a performer uses more than the allotted time. Traditional dances cannot be completely performed within these time limits, so entry and exit dances and interlude dances have had to be cut.

FOOD FOR THOUGHT

Is "traditional" hula a thing of the past? How has globalization played a role here?

National Park and have played a greater role in the park management system there.

Tourism and Revitalization

Global tourism has had varied effects on indigenous arts. Often, tourist demand for ethnic arts and souvenirs has led to mass production of sculpture or weaving or jewellery of a less high quality than was created before the demand. Tourists' preferences for certain colours has sometimes had an effect on an indigenous art form. For example, red and green are prominent combinations in the textiles of India, but to many European and North American consumers, these colors signify "Christmas." Also, tourists' interests in seeing an abbreviated form of a traditionally long dance or theatre performance has led to the presentation of "cuts" rather than an entire piece. Some scholars say, therefore, that tourism leads to the decline and transformation of indigenous arts in a negative sense. While evidence exists to support this position, evidence exists to support an alternative argument, too. (See the Multiple Cultural Worlds box.)

A water puppet performance in Hanoi, Vietnam. Water puppet shows are far more popular among international tourists than among the Vietnamese.

Often, tourist support for indigenous arts is the sole force maintaining them, since local people in a particular culture may be more interested in foreign music, art, or sports themselves. Vietnamese water puppetry is an ancient performance mode, dating back at least to the Ly Dynasty of 1121 CE (Contreras 1995). Traditionally, water puppet shows took place in the spring during a lull in the farm work, or at special festival times. Now, water puppet shows are performed mainly for foreign tourists in large cities. Vietnamese people tend to prefer imported videos (Brownmiller 1994).

Change in Expressive Culture

Nowhere are forms and patterns of art, play, and leisure frozen in time. Change is universal, and much change is influenced by Western culture. However, influence does not occur in only one direction. African musical styles have transformed the American musical scene since the days of slavery. Japan has provided a strong influence on upper-class garden styles in North America. Cultures in which tradition and conformity have been valued in pottery-making, dress, or theatre may find themselves having to make choices about whether to innovate, and if so, how. Many contemporary artists (including musicians and playwrights) from Latin America to China are fusing ancient and "traditional" motifs and styles with more contemporary themes and messages.

Western interest in indigenous arts as "art" is quite recent, since their esthetic value was not widely recognized until the early twentieth century. Before that, the typical Western reaction to non-Western art was often one of either horror or curiosity (Mitter 1977). Graburn (1993) has analyzed the range of indigenous art in Canada and found a range from traditional activities and products made for internal consumption to those made for external markets.

Given current global exchanges and influences in art and play (especially organized sports), it is not surprising that leisure activities and artistic products and processes have changed to reflect new ideas and tastes as a result of past and present transnational processes.

Colonialism and Syncretism

Western colonialists had dramatic effects on the expressive culture of indigenous peoples with whom they came into contact. In some instances, colonial disapproval of particular art forms and activities resulted in their extinction. For example, when colonialists banned headhunting in various cultures, this change also meant that body decoration, weapon decoration, and other related expressive activities were abandoned. This section provides an in-depth example of how colonial repression of indigenous forms succeeded only temporarily.

Western colonialist powers often acted directly to change certain indigenous art and leisure practices. In the Trobriand Islands, now part of Papua New Guinea, British administrators and missionaries sought to eradicate the frequent tribal warfare as part of its pacification process. One strategy was to replace it with intertribal competitive sports (Leach 1975). In 1903, Reverend Gilmore, a British missionary, introduced the British game of cricket in the Trobriands as a way of promoting a new morality, separate from the former warring traditions. As played in England, cricket involves particular rules of play and a very "proper" look of pure white uniforms. In the early stages of the adoption of cricket in the Trobriands, the game followed the British pattern closely. As time passed and the game spread into more regions, it became increasingly localized. Most importantly, it was merged into indigenous political competition between big-men. Big-men leaders would urge their followers to increase production in anticipation of a cricket match since the matches were followed by a redistributive feast. The British missionaries had discouraged traditional magic in favour of Christianity, but the Trobriand Islanders transferred war-related magic into cricket. For example, spells are used to help one's team win, and the bats are ritually treated in the way that war weapons were. Weather magic is also important. If things are not going well for one's team, a spell to bring rain and force cancellation of the game is a possibility.

In Bermuda, as elsewhere in the West Indies, cricket is "played with elegant skill, studied with scholarly intensity, argued with passionate conviction, and revered with patriotic pride" (F. Manning 1981:617). Participation in cricket festivals is marked by indulgence and festive sociability. These are cultural performances where Blacks dress in "whites" to play a White game they have transformed into a celebration of Black culture. But in Bermuda, where economic power is very much in White hands, the cricket games and related festivals reveal tensions between celebrations of Black culture and economic dependency.

Post-Communist Transitions

Major changes are occurring in the arts in the post-communist states for two reasons: loss of state financial support and removal of state controls over subject matter and creativity. "A new generation of talented young artists has appeared. Many are looking for something new and different—art without ideology" (Akinsha 1992c:109). Art for art's sake—art as independent from the socialist project—is now possible. A circle of artists called the Moscow Conceptualists has been the dominant "underground" (nonofficial) school of art. These artists focused on political subject matter and poverty. In contrast, the new underground finds its inspiration in nostalgia for the popular culture of the 1950s and 1960s, a pack of Yugoslav chewing gum, or the cover of a Western art magazine. Commercial galleries are springing up, and a museum of modern art in Moscow may become a reality in the near future.

Theatre in China is passing through a difficult transition period with the recent development of some features of capitalism. Since the beginning of the People's Republic in 1949, the arts have gone through different phases, from being suppressed as part of the old feudal tradition to being revived under state control. In the mid-1990s, nearly all of China's theatre companies were in financial crisis (Jiang 1994:72). Steep inflation has meant that actors can no longer live on their pay. Theatre companies are urging their workers to find jobs elsewhere, such as by making movies or videos, but this is not an option for provincial troupes. Traditional theatre troupes are surviving by going on tours. Foreign tourist audiences are one source of support for traditional theatre. Another factor is that audience preferences have changed: "People are fed up with shows that 'educate,' have too strong a political flavor, or convey 'artistic values.' They no longer seem to enjoy love stories, old Chinese legends, or Western-style theater. Most of the young people prefer nightclubs, discos, or karaokes. Others stay at home watching TV" (73). The new materialism in China means that young people want to spend their leisure time having "fun." For the theatre, too, money now comes first. One trend is towards the production of Western plays.

For example, Harold Pinter's *The Lover* was an immediate success when it was performed in Shanghai in 1992. Why was it so successful?

> *Sex is certainly a big part of the answer. Sex has been taboo in China for a long time; it is still highly censored in theater and films. The producers warned, "no children," fueling speculation about a possible sex scene.... Actually,* The Lover *contains only hints of sexuality, but by Chinese standards the production was the boldest stage show in China. The actress's alluring dress, so common in the west, has seldom, if ever, been seen by Chinese theatregoers. Also, there was lots of bold language—dialog about female breasts, for example. (75–76)*

Another important feature is the play's focus on private life, on interiority, thoughts, and feelings. This emphasis corresponds with increasing interest in private lives in China. Change in the performing arts in China is being shaped by underlying changes in the global and local political economy.

What is art and how does cultural anthropology study it?

One of the first questions that cultural anthropologists raise about art is the narrowness of Western definitions. In this, anthropologists share with philosophers, art critics, and others an interest in defining the category of art versus non-art. Anthropologists choose a broad definition that can take into account cross-cultural variations. In the anthropological perspective, therefore, all cultures have art and all cultures have a concept of what good art is. Franz Boas, a founding figure in the anthropology of art, insisted that art should be studied in its social context and that attention should be given to the process of making art and the artist, not just the finished product. Ethnographers document the ways art relates to many aspects of culture: economics, politics, human development and psychology, healing, social control, and entertainment. Art may serve to reinforce social patterns, but it may also be a vehicle of protest and resistance. In state societies, people began collecting art objects in museums. Later, ethnographic museums were established in Europe as the result of scientific and colonialist interest in learning about other cultures. Anthropologists study museum displays as yet another reflection of cultural values as well as a site of formation of perceptions and values.

What do play and leisure activities tell us about culture?

Anthropological studies of play and leisure also pay attention to these activities within their cultural context. Games can be seen to reflect and reinforce dominant social values and have thus been analyzed as cultural microcosms. Sports and leisure activities, while done for nonutilitarian purposes, are often tied to economic and political interests. In some cultures, sports are also related to religion and spirituality.

How is expressive culture changing in contemporary times?

Major forces of change in expressive culture include Western colonialism and international tourism. In some cases, outside forces have led to the extinction of local forms, while in other cases outside forces have promoted continuity or the recovery of practices that had been lost. The effects of change are not always on the "receiving" culture's side, however, because art and play in colonial powers and in contemporary core states have also changed through exposure to other cultures.

Core Concepts

art, p. 336

blood sports, p. 350

ethno-esthetics, p. 337

ethnomusicology, p. 341

expressive culture, p. 336

fine art, p. 336

folk art, p. 336

repatriation, p. 346

theatre, p. 342

Suggested Readings

Michael Ames, *Cannibal Tours and Glass Boxes: The Anthropology of Museums*. Vancouver: University of British Columbia Press, 1992. Written by the director of the Museum of Anthropology at UBC, this book wrestles with the role of anthropology in creating concepts of natives, native art, and the use of museums in these constructions.

John Miller Chernoff, *African Rhythm and African Sensibility: Aesthetics and African Musical Idioms*. Chicago: University of Chicago Press, 1979. This book describes shared features of music style and musical performance throughout Africa, and presents links to key African cultural values.

Eugene Cooper and Yinho Jiang (contributor), *The Artisans and Entrepreneurs of Dongyang County: Economic Reform and Flexible Production in China*. Armonk, NY: M. E. Sharpe, 1998. This ethnography links attention to economic change and artistic change in China through its description of traditional and contemporary woodcarving in two villages and one town.

Nelson H. H. Graburn, ed., *Ethnic and Tourist Arts: Cultural Expressions from the Fourth World*. Berkeley: University of California Press, 1976. Organized regionally, 20 chapters explore the survival, revival, and reinvention of the arts of indigenous peoples in North America, Mexico and Central America, South America, Asia, Oceania, and Africa. Graburn's introduction to the book and his introductory essays preceding each section provide theoretical and comparative insights.

Jay R. Mandle and Joan D. Mandle, *Caribbean Hoops: The Development of West Indian Basketball*. Amsterdam: Gordon and Breach Publishers, 1994. This concise description and analysis of the emergence of basketball (mainly men's basketball) as a popular sport in several Caribbean nations also explores regional differences within the Caribbean.

Timothy Mitchell, *Blood Sport: A Social History of Spanish Bullfighting*. Philadelphia: University of Pennsylvania Press, 1991. Based on fieldwork and archival study, this book presents a well-rounded view of bullfighting within the context of annual Spanish village and national fiestas, consideration of the role of the matador in society, and a psychosexual interpretation of the bullfight, with comparison to blood sports in ancient Rome.

Stuart Plattner, *High Art Down Home: An Economic Ethnography of a Local Art Market*. Chicago: University of Chicago Press, 1996. Based on participant observation and interviews with artists, art dealers, and collectors in St. Louis, Missouri, this book explores concepts of value related to contemporary art and constraints that the market places on artists.

Your *Cultural Anthropology*, Second Canadian Edition Media Edition CD-ROM contains many Web sites relevant to this chapter. Use it to explore the Web and to expand your knowledge of anthropology.

Chapter 15

People on the Move

Religion provides an important source of social cohesion and psychological support for many new immigrant groups. Places of worship attract both worshippers and cultural anthropologists interested in learning how religion fits into migrants' adaptation.

Key Questions

What are the reasons for migration?

What is a displaced person?

How are new immigrants contributing to transnational connections and multiculturalism?

*T*he current generation of North American youths will experience more moves during their lives than previous generations. University graduates are likely to change jobs an average of eight times during their careers, and these changes may require relocation. Ecological, economic, familial, and political factors are causing population movements at seemingly all-time high levels. Research in anthropology has shown, however, that frequent moves during a person's life and mass movements of peoples are nothing new; they have occurred throughout human evolution. Foragers and pastoralists relocate frequently as a normal part of their lives. Population movements account for the past and present dispersion of the world's cultures:

> When we look at population maps of any part of the world, we are looking at the results of migration. Some maps represent major permanent moves, such as the spread of Native Americans from the Bering Sea to Tierra del Fuego, or the spread of Bantu-speaking peoples into the southern half of the African continent. Major moves may be brought on by necessity (the potato famine in Ireland), by population pressure (as befell the San and the Khoi), or by extreme force (the African diaspora in which ten million people were removed from their home communities and scattered throughout the New World). (du Toit 1990:305)

Migration is the movement of a person or people from one place to another (Kearney 1986:331). It is related to other aspects of life such as job and family status, and it may also affect mental health and social relationships. Thus, many academic subjects and professions are relevant here. Historians; economists; political scientists; sociologists; and scholars of religion, literature, art, and music have studied migration. Migration is one of three core areas of demography, along with fertility and mortality. The professions of law, medicine, education, business, architecture, urban planning, public administration, and social work have specialties that focus on the process of migration and the period of adaptation following a move. Experts working in these areas share with anthropologists an interest in such issues as people who migrate, causes of migration, processes of migration, psychosocial adaptations to new locations, and implications for planning and policy.

Anthropology and Migration

The subject matter of migration is related to all four fields of general anthropology. Archaeologists have reconstructed population movements through space and history and examined their relation to language change. They have studied urban growth in the past, much of which is accounted for by migration of people from the countryside to the city. Physical anthropologists examine migratory patterns of nonhuman primates and attempt to understand the reasons for movements of groups, especially in relation to carrying capacity of the environment. They have conducted nutritional and medical assessments of human populations in different environments, comparing, for example, foragers to settled populations. Linguistic anthropology is concerned with second language acquisition among migrants. Because the movement of people is interrelated with so many other aspects of culture, many chapters of this book have included information on migrant groups in relation to their subject matter.

Cultural anthropologists have addressed a wide range of issues related to migration, and it is their work that forms the basis of this chapter. They have studied *why* people move as well as their adjustments to living in a new place, especially the challenges and opportunities of maintaining their culture or constructing a new cultural identity. Given the breadth of migration studies, cultural anthropologists have used the full range of methods available, from individual life histories to large-scale surveys. Three differences distinguish migration studies in cultural anthropology. First, anthropologists studying migration are more likely to have fieldwork experience in more than one location in order to understand the places of origin and destination. Maxine Margolis (1994), for example, first did fieldwork in Brazil, then later studied Brazilian immigrants in New York City. Second, a greater emphasis on using macro and micro perspectives characterizes anthropology's approach to migration studies. Studying migration has challenged traditional cultural anthropology's focus on one village or neighbourhood and created the need to take into account national and

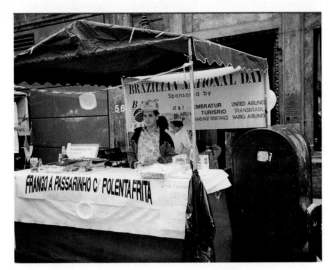

A food vendor at the Brazilian Independence Day street festival celebrated on West 46th Street in New York, an area known as "Little Brazil."

global economic, political, and social forces (Basch, Glick Schiller, and Szanton Blanc 1994; Lamphere 1992). Third, anthropologists who work with migrants are more likely to be involved in assisting them, often in resettlement work. Doreen Indra became the director of a large agency for Southeast Asian refugees because of her interest in refugee resettlement; as a professor of anthropology at the University of Lethbridge, she also published extensively on refugee research (Indra 1988).

What Is Migration?

Migration, or a spatial move, also involves cultural change, to varying degrees. A new situation requires individuals to learn new rules, roles, and expectations and adjust to them. Migration encompasses many categories depending on the distance of the move, its purpose, duration, degree of voluntarism (was the move forced or more a matter of choice?), and the migrant's status in the new destination. There is a major difference between **internal migration** (movement within national boundaries) and

international migration. Moving between nations is likely to create more challenges both in the process of relocation and in adjustment after arrival.

Internal Migration

Rural-to-urban migration was the dominant stream of internal population in most countries during the twentieth century. A major reason for people migrating to urban areas is the availability of work. According to the **push-pull theory** of labour migration, rural areas are increasingly unable to support population growth and rising expectations about the quality of life (the push factor). At the same time, cities (the pull factor) attract people, especially youth, for employment and lifestyle reasons. The push-pull model makes urban migration sound like a simple function of the rational decision making of freely choosing human agents who have information on the costs and the benefits of rural versus urban life, weigh that information, and then opt for going or staying (recall the approach to understanding culture that emphasizes human agency, Chapter 1). But many instances of urban migration are more the result of structural forces (economic need or political factors such as war) that are beyond the control of the individual (see the Multiple Cultural Worlds box on page 362).

The anonymity and rapid pace of city life and the likelihood of "psychosocial discontinuity" caused by relocation pose special challenges for migrants from rural areas. Research has shown that urban life increases the risk of *hypertension* (elevated blood pressure through stress or tension), and hypertension is related to coronary heart disease. For example, an anthropological study of urban migrants in comparison to rural dwellers in the Philippines found that hypertension, as defined by high blood pressure, is more prevalent in urban migrant populations than in settled rural groups (Hackenberg et al. 1983). This finding applied to both men and women. (Other social factors such as income level, education, age at migration, and social support systems can be important in affecting health outcomes of migration.) The relationship between elevated health risks resulting from psychosocial adjustment problems in rural-urban migration exists among international immigrant groups as well, for example, among Samoans living in California (Janes 1990).

Urban Labour Migration of Girls in Ghana

Child fostering is common throughout sub-Saharan Africa. Parents foster out children to enhance their chances for formal education or to help them learn a skill such as marketing through apprenticeship. The predominant direction of fostering is from rural to urban areas and from poorer to better-off families. Roger Sanjek (1990b) conducted a study of household composition in Adabraka, a middle-class neighbourhood in Ghana's capital city

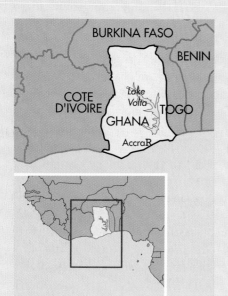

of Accra. The neighbourhood comprises people of different Ghanaian ethnic groups, but most are from the southern region, Christian, literate, and "modern." Child fostering is common. Of 40 adults in the study, more than half had been fostered, with the proportion higher among women than men.

About one-fourth of the resident children in the fieldwork neighbourhood were in-fostered. Striking gender differences emerge in this group of in-fostered children. First, there were twice as many girls as boys. School attendance rates were biased towards boys: All of the 17 boys were attending school, but only 4 of the 31 girls were. The others worked as maids or assisted in market trade. As a whole, 80 per cent of the children were kin of their sponsors, but this percentage was only 50 per cent for girls. Girls sponsored by kin are less likely to be mistreated than other girls. Maids who are not kin are secured by making a cash payment to the parents. Payments to the girl are at the discretion of the "employer." All maids help in cooking and housecleaning. They may also assist in selling items from in front of their employer's

building. Market helpers transport goods, take care of the trade location when the market woman is off on business or shopping, and run errands in the marketplace.

The number of girl maids and helpers in Accra as a whole is in the tens of thousands. This form of "hidden" child labour migration provides cheap labour for the better-off urban population. It subsidizes the education of city boys and girls by replacing their labour contribution to the household. Does urban fostering of poor rural girls offer them a path to social mobility? The research findings contradict this as a general conclusion. Rather, the labour of these girls is tapped mainly to benefit others, and "the life chances of many Ghanaian girls have been used up by the time they are 8 or 9 years old" (58).

FOOD FOR THOUGHT

Can you provide further interpretation of this illustration by reference to class and gender?

International Migration

International migration has grown in volume and significance since 1945, especially since the mid-1980s (Castles and Miller 1993). No one knows how many international migrants there are, although it is estimated that nearly 2 per cent of the world's population lives abroad (thus, the vast majority resides in their home countries). This amounts to about 100 million people, including legal and

illegal immigrants. Migrants who move for work-related reasons constitute the majority of people in this category. At least 35 million people from developing countries have migrated to the industrialized countries in the past three decades. International migration is likely to be one of the key factors in global social change through the first decade of the twenty-first century. Driving forces behind this trend are economic and political changes that affect labour demands and human welfare.

The "classic" countries of early international immigration are the United States, Canada, Australia, New Zealand, and Argentina. The first waves of European immigrants largely destroyed and dispossessed the indigenous peoples in each case. These countries' populations are now formed mainly of descendants of the European immigrants. The immigration policies of these nations in the early twentieth century have been labelled "White immigration" because they explicitly limited non-White immigration (Ongley 1995). In the 1960s in Canada, for instance, changes made immigration policies less racially discriminatory and more focused on skills and experience. Through the 1980s, further liberalization occurred and family reunification provisions were widened. In Canada, a combination of changing labour needs and interest in improving its international image prompted these reforms. During the 1980s, increased refugee flows inspired greater attention to humanitarian concerns.

During the 1980s and the 1990s, the United States and Canada experienced large-scale immigration from new sources—Asia, Mexico, Latin America, and the Caribbean (Castles and Miller 1993). In addition, new destination countries have joined these "classic" countries. Long-time areas of out-migration of northern, western, and southern Europe are now receiving many immigrants (often refugees from Asia). Some Central European states, such as Hungary, Poland, and Czechoslovakia, are new migrant destinations. Population flows in the Middle East are complex, with some nations such as Turkey experiencing substantial movements in both directions. Millions of Turks have emigrated to Germany, while ethnic Turks in places such as Bulgaria have returned to Turkey. Turkey has also received Kurdish and Iranian refugees. Several million Palestinian refugees now live mainly in Jordan and Lebanon. Israel has attracted Jewish immigrants from Europe, northern Africa, the United States, and most recently the former Soviet Union, through its attempt to build a Jewish nation. The Persian Gulf states draw thousands of labour migrants from elsewhere in the Middle East and Asia. Throughout Africa, labour migrants frequently go to their former colonial countries—for example, Moroccan and Algerian migrant workers go to France—and millions of refugees live outside their native countries. Industrialized Asian nations have also become immigration destinations. The complicated stratification of migration in and out of South American countries involves refugees and foreign workers entering Venezuela, Brazil, the Dominican Republic, and Argentina, and out-migration from Haiti, the Dominican Republic, and Mexico.

Categories of Migrants
Labour Migrants

Thousands of people migrate to work for a specific period of time. They do not intend to establish permanent residence and are often explicitly barred from doing so. This form of migration, when legally contracted, is called **wage labour migration.** The period of work may be brief or it may last several years, as among rural Egyptian men who go to other Middle Eastern countries to work for an average period of four years (Brink 1991). Asian women are the fastest growing category among the world's 35 million migrant workers (International Labour Office 1996:16–17). About 1.5 million Asian women are working abroad; most are in domestic service jobs, and some work as nurses and teachers. Major sending countries are Indonesia, the Philippines, Sri Lanka, and Thailand. Main receiving countries are Saudi Arabia and Kuwait, and to a lesser degree, Hong Kong, Japan, Taiwan, Singapore, Malaysia, and Brunei. Such women are usually alone and are not allowed to marry or have a child in the country where they are temporary workers. International migrant workers are sometimes illegally recruited and thus have no protection in their working conditions. The illegal recruitment of female prostitutes, a growing problem worldwide, is especially serious in Thailand, where young women are offered the prospect of migrating to Europe and North America under pretenses of receiving work, for example, as restaurant hostesses.

Circular migration refers to a common form of labour migration involving movement in a regular pattern between two or more places. Circular migration may occur either within or between nations. In the latter case, it is also referred to as **transnational migration.** The undocumented workers who go back and forth between Mexico and the United States each year are international circular migrants (Chavez 1992), as are many Haitian cane-cutters who work in the Dominican Republic (see the Critical Thinking box on pages 364 and 365). Internal circular migrants include, for example, female domestic

Haitian Cane-Cutters in the Dominican Republic—Two Views on Human Rights

The circulation of male labour from villages in Haiti to sugar estates in the Dominican Republic is the oldest and perhaps the largest continuing population movement within the Caribbean region (Martínez 1996). Beginning in the early twentieth century, Dominican sugar cane growers began to recruit Haitian workers, called *braceros*. Between 1952 and 1986, an agreement between the two countries' governments regulated and organized labour recruitment. Since then, recruitment became a private matter, with men crossing the border on their own or with recruiters working in Haiti without official approval.

Many studies and reports have addressed the system of labour recruitment from Haiti to the Dominican Republic. Two competing views exist. The human rights activists (View 1) focus on evidence of forced and fraudulent labour recruitment and take the position that this system violates the human rights of the Haitian labourers and is neo-slavery. The academics (View 2), while not completely unified in their views, use ethnographic data to support their position that it is inaccurate to consider the *braceros* as slaves because they have evidence that, more often, *braceros* migrate voluntarily.

VIEW 1

Interviews with Haitian *braceros* in the Dominican Republic have exposed a consistent pattern of labour rights abuses:

> Men and boys as young as seven in rural Haiti are accosted by Haitian Creole-speaking recruiters making promises of easy, well-paid employment in the Dominican Republic. Those who agree are taken to the frontier on foot and are either taken directly to a farm in the Dominican Republic or perhaps more often are turned over by the recruiter to Dominican soldiers for a fee of a few pesos per recruit. Inside the Dominican Republic, soldiers and policemen also detain undocumented Haitians at highway checkpoints and in roundups conducted mostly in rural areas. Contrary to common international practice, the Dominican authorities generally do not deport undocumented Haitian entrants but hand them over, again for a fee, to agents of state-owned sugar estates, for shipment to company compounds. The recruits are transported from the frontier under armed military guard in buses that stop infrequently on the way east to minimize the risk of their Haitian passengers absconding.

> Once on the sugar estates, the recruits are given only one means of earning money for survival, cutting sugar cane. Cutting cane is very physically debilitating labour, and in the Dominican Republic only the strongest and most experienced cane cutters can earn more than the equivalent of US$2 a day. Given the horrible labour conditions on the estates and the availability of lighter and better-paying work elsewhere in the Dominican Republic, it is not surprising that cane growers take measures to try to prevent their Haitian recruits from leaving. For example, armed guards patrol estate grounds on the lookout for any bracero who tries to leave in the night.

> At work, too, the braceros are subjected to open coercion. On ordinary work days, they are obliged to go out to the cane fields before dawn, sometimes even if they are too sick to work. Company overseers may also force them to work on Sundays or after dark, to help ensure a constant supply of cane to the mill.... As if all these abuses were not bad enough, a many-branched system of pay reductions and petty corruption deprives the braceros of a large fraction of the wages to which they are legally entitled. Many Haitians on the sugar estates say they have never been able to save enough money to return home. (19–29)

VIEW 2

Anthropological studies based on long-term fieldwork in Haiti provide observations that appear to contradict the neo-slavery interpretation. They find instead that most Haitian labour migrants cross the border to the Dominican Republic of their own volition. Samuel Martínez comments that "Recruitment by force in Haiti seems virtually unheard of. On the contrary, if this is a system of slavery, it may be the first in history to have to turn away potential recruits" (20). Some recruits have even paid bribes to be hired. Most people, even young people, are aware of how terrible the working conditions are in the Dominican Republic. They therefore choose to go, understanding what they will face. Repeat migration is common and is also taken as evidence of free choice. In the cane fields, the major means of maintaining labour discipline is not force but wage incentives: The piece-work system ensures long and hard work. The life histories of *braceros* show that many of them move from one sugar estate to another, discrediting the view of the estates as being like "concentration camps."

Martínez adds a more focused understanding to View 2 by giving emphasis to the importance of the driving force of poverty in shaping the *braceros'* decisions to migrate. In this way, we can see, perhaps, a link between View 1 and

View 2, since "neo-slavery" could be defined to include economic systems in which choice is so severely limited by economic needs that "freedom" is scarcely a factor in decision making:

Both economically and legally, the bracero finds his freedoms narrowly restricted...poverty and the dearth of income opportunities and credit at home for the young, land-poor, and the unskilled leave many rural Haitians little or no choice about whether to emigrate. For example, the prevailing wage for a six-to-eight hour "day" of farm labor in rural Haiti is less than one dollar. Even at this wage, paid employment for poorer folk is scarce, because few Haitian farmers have the means to hire much labor.... Faced with such daunting obstacles to economic advancement at home, a man who lacks money, social support, and human capital to go to a more desirable urban or overseas destination may turn to the Dominican Republic, in hope of bringing home at least a small cash surplus. The typical migrant brings home savings of US$25 to $75, but many fail to save even this much. The fact that such meager and uncertain

A Haitian migrant labourer. It is a matter of academic debate as to how much choice such a labourer has in terms of whether he will migrate to the neighbouring Dominican Republic for short-term work cutting cane, given the fact that he cannot find any kind of work in Haiti.]

rewards exert an important attraction suggests that most migrants leave home not so much to optimize their incomes as to grasp at any chance that may present itself...poverty drives dependent young men and male heads of poorer households to go to the Dominican Republic and thus opens the door to the labor rights abuses so amply documented. (21–22)

Source: Samuel Martínez 1996. Reproduced by permission of the American Anthropological Association from *American Anthropologist* 98:1, March 1996. Not for further reproduction.

CRITICAL THINKING QUESTIONS

How might the research methods of the activists and the academic anthropologists differ?

How do these differences influence their results? Is either perspective more "biased" than the other in terms of presenting an accurate picture of the bracero system?

What does each view offer in terms of policy reform?

workers throughout Latin America and the Caribbean. These women have their permanent residence in rural areas, but work for long periods of time in the city for better-off people. They tend to leave their children in the care of their mother in the country and send regular remittances for their support.

Displaced Persons and Refugees

Displaced persons are people who, for one reason or another, are "evicted from their houses, farms, and communities and forced to find a living elsewhere"

(Guggenheim and Cernea 1993:1). Colonialism, slavery, war, persecution, natural disasters, and large-scale mining and dam-building are major causes of population displacement. **Refugees**, a category of displaced persons, are forced to relocate because they are victims or potential victims of persecution because of race, religion, nationality, ethnicity, gender, or political views (Camino and Krulfeld 1994:vii). In contrast to much labour migration, migration caused by these factors is involuntary and often traumatic. The manner in which displaced persons are relocated has serious impacts on how well they will adjust to their new lives. Displaced persons in general have little choice about when and where they move, with refugees typically having the least of all.

Refugees constitute a large and growing category of displaced persons. The United Nations High Commissioner for Refugees (UNHCR) estimates a figure of over 22 million refugees worldwide (1997). The lack of accurate data is compounded by political interests seeking, in some cases, to inflate numbers, and in others, to deflate numbers (see the Multiple Cultural Worlds box). In the past, most refugees have left their homes for political or economic reasons. The Love Canal residential area in western New York state and the Chernobyl area created a new subcategory of displaced persons called **ecological refugees,** or people who have to relocate because their home area has become unfit for habitation

MULTIPLE CULTURAL WORLDS

Palestinian Refugees in Lebanon—Uncounted and Unwanted

Hundreds of thousands of Palestinians fled or were driven from their homes during the 1948 war (Zureik 1994). They went mainly to Jordan, the West Bank/East Jerusalem, Gaza, Lebanon, Syria, and other Arab states. Jordan and Syria have granted Palestinian refugees equal rights. Their situation in Lebanon is much worse because Lebanon refuses to grant them the right to settle there.

No official census count exists for the number of Palestinians who entered Lebanon following the 1948 formation of Israel. Estimates vary from about 200 000 to 600 000 (Salam 1994). The lower count is claimed to be accurate by the Israelis in order to downgrade the importance of the refugee problem. The higher count is favoured by both the Palestinians, to highlight the seriousness of their plight, and the Lebanese government, to emphasize its inability to absorb them. According to a 1987 estimate, only 30 000 had become Lebanese citizens. The rest are caught between resettlement and **repatriation** (return to one's homeland).

The Lebanese government does not extend civil rights, including the right to work or own property, to the Palestinians (*The Economist* 1995:4). The refugees are excluded from public services, including health and education. They are spatially restricted to a limited number of camps, which are threatened by expansion and development in Beirut. Palestinians believe that the Lebanese are trying to force them to migrate out, but they cannot go back to Israel. Israel refuses them "right of return" (Salam 1994). The right of return says that

- refugees who wish to return home and live at peace should be allowed to do so;
- they may accept either repatriation or compensation for losses; and
- they have the right to compensation for damages suffered regardless of whether they wish to return.

The right of return, considered a basic human right in the West since the time of the Magna Carta, is included in the United Nations General Assembly Resolution 194 passed in 1948. The right of return was elevated by the United Nations in 1974 to an "inalienable right." Israel responds to Palestinian claims by saying that their acceptance of Jewish immigrants from Arab countries constitutes an exchange. Some scholars and government officials say that the 1948 exodus from Israel was either voluntary or largely instigated by leaders of neighbouring Arab countries—thus the Palestinians, they claim, were not true "refugees." Egypt and several Gulf states are following Lebanon's lead and denying rights to Palestinians. These governments consider the Palestinian presence a threat to internal stability.

FOOD FOR THOUGHT

Several cultures are involved in the specific case described here. Which cultures appear to have greater power in making decisions about the Palestinians? Can you think of another situation in which refugee populations are relatively "voiceless"?

from pollution, a nuclear disaster, or environmental devastation from war.

Canada became a signatory to the United Nations Convention on Refugees in 1969, some 18 years after it was drawn up. The Immigration Act of 1976 incorporated into law Canada's responsibility towards the humane treatment of refugee claimants. Since that time, thousands of refugees resettle in Canada each year. Some arrive at the border claiming refugee status and are given a hearing to determine whether they meet the criteria as refugee claimants. Some are resettled directly from refugee camps, as UNHCR-defined convention refugees or members of a designated class identified on humanitarian grounds. Some are government sponsored; others are sponsored by groups. Privately sponsored refugee resettlement is organized by sponsorship agreements between a consortium of interested groups, often including religious institutions. Both government and private sponsorships offer advantages and disadvantages to the newcomer. Canada's record of upholding its international obligations to refugees was recognized in 1986, when the United Nations awarded the Nansen medal for efforts on behalf of refugees to Canada, an honour that previously had only been given to individuals (Beiser 1999:41).

Cultural anthropologists have done substantial research with refugee populations, especially those related to war (Camino and Krulfeld 1994; Hirschon 1989; Manz 1988; Gilad 1990; Chan and Indra 1987; Dorais, Pilon-Le, and Huy 1987; Tepper 1980). They have helped discover the key factors that ease or increase relocation stresses. One major issue is the extent to which the new location resembles or differs from the home place in several features such as climate, language, and food (Muecke 1987). Generally, the more different the places of origin and destination are, the greater will be the adaptational demands and stress. Other major factors are the refugee's ability to get a job equivalent to his or her training and experience, the presence of family members, and whether people in the new location are welcoming or hostile to the refugees.

The relatively successful case of Karelian refugee resettlement following World War II illustrates these points. One of the largest movements following the war was the displacement of over 400 000 Finnish Karelians from their homeland in eastern Finland because the area was ceded by Finland to the Soviet Union (Mustanoja and Mustanoja 1993). The resettlement plan for these people was successful for the following reasons: It provided land to farmers quickly; it involved household welfare support during the time of transition; entire villages were resettled together as much as possible; new social organizations were formed to facilitate adaptation; and there was cultural similarity between the Karelians and the local Finnish population in the resettlement area. Important shared cultural features included farming practices, religion, and women's status.

Institutional Migrants

Institutional migrants include people who move into a social institution, either voluntarily or involuntarily. They include monks and nuns, retirees, prisoners, and boarding school or college students. This section considers only some examples of students as a category of migrants.

Studies of student adjustment reveal similarities with many other forms of migration, especially in terms of risks for mental stress. Ethnographic research conducted among adolescent boarding school children in Ambanja, a town in Madagascar, showed that girls experience more adjustment strains than boys (Sharp 1990). Ambanja is a "booming migrant town" characterized by rootlessness and anomie. Boarding school children in this town constitute a vulnerable group because they have left their families and come alone to the school. Many of the boarding school girls, who were between the ages of 13 and 17, experienced bouts of spirit possession. Local people say that it is the "prettiest" girls that become possessed. The data on possession patterns showed, instead, that possession is correlated with a girl's being unmarried and pregnant. Many of these school girls become the mistresses of older men, who shower them with expensive gifts such as perfume and gold jewellery. Such girls attract the envy of both other girls and school boys, who are being passed over in favour of adult men. Thus, the girls have little peer support among their schoolmates. If a girl becomes pregnant, school policy requires that she be expelled. If the baby's father refuses to help her, she faces severe hardship. Her return home will be a great disappointment to her parents. Within this context, a girl's spirit possession may be understood as an expression of distress. Through the spirits, girls act out their difficult position between country and city and girlhood and womanhood.

International students also face serious challenges of spatial and cultural relocation. Like the school girls of Madagascar, they are at greater risk of adjustment stress than are local students. Many international students report mental health problems to varying degrees depending on age, marital status, and other factors. Spouses who accompany international students also suffer the strains of dislocation. The issue of international student adjustment is of increasing importance in Canada, where about 100 000 international students are enrolled in institutions of higher education, and that number is growing (Shik 1995).

Spouse/Partner Migration

When a relationship is initiated, patrilocal or matrilocal rules about residence may mean that one partner relocates while the other stays in place. The preponderance of patrilocal residence cross-culturally means that in heterosexual unions, women more often have a greater adjustment burden than men. In international marriage migration, one partner or both may lack language abilities and have poor job prospects. Staying at or near one's home location is relatively empowering because it allows the person to capitalize on local knowledge (of agricultural conditions or the best places to gather food) and social support. "Mail-order brides," women whose marriage to a North American is arranged through a mail-order service, are particularly at risk of difficult adjustments. The new husband typically has expectations of a subservient and dependent wife. The wife's expectations may not match her husband's, and she may be unable to find wage-paying work that would increase her autonomy. Frequent reports of wife abuse in "mail-order marriages" have brought attention to this system, although no clear solutions have emerged.

The New Immigrants

The term **new immigrants** refers to international migrants who have moved after the 1960s. New immigrants worldwide include increasing proportions of refugees, many of whom are destitute and desperate for asylum. Three trends are apparent in the new international migration of the last decade, and they are likely to continue:

- *Globalization:* More countries are involved in international migration, leading to increased cultural diversity in sending and receiving countries.

- *Acceleration:* Quantitative growth of migration has occurred in all major regions of the world. In the 1990s the majority of new immigrants came to Canada from Europe and South and Southeast Asia.

- *Feminization:* Women are playing a greater role in migration to and from all regions and in all types of migration, with some forms having a majority of women.

These three trends merit scholarly attention and raise new issues for policy-makers and international organizations as the cultural practices of immigrant groups and the areas of destination increasingly come in contact and, sometimes, in conflict, with each other (see the Multiple Cultural Worlds box).

In Canada, the category of "new immigrants" refers to people who arrived following the development of the Immigration Regulations of 1967. The regulations made it possible for far more people from developing countries to enter Canada, especially if they were professionals or trained in some desired skill. Later, the "family reunification" provision allowed permanent residents and naturalized citizens to bring in close family members. Most of the new immigrants to Canada are from Asia, Latin America, and the Caribbean, although increasing numbers are from Eastern Europe, especially Russia.

Canada provides temporary employment visas to allow migrant labourers to work in Canada for up to 12 months. Visas are also required by international students studying in Canada, who may stay for the period of their studies. Visa students may work in some limited contexts associated with their studies. Persons immigrating to Canada apply for landed immigrant status or permanent residence leading to citizenship after three years in the country. Canada's immigration policy tries to balance humanitarian concerns for refugee claimants, family reunification, and the perceived need to attract highly skilled and educated persons.

The New Immigrants from Latin America and the Caribbean

Since the 1960s, substantial numbers of people from Mexico, Central and South America, and the Caribbean

The New Immigrants and Female Circumcision in Canada

Canada recognizes the principle that fear of the practice of female circumcision (see Chapter 6) is a reason for being given refugee status (Berg 1997). In 1994 a woman from Somalia was given refugee status in Canada because of the fear she had for her daughters. If the family returned to Somalia, her children would have been subjected to this practice. Estimated rates of female circumcision in Somalia and Ethiopia are 90 per cent; in Egypt, 50 per cent. This suggests that many young girls would undergo this invasive operation if they remained in countries where this is a common practice.

Canada along with England, France, Belgium, Denmark, Switzerland, and Sweden have made female circumcision illegal. Under Canadian law, it is considered a form of child abuse and aggravated assault (21). Medical associations in most Canadian provinces have strict penalties for practitioners who perform female circumcision and reinfibulation after childbirth. They have also begun educational efforts in communities where the practice is most likely, in the hopes of discouraging the practice rather than punishing parents.

The World Health Organization called for an eradication of the practice by 2000, and UNICEF identifies it as a violation of the rights of the child. No one expects these pronouncements to end the practice, but advocacy groups may use these statements as a guide for changing a long-established practice. Advocacy groups are active in both the countries of origin and among immigrant groups in Canada.

FOOD FOR THOUGHT

Should people be allowed to practise female circumcision when they immigrate in spite of the disapproval of the medical community in their new country?

---

have come to Canada. Major flows come from the Caribbean islands of Jamaica, Barbados, Cuba, and Haiti, among others. This is partly a result of the change in Canada's immigration policy in the 1960s, which had previously excluded people from areas outside Europe (Avery 1995:197). In addition to immigrant and refugee flows, many people came from Mexico and the Caribbean as seasonal farm labourers working in deplorable conditions for little pay. Some of these people work in the tobacco and fruit orchards of southern Ontario.

Chain Migration of Haitians Haitian immigrants and refugees are clustered mainly in Quebec, particularly Montreal, attracted to the province because of their familiarity with French and their desire to be in a francophone environment. Early Haitian immigrants to Quebec in the 1950s were well-educated and skilled people who pursued careers in academia and the professions. By the 1970s, Haitians with rural backgrounds began coming in large numbers to Quebec to take employment in factories, construction, and the service industry (Dejean 1980). Once established in their new home, many Haitians began sponsoring their relatives as immigrants, as allowed under Canadian law. The process by which a first wave of migrants then attracts relatives and friends to join them in the destination place is

called **chain migration.** Many Haitians in Quebec work in construction and factories. Women in the community also work in the factories, although a smaller number work as domestics or in the service sectors. To assist in adaptation, the Haitians in Quebec established several self-help associations to deal with immigration issues and general problems of integrating into Quebecois society (Hess and Smith 1984:78).

Many second-generation Haitian youth find that racism is a constant part of life in Canada. Facing problems of academic performance, high unemployment rates, racism from the police, and resistance from school staff, Haitian youth come to depend on each other, and find all of their friends and colleagues are of Haitian descent or are other Blacks. Racism affects the way they participate in society and how well they do in school. These young people who were born in Quebec and expected to be integrated into Quebecois society instead experience exclusion and domination, and find racial tensions pervasive in everyday life (Potvin 1999:48–50).

Caribbean Women: Strategies for Survival A large portion of recent immigration to Canada was from the Caribbean in the 1980s. Yvonne Bobb Smith (1999) describes how many Caribbean women never lose the sense that "home" is in the islands,

Anthropologist Wenona Giles writes about the life of a first generation Portuguese immigrant to Canada.

Six months after Rosa arrived in Canada, her sister-in-law found her a job in a plastic bottle factory in Toronto. She couldn't speak English in those days, and because she worked with other Portuguese women in the factory, she didn't learn to speak English there and still doesn't. Even though she "earned good money," she was taken aback at the realization that she would have to pay for child care in Canada, which she found expensive. By doing shift work and catching a few hours sleep here and there, she was able to share child care with her husband:

When I got home in the morning he [her husband] would have left just a bit before and I kept awake until around eight when I could wash my son, dress him, and take him to school. And then I'd sleep a bit until eleven and I'd get up to go and get him for lunch. And then I'd take him to school, come back and go back to bed and then have to get up at up at three and go get him again.

It was a struggle for Rosa and her husband to care for their family and personal needs and also to show up at their factories ready to work. She sometimes felt that her own life was of no interest to her employer. She raised questions about the strength of the union at the bottle factory to address these issues:

In the factory it was like this—we used to talk a lot that we'd go on strike, we'd vote but once we got there [to the union meeting], everybody would keep their mouth shut. They'd approve everything.

Most of the workers could not understand the proceedings of these meetings since they were held in English. Rosa concluded that it was "a company union":

The union was not that much on the side of the workers. They also knew that the people couldn't speak English and couldn't defend themselves. Those meetings were in English and we couldn't understand a thing.

Rosa was eventually injured in the bottle factory and went on worker's compensation. She later took employment at an athletic club. She prefers life in Canada because she enjoys membership in a Portuguese political club and a theatre group, activities not available to women in Portugal. In other ways, things in Canada and Portugal would have been much the same. For example, her employment status would have been similar back home.

Source: Excerpt from *Portuguese Women in Toronto: Gender, Immigration, and Nationalism.* pages 68–70 by Wenona Giles. University of Toronto Press. 2002.

whether Jamaica, St. Lucia, or Trinidad. Smith posits three strategies for their survival in a society where racist insults are a constant part of the social environment for people from the Caribbean (Henry 1987). They see education as the first strategy in opening the door to better employment and a more satisfying role in the community. The second strategy is networking, building links with other men and women of the diaspora—the movement of Black Caribbean people to industrial nations like Canada, the United States, and the United Kingdom. The links may be established though casual meetings that eventually develop into strong, warm friendships. The third strategy is community activism. Caribbean women in Canada have founded or are involved in several community organizations that support and promote causes important to Caribbean immigrant groups and other minorities, including the National Congress of Black Women of Canada, Black Theatre Canada, and the Coalition of Visible Minority Women of Ontario (Y. Smith 1999:163).

The New Immigrants from East Asia

Monster Houses: The Arrival of Hong Kong Chinese in Canadian Neighbourhoods

The arrival of large numbers of new immigrants in any community causes apprehension and concern, especially when the new arrivals have substantially different languages and customs from the resident populations. The arrival of Hong Kong Chinese in Canada in the late 1980s and early 1990s met with some negative reactions from the predominantly White Canadian population.

In anticipation of the transfer of Hong Kong to China in 1997, about 60 000 Hong Kong Chinese left for Canada, New Zealand, the United Kingdom, the United States, and Singapore. Since 1987, Hong Kong has been the single largest source of immigrants to Canada. Many of these immigrants entered Canada under the Business or Independent categories, meaning they had substantial amounts of capital to invest, although most that came to Canada saw the country as a safe haven, not as a place to make great economic progress (J. Smart 1994). These people were called "astronauts" because they were in the air most of the time travelling between their homes in Canada and their businesses in Hong Kong. These immigrants wanted to obtain property in neighbourhoods that were safe and had good educational resources for their children. In the early 1990s, a 1000-square-foot apartment in Hong Kong could be sold for C$800 000, thus many of these Hong Kong immigrants could afford to buy homes in any one of Canada's most exclusive neighbourhoods.

Anthropologists point out that stories inhabitants tell about neighbourhoods help create the identity of particular places. Since different stories may be told about a place by different people, places can have ambiguous or multiple meanings (Rodman 1992). For example, neighbourhoods are seen as downtrodden slums or as vibrant inner-city communities, depending on differing perspectives. In this way, many upscale Canadians told stories about their neighbourhoods, voicing their opposition to Hong Kong Chinese buying homes next door (Smart and Smart 1996). Comments from people living in upscale neighbourhoods like Toronto's Bridle Path and Vancouver's Shaugnessy indicate that the story to be told was one of opposition to developers and *nouveau riche* who wanted to tear down the neighbourhood's grand old homes and put up monster homes decorated with intrusive stone statues of lions. Long-time residents may not directly refer to the Hong Kong Chinese, but the implication was that the developers building monster homes are immigrants or their agents. The immigrants had to be kept in their place even though their wealth gave them access to the most exclusive parts of a privileged community. Neighbourhoods sought to put bylaws in place that would preserve the character of the place. In Shaugnessy, this meant maintaining English landscape tastes that would necessarily exclude stone lions and other perceived garish elements of Asian design. These bylaw changes suggest that these stories are not about neighbourhood integrity, but are rather stories being told to exclude a certain group of people.

The New Immigrants from Southeast Asia

Three Patterns of Adaptation among the Vietnamese Over one and a quarter million refugees have left Vietnam since the 1970s. Although most were relocated to the United States, many went to Canada,

Australia, France, Germany, and Britain (S. Gold 1992). For example, in the period between 1979 and 1981, Canada accepted 60 000 Southeast Asian refugees. Vietnamese immigrants in Canada constitute a significant Asian minority. Three distinct subgroups are the 1975-era elite, the boat people, and the ethnic Chinese. While they interact frequently, they have retained distinct patterns of adaptation.

The first group avoided many of the traumatic elements of flight. They were U.S. employees and members of the South Vietnamese government and military. They left before having to live under the communist regime, and they spent little time in refugee camps. A few of these came to Canada, especially to Quebec.

The boat people began to enter Canada after the outbreak of the Vietnam-China conflict of 1978. Mainly of rural origin, they lived for three years or more under communism, working in re-education camps or "new economic zones." Their exit, either by overcrowded and leaky boats or on foot through Cambodia, was dangerous and difficult. Over 50 per cent died on the way. Those who survived faced many months in refugee camps in Thailand, Malaysia, the Philippines, or Hong Kong before being admitted to Canada. Many more males than females escaped as boat people; thus, they are less likely to have arrived with intact families. They were less well educated than the earlier wave, half had no competence in English or French, and they faced a depressed economy. They have had a much more difficult time adjusting to life in Canada than the 1975-era elite.

The Sino-Vietnamese, traditionally a distinct and socially marginalized class of entrepreneurs in Vietnam, arrived mainly as boat people. Many of these immigrants have successfully used contacts in the overseas Chinese community and have been able to re-establish their roles as entrepreneurs.

No Vietnamese had lived in the prairie city of Lethbridge, Alberta, before 1979 (Indra 1988). The adaptation of Vietnamese and Sino-Vietnamese to this environment has been relatively successful. The Sino-Vietnamese, are able to connect with other Chinese in the community and therefore maintain their cultural identity. In addition, the Sino-Vietnamese have been better able to reconstitute their core families. The Vietnamese in Lethbridge have been less able to adjust, finding it more difficult to re-establish families and feeling a strong attachment to Vietnam as it once was. Despite their being marginally employed, all Vietnamese in Lethbridge had a positive self-concept and even after 10 years, people had kept contact with their sponsors in the community.

Khmer Refugees' Interpretation of Their Suffering

Since the late 1970s, approximately 20 000 people from Cambodia have come to Canada as refugees from the Pol Pot regime. These people survived years of political repression, a difficult escape, and time in a refugee camp before arriving in Canada. One question anthropologists ask is how people who have been through such terror and loss reconstruct their understanding of how the world works and their place in it. In Canada, many Cambodians, or Khmer, are from rural backgrounds and have beliefs in spirits called *neak ta*. Physical complaints are often blamed on these spirits. Some women refugees were possessed by the spirits of those who were murdered or not given proper burial rites, a common occurrence during the Pol Pot years. One cure for this state is giving food to Buddhist monks on behalf of the distressed spirit. Or consultation may be sought with a traditional healer, known as a *Khmer kru*. In this way, the possession can be resolved; but if monks or a traditional healer are not available, the suffering may be expressed in "physical ailments, social withdrawal and mental illness" (McLellan 1996:246). In Ontario, where most Khmer live in Canada, no programs have focused on the particular problems suffered by this population, despite widespread knowledge about the nature of the Pol Pot regime and the stresses this population has endured.

The New Immigrants from South Asia

The Sikhs in British Columbia: Maintaining Their Religious Identity

Sikhs began coming to British Columbia in the early twentieth century, but they did not arrive in large numbers until the 1960s and 1970s, when Canada's immigration laws were relaxed. Annamma Joy studied the Sikhs in the Okanagan Valley in the interior of British Columbia, an area famous for apple growing (1989). Many of the Sikhs had come to the valley on the recommendation of friends and relatives, an example of chain migration. Most had been successful farmers in India and hoped to be able to live well in Canada, purchasing houses and cars. Many worked in the sawmills of the northern Okanagan. Male Sikhs suffered severe criticism from non-Sikh co-workers because of the visible symbols of their religion—beards and turbans. Even when Sikhs gave in to pressure, by shaving their beards and no longer wearing the turban, they were still subject to prejudice. The Sikhs were recognized as good workers by management, but were seen as a threat by other community members.

The male practices of wearing the turban, having unshorn hair, and carrying the *kirpan* (sword) are important features of the Sikh religion. The bangle, the breeches, and the comb symbolize maintaining a balance between the uncontrollable nature of power and sexual virility and discipline and restraint. The unshorn hair is a symbol of power and virility, which is restrained by the comb, while the *kirpan* is restrained by the bangle. The *kirpan* is also important in the baptism of Sikhs. It is usually kept in the home, but some Sikhs feel they have the right to carry it, a practice which sometimes causes difficulties with various jurisdictions. Since 1976, Canadian law has allowed Sikhs to carry the *kirpan,* provided it is for religious purposes.

The New Immigrants from Eastern Europe

The breakup of the Soviet Union into 15 separate countries spurred the movement of over nine million people throughout eastern Europe and Central Asia. Many of these immigrants are people of Slavic descent who had lived in Central Asia during the time of the former Soviet Union and are seeking to return to their homelands. Another large category includes people who were forcibly relocated to Siberia or Central Asia. Many Soviet Germans have migrated from Siberia to Germany, and Crimean Tatars are shifting from Uzbekistan back to Crimea. Since 1988, people from the former Soviet Union have been the largest refugee nationality to enter the United States (Littman 1993, cited in S. Gold 1995).

Soviet Jews: Refugees Fleeing Religious Persecution

A sizable proportion of the refugees from the former Soviet Union are Soviet Jews. They have relocated to Israel, some countries of western Europe, and North America. The largest number of Soviet Jews live in Israel; since the mid-1960s, about 325 000 have settled in the United States and over 60 000 in Canada. Steven Gold (1995) has studied different refugee groups in California for many years and speaks from a compar-

Immigrants learning English at an adult school.

professionals, such as doctors and dentists, are unable to pass their licensing exams and are forced to accept menial labour jobs far beneath their qualifications. This is especially true for women emigres who were employed, often as professionals, in the Soviet Union, but who can find no work other than housecleaning or babysitting. Another major challenge relates to marriage options. Cultural norms promote interethnic marriage; however, the number of Soviet Jews in the marriage pool is small. As a result, marriage brokerage businesses have developed that pair young women in Russia with established emigres in North America.

Bosnian Refugees: Rebuilding Their Lives after War

The Serbian policy of ethnocide or "ethnic-cleansing" in the former Yugoslavia involved the claiming of territory and driving out of all "non-Serbs" through outright murder, mass rape of women, imprisonment, and torture (Stiglmayer 1994). The recent war in Bosnia and Herzegovina created the greatest refugee crisis in Europe since World War II. More than three million former Yugoslavians were displaced. Of these, about 13 000 were resettled in the United States by 1994. They are thus the most recent refugee arrivals. They share with other refugees from war and violence the memories of extreme suffering and loss experienced within the context of direct genocide (see the Multiple Cultural Worlds box on page 374).

ative perspective when he points out unique features of the experience of Soviet Jewish refugees. First, their origins in the Soviet Union accustomed them to the fact that the government controlled almost every aspect of life, "from the production of butter and the administration of summer camps to the shaping of ideology" (xi). These emigres are used to a wide range of government services, including jobs, housing, daycare, and other basic needs. They have had to find new ways of meeting these needs in a market economy. Second, Soviet Jews, as White Europeans, are members of the dominant racial majority group in the United States. While Soviet Jews have suffered centuries of discrimination in eastern Europe, they are much closer to the racial mainstream in the United States. Third, they have access to established and prosperous communities of American Jews. They have well-connected sponsors when they arrive. Most other new immigrant groups do not have these advantages.

The economic downturn of the 1990s, however, prompted a wave of anti-immigrant sentiment of which Soviet Jewish immigrants are "keenly aware" (xiii). Soviet Jewish immigrants face other challenges as well. Depending on their area of relocation, many have a difficult time finding a job commensurate with their education and previous work in the Soviet Union. In Canada, many Soviet Jewish immigrants who were highly skilled

The Politics and Policies of Inclusion and Exclusion

National immigration policies that set quotas on the quantity and types of immigrants welcomed and determine how they are treated are largely dictated by political and economic interests. Even in the cases of seemingly humanitarian quotas, governments undertake a cost-benefit analysis of how much will be gained and how much will be lost. Politically, governments show either their

Bosnian Refugees' Trauma Testimonies

Refugee survivors of violence are especially at risk to suffer from various mental health problems, including what Western psychiatrists term PTSD (post-traumatic stress disorder). PTSD can include symptoms such as depression, anxiety, sleep disorders, and changes in personality. In terms of treating refugee survivors in North America, several approaches have been used including the testimony method in conjunction with therapy such as support groups. One study of 20 Bosnian refugees who are now settled in the United States sheds light on the positive effects of having survivors narrate their "trauma testimonies," which are accounts of their experiences of terror and suffering (Weine et al. 1994). The testimony method involves asking the individual "to tell in detail the story of what happened to them and recording their narrative account verbatim…many clinicians agree that having individuals tell the story of their traumatic experiences in a safe and caring interpersonal setting helps them to live better with traumatic memories" (536–537).

Ten of the refugees in the study were male and 10 were female. They belonged to six families and ranged in age from 13 to 62 years. All but one were Muslims, and all adults were married and had worked either inside or outside the home. Analysis of the testimony showed that all had experienced a high number of traumatic events, with the frequency increasing with a person's age. The number of traumatic events in the narratives did not differ by gender, but the qualitative aspects of the trauma did:

> Adult men were more likely to be separated from their families and to be held in concentration camps where they suffered extreme deprivation and atrocities. Adult women (as well as adolescents of both genders) were often held briefly in detention camps and then they spent months fleeing from capture or being held in occupied territory where they were subjected to violence. (537)

> Almost all the refugees experienced the destruction of their homes, forced evacuation, food and water deprivation, disappearance of family members, exposure to acts of violence or death, detainment in a refugee camp, and forced emigration: "Nearly all the refugees emphasized the shock that came with the sudden occurrence of human betrayal by neighbors, associates, friends, and relatives." (538)

The testimonies document the genocidal nature of the traumas directed at the entire Muslim Bosnian population. The traumas experienced were "extreme, multiple, repeated, prolonged and communal." (539) Some of the survivors carry with them constant images of death and atrocity. One man describes them as "films" that play in his head. In contrast, others have lost their memories of the events, and one woman was later unable to remember the trauma story she told three weeks earlier: "All kinds of things come together. Being expelled. Things we lost. Twenty years of work—then suddenly being without anything…. All the memories come at the same moment and it's too much." (541)

The massiveness of their suffering, the psychiatrists report, extends beyond the bounds of the current diagnostic category of PTSD.

FOOD FOR THOUGHT

The Bosnian refugees described here have experienced severe traumas. Do you have any experiences that even remotely resemble these events in your life? Do you know anyone who has? How do you think you would react to such changes?

support or disapproval of other governments through their immigration policies. One of the most obvious economic factors affecting policy is labour flow. Cheap, even illegal, immigrant labour is used around the world to maintain profits for businesses and services for the better-off. Flows of such labour undermine labour unions and the status of established workers.

In Canada, immigration law determines who will be allowed entry and what benefits the government will allow them. The focus on cheap labour was dominant at the beginning of the twentieth century in Canada. The large extraction industries of lumbering and mining, along with the railroads, demanded large numbers of cheap labourers. Business in Canada overrode government concerns about foreign labour even when many residents of Canada complained about the influx of foreigners, mainly southern and eastern Europeans (Avery 1995). Government regulations on immigrants from Asia were more restrictive. For example, the Chinese were subject to an entry tax in 1885, and in 1923 were specifically forbidden to enter Canada. Canada still continues some restrictive policies. In 1995, the government introduced a $975 landing fee for every adult immigrant and refugee applying for permanent residence (in 2002 the fee for refugees was discontinued). Officially, this policy was put in place to offset the costs to the government of settlement programs. But many immigrant and refugee advocates perceive it as an unfair burden on immigrants and refugees struggling to become established in a new country.

National immigration policies are played out in local communities. In some instances, local resentments are associated with a so-called **lifeboat mentality,** which seeks to limit enlarging a particular group because of perceived resource constraints.

Influxes of immigrants who compete for jobs have led to hostility in many parts of Europe and North America. Some observers have labelled this *working-class racism* because it emerges out of competition with immigrants for jobs and other benefits (J. Cole 1996). The number of immigrants has grown substantially in southern Italy since the early 1980s. In the city of Palermo, with a total population of 800 000, there are now between 15 000 and 30 000 immigrants from Africa, Asia, and elsewhere. Does the theory of working-class racism apply to the working class in Palermo? Two conditions seem to predict that it would: large numbers of foreign immigrants and a high rate of unemployment. However, instead of expressing racist condemnation of the immigrants, working-class residents of Palermo accept the immigrants as fellow poor people. One critical factor may be the lack of competition for jobs, which derives from the fact that working Palermitans and immigrants occupy different niches. Immigrant jobs are less desirable, more stigmatized, and less well-paying. African immigrant men work in bars and restaurants, as building cleaners, or as itinerant street vendors. African and Asian women work as domestic servants in the better-off neighbourhoods. Sicilians do refer to immigrants by certain racial/ethnic names, but they seem to be used interchangeably and imprecisely. For example, a common term for all immigrants, Asian or African, is *turchi,* which means *Turks.* The word can be applied teasingly to a Sicilian as well and in conversation may connote alarm as in "Mom, the Turks!" Other loosely applied terms are the Italian words for Moroccans, Blacks, and Tunisians. In a questionnaire given to school children, the great majority agreed with the statement that "a person's race is not important." The tolerance among Palermo's working class may be only temporary. Nonetheless, it suggests that researchers take a closer look at cases elsewhere that assume working-class racism against immigrants.

Recent politically conservative trends in the United States have succeeded in rolling back more progressive policies about immigration and minorities. Police raids in areas known to have many undocumented migrants have brought mass expulsion. Reversals of affirmative action in college admissions, initiated in California in the late 1990s, have gained widespread support among "nativist" Americans. This lifeboat mentality of exclusiveness and privilege is held mainly by the dominant White majority and others who have "made it."

However, political and economic considerations about immigration exist within broad frameworks, such as "melting pot ideology" or "multiculturalism." While the United States refers to the melting pot that assimilates newcomers, Canada's official multiculturalism policy, incorporated into law by the Multiculturalism Act of 1988, encourages individuals and communities to maintain linguistic and cultural diversity.

Key Questions Revisited

What are the reasons for migration?

Reasons for migration include the search for productive resources, for marriage and other domestic partnerships, or because of "push" factors such as warfare or natural disasters. People's adjustment to their new situations depends on the degree of voluntarism involved in the move, the degree of cultural difference between the place of origin and the destination, and how closely expectations about the new location are met especially in terms of making a living and establishing social ties.

What is a displaced person?

Displaced persons are one of the fastest growing categories of migrants. Refugees, fleeing from political persecution, warfare, displacement by development projects, and ecological problems constitute an increasing number of all migrants. They face the most serious adjustment challenges since they often leave their home countries with few material resources and frequently have experienced much psychological suffering.

How are new immigrants contributing to transnational connections and multiculturalism?

Worldwide, new immigrants are contributing to growing transnational connections and the formation of increasingly multicultural populations within states. In Canada, the three largest non-European immigrant groups in the 1990s were from Hong Kong, India, and the Philippines. By the year 2004, 20 per cent of Canada's population will be visible minorities, most of them making up half the population of Canada's three largest cities, Toronto, Montreal, and Vancouver. Immigrant groups throughout the world are likely to face certain forms of discrimination in their new destinations, although the degree to which it occurs varies depending on perceived resource competition from already settled residents.

Core Concepts

chain migration, p. 370
circular migration, p. 363
displaced persons, p. 365
ecological refugees, p. 366
internal migration, p. 361
international migration, p. 361
lifeboat mentality, p. 375
migration, p. 360
new immigrants, p. 368
push-pull theory, p. 361
refugees, p. 365
repatriation, p. 366
transnational migration, p. 363
wage labour migration, p. 363

Suggested Readings

Linda Basch, Nina Glick Schiller, and Christina Szanton Blanc, *Nations Unbound: Transnational Projects, Postcolonial Predicaments, and Deterritorialized Nation-States*. Langhorne, PA: Gordon and Breach Science Publishers, 1994. Eight chapters explore theoretical issues in transnational migration and present detailed analysis of cases of migration from the Caribbean including St. Vincent, Grenada, and Haiti.

Morton Beiser, *Strangers at the Gate: The "Boat People's" First Ten Years in Canada*. Toronto: University of Toronto Press, 1999. This volume aims to inform the Canadian public about the impact of refugees on Canada, and shows how these newcomers have struggled, without making extensive use of health and social services.

Colin Clarke, Ceri Peach, and Steven Vertovic, eds., *South Asians Overseas: Migration and Ethnicity*. New York: Cambridge University Press, 1990. The text includes 15 chapters plus introductory essays that place the case studies in a broader context. Chapters are divided into two sections: South Asians in colonial and post-colonial contexts and South Asians in contemporary Western countries and the Middle East.

W. Giles, H. Moussa, and P. Van Esterik, eds., *Development and Diaspora: Gender and the Refugee Experience*. Dundas, ON: Artemis Enterprises, 1996. Chapters in this edited volume explore the relation between gender, development, and the movements of refugees, and include an examination of the resettlement process.

Sherri Grasmuck and Patricia R. Pessar, *Between Two Islands: Dominican International Migration*. Berkeley: University of California Press, 1991. Based on fieldwork in the Dominican Republic and New York City, this volume focuses on social ties and networks facilitating migration from rural areas in the Dominican Republic to Santo Domingo and from the Dominican Republic to the United States, and how employment opportunities shape the migration experience.

P. Magocsi, ed., *Encyclopedia of Canada's Peoples*. Toronto: University of Toronto Press, 1999. Edited by the director of the Multicultural History Society of Ontario, this massive book gathers complex information on about 130 peoples that make up Canadian society, including details about their origins, settlement, and intergroup dynamics.

Beatriz Manz, *Refugees of a Hidden War: The Aftermath of Counterinsurgency in Guatemala*. Albany: State University of New York Press, 1988. This study was conducted to assess whether conditions would allow the return to Guatemala of 46 000 Indian peasant refugees living in camps in Mexico. It gives attention to aspects of family and community life in the camps and in resettled villages in Guatemala, where the Indians face discrimination and harassment from the military.

Jennifer Robertson, *Native and Newcomer: Making and Remaking a Japanese City*. Berkeley: University of California Press, 1991. This text studies the social and symbolic adjustments of native residents of Kodaira city and the many residents who moved to Kodaira beginning in the 1950s. Detailed attention is given to the role of a community festival in expressing links between the natives and newcomers, while also stating and maintaining group boundaries.

 Your *Cultural Anthropology*, Second Canadian Edition Media Edition CD-ROM contains many Web sites relevant to this chapter. Use it to explore the Web and to expand your knowledge of anthropology.

Chapter 16

Development Anthropology

CHAPTER OUTLINE

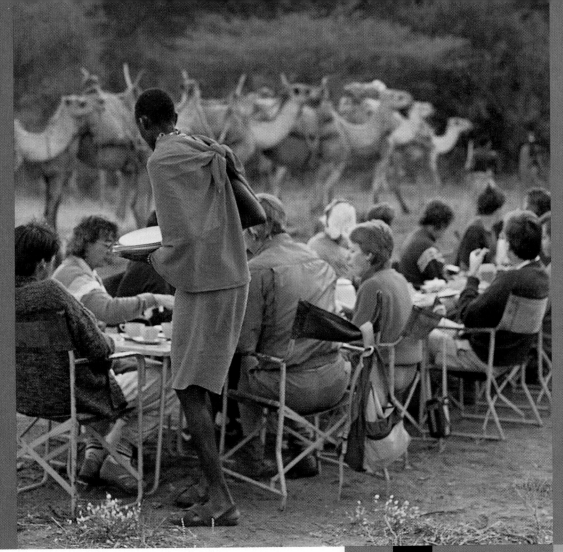

International tourism is a huge and growing part of the global and local economies of many countries. Tourists are increasingly interested in "cultural" tourism through which they are able to see and participate in certain aspects of the culture they visit. Safari tour groups in Africa, as in the case of a trip to Maasailand shown here, combine exposure to wildlife and Maasai culture.

Key Questions

How does anthropology study change?

What are the most common approaches to development?

What does anthropology contribute to understanding some major issues in development?

*T*he usual goal of cultural anthropology is to provide informed description and analysis, with minimal influence on the people being studied. In applied anthropology, in contrast, the goal is to use knowledge to provide solutions to practical problems. (As mentioned in Chapter 1, all of anthropology's four fields have applied aspects.) Development anthropology seeks to understand how cultures change and how anthropologists can inform and transform the process of **international development,** directed change to achieve improved levels of human welfare in so-called developing countries, often through promoting economic growth.

In the first part of the chapter, we consider general processes of cultural change and then review approaches in international development and anthropological views and findings related to them. In the second part of the chapter, we examine three interrelated issues of great contemporary concern: women and development, indigenous peoples and development, and human rights.

Anthropology and the Study of Change

All cultures change, but the causes and processes of change are varied. Cultural change can be intentional or accidental, forward-looking or backward-looking, rapid or gradual, obvious or nearly invisible, beneficial or harmful. Physical anthropology's interest in human evolution has long prompted a view of change that goes back millions of years into prehistory, even before the time when humans emerged. Archaeology's study of human cultural remains encompasses both prehistory and history, as does the work of linguistic anthropologists in reconstructing the evolution of language.

In contrast to these three fields, early work in cultural anthropology took a **synchronic** view in describing a particular culture at one point in time, with minimal or no attention to its past. This approach led to a static view of culture, fixed in what was called the "ethnographic present," a phrase referring to the period during which the anthropologist was in the field. Such cultural "snapshots" were erroneously assumed to have enduring validity until the 1970s, when anthropologists realized how dated these ethnographies were. Because cultural anthropology was originally devoted to conducting synchronic studies, its theories and methods have been revised to

account for change. Much current work is being done to improve **diachronic analysis** (analysis through time).

According to materialist anthropologists, the first step in theorizing about and researching change is to examine the infrastructural base (modes of production and reproduction), its links with transformations in political and power structures, and finally the way production and power influence ideology. The logic is that the deepest causal explanations are to be found in the base rather than in social structure and superstructure. Of course, social structure and ideas (superstructure) cause change as well. For example, higher education changes one's knowledge level and can lead to a better-paying job. In this example, it appears that change in the superstructure causes change in infrastructure. However, the cultural materialist would suggest a closer look towards the possible infrastructural factors that led, in the first place, to the person being able to get a higher education. In sum, a holistic, cultural materialistic view of change attempts to encompass all aspects of change, but gives priority to looking at material causal factors and outcomes. Within this broad framework of change, two basic processes are at work: invention and diffusion.

Invention

The invention of a new device or process may prompt cultural change. Inventions usually evolve gradually, through step-wise experimentation and accumulation of knowledge, but some appear rather suddenly. We can all name many technological inventions that have created cultural change, for example the printing press, gun powder, polio vaccine, and satellite communication.

Research by cultural anthropologists and other social scientists shows that not all inventions have positive social outcomes. Even innovations inspired by a socially positive goal often turn out to have mixed or even negative effects (see the Critical Thinking box). Along these lines, cultural anthropologists have made substantial contributions to improving development projects by telling the stories of those negatively affected by change (examples of this approach are provided throughout this chapter).

Diffusion

Diffusion is the spread of technology and ways of behaving and thinking through contact. It is logically related to invention because useful new discoveries are

Social Effects of the Green Revolution

Agricultural research scientists of the 1950s, inspired by the laudable goal of eliminating world hunger, developed high-yielding genetic variations of wheat, rice, and corn. These high-yielding varieties (HYV) of seeds were promoted to farmers throughout the developing world as part of the "Green Revolution" that would feed the world by boosting production. In most places where Green Revolution agricultural practices were adopted, grain production did increase. Was world hunger conquered? The answer is no because world hunger is not merely a problem of production; it also involves distribution.

Analyses of the social impact of the Green Revolution in India reveal that one of its results was to increase disparities between the rich and the poor (Frankel 1971). How did this happen? Green Revolution agriculture requires several expensive inputs: purchased seeds (HYV seeds cannot be harvested from the crop and saved until the next year since they are hybridized), the heavy use of commercial fertilizers, and the need for dependable irrigation sources. Thus, farmers who could use HYV seeds successfully were, in the first place, better off because the innovation was selected for those who could afford such inputs. Small farmers who tried planting HYV seeds but could not provide these inputs experienced crop failure, went deeper into debt, and ended up having to sell the small amounts of land they had. Larger and better-off farmers took advantage of these new openings in the land market to accumulate more land and expand their holdings. With the acquisition of tractors and other mechanized equipment, large farmers became even more productive. Small farmers were unable to compete and continued to be squeezed out financially. They became hired day labourers, dependent on seasonal employment by large farmers, or they migrated to cities where they became part of the urban underclass.

Looking at the Green Revolution from a critical thinking perspective, we may see more clearly whose interests were served, whether this was the original intention or not. The big winners included the companies involved in selling chemical fertilizers (largely petroleum-based) and HYV seeds, companies that manufacture and sell mechanized farm equipment, the larger farmers whose income levels improved, and the research scientists themselves who gained funding for their research and world fame for their discoveries. In retrospect, it is difficult to imagine that early planners in the 1950s could have been so naive as to not realize who they would be helping and who they might end up hurting.

CRITICAL THINKING QUESTIONS

Is it likely that the original innovators of HYV grains considered what social transformations might occur in developing country agriculture as a result of their invention?

Would they have been likely to stop their research if they had realized that it would lead to the "rich getting richer and the poor getting poorer"? Should they have done so?

How does this example reflect the current debates about genetically modified food?

likely to spread. Diffusion can occur in several ways. First, in mutual borrowing, two roughly equal societies exchange elements of their culture with each other. For example, the United States exported rock and roll music to England and England exported the Beatles to the United States. Second, diffusion may occur between unequal societies and involve a transfer from a dominant culture to a less powerful culture. This process may occur through force or more subtly through education or marketing processes that promote adoption of new practices and beliefs. For example, through volunteer groups such as CUSO or WUSC (World University Service of Canada), many North American products, practices, and beliefs are spread to developing countries. Third, a more powerful culture may appropriate aspects of a less powerful culture (the latter process is called *cultural imperialism*). For example, the Tower of London in England is full of priceless jewels from India.

In each of these types of diffusion, the result is some degree of **acculturation,** or change in one culture as a result of contact with another culture. At one extreme, a culture may become so completely acculturated that it has become **assimilated,** no longer distinguishable as having a separate identity. In many cases, cultural change through diffusion has led to extreme change in the "receiving" culture, which becomes **deculturated,** or extinct. Such deculturation has occurred among many indigenous peoples as the result of the introduction of new technology (see the Multiple Cultural Worlds box). Other responses to acculturative influences include re-

Services for photocopying and sending faxes, invented in the West, have been recently diffused to most parts of the world, including the formerly remote capital of India's Andaman Islands, Port Blair. A popular restaurant at the same location also demonstrates the diffusion of cuisine: South Indian, Chinese, and Continental.

sistance, rejection, or partial acceptance of something new with reformulation and reshaping, like cricket in the Trobriands (see Chapter 14). The study of international development is, in fact, concerned with the dynamics and results of a particular form of change—the adoption of Western goods, behaviour, and values through processes such as neocolonialism, globalization, and international assistance projects.

Approaches to Development

In this section we consider the most common approaches to international development, and how development is carried out by various kinds of organizations—large-scale and grassroots. We look closely at the development project as the main mechanism of development organizations for bringing about change. Special methods used by anthropologists who work in the field of development are then discussed.

Theories of Cultural Change

Two theories of cultural change dominate the thinking of global leaders and local entrepreneurs in out-of-the-way settings: modernization theory and growth-oriented development. These concepts are heavily influenced by Western economics. In contrast to these two theories, we also consider three additional approaches to development.

Modernization **Modernization theory** refers to change marked by industrialization, consolidation of the nation-state, bureaucratization, market economy, technological innovation, literacy, and options for social mobility. It derives from a period in Western European history beginning in the seventeenth century, which emphasized the importance of secular rationality and the inevitable advance of scientific thinking (Norgaard 1994). Modernization appears as almost an inevitable process that will, given the insights of science and rationality, spread throughout the world and lead to improvement in people's lives everywhere. Overall, the emphasis of modernization is on material progress and individual betterment.

Supporters and critics of modernization are found in both rich and poor countries. Supporters claim that the benefits of modernization (improved transportation; electricity; domestic comforts such as air conditioning; and technology such as washing machines, biomedical health care, and telecommunications) are worth the costs—whether those costs are calculated in terms of environmental or social costs. Other scholars in many disciplines—from literary studies to anthropology—regard modernization as a failure. Most cultural anthropologists are critics of modernization as a general process of social change because it leads to increased social inequality, the destruction of indigenous cultures, ecological ruin, and the overall decline in global cultural diversity. Selected aspects of modernity, however, such as electricity and antibiotics may be accepted as positive. In spite of strong cautionary critiques from anthropologists and environmentalists about the negative impacts of modernization, nations around the world have not slowed their attempts to achieve it.

Growth-Oriented Development
Since World War II, an enormous amount of financial, technical, and material assistance has been provided to developing coun-

Snowmobiles and Sami Reindeer Herding

How does adoption of a new belief or practice benefit or harm a particular culture and its various members? This question is difficult to answer, but it must always be asked. A classic study of the "snowmobile disaster" among a Sami group in Finland offers a careful response to this question in a context of rapid technological diffusion (Pelto 1973). In the 1950s, the Sami of Finland (previously referred to by outsiders as Lapps, which, in the Sami language, is a derogatory term) had an economy based on fishing and reindeer herding, which provided most of the diet. Reindeer had several other important economic and social functions. They were used as draught animals, especially for hauling wood for fuel. Their hides were made into clothing and their sinews used for sewing. Reindeer were key items of exchange, both in external trade and internal gift-giving. A child was given a reindeer to mark the appearance of its first tooth. When a couple became engaged, they exchanged a reindeer with each other to make the commitment. Reindeer were the most important wedding gift. Each summer the herds were let free and then rounded up in the fall, a time of communal festivity.

By the 1960s, all this had changed because of the introduction of the snowmobile. Previously, the men had tended the reindeer herds on skis. Introduction of snowmobiles in herd management had several results. The herds were no longer kept closely domesticated for part of the year, during which they became tame. Instead they were allowed to roam freely all year and thus became wilder. On snowmobiles, the men would cover larger amounts of territory at round-up time to bring in the animals, and sometimes several roundups occurred instead of one.

Herd size declined dramatically. Reasons for the decline included the stress caused to the reindeer by the extra distance travelled during roundups, the multiple roundups instead of a single one, and the fear aroused by the noisy snowmobiles. Roundups were now held at a time when the females were near the end of their pregnancy, another factor causing reproductive stress. As the number of snowmobiles increased, the number of reindeer decreased.

Another economic change involved dependence on outside resources through links to the cash economy. Cash was needed to purchase a snowmobile, gasoline, and to pay for parts and repairs. This delocalization of the economy led to social inequality, which had not existed previously:

- The cash cost of effective participation in herding exceeded the resources of some families, who had to drop out of serious participation in herding.
- The use of snowmobiles changed the age pattern of reindeer herding in favour of youth over age; thus, older herders were squeezed out.
- The snowmobile pushed many Sami into debt.
- The dependence on cash and indebtedness forced many Sami to migrate to cities for work.

Pertti Pelto, the anthropologist who documented this case, terms these transformations a "disaster" for Sami culture. He offers some recommendations that might be helpful for the future: The lesson of the Sami, and other groups, should be presented to other communities before they adopt new technology so they understand better the potential consequences; any group facing change should have a chance to weigh evidence on the pros and cons and make an informed judgment, something that the Sami had no chance to do. Pelto's work is thus one of the early warnings from anthropology about the need for **social impact assessments** to gauge the potential social costs and benefits of particular innovations before the change is undertaken.

FOOD FOR THOUGHT

Are their any parallels in the way snowmobiles influenced the subsistence patterns of the Inuit?

Can you suggest what technological and cultural changes might have accompanied the "Distant Early Warning" radar system in the Canadian Arctic following World War II? Or Nunavut's launch into self-government in 1999?

tries through bilateral and multilateral agencies. By the middle of the twentieth century, most countries had obtained political independence, but many were in a state of economic dependence. Most wanted to increase their economic productivity, but many lacked the institutional capacity, skills, and capital. One can think of development as the attempt, through conscious planning and intervention, to increase economic productivity in the developing world. Investments in economic growth in some sectors of the population were thought to support (through the "trickle-down" effect) wider achievement of improved human welfare, such as health and education.

Since the 1950s, many industrialized countries have emphasized economic development in their foreign aid packages, especially the transfer of Western economic expertise (in the form of advisers) and technology (such as agricultural equipment) to developing countries. Promoting growth-oriented development in poor nations, as followed by most large-scale development organizations, includes two major economic strategies:

1. Increasing economic productivity and trade through, for example, new forms of agriculture, irrigation, and markets.
2. Reducing government expenditures on public services such as schools and health in order to reduce debt and reallocate resources to uses perceived to be more directly related to increased production; this strategy, called **structural adjustment,** has been vigorously promoted by the World Bank since the 1980s.

The growth-oriented development approach is being powerfully spread throughout the world under the current intensified pattern of economic and political globalization. As noted in Chapter 1, cultural anthropologists have recently taken up the research challenge presented by intensified globalization to study its effects on local cultures.

Distributional Development In contrast to the growth-oriented development approach, the distributional development approach views poverty as the result of global economic and political factors, such as world trade imbalances between nations and unequal distribution of entitlements within nations and communities (recall the discussion of entitlements in Chapter 4). This approach rejects the claim of other approaches that poverty is caused by some inadequacy on the part of poor people or poor countries themselves (Rahnema 1992). Growth-oriented strategies without concern for distribution often result in increased social inequality with the "rich getting richer and the poor getting poorer."

The distributional approach takes a critical view of structural adjustment promoted in the growth-oriented approach because it worsens the welfare of the poor by reducing public services. Advocates of the distributional approach insist on the need to readjust access to crucial resources such as food within countries in order to allow the poor to have a greater ability to produce and provide for their own needs.

Within a particular country, the distributional approach involves the following strategies that differ markedly from the growth-oriented approach (Gardner and Lewis 1996):

• *Entitlement assessment:* This step produces an understanding of who has access to which life-supporting resources. Entitlement assessment asks how access to these resources is organized and how decision-making power is distributed in the community. Entitlement differences are often related to race, gender, class, and age. Particular groups are not always disadvantaged to the same degree in all contexts. Women-headed households, for example, are often, but not always, disadvantaged, and male-headed households are not necessarily advantaged.

• *Assessment of the cultural effects of development:* This stage is related to entitlement assessment, but it adds the dimension of determining the effects of outside intervention on basic entitlements. Assessing a resettlement project, for example, requires information about access to resources, organization of work, and household organization in the original location and the relocation site. This assessment highlights, again, the social complexity involved in development impact assessment and helps overcome the tendency of outside planners to homogenize "the poor."

• *Redistribution of crucial resources, especially land:* While generally unpopular with rich and powerful members of society, successful land reform programs have been undertaken by some nations, such as Japan and Taiwan. Such programs require substantial political will to achieve success.

• *Assistance programs:* As carried out in welfare states, such programs may serve as forms of redistribution. Health and education services, for example, seek to raise the quality of "human capital" without a radical redistribution of productive resources. Eventually, the recipients would be expected to gain independence from such assistance.

Many neoliberal economists argue on economic grounds that redistribution is not a realistic or a feasible strategy. Nevertheless, anthropologists have reported many cases in which the redistribution model has worked. One instance of successful development through redistribution comes from India's southern state of Kerala.

Anthropological research in Nadur village, Kerala, posed the question of whether redistribution was an effective and realistic development strategy (Franke 1993). The answer is *yes*. Kerala's per capita income is low in comparison to the rest of India and to the rest of the world. Yet, while income remained low and stagnant, substantial material improvements occurred in many people's lives, including some of the poorest of the poor. How did this happen? Redistribution was not the result of a socialist revolution; it took place through democratic channels—protests and pressure on the government by people's groups and labour unions. These groups forced the state to reallocate land ownership, shifting some land to the landless and thereby reducing inequality (although not eradicating it completely). In other instances, people pressured government leaders to improve village conditions by improving the schools, providing school lunches for poor children, and increasing attendance by *dalit* children. Throughout the 1960s and 1970s, Nadur village became a better place to live, for many people.

Human Development Yet another alternative to the "growth-first" strategy is called **human development,** an approach of first investing in human welfare. The United Nations coined this term in order to emphasize the need for improvements in human welfare in terms of health, education, and personal security and safety. According to this approach, improvements in human welfare will lead to overall development of the nation. We know that the reverse is not true: The level of economic growth of a country (or region within a country) is not necessarily correlated with its level of human development. Obviously, the relationship between poverty and development is more complex. Some poor countries, and areas within countries such as India's Kerala state, have achieved higher levels of human development than their GNP or GDP would predict. Thus, economic growth need not be considered an end in itself. The goal of development should be an improved level of human welfare.

Sustainable Development Sustainable development, a fourth approach, questions the pursuit of economic growth in terms of its long-term viability, both environmentally and financially. According to this approach, the economic growth achieved by the wealthy nations has occurred at great cost to the environment and cannot be sustained at its present level. Since the 1980s, **sustainable development,** or forms of development that do not destroy nonrenewable resources and are financially supportable by the host country, has gained prominence in international development. This approach emphasizes meeting the needs of the present without compromising the ability of future generations to meet their needs. The Canadian International Development Agency (CIDA) sustainable development program stresses preserving biodiversity, avoiding environmental degradation, and considering equity and social justice issues.

Institutional Approaches to Development

Cultural anthropologists have become increasingly aware of the importance of examining the institutions and organizations involved in international development. This knowledge will help cultural anthropologists have a greater impact on how development is done. They have studied the management systems of large-scale institutions such as the United Nations agencies and the World Bank as well as "local" management systems found in diverse settings; they have also examined internal hierarchies and inequalities, social interactions, symbols of power, and development discourse within the institutions themselves. This section first describes some of the major development institutions and then discusses smaller grassroots organizations.

Large-Scale Institutions Large-scale development institutions can be separated into the *multilaterals* (those that include several nations as donors) and the *bilaterals* (those that involve a relationship between only two countries, a donor and a recipient). The major multilaterals include the United Nations and the World Bank, each constituting a vast and complex social system. The United Nations, established in 1945, includes some 188 member states, each contributing an amount of money, and each given one vote in the General Assembly. The United States would have lost its voting rights in the General Assembly in January of 2000 if it had not paid a portion of its dues. According to the United Nations Secretariat, the United States owes $1.1 billion in unpaid UN dues (as of February 2002). Table 16.1 shows the major development agencies within the United Nations and their functions.

The World Bank is supported by contributions from member countries. Founded in 1944 at a conference

TABLE 16.1 Major Agencies within the United Nations Related to International Development

AGENCY	HEADQUARTERS	FUNCTION
UNDP (The United Nations Development Program)	New York City	UNDP provides many different services designed to help a country in planning and managing its own development through executing agencies: groundwater and mineral exploration, computer and satellite technology, seed production and agricultural extension, and research.
FAO (The Food and Agricultural Organization)	Rome, Italy	FAO implements agricultural field projects that receive funding from the UNDP as well as "host governments." It monitors global food stocks and factors affecting food prices to ensure food security.
WHO (The World Health Organization)	Geneva, Switzerland	WHO has four goals: developing and organizing personnel and technology for disease prevention and control; eradication of major tropical diseases; immunization of all children against major childhood diseases; and establishing primary health care services.
UNICEF (The United Nations Children's Emergency Fund)	Joint headquarters New York City and Geneva, Switzerland	UNICEF, with nearly 90 field offices in developing countries, is concerned with basic health care and social services for children. UNICEF receives about three-fourths of its funding from UN member governments and the other one-fourth from the general public.
UNESCO (The United Nations Educational, Scientific, and Cultural Organization)	Paris, France	UNESCO is dedicated to enhancing world peace and security through education, science, and culture, and to promoting respect for human rights, the rule of law, and fundamental freedoms. One of UNESCO's practical concerns is to promote literacy.
UNHCR (The United Nations High Commission for Refugees)	Geneva, Switzerland	UNHCR is dedicated to promoting the rights and safety of refugees. It coordinates international efforts to solve refugee dilemmas.
UNIFEM (The United Nations International Development Fund for Women)	New York City	UNIFEM promotes projects directed towards raising the status of women. It supports initiatives that promote the political, social, and economic empowerment of women, and gender equality, and it ensures that women's issues are coordinated within the UN development system.
UNFPA (The United Nations Fund for Population Activities)	New York City	UNFPA supports family planning projects and projects that improve reproductive health. It helps formulate policies related to global and national population issues.

Source: Hancock 1989.

called by President Roosevelt in Bretton Woods, New Hampshire, "the Bank" is dedicated to promoting the concept of economic growth and expanded purchasing power throughout the world (B. Rich 1994). The main strategy is to promote international investment through loans. The World Bank is guided by a Board of Governors made up of the finance ministers of member countries. Rather than following the United Nation's approach of one country–one vote, in the World Bank system, the number of votes is based on the size of a country's fi-

nancial commitment: "There is no pretense of equality— the economic superpowers run the show" (Hancock 1989:51).

Two major units within the World Bank are the International Bank for Reconstruction and Development (IBRD) and the International Development Association (IDA). Both are administered at the World Bank headquarters in Washington, D.C. They both lend for similar types of projects and often in the same country, but their conditions of lending differ. The IBRD provides loans to the poorest nations, which are generally regarded as "bad risks" on the world commercial market. Thus, the IBRD is a source of interest-bearing loans to countries that otherwise would not be able to borrow. The IBRD does not allow rescheduling of debt payments. It has recorded a profit every year of its existence, so it stands in an interesting position as a profit-making aid institution. Most of its loans support large infrastructure projects and, more recently, sectoral development in health and education. The IDA is the "soft-loan" side of the World Bank because it provides interest-free loans (although there is a 0.75 per cent annual "service charge") and a flexible repayment schedule averaging between 35 and 40 years (B. Rich 1994:77). These concessional loans are granted to the poorest countries for projects of high development priority. The International Monetary Fund (IMF), also created in 1944, monitors the monetary policies of member nations, and provides credit for member countries experiencing temporary balance of payments deficits.

Critics of the World Bank and the IMF have emerged from many directions, including politicians, scholars, and people whose lives have been affected negatively by their projects. Politicians in the United States who oppose foreign aid to developing countries in any form point to the overlapping and wasteful organization of some United Nations institutions and the fact that they seem to have accomplished too little in comparison to the funds required by member countries to support them. Others argue that, too often, the projects supported by these institutions have failed to help the poor, but instead provide thousands of jobs for the people in their employment and are good business investments for first-world countries. Such critics point especially to the biased lending and aid policies that are shaped more by political factors than by economic need.

Some prominent bilateral institutions include CIDA, the United States Agency for International Development (USAID), the United Kingdom's Department for International Development (DFID), the Swedish Agency for International Development (Sida), and the Danish Organization for International Development (DANIDA). These agencies vary in terms of the proportion of aid disbursed as loans that have to be repaid or as grants that do not require repayment. Another variation is whether the loans or grants are "tied" to supporting specific projects that also provide for substantial donor country involvement in providing goods, services, and expertise versus

being "untied," or allowing the recipient country the freedom to decide how to use the funds. The USAID generally offers more aid in the form of loans than grants, and more in tied than untied aid, especially in comparison to the bilateral agencies of Sweden, the Netherlands, Canada, and Norway. Another difference among the bilaterals is the proportion of their total assistance that goes to the poorest of countries. The United Kingdom's DFID sends more than 80 per cent of its aid to the poorest countries, while the largest chunk of U.S. foreign aid goes to Egypt and Israel. Canada's Official Development Assistance (ODA) used to be motivated by a moral obligation to help those who are oppressed or live in poverty. However, around 1994, priorities shifted to projects that support trade rather than targeting the poorest countries. Nevertheless, Canada seldom uses ODA to secure support for foreign policy objectives (Morrison 2000:22). Table 16.2 lists CIDA's ODA priorities.

Emphasis on certain types of aid also varies from bilateral institution to bilateral institution. Cuba has long played a unique role in bilateral aid, although this fact is scarcely known in the United States. Rather than offering assistance for a wide range of development projects, Cuba has concentrated on health-related assistance for training health care providers and promoting preventive health care (Feinsilver 1993). Most of Cuba's development assistance goes to socialist countries, including many in Africa.

Grassroots Approaches

Many countries have experimented with what are sometimes called "grassroots" approaches to development, or locally initiated "bottom-up" projects. This alternative to "top-down" development as pursued by the large-scale agencies described in the previous section is more likely to be culturally appropriate, locally supported through participation, and successful.

During the 1970s, Kenya sponsored a national program whereby the government committed itself to provide teachers to local communities that built schools (Winans and Haugerud 1977). This program was part of Kenya's promotion of *har-ambee*, or self-help, in many sectors, including health, housing, and schooling. Local people's response to the schooling program, especially, was overwhelmingly positive. They turned out in large numbers to build schools, which was their part of the bargain. Given the widespread construction of schools, the government found itself hard pressed to respond to its end

TABLE 16.2　CIDA's ODA Priorities

Canada's Official Development Assistance (ODA) program concentrates resources on the following six priorities:

- *Basic human needs:* To support efforts to provide primary health care, basic education, family planning, nutrition, water and sanitation, and shelter. Canada will continue to respond to emergencies with humanitarian assistance. Canada will commit 25 per cent of its ODA to basic human needs as a means of enhancing its focus on addressing the security of the individual.
- *Gender equity:* To support the achievement of equality between women and men to ensure sustainable development.
- *Infrastructure services:* To help developing countries to deliver environmentally sound infrastructure services, with an emphasis on poorer groups and on capacity building.
- *Human rights, democracy, good governance:* To increase respect for human rights, including children's rights; to promote democracy and better governance; and to strengthen both civil society and the security of the individual.
- *Private sector development:* To promote sustained and equitable economic growth by supporting private sector development in developing countries.
- *Environment:* To help developing countries protect their environment and contribute to addressing global and regional environmental issues.

Source: CIDA 2001.

development efforts through non-governmental organizations (NGOs) emerged. This trend prompted the formation of many NGOs in developing countries that often became partners with bilateral agencies to develop and support local projects. For example, the Canada Fund in Thailand supports Thai NGOs that give small seed grants to grassroots organizations in rural Thailand. In India, CIDA collaborated with government agencies and NGOs to support a Tree Grower's Cooperative in three states undergoing rapid deforestation.

The Development Project

Development organizations, whether they are large multilaterals or small, local NGOs, all rely on the concept of the development project as the specific set of activities that put policies into action. For example, let's say a government sets a policy of increased agricultural production by a certain percentage within a certain period. Development projects put in place to achieve the policy goal might include the construction of a specified number of irrigation canals that would supply water to a number of farmers. Development projects have a basic **project cycle**, or the full process of a project from initial planning to completion (Cernea 1985). These steps include:

- *Project identification:* Selecting a project to fit a particular purpose.

- *Project design:* Preparing the details of the project.

- *Project appraisal:* Assessing the project's budgetary aspects.

- *Project implementation:* Putting the project into place.

- *Project evaluation:* Assessing whether the project goals were fulfilled.

Since the 1970s, anthropologists have been hired to offer insights into the project cycle at different stages, and with differing impacts. In the early phase of involvement, anthropologists tended to be primarily hired to do project evaluations, the last step in the project cycle, to see whether the project had achieved its goals. Unfortunately, many evaluations reported the projects to be dismal failures. Some of the most frequent findings were: (1) The target group, such as the poor or women, had not been "reached," but instead project ben-

of the bargain: paying the teachers' salaries. This program shows that self-help movements can be highly successful in terms of mobilizing local contributions, if the target—in this case, children's education—is something that is highly valued.

Many non-governmental, grassroots organizations have existed for several decades. Prominent international examples include Oxfam, CARE, and Feed the Children. Churches also sponsor grassroots development. In Bangladesh, for example, the Lutheran Relief Agency has played an important role in helping local people provide and maintain small-scale infrastructure projects such as village roads and canals.

With the push towards privatization in the 1980s in North America and Britain, an emphasis on supporting

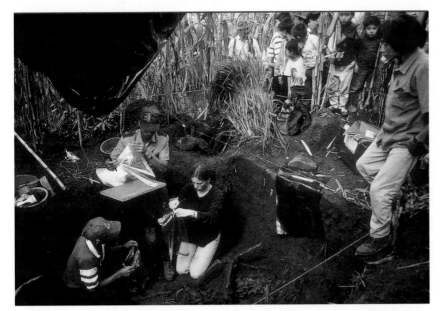

CIDA's project with a Montreal-based NGO investigates a 1982 massacre in Guatemala. This project reflects CIDA's development priorities concerning human rights, democracy, and good governance.

efits had gone to some other group; (2) the project was inappropriate for the context; and (3) the intended beneficiaries were actually worse off after the project than before (as in the case of dam construction, for example).

Jim Freedman (2000), a Canadian anthropologist who has worked as a consultant for bilateral (CIDA) and multilateral (United Nations) organizations, conducted a baseline study and an impact study of an irrigation and salinity control project in northern Pakistan. The project cycle provides part of the story about the results, but he goes beyond the project cycle to analyze the impact on the people most affected by the project—the freedom-loving Pathans, people whose ancestral roots lie in stateless, semi-nomadic life. Freedman summarizes the steps of the project cycle:

- *Project identification:* Renovate a water delivery system and reduce soil salination.

- *Project design:* An underground drainage system would be provided to control salination, which would increase food production and result in higher incomes for local farmers.

- *Project appraisal:* The budget was negotiated between CIDA, the World Bank, and the government of Pakistan.

- *Project implementation:* The drains were built, food production (wheat, sugarcane, and maize) increased modestly (around 5 per cent over 10 years), but during the process of building the system, some small farmers were displaced.

- *Project evaluation:* The project assumed that the cost to small farmers was a small price to pay for the value of the improved technology to the more productive farmers (200–208).

Freedman drew much broader conclusions about the interconnections between prosperity and democracy from the experience of working with this project. He observed that economic growth undermined social equity; and social and economic inequities undermined economic growth, a condition for democracy. What was missing from the project was a consideration of the effect of widening income disparities in the project villages and resultant shifts in power relations. The improved irrigation allowed landlords to increase their power over land and over their tenants who became even more dependent on the protection of their patrons. The resulting factions intensified the conflict between rival landlords. Although the landlords increased their personal wealth, this did not translate into increased well-being for the villages, where disparities in wealth doubled or tripled (Freedman 2000).

One reason development initiatives often failed was that projects were typically identified and designed by Western economists located in cities far from the intended project site. These experts applied a "universal" formula, with little or no attention to the local cultural context. In other words, projects were designed by "people-distant" and culturally uninformed economists and planners, but were evaluated by "people-close" and culturally informed anthropologists. By demonstrating the weaknesses in project planning that led to failed projects, and the need to take local cultural context into account in projects, cultural anthropologists gained a reputation in development circles as trouble-makers and "nay-sayers."

Cultural anthropologists worked during the 1980s and 1990s to find a greater role earlier on in the project cycle, especially at the project identification and design stages. Although still far less powerful than economists in defining development policy in the large-scale multilaterals, a few anthropologists have made notable strides in this direction, including having leadership roles in development organizations. Their role as watch-dogs and critics should not be discounted because it serves an important function in drawing attention to new and continuing problems.

We now have nearly 50 years of data on development projects that can be analyzed in order to reveal key factors contributing to project success or failure. Results of a few selected studies are reviewed here in terms of their insights on, first, project design and, then, project implementation.

A comparative study (Kottak 1985) reviewed evaluations of 68 development projects to see if the economic success of projects was related to **socio-cultural fit,** or how well a project meshes with the local culture and population. Results showed a strong correlation between the two factors. Through the years, anthropologists have provided many examples of projects that were culturally inappropriate; all were a waste of time and money. A project to improve nutrition and health in the South Pacific involved the transfer of large quantities of American powdered milk to an island community. The inhabitants, however, were lactose intolerant (unable to digest raw milk) and everyone soon had diarrhea. Realizing what caused this outbreak, the people used the powdered milk to whitewash their houses. Beyond wasting resources, inappropriately designed projects can result in the exclusion of the intended beneficiaries, such as when a person's signature is required among people who cannot write, or a photo identification card is requested from Muslim women, whose faces should not be shown in public. One role for anthropologists is to expose areas of non-fit and provide insights about how to achieve socio-cultural fit and enhance project success rates.

The Anthropological Critique of Development

The early decades of development anthropology were dominated by what can be called **traditional development anthropology (TDA).** In TDA, the anthropologist accepts the role of helping to make modernization-development work better. This can be called the "add an anthropologist and stir" approach to development. It is an option that economists and others realize can help make their plans more effective. For example, an anthropologist familiar with a local culture could provide information about what kinds of consumer goods would be desired by the people, or what might induce them to relocate with less resistance. This kind of participation by anthropologists could be either positive or negative for the local people, depending on the project being undertaken.

Anthropologists have expressed concern that helping make large-scale development projects work can be disastrous for local people and their environments (Bodley 1990; Horowitz and Salem-Murdock 1993; Taussig 1978). The awareness of the socially negative impact of many supposedly positive development projects has led to the emergence of critical development anthropology (CDA). In this approach, the anthropologist does not simply accept a supportive role, but rather takes on a critical-thinking role. The question is not: What can we do to make this project successful? Instead, the anthropologist asks: Is this a good project from the perspective of the people affected? After long and careful thinking, if the answer is *yes,* then that is a green light for a supportive role. If careful thinking reveals areas where revisions in the project would make it beneficial, then the anthropologist tries to intervene with this information. If all evidence suggests that the project will harm the target population, either in the short run or the long run, then the anthropologist should assume the role of whistle-blower and either try to stop the project completely or substantially change the design.

Methods in Development Anthropology

Many full-scale anthropological studies of cultural change and development are based on long-term fieldwork and standard research methods as described in Chapter 2. However, often a development agency needs input from an anthropologist that requires faster turnaround than what long-term fieldwork would allow. Specialized methods have emerged to respond to the short time frame and provide answers to the often specific questions at hand in a way that planners and policy-makers can use. Research in development anthropology is different from standard long-term fieldwork in three ways:

1. It has a more focused, less holistic research agenda.
2. It makes more use of multidisciplinary research teams.
3. It relies on specialized methods, such as rapid research methods and participatory research methods.

These three differences relate to the need to gather dependable data within a relatively short time period. Choosing the research focus is crucial and best achieved when the researchers already have some familiarity with the culture. The addition of multiple researchers working on different aspects of the problem from different angles at the same time can intensify the research process and help make up for the shorter duration for observation. The particular approaches that development anthropologists have found useful in responding to the need for short urnaround time in generating research results are discussed next.

Rapid Research Methods **Rapid research methods (RRMs)** are research methods designed to provide focused cultural data in a short time period (Chambers 1983). They include strategies such as going to the field with a prepared checklist of questions, conducting focus group interviews (talking to several people at the same time rather than one by one), and conducting "transect" observations (walking through a specific area with key informants and asking for explanations along the way) (Bernard 1995:139–140). When used correctly, RRMs can provide useful data for assessing the problems and opportunities related to development, particularly when several methods are used together, and when researchers work in teams.

An effective mix of RRMs was used for pre-project planning in rural Bali (Mitchell 1994). The research sought to identify environmental and social stresses that might be caused by economic development and then make recommendations to the government in preparing its next five-year development plan. A Canadian university and an Indonesian university designed an eight-village study to provide data on ecological, economic, and social features. Each village was studied by a four-member team. Teams consisted of Indonesian and Canadian researchers, both men and women. All team members could speak Bahasa Indonesian (the national language) and at least one could also speak Bahasa Bali (the local language). Researchers lived in the village for four weeks. The teams used several methods for data collection: background data from provincial documents and village records; and interviews with key informants representing the village administration, religion, women, youth, school teachers, health clinic personnel, and agricultural extension workers. Household interviews were conducted with 15 men and 15 women from different neighbourhoods in the village, and with a sample of primary school children. Other observations included general conditions of the village and villagers' daily activities. For each village, the research generated a fairly rich profile of relevant biophysical features; production and marketing; local government; health and welfare; and expressive culture. Their findings offered a range of issues for the government's consideration, including the apparent environmental and social stresses being caused by external development such as urbanization and tourism.

Participatory Research Methods Building on the RRM approach, in the late 1980s, a more recent method has emerged involving the local people, called **participatory research methods (PRMs).** PRMs respond to the growing awareness that when the population is involved in a development project, it is more likely to be successful in the short run and sustainable over the long run (Kabutha, Thomas-Slayter, and Ford 1993:76). Participatory research rests heavily on the anthropological assumption that local knowledge should not be bypassed, but instead should be the foundation of development work. Participatory research involves key community members in all stages of the research.

The best PRM work teaches local people how to collect and analyze important kinds of data themselves. For example, local people know about such things as field size and soil quality. Barely literate villagers understand seasonal changes and can therefore participate in considering alternative strategies for improving food supplies during lean times. Such people can learn how to prepare maps and charts that will be used in project identification. Besides sheer data gathering and analysis, a crucial feature of PRM is feedback from community members in project selection and project evaluation. Local people can be trained to carry on data collection and analysis after the team has left the village. Two important effects of PRM are the fostering of local autonomy in planning and a greater chance that the projects put in place will be maintained and adjusted to changing conditions.

Issues in Development

This section considers three interrelated issues in international development: women and development, indigenous peoples, and human rights. The first two issues emphasize particular categories of people who have been affected by international development in various ways. They are discussed in more detail because they illustrate key concepts used throughout this book: gender and social inequality. The issue of human rights crosses all social categories including indigenous peoples, ethnic minorities, women, men, and children.

Women and Development

Women constitute about half of every population, yet many live as "subordinates" in household configurations with more dominant group members. In the mid-1970s, gender inequity was recognized as a serious constraint to development. Emphasis on women and development—and later gender and development (Rathgeber 1990)—in multilateral and bilateral assistance programs, national governments, and NGOs encouraged policies that made gender equity a goal of development, a goal that should transform the concept of development itself. Development has also resulted in women losing power in their communities as well as former rights to property (recall the Multiple Cultural Worlds box on Malay women farmers in Chapter 3). One reason is that matrilineal kinship, a system that keeps property in the female line, is in decline throughout the world, often as a result of Westernization and modernization. Another is that Western experts have chosen to deal with men in the context of development projects.

In this section, we consider evidence that much activity in international development has been biased in favour of men to the detriment of women. We then turn to examples in which some women's groups are taking de-velopment into their own hands and making it work for their welfare.

The Male Bias in Development Women have been affected by development differently than men, within the same community and even household, because development has been pursued in an androcentric (male-centred) way. In the 1970s, researchers began to write about the male bias of projects that completely bypassed women as beneficiaries or targeted men for such new initiatives as growing cash crops or learning about new technologies (Boserup 1970; Tinker 1976). This male bias in development contributed to increased gender inequality and hierarchy by giving men greater access to new sources of income and depriving women of their traditional economic roles. The development experts' image of a farmer, for example, was male, not female. Women's projects focused on the domestic, ignoring their often important economic roles. Thus, women's projects were typically concerned with infant feeding patterns, child care, and family planning, and, over time, this has led to the increased "domestication" of women worldwide (Rogers 1979). For example, University of Windsor anthropologist Lynne Phillips found in her research on rural Ecuadorian women (1998) that development discourses may inadvertently homogenize women's own interpretations of their situations. Terms such as the "feminization of agriculture" may flatten the complexity of women's lives. Her research is a reminder that women in societies exposed to development programs may not necessarily experience development in ways envisioned by policy-makers or by development critics.

The male bias in development also created an increased rate of project failure. In the West African nation of Burkina Faso, for example, a reforestation project targeted men as the sole participants, whose tasks would include planting and caring for the trees. Unfortunately, cultural patterns there dictate that men do not water plants; women do. So the men planted the seedlings and left them. Since the women were not included as project participants, the new young trees that were planted simply died.

Exclusion of women from positive forms of development continues to be a problem, in spite of over 20 years of work attempting to place and keep women on the development agenda. An example of a new development issue is gender-based violence. The problem is gaining attention even among the large multilaterals, where experts now realize that women cannot participate in a development program if they fear their husbands will beat them for leaving the house. In September 1992, the United Nations Commission on the Status of Women formed a working group that drafted a declaration against violence against women (Heise, Pitanguy, and Germain 1994). The declaration was adopted by the General Assembly in 1993. Article 1 of the declaration states that violence against women includes "any act of gender-based violence that results in, or is likely to result in, physical, sexual or psychological harm or suffering to women, including threats of such acts, coercion or arbitrary deprivations of liberty, whether occurring in public or private life" (Economic and Social Council 1992). This definition cites "women" as the focus of concern, but it includes girls as well (see Table 16.3). A weakness of programs that address issues of violence against girls and women is that they tend to deal with their effects, not the causes, often with disastrous results. For example, they may seek to increase personal security of women and girls in refugee camps by augmenting the number of guards at the camp when, in fact, it is often the guards who abuse refugee females.

Women Organizing for Change There is a growing global consensus on gender issues, partly based on the use of "international instruments" to push the agenda for gender equity at the national level. Both multilaterals and bilaterals have cooperated in projects such as the Decade for Women (1975–1985) with the United Nations Commission on the Status of Women. International meetings on women's issues, particularly the Platform for Action from Nairobi (1985) and Beijing (1995) helped national groups and NGOs to use international instruments for women's advancement, such as the Convention on the Elimination of all Forms of Discrimination against Women (CEDAW). These meetings and conventions provided opportunities to raise the profile of gender equity issues.

In many countries, women have made substantial gains in improving their status and welfare through forming organizations. These organizations range from "mothers' clubs" that provide communal child care to lending and credit organizations that provide women with the opportunity to start their own businesses. Some are local and small-scale, others are global in reach, such as Women's World Banking, an international organization that grew out of credit programs for poor working women in India.

In the 1990s, micro-finance became the leading development strategy adopted by governments and NGOs for alleviating poverty and empowering the poor, especially women. As the limits of a welfare-oriented approach to development are now well recognized by large institutions, micro-finance initiatives similar to South Asia's Grameen Bank model promote income-generating projects for the poor by providing access to low-interest credit or loans, and organizing savings activities. Because of women's higher repayment rates and preference for spending on family welfare, many of these programs target women specifically to increase program cost efficiency and to achieve more effective poverty alleviation.

How does micro-finance work? Groups of individuals organize themselves into groups of five to fifteen trusted friends and neighbours. Each village may support five to ten groups. For a four- to six-month trial period, groups meet weekly to contribute an agreed-upon amount of savings to their group fund. In this initial stage

TABLE 16.3 Gender-Based Violence against Girls and Women throughout the Life Cycle	
Prebirth	Sex-selective abortion, battering during pregnancy, coerced pregnancy
Infancy	Infanticide, emotional and physical abuse, deprivation of food and medical care
Girlhood	Child marriage, genital mutilation, sexual abuse by family members and strangers, deprivation of food and medical care, child prostitution
Adolescence	Dating and courtship violence, forced prostitution, rape, sexual abuse in the workplace, sexual harassment
Adulthood	Partner abuse and rape, partner homicide, sexual abuse in the workplace, sexual harassment, rape
Old Age	Abuse and neglect of widows, elder abuse

Source: Adapted from Heise, Pitanguy, and Germain 1994:5.

Grameen Bank, a development project that began in Bangladesh to provide small loans to poor people, is one of the most successful examples of improving human welfare through "micro-credit." Professor Muhammad Yunnus (centre) founded Grameen Bank and continues to be a source of charismatic leadership for it.

opportunities and constraints offered by this new project. In the first year of operation, the micro-finance program was very popular, particularly among farmers and craftspeople who do not have access to the formal banking sector because of their lack of collateral. They welcome the opportunity to obtain loans at interest rates of 15 per cent per year—well below rates offered by local money-lenders (120 per cent per year) and those available through the formal banking sector (21 to 26 per cent per year). Realizing the limitations of a credit-only approach that simply gives loans to raise household income, this program also encourages members to contribute to pooled group savings from which they can make small personal loans. Milgram cautions, however, that many women still hesitate to take loans from the banking cooperative, fearing they might fall behind in their repayments.

of operation, they can borrow small amounts from their pooled group savings for household consumption purposes, such as medical and education costs. After successfully operating for this time period, and passing a test on the principles of the program, members complete simplified application forms to obtain larger loans from the banking cooperative supported and subsidized by a development agency. Loans are allocated in predetermined amounts repayable within the year in 50 weekly installments, and they increase when previous loans are repaid in full. Material collateral is replaced by social collateral in the form of organized peer pressure by group members and by bank workers.

Lynne Milgram's ethnographic research in the upland provinces of northern Luzon, Philippines (1999), documents how Ifugao women meet their households' needs by combining different forms of wage work, such as agriculture, crafts, and trading. In 1997, a new micro-finance initiative developed a local system of village savings-and-loan groups and connected them to local banking cooperatives. Milgram's work analyzes how women use the

Another community-based credit system in Mozambique, southern Africa helps farm women buy seeds, fertilizers, and supplies on loan (Clark 1992:24). When the loan program was first started, 32 farm families in the village of Machel formed themselves into seven solidarity groups, each with an elected leader. The woman-headed farmer groups managed irrigation more efficiently and conferred on how to minimize use of pesticides and chemical fertilizers. Through their efforts, the women quadrupled their harvests and were able to pay off their loans. Machel women then turned their attention to getting additional loans to improve their herds and to buy a maize mill. Overall, in the midst of poverty, military conflict, the lack of government resources, and a drought, the project and the organization it fostered allowed many women farmers to increase their economic and household security.

A more informal system of social networks has emerged to help support poor women vendors in San Cristobal, Mexico (Sullivan 1992). Many of the vendors around the city square are women, and most of them have been expelled from highland Chiapas because of political conflicts there. The women vendors manufacture and sell goods to tourists and thereby provide an important portion of household income. In the city, they find support in an expanded social network that compensates for the loss of support from the extensive *compradrazgo* (god-parenthood system) of the highlands, which has broken down because of out-migration. Instead, the vendors have established networks encompassing relatives, neighbours, and church members, as well as other vendors, regardless of religious, political, economic, or social background.

These networks first developed in response to a series of rapes and robberies that began in 1987. The perpetrators were persons of power and influence, and so the women never pressed charges. Mostly single mothers and widows, they adopted a defensive strategy of self-protection: They began to group together during the slow period each afternoon. They travel in groups and carry sharpened corset bones and prongs: "If a man insults one of them, the group surrounds him and jabs him in the groin" (39–40). If a woman is robbed, the other women surround her, comfort her, and help contribute something towards her loss. The mid-afternoon gatherings have developed into support groups that provide financial assistance, child care, medical advice, and job skills. They have also publicly, and successfully, demonstrated against city officials' attempts to prevent them from continuing their vending. Through their organizational efforts, these women refugees from highland Chiapas have brought about important improvements in their lives.

Indigenous Peoples and Development

This section first raises the question of who indigenous peoples are. We next consider findings about how indigenous peoples have been victimized by many aspects of growth-oriented development (as they were with colonialism before it) and then look at examples of how many indigenous groups are taking development into their own hands.

Who Are Indigenous Peoples? The term **indigenous peoples** refers to groups of people who are the original inhabitants of a particular territory (Bodley 1990). Often, indigenous peoples now take the name of "First Peoples," or in Canada "First Nations peoples," as a way of self-definition as original claimants to a place. This naming practice highlights one of the major problems facing most indigenous peoples today: the fact that they have lost, and are losing, claim to their ancestral lands in the face of encroachment from outsiders.

The United Nations distinguishes between indigenous peoples and minority groups such as the Rom, the Tamils of Sri Lanka, or Sikhs in Canada, for example. While this distinction is useful in some ways, it should not be taken as a hard-and-fast difference since some groups cannot be defined as either and some groups seem to fit in both categories (Maybury-Lewis 1997; Plant 1994). It is most useful to think of all these groups as forming a continuum from more clearly indigenous groups, such as the Inuit, to minority/ethnic groups that may not be geographically "original" to a place but that share many problems with indigenous peoples as a result of being encapsulated and marginalized within a majority culture.

Indigenous peoples differ from most national minorities by the fact that they often occupy (or occupied) remote areas and were, until the era of colonial expansion, less affected by outside interests. Now governments and international businesses have recognized that their lands often contain valuable natural resources such as natural gas and timber in Canada and gold in Papua New Guinea and the Amazon. Different governments have paid varying degrees of attention to "integrating" indigenous peoples into "mainstream" culture in the interests of fostering nationalism at the expense of pluralism.

Accurate demographic statistics on indigenous peoples are difficult to obtain (Kennedy and Perz 2000). There are often questions about who should be counted as indigenous and in some cases, there are political implications to the collecting of statistics. Governments may not bother to conduct a census of indigenous peoples, or if they do, they may report undercounts of indigenous peoples in order to downplay recognition of their very existence as a group (Baer 1982:12). A few island populations in India's Andaman Islands in the Bay of Bengal remain uncounted because Indian officials cannot gain access to them (Singh 1994). Given the difficulties involved in defining and counting indigenous peoples, therefore, it is possible only to provide very rough information on their number. It is estimated that, globally, indigenous peoples make up about 5 per cent of

TABLE 16.4   Population Estimates of Indigenous Peoples

Western Hemisphere
  less than 1 million in Canada
  1.75 million in the United States
  less than 13 million in Mexico and Central America
  16 million in South America

Europe
  60 000 in Greenland
  60 000 in Norway, Sweden, Finland, and Russia
  28 million within the former Soviet Union

Middle East
  5 million

Africa
  14 million

Asia
  52 million in India
  31 million in China (the government terms them
    national minorities)
  26.5 million in Southeast Asia
  50 000 in Japan and the Pacific combined
  550 000 in Australia and New Zealand combined

Total: About 5 per cent of the world's total population.

Source: Maybury-Lewis 1997:10–11.

the total world population. (Bodley 1990:365; Lee and Daly 1999). (See Table 16.4.)

Marginalization of Indigenous Peoples

Many indigenous peoples and their cultures have been exterminated completely as a result of contact with outsiders (recall the discussion of diseases of colonial contact in Chapter 7). Besides death and decline through contagious disease, political conflicts within indigenous peoples' territory often threaten their survival. In the Peruvian Andes, armed conflict between the Peruvian guerrillas called the Shining Path, drug traffickers, and U.S.-backed police and army units has taken a heavy toll on indigenous groups.

First Peoples have also suffered from intentional efforts to take over their land by force, to prevent them from practising their traditional lifestyle (including using their own languages, see the Voices box), and to integrate them into the state. John Bodley (1988) has examined the effects of loss of autonomy for indigenous peoples that results from the unwillingness of the state to tolerate the presence of politically sovereign tribes within its boundaries. States intervene to prevent and quell armed resistance by indigenous peoples, even though such resistance may be critical to the maintenance of indigenous culture and the people's welfare. Indicators that an indigenous group has lost its autonomy are: inability to expel outside intruders or use force to regulate its internal affairs; introduction of formal schooling and national court systems; appointment of state-sanctioned political leaders; the institution of compulsory military service; and enforcement of payment of taxes. These changes undermine the previous quality of life and set in motion changes that indirectly lead to the people's further impoverishment.

An anthropological analysis of government policies in Thailand for development of the highlands reveals the complex interplay between outside interests and the welfare of the *chao khao,* or "hill people" (Kesmanee 1994). The hill people include the Karen, Hmong, Mien, Lahu, Lisu, Akha, and others, totalling about half a million people or 1 per cent of the total Thai population. There's international pressure for the hill people to replace opium cultivation with other cash crops. The Thai government's main concerns are with political stability and national security in this area, which borders on Myanmar (Burma) and Laos. It therefore has promoted development projects to establish more connections between the highlands and the lowlands through transportation and marketing. Thus far, efforts to find viable substitute crops especially among the Hmong, who have traditionally been most dependent on opium as a cash crop, have been unsuccessful. Crops that have been introduced have required extensive use of fertilizers and pesticides, which have greatly increased environmental pollution. Efforts have been made to relocate hill horticulturalists to the plains, but there they have been provided plots with poor soil and the economic status of the people has declined. In the meantime, commercial loggers have gained access to the hills and done more damage to the forests than the traditional patterns of shifting horticulture. Increased penetration of the hill areas by lowlanders, international tourism, and communications have also promoted the increase of HIV/AIDS rates, prostitution, and opium addiction throughout the area. As a result, hill people are threatened both with the

Deborah Decontie, "My Algonquin Vocabulary"

The following essay was written by 14-year-old Deborah Decontie, an Algonquin, in an English class at the Kitigan Zibi School in Maniwaki, Quebec. It was first published in *Turtle Quarterly* magazine, in Spring/Summer 1993.

> *Kitigewinini obimiwidon toshanabo-atagan was the first sentence I learned to speak in Algonquin, my Native language. I remember learning it in Grade one and being very happy about my little accomplishment. I was taught Algonquin since I was in Nursery. I was just learning the basics such as my numbers and colors and then words I could use everyday, like* "please" *and* "thank you." *Progressively, I began to learn more.*
>
> *In spite of my Algonquin lessons, my vocabulary is very limited. Allow me to explain "limited." "Limited" in the sense that if someone would come up to me and start talking to me in Algonquin I would not understand a word he or she said. "Limited" in the sense that I had to ask someone how to spell the sentence mentioned at the onset. "Limited" in the sense that I cannot tell someone something in Algonquin that he or she would understand or that would be understood clearly. So, my Algonquin vocabulary is very "limited" and perhaps it's my fault or perhaps it's not. The purpose of this essay is not to point the finger at anyone. However, I do realize that I do not know my language and I can honestly say that I regret not having put more of an effort to learn it. So I'm writing this essay from my viewpoint, my perspective, as a fourteen-year-old Algonquin girl who lives on an Algonquin reserve, and goes to an Algonquin school, and does not know her language.... Maybe someday I can rewrite this essay in my Native language.*

Source: Hirschfelder 1995:80–81.

loss of their land and with the loss of their cultural identity. Solving this problem requires a major change in how development is being approached by international agencies and the Thai government.

The situation in Thailand is not unique. In case after case, indigenous peoples have been subjected to loss of the rights they once had, increased impoverishment, and widespread despair. While active resistance to their disenfranchisement has taken place throughout history, it appears that more effective and highly organized forms of protest and reclamation of rights have become prominent since the 1980s. Many indigenous groups have acquired legal advice and expertise and have confronted power-holders in world capitals, insisting on changes. One of the most basic claims of all groups is recognition of their land rights.

Indigenous Peoples' Advocacy Much evidence attests to the value of "development from within," or advocacy efforts to increase peoples' welfare and livelihood promoted by indigenous organizations rather than exogenous organizations. Basic components of indigenous peoples' development include rights to resources, local initiatives in planning through local organizations, and local leadership. The following sections consider resource issues (especially land) and indigenous organizations for change.

The many land and resource claims being made by indigenous peoples are a direct response to their earlier losses and a major challenge to many states. Depending on how these disputes are resolved, they can be a basis for conflicts, ranging from fairly benign litigation to attempts at secession (Plant 1994).

The majority of Latin America's indigenous peoples are small peasant farmers or landless labourers working on commercial farms. Yet, no Latin American country government provides protection against encroachment on the land of farm families. Throughout Latin America, increasing numbers of indigenous peoples have been forced off the land and have had to seek wage labour. Those who remain live in extreme poverty. In response, a strong resurgence of activity by indigenous peoples and groups that support them has occurred in the 1990s (Plant 1994). Some of this activity has taken the form of physical resistance. Violence continues to erupt between indigenous peoples and state-supported power structures, especially in the southern Mexican state of Chiapas, with recurrent massacres of indigenous peoples occurring since the 1990s.

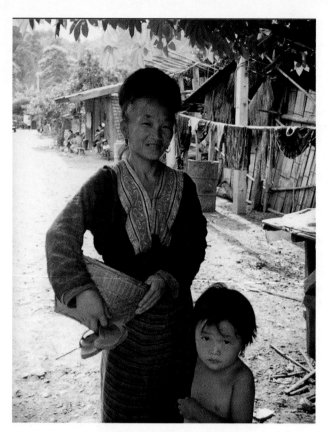

A Hmong woman and child. The Hmong people of highland Southeast Asia have suffered decades of war in their homeland. Many Hmong from Laos have entered the United States and Canada as refugees.

Indigenous claims and pressures have had some positive effects, with Bolivia, Brazil, Colombia, and Paraguay adopting new legislation about indigenous lands. In these countries, however, more achievements have been made in demarcating lands of the forest-dwelling people of the Amazon compared to the highland, horticultural groups. Brazil's early policies provided for reservations, granting indigenous peoples' use of the land. Unfortunately, this did not include ownership because they were considered to be "minors" and thus not entitled to own property. Recently, even these meagre advances in Brazil have been rolled back by new government policies unfavourable to the indigenous peoples. Peru, in contrast to Brazil, titled large areas of forest lands to communal ownership by indigenous groups. However, free access to these areas is allowed for oil and mineral exploration, so the meaning of holding a "title" is no protection against encroachment and environmental destruction.

In Canada, the law distinguishes between two different types of Aboriginal land claims—specific and comprehensive (Plant 1994). The "specific claims" concern problems arising from previous agreements or treaties, and are moving through the courts. In "comprehensive claims," no treaties or agreements have been made. Many of the former claims have led to monetary compensation. In the latter category, government interests in oil and mineral exploration have led to negotiations with indigenous peoples seeking to have their native claims either relinquished or redefined. So far, of the 46 comprehensive claims filed, only four have been settled. In some provinces, especially British Columbia, current claims affect most of the province. One recent land claim case has been settled after 112 years of bargaining. A historic land-claim treaty gives the Nisga'a of British Columbia $235 million in cash, 2000 square kilometres of land, and self-government powers.

Anthropologists played a role in the 1975 James Bay and Northern Quebec Agreement. The James Bay Cree Project provided the Cree and the Quebec government with information that helped settle the land claim (Salisbury 1986). Traditional hunting and fishing lands of several thousand Cree and Inuit were to be affected by a large hydroelectric project. It was agreed that the indigenous peoples would receive $225 million in partial compensation for their original title. A reserve was set aside for hunting, fishing, and trapping, but the agreement said that the government of Quebec and several corporations had the right to develop resources on those lands. In 1989, the Quebec government renewed its interest in hydroelectric development. The Great Whale River project would have threatened the livelihood and environment of the Cree in the area, and they successfully opposed the project on the grounds of global concerns about pollution and the protection of natural environments (Adelson 1998).

Most Asian countries have been reluctant even to recognize the concept of special land rights of indigenous peoples (Plant 1994). In Bangladesh, for example, settlers from the crowded plains have encroached on the formerly protected area of the Chittagong Hill Tracts. Non-indigenous settlers now occupy the most fertile land. A large hydroelectric dam built in 1963 displaced

Matthew Coon Come, Grand Chief of the Assembly of First Nations, and former chief of the Cree Council of Quebec, was a key figure in the successful fight against the James Bay II hydroelectric development project. The Great Whale River project would have flooded large areas, including traditional Cree hunting grounds.

Mauritania, and their prospects are grim. As elsewhere, resistance movements spring up, but states and local power interests move quickly to quell them. The death of Ogoni leader Ken Saro-Wiwa in 1995 is a stunning example of the personal price of resistance (Sachs 1996). Saro-Wiwa, a Nigerian writer, Nobel Peace Prize nominee, and supporter of minority people's rights, was executed by Nigerian military rulers. He had vigorously spoken out against the Nigerian regime and the oil development being pursued in Ogoniland by Royal/Dutch Shell. As president and spokesperson for the Movement for the Survival of the Ogoni People (MOSOP), he had asked the government to respect the Ogoni people's right to self-determination. He also had asked Shell to clean up oil spills and toxic waste pits that had ruined Ogoni farming and fishing communities along the Niger River delta. His message is one that applies worldwide: States tend to impose the costs of their economic growth on the people least able to cope with it—impoverished minorities—and then apply violent means of repression if such people raise serious objections to their treatment.

100 000 hill dwellers because they could no longer practise horticulture in the flooded areas. A minority received financial aid, but most did not. Tribal opposition groups began emerging, and conflict, although suppressed in the news, has been ongoing for decades. Other Asian sites of contestation with the state over land and resources in Asia include the Moros of the southern Philippines, and the people of Irian Jaya in western Papua New Guinea.

In Africa, political interests of state governments in establishing and enforcing territorial boundaries have created difficulties for indigenous peoples, especially pastoralists who are, for example, accustomed to moving their herds freely. Pastoralists in the Sahel region of Africa have been particularly affected by this process. Many formerly autonomous pastoralists have been transformed into refugees living in terrible conditions. The Tuareg people, for example, have traditionally lived and herded in a territory crossing what are now five different nations: Mali, Niger, Algeria, Burkina Faso, and Libya (Childs and Chelala 1994). Given political conflict in the region, thousands of Tuareg people live in exile in

Many indigenous peoples have formed their own organizations for change in order to promote "development from within." In Mali, West Africa, a group named Tassaght ("The Link") is an example of an NGO established by indigenous peoples in response to a crisis. It began in 1985 when its founders, the Tamacheq people, obtained a grant to provide assistance to Tamacheq refugees stricken with drought. Tassaght was a facilitating organization:

Translating, coordinating logistics and conducting research, the staff gained credibility within the NGO community and eventually obtained funding from several international partners. Tassaght developed a reputation for the use of action research methods. The staff would first speak with settlement residents and the displaced popu-

lations around the city of Gao to better understand the dilemmas and possible solutions. Information from these meetings determined the direction of development projects to improve literacy, agriculture, cereal storage, and herd management. (Childs and Chelala 1994:20)

The Assembly of First Nations, formed in Canada in 1982, has become the unofficial spokesperson for many First Nations groups, presenting a united front on constitutional issues and self-government (Frideres 1998). Skilled in lobbying and the law, this group fights for Aboriginal rights guaranteed under the Canadian constitution. These groups are taken more seriously today because Aboriginal issues are viewed as a threat to national security (Tanner 1983). In this era of rapid Internet access, many indigenous groups are taking advantage of new forms of communication in order to maintain links with each other over large areas. For example, the Inuit Tapiriit Kanatami of Canada, founded in 1971, is a national organization representing 41 100 Inuit. The federal government provided them with funding to create a Web site designed to allow the "national voice" of the Inuit to reach an international audience, encourage understanding and learning about the Inuit, and provide a virtual community linking Inuit groups and organizations across the Arctic such as the Labrador Inuit Association (LIA), representing 5000 Inuit of Labrador; Makivik Corporation, representing 9000 Inuit of Nunavik; Inuvialuit Regional Corporation, representing 5000 Inuit of the western Arctic; and the Nunavut Tunngavik Incorporated, representing 21 500 Inuit of Nunavut. The Grand Council of the Cree has collaborated with the Inuit Tapiriit Kanatami and other organizations over land issues.

Although it is tempting to see hope in the newly emerging forms of resistance, self-determination, and organizing among indigenous peoples, such hope cannot be generalized to all indigenous peoples. Many are making progress and their economic status is improving; others are suffering extreme political and economic repression, with little attention from the rest of the world.

Human Rights and Development

Much of the preceding discussion of women and indigenous peoples links with the question of human rights and development. Anthropologists' cross-cultural research and growing sense of the importance of advocacy as part of their role place them in a key position to speak to issues of global human rights. In considering what cultural anthropologists have to contribute to the issue of human rights, we must first ask some basic and difficult questions:

- What are human rights?
- Is there a universal set of human rights?
- Are local cultural definitions of human rights that clash with those of other groups defensible?

For over 50 years, the United Nations has been promoting human rights through its Universal Declaration of Human Rights and other resolutions. Difficulty in coming to a consensus on defining these rights is based in one sense on a split between capitalist and socialist states. The former emphasize political and civil rights such as freedom of speech as universally important. The latter emphasize socio-economic rights such as employment and fair working conditions. Capitalist states do not always acknowledge such socio-economic rights as universal human rights and socialist states do not always recognize the same political rights. Developing states and indigenous peoples have added their voices, insisting on group rights to self-determination, locally defined paths of social change, and in some African states freedom from hunger. As Ellen Messer (1993) says, "[N]o state would go on record as being opposed to human rights.... Yet those from different states, and from different political, cultural, and religious traditions, continue to disagree on which rights have universal force and who is protected under them" (223).

As culturally diverse groups seek to define and claim their rights around the increasingly globalized world, we are all faced with the challenge of considering contending positions. (See the Multiple Cultural Worlds box.)

Human Rights: A Cross-Cultural Perspective This section looks at two cases where international development and human rights are linked. In the first case, we find ties between large-scale development institutions and military control in the Philippines, through which violations of local people's human rights have occurred. In the second case, we address the question of environmental destruction as a human and cultural rights violation.

An in-depth study of social conditions among the Ifugao, indigenous peoples of the highland region of northern Luzon, the Philippines, reveals the important,

Human Rights versus Animal Rights: The Case of the Grey Whale

Human rights have recently been interpreted to mean that cultural groups have the right to practice their cultural traditions. However, debates about cultural rights and human rights are complex, and may be further complicated by consideration of animal rights.

In the spring of 1999, members of the Makah Tribe, a Native American group living in Washington state, undertook a revival of their traditional practice of hunting grey whales (Winthrop 2000). Like many other native people of the Pacific Northwest, the Makah's traditional economy depended on fish, shellfish, and marine mammals. A treaty of 1855 provides the Makah with the right to hunt whales and seals. The practice died out, however, in the twentieth century due to dwindling supplies as a result of commercial overhunting. In 1982, the International Whaling Commission (IWC) imposed a ban on all commercial whaling, but allowed continued whale hunting for subsistence purposes. In 1994,

the grey whale population had recovered and it was taken off the endangered list. The IWC allocated the Makah the right to harvest 20 whales during the period from 1998 to 2002.

When, under this new plan, the Makah killed a 30 tonne, 10 metre whale in May 1999, the Makah watching the event cheered. The animal rights activists at the scene, in contrast, protested and said this occasion should have been one of mourning and not celebration.

The Nuu-Chah-Nulth of Vancouver Island saw the whaling as a potential treaty issue, but voiced concern that it would pit Aboriginal rights against environmental rights. While the Makah see the revival of whale hunting as a sign of cultural revival, some animal rights activists say that the way the hunt is being carried out is not culturally authentic (the Makah first harpoon the whale and then use a rifle to kill it, for example) and thus the claim of whale hunting as a traditional cultural right is not legitimate.

Environmental groups argued that cultural rights to whaling could be the "thin wedge" that opens up commercial whaling in countries such as Japan and Norway that also claim cultural rights to whaling. Other protests are motivated by ecological concerns for preservation of the species against extinction, supporting a concept of animal, especially mammalian, rights to life. The First Nations Environmental Network based in Tofino, Vancouver Island, is opposed to whale hunting, arguing that the act of killing whales cannot be justified spiritually or morally (Lamirande 1999).

FOOD FOR THOUGHT

What other practices described in this book could illustrate the tension between human rights and cultural rights? Compare this case with other examples of human versus animal rights. Where do you stand in these debates and what is the basis for your position?

---

negative role of the militarization of everyday life for the Ifugao (Kwiatkowski 1998). The military presence is felt everywhere—in schools, clinics, and, especially, at sites of large development projects such as dams. The military presence is there to ensure that people adhere to its principles and do not participate in what would be considered by the military to be subversive activities. Military force has been used to suppress local resistance to dams funded by the World Bank, resulting in numerous human rights violations, including torture, killings, imprisonment, and harassment of Cordillera people for suspected subversive activities (Drucker 1987). Members of a local NGO that support more appropriate, small-scale forms of development that would benefit more people in the area have been harassed by the military. The case of the Ifugao in northern Luzon illustrates how the powerful interests of state governments and international development in-

stitutions join together to promote their plans and projects and violate human rights along the way.

Development that leads to environmental degradation, such as pollution, deforestation, and erosion, can also be considered a form of human rights violation. Slain Ogoni leader Ken Saro-Wiwa made this point eloquently in a 1992 speech to the United Nations Working Group on Indigenous Populations:

Environmental degradation has been a lethal weapon in the war against the indigenous Ogoni people...Oil exploration has turned Ogoni into a wasteland: lands, streams, and creeks are totally and continually polluted; the atmosphere has been poisoned, charged as it is with hydrocarbon vapors, methane, carbon monoxide, carbon dioxide, and soot emitted by gas which has been flared 24 hours a day for 33 years in close proximity to human habitation...The rainforest has fallen to the axe of the multinational companies...the Ogoni countryside is no longer a source of fresh air and green vegetation. All one sees and feels around is death. (quoted in Sachs 1996:13–16)

Many social scientists now argue, along with Saro-Wiwa, that such forms of development violate human rights since they undermine a people's way of life and threaten their continued existence (Johnston 1994).

Cultural Anthropology and Human Rights: A Role for the Future During the past few decades, cultural anthropologists have played an important role in defining and exposing a wide range of human rights abuses around the world. While this role as "whistle-blower" can promote positive change, it is also important that cultural anthropologists participate more actively in advocacy work directed towards the prevention of human rights abuses. Exactly how cultural anthropologists can contribute to prevention is a challenge that still faces the discipline since the traditional roots of cultural anthropology in studying what is—rather than what might be, or, in this case, what should not be—remain strong. Anthropology's continuing dialogue on human rights and cultural diversity should help promote greater understanding and tolerance (Shweder, Minow, and Markus 2000).

As the only discipline concerned with both individual and collective rights and responsibilities, human interaction with the natural environment, people's patterns of production and consumption, family structures and political organizations, language, expressive culture, and religious beliefs, anthropology is a field of study that can speak and act to advocate for increased respect for local knowledge and cultural diversity.

How does anthropology study change?

Cultural anthropologists have become seriously involved in the study of change mainly since the mid-twentieth century. Since that time, many cultural anthropologists have contributed to theoretical debates about how change occurs and what the role of anthropological knowledge should be in contributing to culturally appropriate forms of change. Major processes of change are invention and diffusion. In contemporary times, modernization has been a powerful model of change which involves diffusion of Western technologies and values to non-Western contexts. After World War II, the term *development* became increasingly important as a form of modernization that emphasizes improved living standards.

What are the most common approaches to development?

Several theories, or approaches, of development exist, including growth-oriented development, distributional development, human development, and sustainable development. Institutional approaches to development, whether pursued by large-scale or grassroots organizations, tend to rely on the development project as a vehicle of local change. Cultural anthropologists have been hired as consultants on development projects, typically at the end of the project cycle to provide evaluations. More recently, some anthropologists have pushed for their involvement earlier in the project cycle so that cultural knowledge can be used in project planning to avoid many of the common errors. In order to provide relevant information often in a short time frame, cultural anthropology has adapted its traditional methods of long-term participant observation. Rapid and participatory research methods are intended to maximize data gathering during a short period with awareness of the limitations involved.

What does anthropology contribute to understanding some major issues in development?

The status of indigenous peoples, the role of women in development, and the complex issue of defining and protecting human rights are three urgent and interrelated areas in international development that have attracted anthropological research and thinking. Research on the impact of growth-oriented, large-scale development shows that many indigenous peoples and women have suffered decline in their entitlements and level of living. Often, such losses are tied to violence and environmental degradation in their homelands. Such tragic occurrences lead directly to the question of what human rights are and how development affects them. Cultural anthropologists contribute insights from different cultures about perceptions of basic human and cultural rights and may be able to help prevent human rights abuses in the future.

Core Concepts

acculturation, p. 381
assimilated, p. 381
critical development
    anthropology (CDA),
    p. 390
deculturated, p. 381
diachronic analysis,
    p. 380

diffusion, p. 380
human development,
    p. 385
indigenous peoples, p.
    395
international
    development, p. 380

modernization theory,
    p. 382
participatory research
    methods (PRMs),
    p. 391
project cycle, p. 388
rapid research methods
    (RRMs), p. 391
social impact assessment,
    p. 383

socio-cultural fit, p. 390
structural adjustment,
    p. 384
sustainable development,
    p. 385
synchronic, p.380
traditional development
    anthropology (TDA),
    p. 390

Suggested Readings

Thomas W. Collins and John D. Wingard, eds., *Communities and Capital: Local Struggles against Corporate Power and Privatization*. Athens, Georgia: The University of Georgia Press, 2000. Nine case studies of local resistance against large capitalist forces follow an introductory chapter that sets the stage. Cases include clam farmers of North Carolina, a fishing community in Malaysia, and banana growers in Belize.

H. Dagenais and D. Piché eds., *Women, Feminism and Development/Femmes, Féminisme et Développement*. Montreal and Kingston: McGill-Queen's University Press, 1994. This book contains French and English language chapters on development issues in Canada and internationally. The papers were first presented at a conference for the Canadian Research Institute for the Advancement of Women (CRIAW), and highlight feminist contributions to the theory and practice of development.

Jim Freedman, ed., *Transforming Development: Foreign Aid for a Changing World*. Toronto: University of Toronto Press, 2000. Fourteen essays on the changing context of Canadian aid arranged around seven themes. Most authors favour the redefinition of development assistance and criticize Canada's reduction in humanitarian-motivated aid to the poorest countries.

Dolores Koenig, Tieman Diarra, Moussa Sow, and Ousmane Diarra, *Innovation and Individuality in African Development: Changing Production Strategies in Rural Mali*. Ann Arbor: University of Michigan Press, 1998. This ethnography of change looks at the history of Malian rural production, agricultural resources, and crop production, and how lessons learned contribute to an improved anthropology of development.

David H. Lempert, Kim McCarthy, and Craig Mitchell, *A Model Development Plan: New Strategies and Perspectives*. Westport, CT: Praeger, 1995. A group of university students from different disciplines (including one anthropologist, Lempert) spent six weeks in Ecuador, visiting nearly every province and studying development issues there as the basis for their development plan for Ecuador. A preface explains the background of the project. The rest of the volume consists of a detailed presentation of the plan.

Richard J. Perry, *From Time Immemorial: Indigenous Peoples and State Systems*. Austin: University of Texas Press, 1996. This book provides a comparative examination of the history and status of indigenous peoples of Mexico, the United States, Canada, and Australia. The conclusion offers findings about state policies, state violence, resistance of the indigenous peoples, and efforts at self-determination.

Richard Reed, *Forest Dwellers, Forest Protectors: Indigenous Models for International Development*. Part of the *Cultural Survival Studies in Ethnicity and Change* Series. Boston: Allyn and Bacon, 1997. This is a fieldwork-based study of the Guaraní, indigenous peoples of Paraguay and Brazil, now occupying one of the world's largest remaining subtropical rain forests. Chapters consider social organization and production and consumption patterns. The text focuses on Guaraní practices and their ideas about use of forest resources.

Kalima Rose, *Where Women Are Leaders: The SEWA Movement in India*. Atlantic Highlands, NJ: Zed Books, 1992. Although not written by an anthropologist, this in-depth case study of a pioneering credit scheme for poor women of India stands as a useful contribution to the "success story" literature. The book provides a history of the Self-Employed Women's Association (SEWA) and chapters describing different strategies of SEWA and its expansion throughout India and globally.

Joan Ryan, *Doing Things the Right Way*. Calgary: University of Calgary Press, 1995. Using participatory action research, the research team documented Dogrib systems of traditional justice. The work has implications for native self-government, constitutional rights, and First Nations legal systems.

Michael French Smith, *Hard Times on Kairiru Island: Poverty, Development and Morality in a Papua New Guinea Village*. Honolulu: University of Hawaii Press, 1994. This is a fieldwork-based analysis of local understandings of poverty and development on a small island off the north coast of Papua New Guinea. Special attention is given to the stresses involved when the indigenous reciprocity economy meets up with profit-oriented capitalism.

Your *Cultural Anthropology*, Second Canadian Edition Media Edition CD-ROM contains many Web sites relevant to this chapter. Use it to explore the Web and to expand your knowledge of anthropology.

References

Abler, Thomas S. 1992 Scalping, Torture, Cannibalism, and Rape: an Ethnohistorical Analysis of Conflicting Cultural Values in War. *Anthropologica* xxxiv:3–20.

Abu-Lughod, Lila. 1993 *Writing Women's Worlds: Bedouin Stories.* Berkeley: University of California Press.

Adams, Kathleen M. 1984 Come to Tana Toraja, "Land of the Heavenly Kings": Travel Agents as Brokers in Ethnicity. *Annals of Tourism Research* 11:469–485.

Adams, Vincanne. 1988 Modes of Production and Medicine: An Examination of the Theory in Light of Sherpa Traditional Medicine. *Social Science and Medicine* 27:505–513.

Adelson, Naomi. 1998 Health Beliefs and the Politics of Cree Well-Being. *Health* 2(1):5–22.

___. 2000 *"Being Alive Well": Health and the Politics of Cree Well–being.* Toronto: University of Toronto Press.

Adlam, Robert. 2000 Fish Talk. *Anthropologica* 44(1):99–111.

Agar, Michael. 1994 *Language Shock: Understanding the Culture of Conversation.* New York: William Morrow and Company, Inc.

Ahmadu, Fuambai. 2000 Rites and Wrongs: An Insider/Outsider Reflects on Power and Excision. In *Female "Circumcision" in Africa: Culture, Controversy, and Change,* ed. Bettina Shell-Duncan and Ylva Hernlund, 283–312. Boulder, CO: Lynne Reiner Publishers.

Akinsha, Konstantin. 1992a Russia: Whose Art Is It? *ARTNews* 91(5):100–105.

___. 1992b Whose Gold? *ARTNews* 91(3):39–40.

___. 1992c After the Coup: Art for Art's Sake? *ARTNews* 91(1):108–113.

Allison, Anne. 1994 *Nightwork: Sexuality, Pleasure, and Corporate Masculinity in a Tokyo Hostess Club.* Chicago: University of Chicago Press.

Alter, Joseph S. 1992 The Sannyasi and the Indian Wrestler: Anatomy of a Relationship. *American Ethnologist* 19(2):317–336.

Ames, David. 1959 *Wolof Co–operative Work Groups. In Continuity and Change in African Cultures,* ed. William R. Bascom and Melville J. Herskovits, 224–237. Chicago: University of Chicago Press.

Ames, Michael. 1992 *Cannibal Tours and Glass Boxes: The Anthropology of Museums.* Vancouver: University of British Columbia Press.

Anderson, Benedict. 1991 [1983] *Imagined Communities: Reflections on the Origin and Spread of Nationalism.* New York: Verso.

Anderson, Richard L., and Karen L. Field. 1993 Chapter Introduction to *Art in Small–Scale Societies: Contemporary Readings,* ed. Richard L. Anderson and Karen L. Fields, 247. Englewood Cliffs, NJ: Prentice Hall.

Antze, Paul, and Michael Lambek, eds. 1996 *Tense Past: cultural essays in trauma and memory.* New York: Routledge.

Appadurai, Arjun. 1986 Introduction: Commodities and the Politics of Value. In *The Social Life of Things: Commodities in Cultural Perspective,* ed. Arjun Appadurai, 3–63. New York: Cambridge University Press.

Applbaum, Kalman D. 1995 Marriage with the Proper Stranger: Arranged Marriage in Metropolitan Japan. *Ethnology* 34(1):37–51.

Ardrey, Robert. 1961 *African Genesis.* New York: Atheneum.

Ariès, Philippe. 1962 *Centuries of Childhood: A Social History of Family Life.* Trans. Robert Baldick. New York: Vintage Books.

Armstrong, Douglas V. 1990 *The Old Village and the Great House: An Archaeological and Historical Examination of Drax Hall Plantation, St. Ann's Bay, Jamaica.* Chicago: University of Illinois Press.

Arnup, Katherine. 2000 Living in the Margins: Lesbian Families and the Law. In *Open Boundaries: A Canadian Women's Studies Reader,* ed. Barbara A. Crow and Lise Gotell, 205–214. Toronto: Prentice-Hall Canada Inc.

Asad, Talal, ed. 1973 *Anthropology and the Colonial Encounter.* London: Ithaca Press.

Asch, Michael. 1997 *Aboriginal Treaty Rights in Canada: Essays on Law, Equality and Responsibility for Difference.* Vancouver: UBC Press.

Attwood, Donald W. 1992 *Raising Cane: The Political Economy of Sugar in Western India.* Boulder: Westview Press.

Avery, Donald H. 1995 *Reluctant Host: Canada's Response to Immigrant Workers, 1896–1994.* Toronto: McClelland & Stewart Inc.

Awe, Bolanle. 1977 The Iyalode in the Traditional Yoruba Political System. In *Sexual Stratification: A Cross–Cultural View,* ed. Alice Schlegel, 144–160. New York: Columbia University Press.

Bachnik, Jane M. 1983 Recruitment Strategies for Household Succession: Rethinking Japanese Household Organisation. *Man* 18:160–182.

Baer, Lars–Anders. 1982 The Sami: An Indigenous People in Their Own Land. In *The Sami National Minority in Sweden,* ed. Birgitta Jahreskog, 11–22. Stockholm: Almqvist & Wiksell International.

Barber, Pauline. 1997 Transnationalism and the Politics of "Home" for Philippine Domestic Workers. *Anthropologica* 39(1–2):39–52.

Bardhan, Pranab. 1974 On Life and Death Questions. *Economic and Political Weekly* Special Number 9(32–34):1293–1303.

Barfield, Thomas J. 1993 *The Nomadic Alternative.* Englewood Cliffs, NJ: Prentice-Hall.

___. 1994a Establishing Legitimacy through Warfare in Archaic and Modern States. Paper presented at the annual meeting of the American Anthropological Association, Atlanta.

___. 1994b Prospects for Plural Societies in Central Asia. *Cultural Survival Quarterly* 18(2 & 3):48–51.

Barker, J. 1987 T.F. McIlwraith and Anthropology at the University of Toronto, 1925–1963. *Canadian Review of Sociology and Anthropology* 24:252–268.

Barlett, Peggy F. 1980 Reciprocity and the San Juan Fiesta. *Journal of Anthropological Research* 36:116–130.

___. 1989 Industrial Agriculture. In *Economic Anthropology,* ed. Stuart Plattner, 253–292. Stanford: Stanford University Press.

Barnard, Alan, and Anthony Good. 1984 *Research Practices in the Study of Kinship.* New York: Academic Press.

Barndt, Deborah, ed. 1999 *Women Working the NAFTA Food Chain: Women, Food and Globalization.* Toronto: Second Story Press.

Baron, Stephen W. 2001 Street youth labour market experiences and crime. *Canadian Review of Sociology and Anthropology* 38(2)189–215.

Barrett, Stanley R. 1987 *Is God a Racist?* Toronto: University of Toronto Press.

Barth, Frederik. 1993 *Balinese Worlds.* Chicago: University of Chicago Press.

Basch, Linda, Nina Glick Schiller, and Christina Szanton Blanc. 1994 *Nations Unbound: Transnational Projects, Postcolonial Predicaments, and Deterritorialized Nation–States.* Langhorne, PA: Gordon and Breach Science Publishers.

Basso, Keith. H. 1972 [1970] "To Give Up on Words": Silence in Apache Culture. In *Language and Social Context,* ed. Pier Paolo Giglioni, 67–86. Baltimore: Penguin Books.

Beals, Alan R. 1980 *Gopalpur: A South Indian Village.* Fieldwork edition. New York: Holt, Rinehart and Winston.

Beatty, Andrew. 1992 *Society and Exchange in Nias.* New York: Oxford University Press.

Beck, Lois. 1986 *The Qashqa'i of Iran.* New Haven: Yale University Press.

Becker, Gary S. 1964 *Human Capital: A Theoretical and Empirical Analysis, with Special Reference to Education.* New York: National Bureau of Economic Research.

Beeman, William O. 1993 The Anthropology of Theater and Spectacle. *Annual Review of Anthropology* 22:363–393.

Beiser, Morton. 1999 *Strangers at the Gate: The "Boat People's" First Ten Years in Canada.* Toronto: University of Toronto Press.

Benedict, Ruth. 1959 [1934] *Patterns of Culture.* Boston: Houghton Mifflin Company.

___. 1969 [1946] *The Chrysanthemum and the Sword: Patterns of Japanese Culture.* Rutland, VT: Charles E. Tuttle Company.

Berg, Karen. 1997 Female Genital Mutilation: Implications for Social Work. *The Social Worker* 65:16–25.

Berlin, Elois Ann, and Brent Berlin. 1996 *Medical Ethnobiology of the Highland Maya of Chiapas, Mexico: The Gastrointestinal Diseases.* Princeton: Princeton University Press.

Bernal, Martin. 1987 *Black Athena: The Afroasiatic Roots of Classical Civilization.* New Brunswick, NJ: Rutgers University Press.

Bernard, H. Russell. 1995 *Research Methods in Cultural Anthropology: Qualitative and Quantitative Approaches.* 2nd edition. Newbury Park, CA: Sage Publications.

Berreman, Gerald D. 1963 *Hindus of the Himalayas.* Berkeley: University of California Press.

___. 1979 [1975] Race, Caste, and Other Invidious Distinctions in Social Stratification. In *Caste and Other Inequities: Essays on Inequality,* ed. Gerald D. Berreman, 178–222. New Delhi: Manohar.

Best, David. 1986 Culture Consciousness: Understanding the Arts of Other Cultures. *Journal of Art & Design Education* 5(1&2):124–135.

Beyene, Yewoubdar. 1989 *From Menarche to Menopause: Reproductive Lives of Peasant Women in Two Cultures.* Albany: State University of New York Press.

Bhardwaj, Surinder M. 1973 *Hindu Places of Pilgrimage in India: A Study in Cultural Geography.* Berkeley: University of California Press.

Bialystok, Ellen, and Shilpi Majumder. 1998. The Relationship between Bilingualism and the Development of Cognitive Processes in Problem Solving. *Applied Psycholinguistics* 19(1):69–85.

Bibeau, Gilles. 1988 A Step Toward Thick Thinking: From Webs of Significance to Connections across Dimensions. *Medical Anthropology Quarterly* 2(4):402–416.

Billig, Michael S. 1992 The Marriage Squeeze and the Rise of Groomprice in India's Kerala State. *Journal of Comparative Family Studies* 23:197–216.

Bird, Sharon R. 1996 Welcome to the Men's Club: Homosociality and the Maintenance of Hegemonic Masculinity. *Gender & Society* 10(2): 120–132.

Bird–David, Nurit. 1993 Tribal Metaphorization of Human–Nature Relatedness: A Comparative Analysis. In *Environmentalism: The View from Anthropology,* ed. Kay Milton, 112–125. New York: Routledge.

Blackwood, Evelyn. 1995 Senior Women, Model Mothers, and Dutiful Wives: Managing Gender Contradictions in a Minangkabau Village. In *Bewitching Women: Pious Men: Gender and Body Politics in Southeast Asia,* ed. Aihwa Ong and Michael Peletz, 124–158. Berkeley: University of California Press.

Blaikie, Piers. 1985 *The Political Economy of Soil Erosion in Developing Countries.* New York: Longman.

Blanchard, Ray, Kenneth J. Zucker, Susan J. Bradley, and Caitlin S. Hume. 1995 Birth Order and Sibling Sex Ratio in Homosexual Male Adolescents and Probably Prehomosexual Feminine Boys. *Developmental Psychology* 31(1):22–30.

Blau, Peter M. 1964 *Exchange and Power in Social Life.* New York: Wiley.

Bledsoe, Caroline H. 1983 Stealing Food as a Problem in Demography and Nutrition. Paper presented at the annual meeting of the American Anthropological Association.

Bledsoe, Caroline H., and Helen K. Hirschman. 1989 Case Studies of Mortality: Anthropological Contributions. Proceedings of the International Union for the Scientific Study of Population, XXIst International Population Conference, 331–348. Liége: International Union for the Scientific Study of Population.

Blood, Robert O. 1967 *Love Match and Arranged Marriage.* New York: Free Press.

Bodley, John H. 1988 *Tribal Peoples and Development Issues: A Global Overview.* Mountain View, CA: Mayfield Publishing Company.

___. 1990 *Victims of Progress.* 3rd edition. Mountain View, CA: Mayfield Publishing Company.

Bogin, Barry. 1988 *Patterns of Human Growth.* New York: Cambridge University Press.

Bohannan, Paul. 1955 Some Principles of Exchange and Investment among the Tiv. *American Anthropologist* 57(1):60–70.

Bollman, R., and P. Smith. 1988 Integration of Canadian Farm and Off-Farm Markets and the Off-Farm Work of Farm Women, Men, and Children. In *The Political Economy of Agriculture in Western Canada,* ed. G.S. Basran and D.A. Hay, Toronto: Garamond Press.

Boserup, Ester. 1970 *Woman's Role in Economic Development.* New York: St. Martin's Press.

Bourdieu, Pierre. 1984 *Distinction: A Social Critique of the Judgement of Taste.* Trans. Richard Nice. Cambridge: Harvard University Press.

Bourgois, Philippe I. 1995 *In Search of Respect: Selling Crack in El Barrio.* New York: Cambridge University Press.

Bourgois, Philippe I. 1995 Families and Children in Pain in the U.S. Inner City. In *Small Wars: The Cultural Politics of Childhood,* ed. Nancy Scheper-Hughes and Carolyn Sargent, 331–351. Berkeley: University of California Press.

Bourgois, P., and J. Bruneau. 2000. Needle Exchange, HIV infection and the Politics of Science: Confronting Canada's Cocaine Infection Epidemic with Participant Observation. *Medical Anthropology* 18(4): 325–350.

Bowen, Anne M., and Robert Trotter II. 1995 HIV Risk in Intravenous Drug Users and Crack Cocaine Smokers: Predicting Stage of Change for Condom Use. *Journal of Consulting and Clinical Psychology* 63:238–248.

Bowen, John R. 1992 On Scriptural Essentialism and Ritual Variation: Muslim Sacrifice in Sumatra. *American Ethnologist* 19(4):656–671.

___. 1998 *Religions in Practice: An Approach to the Anthropology of Religion.* Boston: Allyn and Bacon.

Brana–Shute, Rosemary. 1976 Women, Clubs, and Politics: The Case of a Lower-Class Neighborhood in Paramaribo, Suriname. *Urban Anthropology* 5(2):157–185.

Brenneis, Donald, and Laura Lein. 1977 "You Fruithead": A Sociolinguistic Approach to Children's Dispute Settlement. In Child Discourse, ed. Susan Ervin–Tripp and Claudia Methcell-Kernan, 49–65. New York: Academic Press.

Briggs, Jean L. 1970 *Never in Anger.* Cambridge, MA: Harvard University Press.

Brink, Judy H. 1991 The Effect of Emigration of Husbands on the Status of Their Wives: An Egyptian Case. *International Journal of Middle East Studies* 23:201–211.

Brinton, Mary C. 1993 *Women and the Economic Miracle: Gender and Work in Postwar Japan.* Berkeley: University of California Press.

Brison, Karen J., and Stephen C. Leavitt. 1995 Coping with Bereavement: Long–Term Perspectives on Grief and Mourning. *Ethos* 23:395–400.

Brodkin, Karen. 2000 Global Capitalism: What's Race Got to Do with It? *American Ethnologist* 27:237–256.

Brooks, Alison S., and Patricia Draper. 1998 [1991] Anthropological Perspectives on Aging. In *Anthropology Explored: The Best of AnthroNotes,* ed. Ruth Osterweis Selig and Marilyn R. London, 286–297. Washington, DC: Smithsonian Press.

Broude, Gwen J. 1988 Rethinking the Couvade: Cross-Cultural Evidence. *American Anthropologist* 90(4):902–911.

Brown, Carolyn Henning. 1984 Tourism and Ethnic Competition in a Ritual Form: The Firewalkers of Fiji. *Oceania* 54:223–244.

Brown, Judith K. 1970 A Note on the Division of Labor by Sex. *American Anthropologist* 72(5):1073–1078.

___. 1975 Iroquois Women: An Ethnohistoric Note. In *Toward an Anthropology of Women,* ed. Rayna R. Reiter, 235–251. New York: Monthly Review Press.

___. 1978 The Recruitment of a Female Labor Force. *Anthropos* 73(1/2):41–48.

___. 1982 Cross-Cultural Perspectives on Middle–Aged Women. *Current Anthropology* 23(2):143–156.

___. 1992 Introduction: Definitions, Assumptions, Themes, and Issues. In *Sanctions and Sanctuary: Cultural Perspectives on the Beating of Wives,* ed. Dorothy Ayers Counts, Judith K. Brown, and Jacquelyn C. Campbell, 1–18. Boulder: Westview Press.

Brown, Peter J., Marcia C. Inhorn, and Daniel J. Smith. 1996 Disease, Ecology, and Human Behavior. In *Medical Anthropology: Contemporary Theory and Method,* ed. Carolyn F. Sargent and Thomas M. Johnson, 183–218. Connecticut: Praeger Publishers.

Browner, Carole H. 1986 The Politics of Reproduction in a Mexican Village. *Signs: Journal of Women in Culture and Society* 11(4):710–724.

Browner, Carole H., and Nancy Ann Press. 1995 The Normalization of Prenatal Diagnostic Screening. In *Conceiving the New World Order: The Global Politics of Reproduction,* ed. Faye D. Ginsberg and Rayna Rapp, 307–322. Berkeley: University of California Press.

___. 1996 The Production of Authoritative Knowledge in American Prenatal Care. *Medical Anthropology Quarterly* 10(2):141–156.

Brownmiller, Susan. 1994 *Seeing Vietnam: Encounters of the Road and Heart.* New York: HarperCollins.

Bruce, Judith, and Daisy Dwyer. 1988 Introduction to In *A Home Divided: Women and Income in the Third World,* ed. Daisy Dwyer and Judith Bruce, 1–19. Stanford: Stanford University Press.

Brumberg, Joan Jacobs. 1988 *Fasting Girls: The Emergence of Anorexia Nervosa as a Modern Disease.* Cambridge: Harvard University Press.

Brumfiel, Elizabeth M. 1994a Ethnic Groups and Political Development in Ancient Mexico. In *Factional Competition and Political Development in the New World,* ed. Elizabeth M. Brumfiel and John W. Fox, 89–102. New York: Cambridge University Press.

Bruner, Edward M. 1991 The Transformation of Self in Tourism. *Annals of Tourism Research* 18:238–250.

Bunzel, Ruth. 1972 [1929] *The Pueblo Potter: A Study of Creative Imagination in Primitive Art.* New York: Dover Publications.

Butler, Shelley. 1999 *Contested Representations: Revisiting "Into the Heart of Africa."* Amsterdam: Gordon and Breach.

Calhoun, Craig, Donald Light, and Suzanne Keller. 1994 *Sociology.* 6th edition. New York: McGraw Hill.

Call, Vaughn, Susan Sprecher, and Pepper Schwartz. 1995 The Incidence and Frequency of Marital Sex in a National Sample. *Journal of Marriage and the Family* 57:639–652.

Cameron, Deborah. 1997 Performing Gender Identity: Young Men's Talk and the Construction of Heterosexual Masculinity. In *Language and Masculinity,* ed. Sally Johnson and Ulrike Hanna Meinhof. Oxford: Blackwell.

Cameron, Mary M. 1995 Transformations of Gender and Caste Divisions of Labor in Rural Nepal: Land, Hierarchy, and the Case of Women. *Journal of Anthropological Research* 51:215–246.

Camino, Linda A., and Ruth M. Krulfeld, eds. 1994 *Reconstructing Lives, Recapturing Meaning: Refugee Identity, Gender and Culture Change.* Basel: Gordon and Breach Publishers.

Cancian, Frank. 1989 Economic Behavior in Peasant Communities. In *Economic Anthropology,* ed. Stuart Plattner, 127–170. Stanford: Stanford University Press.

Caplan, Pat. 1987 Celibacy as a Solution? Mahatma Gandhi and Brahmacharya. In *The Cultural Construction of Sexuality,* ed. Pat Caplan, 271–295. New York: Tavistock Publications.

Caputo, Virginia. 2001 Telling Stories from the Field: Children and the Politics of Ethnographic Representation. *Anthropologica* 43(2):179–189.

Carneiro, Robert L. 1994 War and Peace: Alternating Realities in Human History. In *Studying War: Anthropological Perspectives,* ed. S. P. Reyna and R. E. Downs, 3–27. Langhorne, PA: Gordon and Breach Science Publishers.

Carroll, M. 1984 On the Psychological Origins of the Evil Eye: A Kleinian View. *Journal of Psychoanalytic Anthropology* 8(4):360–382.

Carstairs, G. Morris. 1967 *The Twice Born.* Bloomington: Indiana University Press.

Carsten, Janet. 1995 Children in Between: Fostering and the Process of Kinship on Pulau Langkawi, Malaysia. *Man* (N.S.) 26:425–443.

Carsten, Janet, ed. 2000 *Cultures of Relatedness: New Approaches to the Study of Kinship.* New York: Cambridge University Press.

Carter, William E., Mauricio Mamani P., and José V. Morales. 1981 Medicinal Uses of Coca in Bolivia. In *Health in the Andes,* ed. Joseph W. Bastien and John M. Donahue. Washington, DC: American Anthropological Association.

Carver, Cynthia. 1981 The Delivers: A Woman Doctor's Reflections on Medical Socialization. In *Childbirth, alternative to medical control,* ed. S. Romalis. Austin: University of Texas Press.

Cassell, Joan. 1991 *Expected Miracles: Surgeons at Work.* Philadelphia: Temple University Press.

Castles, Stephen, and Mark J. Miller. 1993 *The Age of Migration: International Population Movements in the Modern World.* New York: The Guilford Press.

Cátedra, María. 1992 *This World, Other Worlds: Sickness, Suicide, Death and the Afterlife among the Vaqueiros de Alzada of Spain.* Chicago: University of Chicago Press.

Cavalli–Sforza, L., P. Menozzi, and A. Piazza. 1994 *History and Geography of Human Genes.* Princeton: Princeton University Press.

Cernea, Michael M. 1985 Sociological Knowledge for Development Projects. In *Putting People First: Sociological Variables and Rural Development,* ed. Michael M. Cernea, 3–22. New York: Oxford University Press.

Chagnon, Napoleon. 1992 *Yanomamö.* 4th edition. New York: Harcourt Brace Jovanovich.

Chalk, Frank, and Kurt Jonassohn. 1986 Conceptualizations of Genocide and Ethnocide. In *Famine in Ukraine: 1932–1933,* ed. Roman Serbyn and Bohdan Krawchenko, 179–190. Edmonton: University of Alberta, Canadian Institute of Ukrainian Studies.

Chambers, Robert. 1983 *Rural Development: Putting the Last First.* Essex, United Kingdom: Longman.

Chan, K.B., and Doreen Indra, eds. 1987 *Uprooting, loss and adaptation: The resettlement of Indochinese refugees in Canada.* Ottawa: Canadian Public Health Association.

Chanen, Jill Schachner. 1995 Reaching Out to Women of Color. *ABA Journal* 81 (May):105.

Chant, Sylvia. 1985 Single-Parent Families: Choice or Constraint? The Formation of Female-Headed Households in Mexican Shanty Towns. *Development and Change* 16:635–656.

Chavez, Leo R. 1992 *Shadowed Lives: Undocumented Immigrants in American Society.* New York: Harcourt Brace Jovanovich.

Cherlin, Andrew J. 1996 *Public and Private Families: An Introduction.* New York: McGraw-Hill Inc.

Cherlin, Andrew, and Frank F. Furstenberg Jr. 1992 [1983] The American Family in the Year 2000. In *One World, Many Cultures,* ed. Stuart Hirschberg, 2–9. New York: Macmillan Publishing Company.

Cheung, Sidney C. H. 1998 Being Here, Searching "There": *Hon Para* as a Virtual Community. In *On the South China Track: Perspectives on Anthropological Research and Teaching,* ed. Sidney C. H. Cheung, 131–148. Hong Kong: Hong Kong Institute of Asia–Pacific Studies, The Chinese University of Hong Kong.

Childs, Larry, and Celina Chelala. 1994 Drought, Rebellion and Social Change in Northern Mali: The Challenges Facing Tamacheq Herders. *Cultural Survival Quarterly* 18(4):16–19.

Chiñas, Beverly Newbold. 1992 *The Isthmus Zapotecs: A Matrifocal Culture of Mexico.* New York: Harcourt, Brace, Jovanovich.

Chowdhury, Najma, Barbara J. Nelson, with Kathryn A. Carver, Nancy J. Johnson, and Paula O'Laughlin. 1994 Redefining Politics: Patterns of Women's Political Engagement from a Global Perspective. In *Women and Politics Worldwide,* ed. Barbara J. Nelson and Najma Chowdhury, 3–24. New Haven: Yale University Press.

Christie, Nils. 1996 Punishment. In *The Social Science Encyclopedia,* ed. Adam Kuper and Jessica Kuper, 708–709. New York: Routledge.

Church, Jon, Vernon Curran, and Shirley Solberg. 2000 "Voices and Faces": A Qualitative Study of Rural Women and a Breast cancer Self–Help Group via Audio Teleconferencing Network. *Centers of Excellence for Women's Health Research Bulletin* 1(1):22–23.

Clark, Gracia. 1992 Flexibility Equals Survival. *Cultural Survival Quarterly* 16:21–24.

Clark, Sam, Elizabeth Colson, James Lee, and Thayer Scudder. 1995 Ten Thousand Tonga: A Longitudinal Anthropological Study from Southern Zambia, 1956–1991. *Population Studies* 49:91–109.

Clay, Jason W. 1990 What's a Nation: Latest Thinking. *Mother Jones* 15(7):28–30.

Clifford, James. 1988 *The Predicament of Culture: Twentieth–Century Ethnography, Literature and Art.* Cambridge: Harvard University Press.

____.1997 *Routes: Travel and Translation in the Late Twentieth Century.* Cambridge: Cambridge University Press.

Cleveland, David A. 2000 Globalization and Anthropology: Expanding the Options. *Human Organization* 59:370–374.

Cohen, Mark Nathan. 1989 *Health and the Rise of Civilization.* New Haven, CT: Yale University Press.

Cohen, Mark Nathan, and George J. Armelagos, eds. 1984 *Palaeopathology at the Origins of Agriculture.* New York: Academic Press.

Cohen, Mark Nathan, and Sharon Bennett. 1993 Skeletal Evidence for Sex Roles and Gender Hierarchies in Prehistory. In *Sex and Gender Hierarchies,* ed. Barbara Diane Miller, 273–296. New York: Cambridge University Press.

Cohn, Bernard S. 1971 *India: The Social Anthropology of a Civilization.* New York: Prentice-Hall.

Cole, Douglas. 1985 *The Scramble for Northwest Coast Artifacts.* Seattle: University of Washington Press.

Cole, Jeffrey. 1996 Working-Class Reactions to the New Immigration in Palermo (Italy). *Critique of Anthropology* 16(2):199–220.

Comaroff, John L. 1987 Of Totemism and Ethnicity: Consciousness, Practice and Signs of Inequality. *Ethnos* 52(3–4):301–323.

Contreras, Gloria. 1995 Teaching about Vietnamese Culture: Water Puppetry as the Soul of the Rice Fields. *The Social Studies* 86(1):25–28.

Corbey, Raymond. 2000 *Arts premiers* in the Louvre. *Anthropology Today* 16:3–6.

Cornell, Laurel L. 1989 Gender Differences in Remarriage after Divorce in Japan and the United States. *Journal of Marriage and the Family* 51:45–463.

Cornia, Giovanni Andrea. 1994 Poverty, Food Consumption, and Nutrition During the Transition to the Market Economy in Eastern Europe. *American Economic Review* 84(2):297–302.

Counihan, Carole M. 1985 Transvestism and Gender in a Sardinian Carnival. *Anthropology* 9(1 & 2):11–24.

Coward, E. Walter, Jr. 1976 Indigenous Organisation, Bureaucracy and Development: The Case of Irrigation. *The Journal of Development Studies* 13(1):92–105.

____. 1979 Principles of Social Organization in an Indigenous Irrigation System. *Human Organization* 38(1):28–36.

Crapanzano, Vincent. 1980 *Tuhami: Portrait of a Moroccan.* Chicago: University of Chicago Press.

Crawford, C. Joanne. 1994 Parenting Practices in the Basque Country: Implications of Infant and Childhood Sleeping Location for Personality Development. *Ethos* 22(1):42–82.

Cronin, Michael P. 1995 The Love Hotel. *Inc. Technology* 17(4):116.

Cruickshank, Julia. 1990 *Life Lived Like a Story: Life Stories of three Yukon elders.* Vancouver: University of British Columbia Press.

Culhane Speck, Dara. 1987 *An Error in Judgement.* Vancouver: Talon Books.

Cunningham, Lawrence S. 1995 Christianity. In *The HarperCollins Dictionary of Religion,* ed. Jonathan Z. Smith, 240–253. New York: HarperCollins.

Dalby, Liza Crihfield. 1983 *Geisha.* New York: Vintage Books.

___. 1993 *Kimono: Fashioning Culture.* New Haven: Yale University Press.

Daly, Mary. 1978 *Gyn/Ecology: The Metaethics of Radical Feminism.* Boston: Beacon Press.

Daly, Martin, and Margo Wilson. 1984 A Sociological Analysis of Human Infanticide. In *Infanticide: Comparative and Evolutionary Perspectives,* ed. Glenn Haustafer and Sarah Blaffer Hrdy, 487–502. New York: Aldine Publishing Company.

Dando, William A. 1980 *The Geography of Famine.* New York: John Wiley and Sons.

Danforth, Loring M. 1989 *Firewalking and Religious Healing: The Anestenaria of Greece and the American Firewalking Movement.* Princeton: Princeton University Press.

Dannhaeuser, Norbert. 1989 Marketing in Developing Urban Areas. In *Economic Anthropology,* ed. Stuart Plattner, 222–252. Stanford: Stanford University Press.

Darnell, Regna. 1970 The Kaska Aesthetic of Speech Use. *Western Canadian Journal of Anthropology* 1(1).

___. 1998 Toward a History of Canadian Departments of Anthropology: Retrospect, Prospect and Common Cause. *Anthropologica* xl(2):153–168.

Das, Veena. 1984 Anthropological Knowledge and Collective Violence: The Riots in Delhi, November 1984. *Anthropology Today* 1:4–6.

Dasgupta, Satadal, Christine Weatherbie, and Rajat Subhra Mukhopadhaya. 1993 Nuclear and Joint Family Households in West Bengal Villages. *Ethnology* 32(4):339–358.

Daugherty, Mary Lee. 1997 [1976] Serpent–Handling as Sacrament. In *Magic, Witchcraft, and Religion,* ed. Arthur C. Lehmann and James E. Myers, 347–352. Mountain View, CA: Mayfield Publishing Company.

Davis, Dona. 1984 Medical Misinformation: Communication between Outport Newfoundland Women and their Physicians. *Social Science and Medicine* 18(3):273–278.

___. 1989 The Variable Character of Nerves in a Newfoundland Fishing Village. *Medical Anthropology* 11:63–78.

Davis, Susan Schaefer, and Douglas A. Davis. 1987 *Adolescence in a Moroccan Town: Making Social Sense.* New Brunswick: Rutgers University Press.

Davis–Floyd, Robbie E. 1987 Obstetric Training as a Rite of Passage. *Medical Anthropology Quarterly* 1:288–318.

___. 1992 *Birth as an American Rite of Passage.* Berkeley: University of California Press.

Davison, Jean, and Martin Kanyuka. 1992 Girls' Participation in Basic Education in Southern Malawi. *Comparative Education Review* 36(4):446–466.

de Athayde Figueiredo, Mariza, and Dando Prado. 1989 The Women of Arembepe. *UNESCO Courier* 7:38–41.

Deaton, Angus. 1987 The Allocation of Goods within the Household: Adults, Children, and Gender. In *Living Standards Measurement Study. Working Paper No. 39.* Washington, DC: The World Bank.

Dejean, Paul. 1980 *The Haitians in Quebec: A Sociological Profile.* Ottawa: The Tecumseh Press.

De Koninck, Rodolphe. 1992 *Malay Peasants Coping with the World: Breaking the Community Circle?* Singapore: Institute of Southeast Asian Studies.

Delaney, Carol. 1988 Mortal Flow: Menstruation in Turkish Village Society. In *Blood Magic: The Anthropology of Menstruation,* ed. Timothy Buckley and Alma Gottlieb, 75–93. Berkeley: University of California Press.

Devereaux, George. 1976 *A Typological Study of Abortion in Primitive Societies: A Typological, Distributional, and Dynamic Analysis of the Prevention of Birth in 400 Preindustrial Societies.* New York: International Universities Press.

Diamond, Jared. 1994 [1987] The Worst Mistake in the History of the Human Race. In *Applying Cultural Anthroplogy: A Reader,* ed. Aaron Podolefsky and Peter J. Brown, 105–108. Mountain View, CA: Mayfield Publishing Company.

Dickemann, Mildred. 1975 Demographic Consequences of Infanticide in Man. *Annual Review of Ecology and Systematics* 6:107–137.

___. 1984 Concepts and Classification in the Study of Human Infanticide: Sectional Introduction and Some Cautionary Notes. In *Infanticide: Comparative and Evolutionary Perspectives,* ed. Glenn Hausfater and Sarah Blaffer Hrdy, 427–438. New York: Aldine Publishing Company.

Dikötter, Frank. 1998 Hairy Barbarians, Furry Primates and Wild Men: Medical Science and Cultural Representations of Hair in China. In *Hair: Its Power and Meaning in Asian Cultures,* ed. Alf Hiltebeitel and Barbara D. Miller, 1–74. Albany: State University of New York Press.

Divale, William T. 1974 Migration, External Warfare, and Matrilocal Residence. *Behavior Science Research* 9:75–133.

Divale, William T., and Marvin Harris. 1976 Population, Warfare and the Male Supremacist Complex. *American Anthropologist* 78:521–538.

Donlon, Jon. 1990 Fighting Cocks, Feathered Warriors, and Little Heroes. *Play & Culture* 3:273–285.

Dorais, Louis-Jacques 1979 Language and Society. In *Challenging Anthropology,* ed. D. Turner and G. Smith. Toronto: McGraw-Hill Ryerson Ltd.

Dorais, Louis-Jacques, Lise Pilon–Le, and Nguyen Huy. 1987 *Exile in a Cold Land: A Vietnamese Community in Canada.* New Haven, CT: Yale Southeast Asian Studies.

Dorgan, Howard. 1989 *The Old Regular Baptists of Central Appalachia: Brothers and Sisters in Hope.* Knoxville: The University of Tennessee Press.

Douglas, Mary. 1962 The Lele: Resistance to Change. In *Markets in Africa,* ed. Paul Bohannan and George Dalton, 211–233. Evanston: Northwestern University Press.

___. 1966 *Purity and Danger: An Analysis of Concepts of Pollution and Taboo.* New York: Penguin Books.

Douglas, Mary, and Baron Isherwood. 1979 *The World of Goods: Towards an Anthropology of Consumption.* New York: W. W. Norton and Company.

Downe, Pamela. 1997 Constructing a Complex of Contagion: The Perceptions of AIDS among Working Prostitutes in Costa Rica. *Social Science and Medicine* 44(10):1575–1583.

___. 1999 Laughing When it Hurts: Humor and Violence in the Lives of Costa Rican Prostitutes. *Women's Studies International Forum* 22(1):63–78.

___. 2001 Playing with Names: How children create Identities of Self in Anthropological Research. *Anthropologica* 43(2):165–177.

Drake, Susan P. 1991 Local Participation in Ecotourism Projects. In *Nature Tourism: Managing for the Environment,* ed. Tensie Whelan, 132–155. Washington, DC: Island Press.

Dreifus, Claudia. 2000 Saving the Orangutan, Preserving Paradise. *The New York Times,* March 21:D3.

Drucker, Charles. 1987 Dam the Chico: Hydropower, Development and Tribal Resistance. In *Tribal Peoples and Development Issues: A Global Overview,* ed. John H. Bodley, 151–165. Mountain View, CA: Mayfield Publishing Company.

Dube, S. C. 1967 *Indian Village.* New York: Harper & Row.

Dunk, Thomas W. 1991 *It's a Working Man's Town: Male Working Class Culture.* Montreal and Kingston: McGill-Queen's University Press.

Duranti, Alessandro. 1994 *From Grammar to Politics: Linguistic Anthropology in a Western Samoan Village.* Berkeley: University of California Press.

Durkheim, Émile. 1951 [1897] *Suicide: A Study in Sociology.* New York: The Free Press.

___. 1965 [1895] *On the Division of Labor in Society.* Trans. G. Simpson. New York: The Free Press.

___. 1966 [1895] *The Elementary Forms of the Religious Life.* New York: The Free Press.

Durning, Alan Thein. 1993 Are We Happy Yet? How the Pursuit of Happiness is Failing. *The Futurist* 27(1):20–24.

du Toit, Brian M. 1990 People on the Move: Rural-Urban Migration with Special Reference to the Third World: Theoretical and Empirical Perspectives. *Human Organization* 49(4):305–320.

Dyson, Tim, and Mick Moore. 1983 On Kinship Structure, Female Autonomy, and Demographic Behavior in India. *Population and Development Review* 9(1):35–60.

Earle, Timothy. 1991 The Evolution of Chiefdoms. In *Chiefdoms, Power, Economy, and Ideology,* ed. Timothy Earle, 1–15. New York: Cambridge University Press.

Eck, Diana L. 1985 *Darson: Seeing the Divine Image in India.* 2nd edition. Chambersburg, PA: Anima Books.

Eckel, Malcolm David. 1995 Buddhism. In *The HarperCollins Dictionary of Religion,* ed. Jonathan Z. Smith, 135–150. New York: HarperCollins.

Economic and Social Council. 1992 *Report of the Working Group on Violence against Women.* Vienna: United Nations. E/CN.6/WG.2/1992/L.3.

The Economist. 1994 Ghana: For Love of Gadgets. November 26:45.

___. 1995 Unwanted, Uncounted. June 24:33.

Edwards, Elizabeth, ed. 1992 *Anthropology and Photography 1860–1920.* New Haven: Yale University Press.

Edwards, John. 1998 *Language in Canada.* Cambridge: Cambridge University Press.

Elder, Joseph W. 1970 Rajpur: Change in the Jajmani System of an Uttar Pradesh Village. In *Change and Continuity in India's Caste System,* ed. K. Ishwaran, xx. New York: Columbia University Press.

Ember, Carol R. 1983 The Relative Decline in Women's Contribution to Agriculture with Intensification. *American Anthropologist* 85(2):285–304.

Entwisle, Barbara, Gail E. Henderson, Susan E. Short, Jill Bouma, and Zhai Fengying. 1995 Gender and Family Businesses in Rural China. *American Sociological Review* 60:36–57.

Esman, Milton. 1996 Ethnic Politics. In *The Social Science Encyclopedia,* ed. Adam Kuper and Jessica Kuper, 259–260. New York: Routledge.

Estioko-Griffin, Agnes. 1986 Daughters of the Forest. *Natural History* 95:36–43.

Estioko-Griffin, Agnes, Madeleine J. Goodman, and Bion Griffin. 1985 The Compatibility of Hunting and Mothering among the Agta Hunter-Gatherers of the Philippines. *Sex Roles* 12: 1199–1209.

Estrin, Saul. 1996 Co–operatives. In *The Social Science Encyclopedia,* ed. Adam Kuper and Jessica Kuper, 138–139. Routledge: New York.

Etienne, Mona, and Eleanor Leacock, eds. 1980 *Women and Colonization: Anthropological Perspectives.* New York: Praeger.

Evans-Pritchard, E. E. 1951 *Kinship and Marriage among the Nuer.* Oxford: Clarendon.

___. 1965 [1947] *The Nuer: A Description of the Modes of Livelihood and Political Institutions of a Nilotic People.* New York: Oxford University Press.

Everett, Daniel. 1995 Personal communication.

Fabian, Johannes. 1995 Ethnographic Misunderstanding and the Perils of Context. *American Anthropologist* 97(1):41–50.

Fabrega, Horacio, and Barbara D. Miller. 1995 Adolescent Psychiatry as a Product of Contemporary Anglo-American Society. *Social Science and Medicine* 40(7):881–894.

Fadiman, Anne. 1997 *The Spirit Catches You and You Fall Down: A Hmong Child, Her American Doctors, and the Collusion of Two Cultures.* New York: Farrar, Straus and Giroux.

Farmer, Paul. 1990 Sending Sickness: Sorcery, Politics, and Changing Concepts of AIDS in Rural Haiti. *Medical Anthropology Quarterly* 4:6–27.

Fedigan, L. 1992 *Primate Paradigms: Sex Roles and Social Bonds.* Chicago: University of Chicago Press.

Feinsilver, Julie M. 1993 *Healing the Masses: Cuban Health Politics at Home and Abroad.* Berkeley: University of California Press.

Feldman-Savelsberg, Pamela. 1995 Cooking Inside: Kinship and Gender in Bangangté Idioms of Marriage and Procreation. *American Ethnologist* 22(3):483–501.

Fernando, Andy. 1995 *Native Heritage: Personal Accounts by American Indians 1790 to the Present,* ed. Arlene Hirschfelder, 222–224. New York: MacMillan.

Ferguson, James. 1994 *The Anti–Politics Machine: "Development," Depoliticization, and Bureaucratic Power in Lesotho.* Minneapolis: University of Minnesota Press.

Ferguson R. Brian. 1990 Blood of the Leviathan: Western Contact and Amazonian Warfare. *American Ethnologist* 17(1):237–257.

Firestone, M. 1985 The "Old Hag": Sleep Paralysis in Newfoundland. *Journal of Psychoanalytic Anthropology* 8(1):47–66.

Fiske, John. 1994 Radical Shopping in Los Angeles: Race, Media and the Sphere of Consumption. *Media, Culture & Society* 16:469–486.

Fluehr-Lobban, Carolyn. 1994 Informed Consent in Anthropological Research: We Are Not Exempt. *Human Organization* 53(1):1–10.

Folbre, Nancy. 1986 Cleaning House: New Perspectives on Households and Economic Development. *Journal of Development Economics* 22:5–40.

Fonseca, Isabel. 1995 *Bury Me Standing: The Gypsies and Their Journey.* New York: Alfred A. Knopf.

Fortune, Reo F. 1959 [1932] *Sorcerers of Dobu: The Social Anthropology of the Dobu Islanders of the Western Pacific.* New York: E. P. Dutton & Co.

Foster, George. 1965 Peasant Society and the Image of the Limited Good. *American Anthropologist* 67:293–315.

Foster, George M., and Barbara Gallatin Anderson. 1978 *Medical Anthropology.* New York: Alfred A. Knopf.

Foucault, Michel. 1977 *Discipline and Punish: The Birth of the Prison.* New York: Pantheon Books.

Fox, Robin. 1995 [1978] *The Tory Islanders: A People of the Celtic Fringe.* Notre Dame: University of Notre Dame Press.

Franke, Richard W. 1993 *Life is a Little Better: Redistribution as a Development Strategy in Nadur Village, Kerala.* Boulder: Westview Press.

Frankel, Francine R. 1971 *India's Green Revolution: Economic Gains and Political Costs.* Princeton: Princeton University Press.

Fratkin, Elliot. 1998 *Ariaal Pastoralists of Kenya: Surviving Drought and Development in Africa's Arid Lands.* Boston: Allyn and Bacon.

Fratkin, Elliot, Kathleen Galvin, and Eric A. Roth, eds. 1994 *African Pastoralist Systems: An Integrated Approach.* Boulder: Westview Press.

Frazer, Sir James. 1978 [1890] *The Golden Bough: A study in Magic and Religion.* New York: Macmillan.

Freed, Stanley A., and Ruth S. Freed. 1969 Urbanization and Family Types in a North Indian Village. *Southwestern Journal of Anthropology* 25:342–359.

Freedman, J. 2000 A Case for Equity. In *Transforming Development: Foreign Aid for a Changing World,* ed. J. Freedman. Toronto: University of Toronto Press.

Freeman, Derek. 1983 *Margaret Mead and Samoa: The Making and Unmaking of an Anthropological Myth.* Cambridge, MA: Harvard University Press.

Freeman, James A. 1981 A Firewalking Ceremony that Failed. In *Social and Cultural Context of Medicine in India,* ed. Giri Raj Gupta, 308–336. New Delhi: Vikas Publishing House.

___. 1989 *Hearts of Sorrow: Vietnamese-American Lives.* Stanford: Stanford University Press.

Fricke, Thomas. 1994 [1984] *Himalayan Households: Tamang Demography and Domestic Processes.* New York: Columbia University Press.

Frideres, James S. 1998 *Aboriginal Peoples in Canada: Contemporary Conflicts.* 5th edition. Scarborough, Ontario: Prentice Hall Allyn and Bacon Canada.

Friedl, Ernestine. 1975 *Women and Men: An Anthropologist's View.* New York: Holt, Rinehart, and Winston.

___. 1986 Fieldwork in a Greek Village. In *Women in the Field: Anthropological Experiences,* ed. Peggy Golde, 195–220. Berkeley: University of California Press.

Frisch, Rose. 1978 Population, Food Intake, and Fertility. *Science* 199:22–30.

Fuller, Christopher J. 1976 *The Nayars Today.* New York: Cambridge University Press.

Furst, Peter T. 1989 The Water of Life: Symbolism and Natural History on the Northwest Coast. *Dialectical Anthropology* 14:95–115.

Gable, Eric. 1995 The Decolonization of Consciousness: Local Skeptics and the "Will to Be Modern" in a West African Village. *American Ethnologist* 22(2):242–257.

Gage–Brandon, Anastasia J. 1992 The Polygyny-Divorce Relationship: A Case Study of Nigeria. *Journal of Marriage and the Family* 54:282–292.

Galdikas, Birute. 1995 *Reflections of Eden: My Years with the Orangutans of Borneo.* Boston: Little, Brown.

Gardiner, Margaret. 1984 *Footprints on Malekula: A Memoir of Bernard Deacon.* Edinburgh: The Salamander Press.

Gardner, Katy, and David Lewis. 1996 *Anthropology, Development and the Post-Modern Challenge.* Chicago: Pluto Press.

Garland, David. 1996 Social Control. In *The Social Science Encyclopedia,* ed. Adam Kuper and Jessica Kuper, 780–783. Routledge: New York.

Geertz, Clifford. 1966 Religion as a Cultural System. In *Anthropological Approaches to the Study of Religion,* ed. Michael Banton, 1–46. London: Tavistock.

Gibb, Camilla. 2002 Deterritorialized People in Hyperspace: Creating and Debating Harari Identity over the Internet. *Anthropologica* 44(1):55–67.

Gilad, Lisa. 1990 *The Northern Route.* St. John's, Newfoundland: Memorial University.

Gill, Lesley. 1993 "Proper Women" and City Pleasures: Gender, Class, and Contested Meanings in La Paz. *American Ethnologist* 20(1):72–88.

Gilman, Antonio. 1991 Trajectories towards Social Complexity in the Later Prehistory of the Mediterranean. In *Chiefdoms: Power, Economy and Ideology,* ed. Timothy Earle, 146–168. New York: Cambridge University Press.

Ginsberg, Faye D., and Rayna Rapp. 1991 The Politics of Reproduction. *Annual Review of Anthropology* 20:311–343.

Gittelsohn, Joel. 1991 Opening the Box: Intrahousehold Food Allocation in Rural India. *Social Science and Medicine* 33(10):1141–1154.

Glasser, Irene, and Rae Bridgeman. 1999 *Braving the Street: The Anthropology of Homelessness.* New York: Berghahn Books.

Glínski, Piotr. 1994 Environmentalism among Polish Youth: A Maturing Social Movement? *Communist and Post–Communist Studies* 27(2):145–159.

Gliotto, Tom. 1995 Paradise Lost. *People Weekly* 43(17):70–76.

Gluckman, Max. 1955 *The Judicial Process among the Barotse of Northern Rhodesia.* Manchester: Manchester University Press.

___. 1963 *Politics, Law and Ritual in Tribal Africa.* London: Cohen and West.

Gmelch, George. 1997 [1971] Baseball Magic. In *Magic, Witchcraft, and Religion,* ed. Arthur C. Lehmann and James E. Myers, 276–282. Mountain View, CA: Mayfield Publishing Company.

Godelier, Maurice. 1971 "Salt Currency" and the Circulation of Commodities among the Baruya of New Guinea. In *Studies in Economic Anthropology,* ed. George Dalton, 52–73. Anthropological Studies No. 7. Washington, DC: American Anthropological Association.

Gold, Ann Grodzins. 1988 *Fruitful Journeys: The Ways of Rajasthani Pilgrims.* Berkeley: University of California Press.

Gold, Stevan J. 1992 *Refugee Communities: A Comparative Field Study.* Newbury Park: Sage Publications.

___. 1995 *From the Workers' State to the Golden State: Jews from the Former Soviet Union in California.* Boston: Allyn and Bacon.

Golde, Peggy, ed. 1986 *Women in the Field: Anthropological Experiences.* 2nd edition. Berkeley: University of California Press.

Goldstein, Melvyn C. 1987 When Brothers Share a Wife. *Natural History* 96:38–49.

Goldstein, Melvin C., and Cynthia M. Beall. 1994 *The Changing World of Mongolia's Nomads.* Berkeley: University of California Press.

Goldstone, Jack. 1996 Revolutions. In *The Social Science Encyclopedia,* ed. In Adam Kuper and Jessica Kuper, 740–743. New York: Routledge.

González, Nancie L. 1970 Toward a Definition of Matrifocality. In *Afro-American Anthropology: Contemporary Perspectives,* Norman E. Whitten, Jr. and John F. Szwed. New York: The Free Press.

Goodall, Jane. 1971 *In the Shadow of Man.* Boston: Houghton–Mifflin.

___. 1986 *The Chimpanzees of Gombe: Patterns of Behavior.* Cambridge, MA: Harvard University Press.

Goody, Jack. 1976 *Production and Reproduction: A Comparative Study of the Domestic Domain.* New York: Cambridge University Press.

___. 1977 *Cooking, Cuisine and Class: A Study of Comparative Sociology.* New York: Cambridge University Press.

___. 1993 *The Culture of Flowers.* New York: Cambridge University Press.

___. 1996 Comparing Family Systems in Europe and Asia: Are There Different Sets of Rules? *Population and Development Review* 22:1–20.

Goody, Jack, and Stanley J. Tambiah. 1973 *Bridewealth and Dowry.* New York: Cambridge University Press.

Gough, E. Kathleen. 1959 The Nayars and the Definition of Marriage. *Journal of the Royal Anthropological Institute* 89:23–34.

Graburn, Nelson. 1993 Ethnic arts of the Fourth World: The View from Canada. In *Imagery and Creativity: Ethnoaesthetics and Art Worlds in the Americas,* ed. D. Whitten and N. Whitten. Tucson: University of Arizona Press.

____. 1998 Weirs in the River of Time: The Development of Historical Consciousness among Canadian Inuit *Museum Anthropology* 22(1):18–32.

Graburn, Nelson H. H., ed. 1976 *Ethnic and Tourist Arts: Cultural Expressions from the Fourth World.* Berkeley: University of California Press.

Graham, Elizabeth. 1998 Mission Archaeology. *Annual Review of Anthropology* 27:25–62.

Greenhalgh, Susan. 1994 Controlling Births and Bodies in Village China. *American Ethnologist* 21(1):3–30.

Greenough, Paul R. 1982 *Prosperity and Misery in Modern Bengal: The Famine of 1943–44.* New York: Oxford University Press.

Gregor, Thomas. 1981 A Content Analysis of Mehinaku Dreams. *Ethos* 9:353–390.

____. 1982 No Girls Allowed. *Science* 82.

Gremillion, Helen. 1992 Psychiatry as Social Ordering: Anorexia Nervosa, a Paradigm. *Social Science and Medicine* 35(1):57–71.

Grenier, Guillermo J., Alex Stepick, Debbie Draznin, Aileen LaBorwit, and Steve Morris. 1992 On Machines and Bureaucracy: Controlling Ethnic Interaction in Miami's Apparel and Construction Industries. In *Structuring Diversity: Ethnographic Perspectives on the New Immigration,* ed. LouiseLamphere, 65–94. Chicago: University of Chicago Press.

Grinker, Roy Richard. 1994 *Houses in the Rainforest: Ethnicity and Inequality among Farmers and Foragers in Central Africa.* Berkeley: University of California Press.

Gross, Daniel R. 1984 Time Allocation: A Tool for the Study of Cultural Behavior. *Annual Review of Anthropology* 13:519–558.

Gross, Daniel R. George Eiten, Nancy M. Flowers, Francisca M. Leoi, Madeleine Lattman Ritter, and Dennis W. Werner. 1979 Ecology and Acculturation among Native Peoples of Central Brazil. *Science* 206(30):1043–1050.

Gross, Daniel R., and Barbara A. Underwood. 1971 Technological Change and Caloric Costs. *American Anthropologist* 73:725–740.

Gruneau, Richard S., and David Whitson. 1993 *Hockey Night in Canada: sport, identities, and cultural politics.* Toronto: Garamond Press.

Guggenheim, Scott E., and Michael M. Cernea. 1993 Anthropological Approaches to Involuntary Resettlement: Policy, Practice, and Theory. In *Anthropological Approaches to Resettlement: Policy, Practice, and Theory,* ed. Michael M. Cernea and Scott E. Guggenheim, 1–12. Boulder: Westview Press.

Gugler, Josef. 1988 The Urban Character of Contemporary Revolutions. In *The Urbanization of the Third World,* ed. Josef Gugler, 399–412. New York: Oxford University Press.

Gulliver, P.H., and M. Silverman. 1995 *Merchants and Shopkeepers: A Historical Anthropology of an Irish Market Town, 1200–1991.* Toronto: University of Toronto Press.

Gupta, Akhil, and James Ferguson, eds. 1997 *Anthropological Locations: Boundaries and Grounds of Field Science.* Berkeley: University of California Press.

Guyer, Jane. 1988 Dynamic Approaches to Domestic Budgeting: Cases and Methods from Africa. In *A Home Divided: Women and Income in the Third World,* ed. Daisy Dwyer and Judith Bruce, 155–172. Stanford: Stanford University Press.

Haas, J., and W. Shaffir. 1982. Ritual Evaluation of Competence: The Hidden Curriculum of Professionalization in an Innovative Medical School Program. *Work and Occupations* 9(2):131–154.

Hackenberg, Robert A., et al. 1983 Migration, Modernization and Hypertension: Blood Pressure Levels in Four Philippine Communities. *Medical Anthropology* 7(1):45–71.

Hackenberg, Robert A. 2000 Advancing Applied Anthropology: Joe Hill in Cyberspace-Steps Toward Creating "One Big Union." *Human Organization* 59:365–369.

Hacker, Andrew. 1992 *Two Nations: Black and White, Separate, Hostile, Unequal.* New York: Ballantine Books.

Hagey, Rebecca. 1984 The Phenomenon, the Explanations and the Responses: Metaphors Surrounding Diabetes in Urban Canadian Indians. *Social Science and Medicine* 18:265–272.

Hakamies-Blomqvist, Liisa. 1994 Aging and Fatal Accidents in Male and Female Drivers. *Journal of Gerontology [Social Sciences]* 49(6):5286–5290.

Hale, Horatio. 1883 *Iroquois Book of Rites.* Philadelphia: D.G. Brinton.

Hall, Thomas D. 1996 World System Theory. In *The Social Science Encyclopedia,* ed. Adam Kuper and Jessica Kuper, 922–923. New York: Routledge.

Hammerlsey, Martyn. 1992 *What's Wrong with Ethnography: Methodological Explorations.* London: Routledge.

Hammond, Peter B. 1966 *Yatenga: Technology in the Culture of a West African Kingdom.* New York: The Free Press.

Hancock, Graham. 1989 *Lords of Poverty: The Power, Prestige, and Corruption of the International Aid Business.* New York: The Atlantic Monthly Press.

Handwerker, W. Penn. 1990 Politics and Reproduction: A Window on Social Change. In *Births and Power: Social Change and the Politics of Reproduction,* ed. Penn W. Handwerker, 1–38. Boulder: Westview Press.

Harner, Michael. 1977 The Ecological Basis of Aztec Sacrifice. *American Ethnologist* 4:117–135.

Harris, Marvin. 1968. *The Rise of Anthropological Theory.* New York: Thomas Y. Crowell Company.

___. 1971 *Culture, Man and Nature*. New York: Thomas Y. Crowell Company.

___. 1974 *Cows, Pigs, Wars and Witches: The Riddles of Culture*. New York: Random House.

___. 1975 *Culture, People, Nature: An Introduction to General Anthropology*. 2nd edition. New York: Thomas Y. Crowell Company.

___. 1977 *Cannibals and Kings: The Origins of Culture*. New York: Random House.

___. 1981 *America Now: The Anthropology of a Changing Culture*. New York: Simon and Schuster.

___. 1989 *Our Kind: Who We Are, Where We Came From and Where We Are Going*. New York: HarperCollins.

___. 1993 The Evolution of Human Gender Hierarchies: A Trial Formulation. In *Sex and Gender Hierarchies*, ed. Barbara D. Miller, 57–80. New York: Cambridge University Press.

___. 1995 *Cultural Anthropology*. 4th edition. New York: HarperCollins.

Harris, Marvin, and Eric B. Ross. 1987 *Death, Sex and Fertility*. New York: Columbia University Press.

Harrison, Simon. 1993 The Commerce of Cultures in Melanesia. *Man* 28:139–158.

Hart, C. W. M., Arnold R. Pilling, and Jane C. Goodale. 1988 *The Tiwi of North Australia*. New York: Holt, Rinehart, and Winston.

Hartmann, Betsy. 1987 *Reproductive Rights and Wrongs: The Global Politics of Population Control and Reproductive Choice*. New York: Harper & Row.

Hastrup, Kirsten. 1992 Anthropological Visions: Some Notes on Visual and Textual Authority. In *Film as Ethnography*, ed. Peter Ian Crawford and David Turton, 8–25. Manchester: University of Manchester Press.

Heider, Karl. 1976 Dani Sexuality: A Low Energy System. *Man* 11:188–201.

Heise, Lori L., Jacqueline Pitanguy, and Adrienne Germain. 1994 *Violence against Women: The Hidden Health Burden*. *World Bank Discussion Paper No. 255*. Washington, DC: The World Bank.

Helleiner, Jane 2001 "The Right Kind of Children": Childhood, Gender and Race in Canadian Postwar Political Discourse. *Anthropologica* 43(2):143–152.

Henry, Francis. 1984 *Victims and Neighbors: A Small Town in Nazi Germany Remembered*. South Hadley, Mass.: Bergin and Garvey.

___. 1987 Caribbean Migration to Canada: Prejudice and Opportunity. In The Caribbean Exodus, ed. Barry Levine. New York: Greenwood Publishing Group.

Henry, Francis, and Carol Tator. 2002 *Discourses of Domination: Racial Bias in the Canadian English-Language Press*. Toronto: University of Toronto Press.

Herdt, Gilbert. 1987 *The Sambia: Ritual and Gender in New Guinea*. New York: Holt, Rinehart and Winston.

Hess, S., C. Smith, and Y. Ternar. 1984 *Repression and Exile: A Study of Salvadoran, Guatemalan, and Haitian refugees in Montreal*. Montreal: McGill University Press.

Hewlett, Barry S. 1991 *Intimate Fathers: The Nature and Context of Aka Pygmy Paternal Care*. Ann Arbor: The University of Michigan Press.

Heyneman, D. 1984 Development and Disease: A Dual Dilemma. *Journal of Parasitology* 70:3–17.

Hiatt, Betty. 1970 Woman the Gatherer. In *Woman's Role in Aboriginal Society*, ed. Fay Gale, 2-28. Canberra: Australian Institute of Aboriginal Studies.

Higginbotham, N., D. Willms, and N. Sewankambo 2001 Transdisciplinary Work in the Community. In *Health Social Science: A Transdisciplinary and Complexity Perspective*, ed. N. Higginbotham, G Albrecht, and L. O'Connor. South Melbourne, Australia: Oxford University.

Hill, Jane H., and Bruce Mannheim. 1992 Language and World View. *Annual Review of Anthropology* 21:381–406.

Hiltebeitel, Alf. 1988 *The Cult of Draupadi: Mythologies from Gingee to Kuruksetra*. Chicago: The University of Chicago Press.

___. 1995 Hinduism. In *The HarperCollins Dictionary of Religion*, ed. Jonathan Z. Smith, 424–440. New York: HarperCollins Publishers.

Hirschfelder, Arlene, ed. 1995 *Native Heritage: Personal Accounts by American Indians 1790 to the Present*. New York: Macmillan.

Hirschon, Renee. 1989 *Heirs of the Catastrophe: The Social Life of Asia Minor Refugees in Piraeus*. New York: Oxford University Press.

Hodge, Robert W., and Naohiro Ogawa. 1991 *Fertility Change in Contemporary Japan*. Chicago: The University of Chicago Press.

Hogan, Dennis P. and Takashi Mochizuki. 1988 Demographic Transitions and the Life Course: Lessons from Japanese and American Comparisons. Journal of Family History 13(3):291–305.

Holmes, Paula Elizabeth. 2001 The Narrative Repatriation of Blessed Kateri Tekakwitha.*Anthropologica* 43(1):87–103.

Horowitz, Irving L. 1967 *The Rise and Fall of Project Camelot: Studies in the Relationship between Social Science and Practical Politics*. Boston: MIT Press.

Horowitz, Michael M., and Muneera Salem-Murdock. 1993 Development-Induced Food Insecurity in the Middle Senegal Valley. *GeoJournal* 30(2):179–184.

Hostetler, John A., and Gertrude Enders Huntington. 1992 *Amish Children: Education in the Family, School, and Community*. New York: Harcourt Brace Jovanovich.

Howell, Nancy. 1979 *Demography of the Dobe !Kung*. New York: Academic Press.

___. 1986 Feedbacks and Buffers in Relation to Scarcity and Abundance: Studies of Hunter–Gatherer Populations. In *The State of Population Theory: Forward from Malthus*, ed. David Coleman and Roger Schofield, 156–187. New York: Basil Blackwell.

___. 1990 *Surviving Fieldwork: A Report of the Advisory Panel on Health and Safety in Fieldwork*. Washington, DC: American Anthropological Association.

Humphrey, Caroline. 1978 Women, Taboo and the Suppression of Attention. In *Defining Females: The Nature of Women in Society*, ed. Shirley Ardener, 89–108. New York: John Wiley and Sons.

Hunte, Pamela A. 1985 Indigenous Methods of Fertility Regulation in Afghanistan. In *Women's Medicine: A Cross–Cultural Study of Indigenous Fertility Regulation*, ed. Lucile F. Newman, 44–75. New Brunswick: Rutgers University Press.

Hutchinson, Sharon E. 1996 *Nuer Dilemmas: Coping with Money, War, and the State*. Berkeley: University of California Press.

Hutter, Michael. 1996 The Value of Play. In *The Value of Culture: On the Relationship between Economics and the Arts*, ed. Arjo Klamer, 122–137. Amsterdam: Amsterdam University Press.

Illo, Jeanne Frances I. 1985 Who Heads the Household? Women in Households in the Philippines. Paper presented at the Women and Household Regional Conference for Asia, New Delhi.

Indra, Doreen M. 1988 Self-Concept and Resettlement: Vietnamese and Sino-Vietnamese in a Small Prairie City. In *Ten Years Later: Indochinese Communities in Canada*, ed. Louis-Jacques Dorais, Kwok B. Chan, and Doreen M. Indra. Montreal: Canadian Asian Studies Association.

Inhorn, Marcia C., and Peter J. Brown, eds., 1997 *The Anthropology of Infectious Disease: International Health Perspectives-(theory and practice in medical anthropology and international health)*. Malaysia: Gordon and Breach Publishers.

International Labour Office. 1996 Female Asian Migrants: A Growing But Vulnerable Workforce. *World of Work* 15:16–17.

Janes, Craig R. 1990 *Migration, Social Change, and Health: A Samoan Community in Urban California*. Stanford: Stanford University Press.

___. 1995 The Transformations of Tibetan Medicine. *Medical Anthropology Quarterly* 9(1):6–39.

Jankowski, Martín Sánchez. 1991 *Islands in the Street: Gangs and American Urban Society*. Berkeley: University of California Press.

Jayawardena, Kumari. 1984 The Plantation Sector in Sri Lanka: Recent Changes in the Welfare of Children and Women. *World Development* 12(3):317–328.

Jefremovas, Villia. 1997 Contested Identities: Power and the Fictions of Ethnicity, Ethnography and History in Rwanda. *Anthropologica* xxxix(1–2):91–104.

Jentoft, Sven, and Anthony Davis. 1993 Self and Sacrifice: An Investigation of Small Boat Fisher Individualism and Its Implication for Producer Cooperatives. *Human Organization* 52(4):356–367.

Jiang, David W. 1994 Shanghai Revisited: Chinese Theatre and the Forces of the Market. *The Drama Review* 38(2):72–80.

Jinadu, L. Adele. 1994 The Dialectics of Theory and Research on Race and Ethnicity in Nigeria. In *"Race," Ethnicity and Nation: International Perspectives on Social Conflict*, ed. Peter Ratcliffe, 163–178. London: University of College London Press.

Johnson, Walter R. 1994 *Dismantling Apartheid: A South African Town in Transition*. Ithaca: Cornell University Press.

Johnston, Barbara Rose. 1994 Environmental Degradation and Human Rights Abuse. In *Who Pays the Price?: The Sociocultural Context of Environmental Crisis*, ed. Barbara Rose Johnston, 7–16. Washington, DC: Island Press.

Jonaitis, Aldona. 1995 *A Wealth of Thought: Franz Boas on Native American Art*. Seattle: University of Washington Press.

Jones, Anna Laura. 1993 Exploding Canons: The Anthropology of Museums. *Annual Review of Anthropology* 22:201–220.

Joralemon, Donald. 1982 New World Depopulation and the Case of Disease. *Journal of Anthropological Research* 38:108–127.

___. 1999 *Health and Disease: The Anthropological View*. Boston: Allyn and Bacon.

Jordan, Brigitte. 1983 *Birth in Four Cultures*. 3rd edition. Montreal: Eden Press.

Joseph, Suad. 1994 Brother/Sister Relationships: Connectivity, Love, and Power in the Reproduction of Patriarchy in Lebanon. *American Ethnologist* 21:50–73.

Jourdan, Christine. 1995 Masta Liu. In *Youth Cultures: A Cross–Cultural Perspective*, ed. Vered Amit-Talai and Helena Wulff 202–222. New York: Routledge.

Joy, Annamma. 1989 *Ethnicity in Canada*. New York: AMS Press Inc.

Kaberry, Phyllis. 1952 *Women of the Grassfields: A Study of the Economic Position of Women in Bamenda, British Cameroons*. London: Her Majesty's Stationery Office.

Kabutha, Charity, Barbara P. Thomas–Slaytor, and Richard Ford. 1993 Participatory Rural Appraisal: A Case Study from Kenya. In *Rapid Appraisal Methods*, ed. Krishna Kumar, 176–211. Washington, DC: The World Bank.

Kahn, Miriam. 1995 Heterotopic Dissonance in the Museum Representation of Pacific Island Cultures. *American Anthropologist* 97(2):324–338.

Kapchan, Deborah A. 1994 Moroccan Female Performers Defining the Social Body. *Journal of American Folklore* 107(423):82–105.

Katz, Nathan, and Ellen S. Goldberg. 1989 Asceticism and Caste in the Passover Observances of the Cochin Jews. *Journal of the American Academy of Religion* 57(1):53–81.

Katz, Richard. 1982 *Boiling Energy: Community Healing among the Kalahari Kung.* Cambridge: Harvard University Press.

Kaufert, Patricia. 1986 The Menopausal Transition; the Use of Estrogen. *Canadian Journal of Public Health* 77(1):86–91.

Kaufert, P., and J. O'Neil. 1990. Cooptation and Control: The Reconstruction of Inuit Birth. *Medical Anthropology Quarterly* 4(4):427–442.

Kearney, Michael. 1986 From the Invisible Hand to Visible Feet: Anthropological Studies of Migration and Development. *Annual Review of Anthropology* 15:331–361.

Keenan, Elinor. 1974 Norm-Makers and Norm–Breakers: Uses of Speech by Women and Men in a Malagasy Community. In *Explorations in the Ethnography of Speaking,* ed. Richard Bauman and Joel Sherzer. New York: Cambridge University Press.

Kelley, Heidi. 1991 Unwed Mothers and Household Reputation in a Spanish Galician Community. *American Ethnologist* 18:565–580.

Kendall, Laurel. 1996 *Getting Married in Korea: Of Gender, Morality, and Modernity.* Berkeley: University of California Press.

Kennedy, David P., and Stephen G. Perz. 2000 Who Are Brazil's Indígenas? Contributions of Census Data Analysis to Anthropological Demography of Indigenous Populations. *Human Organization* 59:311–324.

Kerns, Virginia. 1992 Preventing Violence against Women: A Central American Case. In *Sanctions and Sanctuary: Cultural Perspectives on the Beating of Wives,* ed. Dorothy Ayers Counts, Judith K. Brown, and Jacquelyn C. Campbell, 125–138. Boulder: Westview Press.

Kesmanee, Chupinit. 1994 Dubious Development Concepts in the Thai Highlands: The Chao Khao in Transition. *Law & Society Review* 28:673–683.

Kideckel, David A. 1993 *The Solitude of Collectivism: Romanian Villagers to the Revolution and Beyond.* Ithaca: Cornell University Press.

King, Ruth. 1998 Language in Ontario. In *Language in Canada,* ed. J. Edwards. Cambridge: Cambridge University Press.

Kitchell, Anne, Erin Hannan, and Willett Kempton. 2000 Identities through Stories: Story Structure and Function in Two Environmental Groups. *Human Organization* 59:96–105.

Klass, Perri. 1987 *A Not Entirely Benign Procedure: Four Years as a Medical Student.* New York: Penguin Books.

Kleinman, Arthur. 1988 *Illness Narratives.* New York: Basic Books.

Kneen, B. 1999 *Farmageddon: Food and the Culture of Biotechnology.* Gabriola Island: New Society Publishers.

Knott, Kim. 1996 Hindu Women, Destiny and Stridharma. *Religion* 26:15–35.

Kolenda, Pauline M. 1968 Region, Caste, and Family Structure: A Comparative Study of the Indian "Joint" Family. In *Structure and Change in Indian Society,* ed. Milton Singer and Bernard S. Cohn, 339–396. New York: Aldine.

____. 1978 *Caste in Contemporary India: Beyond Organic Solidarity.* Prospect Heights, IL: Waveland Press.

Kondo, Dorinne. 1997 *About Face: Performing Race in Fashion and Theatre.* New York: Routledge.

Konner, Melvin. 1987 *Becoming a Doctor: The Journey of Initiation in Medical School.* New York: Penguin Books.

____. 1989 Homosexuality: Who and Why? *The New York Times Magazine,* April 2:60–61.

Kottak, Conrad Phillip. 1985 When People Don't Come First: Some Sociological Lessons from Completed Projects. In *Putting People First: Sociological Variables and Rural Development,* ed. Michael M. Cernea, 325–356. New York: Oxford University Press.

____. 1992 *Assault on Paradise: Social Change in a Brazilian Village.* New York: McGraw Hill.

Krantzler, Nora J. 1987 Traditional Medicine as "Medical Neglect": Dilemmas in the Case Management of a Samoan Teenager with Diabetes. In *Child Survival: Cultural Perspectives on the Treatment and Maltreatment of Children,* ed. Nancy Scheper-Hughes, 325–337. Boston: D. Reidel.

Kroeber, A. L., and Clyde Kluckhohn. 1952 *Culture: A Critical Review of Concepts and Definitions.* New York: Vintage Books.

Kuipers, Joel C. 1990 *Power in Performance: The Creation of Textual Authority in Weyéwa Ritual Speech.* Philadelphia: University of Pennsylvania Press.

____. 1991 Matters of Taste in Weyéwa. In *The Varieties of Sensory Experience: A Sourcebook in the Anthropology of the Senses,* ed. David Howes, 111–127. Toronto: University of Toronto Press.

Kumar, Sanjay. 1996 Largest–ever World Bank Loan Mistrusted in India. *The Lancet* 347(April 20):1109.

Kurin, Richard. 1980 Doctor, Lawyer, Indian Chief. *Natural History* 89(11):6–24.

Kwiatkowski, Lynn M. 1998 *Struggling with Development: The Politics of Hunger and Gender in the Philippines.* Boulder: Westview Press.

Labov, William. 1966 *The Social Stratification of English in New York City.* Washington, DC: Center for Applied Linguistics.

Ladányi, János. 1993 Patterns of Residential Segregation and the Gypsy Minority in Budapest. *International Journal of Urbana and Regional Research* 17(1):30–41.

Laderman, Carol. 1988 A Welcoming Soil: Islamic Humoralism on the Malay Peninsula. In *Paths to Asian Medical Knowledge,* ed. Charles Leslie and Allan Young, 272–288. Berkeley: University of California Press.

LaFleur, William.1992 *Liquid Life: Abortion and Buddhism in Japan.* Princeton: Princeton University Press.

Lakoff, Robin. 1973 Language and Woman's Place. *Language in Society* 2:45–79.

___. 1990 *Talking Power: The Politics of Language in Our Lives.* New York: Basic Books.

Laliberte, Ron, and Vic Satzewich. 1999 Native Migrant Labour in the Southern Alberta Sugar-Beet Industry: Coercion and Paternalism in the Recruitment of Labour. *The Canadian Review of Sociology and Anthropology* 36:65.

Lambek, Michael. 1993 *Knowledge and Practice in Mayotte: Local Discourses of Islam, Sorcery, and Spirit Possession.* Toronto: University of Toronto Press.

Lamirande, T. 1999 Whale for the Killing: controversy erupts after Washington natives pursue a tradition. *First Perspectives* 8(6).

Lamphere, Louise. 1992 Introduction: The Shaping of Diversity. In *Structuring Diversity: Ethnographic Perspectives on the New Immigration,* ed. Louise Lamphere. Chicago: The University of Chicago Press.

Landes, Ruth. 1938 The Abnormal among the Ojibwa Indians. *Journal of Abnormal and Social Psychology* 33:14–33.

Landy, David 1985 Pibloktoq (Hysteria) and Inuit Nutrition: Possible Implication of Hypervitaminosis A. *Social Science and Medicine* 21(2):173–185.

Lansing, J. Stephen. 1995 *The Balinese.* Toronto: Harcourt Brace College Publishers.

Larsen, Clark Spenser, and George R. Milner. 1994 Bioanthropological Perspectives on Postcontact Traditions. In *In the Wake of Contact: Biological Responses to Conquest,* ed. Clark Spenser Larsen and George R. Milner, 1–8. New York: Wiley-Liss.

Laughlin, C. 1989 Brain, Culture and Evolution: Some Basic Issues in Neuroanthropology. In *A Different Drummer: Readings in Anthropology with a Canadian Perspective,* ed. B. Cox, J. Chevalier, and V. Blundell. Ottawa: Department of Sociology and Anthropology.

Laumann, Edward O., John H. Gagnon, Robert T. Michael, and Stuart Michaels. 1994 *The Social Organization of Sexuality: Sexual Practices in the United States.* Chicago: The University of Chicago Press.

Leach, Jerry W. 1975 *Trobriand Cricket: An Ingenious Response to Colonialism.* Video. Berkeley: University of California Extension Media.

Leacock. Eleanor. 1978 Women's Status in Egalitarian Society: Implications for Social Evolution. *Current Anthropology* 19(2):247–255.

___. 1993 Women in Samoan History: A Further Critique of Derek Freeman. In *Sex and Gender Hierarchies,* ed. Barbara D. Miller, 351–365. New York: Cambridge University Press.

Lebra, Takie. 1976 *Japanese Patterns of Behavior.* Honolulu: University of Hawaii Press.

Lee, Gary R., and Mindy Kezis. 1979 Family Structure and the Status of the Elderly. *Journal of Comparative Family Studies* 10:429–443.

Lee, Raymond M., and Claire M. Renzetti. 1993 *Researching Sensitive Topics.* Newbury Park, CA: Sage Publications.

Lee, Richard Borshay. 1969 Eating Christmas in the Kalahari. *Natural History* December.

___. 1979 *The !Kung San: Men, Women, and Work in a Foraging Society.* New York: Cambridge University Press.

Lee, Richard, and Richard Daly, eds. 1999 *The Cambridge Encyclopaedia of Hunters and Gatherers.* Cambridge: Cambridge University Press.

Lein, Laura, and Donald Brenneis. 1978 Children's Dispute in Three Speech Communities. *Language in Society* 7:299–323.

Lempert, David. 1996 *Daily Life in a Crumbling Empire.* 2 volumes. New York: Columbia University Press.

Lepowsky, Maria. 1993 *Fruit of the Motherland: Gender in an Egalitarian Society.* New York: Columbia University Press.

Lerer, Leonard. 1998 Who Is the Rogue? Hunger, Death, and Circumstance in John Mampe Square. In *Small Wars: The Cultural Politics of Childhood,* ed. Nancy Scheper-Hughes and Carolyn Sargent, 228–250. Berkeley: University of California Press.

Levinson, David. 1989 *Family Violence in Cross–Cultural Perspective.* Newbury Park, CA: Sage Publications.

Lévi-Strauss, Claude. 1967 *Structural Anthropology.* New York: Anchor Books.

___. 1968 *Tristes Tropiques: An Anthropological Study of Primitive Societies in Brazil.* New York: Atheneum.

___. 1969 [1949] *The Elementary Structures of Kinship.* Boston: Beacon Press.

Levy, Jerrold E., Eric B. Henderson, and Tracy J. Andrews. 1989 The Effects of Regional Variation and Temporal Change in Matrilineal Elements of Navajo Social Organization. *Journal of Anthropological Research* 45(4):351–377.

Lew, Irvina. 1994 Bathing as Science: Ancient Sea Cures Gain Support from New Research. *Condé Nast Traveler* 29(12):86–90.

Lewin, Ellen. 1993 *Lesbian Mothers: Accounts of Gender in American Culture.* Ithaca: Cornell University Press.

Lewis, Oscar. 1966 The Culture of Poverty. *Scientific American.* 215:19–25.

Leynaud, Emile. 1961 Fraternités d'âge et sociétés de culture dans la Haute-Vallée du Niger. *Cahiers d'Etudes Africaines* 6:41–68.

Leyton, Elliot. 1996 *Men of Blood: Murder in Everyday Life.* Toronto: McClelland & Stewart Inc.

Lindenbaum, Shirley. 1979 *Kuru Sorcery: Disease and Danger in the New Guinea Highlands.* Mountain View, CA: Mayfield Publishing Company.

Linnekan, Jocelyn. 1990 *Sacred Queens and Women of Consequence: Rank, Gender, and Colonialism in the Hawaiian Islands.* Ann Arbor: University of Michigan Press.

Little, Kenneth. 1966 The Strange Case of Romantic Love. *The Listener* 7(April).

___. 1991 On Safari; The Visual Politics of a Tourist Representation. In *The Varieties of Sensory Experience,* ed. D. Howes. Toronto: University of Toronto Press.

Littman, Mark. 1993 Office of Refugee Resettlement Monthly Data Report for September 1992. Washington, DC: Office of Refugee Resettlement.

Lloyd, Cynthia B. 1995 *Household Structure and Poverty: What Are the Connections? Working Papers, No. 74.* New York: The Population Council.

Lock, Margaret. 1993 *Encounters with Aging: Mythologies of Menopause in Japan and North America.* Berkeley: University of California Press.

___. 1996 Deadly Disputes: Ideologies and Brain Death in Japan. In *Organ Transplantation: Meanings and Realities,* ed. S. Youngner, R. Fox and L. O'Connell. Madison: University of Wisconsin Press.

Lock, M., and G. Bibeau. 1995 Healthy Disputes: Some Reflections on the Practice of Medical Anthropology in Canada. *Health and Canadian Society/Santé et Société Canadienne* 1(1):147–175.

Lock, Margaret, and Pamela Wakewich-Dunk. 1990 Nostalgia: Expression of Loss among Greek Immigrants in Montreal. *Canadian Family Physician* 36:253–258.

Lockwood, Victoria S. 1993 *Tahitian Transformation: Gender and Capitalist Development in a Rural Society.* Boulder: Lynne Reiner Publishers.

Loker, William. 1993 Human Ecology of Cattle-Raising in the Peruvian Amazon: The View from the Farm. *Human Organization* 52(1):14–24.

Louie, Andrea. 2000 Re-territorializing Transnationalism: Chinese Americans and the Chinese Motherland. *American Ethnologist* 27:645–669.

Lovell, N., and P. Lai. 1994 Lifestyle and Health of Voyageurs in the Canadian Fur Trade. In *Strength in Diversity: A Reader in Physical Anthropology,* ed. A.Herring and L.Chan. Toronto: Canadian Scholars Press.

Lovisek, J., T. Holzkamm, and L. Waisberg. 1997 Fatal Errors: Ruth Landes and the Creation of the "Atomistic Ojibwa". *Anthropologica* 39(1–2):133–145.

Low, Setha M. 1995 Indigenous Architecture and the Spanish American Plaza in Mesoamerica and the Caribbean. *American Anthropologist* 97(4):748–762.

Lu, Hanchao. 1995 Away from Nanking Road: Small Stores and Neighborhood Life in Modern Shanghai. *Journal of Asian Studies* 54(1):93–123.

Luhrmann, Tanya M. 1989 *Persuasions of the Witch's Craft: Ritual Magic in Contemporary England.* Cambridge: Harvard University Press.

Lutz, Catherine A. 1988 *Unnatural Emotions: Everyday Sentiments on a Micronesian Atoll and Their Challenge to Western Theory.* Chicago: University of Chicago Press.

MacDonald, George, and Stephen Alsford. 1989 *A museum for a golbal village: The Canadian Museum of Civilization.* Hull, Quebec: Canadian Museum of Civilization.

MacDonald, M. 2001. Postmodern Negotiations with Medical Technology: The role of Midwifery Clients in the New Midwifery in Canada. *Medical Anthropology* 20:245–276.

Maclachlan, Morgan. 1983 *Why They Did Not Starve: Biocultural Adaptation in a South Indian Village.* Philadelphia: Institute for the Study of Human Issues.

MacLeod, Arlene Elowe. 1992 Hegemonic Relations and Gender Resistance: The New Veiling as Accommodating Protest in Cairo. *Signs: The Journal of Women in Culture and Society* 17(3):533–557.

Magliore, Sam. 1983 Evil Eye or Delusions: On the "Consistency" of Folk Models. *Medical Anthropology Quarterly* 14(2):4–9.

Malinowski, Bronislaw. 1929 *The Sexual Life of Savages.* New York: Harcourt, Brace & World.

___. 1961 [1922] *Argonauts of the Western Pacific.* New York: E. P. Dutton & Co.

___. 1961 [1926] *Crime and Custom in Savage Society.* Paterson, NJ: Littlefield, Adams & Co.

Mamdani, Mahmoud. 1972 *The Myth of Population Control: Family, Caste, and Class in an Indian Village.* New York: Monthly Review Press.

Manning, Frank. 1981 Celebrating Cricket: The Symbolic Construction of Caribbean Politics. *American Ethnologist* 8:616–632.

Manning, Frank, ed. 1983 Consciousness and Inquiry: Ethnology and Canadian Realities. Canadian Ethnology Service, Paper No. 89e, Ottawa: National Museum of Man.

Manz, Beatriz. 1988 *Refugees of a Hidden War: The Aftermath of Counterinsurgency in Guatemala.* Albany: State University of New York Press.

Marano, L. 1982 Windigo Psychosis: The Anatomy of an Emic–Etic Confusion. *Current Anthropology* 23(4):385–397.

March, Kathryn S., and Rachelle L. Taqqu. 1986 *Women's Informal Associations in Developing Countries: Catalysts for Change?* Boulder: Westview Press.

Margolis, Maxine. 1984 *Mothers and Such: Views of American Women and Why They Changed.* Berkeley: University of California Press.

___. 1994 *Little Brazil: An Ethnography of Brazilian Immigrants in New York City.* Princeton: Princeton University Press.

Margolis, Maxine L., and Marigene Arnold. 1993 Turning the Tables? Male Strippers and the Gender Hierarchy in America. In *Sex and Gender Hierarchies,* ed. Barbara D. Miller, 334–350. New York: Cambridge University Press.

Marotz-Baden, Ramona, and Claudia Mattheis. 1994 Daughters–in–Law and Stress in Two–Generation Farm Families. *Family Relations* 43:132–137.

Marriott, McKim. 1965 *Caste Ranking and Community Structure in Five Regions of India and Pakistan.* Poona, India: Deccan College.

Marshall, Ingeborg. 1996 *A History and Ethnography of the Beothuk.* Montreal: McGill-Queen's University Press.

Marshall, Robert C. 1985 Giving a Gift to the Hamlet: Rank, Solidarity and Productive Exchange in Rural Japan. *Ethnology* 24:167–182.

Martin, Emily. 1987 *The Woman in the Body: A Cultural Analysis of Reproduction.* Boston: Beacon Press.

Martin, M. Kay, and Barbara Voorhies. 1975 *Female of the Species.* New York: Columbia University Press.

Martin, Richard C. 1995 Islam. In *The HarperCollins Dictionary of Religion,* ed. Jonathan Z. Smith, 498–513. New York: HarperCollins.

Martínez, Samuel. 1996 Indifference with Indignation: Anthropology, Human Rights, and the Haitian Bracero. *American Anthropologist* 98(1):17–25.

Marx, Karl, and Friedrich Engels. 1964 [1848] *The Communist Manifesto.* New York: Monthly Review Press.

Massiah, Joycelin. 1983 *Women as Heads of Households in the Caribbean: Family Structure and Feminine Status.* Paris: UNESCO.

Mathabane, Mark. 1986 *Kaffir Boy: The True Story of a Black Youth's Coming of Age in Apartheid South Africa.* New York: Plume.

Mathews, Holly F., Donald R. Lannin, and James P. Mitchell. 1994 Coming to Terms with Advanced Breast Cancer: Black Women's Narratives from Eastern North Carolina. *Social Science and Medicine* 38:789–800.

Mauss, Marcel. 1967 [1925] *The Gift: Forms and Functions of Exchange in Archaic Societies.* New York: W. W. Norton & Company.

Maybury-Lewis, David. 1997 *Indigenous Peoples, Ethnic Groups, and the State.* Boston: Allyn and Bacon.

Mayer, Adrian. 1960 *Caste and Kinship in Central India: A Village and Its Region.* Berkeley: University of California Press.

McCaghy, Charles H., and Charles Hou. 1994 Family Affiliation and Prostitution in a Cultural Context: Career Onsets of Taiwanese Prostitutes. *Archives of Sexual Behavior* 23:251–265.

McCoid, Catherine Hodge, and LeRoy D. McDermott. 1996 Toward Decolonizing Gender: Female Vision in the Upper Paleolithic. *American Anthropologist* 98(2):319–326.

McCracken, Grant. 1996 *Big Hair: A Journey into the Transformation of Self.* Woodstock, NY: The Overlook Press.

McDermott, LeRoy D. 1996 Self-Representation in Upper Paleolithic Female Figurines. *Current Anthropology* 37:227–275.

McDonald, G., and S. Alford. 1989 *Museum for the Global Village.* Hull, Quebec: Canadian Museum of Civilization.

McElroy, Ann, and Patricia K. Townsend. 1996 *Medical Anthropology in Ecological Perspective.* 3rd edition. Boulder: Westview Press.

McGrew, William C. 1998 Culture in Nonhuman Primates? *Annual Review of Anthropology* 27:301–328.

McKenna, James. 1993 Rethinking Healthy Infant Sleep. *Breastfeeding Abstracts* 12(3):27.

M'Closkey, Kathy. 1994 Marketing Multiple Myths: The Hidden History of Navajo Weaving. *Journal of the Southwest* 36(3):185–220.

___. 1996 Art or Craft?: The Paradox of the Pangnirtung Weave Shop. In *Women of the First Nations: Power, Wisdom and Strength,* ed. Christine Miller and Patricia Chuchryk, 113–126. Winnipeg: University of Manitoba Press.

McLellan, Janet. 1996 Silent Screams and Hidden Pain: Barriers to the Adaptation and Integration of Cambodian Women Refugees in Ontario. In *Development and Diaspora: Gender and the Refugee Experience,* ed. Wenona Giles, Helene Moussa, and Penny Van Esterik. Dundas, ON: Artemis Enterprises.

McLuhan, Marshall. 1964 *Understanding Media: The extensions of man.* New York: McGraw–Hill.

McMahon, April M. S. 1994 *Understanding Language Change.* New York: Cambridge University Press.

Mead, Margaret. 1961 [1928] *Coming of Age in Samoa: A Psychological Study of Primitive Youth for Western Civilization.* New York: Dell Publishing Company.

___. 1963 [1935] *Sex and Temperament in Three Primitive Societies.* New York: William Morrow.

___. 1977 *Letters from the Field 1925–1975.* New York: Harper & Row.

___. 1986 Field Work in the Pacific Islands, 1925–1967. In *Women in the Field: Anthropological Experiences,* ed. Peggy Golde, 293–331. Berkeley: University of California Press.

Mealing, S.R., ed. 1963 *The Jesuit Relations and allied documents; a selection.* Toronto: McClelland & Stewart.

Meigs, Anna S. 1984 *Food, Sex, and Pollution: A New Guinea Religion.* New Brunswick: Rutgers University Press.

Mencher, Joan P. 1965 The Nayars of South Malabar. In *Comparative Family Systems,* ed. Meyer F. Nimkoff, 163–191. Boston: Houghton Mifflin Company.

___. 1974 The Caste System Upside Down, or The Not–So–Mysterious East. *Current Anthropology* 15(4):469–49.

Mernissi, Fatima. 1987 *Beyond the Veil: Male–Female Dynamics in Modern Muslim Society.* Revised edition. Bloomington: Indiana University Press.

___. 1995 *Dreams of Trespass: Tales of a Harem Girlhood.* New York: Addison–Wesley.

Merry, Sally Engle. 1992 Anthropology, Law, and Transnational Processes. *Annual Review of Anthropology* 21:357–379.

Messer, Ellen. 1993 Anthropology and Human Rights. *Annual Review of Anthropology* 22:221–249.

Meyerhoff, Miriam. 1999 *Sorry* in the Pacific: Defining Communities, Defining Practice. *Language in Society* 28:225–238.

Michaelson, Evalyn Jacobson, and Walter Goldschmidt. 1971 Female Roles and Male Dominance among Peasants. *Southwestern Journal of Anthropology* 27:330–352.

Milgram, B. Lynne. 1999 Crafts, Cultivation and Household Economies: Women's Work and Positions in Ifugao, Upland Philippines. In *Research in Economic Anthropology,* ed. Barry Issac. Greenwich, CT.: JAI Press.

Miller, Barbara D. 1997 [1981] *The Endangered Sex: Neglect of Female Children in Rural North India.* Ithaca, NY: Cornell University Press.

___. 1987a Social Patterns of Food Expenditure among Low-Income Jamaicans. In *Papers and Recommendations of the Workshop on Food and Nutrition Security in Jamaica in the 1908s and Beyond,* ed. Kenneth A. Leslie and Lloyd B. Rankine, 13–33. Kingston, Jamaica: Caribbean Food and Nutrition Institute.

___. 1987b Female Infanticide and Child Neglect in Rural North India. In *Child Survival: Anthropological Perspectives on the Treatment and Maltreatment of Children,* ed. Nancy Scheper-Hughes, 95–113. Boston: D. Reidel Publishing Company.

___. 1993 Surveying the Anthropology of Sex and Gender Hierarchies. In *Sex and Gender Hierarchies,* ed. Barbara D. Miller, 3–31. New York: Cambridge University Press.

Miller, Barbara D., and Showkat Hayat Khan. 1986 Incorporating Voluntarism into Rural Development in Bangladesh. *Third World Planning Review* 8(2):139–152.

Miller, Barbara D., and Carl Stone. 1983 The Low-Income Household Expenditure Survey: Description and Analysis. Jamaica Tax Structure Examination Project, Staff Paper No. 25. Syracuse, NY: Metropolitan Studies Program, Syracuse University.

Millett, Kate. 1994 *The Politics of Cruelty: An Essay on the Literature of Political Imprisonment.* New York: Norton.

Mills, Mary Beth. 1995 Attack of the Widow Ghosts: Gender, Death, and Modernity in Northeast Thailand. In *Bewitching Women, Pious Men: Gender and Body Politics in Southeast Asia,* ed. Aihwa Ong and Michael G. Peletz, 244–273. Berkeley: University of California Press.

Millward, Hugh. 1996. Greater Halifax: Public Policy Issues in the Post 1960 Period. *Canadian Journal of Urban Research* 5(1):1–17.

Milton, Katharine. 1992 Civilization and Its Discontents. *Natural History* 3/92:37–92.

Miner, Horace. 1965 [1956] Body Ritual among the Nacirema. In *Reader in Comparative Religion: An Anthropological Approach,* ed. William A. Lessa and Evon Z. Vogt, 414–418. New York: Harper & Row.

Mines, Mattison. 1994 *Public Faces, Private Voices: Community and Individuality in South India.* Berkeley: University of California Press.

Mintz, Sidney. 1985 *Sweetness and Power: The Place of Sugar in Modern History.* New York: Penguin Books.

Mir-Hosseini, Ziba. 1993 *Marriage on Trial: A Study of Islamic Family Law: Iran and Morocco Compared.* New York: I. B. Tauris & Co. Ltd.

Mitchell, Bruce. 1994 Sustainable Development at the Village Level in Bali, Indonesia. *Human Ecology* 22(2):189–211.

Mitter, Partha. 1977 *Much Maligned Monsters: A History of European Reactions to Indian Art.* Chicago: University of Chicago Press.

Modell, Judith S. 1994 *Kinship with Strangers: Adoption and Interpretations of Kinship in American Culture.* Berkeley: University of California Press.

Moerman, Daniel E. 1979 Anthropology of Symbolic Healing. *Current Anthropology* 20:59–80.

___. 1983 General Medical Effectiveness and Human Biology: Placebo Effects in the Treatment of Ulcer Disease. *Medical Anthropology Quarterly* 14:13–16.

___. 1992 Minding the Body: The Placebo Effect Unmasked. In *Given the Body Its Due,* ed. M. Sheets-Johnstone, 69–84. Albany, NY: State University of New York Press.

Morgan, Lewis Henry. 1851 *The League of the [Ho-de-ne-sau, or] Iroquois.* New York: Russell Sage.

Morgan, William. 1977 Navaho Treatment of Sickness: Diagnosticians. In *Culture, Disease, and Healing: Studies in Medical Anthropology*, ed. David Landy, 163–168. New York: Macmillan.

Morris, Rosalind. 1994a *New Worlds from Fragments: Film, Ethnography and the Representation of Northwest Coast Culture.* Boulder: Wesview Press.

___. 1994b Three Sexes and Four Sexualities: Redressing the Discourses on Gender and Sexuality in Contemporary Thailand. *Positions* 2:15–43.

Morrison, David. 2000 Canadian Aid: A Mixed Record and an Uncertain Future. In *Transforming Development: Foreign Aid for a Changing World,* ed. J. Freedman. Toronto: University of Toronto Press.

Morrison, L., S. Guruge, and K. Snarr. 1999 Sri Lankan Tamil Immigrants in Toronto: Gender, Marriage Patterns, and Sexuality. In *Gender and Immigration,* ed. Gregory A. Kelson and Debra L. Delaet, 144–162. London: Macmillan Press.

Mortland, Carol A. 1994 Khmer Buddhism in the United States: Ultimate Questions. In *Cambodian Culture Since 1975: Homeland and Exile,* ed. May M. Ebihara, Carol A. Mortalnd, and Judy Ledgerwood, 72–90. Ithaca: Cornell University Press.

Motyl, Alexander J. 1993 *Dilemmas of Independence: Ukraine After Totalitarianism.* New York: Council on Foreign Relations Press.

Moynihan, Elizabeth B. 1979 *Paradise as a Garden in Persia and Mughal India.* New York: George Braziller.

Muecke, Marjorie A. 1987 Resettled Refugees: Reconstruction of Identity of Lao in Seattle. *Urban Anthropology* 16(3–4):273–289.

Mull, Dorothy S., and J. Dennis Mull. 1987 Infanticide among the Tarahumara of the Mexican Sierra Madre. In *Child Survival: Anthropological Perspectives on the Treatment and Maltreatment of Children,* ed. Nancy Scheper–Hughes, 113–132. Boston: D. Reidel Publishing Company.

Munachonga, Monica. 1988 Income Allocation and Marriage Options in Urban Zambia. In *A Home Divided: Women and Income in the Third World,* ed. Daisy Dwyer and Judith Bruce, 173–194. Stanford: Stanford University Press.

Murcott, Anne. 1993 [1983] "It's a Pleasure to Cook for Him": Food, Mealtimes and Gender in Some South Wales Households. In *Gender in Cross-Cultural Perspective,* ed. Caroline B. Brettell and Carolyn F. Sargent, 77–87. Englewood Cliffs, NJ: Prentice Hall.

Murdock, George Peter. 1965 [1949] *Social Structure.* New York: The Free Press.

Murphy, Yolanda, and Robert F. Murphy. 1985 *Women of the Forest.* New York: Columbia University Press.

Murray, David. 2002 *Opacity: Gender, Sexuality, Race and the Problem of "Identity" in Martinique.* New York: Peter Lang Publishing.

Mustanoja, Ulla Marjata, and Kari J. Mustanoja. 1993 Resettlement after Involuntary Displacement: The Karelians in Finland. In *Anthropological Approaches to Resettlement: Policy, Practice, and Theory,* ed. Michael M. Cernea and Scott E. Guggenheim, 87–108. Boulder: Westview Press.

Myerhoff, Barbara. 1978 *Number Our Days.* New York: Simon and Schuster.

Myers, James. 1992 Nonmainstream Body Modification: Genital Piercing, Branding, Burning, and Cutting. *Journal of Contemporary Ethnography* 21(3):267–306.

Myers–Scotton, Carol. 1993 *Social Motivations for Code–Switching.* New York: Oxford University Press.

Nader, Laura. 1972 Up the Anthropologist-Perspectives Gained from Studying Up. In *Reinventing Anthropology,* ed. Dell Hymes, 284–311. New York: Vintage Books.

___. 1995 Civilization and Its Negotiations. In *Understanding Disputes: The Politics of Argument,* ed. Pat Caplan, 39–64. Providence, RI: Berg Publishers.

Nag, Moni. 1963 *Factors Affecting Human Fertility in Nonindustrial Societies: A Cross-Cultural Study.* New Haven: Human Relations Area Files Press.

___. 1972 Sex, Culture and Human Fertility: India and the United States. *Current Anthropology* 13:231–238.

___. 1983 Modernization Affects Fertility. *Populi* 10:56–77.

Nag, Moni, Benjamin N. F. White, and R. Creighton Peet. 1978 An Anthropological Approach to the Study of the Economic Value of Children in Java and Nepal. *Current Anthropology* 19(2):293–301.

Nagata, Judith. 1984 *The Reflowering of Malaysian Islam: Modern Religious Radicals and Their Roots.* Vancouver: University of British Columbia Press.

Nanda, Serena. 1990 *Neither Man Nor Woman: The Hijras of India.* Belmont, CA: Wadsworth Publishing Company.

___. 1994 *Cultural Anthropology.* Wadsworth, CA: Wadsworth Publishing Company.

Neale, Walter C. 1976 *Monies in Societies.* San Francisco: Chandler & Sharp Publishers, Inc.

Nelson, Sarah. 1993 Gender Hierarchies and the Queens of Silla. In *Sex and Gender Hierarchies,* ed. Barbara D. Miller, 297–315. New York: Cambridge University Press.

Netting, Robert McC. 1989 Smallholders, Householders, Freeholders: Why the Family Farm Works Well Worldwide. In *The Household Economy: Reconsidering the Domestic Mode of Production,* ed. Richard R. Wilk, 221–244. Boulder: Westview Press.

Neusner, Jacob. 1995 Judaism. In *The HarperCollins Dictionary of Religion,* Jonathan Z. Smith, 598–607. New York: HarperCollins.

Ngokwey, Ndolamb. 1988 Pluralistic Etiological Systems in Their Social Context: A Brazilian Case Study. *Social Science and Medicine* 26:793–802.

Nichter, Mark. 1992 Of Ticks, Kings, Spirits and the Promise of Vaccines. In *Paths to Asian Medical Knowledge*, ed. Leslie Charles and Allan Young, 224–253. Berkeley: University of California Press.

___. 1996 Vaccinations in the Third World: A Consideration of Community Demand. In *Anthropology and International Health: Asian Case Studies*, ed. Mark Nichter and Mimi Nichter, 329–365. Amsterdam: Gordon and Breach Publishers.

Nichter, Mark, and Mimi Nichter, eds. 1996 *Anthropology and International Health: Asian Case Studies*. Amsterdam: Gordon and Breach Publishers.

Nichter, Mimi, and Nancy Vuckovic. 1994 Fat Talk: Body Image among Adolescent Girls. In *Many Mirrors: Body Image and Social Relations*, ed. Nicole Sault, 109–131. New Brunswick: Rutgers University Press.

Nicks, Trudy. 1992 Partnerships in Developing Cultural Resources: Lessons from the Task Force on Museums and First Peoples. *Culture* 12(1):87–94.

Nieves, Isabel. 1979 Household Arrangements and Multiple Jobs in San Salvador. *Signs: Journal of Women in Culture and Society* 5:134–142.

Nodwell, Evelyn, and Neil Guppy. 1992 The Effects of Publicly Displayed Ethnicity on Interpersonal Discrimination: Indo–Canadians in Vancouver. *The Canadian Review of Sociology and Anthropology* 29(1):87–99.

Nordstrom, Carolyn, and Antonius C. G. M. Robben, eds. 1995 *Fieldwork under Fire: Contemporary Studies of Violence and Survival*. Berkeley: University of California Press.

Norgaard, Richard B. 1994 *Development Betrayed: The End of Progress and the Coevolutionary Revisioning of the Future*. New York: Routledge.

Obeyesekere, Gananath. 1981 *Medusa's Hair: An Essay on Personal Symbols and Religious Experience*. Chicago: University of Chicago Press.

Ochs, Elinor. 1990 Indexicality and Socialization. In *Cultural Psychology: Essays on Comparative Human Development*, ed. James W. Stigler, Richard A. Shweder, and Gilbert Herdt, 287–308. New York: Cambridge University Press.

Ohnuki–Tierney, Emiko. 1994 Brain Death and Organ Transplantation: Cultural Bases of Medical Technology. *Current Anthropology* 35(3):233–242.

Oinas, Felix J. 1993 Couvade in Estonia. *Slavic & East European Journal* 37(3):339–345.

Okely, Judith. 1993 [1984] Fieldwork in the Home Counties. In *Talking about People: Readings in Contemporary Cultural Anthropology*, ed. William A. Haviland and Robert J. Gordon, 4–6. Mountain View, CA: Mayfield Publishing Company.

Olujic, Maria B. 1998 Children in Extremely Difficult Circumstances: War and Its Aftermath in Croatia. In *Small Wars: The Cultural Politics of Childhood*, ed. Nancy Scheper–Hughes and Carolyn Sargent, 318–330. Berkeley: University of California Press.

Omvedt, Gail. 1995 *Dalit Visions: The Anti–Caste Movement and the Construction of an Indian Identity*. New Delhi: Orient Longman/Tracts for the Times/8.

Ong, Aihwa. 1987 *Spirits of Resistance and Capitalist Discipline: Factory Women in Malaysia*. Albany: State University of New York Press.

___. 1995 State versus Islam: Malay Families, Women's Bodies, and the Body Politic in Malaysia. In *Bewitching Women, Pious Men: Gender and Body Politics in Southeast Asia*, ed. Aihwa Ong and Michael G. Peletz, 159–194. Berkeley: University of California Press.

Ongley, Patrick. 1995 Post–1945 International Migration: New Zealand, Australia and Canada Compared. *International Migration Review* 29(3):765–793.

Ortner, Sherry B. 1974 Is Female to Male as Nature Is to Culture? In *Woman, Culture and Society*, ed. Michelle Zimbalist Rosaldo and Louise Lamphere, 67–88. Stanford: Stanford University Press.

Oxfeld, Ellen. 1993 *Blood, Sweat and Mahjong: Family and Enterprise in an Overseas Chinese Community*. Ithaca: Cornell University Press.

Pahl, Jan. 1980 Patterns of Money Management within Marriage. *Journal of Social Policy* 9(3):313–335.

___. 1983 The Allocation of Money and the Structuring of Inequality within Marriage. *Sociological Review* 31(2):1983.

Painter, Andrew A. 1996 The Telerepresentation of Gender. In *Re–Imaging Japanese Women*, ed. Anne E. Imamura, 46–72. Berkeley: University of California Press.

Pappas, Gregory. 1989 *The Magic City: Unemployment in a Working–Class Community*. Ithaca: Cornell University Press.

Park, Michael Alan. 1996 *Biological Anthropology*. Mountain View, CA: Mayfield Publishing Company.

Parker, Richard G. 1991 *Bodies, Pleasures, and Passions: Sexual Culture in Contemporary Brazil*. Boston: Beacon Press.

Parry, Jonathan P. 1966 Caste. In *The Social Science Encyclopedia*, ed. Adam Kuper and Jessica Kuper, 76–77. New York: Routledge.

Peacock, James L. 1986 *The Anthropological Lens: Harsh Light, Soft Focus*. New York: Cambridge University Press.

Peacock, James L., and Dorothy C. Holland. 1993 The Narrated Self: Life Stories in Process. *Ethos* 21(4):367–383.

Peattie, Lisa Redfield. 1968 *The View from the Barrio*. Ann Arbor: University of Michigan Press.

Pechman, Joseph A. 1987 Introduction: Recent Developments. In *Comparative Tax Systems: Europe, Canada, and Japan*, ed. Joseph A. Pechman, 1–32. Arlington, VA: Tax Analysts.

Pedelty, Mark. 1995 *War Stories: The Culture of Foreign Correspondents*. New York: Routledge.

Peletz, Michael. 1987 The Exchange of Men in 19th-Century Negeri Sembilan (Malaya). *American Ethnologist* 14(3):449–469.

Pelto, Pertti. 1973 *The Snowmobile Revolution: Technology and Social Change in the Arctic*. Menlo Park, CA: Cummings.

Pelto, Pertti, Maria Roman, and Nelson Liriano. 1982 Family Structures in An Urban Puerto Rican Community. *Urban Anthropology* 11:39–58.

Pendergast, David M, Grant D. Jones, and Elizabeth Graham. 1993 Locating Spanish Colonial Towns in the Maya Lowlands: A Case Study from Belize. *Latin American Antiquity* 4(1):59–73.

Phillips, Lynne. 1998 Dissecting Globalization: Women's Space–Time in the Other America. In *Transgressing Borders: Critical Perspectives on Gender, Household, and Culture,* ed. Susan Ilcan and Lynne Phillips. Westport, CT.: Bergin & Garvey.

Piddocke, Stuart. 1969 The Potlatch System of the Southern Kwakiutl: A New Perspective. In *Environment and Cultural Behavior: Ecological Studies in Cultural Anthropology,* ed. Andrew P. Vayda, 130–156. Garden City, NY: The Natural History Press.

Pigg, Stacey. 1996 The Credible and the Credulous: the question of villagers' beliefs in Nepal. *Cultural Anthropology* 11:160–201.

___. 2001 The Politics of Development and the Politics of Health: Contradictions of AIDS Prevention in Nepal. *Anthropologie -et- Societes* 25(1):43–62.

Pillsbury, Barbara. 1990 The Politics of Family Planning: Sterilization and Human Rights in Bangladesh. In *Births and Power: Social Change and the Politics of Reproduction,* ed. W. Penn Handwerker, 165–196. Boulder: Westview Press.

Plant, Roger. 1994 *Land Rights and Minorities.* London: Minority Rights Group.

Plattner, Stuart. 1989 Markets and Marketplaces. In *Economic Anthropology,* ed. Stuart Plattner, 171–208. Stanford: Stanford University Press.

Poirier, Sylvie. 1992 "Nomadic" Rituals: Networks of Ritual Exchange between Women of the Australian Western Desert. *Man* 27:757–776.

Ponting, J. Rick, and Jerilynn Kiely. 1997 Disempowerment: "Justice," Racism, and Public Opinion. In *First Nations in Canada: Perspectives on Opportunity, Empowerment, and Self-Determination,* ed. J. Rick Ponting. Toronto: McGraw–Hill Ryerson.

Pospisil, Leopold. 1979 Legally Induced Cultural Change in New Guinea. In *The Imposition of Law,* ed. Sandra B. Bruman and Barbara E. Harrell-Bond. New York: Academic Press.

Postgate, Nicholas, Tao Wang, and Toby Wilkinson. 1995 The Evidence for Early Writing: Utilitarian or Ceremonial? *Antiquity* 69:459–480.

Potvin, Maryse. 1999 Second Generation Haitian Youth in Quebec: Between the "Real" Community and the "Represented" Community. *Canadian Ethnic Studies* 31(1):43–72.

Pratt, Mary Louise. 1992 *Imperial Eyes: Travel Writing and Transculturation.* London: Routledge.

Price, David H. 1995 Water Theft in Egypt's Fayoum Oasis: Emics, Etics, and the Illegal. In *Science, Materialism, and the Study of Culture,* ed. Martin F. Murphy and Maxine L. Margolis, 96–110. Gainesville: University of Florida Press.

Price, John A. 1979 *Indians of Canada: Cultural Dynamics.* Scarborough, ON: Prentice-Hall of Canada, Ltd.

Prince, Raymond. 1985 The Concept of Culture–Bound Syndromes: Anorexia Nervosa and Brain–Fag. *Social Science and Medicine* 21(2):197–203.

Purdum, Elizabeth D., and J. Anthony Paredes. 1989 *Facing the Death Penalty: Essays on Cruel and Unusual Punishment.* Philadelphia: Temple University Press.

Radcliffe-Brown, A. R. 1964 [1922] *The Andaman Islanders.* New York: The Free Press.

Radin, Paul. 1963 [1920] *The Autobiography of a Winnebago Indian: Life, Ways, Acculturation, and the Peyote Cult.* New York: Dover Publications.

Raheja, Gloria Goodwin. 1988 *The Poison in the Gift: Ritual, Prestation, and the Dominant Caste in a North Indian Village.* Chicago: University of Chicago Press.

Rahnema, Majid. 1992 Poverty. In *The Development Dictionary: A Guide to Knowledge and Power,* ed. Wolfgang Sachs, 159–176. Atlantic Highlands, NJ: Zed Press.

Ramesh, A., C. R. Srikumari, and S. Sukumar. 1989 Parallel Cousin Marriages in Madras, Tamil Nadu: New Trends in Dravidian Kinship. *Social Biology* 36(3–4):248–254.

Ramphele, Mamphela. 1996 Political Widowhood in South Africa: The Embodiment of Ambiguity. *Daedalus* 125(1):99–17.

Rapoport, Tamar, Yoni Garb, and Anat Penso. 1995 Religious Socialization and Female Subjectivity: Religious-Zionist Adolescent Girls in Israel. *Sociology of Education* 68:48–61.

Rapp, Rayna. 1993 Reproduction and Gender Hierarchy: Amniocentesis in America. In *Sex and Gender Hierarchies,* ed. Barbara D. Miller, 108–126. New York: Cambridge University Press.

Rappaport, Roy. 1968 *Pigs for the Ancestors.* New Haven: Yale University Press.

Rathgeber, Eva M. 1990 WID, WAD, GAD: Trends in Research and Practice. *Journal of Developing Areas* 24:489–502.

Rathje, William, and Cullen Murphy. 1992 *Rubbish! The Archaeology of Garbage.* New York: Harper & Row.

Reiner, R. 1996 Police. In *The Social Science Encyclopedia,* ed. Adam Kuper and Jessica Kuper, 619–621. New York: Routledge.

Reyna, Stephen P. 1994 A Mode of Domination Approach to Organized Violence. In *Studying War: Anthropological Perspectives,* ed. S. P. Reyna and R. E. Downs, 29–65. Langhorne, PA: Gordon and Breach Science Publishers.

Rich, Adrienne. 1980 Compulsory Heterosexuality and Lesbian Existence. *Signs* 5:631–660.

Rich, Bruce. 1994 *Mortgaging the Earth: The World Bank, Environmental Impoverishment, and the Crisis of Development.* Boston: Beacon Press.

Riddington, Robin. 1990 *Little Bit Know Something: Stories in a Language of Anthropology.* Iowa City: University of Iowa Press.

Robben, Antonius C. G. M., and Carolyn Nordstrom. 1995 The Anthropology and Ethnography of Violence and Sociopolitical Conflict. In *Fieldwork under Fire: Contemporary Studies of Violence and Survival,* ed. Carolyn Nordstrom and Antonius C. G. M. Robben, 1–25. Berkeley: University of California Press.

Robertson, Carol E. 1987 Power and Gender in the Musical Experiences of Women. In *Women and Music in Cross-Cultural Perspective,* ed. Ellen Koskoff, 225–244. New York: Greenwood Press.

Robertson, Jennifer. 1991 *Native and Newcomer: Making and Remaking a Japanese City.* Berkeley: University of California Press.

Robson, Colin. 1993 *Real World Research: A Resource for Social Scientists and Practitioner-Researchers.* Cambridge, MA: Blackwell Publishers.

Rodman, Margaret. 1992 Empowering Place: Multilocality and Multivocality. *American Anthropologist* 94(3):640–56.

Rodman, Margaret, Patti Hall Hawkins, and Daniel Teramura. 1998 It's Not Over: Vari Hall as Contested Academic Space at York University. *Canadian Journal of Urban Research* 7(1):47–71.

Rogers, Barbara. 1979 *The Domestication of Women: Discrimination in Developing Societies.* New York: St. Martin's Press.

Rohde, J.E. 1982 Mother's Milk and the Indonesian Economy: A Major National Resource. *Journal of Tropical Pediatrics* 28:166–174.

Romalis, Shelly, ed. 1981 *Childbirth, alternative to medical control.* Austin: University of Texas Press.

Rosaldo, Renato. 1980 *Ilongot Headhunting 1883–1974: A Study in Society and History.* Stanford: Stanford University Press.

Roscoe, Will. 1991 *The Zuni Man-Woman.* Albuquerque: University of New Mexico Press.

Rose, Jerome C., Thomas J. Green, and Victoria D. Green. 1996 NAGPRA is Forever: Osteology and the Repatriation of Skeletons. *Annual Review of Anthropology* 25:81–103.

Roseman, Marina. 1987 Inversion and Conjuncture: Male and Female Performance among the Temiar of Peninsular Malaysia. In *Women and Music in Cross-Cultural Perspective,* ed. Ellen Koskoff, 131–149. New York: Greenwood Press.

Rosenberg, Harriet G. 1988 *A Negotiated World: Three Centuries of Change in a French Alpine Community.* Toronto: University of Toronto Press.

Rosenberg, Lisa. 1996 Determination/Despair: Agunot Speak About Their Chains. *Canadian Woman Studies/Les Cahiers De La Femme* 16(4):69–73.

Rosenberger, Nancy. 1992 Images of the West: Home Style in Japanese Magazines. In *Re-made in Japan: Everyday Life and Consumer Taste in a Changing Society,* ed. James J. Tobin, 106–125. New Haven: Yale University Press.

Rosenblatt, Paul C., Patricia R. Walsh, and Douglas A. Jackson. 1976 *Grief and Mourning in Cross-Cultural Perspective.* New Haven: HRAF Press.

Rouland, Norbert. 1994 *Legal Anthropology.* Trans. Philippe G. Planel. Stanford: Stanford University Press.

Rubel, Arthur J., Carl W. O'Nell, and Rolando Collado-Ardón. 1984. *Susto: A Folk Illness.* Berkeley: University of California Press.

Rubin, Gayle. 1975 The Traffic in Women: Notes on the "Political Economy" of Sex. In *Toward an Anthropology of Women,* ed. Rayna R. Rapp, 157–210. New York: Monthly Review Press.

Ryan, Joan. 1995 *Doing Things the Right Way.* Calgary: University of Calgary Press.

Sachs, Aaron. 1996 Dying for Oil. *WorldWatch* June:10–21.

Saggers, Sherry, and Dennis Gray. 1998 *Dealing with Alcohol: Indigenous Usage in Australia, New Zealand and Canada.* New York: Cambridge University Press.

Sahlins, Marshall. 1963 Poor Man, Rich Man, Big Man, Chief. *Comparative Studies in Society and History* 5:285–303.

___. 1972 *Stone Age Economics.* Chicago: Aldine de Gruyter.

Said, Edward W. 1979 [1978] *Orientalism.* New York: Vintage Books.

Saitoti, Tepilit Ole. 1986 *The Worlds of a Maasai Warrior.* New York: Random House.

Salam, Nawaf A. 1994 Between Repatriation and Resettlement: Palestinian Refugees in Lebanon. *Journal of Palestine Studies* 24(1):18–27.

Salisbury, Richard 1983 The Social Structure of an Unorganized Society: Beyond Intentions and Peripheral Boasians. In *Consciousness and Inquiry: Ethnology and Canadian Realities,* ed. F. Manning. Canadian Ethnology Service, Paper No. 89e. Ottawa: National Museum of Man.

___. 1986 *A Homeland for the Cree: Regional Development in James Bay, 1971–1981.* Montreal: McGill-Queen's University Press.

Sanday, Peggy Reeves. 1973 Toward a Theory of the Status of Women. *American Anthropologist* 75:1682–1700.

___. 1986 *Divine Hunger: Cannibalism as a Cultural System.* New York: Cambridge University Press.

___. 1990 *Fraternity Gang Rape: Sex, Brotherhood, and Privilege on Campus.* New York: New York University Press.

Sanders, William B. 1994 *Gangbangs and Drive-Bys: Grounded Culture and Juvenile Gang Violence.* New York: Aldine de Gruyter.

Sanjek, Roger. 1990a A Vocabulary for Fieldnotes. In *Fieldnotes: The Making of Anthropology,* ed. Roger Sanjek, 92–138. Ithaca: Cornell University Press.

___. 1990b Maid Servants and Market Women's Apprentices in Adabraka. In *At Work in Homes: Household Workers in World Perspective,* ed. Roger Sanjek and Shellee Colleen, 35–62. American Ethnological Society Monograph Series, Number 3. Washington, DC: American Anthropological Association.

___. 1994 The Enduring Inequalities of Race. In *Race,* ed. Steven Gregory and Roger Sanjek, 1–17. New Brunswick, NJ: Rutgers University Press.

___. 2000 Keeping Ethnography Alive in an Urbanizing World. *Human Organization* 53:280–288.

Sankoff, D., and S. Laberge. 1978 The Linguistic Market and the Statistical Explanation of Variability. In *Linguistic Variation: Models and Methods,* ed. D. Sankoff, 239–250. New York: Academic Press.

Santiago, Esmeralda. 1993 *When I Was Puerto Rican.* New York: Vintage Books.

Saul, John Ralston. 1997 *Reflections of a Siamese Twin at the End of the Twentieth Century.* Toronto: Viking.

Sault, Nicole L. 1985 Baptismal Sponsorship as a Source of Power for Zapotec Women of Oaxaca, Mexico. *Journal of Latin American Lore* 11(2):225–243.

___. 1994 How the Body Shapes Parenthood: "Surrogate" Mothers in the United States and Godmothers in Mexico. In *Many Mirrors: Body Image and Social Relations,* ed. Nicole Sault, 292–318. Rutgers: Rutgers University Press.

Savishinsky, Joel S. 1974 *The Trail of the Hare: Life and Stress in an Arctic Community.* New York: Gordon and Breach.

___. 1991 *The Ends of Time: Life and Work in a Nursing Home.* New York: Bergin & Garvey.

Scheper-Hughes, Nancy. 1979 *Saints, Scholars, and Schizophrenics: Mental Illness in Rural Ireland.* Berkeley: University of California Press.

___. 1990 Three Propositions for a Critically Applied Medical Anthropology. *Social Science and Medicine* 30(2):189–197.

___. 1993 *Death without Weeping: The Violence of Everyday Life in Brazil.* Berkeley: University of California Press.

Schlegel, Alice. 1995 A Cross Cultural Approach to Adolescence. *Ethos* 23(1):15–32.

Schlegel, Alice, and Herbert Barry III. 1991 *Adolescence: An Anthropological Inquiry.* New York: Free Press.

Schmid, Thomas J., and Richard S. Jones. 1993 Ambivalent Actions: Prison Adaptation Strategies of First-Time, Short-term Inmates. *Journal of Contemporary Ethnography* 21(4):439–463.

Schneider, David M. 1968 *American Kinship: A Cultural Account.* Englewood Cliffs, NJ: Prentice-Hall.

Scott, Colin. 2001 *Aboriginal Autonomy and Development in Northern Quebec and Labrador.* Vancouver: UBC Press.

Scott, James C. 1985 *Weapons of the Weak: Everyday Forms of Peasant Resistance.* New Haven: Yale University Press.

Scrimshaw, Susan. 1984 Infanticide in Human Populations: Societal and Individual Concerns. In *Infanticide: Comparative and Evolutionary Perspectives,* ed. Glenn Hausfater and Sarah Blaffer Hardy, 463–486. New York: Aldine Publishing Company.

Scudder, Thayer. 1973 The Human Ecology of Big Dam Projects: River Basin Development and Resettlement. *Annual Review of Anthropology* 2:45–55.

Sen, Amartya. 1981 *Poverty and Famines: An Essay on Entitlement and Deprivation.* New York: Oxford University Press.

Sen, Mala. 1991 *India's Bandit Queen: The True Story of Phoolan Devi.* New Delhi: Indus/HarperCollins.

Sentumbwe, Nayinda. 1995 Sighted Lovers and Blind Husbands: Experience of Blind Women in Uganda. In *Disability and Culture,* ed. Benedicte Ingstad and Susan Reynolds, 159–173. Berkeley: University of California Press.

Shankman, Paul, and Tracy Bachrach Ehlers. 2000 The "Exotic" and the "Domestic": Regions and Representations in Cultural Anthropology. *Human Organization* 59:289–299.

Sharff, Jagna-Wojcicka. 1995 "We Are All Chickens for the Colonel": A Cultural Materialist View of Prisons. In *Science, Materialism and the Study of Culture,* ed. Martin F. Murphy and Maxine L. Margolis, 132–158. Gainesville: University Press of Florida.

Sharp, Lesley. 1990 Possessed and Dispossessed Youth: Spirit Possession of School Children in Northwest Madagascar. *Culture, Medicine and Psychiatry* 14:339–364.

Shell-Duncan, Bettina, and Ylva Hernlund. 2000 Female "Circumcision" in: Dimensions of the Practice and Debates. In *Female "Circumcision" in Africa: Culture, Controversy, and Change,* ed. Bettina Shell-Duncan and Ylva Hernlund, 1–40. Boulder, CO: Lynne Reiner Publishers.

Shenhav-Keller, Shelly. 1993 The Israeli Souvenir: Its Text and Context. *Annals of Tourism Research* 20:182–196.

Sheriff, Robin E. 2000 Exposing Silence as Cultural Censorship: A Brazilian Case. *American Anthropologist* 102:114–132.

Shibamoto, Janet. 1987 The Womanly Woman: Manipulation of Stereotypical and Nonstereotypical Features of Japanese Female Speech. In *Language, Gender, and Sex in Comparative Perspective,* ed. Susan U. Philips, Susan Steel, and Christine Tanz, 26–49. New York: Cambridge University Press.

Shifflett, Peggy A., and William A. McIntosh. 1986–1987 Food Habits and Future Time: An Exploratory Study of Age-Appropriate Food Habits among the Elderly. *International Journal of Aging and Human Development* 24(1):2–15.

Shik, Angela W.Y. 1995 Visa-00000 Students from Hong Kong: Adaptation and Mental Health. Master of Science dissertation. University of Toronto.

Short, James F. 1996 Gangs. In *The Social Science Encyclopedia,* ed. Adam Kuper and Jessica Kuper, 325–326. New York: Routledge.

Shostak, Marjorie. 1981 *Nisa: The Life and Times of a !Kung Woman.* Cambridge, MA: Harvard University Press.

Shu-Min, Huang. 1993 A Cross-Cultural Experience: A Chinese Anthropologist in the United States. In *Distant Mirrors: America as a Foreign Culture,* ed. Philip R. DeVita and James D. Armstrong, 39–45. Belmont, CA: Wadsworth Publishing Company.

Shweder, Richard A. 1986 Storytelling among the Anthropologists. *The New York Times Book Review,* September 21:1, 38–39.

___. 2000 Martha Minow and Hazel Rose Markus. Introduction. *Daedalus* 129: v–ix.

Silver, Ira. 1993 Marketing Authenticity in Third World Countries. *Annals of Tourism Research* 20:302–318.

Simmons, William S. 1986 *Spirit of the New England Tribes: Indian History and Folklore, 1620–1984.* Hanover, NH: University Press of New England.

Simons, Ronald C., and Charles C. Hughes, eds. 1984 *The Culture-Bound Syndromes: Folk Illnesses of Psychiatric and Anthropological Interest.* Boston: D. Reidel.

Singer, Merrill. 1989 The Coming of Age of Critical Medical Anthropology. *Social Science and Medicine* 28(11):1193–1203.

Singh, K. S. 1994 The Scheduled Tribes. In *Anthropological Survey of India, People of India, National Series Volume III,* ed. K. S. Singh. Delhi: Oxford University Press.

Skinner, G. William. 1964 Marketing and Social Structure in Rural China (Part 1). *Journal of Asian Studies* 24(1):3–43.

___. 1993 Conjugal Power in Tokugawa Japanese Families: A Matter of Life or Death. In *Sex and Gender Hierarchies,* ed. Barbara D. Miller, 236–270. New York: Cambridge University Press.

Skocpol, Theda. 1979 *States and Social Revolutions: A Comparative Analysis of France, Russia, and China.* New York: Cambridge University Press.

Skrobanek, S., Nataya Boonpakdee, and Chutima Jantateero. 1997 *The Traffic in Women: Human Realities of the International Sex Trade.* London: Zed Press.

Slocum, Sally. 1975 Woman the Gatherer: Male Bias in Anthropology. In *Toward an Anthropology of Women,* ed. Rayna R. Reiter, 36–50. New York: Monthly Review Press.

Smart, Alan, and Josephine Smart. 1996 Monster Homes: Hong Kong Immigration to Canada, Urban Conflicts, and Contested Representations of Space. In *City Lives and City Forms: Critical Research and Canadian Urbanism,* ed. Jon Caulfield and Linda Peake. Toronto: University of Toronto Press.

Smart, J. 1994 Business Immigration in Canada: Deception and Exploitation. In *Reluctant Exiles: migration from Hong Kong and the new Overseas Chinese,* ed. R. Skeldon. Armonk, NY: M.E. Sharpe.

Smith, Derek. 2001 'Policy of Aggressive Civilization' and Projects of Governance in Roman Catholic Industrial Schools for Native Peoples in Canada, 1870–95. *Anthropologica* 43(2):253–271.

Smith, Jonathan Z., ed. 1995 *The HarperCollins Dictionary of Religion.* New York: HarperCollins.

Smith, Michael. G. 1966 Political Organization. In *International Encyclopedia of Social Sciences,* 193–202. New York: Macmillan.

Smith, Yvonne Bobb. 1999 There Is No Place Like Home: Caribbean Women's Feminism in Canada. In *Emigre Feminism: Transnational Perspectives,* ed. Alena Heitlinger. Toronto: University of Toronto Press.

Soh, Chunghee Sarah. 1993 *Women in Korean Politics.* 2nd edition. Boulder: Westview Press.

Sperber, Dan. 1985 *On Anthropological Knowledge: Three Essays.* New York: Cambridge University Press.

Spiro, Melford. 1967 *Burmese Supernaturalism: A Study in the Explanation and Reduction of Suffering.* Englewood Cliffs, NJ: Prentice-Hall.

___. 1982 *Buddhism and Society: A Great Tradition and Its Burmese Vicissitudes.* Berkeley: University of California Press.

___. 1990 On the Strange and the Familiar in Recent Anthropological Thought. In *Cultural Psychology: Essays on Comparative Human Development,* ed. James W. Stigler, Richard A. Shweder, and Gilbert Herdt, 47–61. Chicago: University of Chicago Press.

Srinivas, M. N. 1959 The Dominant Caste in Rampura. *American Anthropologist* 1:1–16.

Staats, Valerie. 1994 Ritual, Strategy or Convention: Social Meaning in Traditional Women's Baths in Morocco. *Frontiers: A Journal of Women's Studies* 14(3):1–18.

Stack, Carol. 1974 *All Our Kin: Strategies for Survival in a Black Community.* New York: Harper & Row Publishers.

Stambach, Amy. 2000 *Lessons from Mount Kilimanjaro: Schooling, Community, and Gender in East Africa.* New York: Routledge.

Stannard, David E. 1992 *American Holocaust.* New York: Oxford University Press.

Starr, June. 1978 *Dispute and Settlement in Rural Turkey: An Ethnography of Law.* Leiden, Netherlands: E. J. Brill.

Stein, Gertrude. 1959 *Picasso.* Boston: Beacon Press.

Stephen, Lynn. 1995 Women's Rights are Human Rights: The Merging of Feminine and Feminist Interests among El Salvador's Mothers of the Disappeared (CO–MADRES). *American Ethnologist* 22(4):807–827.

Stephenson, P. 1991 *The Hutterian People.* Lantham: University Press of America.

Stiglmayer, Alexandra, ed. 1994 *Mass Rape: The War against Women in Bosnia-Herzegovina.* Lincoln: University of Nebraska Press.

Stillman, Amy Ku'uleialoha. 1996 Hawaiian Hula Competitions: Event, Repertoire, Performance and Tradition. *Journal of American Folklore* 109(434):357–380.

Stivens, Maila, Cecelia Ng, and Jomo K. S., with Jahara Bee. 1994 *Malay Peasant Women and the Land.* Atlantic Highlands, NJ: Zed Books.

Stocking, George W. Jr., ed. 1985. *Objects and Others: Essays on Museums and Material Culture. History of Anthropology Series, 3.* Madison: University of Wisconsin Press.

Stoler, Ann Laura. 1985 *Capitalism and Confrontation in Sumatra's Plantation Belt, 1870–1979.* New Haven: Yale University Press.

___. 1989 Rethinking Colonial Categories: European Communities and the Boundaries of Rule. *Comparative Studies in Society and History* 31(1):134–161.

Stone, Linda. 1998 *Kinship and Gender: An Introduction.* Boulder, Colorado: Westview Press.

Storper-Perez, Danielle, and Harvey E. Goldberg. 1994 The Kotel: Toward an Ethnographic Portrait. *Religion* 24:309–332.

Story, G., W. Kirwin, and J. Widdowson. eds., 1982 *Dictionary of Newfoundland English.* Toronto: University of Toronto Press.

Strathern, Andrew. 1971 *The Rope of Moka: Big-Men and Ceremonial Exchange in Mount Hagen, New Guinea.* London: Cambridge University Press.

Strathern, Marilyn. 1980 No Nature, No Culture: The Hagen Case. In *Nature, Culture, and Gender,* ed. Carol P. MacCormack and Marilyn Strathern, 174–222. New York: Cambridge University Press.

Stringer, Martin D. 1999 Rethinking Animism: Thoughts from the Infancy of Our Discipline. Journal *of the Royal Anthropological Institute* 5:541–556.

Sullivan, Kathleen. 1992 Protagonists of Change. *Cultural Survival Quarterly* 16:4(Winter):38–40.

Suttles, Wayne. 1991 The Traditional Kwakiutl Potlatch. In *Chiefly Feasts: The Enduring Kwakiutl Potlatch,* ed. Aldona Jonaitis, 71–134. Washington, DC: American Museum of Natural History.

Tambiah, Stanley Jeyaraja. 1985 Animals Are Good to Think and Good to Prohibit. In *Culture, Thought, and Social Action: An Anthropological Perspective,* ed. Stanley Jeyaraja Tambiah, 169–211. Cambridge: Harvard University Press.

Tannen, Deborah. 1990 *You Just Don't Understand: Women and Men in Conversation.* New York: Morrow.

Tanner, A. 1983 *The Politics of Indianness.* St. John's, NF: Institute of Social and Economic Research, Memorial University of Newfoundland.

Tapp, Nicholas. 1989 *Sovereignty and Rebellion: The White Hmong of Northern Thailand.* New York: Oxford University Press.

Taussig, Michael. 1978 Nutrition, Development, and Foreign Aid: A Case Study of U.S.-Directed Health Care in a Colombian Plantation Zone. *International Journal of Health Services* 8(1):101–121.

Tennant, Paul 1990 *Aboriginal Peoples and Politics: The Indian Land Question in British Columbia, 1849–1989.* Vancouver: University of British Columbia Press.

Tepper, Elliot L., ed. 1980 *Southeast Asian Exodus: From Tradition to Resettlement.* Ottawa: Canadian Asian Studies Association.

Thomas, Duncan. 1991 *Gender Differences in Household Resource Allocations. Living Standards Measurement Study, Working Paper No. 79.* Washington, DC: The World Bank.

Thompson, Julia J. 1998 Cuts and Culture in Kathmandu. In *Hair: Its Meaning and Power in Asian Cultures,* ed. Alf Hiltebeitel and Barbara D. Miller, 219–258. Albany: State University of New York Press.

Thompson, Robert Farris. 1971 Aesthetics in Traditional Africa. In *Art and Aesthetics in Primitive Societies,* ed. Carol F. Jopling, 374–381. New York: E. P. Dutton.

Tice, Karin E. 1995 *Kuna Crafts, Gender, and the Global Economy.* Austin: University of Texas Press.

Tiffany, Walter W. 1979 New Directions in Political Anthropology: The Use of Corporate Models for the Analysis of Political Organizations. In *Political Anthropology: The State of the Art,* ed. S. Lee Seaton and Henri J. M. Claessen, 63–75. New York: Mouton.

Tinker, Irene. 1976 The Adverse Impact of Development on Women. In *Women and World Development,* ed. Irene Tinker and Michele Bo Bramsen, 22–34. Washington, DC: Overseas Development Council.

Tobin, Joseph J., ed. 1992 *Re-Made in Japan: Everyday Life and Consumer Taste in a Changing Society.* New Haven: Yale University Press.

Toren, Christina. 1988 Making the Present, Revealing the Past: The Mutability and Continuity of Tradition as Process. *Man (N.S.)* 23:696–717.

Traphagan, John W. 2000 The Liminal Family: return Migration and Intergenerational Conflict in Japan. *Journal of Anthropological Research* 56:365–385.

Trawick, Margaret. 1988 Death and Nurturance in Indian Systems of Healing. In *Paths to Asian Medical Knowledge*, ed. Charles Leslie and Allan Young, 129–159. Berkeley: University of California Press.

___. 1992 *Notes on Love in a Tamil Family.* Berkeley: University of California Press.

Trelease, Murray L. 1975 Dying among Alaskan Indians: A Matter of Choice. In *Death: The Final Stage of Growth,* ed. Elisabeth Kübler-Ross, 33–37. Englewood Cliffs, NJ: Prentice–Hall.

Trigger, Bruce. 1969 *The Huron: Farmers of the North.* New York: Holt, Rinehart and Winston.

___. 1976 *The Children of Aataentsic: A History of the Huron People to 1660.* 2 volumes. Montreal: McGill-Queens University Press.

___. 1996 State, Origins of. In *The Social Science Encyclopedia,* ed. Adam Kuper and Jessica Kuper, 837–838. New York: Routledge.

___. 1997 Loaves and Fishes: Sustaining Anthropology at McGill. *Culture* 17(1–2):89–100.

Trotter, Robert T., II. 1987 A Case of Lead Poisoning from Folk Remedies in Mexican American Communities. In *Anthropological Praxis: Translating Knowledge into Action,* ed. Robert M. Wulff and Shirley J. Fiske, 146–159. Boulder: Westview Press.

Trouillot, Michel-Rolph. 1994 Culture, Color, and Politics in Haiti. In *Race,* ed. Steven Gregory and Roger Sanjek, 146–174. New Brunswick: Rutgers University Press.

Tudiver, S. 1997 Depo-Provera. *Womanly Times* Summer/Fall:1–5,14.

Turner, David. 1977 Windigo Mythology and the Analysis of Cree Social Structure. *Anthropologica* 19(1):63–73.

Turner, Victor W. 1969 *The Ritual Process: Structure and Anti-Structure.* Chicago: Aldine Publishing Company.

___. 1974 Pilgrimage and Communitas. *Studia Missionalia* 23:305–27.

Tylor, Edward Burnett. 1871 *Primitive Culture: Researches into the Development of Mythology, Philosophy, Religion, Art, and Custom.* 2 volumes. London: J. Murray.

Udall, Louise. 1969 *Me and Mine: The Story of Helen Sekaquaptewa.* Tuscon: University of Arizona Press.

Uhl, Sarah. 1991 Forbidden Friends: Cultural Veils of Female Friendship in Andalusia. *American Ethnologist* 18(1):90–105.

United Nations Development Programme. 1994 *Human Development Report 1994.* New York: Oxford University Press.

United Nations High Commissioner for Refugees (UNHCR). 1997 *The State of the World's Refugees: A Humanitarian Agenda.* Oxford: Oxford University Press.

Uphoff, Norman T., and Milton J. Esman. 1984 *Local Organizations: Intermediaries in Rural Development.* Ithaca: Cornell University Press.

Valentine, Lisa Philips. 1995 *Making It Their Own: Ojibwe Communicative Practices.* Toronto: University of Toronto Press.

van der Geest, Sjaak, Susan Reynolds Whyte, and Anita Hardon. 1996 The Anthropology of Pharmaceuticals: A Biographical Approach. *Annual Review of Anthropology* 25:153–178.

van der Kwaak, Anke. 1992 Female Circumcision and Gender Identity: A Questionable Alliance? *Social Science and Medicine* 35(6):777–787.

Van Esterik, John. 1996 Women Meditation Teachers in Thailand. In *Women of Southeast Asia,* ed. Penny Van Esterik. Dekalb, IL: Northern Illinois University.

Van Esterik, Penny. 1989 *Beyond the Breast-Bottle Controversy.* New Brunswick: Rutgers University Press.

___. 1992. *Taking Refuge: Lao Buddhists in North America.* Program for Southeast Asian Studies: Arizona State University.

___. 1995. The Politics of Breastfeeding: An Advocacy Perspective. In *Breastfeeding: Biocultural Perspectives,* ed. Patricia Stuart-Macadam and Katherine A. Dettwyler. New York: Aldine de Gruyter.

___. 1996 Laywomen in Theravada Buddhism. In *Women of Southeast Asia,* ed. Penny Van Esterik, Dekalb, IL: Northern Illinois University.

___. 2000 *Materializing Thailand.* Oxford: Berg Press.

Van Gennep, Arnold. 1960 [1908] *The Rites of Passage.* Chicago: University of Chicago Press.

Van Maanen, John. 1988 *Tales of the Field: On Writing Ethnography.* Chicago: University of Chicago Press.

Veblen, Thorstein. 1953 [1899] *The Theory of the Leisure Class.* New York: Mentor Books.

Velimirovic, Boris. 1990 Is Integration of Traditional and Western Medicine Really Possible? In *Anthropology and Primary Health Care,* ed. Jeannine Coreil and J. Dennis Mull, 751–778. Boulder: Westview Press.

Verdery, Katherine. 1996 *What Was Socialism, and What Comes Next?* Princeton: Princeton University Press.

Verdon, Michel. 1980 The Quebec Stem Family Revisited. In *Canadian Families: Ethnic Variations,* ed. K. Ishwaran. Toronto: McGraw-Hill Ryerson Ltd.

Vickers, Jeanne. 1993 *Women and War.* Atlantic Highlands, NJ: Zed Books.

Vincent, Joan. 1990 *Anthropology and Politics: Visions, Traditions, and Trends.* Tucson: The University of Arizona Press.

____. 1996 Political Anthropology. In *The Social Science Encyclopedia,* ed. Adam Kuper and Jessica Kuper, 624. New York: Routledge.

Vincke, John, Ralph Bolton, Rudolf Mak, and Susan Blank. 1993 Coming Out and AIDS-Related High-Risk Sexual Behavior. *Archives of Sexual Behavior* 22(6):559–586.

Wakin, E. 1992 *Anthropology Goes to War: Professional Ethics and Counterinsurgency in Thailand.* Center for Southeast Asian Studies, Monograph 7. Madison: University of Wisconsin.

Waldram, J., A. Herring, and K. Young. 1995 *Aboriginal Health in Canada: Historical, Cultural and Epidemiological Perspectives.* Toronto: University of Toronto Press.

Walker, Marilyn. 1984 *Harvesting the Northern Wild.* Yellowknife, NWT: The Northern Publishers.

Wallerstein, Immanuel. 1979 *The Capitalist World-Economy.* New York: Cambridge University Press.

Ward, Martha C. 1989 Once Upon a Time. In *Nest in the Wind: Adventures in Anthropology on a Tropical Island,* ed. Martha C. Ward, 1–22. Prospect Heights, IL: Waveland Press.

Warren, Carol A. B. 1988 *Gender Issues in Field Research. Qualitative Research Methods, Volume 9.* Newbury Park, CA: Sage Publications.

Watson, Rubie S. 1986 The Named and the Nameless: Gender and Person in Chinese Society. *American Ethnologist* 13(4):619–631.

____. 1997 Museums and Indigenous Cultures: The Power of Local Knowledge. *Cultural Survival Quarterly* 21(1):24–25.

Waxler-Morrison, N. J. Anderson, and E. Richardson. 1990 *Cross-.cultural Caring: A Handbook for Health Professionals in Western Canada.* Vancouver: University of British Columbia Press.

Webster, Gloria Cranmer. 1991 The Contemporary Potlatch. In *Chiefly Feasts: The Enduring Kwakiutl Potlatch,* ed. Aldona Jonaitis, 227–250. Washington, DC: American Museum of Natural History.

Weine, Stevan M., et al. 1995 Psychiatric Consequences of "Ethnic Cleansing": Clinical Assessments and Trauma Testimonies of Newly Resettled Bosnian Refugees. *American Journal of Psychiatry* 152(4):536–542.

Weiner, Annette. 1976 *Women of Value, Men of Renown: New Perspectives in Trobriand Exchange.* Austin: University of Texas Press.

Weismantel, M. J. 1989 The Children Cry for Bread: Hegemony and the Transformation of Consumption. In *The Social Economy of Consumption, Monographs in Economic Anthropology No. 6,* ed. Henry J. Rutz and Benjamin S. Orlove, 85–99. New York: University Press of America.

White, Douglas R., and Michael L. Burton. 1988 Causes of Polygyny: Ecology, Economy, Kinship, and Warfare. *American Anthropologist* 90(4):871–887.

Whitehead, Tony Larry. 1986 Breakdown, Resolution, and Coherence: The Fieldwork Experience of a Big, Brown, Pretty-talking Man in a West Indian Community. In *Self, Sex, and Gender in Cross-Cultural Fieldwork,* ed. Tony Larry Whitehead and Mary Ellen Conway, 213–239. Chicago: University of Illinois Press.

Whitehead, Tony Larry, and Mary Ellen Conway, eds. 1986 *Self, Sex, and Gender in Cross-Cultural Fieldwork.* Chicago: University of Illinois Press.

Whiting, Beatrice B., and John W. M. Whiting. 1975 *Children of Six Cultures: A Psycho-Cultural Analysis.* Cambridge: Harvard University Press.

Whyte, Martin King. 1993 Wedding Behavior and Family Strategies in Chengdu. In *Chinese Families in the Post–Mao Era,* ed. Deborah Davis and Stevan Harrell, 89–218. Berkeley: University of California Press.

Wiber, M. 1997 *Erect Men, Undulating Women: The Visual Imagery of Gender, "Race" and Progress in Reconstructive Illustrations of Human Evolution.* Waterloo: Wilfred Laurier Press.

Wikan, Unni. 1977 Man Becomes Woman: Transsexualism in Oman as a Key to Gender Roles. *Man* 12(2):304–319.

____. 1982 *Behind the Veil in Arabia: Women in Oman.* Chicago: University of Chicago Press.

____. 2000 Citizenship on Trial: Nadia's Case. *Daedalus* 129:55–76.

Wilde, James. 1988 Starvation in a Fruitful Land. *Time,* December 5:43–44.

Williams, Brett. 1988 *Upscaling Downtown: Stalled Gentrification in Washington, D.C.* Ithaca: Cornell University Press.

____. 1991 Good Guys and Bad Toys: The Paradoxical World of Children's Cartoons. In *The Politics of Culture,* ed. Brett Williams, 109–132. Washington, DC: Smithsonian Institution Press.

____. 1994 Babies and Banks: The "Reproductive Underclass" and the Raced, Gendered Masking of Debt. In *Race,* ed. Steven Gregory and Roger Sanjek, 348–365. Ithaca: Cornell University Press.

Williams, Raymond. 1983 *Keywords: A Vocabulary of Culture and Society.* New York: Oxford University Press.

Wilson, Richard. 1995 *Maya Resurgence in Guatemala: Q'eqchi' Experiences.* Norman, OK: University of Oklahoma Press.

Winans, Edgar V., and Angelique Haugerud. 1977 Rural Self–Help in Kenya: The Harambee Movement. *Human Organization* 36:334–351.

Winland, D. 1992 The Role of Religious Affiliation in Refugee Resettlement: The Case of the Hmong. *Canadian Ethnic Studies* 24(1):96–119.

Winthrop, Rob. 2000 The Real World: Cultural Rights/Animal Rights. *Practicing Anthropology* 22:44–45.

Winzeler, Robert L. 1974 Sex Role Equality, Wet Rice Cultivation, and the State in Southeast Asia. *American Anthropologist* 76(3):563–565.

Wolf, Charlotte. 1996 Status. In *The Social Science Encyclopedia,* ed. Adam Kuper and Jessica Kuper, 842–843. New York: Routledge.

Wolf, Daniel R. 1991 *The Rebels: A Brotherhood of Outlaw Bikers.* Toronto: University of Toronto Press.

Wolf, Eric R. 1966 *Peasants.* Englewood Cliffs, NJ: Prentice-Hall.

___. 1969 *Peasant Wars of the Twentieth Century.* New York: Harper & Row.

___. 1982 *Europe and the People without History.* Berkeley: University of California Press.

Wolf, Margery. 1968 *The House of Lim: A Study of a Chinese Farm Family.* New York: Appleton–Century–Crofts.

Woodrick, Anne C. 1995 Mother-Daughter Conflict and the Selection of Ritual Kin in a Peasant Community. *Anthropological Quarterly* 68(4):219–233.

Woolfson, Peter, Virginia Hood, Roger Secker-Walker, and Ann C. Macaulay. 1995 Mohawk English in the Medical Interview. *Medical Anthropology Quarterly* 9(4):503–509.

Wu, David Y. H. 1990 Chinese Minority Policy and the Meaning of Minority Culture: The Example of Bai in Yunnan, China. *Human Organization* 49(1):1–13.

Xenophanes. 1992 *Xenophanes of Colophon: Fragments: A Text and Translation with a Commentary.* Trans. James H. Lesher. Toronto: University of Toronto Press.

Xenos, Peter. 1993 Extended Adolescence and the Sexuality of Asian Youth: Observations on Research and Policy. East-West Center Reprints, Population Series No. 292. Honolulu: East–West Center.

Xizhe, Peng. 1991 *Demographic Transition in China: Fertility Trends Since the 1950s.* New York: Oxford University Press.

Yang, Mayfair Mei-hui. 1994 *Gifts, Favors and Banquets: The Art of Social Relationships in China.* Ithaca: Cornell University Press.

Yawney, Carole D., and J. Homiak. 2001 Rastafari. In *Encyclopedia of African and African–American Religions,* ed. Stephen D. Glazier. New York: Routledge.

Yinger, John. 1995 Opening Doors: How to Cut Discrimination by Supporting Neighborhood Integration. Center for Policy Research, Policy Brief No. 3.1995. Syracuse, NY: Syracuse University, Maxwell School of Citizenship and Public Affairs.

Young, Michael W. 1983 "Our Name is Women; We are Bought with Limesticks and Limepots": An Analysis of the Autobiographical Narrative of a Kalauna Woman. *Man* 18:478–501.

Young, Michael, and Peter Willmott. 1979 *Family and Kinship in East London.* New York: Penguin Books.

Young, Roger, and Caroline Van Bers. 1991 Death of the Family Farm. *Alternatives* 17(4):22–23.

Zaidi, S. Akbar. 1988 Poverty and Disease: Need for Structural Change. *Social Science and Medicine* 27:119–127.

Zarrilli, Phillip B. 1990 Kathakali. In *Indian Theatre: Traditions of Performance,* ed. Farley P. Richmond, Darius L. Swann, and Phillip B. Zarrilli, 315–357. Honolulu: University of Hawaii Press.

Zenie-Ziegler, Wedad. 1988 *In Search of Shadows: Conversations with Egyptian Women.* London: Zed Books.

Zureik, Elia. 1994 Palestinian Refugees and Peace. *Journal of Palestine Studies* 24(1):5–17.

Index

susto, 171
Windigo psychosis, 172
culture of poverty, 144
culture shock, 41–42
customary law, 275

D
dalit, 252
Daly, Martin, 132
the Dani, 125
Danish Organization for International Development (DANIDA), 387
Das, Veena, 276
data analysis
ethnography, 51–52
qualitative data, 49–51
quantitative data, 51
realist ethnography, 52
reflexive ethnographies, 52
tropes, 50
writing about culture, 51–52
data collection
combining watching and asking, 45
deductive research, 42
discourse, 42
emic approach, 42–43
etic approach, 42–43
field-note diary, 43
historical sources, 47
inductive research, 42
interviews, 44–45
kinship data, 45
life history, 45–46
multiple research methods, 47–48
participant observation, 33–34, 43
qualitative research, 42
quantitative research, 42
questionnaires, 44–45
research methods, 43
team projects, 47–48
texts, 46–47
theoretical considerations, 42–43
time allocation study, 43
triangulation, 47
daughter preference, 126

Davis-Floyd, Robbie, 180
Dawson, Sir John William, 24
De Koninck, Rodolphe, 75
Deacon, Bernard, 54
death
causes of, 132
ethnocide, 137
femicide, 136
genocide, 137
infanticide, 132–134
research on, 131
suicide, 134–136
by violence, 136–137
death and dying, 160
death penalty, 275
Decontie, Deborah, 397
deculturated, 382
deductive research, 42
demographic transition, 122
demography
defined, 120
fertility, 120
migration, 120
mortality, 120
the Dene of Colville Lake, 63
Department for International Development (DFID) (UK), 387
descent
ambilineal descent, 199
bilateral descent, 198–200
defined, 195
double descent, 198
matrilineal descent, 195, 196–198
patrilineal descent, 195, 196
residence patterns, 200
unilineal descent, 195, 198
development. *See* change; international development
development anthropology
critical development anthropology (CDA), 390
methods in, 390–392
participatory research methods (PRMs), 391–392
rapid research methods (RRMs), 391
vs. standard fieldwork, 391

traditional development anthropology (TDA), 390
the development project, 388–390
diachronic analysis, 380
diagnosis, 174–175
dialects, 321–322
diaspora population, 251
diffusion, 381–382
dimorphism, 206
direct entitlements, 94
direct infanticide, 132
discourse, 42, 324–325
discrimination
caste, 254
homosexuality, 22
in immigration policies, 363
disease
colonialism and, 167–169
culture-bound syndromes, 171, 172
defining, 171–172
diseases of development, 169–170
HIV/AIDS, 168
Kyasanur Forest disease (KFD), 170
new infectious diseases, 166–167
psychosocial factors, 175
diseases of development, 169–170
displaced persons, 365–367
displacement, 316
Dispute and Settlement in Rural Turkey (Starr), 271
distributional development, 384–385
divination, 174
divorce
cross-cultural variations, 227–228
and gender, 228–229
Islamic women, 228–229
and kinship patterns, 227–229
lesbian mothers, 229
and polygyny, 228
doctrine, 290, 291
domestic violence, 226

R

race
   apartheid, 98, 248–250
   and consumption, 98–99
   and cultural differentiation, 21
   and fieldwork, 40
   and social stratification, 248–250
racial stratification, 248–250
racism, 247, 250, 346
Radcliffe-Brown, A.R., 9, 260
Radin, Paul, 46
rapid research methods (RRMs), 391
rapport, 37
Ras Tafari, 306
Rastafarianism, 306
"re-studies," 35
realist ethnography, 52
reciprocity, 106
recording research
   field notes, 48
   films, 49
   photography, 49, 50
   tape recordings, 48–49
   videos, 49
redistribution, 106
reflexive ethnographies, 52
reflexive museology, 346
refugees, 365–367
region
   cultural differentiation, 23
   defined, 23
religion
   and abortion, 130–131
   African religions, 306
   animism, 289
   cargo cults, 308
   changes, 306–309
   contested sacred sites, 308
   definitions of, 288
   vs. magic, 288–289
   monotheism, 289
   origin of, theories, 289
   polytheism, 289
   revitalization movements, 307–308
   and suicide, 134
   syncretism, 301, 304

world religions. See world religions
   vs. world view, 288
religious beliefs
   doctrine, 290, 291
   expression of, 290–291
   myth, 290–291
   ritual practices, 293–296
   supernatural forces and beings, 291–293
   varieties of, 289–296
religious freedom, as human right, 308–309
religious persecution, 372–373
religious specialists
   diviners, 298
   other specialists, 298
   palm readers, 298
   priestess, 298
   priests, 298
   prophets, 298
   shamans, 298
   tarot card readers, 298
   witches, 298
remarriage, 208, 209, 230
remittances, 224
repatriation, 347, 366
replacement-level fertility, 122
reproduction
   in agricultural societies, 121–122
   below-replacement-level fertility, 122
   and culture, 120–123
   defined, 120
   in foraging societies, 121
   in industrial societies, 122–123
   replacement-level fertility, 122
reproductive rights, 128
Reproductive Rights and Wrongs (Hartmann), 128
research
   see also data collection; fieldwork
   data analysis. *See* data analysis
   data collection. *See* data collection
   deductive, 42
   inductive, 42
   multi-sited research, 33

multiple research methods, 47–48
   participatory research methods (PRMs), 391–392
   qualitative research, 42
   quantitative research, 42
   rapid research methods (RRMs), 391
   "re-studies," 35
   recording research. *See* recording research
   regional focus, shifts in, 36
   secondary research, 34
   team projects, 47–48
research methods, 43
residence patterns, 200
restricted exchange systems, 204
reverse culture shock, 42
revitalization and tourism, 352–353
revitalization movements, 307–308
revolution, 278
Rich, Adrienne, 155
right of return, 366
rights in people, exchange of, 105
ritual marriage, 203
ritually established sharing bonds, 202
rituals
   cannibalism, 296
   defined, 293
   life-cycle, 293–295
   periodic, 293
   pilgrimage, 295
   of reversal, 295–296
   sacrifice, 296
rituals of reversal, 295–296
Robertson, Jennifer, 37, 50
role, 247
Romania, collectivised agriculture in, 79–80, 251
romantic love, 206–207
Rosaldo, Michelle Zimbalist, 54
Rosenberg, Harriet, 33, 76
Rosenberg, Lisa, 41
Rubin, Gayle, 105

social impact assessments, 383

social inequality
    and exchange, 110–111
    and the law, 275

social stratification
    achieved position, 246
    achieved status, 247
    ascribed position, 246
    ascribed status, 247–254
    and bands, 263
    caste, 247, 252–254
    class, 247
    defined, 246
    dominant caste, 253
    ethnicity, 250–252
    mechanical solidarity, 247
    organic solidarity, 247
    racial stratification, 248–250
    status groups, 246–247

socialism, 72

socialization
    during childhood, 148–151
    language, 320–321
    sexual orientation and childhood experiences, 155

socio-cultural fit, 390

sociolinguistics, 320

Soh, Chunghee Sarah, 261

son preference, 126

South Africa, apartheid in, 98, 248–250

South Asia, new immigrants from, 372

Southeast Asia, new immigrants from, 371–372

Soviet Jews, 372–373

Spain, friendship in, 238

spatial segregation, 254

speaking, ethnography of, 320–321

specialization of law and order tasks, 273

Speck, Dara Culhane, 184

spirit possession, 367

sports, 348–350

spousal abuse, 136

spouse/partner migration, 368

spouse/partner relationships, 225

spouse selection
    exclusion rules, 204–205
    incest taboo, 204–205
    physical ability, 206
    physical appearance, 206
    preference rules, 205–207
    and romance 206–207

Srinivaas, M.N., 253

Stack, Carol, 110, 239

Starr, June, 271

state
    defined, 266
    fractured states, 269–270
    gender and leadership, 267
    in-kind taxation, 267
    nation-state, 269
    origins of, 266–267
    power and politics in democratic states, 268–269
    powers of, 267
    social control in, 273–275
    symbols of state power, 268

status, 247

status groups, 246–247

Stein, Gertrude, 50

stem household, 217

Stoler, Ann, 47, 260

storytelling, 246

stratificational model, 278

street gangs, 241

street youth in Edmonton, 82

structural adjustment, 384

structure, 14

structurism, 14

subaltern peoples, 260

suicide, 134–136

supernatural forces and beings
    animatism, 291
    anthropomorphic, 291–292
    deceased ancestors, 293
    domain specialization, 292
    zoomorphic, 291

superstructure, 14

sustainable development, 385

sustainable systems
    foraging, 64–65
    horticulture, 68–69
    pastoralism, 71

Sweden, consumerism control in, 93

Swedish Agency for International development (Sida), 387

symbol
    and culture, 18–19
    defined, 19
    state power 268

symbolic analysis, 289

symbolic goods, 103–104

symbolic understanding, 314

synchronic view, 380

syncretism, 301, 304, 353

T

taboos
    defined, 100
    food taboos, 100–101
    incest taboo, 105, 204–205
    post-partum taboos, 125

tape recordings, 48–49

Tator, Carol, 330

tax/rent fund, 93

team projects, 47–48

teenage pregnancy as desired condition, 124

Tekakwitha, Kateri, 292

teknonyms, 197

television studies, 328–329

the Temiar, 341

testimony method, 374

Thailand, *chao khao* in, 396

Thatcher, Margaret, 267

theatre, 342–343, 354

theft, 108–109

Tibetan medicine, 250

the Tiwi (Australia), 65–66

the *Tjaralda,* 104

Tomasita Project, 17

tomato production, and globalization, 17

tourism, 350–353

trade, 107

traditional development anthropology (TDA), 390

transnational migration, 365

transnationalism, 34

travel, 350–353

working-class racism, 375
World Bank, 384, 385, 386–387
world economy, and globaliza-
    tion, 61
World Health Organization, 184,
    369
world peace, 270, 281–282
world religions
    Buddhism, 300–301
    Christianity, 303–304
    defined, 299
    Hinduism, 299–300
    Islam, 305
    Judaism, 301–303
    vs. "local religions," 306
    no single monolithic entity, 299
world view, 288
wrestling in India, 349
writing systems, 318–319
Writing Women's Worlds (Abu-
    Lughod), 51

Y
Yang, Mayfair, 102
the Yanomami, 60, 190
Yoruba women, 266
youth gangs, 240–241
youth work groups, 243

Z
Zenié-Ziegler, Wédád, 124
Zinacantan (Mexico), 76
zoomorphic, 291

Photo Credits

Chapter 1
p. 3, Gilles Mingasson, Gamma Liaison; p. 4, Richard Wrangham, AnthroPhoto; p. 6, Spooner/Redmond-Callow, Liaison; p. 10, Stan Washburn, AnthroPhoto; p. 17, Michael Newman, PhotoEdit; p. 19, Barbara Miller; p. 21, Barbara Miller; p. 22, Ruth Bonneville/The Canadian Press/Winnipeg Free Press

Chapter 2
p. 31, Joel Savishinsky; p. 34, Penny and John Van Esterik; p. 36, Courtesy of W. Rodman; p. 40, Liza Dalby; p. 45, Mel Konner, AnthroPhoto; p. 46, Gananath Obeyesekere; p. 48, Michael Horowitz; p. 53, Antonio Ribeiro, Gamma Liaison

Chapter 3
p. 59, Reuters/George Mulala, Archive Photos; p. 62, Joel Savishinsky; p. 65, Reuters/Megan Lewis/Archive Photos; p. 68, Elliot Fratkin; p. 68, Barbara Miller; p. 72, Xinhau-Chine Nou, Gamma Liaison; p. 74, Sean Sprague, Stock Boston; p. 77, Barbara Miller; p. 79, David Kideckel

Chapter 4
p. 89, Roshani Kothari; p. 90, J. Welsh/Royal British Columbia Museum 2307b; p. 93, Kim Newton, Woodfin Camp & Associates; p. 95, Brennan Linsey/The Canadian Press; p. 97, Edward Keller; p. 101, David Austen, Stock Boston; p. 104, © Douglas Mason/Woodfin Camp; p. 106, © Chuck Fishman/Woodfin Camp; p. 107, Barbara Miller; p. 108, Barbara Miller; p. 112, Edward Keller; p. 114, Bill Bachmann, PhotoEdit

Chapter 5
p. 119, Roshani Kothari; p. 122, David & Peter Turnley, CORBIS; p. 124, Stephanie Dinkins, Photo Researchers; p. 127, Kelly-Mooney Photography, CORBIS; p. 128, Barry Iverson, Woodfin Camp & Associates; p. 131, Oliver Pichetti, Gamma Liaison; p. 133, Courtesy of UNICEF; p. 136, Allan Tannenbaum, The Image Works

Chapter 6
p. 141, Jeff Greenberg, PhotoEdit; p. 143, Ken Heyman, Woodfin Camp & Associates; p. 146, Nancy Scheper-Hughes; p. 149, Roshani Kathari; p. 150, Napoleon A. Chagnon, AnthroPhoto; p. 156, The National Anthropological Archive, Smithsonian Institution; p. 158, Barry Hewlett; p. 159, © P. Dury/PubliPhoto/Photo Researchers

Chapter 7
p. 165, B. & C. Alexander, Photo Researchers; p. 166, Peter Menzel, Stock Boston; p. 167, Sean Sprague, Stock Boston; p. 174, Mary Beth Mills/Colby College; p. 176, Irven DeVore, AnthroPhoto; p. 177, Laurel Kendall; p. 178, Courtesy of Ana Ning; p. 183, Vincanne Adams

Chapter 8
p. 189, Sa180oala, Liaison; p. 190, © Napoleon A. Chagnon/AnthroPhoto; p. 201, Reuters/Will Burgess/Archive Photo; p. 204, Canadian Press CP; p. 206, Rick Smolan, Stock Boston; p. 207, Jack Heaton; p. 210, Naboro Komine, Photo Researchers

Chapter 9
p. 215, N. Schiller, Image Works; p. 217, Keren Su, Stock Boston; p. 219, Barbara Miller; p. 221, Thomas L. Kelly, Woodfin Camp & Associates; p. 223, Ellen Oxfeld; p. 224, Reuters/Archive Photos; p. 227, David Wells, Image Works; p. 230, Andy Levin, Photo Researchers

Chapter 10
p. 235, Barbara Miller; p. 241, Mark Richards, PhotoEdit; p. 242, Canadian Press EDMS; p. 243, Charles & Josette Lenars, CORBIS; p. 245, Peter Menzel, Stock Boston; p. 252, Bruno Barbey, Magnum; p. 253, Barbara Miller

Chapter 11
p. 259, Reuters/Jason Reid/Archive Photos; p. 261, Chunghee Sarah Soh; p. 264, Hank Wittemore, Sygma; p. 265, Kal Muller, Woodfin Camp & Associates; p. 268, Jack Heaton; p. 269, Roshani Kothari; p. 270, Daniel Simon, Gamma Liaison; p. 273, © J.F.E. Bloss/AnthroPhoto; p. 274, Barbara Miller; p. 281, UPI/Corbis-Bettmann

Chapter 12
p. 287, Robert Frerck, Woodfin Camp & Associates; p. 291, Simon Hiltebeitel; p. 294, © Annerino/Liaison; p. 296, Lorenzo Pezzatini; p. 300, Jack Heaton; p. 302, Barbara Miller; p. 303, Edward Keller; p. 306, Gerd Ludwig, Woodfin Camp & Associates; p. 307, © Kal Muller, Woodfin Camp & Associates

Chapter 13

p. 313, Eastcott, The Image Works; p. 315, Susan Kuklin, Photo Researchers; p. 319, M. Vautier, Anthropological & Archaeological Museum, Lima, Peru, Woodfin Camp & Associates; p. 321, Michel Ponomareff/PONO-PRESSE; p. 324, Olympia/PhotoEdit; p. 325, Richard Lord, PhotoEdit; p. 326, Olympia, PhotoEdit

Chapter 14

p. 335, Roger Dashow, AnthroPhoto; p. 337, Peabody Museum, Harvard University; p. 338, Courtesy of Judy Chapman; p. 339, Courtesy of Catherine H. McCoid and LeRoy D. McDermott. Reproduced by permission of the American Anthropological Association from American Anthropologist 98:2, June 1996. Not for further reproduction; p. 339, Courtesy of Catherine H. McCoid and LeRoy D. McDermott. Reproduced by permission of the American Anthropological Association from American Anthropologist 98:2, June 1996. Not for further reproduction; p. 342, © Sarala Dandekar/photographer Arbindam Basu; p. 349, X. Zimbardo, Liaison International; p. 352, © John Elk III, Stock Boston

Chapter 15

p. 359, Ruth Krulfeld; p. 361, J.T. Milanich; p. 365, Ed Keller; p. 373, © Michael Grecco/Stock Boston

Chapter 16

p. 379, © Betty Press/Woodfin Camp & Associates; p. 382, Barbara Miller; p. 389, William Rodman/CIDA; p. 394, © Robert Nickelsberg/Gamma Liaison; p. 398, Roshani Kothari; p. 399, str-Clement Allard/Canadian Press

Recommended System and Software Requirements*

Windows
Windows 98, Windows NT 4.0, Windows 2000, Windows XP

Mac OS
Mac OS 9.x, Mac OS X

IBM Compatible
Pentium 233 MHz, 64 MB RAM, 40 MB free hard drive space

Mac OS
PowerPC 604e 266 MHz, G3, G4, 64 MB RAM, 40 MB free hard drive space

SVGA monitor displaying 256 or more colours, 4X or faster CD-ROM, Mouse

Internet Explorer 5.5+ (Recommended) or Netscape 6.0.2+

*Note: This product may run on computers that don't meet the recommended requirements, but performance may be slow or unstable.

"AS IS" LICENSE AGREEMENT AND LIMITED WARRANTY

READ THIS LICENSE CAREFULLY BEFORE USING THIS PACKAGE. BY USING THIS PACKAGE, YOU ARE AGREEING TO THE TERMS AND CONDITIONS OF THIS LICENSE. IF YOU DO NOT AGREE, DO NOT USE THE PACKAGE. PROMPTLY RETURN THE UNUSED PACKAGE AND ALL ACCOMPANYING ITEMS TO THE PLACE YOU OBTAINED THEM. *THESE TERMS APPLY TO ALL LICENSED SOFTWARE ON THE DISK EXCEPT THAT THE TERMS FOR USE OF ANY SHAREWARE OR FREEWARE ON THE DISKETTES ARE AS SET FORTH IN THE ELECTRONIC LICENSE LOCATED ON THE DISK:*

1. **GRANT OF LICENSE and OWNERSHIP:** The enclosed computer programs ("Software") are licensed, not sold, to you by Pearson Education Canada Inc. ("We" or the "Company") in consideration of your adoption of the accompanying Company textbooks and/or other materials, and your agreement to these terms. You own only the disk(s) but we and/or our licensors own the Software itself. This license allows instructors and students enrolled in the course using the Company textbook that accompanies this Software (the "Course") to use and display the enclosed copy of the Software for academic use only, so long as you comply with the terms of this Agreement. You may make one copy for back up only. We reserve any rights not granted to you.

2. **USE RESTRICTIONS:** You may <u>not</u> sell or license copies of the Software or the Documentation to others. You may <u>not</u> transfer, distribute or make available the Software or the Documentation, except to instructors and students in your school who are users of the adopted Company textbook that accompanies this Software in connection with the course for which the textbook was adopted. You may <u>not</u> reverse engineer, disassemble, decompile, modify, adapt, translate or create derivative works based on the Software or the Documentation. You may be held legally responsible for any copying or copyright infringement which is caused by your failure to abide by the terms of these restrictions.

3. **TERMINATION:** This license is effective until terminated. This license will terminate automatically without notice from the Company if you fail to comply with any provisions or limitations of this license. Upon termination, you shall destroy the Documentation and all copies of the Software. All provisions of this Agreement as to limitation and disclaimer of warranties, limitation of liability, remedies or damages, and our ownership rights shall survive termination.

4. **DISCLAIMER OF WARRANTY: THE COMPANY AND ITS LICENSORS MAKE <u>NO</u> WARRANTIES ABOUT THE SOFTWARE, WHICH IS PROVIDED "<u>AS-IS</u>." IF THE DISK IS DEFECTIVE IN MATERIALS OR WORKMANSHIP, YOUR ONLY REMEDY IS TO RETURN IT TO THE COMPANY WITHIN 30 DAYS FOR REPLACEMENT UNLESS THE COMPANY DETERMINES IN GOOD FAITH THAT THE DISK HAS BEEN MISUSED OR IMPROPERLY IN-STALLED, REPAIRED, ALTERED OR DAMAGED. THE COMPANY DISCLAIMS ALL WARRANTIES, EXPRESS OR IMPLIED, INCLUDING WITHOUT LIMITATION, THE IMPLIED WARRANTIES OF MERCHANTABILITY AND FITNESS FOR A PARTICULAR PURPOSE. THE COMPANY DOES NOT WARRANT, GUARANTEE OR MAKE ANY REPRESENTATION REGARDING THE ACCURACY, RELIABILITY, CURRENTNESS, USE, OR RESULTS OF USE, OF THE SOFTWARE.**

5. **LIMITATION OF REMEDIES AND DAMAGES: IN NO EVENT, SHALL THE COMPANY OR ITS EMPLOYEES, AGENTS, LICENSORS OR CONTRACTORS BE LIABLE FOR ANY INCIDENTAL, INDIRECT, SPECIAL OR CON-SEQUENTIAL DAMAGES ARISING OUT OF OR IN CONNECTION WITH THIS LICENSE OR THE SOFTWARE, INCLUDING, WITHOUT LIMITATION, LOSS OF USE, LOSS OF DATA, LOSS OF INCOME OR PROFIT, OR OTHER LOSSES SUSTAINED AS A RESULT OF INJURY TO ANY PERSON, OR LOSS OF OR DAMAGE TO PROP-ERTY, OR CLAIMS OF THIRD PARTIES, EVEN IF THE COMPANY OR AN AUTHORIZED REPRESENTATIVE OF THE COMPANY HAS BEEN ADVISED OF THE POSSIBILITY OF SUCH DAMAGES.** SOME JURISDICTIONS DO NOT ALLOW THE LIMITATION OF DAMAGES IN CERTAIN CIRCUMSTANCES, SO THE ABOVE LIMITATIONS MAY NOT ALWAYS APPLY.

6. **GENERAL:** THIS AGREEMENT SHALL BE CONSTRUED AND INTERPRETED ACCORDING TO THE LAWS OF THE PROVINCE OF ONTARIO. This Agreement is the complete and exclusive statement of the agreement between you and the Company and supersedes all proposals, prior agreements, oral or written, and any other communications between you and the company or any of its representatives relating to the subject matter.

Should you have any questions concerning this agreement or if you wish to contact the Company for any reason, please contact in writing: Customer Service, Pearson Education Canada, 26 Prince Andrew Place, Don Mills, Ontario, M3C 2T8.